graphic
JAVA™ 1.1
MASTERING THE AWT

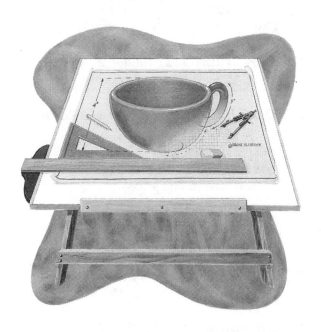

THE SUNSOFT PRESS
JAVA SERIES

▼ **Core Java 1.1,** *Volume 1 - Fundamentals*
Cay S. Horstmann & Gary Cornell

▼ **Core Java 1.1,** *Volume 2 - Advanced Features*
Cay S. Horstmann & Gary Cornell

▼ **Graphic Java 1.1,** *Second Edition*
David M. Geary

▼ **Inside Java Workshop**
Lynn Weaver & Bob Jervis

▼ **Instant Java,** *Second Edition*
John A. Pew

▼ **Java by Example,** *Second Edition*
Jerry R. Jackson & Alan L. McClellan

▼ **Jumping JavaScript**
Janice Winsor & Brian Freeman

▼ **Just Java 1.1,** *Third Edition*
Peter van der Linden

▼ **Not Just Java**
Peter van der Linden

graphic
JAVA™ 1.1
MASTERING THE AWT

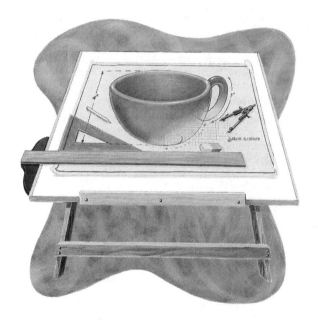

DAVID M. GEARY

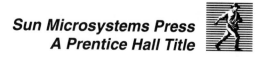

Sun Microsystems Press
A Prentice Hall Title

The publisher offers discounts on this book when ordered in bulk quantities.
For more information, contact: Corporate Sales Department, Phone: 800-382-3419;
Fax: 201-236-7141; E-mail: corpsales@prenhall.com; or write: Prentice Hall PTR,
Corp. Sales Dept., One Lake Street, Upper Saddle River, NJ 07458.

Editorial/production supervision: *Patti Guerrieri*
Cover design director: *Jerry Votta*
Cover designer: *Anthony Gemmellaro*
Cover illustration: *Karen Strelecki*
Manufacturing manager: *Alexis R. Heydt*
Marketing manager: *Stephen Solomon*
Acquisitions editor: *Gregory G. Doench*
Sun Microsystems Press publisher: *Rachel Borden*

10 9 8 7 6 5 4 3 2 1

ISBN 0-13-863077-1

Sun Microsystems Press
A Prentice Hall Title

For RoyBoy

Contents

Chapter 4
Inheritance-Based Event Handling (AWT 1.02 and Before), 65

Chapter 6

The AWT Component Class, 149

Chapter 7

Basic Components: Labels, Buttons, Canvases, and Panels, 181

Chapter 15
Lightweight Components, 475

Chapter 16
Clipboard and Data Transfer, 503

Part 3   **Appendixes**

Preface to the Second Edition

The AWT has undergone an amazing metamorphosis between 1.02 and 1.1. The 1.1 version of the AWT has been fitted with an industrial-strength event model, and support has been added for: lightweight components, clipboard and data transfer, printing, desktop colors and mouseless operation. Many shortcomings of the original AWT have been dealt with in the 1.1 release; for example, the AWT now sports both popup menus[1] and a scrollpane[2].

Perhaps more importantly, however, the 1.1 version of the AWT is much more solid than the 1.02 version. The 1.1 AWT, with the exception of a few bugs here and there, performs as advertised.

Perhaps the most exciting addition to the 1.1 AWT is support for lightweight components. Lightweight components are less resource intensive than their heavyweight counterparts, and can be transparent with an irregular (non-rectangular) border. Although the 1.1 AWT provides the infrastructure for implementing custom lightweight components, it does not provide any specific lightweight components. In a future release, the AWT will provide lightweight versions of all of the existing (heavyweight) components.

1.   See "Popup Menus" on page 320.
2.   See "java.awt.ScrollPane" on page 256.

The second edition of *Graphic Java* is based on the 1.1.2 version of the AWT. 1.1.1 and 1.1.2 were both bug fix releases; the latter hit the streets just as we went to press.

AWT/GJT Coverage

For the second edition of Graphic Java we wanted to deemphasize discussion of the Graphic Java Toolkit. Some of the feedback we received from the first edition of *Graphic Java* was that the book leaned too much towards the GJT with not enough explicit coverage of the AWT.

We have worked hard to remedy this the second time around, by adding 10 new chapters spanning 350 pages, all of which deal exclusively with the AWT:

- *Delegation-Based Event Model (AWT 1.1 and Beyond)*
- *The AWT Component Class*
- *Basic Components: Labels, Buttons, Canvases, and Panels*
- *Item Selectables: Checkboxes, Choices, and Lists*
- *Text Components*
- *Scrolling: Scrollbars and Scrollpanes*
- *Windows, Frames, and Dialogs*
- *Lightweight Components*
- *Clipboard and Data Transfer*
- *System Colors, Mouseless Operation, and Printing*

Instead of being split evenly between AWT and GJT coverage, as was the case with the first edition, 70% of *Graphic Java* is now devoted exclusively to the AWT. Also much of the original coverage of the AWT that employed the GJT to illustrate concepts has been rewritten so that it no longer uses GJT components.

Layout manager coverage has been signficiantly beefed up. In our relentless pursuit to provide you with the best `GridBagLayout` discussion on the planet, 30 new pages dedicated to `GridBagLayout` have been added to the layout manager chapter[3].

All of the chapters covering the GJT have been updated, and a good percentage have been rewritten from the ground up, such as the chapter on GJT dialogs.

---

3.   See "The GridBagLayout Layout Manager" on page 403.

The Graphic Java Toolkit (GJT)

The Graphic Java Toolkit[4] has undergone significant changes. The GJT's event handling, of course, has been updated to the new event model while other new features of 1.1, such as system colors, have been incorporated into the GJT.

The sprite animation package has been refactored[5]. Sprites are now lightweight components that are animated on a playfield that is an extension of the new `DoubleBufferedContainer` class[6], whose forte is displaying lightweight components. A fair percentage of the GJT custom components are now lightweights.

The convenience dialogs have been revamped: they can now display a picture and a panel side-by-side[7].

Then there are new components: splash screens, bubble help, toolbox, work dialog, color and cursor choices, etc.

We tried to maintain the public interfaces of the original GJT whenever possible, but in some cases we had to make modifications. If you have code that uses the original GJT, it should be a fairly simple matter to slip in the 1.1 version of the GJT, provided that you are using the 1.1 JDK, of course.

GJT JavaBeans

The Graphic Java Toolkit will soon be available in a JAR. Watch `comp.lang.java.announce` for details.

For Mac Users

Graphic Java now supports the Macintosh!

The CD in the back of the book comes complete with a 1.02 version of the GJT, along with project files for both CodeWarrior and Cafe on the Macintosh. The 1.1 JDK for the Mac was not out when we went to press.

We were pleasantly suprised with the GJT on the Mac. Certainly the state of Java affairs on the Macintosh is greatly improved since the first edition of Graphic Java, and we have confidence that the 1.1 JDK on the Mac will prove to be solid as well.

---

4. The GJT is introduced in "Introducing the Graphic Java Toolkit" on page 559.
5. See "Sprite Animation" on page 809.
6. See "DoubleBufferedContainer" on page 489.
7. See "Dialogs" on page 715.

So if you are a Mac user, here's the bottom line. All of the code discussed in *Graphic Java* has been implemented under 1.1, and therefore will not work on the Mac until the Mac 1.1 JDK comes out. When the Mac 1.1 JDK comes out, all of the code presented in *Graphic Java* should run as advertised on the Mac. The 1.02 version of the GJT is provided for those that want to get their feet wet using the 1.02 JDK, and also for anyone unfortunate enough to be unable to upgrade to 1.1.

Finally, we should note that we couldn't resist putting some Mac screenshots of GJT unit tests in the second half of the book. We should note that such screenshots are applets running under the 1.02 AWT on the Mac, and not under the 1.1 AWT as are the rest of the screenshots in the book.

Preface

Graphic Java is meant, first and foremost, to help you *master* the AWT. Both fundamental and advanced concepts of the AWT are fully explored in the pages that lie ahead. Each AWT component is examined in detail, and AWT Tips are provided to illuminate some of the AWT's dark corners. More than 50 custom components are dissected. We aim to leave no stone unturned.

What You'll Find Inside

After reading *Graphic Java*, you will have a thorough grasp of how the AWT is designed, and how to best take advantage of that design. The following is a sample of the coverage provided in the pages that lie ahead.

Peers

You will understand the peer architecture of the AWT, along with the pros and cons of the peer approach. For instance, you'll know which `Component` methods behave differently if invoked before a component's peer has been created, and what to do about it.

Clipboard and Data Transfer

You'll understand the data transfer model employed by the AWT, and how to utilize both local clipboards and the system clipboard. While the AWT only provides the ability to transfer strings to and from a clipboard, *Graphic Java* shows you how to put other data types on the clipboard, with examples of transferring both images and custom components.

Lightweight Components

In addition to being able to implement lightweight custom components, you'll also know how to drag them across a double buffered container, and even how to animate them on a playfield. You will understand how double buffering works, and why lightweight components should be displayed in a double buffered container. You will know the pitfalls of placing lightweight components in a container, and why lightweight containers must be manually fitted with a layout manager.

Layout Managers

You will have a complete grasp of layout managers, including the behemoth, `GridBagLayout`, and you will be able to implement custom layout managers with ease. You will understand how to force a container to layout its components, and why it is sometimes necessary to do so.

Internationalization and Serialization

You'll be able to internationalize a graphical user interface, and serialize both AWT components and their event listeners.

Scrolling

You will be able to scroll any number of components in a container by using a scrollpane. You'll also understand the limitations of the scrollpane class and why it is sometimes necessary to have a peerless scrolling framework. Of course, we'll discuss the implementation of such a scrolling framework from the Graphic Java Toolkit, which you are free to use for your own purposes.

Custom Components and Graphic Java

When discussing standard AWT components, we strive to take you one step further, usually by discussing the implementation of a custom component. For instance, when we cover windows, we will discuss the implementation of a splash screen, and when we explore text components, we'll look at field validation, both exit validation and on-the-fly validation. In addition to discussing dialogs in detail, five custom dialogs are examined.

The Graphic Java Toolkit

The Graphic Java Toolkit (GJT) is a collection of more than 45 custom components built using the AWT. The GJT is not a replacement for the AWT—instead it provides custom components that are not found in the AWT. The GJT is freely available; you can download it from:

```
http://www.sun.com/books/books/Geary/Geary.html
```

The GJT can be used in any product, even a commercial endeavour, as long as it is not sold as a standalone toolkit. See the license that comes on the CD for the legal details. See "Introducing the Graphic Java Toolkit" on page 559 for an introduction to the GJT.

Strategic Importance of Custom Components

All in all, more than 50 custom components are discussed in the pages ahead, such as: splash screens, bubble help, rubberbanding, sprite animation, image buttons, toolbars, custom dialogs, etc. The custom components are meant to illustrate the ins and outs of implementing custom components, while also providing you with a set of components you can use right alongside the components provided by the AWT.

Graphic Java Content

The 1.1 event model, lightweight components, clipboard and data transfer, desktop colors, mouseless operation, and printing are all thoroughly covered. You'll also find extensive coverage of scrolling, menus (including popup menus), image manipulation, graphics, fonts and fontmetrics, dialogs, text components, etc.

Extending the AWT

In Part 2 of the book, we present the Graphic Java Toolkit (GJT). In all, there are over 45 custom components in the GJT. Among these are components such as:

- Image buttons and toolbars
- Separators and bargauges
- Etched and three-dimensional rectangles and borders
- Image and component scrollers
- Rubberbands
- Convenience dialogs

The GJT also includes image filters and a package of classes for developing sprite animations. You are welcome to use and incorporate the GJT into your own program development.

In describing these custom components, we highlight lessons learned and reveal tricks of the trade for those who'll be developing their own custom components. Along the way, we hope to encourage good programming practices, using Java's object-oriented features to develop elegant, maintainable, and readable code. And we try to do these things in practical terms, so that you can see and learn from examples of real programs.

Audience

This book is written for object-oriented developers working in Java. There are numerous books explaining details of the Java language and how it works vis-a-vis Visual Basic, C, C++, etc. We leave details of how Java works to those books. If you are new to Java, you might want one of those books alongside *Graphic Java*.

The Graphic Java Toolkit

The CD that accompanies this book includes:

- The complete source code for the Graphic Java Toolkit.
- Unit test applets for all GJT components, including HTML files for unit test applets.
- HTML documentation for all GJT classes
- Numerous image files in `.gif` format developed by Pixelsite

Virtually all these programs are discussed throughout the book. Feel free to borrow, adapt, or extend these for your own purposes.

The Graphic Java Toolkit Package Structure

Table P-1 shows the GJT package structure.

Table P-1 GJT Package Structure

Package	Contents
gjt	This package contains the source files for many of the custom components discussed in *Graphic Java*.
gjt.animation	This package contains a set of classes that support sprite animation.
gjt.image	This package contains a set of classes that provide support for image manipulation such as bleaching or dissolving images.
gjt.test	This package contains source code for all the component unit tests discussed in *Graphic Java*.
gjt.rubberband	This package contains a set of classes that support rubberbanding—stretching lines and shapes over a backdrop without affecting the backdrop.

Internet Sources of Information

There are several online sources of information on Java. You can find online guides and tutorials on Sun's home page:

`http://java.sun.com/`

There is an active net newsgroup dedicated to Java:

`comp.lang.java`

There is also a mailing list where Java aficionados exchange ideas, questions, and solutions. For information about the mailing list, look on the World Wide Web at:

`http://java.sun.com/mail.html`

From these newsgroups and web sites, you'll be able to locate countless other resources, tutorials, Frequently-Asked-Questions (FAQs), and online magazines dedicated to Java.

For updates about this book and information about other books in the SunSoft Press Java Series, look on the web at:

`http://www.sun.com/books/books/Geary/Geary.html`

For some of the coolest looking graphics on the planet, take a look at:

`http://www.pixelsight.com:80/PS/pixelsite/pixelsite.html`

Conventions Used in This Book

Table P-2 shows the coding conventions used in this book.

Table P-2 Coding Conventions

Convention	Example
Class names have initial capital letters.	`public class LineOfText`
Method names have initial lowercase and the rest of the words have an initial capital letter.	`public int getLength()`
Variable names have initial lowercase and the rest of the words have an initial capital letter.	`private int length` `private int bufferLength`
`static` variables begin with an underscore.	`protected static int _defaultSize = 2;`

Note that, for the most part, we refer to methods without their arguments; however, we include the arguments when the discussion warrants including them.

Table P-3 shows the typographic conventions used in this book.

Table P-3 Typographic Conventions

Typeface or Symbol	Description
💿	Indicates that the accompanying code, command, or file is available on the CD that accompanies this book.
`courier`	Indicates a command, file name, class name, method, argument, Java keyword, HTML tag, file content, or code excerpt.
`bold courier`	Indicates a sample command-line entry.
italics	Indicates definitions, emphasis, a book title, or a variable that you should replace with a valid value.

Acknowledgments

I'd like to thank the many folks that have had a hand in *Graphic Java*. From co-workers to publishers to reviewers, to those that have filed bug reports and errata, you have all made this book better in some fashion.

Rachel Borden and John Bortner of Sun Microsystems Press, along with Greg Doench and Patti Guerrieri from Prentice Hall, have all bent over backwards to go above and beyond the call time after time. Lisa Iarkowski, Gail Cocker-Bogusz and Mary Treacy have all had a hand in one facet of the book or another.

Mary Lou Nohr, our editor, has once again done a splendid job of pointing out things like omitting commas before conjunctions in sentences with compound predicates. Her keen eye is greatly appreciated.

Thanks to the AWT team, especially Amy Fowler and Thomas Ball, who are always quick to answer my questions. The AWT team is a great group of folks who are doing an awesome job with the AWT. We should all be grateful to them for the work they did in transforming the AWT into a solid, industrial-strength toolkit.

Our immense appreciation goes to Keith Ohlfs of Pixelsite for granting permission to use all the cool images. You can see more of Keith's handiwork at:

```
http://www.pixelsight.com:80/PS/pixelsite/pixelsite.html
```

If you are a Mac user, then you'll appreciate the efforts of Wally Wedel, who put together the Mac files on the CD. Wally did an awesome job of tweaking the GJT on the Mac, in addition to running and documenting the results of unit tests under a number of different IDEs and browsers. Wally also provides some introductory material concerning the GJT and the Mac that can be viewed in your web browser. See "The Graphic Java CD-ROM" on page 851.

Thanks to Bob Sutherland for sending me email concerning `GridBagLayout` that eventually turned into the `GridBagLab` applet provided on the CD and discussed in "GridBagLab" on page 424.

A number of folks doggedly tracked down errata from the first edition. Specifically, Rick Mudgrige, Kevin Raulerson and Kevin Lewis unearthed more than their share of errata. The more dirt the readers of Graphic Java can dig up, the better the next edition will be.

Thanks to Peter Rivera and Rob Gordon for their insightful comments on the second edition.

Finally, I'd like to say a special thank you to Ashley Anna Geary, who is a bug finder extrordinaire—more software developers should have 8-year olds test their software. And to my wife Lesa, who endures the clicking of keys well into the night.

PART ONE

Exploring the Abstract Window Toolkit

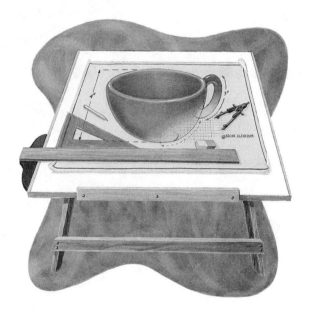

CHAPTER 1

Introduction

The Abstract Window Toolkit

Developing Java™ applets and graphical applications requires working with the Abstract Window Toolkit to some degree. Commonly referred to as the *AWT*, the Abstract Window Toolkit is part of the freely distributed Java Development Kit (JDK).

The AWT provides basic user interface components, such as buttons, lists, menus, textfields, etc. AWT components are platform independent and are primarily used to build graphical user interfaces. In addition, the AWT also provides an event handling mechanism, support for clipboard and data transfer, and image manipulation. The AWT is composed of six Java packages, shown in Table 1-1.

Table 1-1 AWT Packages

AWT Package	Description
java.awt	Basic component functionality.
java.awt.datatransfer	Clipboard and data transfer support.
java.awt.event	Event classes and listeners.
java.awt.image	Fundamental image manipulation classes.
java.awt.peer	Peer interfaces for component peers.
java.awt.test	A single applet that tests a limited subset of AWT functionality.

The original AWT was a limited and buggy toolkit that was meant to support small applets only. The current (1.1) release of the AWT is vastly improved over the original. With a redesigned event handling model, support for clipboard and data transfer, printing and mouseless operation, the AWT is now much more comparable to industrial-strength user interface frameworks such as Parc Place's VisualWorks™ or Borland's Object Windows Library™ (OWL).

Peers and Platform Independence

As the programming interface for applet and graphical application development, the AWT provides a generalized set of classes that can be used without concern for platform-specific windowing issues. This feature is made possible by a set of AWT classes known as *peers*. Peers are native GUI components which are manipulated by the AWT classes[1]. The way peers work and their influence on program development is sometimes confusing, so we'll take a closer look at them here and in subsequent chapters in this book.

The AWT components delegate a great deal of functionality to their peers. For example, when you use the AWT to create an instance of the Menu class, the Java runtime system creates an instance of a menu peer. It is the menu peer that does the real work of displaying and managing the menu behavior. In the case of a menu, the Solaris™ JDK would create a Motif® menu peer; the Windows 95™ JDK would create a Windows 95 menu peer; the Macintosh® JDK would create a Macintosh menu peer, and so on. Figure 1-1 shows how peers fit into the process of displaying components in native windowing systems.

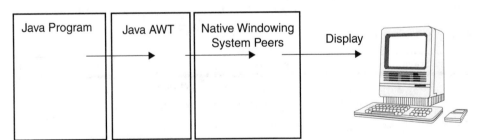

Figure 1-1 Peers at Work
A Java program creates and displays an AWT component, which creates and displays a native component (a peer).

---

1. A future version of the AWT will provide peerless components.

The decision by the Java development team to use a peer approach for portability in the AWT enabled rapid development of a cross-platform window toolkit in the JDK. Using peers obviates the need to reimplement the functionality encapsulated in native windowing components. Additionally, the use of peers enables applets and applications using the AWT to retain the look-and-feel of the native windowing system. (Remember, peers are actually native components.) The Java AWT classes are just wrappers around the peers and delegate functionality to them.

Although using the AWT rarely requires you to deal directly with peers, you might be influenced by their presence. In some ways, the peer approach makes the AWT harder to understand—so much of the implementation is buried in peers that it is sometimes difficult to trace a sequence of actions by looking through the AWT source code.

Components—The Foundation of the AWT

The AWT is a world of components; approximately half of the classes in the AWT are extensions of the `java.awt.Component` class. The `Component` class and its supporting cast are the foundation upon which the AWT is built:

- `Component` class – An abstract class for components such as menus, buttons, labels, lists, and so on.

- `Container` – An abstract class that extends `Component`. Classes derived from `Container`, most notably `Panel`, `Applet`, `Window`, `Dialog`, and `Frame`, can *contain* multiple components.

- `LayoutManager` – An interface that defines methods for positioning and sizing objects within a container. Java defines several default implementations of the `LayoutManager` interface.[2]

- `Graphics` class – An abstract class that defines methods for performing graphical operations in a component. Every component has an associated `Graphics` object.

Figure 1-2 shows a class diagram of the relationships between components, containers, and layout managers.[3]

---

2. The 1.1 version of the AWT also defines a `LayoutManager2` interface for layout managers that attach constraints to the components they lay out.
3. Graphic Java contains many class diagrams that show relationships between classes. "AWT Class Diagrams" on page 847 provides an introduction to class diagrams and a complete set of class diagrams for the AWT.

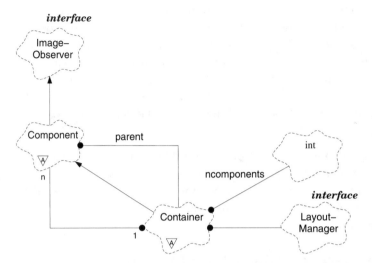

Figure 1-2 Components, Containers and Layout Managers

Components, Containers, and Layout Managers

`Component` and `Container` form a simple, yet fundamental relationship of the AWT: containers may contain components. All containers come equipped with a layout manager[4], which positions and shapes (*lays out*) the container's components. A layout manager's responsibilities are defined by the `java.awt.LayoutManager` and `LayoutManager2` interfaces. Much of the action that takes place in the AWT occurs between components, containers, and their layout managers.

Components

In Java parlance, user interface controls, such as panels, scrollbars, labels, text fields, buttons, and so on are generically referred to as *components* because they all extend `java.awt.Component`. Table 1-2 lists the AWT component classes that are ultimately derived from `java.awt.Component`.

---

4.   Except for the `java.awt.Container` class itself.

Table 1-2 AWT Components

Component	Superclass	Description
Button	Component	A textual button for triggering an action.
Canvas	Component	A canvas for painting graphics.
Checkbox	Component	A checkable boolean component.
Choice	Component	Pop-down menu of textual entries.
Dialog	Window	A window that can be modal.
FileDialog	Dialog	A platform dependent dialog for selecting files.
Frame	Window	Top-level window with titlebar and optional menubar.
Label	Component	Component that displays a string.
List	Component	A scrollable list of textual entries.
Panel	Container	A generic container of components.
Scrollbar	Component	An Adjustable component for scrolling items.
ScrollPane	Container	A scrollable container.
TextArea	TextComponent	A multi-line, scrollable textfield.
TextComponent	Component	Base functionality for TextArea and TextField.
TextField	TextComponent	A single-line component for entering text.
Window	Container	A borderless window with no title.

Figure 1-3 shows each of the standard Java AWT components (with the exception of classes that extend java.awt.Window).

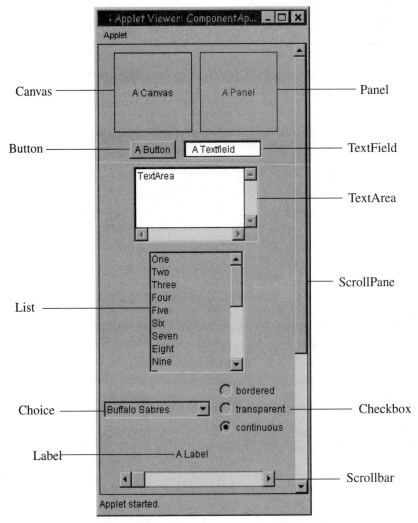

Figure 1-3 AWT Components
The AWT provides a basic set of user interface components.
Components that extend `java.awt.Window` are not shown.

What a Component Gives You

The `java.awt.Component` class is an abstract class that provides a great deal of functionality for the classes that extend it[5]. For example, a `Component` has the following affiliated with it:

- `Graphics` object
- Location
- Size
- Native peer
- Parent container
- Fonts and font dimensions (referred to as font metrics in the AWT)
- Foreground and background colors
- Locale
- Minimum, maximum and preferred sizes

Containers

`java.awt.Container` class is also an abstract class that extends `Component`. A `Container` can contain multiple components. Using containers, you can group related components and treat them as a unit. This simplifies an applet's design and is useful in arranging components on the display. Note that the `Applet` class is a subclass of `Panel`, which extends `Container`, so all applets inherit the ability to contain components.

Table 1-3 lists the AWT containers derived from the `java.awt.Container` class.

Table 1-3 `Container` **Subclasses**

Subclasses	Description
`Applet`	An extension of `Panel`. `Applet` is the superclass of all applets.
`Dialog`	An extension of `Window` that can be modal or nonmodal.
`FileDialog`	A `Dialog` for selecting a file.
`Frame`	An extension of `Window`, `Frame` is the container for an application. A `Frame` may have a menubar, but an `Applet` may not.

---

5. See "The AWT Component Class" on page 149 for a thorough discussion of `java.awt.Component`.

Table 1-3 `Container` Subclasses (Continued)

Subclasses	Description
`Panel`	An extension of `Container`, `Panel` is a simple container.
`ScrollPane`	Scrolls a component.
`Window`	An extension of `Container`, `windows` have no menu or border. `Window` is rarely extended directly; it is the superclass of `Frame` and `Dialog`.

Layout Managers

Containers merely keep track of the components they contain; they delegate the positioning and shaping of their components to a layout manager. The `LayoutManager` interface defines methods for laying out components and calculating the preferred and minimum sizes of their containers. The AWT provides five classes that implement the `LayoutManager` interface[6]:

- `BorderLayout` – Lays out North/South/East/West/Center components
- `CardLayout` – Displays one panel at a time from a deck of panels
- `FlowLayout` – Specifies that components flow left to right, top to bottom
- `GridBagLayout` – Imposes constraints on each component in a grid
- `GridLayout` – Lays out components in a simple grid; components are stretched to fill the grid

We'll discuss layout managers extensively—both the standard AWT layout managers and how to implement custom layout managers. For now, the important point is to understand at a high level how they fit into the big picture of the AWT and applet development.

6.   Actually, the classes listed implement either `LayoutManager` or `LayoutManager2`.

Summary

The AWT is a platform-independent windowing toolkit. It relies on *peers*, which are native windowing components that manage the display of applets and applications. Although their presence influences applet and graphical application development, you do not generally need to deal directly with peers.

There are four main classes in the Java Abstract Window Toolkit: the `Component` class, `Container` class, `Graphics` class, and the `LayoutManager` (and `LayoutManager2`) interfaces.

Containers contain components, and while layout managers position and shape the components contained in a container. These classes and the relationships between them form the foundation of the AWT.

CHAPTER 2

Applets and Applications

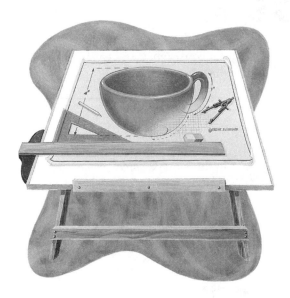

In this chapter, we will cover the basics of developing Java applets and graphical applications. We'll include some simple programs that highlight the key methods used in any applet or graphical application, and we'll discuss the relationship between an applet and the java.awt package. First, we'll take a look at applets, and then we'll go into some detail about applications, noting differences and implications of each as we go along.

Java Applets

Applets are Java programs that execute within a Java-enabled web browser. Most of the graphical support required for an applet to execute is built in to the browser. The implication for applet programmers is that you don't need to worry about creating a frame for the applet to execute in.

Using the appletviewer

Applets are launched by embedding the applet HTML tag in a web page and then viewing that page with a Java-enabled browser or the appletviewer that comes with the Java Development Kit (JDK).

For consistency and ease of illustration, all of the applets in this book are used in the following way:

```
appletviewer applet_name.html
```

In this syntax, *applet_name*.html is a minimal HTML file that can be used as an argument to the `appletviewer`. The HTML file looks like this:

```
<title>Applet Title</title>
<hr>
<applet code="applet_name.class" width=width height=height>
</applet>
<hr>
```

Each applet on the CD included with *Graphic Java* has a corresponding HTML file that can be used as an argument to `appletviewer`. Of course, these applets could also be displayed within a Java-enabled web browser, as long as the web page includes the appropriate HTML `applet` tag to call the applet. The `appletviewer` ignores all but the `applet` HTML tag, so it can be used on any HTML file with an `applet` tag.

The Browser Infrastructure

When applets are executed in a Java-enabled browser, the browser provides a great deal of the infrastructure necessary for an applet's execution. For example, when a web page containing an applet is visited, the browser calls the set of methods required to initialize and start the applet. When the web page containing an applet is no longer displayed, the browser calls methods to terminate the applet's execution.

One point that sometimes confuses developers new to Java is the absence of a `main()` statement in the applet code. In applets, `main()` is unnecessary because control for executing the applet is managed by the browser.

The java.awt.Applet Class

All applets extend `java.applet.Applet` (generically referred to as Applet).
`Applet` extends `java.awt.Panel`, as illustrated in Figure 2-1. Since `Panel` is
an AWT container, it has a default layout manager—a `FlowLayout`, which lays
out the applet's components[1].

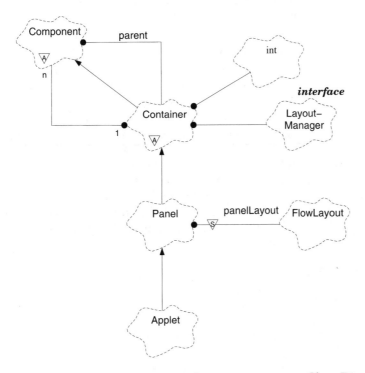

Figure 2-1 `Applet`, `Container`, and `LayoutManager` Class Diagram
An `Applet` is a container with a default, `FlowLayout` layout manager.

Key Applet Methods

The `Applet` class provides a basic set of methods that define the overall behavior
of applets. An applet's execution is controlled by four methods: `init()`,
`start()`, `stop()`, and `destroy()`. You don't typically call these methods

1. See "The FlowLayout Layout Manager" on page 399.

directly—rather, they are invoked automatically either by the browser or the
appletviewer. (Note, however, that these methods are commonly overridden
in classes that classes that extend Applet.) Table 2-1 summarizes their use.

Table 2-1 Commonly Used applet.Applet **Methods**

Key Applet Methods	Description
init()	When a document with an applet is opened, the init() method is called to initialize the applet.
start()	When a document with an applet is opened, the start() method is called after the init() method to start the applet.
stop()	When a document with an applet is no longer displayed, the stop() method is called. This method is always called before the destroy() method is called.
destroy()	After the stop() method has been called, the destroy() method is called to clean up any resources that are being held.

Example 2-1 shows a simple applet and the use of the init(), start(),
stop(), and destroy() methods; these methods are commonly overridden.
StarterApplet overrides them simply to highlight when they are executed.
The start() method also adds a "Starter" label to the applet every time it is
called. Additionally, note that StarterApplet, like all applets, extends the
java.appelt.Applet class.

Example 2-1 Starter Applet

```java
import java.appplet.Applet;
import java.awt.Label;

public class StarterApplet extends Applet {
  private Label label;

  public void init() {
    System.out.println("Applet.init()");
  }
  public void start() {
    System.out.println("Applet.start()");
    label = new Label("Starter");
    add(label);
  }
  public void stop() {
    System.out.println("Applet.stop()");
    remove(label);
  }
  public void destroy() {
    System.out.println("Applet.destroy()");
  }
}
```

This applet could be executed by running `appletviewer` on the following HTML file:

```
<title>Starter Applet</title>
<hr>
<applet code="StarterApplet.class" width=300 height=100>
</applet>
<hr>
```

Figure 2-2 shows the applet window.

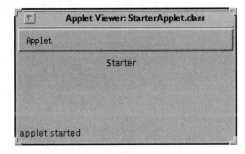

Figure 2-2 A Starter Applet

Starting the `Starter` applet results in the following output:

```
Applet.init()
Applet.start()
```

Exiting the applet results in the following output:

```
Applet.stop()
Applet.destroy()
```

java.awt.Component Display Methods

The `java.awt.Component` class implements methods to update its display: `paint()`, `repaint()`, and `update()`. Table 2-2 summarizes how they work.

Table 2-2 Commonly Used `awt.Component` **Methods**

Component **Display Methods**	**Description**
`paint()`	Paints the component.
`repaint()`	Schedules a call to the component's `update()` method as soon as possible.
`update()`	Is responsible for redrawing the component. The default version redraws the background and calls the `paint()` method.

Java Applications

Applications are invoked from the command line and executed by the `java` interpreter. From the developer's point of view, there are primarily two differences between a Java applet and a Java application:

- An application must include a `main()` method.

- If the application requires a window, it must extend the AWT `Frame` class. A `Frame` is a window in which the application is displayed and, like all containers, comes with a layout manager for positioning and sizing its components.

There is one other notable distinction between a Java application and a Java applet. An application does not have the same security restrictions that an applet does. Whereas untrusted applets cannot write or modify files, an application can perform file I/O. Applications are not constrained by the security restrictions that Java-enabled browsers enforce on applets.

Setting Up an Application

Unlike applets, applications must extend the `Frame` class in order to provide a window in which to run, as in Example 2-2.

Example 2-2 Starter Application

```
import java.awt.Event;
import java.awt.Frame;
import java.awt.event.*;
import java.awt.Label;

public class StarterApplication extends Frame {
  public static void main(String args[]) {
    StarterApplication app = new StarterApplication("Starter
                                                   Application");
    app.setSize(300,100);
    app.show();
    System.out.println("StarterApplication.main()");
  }
  public StarterApplication(String frameTitle) {
    super(frameTitle);
    add   (new Label("Starter", Label.CENTER), "Center");

    addWindowListener(new WindowAdapter() {
       public void windowClosing(WindowEvent event) {
          dispose();
          System.exit(0);
       }
    });
  }
}
```

This is a fairly simple application, but it's worth noting exactly how it works since it is different from the applet on page 16 in several ways. The first thing to note is that the application does not import and extend `java.applet.Applet`. Instead, it imports and extends `java.awt.Frame`.

The next important distinction is that the application implements a `main()` method. All Java applications require a `main()` method, just like a C or C++ program; `main()` is the first method invoked in an application. The `main()` method of `StarterApplication` creates an instance of a `StarterApplication` (a `Frame`), which it resizes and shows. The constructor for the `StarterApplication` class initializes a `StarterApplication` instance.

Finally, a window listener is added to the frame, in order to dispose of the window and exit the application when the window is closed[2].

Displaying Applications

Graphical applications, like all other Java applications, are executed directly by the `java` interpreter. For example, the compiled application in Example 2-2 is executed in the following manner:

```
java StarterApplication
```

The Java interpreter then runs the application, as shown in Figure 2-3.

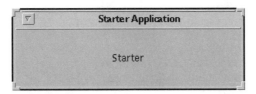

Figure 2-3 A Java Application
The `StarterApplication` implements a `WindowListener` that exits
the application when the user activates the quit menu from the system menu.

Combining Applet and Application Code

There are a number of ways to write a Java program so that it can execute either from within a browser or as a standalone application. One way to do this is to center an `Applet` within a `Frame`, as in Example 2-3.

2.   See "Frames Don't Close By Default" on page 286.

Example 2-3 Combining Applet and Application Code

```java
import java.applet.Applet;
import java.awt.Event;
import java.awt.Frame;
import java.awt.event.*;
import java.awt.Label;

public class StarterCombined extends Applet {
  private Label label;

  public static void main(String args[]) {
    StarterCombinedFrame app = new StarterCombinedFrame("Starter
        Application");
    app.setSize(300,100);
    app.show();
    System.out.println("StarterCombinedFrame.main()");
  }
  public void init() {
    System.out.println("Applet.init()");
  }
  public void start() {
    System.out.println("Applet.start()");
    label = new Label("Starter");
    add(label);
  }
  public void stop() {
    System.out.println("Applet.stop()");
    remove(label);
  }
  public void destroy() {
    System.out.println("Applet.destroy()");
  }
}
class StarterCombinedFrame extends Frame {
  public StarterCombinedFrame(String frameTitle) {
    super(frameTitle);

    StarterCombined applet = new StarterCombined();

    applet.start();
    add (applet, "Center");
    addWindowListener(new WindowAdapter() {
      public void windowClosing(WindowEvent event) {
          dispose();
          System.exit(0);
      }
    });
  }
}
```

The `import` statements import the essential classes needed for both an applet and an application. Putting the `main()` method in the applet class enables the program to be executed with the same argument, whether it is going to run as an applet or as an application. For example, the following command would execute it as an application:

```
java StarterCombined
```

Using the `appletviewer` on the following HTML file would execute the code as an applet:

```
<title>Starter Combined Test</title>
<hr>
<applet code="StarterCombined.class" width=300 height=100>
</applet>
<hr>
```

If the program is run as an applet, the `main()` method is completely ignored; instead, the browser or `appletviewer` invokes the `init()` and `start()` methods to start the applet.

`StarterCombinedFrame` provides a `Frame` for the application to run in. StarterCombinedFrame creates an instance of the applet, which is created and centered in the `Frame`.

Summary

Both applets and applications are executed by the Java `java` interpreter. Applications must create their own frame, whereas while applets run in the frame provided by the Java-enabled web browser or `appletviewer`. As a result, applications must handle window closing events, while an applet's execution is controlled by the browser or `appletviewer`. Applications are free to read and write files, but untrusted applets are not permitted to do so.

CHAPTER

3

Graphics, Colors, and Fonts

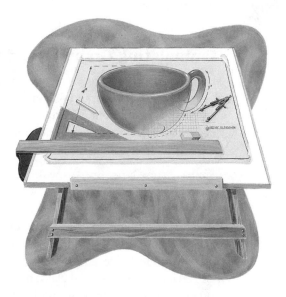

This chapter introduces the Java AWT `Graphics` class. The `Graphics` class provides graphical support for components ranging from painting and filling shapes to drawing images and strings to manipulation of graphical regions. AWT programmers are typically involved with the `Graphics` class before they know it, so this chapter illustrates some of the nuances of using the `Graphics` class. Additionally, we will introduce the AWT `Color`, `Font`, and `FontMetrics` classes.

This chapter introduces four custom components (`DrawnRectangle`, `EtchedRectangle`, `ThreeDRectangle`, and `LabelCanvas`) from the Graphic Java Toolkit (GJT). These custom components extend the AWT, but the focus in this chapter is less on extending the AWT and more on the specific use of the `Graphics`, `Color`, `Font`, and `FontMetrics` classes. Rather than provide arbitrary examples to highlight the use of these AWT classes, we've chosen to discuss custom components from the GJT. (Other custom components in the Graphic Java Toolkit are discussed in *Extending the AWT—The Graphic Java Toolkit*.)

Manipulating Graphics and Color

The `java.awt.Graphics` class is an abstract class that defines a collection of abstract methods for drawing, copying, clipping, filling, and clearing graphical regions in a component. Nearly all applets that use the AWT manipulate a `Graphics` object for at least one graphic service. For example, even simple Hello World applets are quick to use a `Graphics` object to display their clever verbiage:

```
public void paint(Graphics g) {
  g.drawString("Hello Graphic Java World", 75, 100);
}
```

While the AWT contains classes for user interface components such as buttons, menus, dialogs, and so on, it surprisingly does not include anything analogous to purely graphical objects. For example, the AWT does not provide a `Line` class or a `Circle` class. The `Shape` class, the prototypical example of object-oriented case studies[1], is nowhere to be found in the AWT[2].

Instead of providing purely graphical objects, the AWT employs a simpler (albeit less flexible and extensible) model. Each component comes complete with its own `Graphics` object, through which graphical operations can be performed in the component.

The `Graphics` class is a veritable kitchen sink of graphical operations. Its 47 public methods can be used for drawing strings, filling shapes, drawing images, painting with different colors, and much more. All of the graphical operations performed take place in the `Graphics` object associated component.

If you wanted to draw a line in a component, for instance, instead of creating a `Line` object and invoking its `draw()` method, you would obtain the component's `Graphics` object and invoke `Graphics.drawLine()`.

The AWT also includes a `Color` class. For this discussion, we are only interested in using `Color` constants, such as `Color.blue`, `Color.red`, and so on, and in obtaining lighter or darker shades of a color. (The AWT `Color` class is much more interesting when it comes to manipulating images, which we describe in "Images" on page 329.)

1. See Stroustrup, Bjarne. *The C++ Programming Language, section 6.4.2*. Addison-Wesley.
2. This will change in future releases of the AWT—as a matter of fact, the 1.1 version of the AWT contains a `Shape` interface, for future use.

To show in greater detail how to manipulate a `Graphics` object, we're going to present a class from the GJT that draws a rectangle. We'll then discuss extensions of that class to illustrate some finer points, such as how to draw etched and three-dimensional lines for the rectangle's border.

Figure 3-1 shows the various rectangles based on GJT classes we'll present in this chapter.

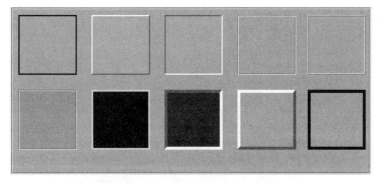

Figure 3-1 Rectangles
The `gjt.*Rectangle` classes in this chapter can be used to draw a variety of rectangles within a component. These classes manipulate a component's `Graphics` object to draw and color a rectangle in a number of different ways.

Drawing a Rectangle

You might have noticed that the AWT does include a `Rectangle` class, which might lead you to believe that we've hoodwinked you in our previous discussion. However, `Rectangle`, `Polygon`, and `Point` classes were added as afterthoughts to the original AWT, and since the original design did not allow for purely graphical objects, these classes wound up without any graphical capabilities. In other words, you cannot draw instances of `awt.Rectangle`, `awt.Polygon`, or `awt.Point`. You can only set and get information about the geometric entity that each represents.

To facilitate examples of a `Graphics` object in action, we'll introduce the handy `gjt.DrawnRectangle`. The `gjt.DrawnRectangle` class is simply a `Rectangle` that can be drawn inside of a component. Instances of `gjt.DrawnRectangle` draw themselves in different line widths and colors and are also able to fill themselves with a color on demand. `gjt.DrawnRectangle` is also the base class for `gjt.EtchedRectangle` and `gjt.ThreeDRectangle`, which we will discuss shortly.

It is worthwhile to note that `gjt.DrawnRectangle` (and the classes that extend it) represent the only custom components in the Graphic Java Toolkit that do not extend the `java.awt.Component` class; that is, they extend `Rectangle` and not `Component`. This fact has no bearing on the concepts we are stressing in this chapter, but it is interesting to note, for example, that `gjt.DrawnRectangle` has a `public void paint()` method that is unrelated to the `public void paint(Graphics g)` method from the `Component` class.

Overview of DrawnRectangle

The `gjt.DrawnRectangle` class paints rectangles with specified line width, line color, and fill color. Figure 3-2 shows two instances of the `gjt.DrawnRectangle` class with varying parameters.

Figure 3-2 Drawn Rectangles
The `gjt.DrawnRectangle` class provides methods for drawing rectangles with varying line widths and colors. `gjt.DrawnRectangle` also includes support for filling and clearing the interior of the rectangle.

The `gjt.DrawnRectangle` class includes four constructors:

❶
```
public DrawnRectangle(Component drawInto) {
    this(drawInto, _defaultThickness, 0, 0, 0, 0);
}
```
❷
```
public DrawnRectangle(Component drawInto, int thick) {
    this(drawInto, thick, 0, 0, 0, 0);
}
```
❸
```
public DrawnRectangle(Component drawInto, int x, int y,
                                          int w, int h) {
    this(drawInto, _defaultThickness, x, y, w, h);
}
```
❹
```
public DrawnRectangle(Component drawInto, int thick,
                      int x, int y, int w, int h) {
```
❺
```
    Assert.notNull(drawInto);
    Assert.notFalse(thick > 0);

    this.drawInto = drawInto;
    this.thick    = thick;
    setBounds(x,y,w,h);
}
```

All the action that's fit to take place in the AWT takes place inside a `Component`; therefore, `gjt.DrawnRectangle` requires you to pass it a `Component` at construction time. The `Component` passed into the `gjt.DrawnRectangle` constructor is assigned to the aptly named `drawInto` member, which is the `Component` into which the rectangle will be drawn. (The `Assert.notNull` in line ❺ ensures that `gjt.DrawnRectangle` won't accept a `null` component. Refer to *Introducing the Graphic Java Toolkit* for more information on the Graphic Java Toolkit utility classes.)

The constructors in lines ❶, ❷, and ❸ call another constructor—the one in line ❹. Using multiple constructors that eventually call just one constructor that does all the work is fairly typical, and we use the technique throughout this book. For example, the statement:

```
this(drawInto, _defaultThickness, 0, 0, 0, 0);
```

in the first constructor actually calls the constructor in line ❹, which sets the `drawInto` component and border thickness and calls the `Rectangle.setBounds()` method. If you use the first constructor and just give it a `Component` for an argument, a `gjt.DrawnRectangle` starts at position 0,0, with a width of 0 and a height of 0. You can also call the constructor in line ❹ explicitly and provide a specific x,y starting position, width, and height.

Before looking at the `gjt.DrawnRectangle` code in Example 3-1 on page 32, it's useful to see an overview of its responsibilities (that is, its public methods), as in Table 3-1.

Table 3-1 `gjt.DrawnRectangle` **Responsibilities**

Methods	Description
`Component component()`	Returns the `Component` drawn into.
`int getThickness()`	Returns the line thickness.
`void setThickness(int thick)`	Sets the line thickness.
`void setLineColor(` `Color lineColor)`	Sets the line color. If not set explicitly, the line color used is three shades darker than the background color of the component being drawn into.
`void setFillColor(` `Color fillColor)`	Sets the color used to fill the rectangle.
`void fill()`	Fills the inside of the rectangle with the current fill color. (It does not obliterate the border of the rectangle.)
`Color getLineColor()`	Returns the current line color.
`Color getFillColor()`	Returns the current fill color.

Table 3-1 gjt.DrawnRectangle **Responsibilities (Continued)**

Methods	Description
Rectangle getInnerBounds()	Returns the boundary inside the border of the rectangle.
void paint()	Paints the rectangle inside the associated component.
void clearInterior()	Clears the interior of the rectangle.
void clearExterior()	Erases the lines of the rectangle.
void clear()	Erases the border of the rectangle and clears the rectangle's interior.
String toString()	Returns a String containing information about the DrawnRectangle.
String paramString()	Reports values for specific parameters such as DrawnRectangle's color, line thickness, and line color.

The associations (that is, class members) for gjt.DrawnRectangle are listed in Table 3-2.

Table 3-2 gjt.DrawnRectangle **Associations**

Variable	Description
protected static int _defaultThickness	Defines the default thickness as 2 pixels.
protected Component drawInto	Defines the component to be drawn into.
private int thick;	Line thickness.
private Color lineColor	Line color.
private Color fillColor	Fill color.

Before looking at the gjt.DrawnRectangle class in its entirety, we're going to pull out sections of it to specifically highlight some of its graphical operations and color manipulation, including:

- Obtaining a component's Graphics object
- Obtaining a component's background color
- Obtaining a darker or brighter shade of a color
- Filling a rectangle in a component
- Drawing lines in a component

Now let's look at how the Graphics object and color are manipulated by the gjt.DrawnRectangle class.

Obtaining a Component's Graphics Object

Every component has a Graphics object affiliated with it. To manipulate a Graphics object first requires obtaining a handle by which to access it. This is accomplished by using the getGraphics() method in the Component class. In the DrawnRectangle class, we obtain a handle on the Graphics object affiliated with drawInto (a Component):

```
Graphics g = drawInto.getGraphics();
```

You'll notice in the gjt.DrawnRectangle class that whenever we want to perform graphical operations in the drawInto component, we first obtain the Graphics object affiliated with drawInto. The Graphics object can then be manipulated in a variety of ways, as it is in the gjt.DrawnRectangle class paint(), clearExterior(), and fill() methods.

Disposing of a Graphics Object

Graphics objects obtained by a call to getGraphics() must be disposed of in order to reclaim system resources associated with the native graphics context. Disposing of a graphics object is accomplished by invoking Graphics.dispose(). While Java has garbage collection, there are a couple of places in the AWT where it is up to you to dispose of system resources, and this is one of them[3].

Notice that we explicitly specified that only graphics objects obtained by a call to getGraphics() need to be disposed by invoking Graphics.dispose(). Graphics objects that are passed to Component methods, such as Component.paint() and Component.update() do not need to be disposed of—they are automatically disposed of by the Component class itself after the call to paint() returns.

Obtaining a Component's Background Color

The Component.getBackground() method returns the component's current background color. In the gjt.DrawnRectangle class, the getFillColor() method invokes the drawInto component's getBackground() method:

```
public Color getFillColor() {
  if(fillColor == null)
    fillColor = drawInto.getBackground();
  return fillColor;
}
```

3. Windows and dialogs must also be disposed of. See "Windows, Frames, and Dialogs" on page 273.

If the fill color has not been explicitly set, getFillColor() calls the drawInto component's getBackground() method to obtain the current background color and sets it to the fillColor member of the DrawnRectangle.

Obtaining a Shade of a Color

The key to obtaining a darker shade of a color is to use the darker() method from the Color class. Conversely, there is a corresponding brighter() method also available in the Color class. You can obtain incrementally darker or brighter shades of a color by repeatedly calling either the darker() or brighter() methods, respectively. The gjt.DrawnRectangle.brighter() method always returns four shades brighter than the current line color:

```
protected Color brighter() {
  return
    getLineColor().brighter().brighter().brighter().brighter();
}
```

OO TIP

Provide Defaults, But Let Clients Override

DrawnRectangle provides default values for both line thickness and line color; however, it also allows clients (and DrawnRectangle extensions) to override those values. Although it does not always make sense to do so, providing defaults that clients can override gives them the best of both worlds; they don't have to deal with such values unless they have a good reason to do so.

Filling a Rectangle

Filling a rectangle relies on the fillRect() and setColor() methods from the Graphics class. Our gjt.DrawnRectangle class has a fill() method that uses both methods to fill a rectangle with the current fill color:

```
public void fill(Color color) {
  Graphics g = drawInto.getGraphics();

  if(g != null) {
    Rectangle r = getInnerBounds();
    g.setColor(color);
    g.fillRect(r.x, r.y, r.width, r.height);
    setFillColor(color);
    g.dispose();
  }
}
```

The `fill()` method invokes `DrawnRectangle.getInnerBounds()`, which returns the boundary *inside* the lines drawn for the rectangle, as illustrated in Figure 3-3.

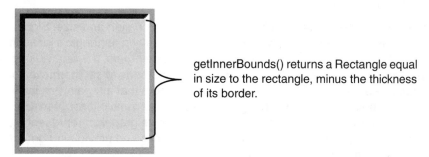

getInnerBounds() returns a Rectangle equal in size to the rectangle, minus the thickness of its border.

Figure 3-3 Calculating the Inner Bounds of a `DrawnRectangle` The `gjt.DrawnRectangle.getInnerBounds()` method creates a new instance of a `Rectangle` with dimensions equal to the area inside its border. (For the sake of illustration, we're using a 3-D rectangle here, even though we haven't discussed it yet. Its broad border lines make it easier to show the inner bounds of the rectangle.)

Once the `fill()` method has obtained the inner bounds of the rectangle, it sets the specified color and fills the rectangle with the `Graphics setColor()` and `fillRect()` methods. The call to `setFillColor()` sets the `DrawnRectangle` `fillColor` to the color passed into `fill()`.

gjt.DrawnRectangle Implementation

Now let's look at the `gjt.DrawnRectangle` implementation. Several general points are worth highlighting. First, notice that it extends the `Rectangle` class:

```
public class DrawnRectangle extends Rectangle {
```

This means that the size and location for a `gjt.DrawnRectangle` can be set, just like a `java.awt.Rectangle`.

OO TIP

Avoid Public Members

java.awt.Rectangle contains public members for its location and size. Since gjt.DrawnRectangle extends java.awt.Rectangle, a drawn rectangle's location or size may be changed by direct manipulation of its members. If java.awt.Rectangle had made its members private and provided methods to set them, we could override those methods in DrawnRectangle to ensure that a repaint() is invoked whenever the size or location changes. Instead, it is possible for a DrawnRectangle's size and/or location to be out of synch with its graphical representation. It is best to always limit access to members of a class and provide set/get methods instead of making members public.

You'll want to pay particular attention in Example 3-1 to the way this class deals with the Graphics object—it's a parameter in several methods—and the Color object, both of which we've already mentioned.

Example 3-1 gjt.DrawnRectangle **Source Code**

```
package gjt;
import java.awt.*;

public class DrawnRectangle extends Rectangle {
  protected static int    _defaultThickness = 2;

  protected Component drawInto;
  private    int        thick;
  private    Color      lineColor, fillColor;

  public DrawnRectangle(Component drawInto) {
      this(drawInto, _defaultThickness, 0, 0, 0, 0);
  }
  public DrawnRectangle(Component drawInto, int thick) {
      this(drawInto, thick, 0, 0, 0, 0);
  }
  public DrawnRectangle(Component drawInto,
                        int x, int y, int w, int h) {
      this(drawInto, _defaultThickness, x, y, w, h);
  }
  public DrawnRectangle(Component drawInto,
                        int thick, int x, int y, int w, int h) {
      Assert.notNull(drawInto);
      Assert.notFalse(thick > 0);

      this.drawInto = drawInto;
```

```
        this.thick    = thick;
        setBounds(x,y,w,h);
    }
    public Component component()           {return drawInto;    }
    public int  getThickness  ()           {return thick;        }
    public void setThickness  (int thick) {this.thick = thick;  }

    public void setLineColor(Color lineColor) {
        this.lineColor = lineColor;
    }
    public void setFillColor(Color fillColor) {
        this.fillColor = fillColor;
    }
    public void fill() {
        fill(getFillColor());
    }
    public Color getLineColor() {
        if(lineColor == null)
            lineColor = SystemColor.controlShadow;
        return lineColor;
    }
    public Color getFillColor() {
        if(fillColor == null)
            fillColor = drawInto.getBackground();
        return fillColor;
    }
    public Rectangle getInnerBounds() {
        return
            new Rectangle(x+thick, y+thick,
                          width-(thick*2), height-(thick*2));
    }
    public void paint() {
        Graphics g = drawInto.getGraphics();
        paintFlat(g, getLineColor());
    }
    private void paintFlat(Graphics g, Color color) {
        if(g != null) {
            g.setColor(color);

            for(int i=0; i < thick; ++i)
                g.drawRect(x+i, y+i, width-(i*2)-1, height-(i*2)-1);

          g.dispose();
        }
    }
    public void clearInterior() {
        fill(drawInto.getBackground());
    }
```

```
public void clearExterior() {
    paintFlat(drawInto.getGraphics(),drawInto.getBackground());
}
public void clear() {
    clearExterior();
    clearInterior();
}
public void fill(Color color) {
    Graphics g = drawInto.getGraphics();

    if(g != null) {
      Rectangle r = getInnerBounds();
      g.setColor(color);
      g.fillRect(r.x, r.y, r.width, r.height);
      setFillColor(color);
      g.dispose();
    }
}
public String toString() {
    return super.toString() + "[" + paramString() + "]";
}
public String paramString() {
    return "color=" + getLineColor() + ",thickness=" +
            thick + ",fillColor=" + getFillColor();
}
protected Color brighter() {
    return
    getLineColor().brighter().brighter().brighter().brighter();
}
}
```

> ## OO TIP
>
> *Think Small*
>
> Take a look at the implementations of DrawnRectangle.clear() and DrawnRectangle.paint(), and see how long it takes you to figure out what each method does. The DrawnRectangle class has a paltry 1.8 lines of code per method, resulting in two very important benefits: It makes each method easy to understand, and it provides a granularity that reduces bugs and simplifies code extension and modification. For instance, take a look at the implementation of DrawnRectangle.getInnerBounds(). This method reports the bounding box inside of the DrawnRectangle (excluding the border). Since the method is only used in DrawnRectangle.fill(Color), it may seem superfluous to put such a simple calculation in its own method. Realize, however, that derived classes and clients of DrawnRectangle will find innerBounds() very useful, and as DrawnRectangle matures, it may very well find a need for innerBounds() in other methods that materialize down the road.

Drawing an Etched Rectangle

Etched rectangles are useful in a number of contexts in graphical user interfaces. The gjt.EtchedRectangle class is an extension of the DrawnRectangle class that manipulates line thickness and shading to make it appear as though its border is etched either in or out.

The gjt.EtchedRectangle class provides methods for drawing etched-in or etched-out borders. Figure 3-4 shows instances of both an etched-in and etched-out gjt.EtchedRectangle.

Figure 3-4 Etched Rectangles
The gjt.EtchedRectangle class extends gjt.DrawnRectangle and overrides paint() to draw etched borders.

Table 3-3 lists the responsibilities of the `gjt.EtchedRectangle` class.

Table 3-3 `gjt.EtchedRectangle` **Responsibilities**

Methods	Description
`void etchedIn()`	Sets the etching value to `Etching.IN`.
`void etchedOut()`	Sets the etching value to `Etching.OUT`.
`boolean isEtchedIn()`	Returns `true` if etched in, false if etched out.
`void paint()`	Draws an etched border.
`void paintEtchedIn()`	Calls `etchedIn()` and passes appropriate color values to `paintEtched()`.
`void paintEtchedOut()`	Calls `etchedOut()` and passes appropriate color values to `paintEtched()`.
`String paramString()`	Reports values for the etched rectangle's line color, thickness, bounds, and whether it is etched in or out.

Example 3-2 shows the code for the `gjt.EtchedRectangle` class in its entirety; then we highlight specifically how it:

- Paints an etched-in border

- Paints an etched-out border

Note that the `paint()` method calls appropriately named methods for painting etched in and etched out, depending upon the current state of the `gjt.EtchedRectangle`. Also, pay attention to the use of the `DrawnRectangle.brighter()` method, which is used for shading the rectangle borders to create the etched effect. (The `Etching` and `ThreeDBorderStyle` classes referenced in this program are simply GJT classes that implement type-safe constants. Refer to *Introducing the Graphic Java Toolkit* for a discussion of the Graphic Java Toolkit utility classes.)

Example 3-2 `gjt.EtchedRectangle` **Class Source Code**

```
package gjt;

import java.awt.*;

public class EtchedRectangle extends DrawnRectangle {
   protected static Etching _defaultEtching = Etching.IN;
   private Etching etching;

   public EtchedRectangle(Component drawInto) {
      this(drawInto, _defaultEtching,
         _defaultThickness, 0, 0, 0, 0);
```

```
}
public EtchedRectangle(Component drawInto, int thickness) {
    this(drawInto, _defaultEtching, thickness, 0, 0, 0, 0);
}
public EtchedRectangle(Component drawInto, int x, int y,
                                          int w, int h) {
    this(drawInto, _defaultEtching,
        _defaultThickness, x, y, w, h);
}
public EtchedRectangle(Component drawInto, int thickness,
                                          int x, int y,
                                          int w, int h) {
    this(drawInto, _defaultEtching, thickness, x, y, w, h);
}
public EtchedRectangle(Component drawInto, Etching etching,
                       int thickness, int x, int y,
                       int w, int h) {
    super(drawInto, thickness, x, y, w, h);
    this.etching = etching;
}
public void    etchedIn  () { etching = Etching.IN;        }
public void    etchedOut () { etching = Etching.OUT;       }
public boolean isEtchedIn() { return etching == Etching.IN;}

public void paint() {
    if(etching == Etching.IN) paintEtchedIn();
    else                      paintEtchedOut();
}
public void paintEtchedIn() {
    Graphics g = drawInto.getGraphics();
    if(g != null)
        paintEtched(g, getLineColor(), brighter());

    etchedIn();
}
public void paintEtchedOut() {
    Graphics g = drawInto.getGraphics();
    if(g != null)
        paintEtched(g, brighter(), getLineColor());

    etchedOut();
}
public String paramString() {
    return super.paramString() + "," + etching;
}
private void paintEtched(Graphics g,
                         Color topLeft,
                         Color bottomRight) {
```

```
int  thickness = getThickness();
int  w = width  - thickness;
int  h = height - thickness;

g.setColor(topLeft);

for(int i=0; i < thickness/2; ++i)
   g.drawRect(x+i, y+i, w, h);

g.setColor(bottomRight);

for(int i=0; i < thickness/2; ++i)
   g.drawRect(x+(thickness/2)+i,
              y+(thickness/2)+i, w, h);

   g.dispose();
  }
}
```

Painting Etched-in and Etched-out Borders

By default, an instance of gjt.EtchedRectangle paints itself *etched in*. The state of its etching can be changed by calling the etchedIn() and etchedOut() methods; however, only the state is changed and the EtchedRectangle does not repaint itself. To change the state and repaint in one fell swoop, you can use the paintEtchedIn() and paintEtchedOut() methods. For instance, paintEtchedIn() looks like this:

```
public void paintEtchedIn() {
  Graphics g = drawInto.getGraphics();

  if(g != null)
     paintEtched(g, getLineColor(), brighter());

  etchedIn();
}
```

The call to paintEtched() includes parameters for the topLeft color and bottomRight color of the rectangles to be drawn. The call to etchedIn() simply sets the state to Etching.IN.

paintEtchedOut() is a mirror image of paintEtchedIn(). It switches the values of the topLeft and bottomRight arguments to paintEtched() and then sets the state to Etching.OUT.

```
public void paintEtchedOut() {
  Graphics g = drawInto.getGraphics();
```

```
    if(g != null)
        paintEtched(g, brighter(), getLineColor());

  etchedOut();
}
```

Notice that neither `paintEtchedIn()` nor `paintEtchedOut()` calls `dispose()` on the graphics object obtained by invoking `Component.getGraphics()` because `paintEtched()` disposes of the graphics context it is passed, as we shall soon discover.

The `paintEtchedIn()` and `paintEtchedOut()` methods rely on the private `paintEtched()` method to draw rectangles and to manipulate the line shading appropriately. This observation leads to the next topic, which is how the `EtchedRectangle.paintEtched()` method achieves its etching effect.

The trick used in `paintEtched()` to create the etching effect is to draw two rectangles, one slightly offset from the other and then to draw each rectangle's border in slightly different shades. Figure 3-5 shows how this technique is used in the `gjt.EtchedRectangle` class.

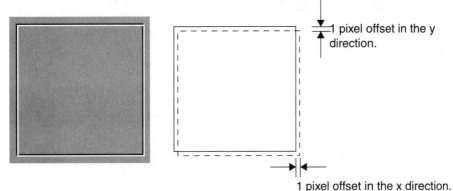

Figure 3-5 Achieving an Etched Effect
The `gjt.EtchedRectangle` achieves its etched effect by drawing two rectangles, one slightly offset from the other, in different shades of the same color.

Here's the `paintEtched()` method that paints either etched-in or etched-out:

```
private void paintEtched(Graphics g,
                         Color topLeft,
                         Color bottomRight) {
  int  thickness = getThickness();
  int  w = width  - thickness;
  int  h = height - thickness;
```

```
    g.setColor(topLeft);

    for(int i=0; i < thickness/2; ++i)
       g.drawRect(x+i, y+i, w, h);

    g.setColor(bottomRight);

    for(int i=0; i < thickness/2; ++i)
       g.drawRect(x+(thickness/2)+i,
                  y+(thickness/2)+i, w, h);

    g.dispose();
  }
```

For an etched-in effect, the lines in the first rectangle are drawn in the current line color, and the offset rectangle's lines are drawn in a brighter color. For an etched-out effect, it is just the opposite. Finally, notice that paintEtched() disposes of the graphics context it is passed, which frees paintEtchedIn() and paintEtchedOut() from that responsibility.

Drawing a 3-D Rectangle

The ability to draw a three-dimensional rectangle is another useful feature in the applet developer's toolkit. Note that we could use the draw3DRect() method from the Graphics class to draw 3-D rectangles, but we want more flexibility in choosing the border thickness and more robust default behavior than draw3DRect() provides. In particular, the Graphics.draw3DRect() method always draws a rectangle whose borders are only one pixel thick, and it creates discernible 3-D shading only when the color is set to lightGray.

The gjt.ThreeDRectangle class provides methods for drawing raised or inset borders, which achieve a 3-D visual effect. Figure 3-6 shows use of ThreeDRectangle to create 3-D borders of varying thickness.

Figure 3-6 Three-Dimensional Rectangles
The `gjt.ThreeDRectangle` class extends `DrawnRectangle` and overrides `paint()` to paint a three-dimensional border.

Table 3-4 lists the responsibilities of a `gjt.ThreeDRectangle`.

Table 3-4 `gjt.ThreeDRectangle` **Responsibilities**

Methods	Description
`void paint()`	Calls either `paintRaised()` or `paintInset()`, depending on the current state of the rectangle. This dictates whether the rectangle is drawn raised or inset.
`void raise()`	Sets the border style to `ThreeDBorderStyle.RAISED` for the next call to `paint()`.
`void inset()`	Sets the border style to `ThreeDBorderStyle.INSET` for the next call to `paint()`.
`boolean isRaised()`	Returns the current state of the border.
`String paramString()`	Returns a string of `DrawnRectangle` parameters.
`void paintRaised()`	Draws rectangle borders with the top and left lines brighter than the bottom and right lines.
`void paintInset()`	Draws rectangle borders with the bottom and right lines brighter than the top and left lines.

Example 3-3 lists the source code for the `gjt.ThreeDRectangle` class. `gjt.ThreeDRectangle` overrides `paint()` to paint a 3-D border. We'll first show the entire class and then highlight specifically how it:

- Paints a raised 3-D border

- Paints an inset 3-D border

You'll probably notice that `gjt.ThreeDRectangle` is very similar to `gjt.EtchedRectangle`. They are structured similarly, and both override `paint()` to produce etching and three-dimensional effects.

Example 3-3 `gjt.ThreeDRectangle` **Class Source Code**

```
package gjt;

import java.awt.*;

public class ThreeDRectangle extends DrawnRectangle {
  protected static BorderStyle
                    _defaultState = BorderStyle.RAISED;

  private BorderStyle state;

  public ThreeDRectangle(Component drawInto) {
    this(drawInto, _defaultState,
        _defaultThickness, 0, 0, 0, 0);
  }
  public ThreeDRectangle(Component drawInto, int thickness) {
    this(drawInto, _defaultState, thickness, 0, 0, 0, 0);
  }
  public ThreeDRectangle(Component drawInto,
                    int x, int y, int w, int h) {
    this(drawInto,
        _defaultState, _defaultThickness, x, y, w, h);
  }
  public ThreeDRectangle(Component drawInto, int thickness,
                                    int x, int y,
                                    int w, int h) {
    this(drawInto, _defaultState, thickness, x, y, w, h);
  }
  public ThreeDRectangle(Component drawInto,
                    BorderStyle state,
                    int thickness, int x, int y,
                    int w, int h) {
    super(drawInto, thickness, x, y, w, h);
    this.state = state;
  }
```

```java
public void paint() {
   if(state == BorderStyle.RAISED) paintRaised();
   else                            paintInset ();
}
public void raise() { state = BorderStyle.RAISED; }
public void inset() { state = BorderStyle.INSET;  }

public boolean isRaised() {
    return state == BorderStyle.RAISED;
}
public String paramString() {
    return super.paramString() + "," + state;
}
public void paintRaised() {
   Graphics g = drawInto.getGraphics();

   if(g != null) {
      raise               ();
      drawTopLeftLines     (g, brighter());
      drawBottomRightLines(g, getLineColor());
      g.dispose();
   }
}
public void paintInset() {
   Graphics g = drawInto.getGraphics();

   if(g != null) {
      inset               ();
      drawTopLeftLines     (g, getLineColor());
      drawBottomRightLines(g, brighter());
      g.dispose();
   }
}
private void drawTopLeftLines(Graphics g, Color color) {
    int thick = getThickness();
    g.setColor(color);

   for(int i=0; i < thick; ++i) {
      g.drawLine(x+i, y+i,    x + width-(i+1), y+i);
      g.drawLine(x+i, y+i+1, x+i, y + height-(i+1));
   }
}
private void drawBottomRightLines(Graphics g, Color color) {
   int thick = getThickness();
   g.setColor(color);

   for(int i=1; i <= thick; ++i) {
      g.drawLine(x+i-1, y + height-i,
```

```
                     x + width-i, y + height-i);
            g.drawLine(x + width-i, y+i-1,
                     x + width-i, y + height-i);
      }
    }
}
```

Painting Inset and Raised 3-D Borders

Painting the rectangle borders inset or raised to produce a 3-D effect is another shadowing trick. In the `gjt.ThreeDRectangle` class, two methods implement the painting of raised and inset 3-D borders: `paintRaised()` and `paintInset()`. Here's how they work:

```
public void paintRaised() {
  Graphics g = drawInto.getGraphics();

  if(g != null) {
     raise();
     drawTopLeftLines(g, brighter());
     drawBottomRightLines(g, getLineColor());
     g.dispose();
  }
}
public void paintInset() {
  Graphics g = drawInto.getGraphics();

  if(g != null) {
     inset();
     drawTopLeftLines(g, getLineColor());
     drawBottomRightLines(g, brighter());
     g.dispose();
  }
}
```

Since the 3-D effect is achieved by painting different shades for the top left and bottom right sides of the rectangle, we need a more specific utility than `Graphics.drawRect()`. As a result, `paintRaised()` and `paintInset()` both invoke `drawTopLeftLines()` and `drawBottomRightLines()`, passing each the appropriate shade of the current line color.

`drawTopLeftLines()` and `drawBottomRightLines()` draw individual lines that converge at a 45 degree angle in the corners. Both employ the `Graphics drawLine()` method, as follows:

```
private void drawTopLeftLines(Graphics g, Color color) {
  int thick = getThickness();
  g.setColor(color);
```

```
    for(int i=0; i < thick; ++i) {
        g.drawLine(x+i, y+i,    x + width-(i+1), y+i);
        g.drawLine(x+i, y+i+1, x+i, y + height-(i+1));
    }
}
private void drawBottomRightLines(Graphics g, Color color) {
    int thick = getThickness();
    g.setColor(color);

    for(int i=1; i <= thick; ++i) {
        g.drawLine(x+i-1, y + height-i,
                    x + width-i, y + height-i);
        g.drawLine(x + width-i, y+i-1,
                    x + width-i, y + height-i);
    }
}
```

The AWT currently allows drawing lines only one pixel thick[4]. The `for()` loops draw lines whose thickness is equal to the current thickness of the `ThreeDRectangle`.

Notice that both `paintRaised()` and `paintInset()` are somewhat paranoid that the `Graphics` object returned from `drawInto.getGraphics()` may turn out to be null. They both include this check:

```
    if(g != null) {
```

This may lead you to wonder if you, too, need to check that a `Graphics` object obtained from `Component.getGraphics()` is valid. The answer is, of course, yes and no.

The answer in this case resides in the fact that our custom component is not an extension of `Component`. Remember that `DrawnRectangle` is merely a `Rectangle`. Recall that the `Component void paint(Graphics)` method is invoked by the AWT machinery when it is time for the `Component` to paint itself (recall our discussion of `paint()` in *Drawing a Rectangle* on page 25). Since `gjt.DrawnRectangle` is not a `Component` (it extends the graphically challenged `Rectangle`), its `paint()` method must be called manually. While we know that the AWT would never pass a null `Graphics` object when invoking `paint(Graphics)`, the same cannot be said for `DrawnRectangle.paint()`, since it needs to be invoked manually.

---

4.   This will change with the advent of the Java 2D API.

The moral is this: extensions of `java.awt.Component` are assured that a valid `Graphics` object is passed to methods that are invoked by the AWT machinery, while classes that do not extend `java.awt.Component` should always check the validity of `Graphics` objects passed to their methods.

Exercising the Rectangle Classes

All of the Graphic Java Toolkit custom components include unit tests. This is really a topic for *Extending the AWT—The Graphic Java Toolkit*, in which we talk more about the rationale for unit tests and how the unit tests are structured. Since we're introducing custom components in this chapter to highlight the use of AWT `Graphics` and `Color` objects, we'll discuss unit tests for the GJT rectangle classes here as well. For now, just be aware that the unit test extends `UnitTest` and overrides its `title()` and `centerPanel()` methods.

You've already seen the output from the `DrawnRectangleTest` class to illustrate all the types of borders and rectangles you can draw with the GJT's rectangle classes. Figure 3-7 shows this output again for completeness.

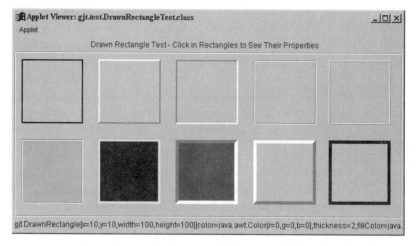

Figure 3-7 `gjt.DrawnRectangle` Unit Test

The unit test code is in Example 3-4 on page 47. The interesting aspect of the unit test is the `DrawnRectangleTestPanel` class, which extends `Panel`. `DrawnRectangleTestPanel` creates new instances of `DrawnRectangle`, `EtchedRectangle`, and `ThreeDRectangle`. All of the rectangles are passed a reference to the `DrawnRectangleTestPanel` instance, which is the component being drawn into. `DrawnRectangleTestPanel.paint()` then paints and fills the rectangles.

As you look through the unit test, pay attention to use of color constants. The `Color` class provides a set of constants that can be used to set the color of your choice. The complete list of color constants is:

- `Color.black`
- `Color.blue`
- `Color.cyan`
- `Color.darkGray`
- `Color.gray`
- `Color.green`
- `Color.lightGray`
- `Color.magenta`
- `Color.orange`
- `Color.pink`
- `Color.red`
- `Color.white`
- `Color.yellow`

Also notice that `DrawnRectangleTest` overrides `MouseListener.mousePressed()` in order to print information about the `gjt.DrawnRectangle` in which the mouse down event occurred. The `gjt.DrawnRectangle` is passed to a shorthand method for printing information about the `gjt.DrawnRectangle` in question.

Example 3-4 and Example 3-5 show the code for the unit test.

Example 3-4 `gjt.test.DrawnRectangleTest` **Class Source Code**

```
package gjt.test;

import java.awt.*;
import java.applet.Applet;
import gjt.*;

public class DrawnRectangleTest extends UnitTest {
  public String title() {
    return "Drawn Rectangle Test - " +
           "Click in Rectangles to See Their Properties";
  }
  public Panel centerPanel() {
```

```
        return new DrawnRectangleTestPanel(this);
   }
}
```

Example 3-5 `gjt.test.DrawnRectangleTestPanel` **Class Source Code**

```java
package gjt.test;

import java.awt.*;
import java.awt.event.*;
import java.applet.Applet;
import gjt.*;

public class DrawnRectangleTestPanel extends Panel
                                implements MouseListener {
   private Applet          applet;
   private DrawnRectangle  drawnFilledOrange,
                           drawnFilledBlue, drawnBlue;
   private EtchedRectangle etchedOut,
                           etchedIn, etchedFilledCyan;
   private ThreeDRectangle thinRaised,
                           thinInset, thickRaised, thickInset;

   public DrawnRectangleTestPanel(Applet applet) {
      this.applet = applet;

      drawnFilledOrange =
          new DrawnRectangle (this, 10,  10,  100, 100);
      drawnFilledBlue =
          new DrawnRectangle (this, 135, 135, 100, 100);
      drawnBlue =
          new DrawnRectangle (this, 505, 135, 100, 100);
      etchedFilledCyan =
          new EtchedRectangle(this, 10,  135, 100, 100);

      etchedIn = new EtchedRectangle(this, 385, 10, 100, 100);
      etchedOut= new EtchedRectangle(this, 505, 10, 100, 100);

      thinRaised = new ThreeDRectangle(this, 135, 10,  100, 100);
      thinInset = new ThreeDRectangle(this, 260, 10,  100, 100);
      thickRaised = new ThreeDRectangle(this, 385, 135, 100, 100);
      thickInset = new ThreeDRectangle(this, 260, 135, 100, 100);

      drawnFilledOrange.setLineColor(Color.black);

      drawnFilledBlue.setLineColor(Color.yellow);
      drawnFilledBlue.setThickness(3);
```

```
      drawnBlue.setLineColor(Color.blue);
      drawnBlue.setThickness(5);

      thickRaised.setThickness(5);
      thickInset.setThickness (5);

      addMouseListener(this);
}
public Dimension getPreferredSize() {
      return new Dimension(610, 270);
}
public void paint(Graphics g) {
      drawnFilledOrange.paint();
      drawnFilledOrange.fill (Color.orange);

      drawnFilledBlue.paint  ();
      drawnFilledBlue.fill  (Color.blue);

      drawnBlue.paint         ();

      etchedIn.paintEtchedIn ();
      etchedOut.paintEtchedOut();

      etchedFilledCyan.paintEtchedIn();
      etchedFilledCyan.fill(Color.cyan);

      thinRaised.paintRaised ();
      thinInset.paintInset    ();

      thickRaised.paintRaised ();

      thickInset.paintInset   ();
      thickInset.fill        (Color.red);
}
public void mouseClicked (MouseEvent event) { }
public void mouseReleased(MouseEvent event) { }
public void mouseEntered (MouseEvent event) { }
public void mouseExited  (MouseEvent event) { }

public void mousePressed(MouseEvent event) {
      int x = event.getPoint().x;
      int y = event.getPoint().y;

      if(drawnFilledOrange.contains(x,y)) show(drawnFilledOrange);
      if(drawnFilledBlue.contains(x,y))  show(drawnFilledBlue);
      if(drawnBlue.contains(x,y))        show(drawnBlue);
      if(etchedIn.contains(x,y))         show(etchedIn);
      if(etchedOut.contains(x,y))        show(etchedOut);
```

```
      if(etchedFilledCyan.contains(x,y))  show(etchedFilledCyan);
      if(thinRaised.contains(x,y))        show(thinRaised);
      if(thickRaised.contains(x,y))       show(thickRaised);
      if(thinInset.contains(x,y))         show(thinInset);
      if(thickInset.contains(x,y))        show(thickInset);
   }
   private void show(DrawnRectangle drawnRectangle) {
      applet.showStatus(drawnRectangle.toString());
   }
}
```

Manipulating Fonts

The AWT includes two classes that support font manipulation: the aptly named `Font` and `FontMetrics` classes. The `Font` class provides a basic set of fonts and font styles. Remember that Java is platform independent, so fonts such as Helvetica, Times Roman, and so on are always mapped to an available font on the native platform. Table 3-5 shows font mappings from Java to the respective supported platforms.

Table 3-5 Java Font Model

Java Font [1]	Maps to Windows Font...	Maps to X Window Font...	Maps to Macintosh Font...
Courier	Courier New	adobe-courier	Courier
Dialog	MS Sans Serif	b&h-lucida	Geneva
DialogInput	MS Sans Serif	b&h-lucidatypewriter	Geneva
Helvetica	Arial	adobe-helvetica	Helvetica
TimesRoman	Times New Roman	adobe-times	Times Roman
Symbol	WingDings	itc-zapfdingbats	Symbol

1. The default font is misc-fixed on X Windows, Arial on Windows 95, and Geneva on Macintosh.

The `Font` class defines font styles in terms of these constants:

- `Font.PLAIN`

- `Font.BOLD`

- `Font.ITALIC`

- `Font.BOLD + Font.ITALIC`

The AWT Font Model

The AWT font model is similar to the one used in the X Window System™. Figure 3-8 shows how font height, ascent, descent, and leading are calculated in the AWT.

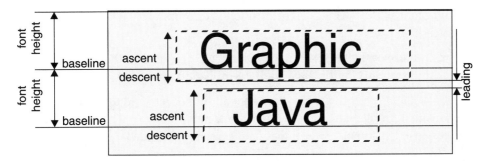

Figure 3-8 The AWT Font Model
The font height is the distance between one baseline and another. The ascent is measured from the baseline to the top of the characters, and the descent is measured from the baseline to the bottom of the characters. The leading is the distance from the descent of one line to the ascent of the next line of text.

The x,y Origin for Drawing Strings

You may remember our use of the `Graphics.drawRect()` method in the `gjt.EtchedRectangle` class earlier in the chapter. The location passed to `drawRect()` represents the upper left-hand corner of the rectangle. In contrast, the location passed to the `Graphics drawString()` method represents the baseline of the characters. Figure 3-9 illustrates how these methods differ.

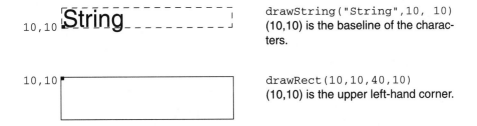

```
drawString("String",10, 10)
```
(10,10) is the baseline of the characters.

```
drawRect(10,10,40,10)
```
(10,10) is the upper left-hand corner.

Figure 3-9 Drawing Strings With the `drawString()` Method
The `drawString()` method uses the baseline as the point of origin. The `drawRect()` method uses the upper left-hand corner as the point of origin.

Overview of gjt.LabelCanvas

The Graphic Java Toolkit includes a `FontDialog` class that enables selecting fonts and changing a font's point size, so we'll defer a detailed discussion of the `Font` class to our chapter on *FontDialog* on page 755. For now, we'll focus more on the use of the `FontMetrics` class, which provides size information about a particular font so that strings can be positioned appropriately within a `Component`.

To introduce use of the `FontMetrics` class, we'll describe another custom component from the Graphic Java Toolkit—`gjt.LabelCanvas`.

With the original AWT, the `Label` component did not respond to mouse events[5], which made it problematic to implement a selectable label. As a result, the GJT provides an extension of `Canvas` that paints a string that can be selected and deselected.

Working With FontMetrics

The `gjt.LabelCanvas` class will help illustrate some nuances of the `FontMetrics` class. In particular, it will show how to obtain a handle on a font's `FontMetrics` and show some detail about positioning strings within a `Component`. Figure 3-10 shows the `LabelCanvas` class in action.

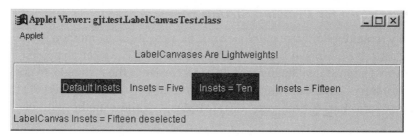

Figure 3-10 `gjt.LabelCanvas`
The `gjt.LabelCanvas` in use. A `LabelCanvas` can be selected and deselected. A `LabelCanvas` generates selection events when it is selected or deselected.

When a `gjt.LabelCanvas` is selected or deselected, it fires an `ItemEvent`. For the unit test, the container of the `LabelCanvas` simply prints information about the selection event:

```
LabelCanvas Standard Insets selected
```

5. This bug has been fixed in the 1.1 release of the AWT. See "Delegation-Based Event Model (AWT 1.1 and Beyond)" on page 93.

```
LabelCanvas Insets = Five selected
LabelCanvas Insets = Ten selected
LabelCanvas Insets = Ten deselected
LabelCanvas Insets = Fifteen selected
LabelCanvas Insets = Fifteen deselected
```

Table 3-6 and Table 3-7 list the `LabelCanvas` class responsibilities and associations, respectively.

Table 3-6 `gjt.LabelCanvas` **Responsibilities**

Methods	Description
`void paint(Graphics g)`	Overrides `Component paint()`. Paints the string according to the selection state.
`void setInsets(Insets insets)`	Sets insets for a `LabelCanvas`.
`Dimension minimumSize()`	Overrides `Component minimumSize()`. Returns `preferredSize()`.
`String getLabel()`	Returns the string representing the label.
`boolean isSelected()`	Returns state of the selection.
`void select()`	Sets selection state to `true`, and repaints.
`void deselect()`	Sets selection state to `false`, and repaints.
`void resize(int w, int h)`	Overrides `Component resize()`. This is a precautionary measure.
`void setBounds(int x, int y, int w, int h)`	Overrides `Component setBounds()`. Centers the string in the canvas.
`Dimension preferredSize()`	Overrides `Component preferredSize()`. Sets preferred size large enough to accommodate the string, plus the size of the insets.

Table 3-7 `gjt.LabelCanvas` **Associations**

Variables	Description
`String label`	The string displayed in the canvas.
`boolean selected`	Tracks the state of the selection.
`Insets insets`	Is set as if we're using a container.
`Point labelLoc`	Specifies the x,y point at which the string should be drawn.

With this overview of how `LabelCanvas` works, let's highlight several ways in which it makes use of the `FontMetrics` class. For those who prefer to see the entire source all at once, we'll also show you the `gjt.LabelCanvas` code in its entirety in "`gjt.LabelCanvas` Class Source Code" on page 57.

Obtaining Font Dimensions

Just as every component has a Graphics object affiliated with it, every Graphics object has a FontMetrics object affiliated with it. The Graphics.getFontMetrics() method returns information about font dimensions.

Accessing a component's FontMetrics is accomplished by obtaining a reference to the component's Graphics object and calling getFontMetrics():

```
Graphics g = getGraphics();
FontMetrics fm = g.getFontMetrics();
```

Dynamically Positioning a String

When it is resized, gjt.LabelCanvas uses its labelLocation() method to recalculate the string's position:

```
public void setBounds(int x, int y, int w, int h) {
    super.setBounds(x, y, w, h);
    labelLoc = labelLocation(getGraphics());
}
```

After the essential call to super.setBounds() is made, the labelLoc position is calculated, based on the size of the string:

```
private Point labelLocation(Graphics g) {
    Dimension    size = size();
    FontMetrics fm   = g.getFontMetrics();
    int x = (size.width/2) - (fm.stringWidth(label)/2);
    int y = (size.height/2) + (fm.getAscent()/2);
    return new Point(x,y);
}
```

As you can see, several of the FontMetrics methods are at work here. After obtaining the FontMetrics object, we use the font width, ascent, and leading to determine the x,y location for drawing the string. First, we determine the x location by subtracting half the width of the component (that is, the Canvas) by the half the width of the label, as illustrated in Figure 3-11.

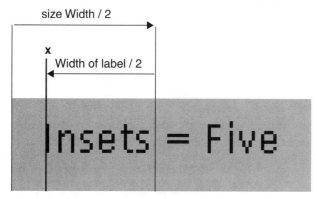

x = (size.width/2) - (fm.stringWidth(label)/2);

Figure 3-11 Determining a String's x Location

Then we determine the y location as in Figure 3-12. As you look at Figure 3-12, remember that the location passed to `Graphics.drawString()` represents the *baseline* of the string's characters.

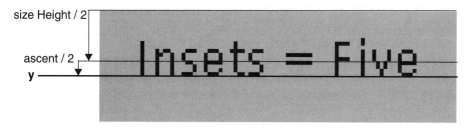

y = (size.height/2) + (fm.getAscent()/2);

Figure 3-12 Determining a String's y Location

Note that we can't just divide the height of the component by 2 to center the string in the vertical direction. While that is the center of the `Canvas`, it will not result in a centered string. We must adjust according to the font ascent to determine the string's baseline.

The `point` returned by the `labelLocation()` method represents the x,y location necessary for drawing a string (refer to page 51). Figure 3-13 shows our final x,y location.

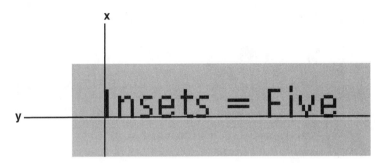

Figure 3-13 Determining a String's x,y Location

Now, based on the `point` returned by `LabelCanvas.labelLocation()`, the `LabelCanvas` can reposition the label's text string appropriately after the canvas has been resized:

```
g.drawString(label, labelLoc.x, labelLoc.y);
```

Drawing a String in Reverse Video

One of the characteristics of a `gjt.LabelCanvas` is that it draws the selected string in reverse video. This is accomplished by the protected `paintSelected()` method:

```
protected void paintSelected(Graphics g) {
    Point labelLoc = labelLocation(g);

    g.setColor(getForeground());
    g.fillRect(0,0,getSize().width-1,getSize().height-1);
    g.setColor(getBackground());
    g.drawString(label, labelLoc.x, labelLoc.y);
}
```

Armed with the information supplied by the `labelLocation()` method, which establishes our drawing position, we simply fill the canvas with the foreground color and draw the string in the background color.

gjt.LabelCanvas Implementation

Now that we've seen some of the particulars of dealing with `FontMetrics` in the `LabelCanvas` class, let's look at the code in its entirety in Example 3-6. There are a couple of items to pay attention to as you look through the code. For example, notice how we override the `Component.getPreferredSize()` method:

```
public Dimension getPreferredSize() {
  FontMetrics fm = getFontMetrics(getFont());
  return new Dimension(
     insets.left + fm.stringWidth(label) +
     insets.right,
     insets.top  + fm.getHeight() +
     insets.bottom);
}
```

Essentially, we obtain the `FontMetrics` and then calculate a preferred size based on the size of the string and the `insets` settings. The `insets` value specifies the *inside* margins of a container. We'll describe insets in detail in our chapter on *Components, Containers, and Layout Managers* [6]. The default `insets` value for `LabelCanvas` is 2 pixels for the top, bottom, left, and right edges of the canvas. The result is that the horizontal preferred size is equal to the width of the string, plus the left and right insets. The vertical preferred size is equal to font height plus the top and bottom insets.

Example 3-6 `gjt.LabelCanvas` **Class Source Code**

```
package gjt;

import java.awt.*;
import java.awt.event.*;
import java.util.Vector;

public class LabelCanvas extends     Component
                          implements ItemSelectable {
  protected boolean selected = false;
  private ItemListener itemListener = null;
  private String    label;
  private Insets    insets   = new Insets(2,2,2,2);
  private Point     labelLoc = new Point(0,0);

  public LabelCanvas(String label) {
     this.label = label;

     addMouseListener(new MouseAdapter() {
        public void mousePressed(MouseEvent event) {
           if(isSelected()) deselect();
           else             select();
        }
```

6. Our use of insets here is somewhat different than that described in "Components, Containers, and Layout Managers" on page 373. Layout managers do not position components inside of a container's insets; here, insets are used to compute the overall size of the `LabelCanvas`.

```
      });
   }
   public void paint(Graphics g) {
      if(selected == true) paintSelected  (g);
      else                 paintDeselected(g);
   }
   public Object[] getSelectedObjects() {
      Object[] objs = null;

      if(isSelected()) {
         objs = new LabelCanvas[1];
         objs[0] = this;
      }
      return objs;
   }
   public void setInsets(Insets insets) {
      this.insets = insets;
      repaint();
   }
   public String getLabel() {
      return label;
   }
   public void setLabel(String label) {
      this.label = label;
   }
   public boolean isSelected() {
      return selected;
   }
   public void select() {
      selected = true;
      repaint();
      processItemEvent();
   }
   public void deselect() {
      selected = false;
      repaint();
      processItemEvent();
   }
   public void setSize(int w, int h) {
      setBounds(getLocation().x, getLocation().y, w, h);
   }
   public void setBounds(int x, int y, int w, int h) {
      super.setBounds(x, y, w, h);
      Graphics g = getGraphics();
      if(g != null) {
         labelLoc = labelLocation(getGraphics());
         g.dispose();
      }
```

```
    }
    public Dimension getMinimumSize() {
        return getPreferredSize();
    }
    public Dimension getPreferredSize() {
        FontMetrics fm = getFontMetrics(getFont());
        return new Dimension(
            insets.left + fm.stringWidth(label) +
            insets.right,
            insets.top  + fm.getHeight() +
            insets.bottom);
    }
    protected void paintSelected(Graphics g) {
        Point labelLoc = labelLocation(g);

        g.setColor(getForeground());
        g.fillRect(0,0,getSize().width-1,getSize().height-1);
        g.setColor(getBackground());
        g.drawString(label, labelLoc.x, labelLoc.y);
    }
    protected void paintDeselected(Graphics g) {
        g.drawString(label, labelLoc.x, labelLoc.y);
    }
    protected String paramString() {
        return super.paramString() + ",text=" + label +
               (isSelected() ? " selected" : " not selected");
    }
    protected Point labelLocation(Graphics g) {
        Dimension   size = getSize();
        FontMetrics fm   = g.getFontMetrics();

        int x = (size.width/2) - (fm.stringWidth(label)/2);
        int y = (size.height/2) + (fm.getAscent()/2) -
                                  fm.getLeading();
        return new Point(x,y);
    }
    protected void processItemEvent() {
        if(itemListener != null) {
            if(isSelected()) {
                itemListener.itemStateChanged(
                    new ItemEvent(this,
                                  ItemEvent.ITEM_STATE_CHANGED,
                                  this,
                                  ItemEvent.SELECTED));
            }
            else {
                itemListener.itemStateChanged(
                    new ItemEvent(this,
```

```
                        ItemEvent.ITEM_STATE_CHANGED,
                        this,
                        ItemEvent.DESELECTED));
            }
        }
    }
    public synchronized void addItemListener(ItemListener l) {
        itemListener = AWTEventMulticaster.add(itemListener, l);
    }
    public synchronized void removeItemListener(ItemListener l) {
        itemListener = AWTEventMulticaster.remove(
                    itemListener, l);
    }
}
```

Exercising the LabelCanvas

Now that you've seen some details about using the FontMetrics class and had
a chance to look at the gjt.LabelCanvas code, let's see the LabelCanvas in
action. First of all, look at Figure 3-10, which shows our unit test implementation
of the gjt.LabelCanvas class.

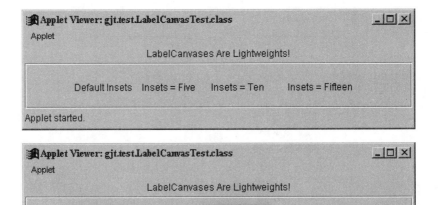

Figure 3-14 gjt.LabelCanvas Unit Test
The bottom picture shows selected gjt.LabelCanvas instances.

Example 3-7 shows the unit test code that puts the `gjt.LabelCanvas` to work. Notice that each instance of `gjt.LabelCanvas` is constructed with different insets. Also notice that LabelCanvasTestPanel implements the `ItemListener` interface so that it can respond to item events fired by its contained label canvases. See "Delegation-Based Event Model (AWT 1.1 and Beyond)" on page 93 for an in-depth look at event sources and listeners.

Example 3-7 `gjt.test.LabelCanvasTest` **Class Source Code**

```
package gjt.test;
import java.applet.Applet;
import java.awt.Event;
import java.awt.Panel;
import java.awt.Insets;
import java.awt.Graphics;
import gjt.LabelCanvas;
import gjt.Util;
import java.awt.event.*;

public class LabelCanvasTest extends UnitTest {
  public String title() {
     return "LabelCanvases Are Lightweights!";
  }
  public Panel centerPanel() {
     return new LabelCanvasTestPanel(this);
  }
}
class LabelCanvasTestPanel extends     Panel
                        implements ItemListener {
  static private Applet applet;
  LabelCanvas def      = new LabelCanvas("Default Insets");
  LabelCanvas five     = new LabelCanvas("Insets = Five");
  LabelCanvas ten      = new LabelCanvas("Insets = Ten");
  LabelCanvas fifteen = new LabelCanvas("Insets = Fifteen");

  static public void broadcastSelection(LabelCanvas canvas) {
     String s = null;

     if(canvas.isSelected())
        s = "LabelCanvas " + canvas.getLabel() +
                        " selected";
     else
        s = "LabelCanvas " + canvas.getLabel() +
                        " deselected";
     applet.showStatus(s);
     System.out.println(s);
```

```
      canvas.repaint();
   }
   public LabelCanvasTestPanel(Applet applet) {
      this.applet = applet;

      five.setInsets    (new Insets(5,5,5,5));
      ten.setInsets     (new Insets(10,10,10,10));
      fifteen.setInsets(new Insets(15,15,15,15));

      add(def);
      add(five);
      add(ten);
      add(fifteen);

      def.addItemListener     (this);
      five.addItemListener    (this);
      ten.addItemListener     (this);
      fifteen.addItemListener(this);
   }
   public void itemStateChanged(ItemEvent event) {
      LabelCanvas canvas = (LabelCanvas)event.getSource();
      broadcastSelection(canvas);
   }
}
```

Summary

This chapter covers the basics of using the Graphics, Color, and FontMetrics classes in the Java AWT. In particular, we have illustrated how to obtain a component's Graphics object, how to draw lines and rectangles, and how to fill rectangles. The Graphic Java Toolkit custom components described in this chapter also illustrate how to obtain brighter or darker shades of a color, along with the use of color constants. Lastly, we've introduced the AWT font model, and presented another GJT custom component (gjt.LabelCanvas) to illustrate the use of the java.awt.FontMetrics class. There are other corners of the Graphics, Color, Font, and FontMetrics classes worth exploring, and we do that in later chapters that focus on custom components. Particularly, the *FontDialog* chapter illustrates manipulation of font styles and sizes, while the *Sprite Animation* chapter covers more advanced usage of the Graphics class.

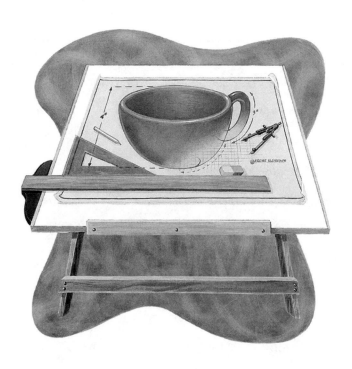

CHAPTER
4

Inheritance-Based Event Handling (AWT 1.02 and Before)

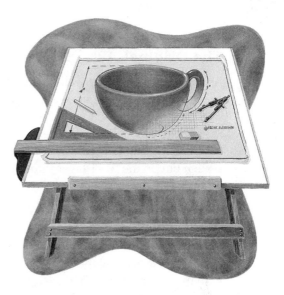

This chapter covers the original AWT event model. With the advent of the 1.1 version of the JDK, the AWT has introduced a much improved event model. We've left this chapter in Graphic Java, solely due to the fact that the 1.1 version of the AWT still supports the old model. However, at some point in a future release of the AWT, the old model will cease to be supported. So, unless you are supporting code that uses the old model and are looking for information concerning the old model, we suggest that you skip this chapter and turn to the next, which discusses the new event model at length. We have also added a section at the end of this chapter that discusses the shortcomings of the original model and how they are rectified by the new model. This chapter will be removed in a subsequent version of Graphic Java.

Modern graphical user interfaces are typically event driven, meaning they spend much of their time idling, waiting for an event to occur; when an event occurs, an event handler responds to the event. Applets and applications developed using the AWT are no different, so in this chapter, we introduce event handling in AWT components and offer advice on a variety of points, including when to override event handling methods and when to handle an event or pass it on. We also introduce several applets to illustrate event handling techniques, such as sensing double clicks, managing action events, and generating and delivering events to custom components.

The Original AWT Event Model

As is the case with nearly all object-oriented user interface toolkits, the AWT is event driven. Actually, since the AWT uses a peer approach, the underlying event subsystem is native to the platform on which an applet or application is running. So, for instance, if an applet is executed under Motif, it uses the X Window event handling system. Our focus, however, is not on the underlying native event system but on the AWT layer through which we respond to events.

It should be noted that this chapter pertains to the original, inheritance-based event model, for AWT 1.0 and AWT 1.02. The 1.1 version of the AWT has a new event model that is delegation based instead of inheritance based and is much improved over the original model. We suggest that you use the new event model instead of the original model. The 1.1 version of the AWT is backward compatible with the original event model, and therefore we have chosen to leave this chapter, which was in the first edition of Graphic Java, intact.

The delegation event model is discussed in the next chapter. If you must use the 1.02 version of the AWT, then this chapter is for you; if you are able to move to the 1.1 version, then you should skip to the next chapter.

Overriding Event Handling Methods

Essentially, event handling using the original AWT event model is a fairly simple proposition: when an event occurs inside a component, a method of that component is invoked. If you want the component to respond to an event, you simply override the appropriate method. For instance, a component's `void setSize(int w, int h)` method is invoked when the component is resized. If you wanted to take some action when a resize event occurs, you would override `setSize()` and take care of business. There are a number of component methods which, like `setSize()`, are called in response to some event. Table 4-1 shows a partial list of such methods.

Table 4-1 Event-Driven Methods Used in Components

Method	Event
Component Methods Frequently Overridden	
`void setSize(int w,int h)`	Component has been resized.
`void setbounds(int x,int y,int w,int h)`	Component resized and/or moved.
`void paint(Graphics g)`	Component needs to be painted.
`void update(Graphics g)`	By default erase, then repaint.

Table 4-1 Event-Driven Methods Used in Components (Continued)

Method	Event
`void addNotify()`	Peer created.
Component Methods Infrequently Overridden	
`void setLocation(int x, int y)`	Component moved to x,y location.
`void layout()`	Component needs to be laid out.
`void validate()`	If invalid, lay out.

It is common to override the first group of methods in Table 4-1 when developing custom components. The methods in the second group in the table represent more obscure events, such as when a component needs to be laid out (we discuss layout managers in detail in *Components, Containers, and Layout Managers*). It is rarely necessary to override the methods associated with these events. Of course, by overriding any of the methods in Table 4-1, you are rewriting what the component does by default. As a result, you will often see event handler methods that call the superclass version before adding embellishments:

```
public addNotify() { // Default version creates the peer object.
  super.addNotify(); // Peer is created only after this call.
  // Now we are guaranteed that things like the Component's
  // Graphics are available, since the peer has been created
}
```

Propagated Events

The events discussed above occur in a component and are handled (or ignored) by the component in which the event occurred. Such events are of concern only to the component in which they occurred.

A second group of events is referred to as *propagated* events; whenever a propagated event occurs in a component, the component's `handleEvent(Event)` method is invoked. The component's `handleEvent()` method may choose to propagate the event to its container or handle the event entirely on its own.

Note the distinction between propagated events and the events listed in Table 4-1. Propagated events are always handled by a component's `handleEvent()` method, which is passed a `java.awt.Event`. Propagated events may be propagated to the component's container; if so, the container's `handleEvent()` method is invoked and the `java.awt.Event` is passed along.

Since propagated events involve a `java.awt.Event`, they are generically referred to as AWT events. The rest of this chapter will only be concerned with such events.

Event Type Constants

Every `java.awt.Event` has an `id` field whose value indicates the type of event that has occurred. Typically, the first thing a component's `handleEvent()` method does is to check the event's `id` field to determine the type of event. For instance, a `handleEvent()` method concerned with mouse events might look something like this:

```
public boolean handleEvent(Event event) {
    if(event.id == Event.MOUSE_DOWN) {
        // react to mouse down
        return true; // event fully handled, do not propagate
    }
    else if(event.id == Event.MOUSE_UP) {
        // react to mouse up
        return true; // event fully handled, do not propagate
    }
    // let superclass handle event and decide to propagate
    return super.handleEvent(event);
}
```

Notice that this example returns `true` if the event is a mouse up or mouse down event, signifying that we have fully handled the event and therefore do not wish to propagate the event to the component's container. If the event is not a mouse up or mouse down, we give the superclass a chance to handle the event. If we were to return `false`, the event would be propagated directly to the component's container and the superclass would never have a chance to handle the event. Therefore, it is always a good idea to have overridden `handleEvent()` methods return `super.handleEvent(event)` if they have not fully handled the event, instead of propagating the event directly to the component's container.

AWT TIP ...

Avoid Returning false From a handleEvent() Method

Returning false from a handleEvent() method propagates the event to the component's container without giving the component's superclass a chance to process the event. Therefore, it is a good idea to avoid returning false from a handleEvent() method. Instead, if a class has not fully handled a particular event, it should always give its superclass a chance to process the event and let the superclass decide whether to propagate the event to the component's container. Even if you know that your superclass is not interested in a particular type of event, there are no guarantees that the superclass will not be modified in the future to process an event that you are not interested in.

Table 4-2 shows the complete list of `java.awt.Event` type constants.

Table 4-2 `java.awt.Event` **Constants**

Event Constants
Window Event Constants
WINDOW_DESTROY
WINDOW_EXPOSE
WINDOW_ICONIFY
WINDOW_DEICONIFY
WINDOW_MOVED
Keyboard Event Constants
KEY_PRESS
KEY_RELEASE
KEY_ACTION
KEY_ACTION_RELEASE
Mouse Event Constants
MOUSE_DOWN, MOUSE_UP
MOUSE_MOVE
MOUSE_ENTER, MOUSE_EXIT
MOUSE_DRAG
Scrollbar Event Constants
SCROLL_LINE_UP, SCROLL_LINE_DOWN
SCROLL_PAGE_UP, SCROLL_PAGE_DOWN
SCROLL_ABSOLUTE

Table 4-2 `java.awt.Event` **Constants (Continued)**

Event Constants
List Event Constants
`LIST_SELECT, LIST_DESELECT`
Action Event Constants
`ACTION_EVENT`
`LOAD_FILE`
`SAVE_FILE`
`GOT_FOCUS, LOST_FOCUS`

Propagated Event Handler Methods

Checking against the `id` field of an event to decipher the type of event in overridden `handleEvent()` methods is rather ugly and requires keeping track of all the event constants listed in Table 4-2, which is not very object-oriented[1]. As a result, `java.awt.Component` implements a `handleEvent()` method that deciphers the type of event and invokes one of a number of convenience methods. Table 4-3 lists all of the convenience methods that are invoked by `java.awt.Component.handleEvent()`.

Table 4-3 Propagated Event Handler Convenience Methods

Method	Event
`boolean action (Event, Object)`	An action event.
`boolean mouseUp (Event,int,int)`	Mouse up.
`boolean mouseDown (Event,int,int)`	Mouse down.
`boolean mouseDrag (Event,int,int)`	Mouse drag.
`boolean mouseMove (Event,int,int)`	Mouse move.
`boolean mouseEnter (Event,int,int)`	Mouse entered component.
`boolean mouseExit (Event,int,int)`	Mouse exited component.
`boolean keyUp (Event,int)`	Key up.
`boolean keyDown (Event,int)`	Key down.
`boolean gotFocus (Event,Object)`	Component has focus.
`boolean lostFocus (Event,Object)`	Component lost focus.

---

1. See Meyer, Bertrand. *Object Oriented Software Construction*, section 10.2.2. Prentice Hall, 1988.

When handling propagated events, you can choose to do one of the following:

- Override `handleEvent()` and check against the `id` field of the event to determine the type of event

- Override one of the convenience methods listed in Table 4-3

Let's take a look at the implementation of `Component.handleEvent(Event)` in order to see exactly how the convenience methods are invoked:

```
// java.awt.Component.handleEvent()
public boolean handleEvent(Event evt) {
  switch (evt.id) {
    case Event.MOUSE_ENTER:
        return mouseEnter(evt, evt.x, evt.y);

    case Event.MOUSE_EXIT:
        return mouseExit(evt, evt.x, evt.y);

    case Event.MOUSE_MOVE:
        return mouseMove(evt, evt.x, evt.y);

    case Event.MOUSE_DOWN:
        return mouseDown(evt, evt.x, evt.y);

    case Event.MOUSE_DRAG:
        return mouseDrag(evt, evt.x, evt.y);

    case Event.MOUSE_UP:
        return mouseUp(evt, evt.x, evt.y);

    case Event.KEY_PRESS:
    case Event.KEY_ACTION:
        return keyDown(evt, evt.key);

    case Event.KEY_RELEASE:
    case Event.KEY_ACTION_RELEASE:
        return keyUp(evt, evt.key);

    case Event.ACTION_EVENT:
        return action(evt, evt.arg);
    case Event.GOT_FOCUS:
        return gotFocus(evt, evt.arg);
    case Event.LOST_FOCUS:
        return lostFocus(evt, evt.arg);
  }
  return false;
}
```

`java.awt.Component.handleEvent(Event)` simply deciphers the type of event and then invokes a convenience method. All of the convenience methods are implemented in the `Component` class as *no-ops*; they exist solely for you to override them and give them some teeth.

Propagated Events Propagate Outward

Applets often have a fairly complex nested layout in which various extensions of `Panel` are nested within one another and positioned according to the container's layout manager. Indeed, this is the core of AWT development—an art that we explore throughout this book.

Events are propagated from the component in which the event occurred to the outermost container. However, any component along the chain of containers can halt the propagation of the event if its `handleEvent()` method completely handles the event and returns `true`.

Overriding Propagated Event Handlers

As we discussed previously, methods that handle a propagated event return a `boolean` value, which indicates whether the event was handled or not. A `true` return value indicates that the event has been handled and should not be propagated to the component's container. A `false` return value signals that the event has not been handled completely and should be forwarded to the component's container. Table 4-4 summarizes the choices a component has when confronted with a propagated event.

Table 4-4 Component Choices When Handling Propagated Events

A Component Can Do This With a Propagated Event...	Then `handleEvent()`...
Propagate event to its container.	Returns `false`.
Not propagate event to its container.	Returns `true`.
Let superclass handle and decide to propagate.	Returns `super.handleEvent(event)`.

Whether you override `handleEvent()` or override one of the convenience methods listed in Table 4-3 on page 70, you must decide the manner in which you will return from the propagated event handler. In either case, if you have completely handled the event, then you can just return `true`, signifying the event is completely handled and should not be propagated. If you have not completely handled the event, then there are two guidelines to follow, as listed in Table 4-5.

Table 4-5 Event Handling Guidelines

If You Have Not Completely Handled the Event and You Have...	Then...
Overridden `handleEvent()`.	Call `super.handleEvent(event)` and let the superclass determine whether or not to propagate the event.
Overridden one of the convenience methods in Table 4-3.	Return `false` and propagate the event to the component's container.

Let's look at the rationale for these guidelines. First, as we've already mentioned in the AWT Tip on page 69, it's preferable when using `handleEvent()` to leave the decision to propagate the event to the superclass's `handleEvent()`. It is just good practice to give the superclass a chance to handle the event.

However, this doesn't work so neatly with the convenience methods. Consider, for instance, the consequences of returning `super.handleEvent(event)` from one of the convenience methods. If you were to override `mouseDown()`, for example, and return `super.handleEvent()`, you might wind up in an infinite loop. If none of your superclasses override `handleEvent()`, you will invoke `Component.handleEvent()`, which detects the mouse down event and invokes `mouseDown()`, putting you right back where you started. As a rule of thumb, when overriding the convenience methods, it is best to propagate the event directly to the container.

AWT TIP ...

Propagate Unhandled Events From Event Handler Convenience Methods

Event handler convenience methods such as mouseDown() should never return super.handleEvent(event) but should instead directly propagate unhandled events to their container. By default, Component.handleEvent(Event) deciphers the event type and invokes a convenience method, which will result in an infinite loop if super.handleEvent(event) is invoked from the convenience method to begin with.

To highlight AWT event handling in action, we will provide a series of small applets in the rest of this chapter that illustrate various features and nuances of the AWT event model.

Event Modifier Constants

In addition to an `id` field, each `java.awt.Event` also contains a `modifier` field that provides additional information about the event. For example, you might want to know which key or which mouse button triggered an event. The `Event` class defines a handful of constants that provide such information. Table 4-6 lists the `modifier` constants. We'll show how to use these later in this chapter, but it's useful to have them handy for reference.

Table 4-6 Event Modifiers

Event Modifier Constant	Type	Meaning
ALT_MASK	Keyboard	ALT key is down.
ALT_MASK	Mouse Button	Button 2 is pressed.
CTRL_MASK	Keyboard	CONTROL key is down.
DOWN	Function Key	DOWN key is pressed.
END	Function Key	END key is pressed.
F1 - F12	Function Key	FUNCTION key 1 – 12 is pressed.
HOME	Function Key	HOME key is pressed.
LEFT	Function Key	LEFT key is pressed.
META_MASK	Keyboard	META key is down.
META_MASK	Mouse Button	Button 3 is pressed.
PGDOWN	Function Key	PAGE DOWN key is pressed.
PGUP	Function Key	PAGE UP key is pressed.
RIGHT	Function Key	RIGHT key is pressed.
SHIFT_MASK	Keyboard	SHIFT key or caps lock is down.
UP	Function Key	UP key is pressed.

Mouse Button Events

To illustrate handling mouse button events, we'll describe a `MouseSensorApplet`. The `MouseSensorApplet` uses a `BorderLayout` layout manager and places an instance of a `MouseSensorCanvas` in the center of the applet. Remember that an applet is an extension of `Container`, so components can be added to an applet. (Since most of the applets in this chapter simply place a blank canvas inside an applet, we won't show pictures of them unless there's something to illustrate.) The `MouseSensorCanvas` class overrides the `mouseDown()`, `mouseUp()`, and `mouseDrag()` convenience methods from `java.awt.Component`. It also implements a whichMouseButton() method to print the mouse button that initiated the event. Example 4-1 shows the implementation for MouseSensorApplet.

Example 4-1 MouseSensorApplet **Source Code**

```
import java.applet.Applet;
import java.awt.*;

public class MouseSensorApplet extends Applet {
  public void init() {
      setLayout(new BorderLayout());
      add(new MouseSensorCanvas(), "Center");
  }
}
class MouseSensorCanvas extends Canvas {
  public boolean mouseDown(Event event, int x, int y) {
      System.out.println(whichMouseButton(event) + ":  Down");
      return true;
  }
  public boolean mouseUp(Event event, int x, int y) {
      System.out.println(whichMouseButton(event) + ":  Up");
      return true;
  }
  public boolean mouseDrag(Event event, int x, int y) {
      System.out.println(whichMouseButton(event) + ":  Drag");
      return true;
  }
  private String whichMouseButton(Event event) {
      String s = new String("Mouse Button 1");

      if((event.modifiers & Event.META_MASK) != 0)
          s = "Mouse Button 2";
      else if((event.modifiers & Event.ALT_MASK) != 0)
          s = "Mouse Button 3";

      return s;
  }
}
```

Notice that each of our convenience methods (mouseUp(), mouseDown() and mouseDrag()) prints information about the event, with the help of whichMouseButton(). These methods return true, indicating that the event is fully handled and should not be propagated to the container, which in this case is the applet.

The whichMouseButton() method does the work of distinguishing between the different mouse buttons:

```
private String whichMouseButton(Event event) {
  String s = new String("Mouse Button 1");

  if((event.modifiers & Event.META_MASK) != 0)
    s = "Mouse Button 2";
  else if((event.modifiers & Event.ALT_MASK) != 0)
    s = "Mouse Button 3";

  return s;
}
```

In order to detect mouse button 2 and 3, this method simply uses a bitwise AND to combine the `modifiers` field of the event with the AWT `Event` class constants, `ALT_MASK` and `META_MASK`.

Note that we could have overridden `handleEvent()` and checked the `id` field of the event in order to sense mouse button events, but we have chosen to override convenience methods instead.

NOTE: In the JDK 1.0.2 release, there is a bug in the Windows 95 version of the AWT in which a mouse up with button 1 is detected as a mouse up with button 2. [2]

Of Mice and Buttons

Different platforms typically use different types of mice. Macintosh systems normally use a one-button mouse, PCs a two- or three-button mouse, and SPARC® systems a three-button mouse. Java deals with these differences by assuming that all mice have one button. For example, the AWT distinguishes only one mouse up event. Correspondingly, there is only one method (`mouseUp()`) to account for this. There's no `mouseUp1()`, `mouseUp2()`, `mouseUp3()` to account for the different mouse buttons that might initiate an event. This is also the case for mouse events such as a mouse down or mouse drag. In effect, the AWT is developed for the lowest common denominator.

As we've seen in the `whichMouseButton()` method above, the mechanism employed to determine which mouse button triggered an event is to look at the event's `modifier` field. If the `modifier` field ANDed with the `Event.META_MASK` is non-zero, then we know that mouse button 2 initiated the event, while an `ALT_MASK` represents mouse button 3. Therefore, on a system

---

2.   Note to all those left-handers out there: We generically refer to mouse buttons 1, 2, and 3 rather than left, middle, and right. Mouse button 1 represents the primary mouse button.

with a one-button mouse, mouse button 2 can be simulated by holding down the Meta key when clicking the mouse, and mouse button 3 can be simulated by holding down the Alt key.

Monitoring Mouse Events

In the next applet, we'll illustrate monitoring mouse events such as the mouse moving, entering, and exiting an applet. This particular applet—called EventMonitorApplet—also monitors mouse up and down events and prints information about each event. EventMonitorApplet extends the Applet class (as do all applets). It includes an EventPrinter class that checks to see if an event is a mouse event, and if so, its print() method prints which mouse event occurred. The EventMonitorApplet includes an instance of EventPrinter that is both public and static. It is public because both EventMonitor and EventPrinter classes use it. It is static because only one EventPrinter is required. Note that this applet is set up just like the MouseSensorApplet. It creates an applet, sets its layout to BorderLayout, and then positions an instance of a class that extends Canvas in the center of the applet. Example 4-2 shows the EventMonitorApplet in its entirety.

Example 4-2 EventMonitorApplet **Source Code**

```
import java.applet.Applet;
import java.awt.*;

public class EventMonitorApplet extends Applet {
  public static EventPrinter printer = new EventPrinter();

  public void init() {
      setLayout(new BorderLayout());
      add(new EventMonitor(), "Center");
  }
  public boolean handleEvent(Event event) {
      System.out.print("APPLET:  ");
      printer.print(event);
      System.out.println();
      return true;
  }
}
class EventMonitor extends Canvas {
  public boolean handleEvent(Event event) {
      System.out.print("CANVAS:  ");
      EventMonitorApplet.printer.print(event);
      System.out.println();
      return true;
  }
```

```
   }
   class EventPrinter {
     public void print(Event event) {
         String s = null;

         if(event.id == Event.MOUSE_DOWN)      s = "Mouse Down";
         else if(event.id == Event.MOUSE_UP)    s = "Mouse Up";
         else if(event.id == Event.MOUSE_DRAG)  s = "Mouse Drag";
         else if(event.id == Event.MOUSE_MOVE)  s = "Mouse Move";
         else if(event.id == Event.MOUSE_EXIT)  s = "Mouse Exit";
         else if(event.id == Event.MOUSE_ENTER) s = "Mouse Enter";

         if(s != null)
             System.out.print(s);
         else
             System.out.print(event.id);
     }
   }
```

The EventMonitor class, which extends Canvas, expands to fill the entire
applet. (The fact that the EventMonitor canvas expands to consume the entire
applet area is the by-product of adding it centered in a BorderLayout. We'll talk
more about BorderLayout and layout managers in general in *Components,
Containers, and Layout Managers* on page 373.)

EventMonitorApplet and EventMonitor both override the handleEvent()
method, causing two things to occur when a mouse action takes place:

- Calls System.out.print to print APPLET: or CANVAS:, respectively

- Calls the print() method in the EventPrinter class to print the mouse
  event that occurred (e.g., MOUSE_UP, MOUSE_DOWN)

So, when dragging the mouse over the applet, you'll see output similar to this:

```
APPLET:  Mouse Enter
CANVAS:  Mouse Enter
CANVAS:  Mouse Move
CANVAS:  Mouse Move
CANVAS:  Mouse Move
CANVAS:  Mouse Down
CANVAS:  Mouse Up
CANVAS:  Mouse Move
CANVAS:  Mouse Move
CANVAS:  Mouse Exit
APPLET:  Mouse Exit
```

The `EventMonitorApplet` illustrates that events are propagated from the component in which the event occurred to outermost container. Our containment strategy here is easy to expose: We have a `Canvas` (`EventMonitor`) contained inside an `Applet` (`EventMonitorApplet`). Both of them have overridden `boolean handleEvent(Event)`, ready to deal with whatever events come their way.

Of course, the return value of the `EventMonitor handleEvent()` method determines whether `EventMonitorApplet` sees events that were generated in `EventMonitor`. In the previous output, the only events that `EventMonitorApplet` sees are mouse enter and mouse exit events; all the rest are effectively gobbled up by `EventMonitor`. (Note that there is a bug under Windows 95 that results in some events being propagated up to the `EventMonitorApplet`, even though they are never explicitly propagated).

If, for instance, the `EventMonitor handleEvent()` method returned `false`, then events would be passed to the container's (`EventMonitorApplet`) `handleEvent()` method. The applet output would change to look something like this:

```
APPLET:   Mouse Enter
CANVAS:   Mouse Enter
APPLET:   Mouse Enter
CANVAS:   Mouse Move
APPLET:   Mouse Move
CANVAS:   Mouse Down
APPLET:   Mouse Down
CANVAS:   Mouse Up
APPLET:   Mouse Up
CANVAS:   Mouse Down
APPLET:   Mouse Down
CANVAS:   Mouse Up
APPLET:   Mouse Up
CANVAS:   Mouse Move
APPLET:   Mouse Move
CANVAS:   Mouse Exit
APPLET:   Mouse Exit
APPLET:   Mouse Exit
```

Sensing Double Clicking

Sensing that the mouse has been *double-clicked* requires use of the `Event` `clickCount` field. To illustrate this, we've written the `DoubleClickApplet` program, which is set up like the previous event applets in this chapter. Example 4-3 shows the `DoubleClickApplet` code.

Example 4-3 `DoubleClickApplet` **Source Code**

```
import java.applet.Applet;
import java.awt.*;

public class DoubleClickApplet extends Applet {
  public void init() {
      setLayout(new BorderLayout());
      add(new DoubleClickCanvas(), "Center");
  }
}
class DoubleClickCanvas extends Canvas {
  public boolean mouseDown(Event event, int x, int y) {
      if(event.clickCount == 2)
          System.out.println("Double click");
      return true;
  }
}
```

The overridden `mouseDown()` method simply checks to see if the `Event` `clickCount` field equals 2. If so, `mouseDown()` informs us that a double click has occurred. Regardless of whether a double click has occurred or not, `mouseDown()` returns `true` because our simple-minded applet is not prepared to deal with a propagated event.

There's an interesting aside here. Note that the location of the cursor seems to have no bearing upon whether or not `clickCount` is advanced. If you click the mouse at one location and then hastily move to another location and click again, it will register as a double click. This may lead one to the AWT source in search of an algorithm for advancing the `clickCount`; we do have the AWT source, after all. It may be hard to believe at first, but `clickCount` is not set anywhere other than at construction time, when it is set to zero; who, then, is responsible for advancing `clickCount`? The answer lies in the component's peer—the unseen laborer that implements much of the functionality of the AWT. Unless we have the source for the peers, which we do not, then we have no way of ever knowing the exact criterion for advancing `clickCount`.

Action Events

Action events are generated by the following classes:

- `Button`
- `Checkbox`
- `Choice`

- `List`
- `MenuItem`
- `TextField`

All of the components listed above are capable of generating action events, as you can see from Figure 4-1. Note that action events under the original event model do not necessarily equate to an `ActionEvent` under the delegation event model—see "Semantic Events" on page 105.[3]

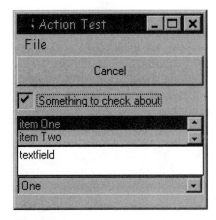

Figure 4-1 Action Events
Action events are events generated by selecting choice items, checkboxes, buttons or menu items, by entering a carriage return in a textfield, or by double-clicking an item in a list.

`ActionTest` creates one of each of these AWT components. The unique characteristic of these AWT components is that *only* `Button`, `Checkbox`, `TextField`, `Choice`, `MenuItem`, and `List` components generate events that are routed through the `Component action()` method. (In contrast, an event from any other component will never result in a call to the `Component action()` method.) Now, let's look at `ActionTest` in Example 4-4 and then discuss the `ActionTest.action()` method.

Example 4-4 `ActionTest` **Source Code**

```
import java.awt.*;

class ActionTest extends Frame {
   Button    button = new Button("Cancel");
```

---

3.   Specifically, checkboxes and choices generate item events instead of action events.

```java
Checkbox   checkbox = new Checkbox("Something to check about");
TextField textfield = new TextField(25);
Choice    choice = new Choice();
List      list = new List();
MenuItem  quitItem = new MenuItem("quit");

static public void main(String args[]) {
   Frame frame = new ActionTest();
   frame.reshape(100,100,200,200);
   frame.show();
}
public ActionTest() {
   super("Action Test");

   MenuBar menubar  = new MenuBar();
   Menu    fileMenu = new Menu("File");

   fileMenu.add("menu item");
   fileMenu.add(quitItem);
   menubar.add(fileMenu);
   setMenuBar(menubar);

   choice.addItem("One");
   choice.addItem("Two");
   choice.addItem("Three");
   choice.addItem("Four");

   list.addItem("item One");
   list.addItem("item Two");
   list.addItem("item Three");
   list.addItem("item Four");
   list.addItem("item Five");
   list.addItem("item Six");

   setLayout(new GridLayout(0,1));
   add(button);
   add(checkbox);
   add(list);
   add(textfield);
   add(choice);
}
public boolean action(Event event, Object what) {
   if(event.target == quitItem) {
       System.exit(0);
   }
   System.out.print(event.target.getClass().getName());
   System.out.println(" " + what.getClass().getName() +
                   "= " + what);
```

```
        return true;
    }
}
```

The `action()` method is passed an `event` and an object we have named `what`. This second argument differs according to the type of component that triggered the event. For example, if `event` is from an instance of `Button`, then `what` will be a `String` containing the label of the button. Table 4-7 shows how the value of the second argument is set, based on the component that generates the `event`.

Table 4-7 Value of the `what` **Argument in the** `action()` **Method**

If the `event` **Is From an Instance of...**	**Then the Second Argument is a...**
`Button`	`String` with the text of label of the button.
`Checkbox`	`Boolean` value, which is `true` if the checkbox is checked and `false` if it is unchecked.
`Choice`	`String` that represents the text displayed in the choice.
`List`	`String` representing the item that was double-clicked.
`MenuItem`	`String` representing the menu item selected.
`TextField`	`String` representing the text in the textfield.

For example, output from the ActionTest application[4] looks like this:

```
java.awt.TextField java.lang.String= text
java.awt.Choice java.lang.String= Three
java.awt.Checkbox java.lang.Boolean= true
java.awt.Button java.lang.String= Cancel
java.awt.MenuItem java.lang.String= menu item
java.awt.List java.lang.String= item One
```

A `TextField` generates an action event *only* after a carriage return. (The 1.0.2 version of the AWT provides no mechanism for being notified when a character other than a carriage return is typed into a textfield.) Action events for `Button`, `CheckBox`, `Choice` or `MenuItem` are generated when each is selected with the mouse. Finally, an action event is generated by double-clicking an item in a `List`.

---

4. ActionTest is an application because it has a menubar, which cannot be added to an applet.

Identifying Components by Label — Just Say No

It is standard AWT practice to check against the labels of certain components (in particular, buttons) to determine the component with which an event is associated. For instance, the following applet displays three buttons and uses the labels of the buttons to determine which one triggered an action event:

```java
import java.applet.Applet;
import java.awt.*;

public class ButtonActionApplet extends Applet {
  public void init() {
      Button buttonOne   = new Button("Button One");
      Button buttonTwo   = new Button("Button Two");
      Button buttonThree = new Button("Button Three");

      add(buttonOne);
      add(buttonTwo);
      add(buttonThree);
  }
  public boolean action(Event event, Object what) {
      if(what.equals("Button One"))
          System.out.println("Button One");
      if(what.equals("Button Two"))
          System.out.println("Button Two");
      if(what.equals("Button Three"))
          System.out.println("Button Three");

      return true;
  }
}
```

While this applet produces the desired effect, namely, it prints the identity of the button activated, it is fraught with difficulties. First of all, the labels of the buttons may very well change over time, causing modification of the action() method each and every time a button has its label changed. This is not a consideration for a toy applet like the one above; however, in the real world it may be unacceptable for a complex applet or application to keep button labels in synch with event handling methods. Furthermore, identifying components by their labels has serious implications for internationalization.

A much better approach is to identify components by reference, instead of their labels, as depicted by the revised applet below:

```java
import java.applet.Applet;
import java.awt.*;
```

```java
public class ButtonActionByRefApplet extends Applet {
    private Button buttonOne   = new Button("Button One");
    private Button buttonTwo   = new Button("Button Two");
    private Button buttonThree = new Button("Button Three");

    public void init() {
        add(buttonOne);
        add(buttonTwo);
        add(buttonThree);
    }
    public boolean action(Event event, Object what) {
        if(event.target == buttonOne)
            System.out.println(buttonOne.getLabel());
        if(event.target == buttonTwo)
            System.out.println(buttonTwo.getLabel());
        if(event.target == buttonThree)
            System.out.println(buttonThree.getLabel());

        return true;
    }
}
```

Notice that we have moved the declarations for the buttons from being local to `init()` to private members of the class. Second, in the `action()` method, we check the target of the event against the button references to identify which button triggered the action event.

This approach ensures that the applet continues to function properly even if we change the labels of the buttons. Note also that we get the label from the buttons themselves to print out the buttons' identity, instead of hardcoding the button labels in the `action()` method.

AWT TIP

Identify Components By Reference, Not By Their Labels

It is standard AWT practice to identify components by their labels when handling certain events. This has some serious implications for maintaining applets and applications, since the methods that identify components must be kept in synch with the component's labels. A better approach is to identify components by reference.

Shortcomings of the Original Event Model

The original event model discussed in this chapter was appropriate for small applets with simple event handling needs, but the model did not scale well for a number of reasons, a few of which we will take the time to briefly explore. The new event model, covered in the next chapter, is delegation-based as opposed to the old model, which was inheritance-based. The inheritance-based model required a component to be extended in order to handle events. Example 4-5 is a simple example of the original event handling mechanism in action; MouseCanvas extends Canvas and overrides handleEvent() to process mouse down events, and mouseUp() to process mouse up events.

Example 4-5 CanvasEventExample—An Example of Inheritance-based Event Model

```
import java.applet.Applet;
import java.awt.*;

public class CanvasEventExample extends Applet {
  public void init() {
    MouseCanvas canvas = new MouseCanvas();
    setLayout(new BorderLayout());
    add(canvas, "Center");
  }
}
class MouseCanvas extends Canvas {
  public boolean handleEvent(Event event) {
    if(event.id == Event.MOUSE_DOWN) {
      System.out.println("Mouse Down!");
      return true;  // event fully handled, don't propagate
    }
    return false;    // event not fully handled, propagate, but
                     // returning false is a bug
  }
  public boolean mouseUp(Event event, int x, int y) {
    System.out.println("Mouse Up!");
    return true;
  }
}
```

Propagation of Events

The original event model required you to determine whether or not an event was propagated to its container, by way of returning a boolean value from overridden event handling methods. handleEvent() and the related convenience methods (such as mouseDown(), mouseUp(), etc.) return a boolean value indicating whether or not the event will be propagated to the component's container. A `true` return value indicates that the event was fully handled by the component and therefore the event is not propagated, whereas `false` means that the event was not fully handled and should be propagated.

Propagation seems like a reasonable design; however, the interaction between propagation and the component hierarchy often resulted in subtle bugs. For instance, our applet in Example 4-5 never has its `mouseUp()` method invoked because we have overridden `handleEvent()`. `Component.handleEvent()` dispatches events to convenience methods (like `mouseUp()`), and since we've overridden `Component.handleEvent()`, that dispatching is no longer invoked. The fix is to have `handleEvent()` return `super.handleEvent(event)`, so that the dispatching can take place, as we've done in Example 4-6.

Example 4-6 CanvasEventExample Revisited

```
import java.applet.Applet;
import java.awt.*;

public class CanvasEventExample extends Applet {
  public void init() {
    MouseCanvas canvas = new MouseCanvas();
    setLayout(new BorderLayout());
    add(canvas, "Center");
  }
}
class MouseCanvas extends Canvas {
  public boolean handleEvent(Event event) {
    if(event.id == Event.MOUSE_DOWN) {
      System.out.println("Mouse Down!");
      return true;  // event fully handled, don't propagate
    }
    return super.handleEvent(event);
  }
  public boolean mouseUp(Event event, int x, int y) {
    System.out.println("Mouse Up!");
    return true;
  }
}
```

As an aside, this is a classic case of inheritance breaking encapsulation. Classes that are unrelated by way of inheritance use each other only by accessing each other's *interface* (public methods). However, classes that are an extension of a (base) class must know a good deal[5] about the *implementation* of the base class they are extending. In this case, extensions of `java.awt.Component` must know that `Component.handleEvent()` dispatches events to convenience methods, in order to determine how to return from overridden `handleEvent()` methods.

Returning `false` instead of `super.handleEvent(event)` is a common error among those new to the AWT. In fact, we felt compelled enough to write an AWT Tip on page 69 warning against the evils of depriving your superclass a crack at handling events.

OO TIP

Prefer Composition Over Inheritance

Instead of extending a class in order to reuse its functionality, it is sometimes preferable to delegate to an enclosed instance of the would-be base class; a technique known as composition. Composition results in less surface area than inheritance because inheritance requires extensions to be intimately familiar with the implementation of their superclass. Composition, on the other hand, requires that the delegator manipulate the delegate via the delegate's public interface (public methods) only, resulting in fewer dependencies and looser coupling between the classes in question.

Inheritance Required

Requiring event handling to be implemented via inheritance can result in a plethora of extensions for functionally identical components that require different event handling algorithms. One can perhaps rightly argue that "plethora" is an exaggeration; however, it is a misplaced use of inheritance that requires you to extend a class in order to change a feature (attributes and/or methods) that varies between individual objects of the same type at runtime—`java.awt.Container` is guilty of this, by requiring you to extend it in order to change its insets. `Component`, by the same token, requires you to override `handleEvent()` (or one of the convenience methods) to handle events. The problem is greatly compounded when the feature is a candidate for frequent change, as is certainly true for event handling.

Embedding Event Handling in Component Classes

With inheritance-based event handling, event handling code becomes hardwired to a single component extension. It is interesting to note that the original designers of the AWT employed the strategy pattern for layout managers, thus decoupling containers from layout management, but neglected to take the same

---

5.   How much one class needs to know about another class is referred to as *surface area*.

approach for event handling. Now, however, with the advent of the delegation-based event model, both layout management and event handling are accomplished by delegating to an object that encapsulates an appropriate algorithm for laying out components and handling events, respectively.

The Responsibility for Routing Events

With inheritance-based delegation, the onus for directing events lies squarely on the shoulders of the component that generates the event. Furthermore, the component in question has little choice as to where to route the event: events could be routed either to the superclass or to the container in which the component resides. With the delegation-based event model, it is the responsibility of event *listeners* to declare themselves interested in certain events associated with a particular component; the events are automatically sent to the listener via the AWT machinery.

The responsibility for routing events should be the purview of objects that are *listeners* of events, rather than objects that *generate* events; if a listener is interested in a button's activation, for instance, the listener should be responsible for registering interest in a particular button's action event—it should not be the responsibility of the button to arrange for events to be routed to the listener.

If the responsibility for routing events is left to the component that generates the event, then the component has to know who is interested in its events at the time the component is developed, which is quite restrictive.

When the responsibility for routing events is shifted from the component to the listener[6], the component knows nothing about who is listening to its events, and therefore the component never needs to be extended for the purpose of routing events to listeners. When the component is responsible for routing events, it also becomes tightly coupled with the classes to whom it routes events. When the listener is responsible for registering interest in events, the component is decoupled from the objects that listen to its events. Such decoupling translates into much more modular code in which it is natural to separate out the user interface classes from the underlying object model.

handleEvent() Switch Statement

Another major drawback with the inheritance-based model was the fact that switch statements within overridden `handleEvent()` methods work fine for simple applets but become a maintenance nightmare in complex surroundings.

---

6.   Strictly speaking, the responsibility for routing events is still shouldered by `java.awt.Component`. However the responsibility for arranging for the event to be routed is the listener's.

Switch statements that switch off an object's type (implied or concrete), are nearly always the result of a faulty object-oriented design. Instead of a switch statement, polymorphism should be employed in order to let the compiler (instead of the developer) decide what functionality to invoke given the type of object[7]. Typically, when a switch statement that switches off object types exists in object-oriented code, it should be refactored so that the constants signifying object types are turned into a hierarchy of classes. The switch statements are then rewritten to simply invoke a method on an object whose type is typically at (or near) the top of the hierarchy of classes. This is exactly what has happened for the 1.1 event model. Instead of integer constants that signify event types in the `Event` class, the delegation-based event model provides a hierarchy of event classes, such as: `AWTEvent, ActionEvent, ComponentEvent, KeyEvent, MouseEvent`, and so forth.

Summary

All applets involving the AWT are event driven. The applets display their components and patiently wait for some event to occur. There's a special group of event handling methods, generically referred to as propagated event handlers because they either handle an event or propagate it up to the container in which the component is displayed. A propagated event handler returns `true` to indicate the event has been completely handled and should not be propagated up to its container; it returns `false` to indicate that the event is to be propagated up to the container. Propagated events always work their way from the innermost component to the outermost container. We've seen that overridden `handleEvent()` methods should never return `false` and directly propagate events to their containers but should instead return `super.handleEvent(event)` to give their superclass a crack at the event and decide whether to propagate the event. Additionally, we have seen that overridden convenience methods, such as `mouseDown()` should not return `super.handleEvent()` because doing so may very well result in an infinite loop.

The AWT `Button, Checkbox, TextField`, and `Choice` components are unique in that they generate events that are routed through a `Component action()` method. This method takes an `Event` argument and an `Object` argument. The latter is set according to the type of `Component` that generated the event.

7.   See Cox, Brad. *Object Oriented Programming An Evolutionary Approach,* chapter 4. Addison-Wesley, 1984.

While it is standard AWT practice to check against the label of certain components to identify the component with which an event is associated, we have advised you to check against object references rather than labels.

Finally, this chapter has covered the original, inheritance-based event model. The 1.1 version of the AWT has a new event model that is delegation based and vastly improved over the original. If possible, you should use the new event model, which is discussed at length in the next chapter.

CHAPTER
5

Delegation-Based Event Model (AWT 1.1 and Beyond)

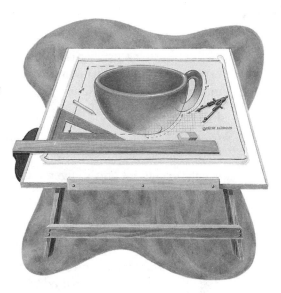

The 1.1 version of the AWT sports a new event model that is delegation-based instead of inheritance-based and is vastly improved over the original model. The 1.1 version of the AWT still supports the old (inheritance-based) event model; however, the old model will be phased out in a future release.

This chapter discusses the new event model in depth. In "Shortcomings of the Original Event Model" on page 86, we discussed some of the drawbacks of the original event model, all of which are addressed by the new model. Applets (and applications) that use the original event model will still continue to work under the new model, however the old API will be eliminated in a future release. For now, compiler warnings are issued if you are still using the old API, and mixing the two event models in a single component is not supported. We strongly suggest that you update your old event handling code to conform to the new model as soon as possible and that you use the new event model for any new development. We give guidelines for doing so in Event Handling Design on page 141.

The Delegation Event Model

The premise behind the delegation event model is simple: *components* fire *events*, which can be listened for and acted upon, by *listeners*. Listeners are registered with a component by invoking one of a number of addXYZListener(XYZListener)

93

methods. After a listener is added to a component, appropriate methods in the listener's interface will be called when events for which the listener has registered interest are fired by the component.

Filtering Events

Under the old model, all events were sent to every component whether the component was interested in the event or not. The new event model filters events; events are only delivered to a component if:

- **A listener interested in the event is added to the component, OR**

- `Component.enableEvents(long mask)` **is invoked, where** `mask` **represents the events to be delivered.**

Regardless of which approach is taken, events associated with either the mask or the type of listener will be fired by the component and either passed along to listeners or made available for overridden event handling methods.

The Big Picture

All of the action, as far as events and listeners are concerned, starts in the `java.util` package. `java.util` comes with a class and an interface— `EventObject` and `EventListener`, respectively, which form the foundation of the 1.1 event model. `EventObject` is a simple class that does nothing more than keep track of its event source, and `EventListener` is a *tagging*[1] interface, which all listeners extend. `EventListener` and `EventObject` anchor hierarchies of listeners and events, respectively. Figure 5-1 shows the event listeners, all of which extend the `java.util.EventListener` interface.

---

1. A tagging interface does not define any methods.

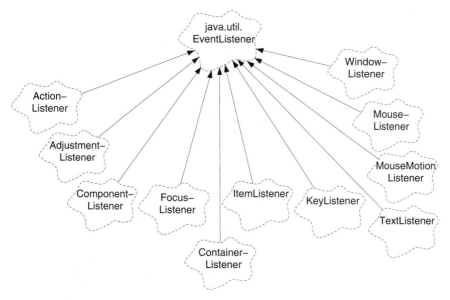

Figure 5-1 Event Listener Interfaces
All of the event listener interfaces shown above reside in the
`java.awt.event` package, except for `java.util.EventListener`.

Figure 5-2 shows the hierarchy of AWT event classes.

`java.util.EventObject` maintains a reference to the source of the event[2], and the `AWTEvent` class keeps track of the ID of the event and whether or not the event is consumed[3]. For the most part, the 1.1 version of the AWT has done away with public variables—access to the source and ID of an event are provided through public accessor methods on the appropriate class—see "AWTEvent and Extensions: Public Methods and Constants" on page 100.

---

2. Note that the event source is of type `Object`, and not `Component`.
3. Consumed events are not passed along to peers. See "Consuming Events" on page 119.

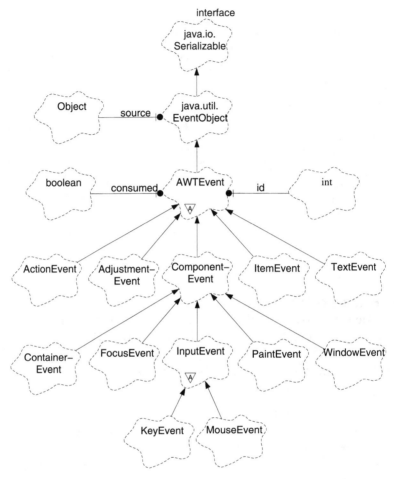

Figure 5-2 AWT Event Class Hierarchy
The 1.1 release of the AWT provides a hierarchy of event classes

Components

Many AWT components are fitted with add*XYZ*Listener(*XYZ*Listener) methods to allow certain types of listeners to register interest in events. For instance, as you can see from Table 5-1, java.awt.Button comes with an addActionListener(ActionListener) method.

In order to handle a particular event for a given component, simply create a listener and pass it to the component's appropriate add*XYZ*Listener() method, and the events in question will automatically be routed to the listener, meaning one of the methods in Table 5-1 will be invoked. Realize that all of the

`java.awt.Component` extensions (`Button`, `Choice`, etc.) inherit the
add*XYZ*`Listener()` methods implemented in the `Component` class. Therefore,
buttons, for instance, can support component, focus, key, mouse, and mouse
motion listeners in addition to action listeners.

Table 5-1 AWT Component Listener Registration Methods

AWT Class/Interface	Listener Registration Methods
`Button`	`void addActionListener(ActionListener)`
`Checkbox`	`void addItemListener(ItemListener)`
`CheckboxMenuItem`	`void addItemListener(ItemListener)`
`Choice`	`void addItemListener(ItemListener)`
`Component`	`void addComponentListener(ComponentListener)`
	`void addFocusListener(FocusListener)`
	`void addKeyListener(KeyListener)`
	`void addMouseListener(MouseListener)`
	`void addMouseMotionListener(MouseMotionListener)`
`Container`	`addContainerListener(ContainerListener)`
`List`	`void addItemListener(ItemListener)`
	`void addActionListener(ActionListener)`
`MenuItem`	`void addActionListener(ActionListener)`
`Scrollbar`	`void addAdjustmentListener(AdjustmentListener)`
`TextArea`	`void addTextListener(TextListener)`
`TextComponent`	`void addTextListener(TextListener)`
`TextField`	`void addActionListener(ActionListener)`
`Window`	`void addWindowListener(WindowListener)`

Note that more than one listener of a particular type can be registered with a
single component. For instance, a button may have a number of action listeners,
all of which listen for action events fired by the button. In such a case, the order in
which events are delivered to the registered listeners is undefined. In practice, this
is usually not a problem, but there are situations where the order of notification is
important. You might think that the order of notification corresponds to the order
in which the listeners are added to the component, but that is not necessarily the
case.

As a matter of fact, we will run across such a situation in "A Rubberband Panel"
on page 648.

AWT TIP ...

Notification Order For Multiple Listeners Is Undefined

If multiple listeners of a particular type are registered with a single component, the order in which the listeners are notified of events is undefined. Although it might seem that the order of notification should correspond to the order in which the listeners are added to the component, that is not necessarily the case. At any rate, you should not rely upon the observed order of notification for multiple listeners, as it may vary from one platform to another.

Focus and Key Events

While all components are capable of firing focus and key events, a component must have keyboard focus in order to fire key or focus events. Canvases and panels, by default, are not interested in obtaining keyboard focus, and therefore will not fire key or focus events. To handle key and/or focus events for a canvas or panel, you must invoke `requestFocus()` on the canvas or panel in question. Once the canvas or panel has keyboard focus, it will fire key and focus events.

Listeners

The `java.awt.event` package defines eleven interfaces for different types of listeners. Each listener interface defines methods that will be invoked when a specific event occurs. For instance, as you can see from Table 5-2, `java.awt.event.ActionListener` defines a lone method: `actionPerformed()`, which is invoked when an *action* event is fired from a component with which the listener has registered interest.

Table 5-2 also lists the corresponding event constant and convenience methods from the old event model to aid you in converting your code to the new model. For example, handling an event under the old event model by checking the `id` field of the event for `ACTION_EVENT` or overriding `action()` gets replaced by an `ActionListener` that has its `actionPerformed()` method invoked when an action event is fired[4].

---

4. There are actually a number of different approaches to take when converting event handling code from the old model to the new. See "Event Handling Design" on page 141.

Table 5-2 java.awt.event Listeners

Interface	Methods	Corresponding Event/Method from 1.02
ActionListener	void actionPerformed(ActionEvent)	ACTION_EVENT/action()
AdjustmentListener	void adjustmentValueChanged(AdjustmentEvent)	N/A
ComponentListener	void componentResized(ComponentEvent)	N/A
	void componentMoved(ComponentEvent)	COMPONENT_MOVED
	void componentShown(ComponentEvent)	N/A
	void componentHidden(ComponentEvent)	N/A
ContainerListener	void componentAdded(ContainerEvent)	N/A
	void componentRemoved(ContainerEvent)	N/A
FocusListener	void focusGained(FocusEvent)	GOT_FOCUS/gotFocus()
	void focusLost(FocusEvent)	LOST_FOCUS/lostFocus()
ItemListener	void itemStateChanged(ItemEvent)	LIST_SELECT, LIST_DESELECT
KeyListener	void keyTyped(KeyEvent)	N/A
	void keyPressed(KeyEvent)	KEY_PRESS/keyDown()
	void keyReleased(KeyEvent)	KEY_RELEASE/keyUp()
MouseListener	void mouseClicked(MouseEvent)	MOUSE_UP/mouseUp()
	void mousePressed(MouseEvent)	MOUSE_DOWN/mouseDown()
	void mouseReleased(MouseEvent)	MOUSE_UP/mouseUp()
	void mouseEntered(MouseEvent)	MOUSE_ENTER/mouseEnter()
	void mouseExited(MouseEvent)	MOUSE_EXIT/mouseExit()
MouseMotion-Listener	void mouseDragged(MouseEvent)	MOUSE_DRAG/mouseDrag()
	void mouseMoved(MouseEvent)	MOUSE_MOVE/mouseMove()
TextListener	void textValueChanged(TextEvent)	N/A
WindowListener	void windowActivated(WindowEvent)	N/A
	void windowDeactivated(WindowEvent)	N/A
	void windowClosing(WindowEvent)	N/A
	void windowClosed(WindowEvent)	WINDOW_DESTROY
	void windowOpened(WindowEvent)	WINDOW_EXPOSE
	void windowIconified(WindowEvent)	WINDOW_ICONIFY
	void windowDeiconified(WindowEvent)	WINDOW_DEICONIFY

Events

Table 5-3 lists the public methods for AWTEvent and its extensions, excluding irrelevant methods such as toString(). The new event model provides classes for events instead of representing events by integer constants, thereby eliminating the switch statement that resided in many overridden handleEvent() methods under the original event model. However, implementing a class for every possible event would result in an overwhelming number of event classes, so some event classes encompass a number of related events. For instance, WindowEvent represents events for activating, deactivating, closing, opening, iconifying and deiconifying windows. As a result, some of the event classes define integer constants for encoding the particular type of event that they represent[5]. These constants, along with other constants defined by the event classes are also listed in Table 5-3.

Table 5-3 AWTEvent and Extensions: Public Methods and Constants

Class	Public Interface	Constants
AWTEvent	int getId()	COMPONENT_EVENT_MASK, FOCUS_EVENT_MASK
		KEY_EVENT_MASK, MOUSE_EVENT_MASK
		MOUSE_MOTION_EVENT_MASK
		WINDOW_EVENT_MASK, ACTION_EVENT_MASK
		ADJUSTMENT_EVENT_MASK, ITEM_EVENT_MASK
ActionEvent	String getActionCommand()	SHIFT_MASK, CTRL_MASK, META_MASK, ALT_MASK
	int getModifiers()	ACTION_FIRST, ACTION_LAST, ACTION_PERFORMED
AdjustmentEvent	Adjustable getAdjustable()	ADJUSTMENT_FIRST, ADJUSTMENT_LAST
	int getValue()	ADJUSTMENT_VALUE_CHANGED
	int getAdjustmentType()	UNIT_INCREMENT, UNIT_DECREMENT
		BLOCK_INCREMENT, BLOCK_DECREMENT, TRACK
ComponentEvent	Component getComponent()	COMPONENT_FIRST, COMPONENT_LAST
		COMPONENT_MOVED, COMPONENT_RESIZED
		COMPONENT_SHOWN, COMPONENT_HIDDEN
ContainerEvent	Container getContainer()	CONTAINER_FIRST
	Component getChild()	CONTAINER_LAST
		CONTAINER_ADDED
		CONTAINER_REMOVED

5. Note that use of these constants can result in switch statements, but the switch statements will be simple and self-contained.

Table 5-3 AWTEvent and Extensions: Public Methods and Constants (Continued)

Class	Public Interface	Constants
FocusEvent	boolean isTemporary()	FOCUS_FIRST, FOCUS_LAST FOCUS_GAINED, FOCUS_LOST
InputEvent	boolean isShiftDown() boolean isControlDown() boolean isMetaDown() boolean isAltDown() long getWhen() int getModifiers() void consume() boolean isConsumed()	SHIFT_MASK, CTRL_MASK, META_MASK, ALT_MASK BUTTON1_MASK, BUTTON2_MASK, BUTTON3_MASK
ItemEvent	ItemSelectable getItemSelectable() Object getItem() int getStateChange()	ITEM_FIRST, ITEM_LAST, ITEM_STATE_CHANGED, SELECTED, DESELECTED
KeyEvent	int getKeyCode() void setKeyCode() void setModifiers() char getKeyChar() void setKeyChar() boolean isActionKey()	KEY_FIRST, KEY_LAST KEY_TYPED, KEY_PRESSED, KEY_RELEASED KEY_ACTION_FIRST, KEY_ACTION_LAST HOME, END, PGUP, PGDN, UP, DOWN F1, F2, F3, F4, F5, F6, F7, F8, F9, F10, F11, F12, PRINT_SCREEN, SCROLL_LOCK, CAPS_LOCK, NUM_LOCK, PAUSE, INSERT, ENTER, BACK_SPACE, TAB, ESCAPE, DELETE
MouseEvent	int getClickCount() int getX() int getY() Point getPoint() void translatePoint(int x, int y) boolean isPopupTrigger()	MOUSE_FIRST, MOUSE_LAST MOUSE_CLICKED, MOUSE_PRESSED, MOUSE_RELEASED, MOUSE_MOVED, MOUSE_ENTERED, MOUSE_EXITED, MOUSE_DRAGGED

Table 5-3 AWTEvent and Extensions: Public Methods and Constants (Continued)

Class	Public Interface	Constants
PaintEvent	Rectangle getUpdateRect() void setUpdateRect(Rectangle)	PAINT_FIRST, PAINT_LAST, PAINT, UPDATE
TextEvent	N/A	TEXT_FIRST TEXT_LAST TEXT_VALUE_CHANGED
WindowEvent	Window getWindow()	WINDOW_FIRST, WINDOW_LAST, WINDOW_OPENED, WINDOW_CLOSING, WINDOW_CLOSED, WINDOW_ICONIFIED, WINDOW_DEICONIFIED

An Action Event Example

Let's start out by writing a simple applet that creates a button and a listener to listen for the button's action events. If we look at Table 5-1 on page 97, we see that Button has an addActionListener(ActionListener) method. From Table 5-2 on page 99, we see that ActionListener defines only the actionPerformed(ActionEvent) method. Our task, therefore, is to create a listener class by implementing the ActionListener interface and then pass an instance of our new listener class to the button's addActionListener() method. Example 5-1 lists our simple applet. When an action event occurs, our listener will have its actionPerformed(ActionEvent) method invoked.

Example 5-1 Action Example—A Button and ActionListener

```
import java.awt.*;
import java.awt.event.*;
import java.applet.Applet;

public class ActionExample extends Applet {
  public void init() {
    Button button = new Button("Activate Me");
    button.addActionListener(new ButtonListener());
    add(button);
  }
}
class ButtonListener implements ActionListener {
  public void actionPerformed(ActionEvent event) {
    System.out.println("Button Activated!");
  }
}
```

A Mouse Event Example

This time around, we'll listen for mouse events from our button. By the way, the new event model distinguishes between mouse events and mouse motion events. Mouse motion events are mouse moved and mouse dragged events, whereas all other mouse events, are, well, they're all other mouse events. Example 5-2 adds a mouse listener to a button and prints out mouse enter and exit events.

Example 5-2 ButtonTest Applet—Implementing the MouseListener Interface

```
import java.awt.*;
import java.awt.event.*;
import java.applet.Applet;

public class ButtonTest extends Applet {
  public void init() {
     Button button = new Button("Press Me");
     button.addMouseListener(new ButtonMouseListener());
     add(button);
  }
}
class ButtonMouseListener implements MouseListener {
  public void mouseEntered(MouseEvent event) {
     System.out.println("Mouse Entered Button");
  }
  public void mouseExited(MouseEvent event) {
     System.out.println("Mouse Exited Button");
  }
  public void mousePressed (MouseEvent event) { }
  public void mouseClicked (MouseEvent event) { }
  public void mouseReleased(MouseEvent event) { }
}
```

Notice that `MouseListener` defines methods for a mouse click and a mouse release. The `mouseClicked()` method is invoked when the mouse button is released immediately following a mouse press. The `mouseReleased()` method is invoked when the mouse button is released following a mouse drag.

Adapters

As you might well imagine, it could become rather tedious to have to implement all the methods associated with one or more listener interfaces if you are only interested in giving meaningful purpose to a small percentage of the methods. For instance, you might have a selectable object that you'd like to be selected with a mouse press; if so, you'd want implement `MouseListener` and override `mousePressed()`. Since an interface is being implemented, however, the other four `MouseListener` methods must be implemented, typically as no-ops, in order for the class to be concrete (nonabstract). The `java.awt.event` package contains classes known as adapters, that implement listener interfaces— `MouseAdapter`, for instance, implements `MouseListener`. The methods in an adapter class all have no-op implementations. Using adapter classes means that instead of implementing an interface and having to code a handful of no-op methods, we can extend a class full of no-ops and selectively override the methods that we're interested in. Example 5-3 is functionally identical to Example 5-2, except that `ButtonMouseListener` extends the `MouseAdapter` class instead of implementing the `MouseListener` interface.

Example 5-3 Extending MouseAdapter Instead of Implementing MouseListener

```java
import java.awt.*;
import java.awt.event.*;
import java.applet.Applet;

public class ButtonTest2 extends Applet {
  public void init() {
    Button    button = new Button("Press Me");
    button.addMouseListener(new ButtonMouseListener());
    add(button);
  }
}
class ButtonMouseListener extends MouseAdapter {
  public void mouseEntered(MouseEvent event) {
    System.out.println("Mouse Entered Button");
  }
  public void mouseExited(MouseEvent event) {
    System.out.println("Mouse Exited Button");
  }
}
```

Table 5-4 lists the adapter classes provided by the AWT, along with the listener interfaces they implement. Notice that there are no adapter classes for `ActionListener`, `AdjustmentListener`, `ItemListener` and `TextListener` because those interfaces define only one method.

Table 5-4 AWT Adapter Classes

Adapter Class	Implements This Interface ...
ComponentAdapter	ComponentListener
ContainerAdapter	ContainerListener
FocusAdapter	FocusListener
KeyAdapter	KeyListener
MouseAdapter	MouseListener
MouseMotionAdapter	MouseMotionListener
WindowAdapter	WindowListener

Semantic Events

The majority of event classes represent low-level events, such as mouse down, key pressed, etc. The AWT also provides *semantic* events, which are higher-level events, such as an action event. Semantic events do not equate to any single low-level input but describe an event that may consist of a number of low-level events.

For instance, if you wheel the mouse (mouse moved) into a `java.awt.Button` (mouse entered), press the mouse button (mouse pressed, and release it inside of the button (mouse clicked), the button will fire an action event. Semantic events are handled in exactly the same manner as low-level inputs; there are four semantic events in `java.awt.event`: `ActionEvent`, `AdjustmentEvent`, `ItemEvent`, and `TextEvent` as you can see from Table 5-5.

Table 5-5 Semantic Events

Semantic Event	Fired By ...	When ...
ActionEvent	Button	button is activated
	List	item is double-clicked
	MenuItem	item is selected
	TextField	enter is typed in field
AdjustmentEvent	Scrollbar	the thumb is moved
ItemEvent	Checkbox	the checkbox is toggled
	CheckboxMenuItem	the menu item is selected
	Choice	item in choice is selected
	List	item in list is selected
TextEvent	TextComponent	the text changes

As you might suspect, an `AdjustmentEvent` is only fired by components that you can adjust—in the 1.1 release of the AWT that would be all classes that implement the `Adjustable` interface, namely, `java.awt.Scrollbar`[6]. Item events are fired by components that have items: `Checkbox`, `CheckboxMenuItem`[7], `Choice`, and `List`. Text events are fired by components that have editable text, which means anything that extends `TextComponent`, namely, `TextField` and `TextArea`. Which components fire action events is not so intuitive—`Button`, `List`, `MenuItem`, and `TextField` all fire action events. Note that `List` and `TextField` fire two different kinds of semantic events: a `List` fires item events when an item in the list is selected, and an action event when an item in the list is double-clicked. A `TextField` fires action events when enter is typed in the field, and fires text events whenever its text is modified.

AWT TIP...

Have Custom Components Fire Semantic Events When Appropriate

Custom components should fire semantic events when appropriate. The exact definitions of semantic events are intentionally left vague—an action event, for example, means different things depending upon the type of component that fires the event. For instance, image buttons should fire action events in a manner similar to the action events fired by a java.awt.Button, while custom components with selectable items should fire item events, Components that are adjustable should fire adjustment events, and components with editable text should fire text events.

Action Events

Figure 5-3 shows an application that handles action events for all of the components that fire them (see Table 5-5 on page 105). We implement two listeners: `ActionWindowListener`, which listens for the closing of the window, and `DebugActionListener`, which simply prints out information about action events as they are fired. Instances of `DebugActionListener` are added to each component, and add an instance of `ActionWindowListener` is added to the frame itself. From there on out, the AWT machinery takes care of business for us.

---

6.   Actually, a package private class, `ScrollPaneAdjustable` also implements `Adjustable`.

7.   We're reaching here—Checkboxes and CheckboxMenuItems have only one item.

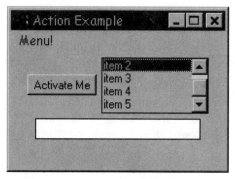

Figure 5-3 Action Events

Action events are generated by double-clicking list items, activating buttons, and entering a carriage return in a textfield or selecting a MenuItem.

Example 5-4 ActionExample2

```java
import java.awt.*;
import java.awt.event.*;

public class ActionExample2 extends Frame {
   private Button    button   = new Button("Activate Me");
   private List      list     = new List();
   private TextField textfield = new TextField(25);
   private MenuItem  menuItem = new MenuItem("Menu menuItem");

   static public void main(String args[]) {
      ActionExample2 f = new ActionExample2();
      f.setBounds(200,200,200,200);
      f.show();
   }
   public ActionExample2() {
      super("Action Example");

      MenuBar mbar = new MenuBar();
      Menu    menu = new Menu("Menu!");

      menu.add(menuItem);
      mbar.add(menu);
      setMenuBar(mbar);

      list.add("item 1");
      list.add("item 2");
      list.add("item 3");
      list.add("item 4");
      list.add("item 5");
```

```
        setLayout(new FlowLayout());
        add(button);
        add(list);
        add(textfield);

        button.addActionListener    (new DebugActionListener());
        list.addActionListener      (new DebugActionListener());
        textfield.addActionListener (new DebugActionListener());
        menuItem.addActionListener  (new DebugActionListener());

        addWindowListener(new ActionWindowListener());
    }
}
class ActionWindowListener extends WindowAdapter {
    public void windowClosing(WindowEvent event) {
        Window window = (Window)event.getSource();
        window.setVisible(false);
        window.dispose();
        System.exit(0);
    }
}
class DebugActionListener implements ActionListener {
    public void actionPerformed(ActionEvent event) {
        System.out.println(event);
    }
}
```

Adjustment Events

Adjustment events are fired by classes that implement the Adjustable interface. Adjustables, as you can surmise from Table 5-6, are objects that maintain an integer value that can be adjusted between settable minimum and maximum values. Adjustables can have their values adjusted by incrementing or decrementing their unit and block increments or by having their value set directly. The exact meaning of unit and block is dependent upon the object that implements the Adjustable interface, but typically a block is defined to be a certain number of units. For example, a text editor would probably define a unit to be a single line of text, and a block would correspond to a page.

The 1.1 version of the AWT contains only one public class that implements the Adjustable interface—java.awt.Scrollbar. Scrollbars can be incremented or decremented by their unit value by activating the scrollbar arrows. They can also be incremented or decremented by their block value by clicking anywhere in the scrollbar outside of the arrows or the slider (thumb) of the scrollbar. The visible value of a scrollbar corresponds to the width of the slider of the scrollbar, and is settable. (See "Scrolling: Scrollbars and Scrollpanes" on page 243.)

Table 5-6 Adjustable Interface

Method	Intent
void setMinimum(int)	Sets minimum value.
void setMaximum(int)	Sets maximum value.
void setUnitIncrement(int)	Sets the unit increment—typically the smallest meaningful increment.
void setBlockIncrement(int)	Sets the block increment—typically defined as a number of units.
void setVisibleAmount(int)	Sets the length of proportional indicator.
void setValue(int)	Sets the current value of adjustable.
int getOrientation()	Returns either Adjustable.HORIZONTAL or Adjustable.VERTICAL.
int getMinimum()	Returns the minimum value the adjustable can take on.
int getMaximum()	Returns the maximum value the adjustable can take on.
int getUnitIncrement()	Returns the unit increment.
int getBlockIncrement()	Returns the block increment.
int getValue()	Returns the current value.
void addAdjustmentListener(AdjustmentListener)	Adds an adjustment listener to adjustable.
void removeAdjustmentListener(AdjustmentListener)	Removes an adjustment listener to adjustable.

java.awt.ScrollPane contains two adjustables[8], to which you can obtain a reference by invoking ScrollPane.getHAdjustable() and ScrollPane.getVAdjustable().

Note that while a scrollpane's adjustables are actually scrollbars, the methods used to access the scrollbars return references to an Adjustable, not a Scrollbar. The reason for this is twofold. First, Scrollbar adds only one public method to the Adjustable interface:[9] setOrientation(). If ScrollPane were to return a reference to a Scrollbar instead of an Adjustable, the orientation of its scrollbars could be modified, which would be highly undesirable. Also, by returning a reference to an Adjustable instead of a

---

8. Which may or may not be visible depending upon what is being scrolled and the scrollbar display policy of the scrollpane.
9. Excluding constructors.

`Scrollbar`, `ScrollPane` hides the implementation of its adjustables, which leaves it free to implement its adjustable components using something other than a scrollbar in the future or on different platforms.

The applet pictured in Figure 5-4 contains a scrollbar and a scrollpane and monitors the firing of adjustment events. The applet is listed in Example 5-5. Whenever the slider of a scrollbar is moved, adjustment events are fired, which we listen for and print out in the `adjustmentValueChanged()` method for our `DebugAdjustmentListener`.

OO TIP

Hide Implementations Of Enclosed Objects By Returning References To Interfaces

It is often the case that objects contain other objects—for instance, a ScrollPane contains two scrollbars for scrolling the contents of the scrollpane. Furthermore, it is sometimes desirable to provide accessors to contained objects. In such a case, it is generally preferable to return a reference to an interface that the enclosed objects implement instead of a reference to the actual class of the enclosed object. Doing so hides the actual implementation of the enclosed objects, which affords the enclosing object the freedom to change the actual class of the enclosed objects (as long as the class implements the interface returned).

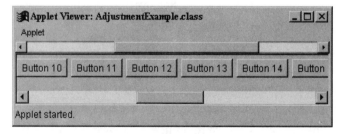

Figure 5-4 Adjustment Events
Adjustment events are fired by the `java.awt.Scrollbar` component, the only adjustable component in the AWT. The bottom scrollbar is part of a scrollpane that scrolls 25 cleverly labeled Buttons. The top scrollbar is a loner.

Example 5-5 AdjustmentExample

```java
import java.awt.*;
import java.awt.event.*;
import java.applet.Applet;

public class AdjustmentExample extends Applet {
  private ScrollPane scroller = new ScrollPane();
  private Scrollbar sbar = new Scrollbar(Scrollbar.HORIZONTAL);

  public void init() {
    setLayout(new BorderLayout());
    sbar.setValues(0,  // value
                   50, // visible
                   0,  // minimum
                   100 // maximum
                   );
    sbar.setLineIncrement(10);
    sbar.setPageIncrement(20);

    add(sbar, "North");
    scroller.add(new ScrollMe(), 0);
    add(scroller, "Center");

    sbar.addAdjustmentListener(new DebugAdjustmentListener());

    DebugAdjustmentListener listener =
          new DebugAdjustmentListener();

    sbar.addAdjustmentListener(listener);
    scroller.getVAdjustable().addAdjustmentListener(listener)
    scroller.getHAdjustable().addAdjustmentListener(listener);
  }
}
class ScrollMe extends Panel {
  public ScrollMe() {
    for(int i=0; i < 25; ++i)
        add(new Button("Button " + i));
  }
}
class DebugAdjustmentListener implements AdjustmentListener {
  public void adjustmentValueChanged(AdjustmentEvent event) {
    Object obj = event.getSource();
    System.out.println(obj.toString());
  }
}
```

Item Events

Our next semantic event application deals with item events. An `ItemEvent` is fired any time you select or deselect an item in an item selectable component—see "Item Selectables: Checkboxes, Choices, and Lists" on page 195. As you can see from Table 5-5 on page 105, item events are fired by the AWT components that contain items: `Checkbox`, `CheckboxMenuItem`, `Choice`, and `List`. Figure 5-5 shows our `ItemExample` applet in action; Example 5-6 shows the source for our applet.

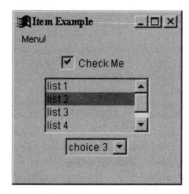

Figure 5-5 Item Events
ItemEvents are fired by components that contain items:
`Checkbox`, `CheckboxMenuItem`, `Choice`, and `List`.

Example 5-6 ItemExample

```java
import java.awt.*;
import java.awt.event.*;
import java.applet.Applet;

public class ItemExample extends Frame {
   private Checkbox   cbox      = new Checkbox("Check Me");
   private Choice     choice    = new Choice();
   private List       list      = new List();
   private CheckboxMenuItem  menuItem =
               new CheckboxMenuItem("Menu menuItem");

   static public void main(String args[]) {
      ItemExample f = new ItemExample();
      f.setBounds(200,200,200,200);
      f.show();
   }
   public ItemExample() {
      super("Item Example");
```

```
    MenuBar mbar = new MenuBar();
    Menu     menu = new Menu("Menu!");

    menu.add(menuItem);
    mbar.add(menu);
    setMenuBar(mbar);

    list.add("list 1");
    list.add("list 2");
    list.add("list 3");
    list.add("list 4");
    list.add("list 5");

    choice.add("choice 1");
    choice.add("choice 2");
    choice.add("choice 3");
    choice.add("choice 4");
    choice.add("choice 5");

    setLayout(new FlowLayout());
    add(cbox);
    add(list);
    add(choice);

    cbox.addItemListener    (new DebugItemListener());
    list.addItemListener    (new DebugItemListener());
    choice.addItemListener  (new DebugItemListener());
    menuItem.addItemListener(new DebugItemListener());
    addWindowListener(new ItemWindowListener());
  }
}
class ItemWindowListener extends WindowAdapter {
  public void windowClosing(WindowEvent event) {
    Window window = (Window)event.getSource();
    window.dispose();
    System.exit(0);
  }
}
class DebugItemListener implements ItemListener {
  public void itemStateChanged(ItemEvent event) {
    Object obj = event.getSource();
    System.out.println(obj.toString());
  }
}
```

Text Events

Our final semantic event applet deals with text events. A `TextEvent` is fired by components that have editable text—`TextField` and `TextArea`, both of which extend `TextComponent`. A `TextEvent` is fired any time a text component's editable text is modified. You can see our applet in action in Figure 5-6—the corresponding source for the applet is listed in Example 5-7.

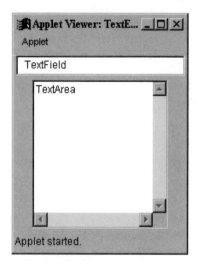

Figure 5-6 Text Events
A `TextEvent` is fired by components that contain editable text: `TextField` and `TextArea` (extensions of `TextComponent`).

Example 5-7 TextExample Applet

```
import java.awt.*;
import java.awt.event.*;
import java.applet.Applet;

public class TextExample extends Applet {
  private TextField textField = new TextField(25);
  private TextArea  textArea  = new TextArea(10, 20);

    public void init() {
        add(textField);
        add(textArea);

        textField.addTextListener(new DebugTextListener());
        textArea.addTextListener(new DebugTextListener());
  }
}
```

```
class DebugTextListener implements TextListener {
  public void textValueChanged(TextEvent event) {
    Object obj = event.getSource();
    System.out.println(obj.toString());
  }
}
```

Inheritance-Based Mechanism

Under certain circumstances, an inheritance-based event handling mechanism *may* be preferable to delegation. For instance, if a class provides some fundamental functionality that is tied to a particular event, an inheritance-based approach might possibly be preferred. The JDK documentation for the event model stresses that the inheritance-based mechanism is to be used sparingly, if at all.

As soon as we've said that, however, we should point out that the inheritance-based mechanism does have its place, in fact, we will encounter a situation where the inheritance-based mechanism *must* be used—see "A Rubberband Panel" on page 648.

AWT TIP ...

Use Inheritance-Based Event Handling Sparingly

The documentation that comes with the 1.1 AWT recommends that you use the inheritance-based mechanism sparingly. As we'll see later on in this chapter, the inheritance-based mechanism can be simulated by listening to yourself, in which case you get nearly all of the benefits associated with the inheritance-based mechanism, while avoiding all of its drawbacks.

Example 5-8 lists the implementation of a button that draws a 3D rectangle around the border of the button when the mouse enters and draws a flat border when the mouse exits, using the inheritance-based feature of the new event model. Under the original event model, we may have chosen to override `mouseEnter()` and `mouseExit()` in order to get the job done. With the new event model, we override `processMouseEvent()`, which must determine the actual type of mouse event and act accordingly.

Just like the old event model, you can choose between overriding a kitchen-sink method that all events get funneled through (`processEvent()`—the equivalent of `handleEvent()`), or you can override one of a number of convenience methods. Example 5-8 overrides `processMouseEvent()`, and Example 5-9 overrides `processEvent()`.

Note that you must call enableEvents(long mask) and specify the type(s) of event(s) that you'd like to be fired from the component (or alternatively add an appropriate event listener to the component), or your overridden methods will never be invoked. This is the one major difference between the old event model and the inheritance-based mechanism in the new model. Figure 5-7 shows our highlight button test applet in action.

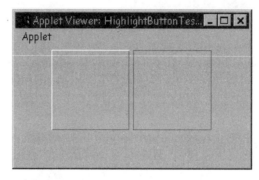

Figure 5-7 HighlightButton Test
Uses inheritance-based event handling to draw a 3D border around a rectangle when the mouse enters (the mouse is in the rectangle on the left). Inheritance-based event handling is supported in the delegation-based event model.

Example 5-8 Inheritance-based Event Handling: Overriding
processMouseEvent()

```
import java.applet.Applet;
import java.awt.*;
import java.awt.event.*;

public class HighlightButtonTest extends Applet {
  public void init() {
     HighlightButton leftButton  = new HighlightButton();
     HighlightButton rightButton = new HighlightButton();

     add(leftButton);
     add(rightButton);
  }
}
class HighlightButton extends Canvas {
  public HighlightButton() {
     // enableEvents() is a protected method, so we can
     // only call it in extensions of Component.  If we
     // added a MouseListener, it would also undam the flow of
     // mouse events from the component
```

```
      enableEvents(AWTEvent.MOUSE_EVENT_MASK);
   }
   public void paint(Graphics g) {
      paintBorder();
   }
   public Dimension getPreferredSize() {
      return new Dimension(100,100);
   }
   public void paintBorder() {
      Graphics g = getGraphics();
      g.setColor(Color.gray);
      g.drawRect(0,0,getSize().width-1,getSize().height-1);
   }
   public void highlight() {
      Graphics g = getGraphics();
      g.setColor(Color.lightGray);
      g.draw3DRect(0,0,getSize().width,getSize().height, true);
   }
   public void unhighlight() {
       paintBorder();
   }
   public void processMouseEvent(MouseEvent event) {
      if(event.getID() == MouseEvent.MOUSE_ENTERED) {
         HighlightButton canvas =
               (HighlightButton)event.getSource();
         canvas.highlight();
      }
      else if(event.getID() == MouseEvent.MOUSE_EXITED) {
         HighlightButton canvas =
               (HighlightButton)event.getSource();
         canvas.unhighlight();
      }
   }
}
```

AWT TIP ...

All Events Are No Longer Delivered to Components

A common mistake when using the inheritance-based mechanism under the new event model is neglecting to call enableEvents(long). Under the old event model, all events were delivered to a component, whether the component was interested in the event or not. The new model is much more selective, only delivering events to components that indicate interest in the particular type of event by calling enableEvent(long) or adding a listener to the component. Therefore, if you must use the inheritance-based mechanism, don't forget to call enableEvents() for events you are interested in.

Example 5-9 illustrates overriding `processEvent()` instead of a convenience
method. Note that we are careful to call `super.processEvent()` after we are
finished processing the events we are interested in because, just like
`handleEvent()` from the old event model, `processEvent()` dispatches events
to convenience methods. If we had, for instance, also overridden
`processKeyEvent()` in Example 5-9 and neglected to invoke
`super.processEvent()`, our overridden `processKeyEvent()` would never
be invoked.

Example 5-9 Inheritance-Based Event Handling: Overriding processEvent()

```java
import java.applet.Applet;
import java.awt.*;
import java.awt.event.*;

public class HighlightButtonTest2 extends Applet {
  public void init() {
     HighlightButton leftButton  = new HighlightButton();
     HighlightButton rightButton = new HighlightButton();
     add(leftButton);
     add(rightButton);
  }
}
class HighlightButton2 extends Canvas {
  public HighlightButton2() {
     enableEvents(AWTEvent.MOUSE_EVENT_MASK);
  }
  public void paint(Graphics g) {
     paintBorder();
  }
  public Dimension getPreferredSize() {
     return new Dimension(100,100);
  }
  public void paintBorder() {
     Graphics g = getGraphics();
     g.setColor(Color.gray);
     g.drawRect(0,0,getSize().width-1,getSize().height-1);
  }
  public void highlight() {
     Graphics g = getGraphics();
     g.setColor(Color.lightGray);
     g.draw3DRect(0,0,getSize().width,getSize().height, true);
  }
  public void unhighlight() {
     paintBorder();
  }
  public void processEvent(AWTEvent event) {
```

```
        if(event.getID() == MouseEvent.MOUSE_ENTERED) {
            HighlightButton canvas =
                (HighlightButton)event.getSource();
            canvas.highlight();
        }
        else if(event.getID() == MouseEvent.MOUSE_EXITED) {
            HighlightButton canvas =
                (HighlightButton)event.getSource();
            canvas.unhighlight();
        }
        super.processEvent(event);   // must do
    }
}
```

Consuming Events

There are times when it would be convenient to block an event from making its way to a component's peer. For instance, GUI builders often have a build mode and a test mode. In build mode it may be desirable to bring up a property sheet when a component is clicked on, while the component should be functional under test mode. The 1.1 event model allows you to consume input events; once consumed, an event is not passed to its native peer. The InputEvent class comes with a consume() method, which causes the event in question to be consumed. Example 5-10 extends java.awt.Button and consumes mouse pressed events, so that the button is not activated when clicked.

Example 5-10 Consuming Mouse Pressed Events

```
import java.applet.Applet;
import java.awt.*;
import java.awt.event.*;

public class ConsumeExample extends Applet {
  public void init() {
    ConsumedButton button =
            new ConsumedButton("Can't Click This");
    add(button);
  }
}
class ConsumedButton extends Button {
  public ConsumedButton(String label) {
    super(label);
    enableEvents(AWTEvent.MOUSE_EVENT_MASK);
  }
  public void processMouseEvent(MouseEvent event) {
    if(event.getID() == MouseEvent.MOUSE_PRESSED) {
        System.out.println("Consuming event!");
```

```
        event.consume();
    }
  }
}
```

Inner Classes

The 1.1 version of the JDK introduces a handy new construct: inner classes. Our intent here is not to provide an in-depth discussion of inner classes—if you are so inclined you can find such a discussion from the Java home page (http://java.sun.com). Instead, we will show how inner classes can be used for handling events.

ThreeDButton

To start off with, we'll implement a simple custom component—ThreeDButton, shown in Example 5-11; you can see our exciting applet in action in Figure 5-8. Note, of course, that our ThreeDButton has no event handling associated with it and, therefore, is always drawn raised. As we go along, we'll add event handling behavior to illustrate various concepts.

Example 5-11 ThreeDButton

```java
import java.applet.Applet;
import java.awt.*;
import java.awt.event.*;

public class ThreeDButtonTest extends Applet {
  public void init() {
    add(new ThreeDButton());
  }
}
class ThreeDButton extends Canvas {
  static public  int BORDER_INSET = 0, BORDER_RAISED = 1;
  int state = BORDER_RAISED;

  public void paint(Graphics g) {
    paintBorderRaised();
  }
  public Dimension getPreferredSize() {
    return new Dimension(100,100);
  }
  public int getState() {
    return state;
  }
  public void paintBorderRaised() {
    Graphics g = getGraphics();
```

```
      g.setColor(Color.lightGray);
      g.draw3DRect(0,0,size().width-1,size().height-1, true);
      state = BORDER_RAISED;
      g.dispose();
   }
   public void paintBorderInset() {
      Graphics g = getGraphics();
      g.setColor(Color.lightGray);
      g.draw3DRect(0,0,size().width-1,size().height-1, false);
      state = BORDER_INSET;
      g.dispose();
   }
}
```

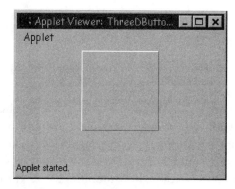

Figure 5-8 ThreeDButton—A Simple Custom Component With No Event Handling.

Encapsulating Event Handling in a Separate Listener Class

Example 5-12 introduces a new class, ThreeDButtonListener, that handles mouse and mouse motion events for a ThreeDButton, similar to the manner in which such events are handled for java.awt.Button.

Example 5-12 ThreeDButtonListener

```
class ThreeDButtonListener extends     MouseAdapter
                           implements MouseMotionListener {
   public void mousePressed(MouseEvent event) {
      ThreeDButton button = (ThreeDButton)event.getSource();
      button.paintBorderInset();
   }
   public void mouseClicked(MouseEvent event) {
      ThreeDButton button = (ThreeDButton)event.getSource();
      button.paintBorderRaised();
   }
   public void mouseReleased(MouseEvent event) {
```

```
      ThreeDButton button = (ThreeDButton)event.getSource();
      button.paintBorderRaised();
   }
   public void mouseDragged(MouseEvent event) {
      ThreeDButton button = (ThreeDButton)event.getSource();
      if(button.contains(event.getX(), event.getY())) {
         if(button.getState() == ThreeDButton.BORDER_RAISED)
            button.paintBorderInset();
      }
      else {
         if(button.getState() == ThreeDButton.BORDER_INSET)
            button.paintBorderRaised();
      }
   }
   public void mouseMoved(MouseEvent event) {
   }
}
```

There are three things to notice about our event handling class:

First, every method (except mouseMoved()) in ThreeDButtonListener must, by invoking java.util.EventObject.getSource(), obtain a reference to the ThreeDButton that fired the event, because each method manipulates the button in some fashion. An alternative implementation would be to have ThreeDButtonListener maintain a reference to the ThreeDButton with which it is associated, as we've done in Example 5-13. Regardless of which approach we take, since ThreeDButtonListener is a top-level class, we must somehow associate the listener to the button on whose behalf it is handling events.

Example 5-13 ThreeDButton Associated With ThreeDButtonListener

```
class ThreeDButtonListener extends     MouseAdapter
                           implements MouseMotionListener {
   private ThreeDButton button;
   public ThreeDButtonListener(ThreeDButton button) {
      this.button = button;
   }
   public void mousePressed (MouseEvent event) {
      button.paintBorderInset();
   }
   public void mouseClicked (MouseEvent event) {
      button.paintBorderRaised();
   }
   public void mouseReleased(MouseEvent event) {
      button.paintBorderRaised();
   }
```

```
public void mouseDragged(MouseEvent event) {
    if(button.contains(event.getX(), event.getY())) {
        if(button.getState() == ThreeDButton.BORDER_RAISED)
            button.paintBorderInset();
    }
    else {
        if(button.getState() == ThreeDButton.BORDER_INSET)
            button.paintBorderRaised();
    }
}
public void mouseMoved(MouseEvent event) {
}
}
```

Second, notice the curious (but bug-free) implementation of
`ThreeDButtonListener.mouseMoved()`. The reason for the no-op
implementation is due to the fact that `ThreeDButtonListener` implements the
`MouseMotionListener` interface and therefore must implement every method
defined in the interface in order to be a concrete (nonabstract) class. This, by the
way, is the lesser of two evils: had `ThreeDButtonListener` extended
`MouseMotionAdapter` and implemented `MouseListener`, we would have had
two no-op methods to implement: `mouseEntered()` and `mouseExited()`.

Listening to Yourself

Third, `ThreeDButtonListener` really has no implementation other than
manipulating the `ThreeDButton` with which it is associated. Perhaps such code
would be better off placed in the `ThreeDButton` class itself, as we've done in
Example 5-14. Now, however, we have three no-op methods because
`ThreeDButton` already extends `Canvas`, and, therefore, we must implement
both the `MouseListener` and `MouseMotionListener` interfaces instead of
extending an adapter class.

Example 5-14 ThreeDButton Listening to Itself

```
class ThreeDButton extends    Canvas
                implements MouseListener, MouseMotionListener{
    static public  int BORDER_INSET = 0, BORDER_RAISED = 1;
    int state = BORDER_RAISED;
    ...
    public void mousePressed (MouseEvent event) {
        paintBorderInset();
    }
    public void mouseClicked (MouseEvent event) {
        paintBorderRaised();
    }
    public void mouseReleased(MouseEvent event) {
```

```
      paintBorderRaised();
   }
   public void mouseDragged(MouseEvent event) {
      if(contains(event.getX(), event.getY())) {
         if(state == ThreeDButton.BORDER_RAISED)
            paintBorderInset();
      }
      else {
         if(state == ThreeDButton.BORDER_INSET)
            paintBorderRaised();
      }
   }
   public void mouseEntered(MouseEvent event) { }
   public void mouseExited (MouseEvent event) { }
   public void mouseMoved  (MouseEvent event) { }
}
```

Although it might make sense to have ThreeDButton handle its own events instead of giving that responsibility to another object, discussed later in the chapter, we're stuck either implementing no-op methods or associating a separate listener class with the component that fires events.

Named Inner Classes

Enter inner classes. Example 5-15 shows an implementation of ThreeDButton that defines two inner classes: ThreeDButtonMouseListener and ThreeDButtonMouseMotionListener. Since inner classes have direct access to the variables and methods defined in their enclosing class[10], there is no need to maintain an association between the listener classes and the button. Also, since the event handling is encapsulated in separate classes, each class can extend an adapter class instead of implementing a listener and having to implement no-op methods in order to satisfy the requirement that concrete classes must implement all methods of the interfaces that they implement.

Example 5-15 ThreeDButton With Inner Classes for Event Handling

```
class ThreeDButton extends Canvas {
   static public  int BORDER_INSET = 0, BORDER_RAISED = 1;
   int state = BORDER_RAISED;

   public ThreeDButton() {
      addMouseListener       (new ThreeDButtonMouseListener());
      addMouseMotionListener(
         new ThreeDButtonMouseMotionListener());
```

10. Inner classes cannot access *private* members of their enclosing class; therefore, state is given package scope (protected would have worked just as well).

```
     }
     class ThreeDButtonMouseListener extends MouseAdapter {
        public void mousePressed (MouseEvent event) {
           paintBorderInset();
        }
        public void mouseClicked (MouseEvent event) {
           paintBorderRaised();
        }
        public void mouseReleased(MouseEvent event) {
           paintBorderRaised();
        }
     }
     class ThreeDButtonMouseMotionListener
              extends MouseMotionAdapter {
        public void mouseDragged(MouseEvent event) {
           if(contains(event.getX(), event.getY())) {
              if(state == ThreeDButton.BORDER_RAISED)
                 paintBorderInset();
           }
           else {
              if(state == ThreeDButton.BORDER_INSET)
                 paintBorderRaised();
           }
        }
     }
   }
   ...
}
```

Anonymous Inner Classes

Notice that with our inner class implementation,
ThreeDButtonMouseListener and ThreeDButtonMouseMotionListener
are very unwieldy names for our event handling classes and really add no value,
except to provide a class name. Inner classes provide some syntactic sugar for
eliminating such names: anonymous classes. Example 5-16 is a rewrite of
Example 5-15 which uses anonymous (as opposed to named) inner classes for
handling mouse events. Anonymous inner classes are defined by inserting a class
body after a new expression—the anonymous inner class is constructed on the fly
and either implements or extends the interface or class, respectively, named in the
new expression.

Example 5-16 ThreeDButton With Anonymous Inner Classes For Event Handling

```
class ThreeDButton extends Canvas {
    static public  int BORDER_INSET = 0, BORDER_RAISED = 1;
    int state = BORDER_RAISED;

    public ThreeDButton() {
        addMouseListener(new MouseAdapter() {
            public void mousePressed (MouseEvent event) {
                paintBorderInset();
            }
            public void mouseClicked (MouseEvent event) {
                paintBorderRaised();
            }
            public void mouseReleased(MouseEvent event) {
                paintBorderRaised();
            }
        });
        addMouseMotionListener(new MouseMotionAdapter() {
            public void mouseDragged(MouseEvent event) {
                if(contains(event.getX(), event.getY())) {
                    if(state == ThreeDButton.BORDER_RAISED)
                        paintBorderInset();
                }
                else {
                    if(state == ThreeDButton.BORDER_INSET)
                        paintBorderRaised();
                }
            }
        });
    }
    ...
}
```

Modifying Default Event Handling Behavior

At this point, the astute reader may observe that we've fused the event handling for `ThreeDButton` to the component class, and therefore `ThreeDButton` must be subclassed in order to modify its event handling algorithm, which was one of the major drawbacks of the old event model. Example 5-17 remedies this by allowing a `ThreeDButton` to be constructed with alternative listeners. Note that we've made the nondefault constructor public, but obviously you are free to change the scope of the constructor to suite your needs.[11]

---

11. In this case, it may actually make sense to allow only subclasses to change the default listeners.

Example 5-17 ThreeDButton With Interchangeable Default Event Handling

```
class ThreeDButton extends Canvas {
  static public  int BORDER_INSET = 0, BORDER_RAISED = 1;
  int state = BORDER_RAISED;

  public ThreeDButton() {
    this(new MouseAdapter() {
      public void mousePressed (MouseEvent event) {
        paintBorderInset();
      }
      public void mouseClicked (MouseEvent event) {
        paintBorderRaised();
      }
      public void mouseReleased(MouseEvent event) {
        paintBorderRaised();
      }
    },
    new MouseMotionAdapter() {
      public void mouseDragged(MouseEvent event) {
        if(contains(event.getX(), event.getY())) {
          if(state == ThreeDButton.BORDER_RAISED)
            paintBorderInset();
        }
        else {
          if(state == ThreeDButton.BORDER_INSET)
            paintBorderRaised();
        }
      }
    });
  }
  public ThreeDButton(MouseListener ml, MouseMotionListener mml) {
    addMouseListener       (ml);
    addMouseMotionListener(mml);
  }
  ...
}
```

Now we've placed the default implementation for handling events in the
component that fires the events without having to implement any no-op methods
or associate a separate listener object with our component—all through the magic
of inner classes. Additionally, the default event handling may be overridden by
clients of the class. Again, this is not always a recommended approach, but in this
case it is a good design.

The last observation that we'll make concerning inner classes is that they provide a mechanism similar to callbacks (function pointers) in C, or blocks in Smalltalk. The difference is that Java uses objects to provide such a mechanism, whereas C provides pointers to functions and Smalltalk provides untyped blocks.

Firing AWT Events From Custom Components

A good percentage of AWT components fire some sort of semantic event. Likewise, many custom components perform one or more actions that could be construed as semantic events. Equipping a custom component to fire semantic events is a fairly common and, thankfully, straightforward task that can be enumerated as follows:

1. Have component implement listener interface if appropriate.

2. Add an appropriate listener member to the class.

3. Implement add*XXX*Listener() and remove*XXX*Listener(). The actual name of the method is unimportant.

4. Implement process*XXX*Event().

Example 5-18 lists the ThreeDButton class modified to fire action events under the same circumstances that java.awt.Button does.

Example 5-18 ThreeDButton That Fires Action Events

```
import java.applet.Applet;
import java.awt.*;
import java.awt.event.*;

public class ThreeDButtonTest extends Applet
                              implements ActionListener {
  public void init() {
    ThreeDButton button = new ThreeDButton();
    button.addActionListener(this);
    add(button);
  }
  public void actionPerformed(ActionEvent event) {
    System.out.println(event.getActionCommand());
  }
}
class ThreeDButton extends Canvas {
  ...
  private ActionListener actionListener = null;
  ...

  public void addActionListener(ActionListener l) {
```

```
      actionListener = AWTEventMulticaster.add(actionListener, l);
   }
   public void removeActionListener(ActionListener l) {
      actionListener =
         AWTEventMulticaster.remove(actionListener, l);
   }
   public void processActionEvent() {
      if(actionListener != null) {
         actionListener.actionPerformed(
            new ActionEvent(this, ActionEvent.ACTION_PERFORMED,
                     "3DButton Action"));
      }
   }
}
```

We've added an `ActionListener` member to `ThreeDButton` and implemented `addActionListener()` and `removeActionListener()`, both of which delegate to the `AWTEventMulticaster`. The `AWTEventMulticaster` implements an efficient event dispatching mechanism; we could have kept track of (for instance) a vector of action listeners that we manage ourselves, but the `AWTEventMulticaster` takes care of that headache for us in a manner that is more efficient than a vector implementation. Whenever a listener is added or removed via the `AWTEventMulticaster`, the multicaster returns a reference to a listener that is the first listener in the chain of listeners (of the appropriate type) that are currently registered with the component in question.

We have also implemented `processActionEvent()`, which invokes `actionPerformed()` on our action listener. Invoking `actionPerformed()` on the lone `actionListener` results in `actionPerformed()` being invoked for every action listener currently registered with our button.

`ThreeDButton.processActionEvent()` constructs an `ActionEvent`, signifying that the button is the source of the event, the type of action event is `ACTION_PERFORMED`, and the action command (a `String` representing the action) is "`3DButton Action`".

`ThreeDButtonTest` implements `ActionListener` and registers itself as an action listener with our button. In addition, it implements `actionPerformed()` and prints out the action command of the button that was the source of the event. It is important to realize that `ThreeDButtonTest` registers itself as an action listener and reacts to action events in exactly the same manner as it would for any AWT component that fires action events.

AWTEventMulticaster Limitations

If you were paying close attention to the above discussion, perhaps you found it somewhat curious that we can invoke `actionPerformed()` on the single `ActionListener` returned by the `AWTEventMulticaster` methods `add()` and `remove()`, and somehow have `actionPerformed()` invoked for every action listener currently registered with our component. This process works because the listener returned by the `AWTEventMulticaster add()` and `remove()` methods is actually an instance of `AWTEventMulticaster`!

`AWTEventMulticaster` implements every listener interface defined in the AWT and overrides all of the associated methods to turn around and invoke the same method for all currently registered listeners. So, for instance, when we invoke `AWTEventMulticaster.add()`, in Example 5-18, the `ActionListener` returned is actually an instance of `AWTEventMulticaster`. When we subsequently invoke `actionPerformed()` on the listener, `AWTEventMulticaster.actionPerformed()` is called, which runs through the list of currently registered action listeners and invokes `actionPerformed()` for each one.

As a result of all this object-oriented tomfoolery, `AWTEventMulticaster` is only useful for the set of events defined by the AWT—if you wish to fire custom events, you must resort to maintaining a list of listeners yourself and ensure that the listeners are notified when your custom events are fired. This, of course, is a segue into our next section.

Firing Custom Events From Custom Components

Firing standard AWT events from custom components is relatively straightforward, as we've seen above. However, implementing custom events and firing them from a custom component is a little tricker. We'll outline the steps involved and then develop a custom component that fires custom events for the sake of illustration.

A Not-So-Contrived Scenario

Let's say that you've been tasked with developing a tree control similar to what you'd find in the Windows 95 Explorer application. For those of you unfamiliar with the Explorer, take a look at Figure 5-9. (A future version of the AWT will provide such a component).

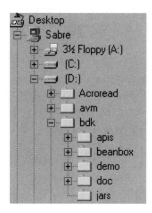

Figure 5-9 The Windows 95 Explorer Tree Control.

Being the good object-oriented developer that you are, you decide to encapsulate the functionality of the plus-minus buttons associated with each node in its own custom component. Furthermore, the plus-minus custom component will fire events whenever it is expanded or contracted, which will serve as notification to any registered listeners that the node has been either expanded or contracted.

If you take a look at the AWT events and listeners, you will find that there are no event/listener pairs that correspond to expansion and contraction.[12] Therefore, a custom event class will need to be implemented in addition to the custom component. So, we have three tasks to accomplish:

- Implement a plus-minus custom component.

- Implement an event representing Expand/Contract events.

- Have the plus-minus component fire events implemented in the previous step when appropriate.

We should note that an alternative approach would be for the plus-minus component to simply fire item events. The `ItemEvent` class defines two constants, `ItemEvent.SELECTED` and `ItemEvent.DESELECTED`, that are used to signify the type of state change for the component in question. We could have used values for the state change other than the selection/deselection values to

---

12. A 1.1 beta version of the AWT specified `ItemEvents` as encompassing expand/contract in addition to select/deselect, but it was thought that expand/contract was not general enough for `ItemEvent` and the feature was therefore pulled.

signify expansion/contraction. However, our intent here is to illustrate firing custom events, so we've chosen the alternative route of implementing a custom event class.

Steps Involved

Of course, the steps outlined above are specific to our plus-minus custom component and a bit too high level, so let's take a look at what's involved in general for developing a custom component that fires custom events:

- Develop a custom event class.

- Develop a listener interface that defines methods for listening to custom events.

  - `void XXXChanged(XXXEvent)`

- Develop an interface that custom components will implement for registering listeners.

  - public void addXXXListener(XXXListener).
  - public void removeXXXListener(XXXListener).
  - public void processXXXEvent(XXXEvent). // fire event to listeners

- Develop a custom component that fires custom events.

  - Implements interface for registering listeners developed in previous step.

Of course, carrying out the steps listed above is easier said than done, so we will implement the plus-minus custom component in order to illustrate how it's done. Note that each step listed above is actually fairly straightforward to implement, but getting your arms wrapped around the task as a whole can take some practice.

Develop a Custom Event Class

A while back[13] we took a look at the `ItemEvent` class and noted that having a `Checkbox` fire an item event seemed to be somewhat of a stretch because a `Checkbox` has but one item (itself). The AWT provides one event/listener pair for components that have selectable items, whether they have one item or more than one item. We'll take the same approach with our expandable event and have it encompass components that have one expandable item, or components that may potentially have more than one expandable item.

---

13. See "Item Events" on page 112.

Following the naming convention established by the AWT events, we'll name our custom event class `ItemExpandEvent`. ItemExpand public methods are listed in Table 5-7.

Table 5-7 `ItemExpandEvent` **Public Methods**

Method	Description
`ItemExpandable getItemExpandable()`	Returns source of the event, which must be an `ItemExpandable`.
`Object getItem()`	Returns the item that was expanded or contracted.
`int getExpandState()`	Returns `ItemExpandState.EXPANDED` or `ItemExpandState.CONTRACTED`.

The implementation of `ItemExpandEvent` is shown in Example 5-19.

Example 5-19 ItemExpandEvent Custom Event

```
import java.awt.AWTEvent;

public class ItemExpandEvent extends AWTEvent {
  public static final int EXPANDED  = 1;
  public static final int CONTRACTED = 2;

  Object item;
  int expandState;

  public ItemExpandEvent(ItemExpandable source, Object item,
                   int expandState) {
    super(source, -1);
    this.item = item;
    this.expandState = expandState;
  }
  public ItemExpandable getItemExpandable() {
     return (ItemExpandable)getSource();
  }
  public Object getItem() {
     return item;
  }
  public int getExpandState() {
     return expandState;
  }
  public String paramString() {
     String s = null;
     switch(expandState) {
       case EXPANDED:  s += "EXPANDED"; break;
```

```
      case CONTRACTED: s += "CONTRACTED"; break;
      default:         s += "unknown expand state";
   }
   return super.paramString() + "[expanded=" + s + "]";
   }
}
```

`ItemExpandEvent` extends `AWTEvent` and as a result inherits the ability to keep track of the source of the event. The source of the event must be an implementation of the `ItemExpandable` interface, as you can see from the `getItemExandable()` implementation.

`ItemExpandEvent` keeps track of the individual item (within the `ItemExpandable`) that was expanded or contracted and also provides access to the source of the event (the `ItemExpandable`).

It is interesting to note that not only will our plus-minus component implement `ItemExpandable`, but in all likelihood the tree control in which it resides would also implement `ItemExpandable`. The difference between the plus-minus component and the tree control is that the plus-minus component has but one expandable item (itself), whereas the tree control has potentially many expandable items (plus-minus or other `ItemExpandable` extensions).

`ItemExpandEvent` provides an accessor method, `getExpandState()` that returns either `ItemExpandEvent.EXPANDED` or `ItemExpandEvent.CONTRACTED`. Note that the expand state must be specified, (along with the `ItemExpandable` and specific object being expanded or contracted) at construction time.

Finally, note that `ItemExpandEvent` provides a `paramString()` method that will print out fascinating information whenever `toString()` is invoked on the event.

Develop a Listener Interface That Defines Methods for Listening for Custom Events

The next thing that we need is an interface for listening to components that fire events of type `ItemExpandEvent`. The `ItemExpandListener` implementation is shown in Example 5-20.

Example 5-20 ItemExpandListener

```
import java.util.EventListener;

public interface ItemExpandListener extends EventListener {
  void itemExpandStateChanged(ItemExpandEvent e);
}
```

As is typically the case, our listener interface is very simple. As is also typically the case, the listener interface extends the `java.util.EventListener` interface. Whenever the expansion state of an item in an `ItemExpandable` changes, the `itemExpandStateChanged()` method of its listeners is invoked.

Define an Interface That Custom Components Will Implement for Registering Listeners

Our plus-minus custom component will implement the `ItemExpandable` interface, which allows item expand listeners to register interest in item expand events and obtain a reference to an array of all currently expanded items. The `ItemExpandable` interface is shown in Example 5-21.

Example 5-21 ItemExpandListener

```
public interface ItemExpandable {
  Object[] getExpandedItems    ();
  void     addExpandListener   (ItemExpandListener l);
  void     removeExpandListener(ItemExpandListener l);
}
```

In addition to enabling listeners to register and unregister, the `ItemExpandListener` interface also provides for returning an array of objects that are currently expanded. When our plus-minus component is expanded, it will return an array with itself as the lone item in the array; when our plus-minus component is contracted, it will return null from `getExpandedItems()`. Other components that implement the `ItemExpandable` interface may contain many expandable objects and therefore may potentially return an array with any number of objects from the `getExpandedItems()` method.

Develop a Custom Component That Fires Custom Events

Our final step involves developing the custom component(s) that fire the custom events. In our case, that would be our plus-minus component, which we'll name `PlusMinus`. The `PlusMinus` class extends `Component`[14] and implements the `ItemExpandable` interface defined above:

```
public class PlusMinus extends    Component
                       implements ItemExpandable {
  protected boolean   expanded     = false;
  private   Object[]  expandedItems = new Object[1];
  private   Vector    listeners    = new Vector();
  ...
  public Object[] getExpandedItems() {
     if(expanded) {
```

14. It's a lightweight component! See "Lightweight Components" on page 475.

```
            expandedItems[0] = this;
            return expandedItems;
        }
        else
            return null;
    }
    public void addExpandListener(ItemExpandListener l) {
        listeners.addElement(l);
    }
    public void removeExpandListener(ItemExpandListener l) {
        listeners.removeElement(l);
    }
...
```

If expanded, the getExpandedItems() method sets the first element of the array to the current instance of PlusMinus; otherwise, it returns null to signify that it is not expanded. Of course, callers of getExpandedItems() must live with the inconvenience of having to dig the instance of PlusMinus out of the first slot in the array, which is the price they pay for the generality of the ItemExpandable interface.

Notice that we're not using the AWTEventMulticaster to broadcast events to listeners as we did when we fired AWT events from custom components in "Firing AWT Events From Custom Components" on page 128. As discussed previously in "AWTEventMulticaster Limitations" on page 130, the AWTEventMulticaster can only be used for the standard events that come with the AWT, and our event is a custom event. As a result, we've taken the easy way out and have kept track of a vector of listeners. Finally, we have PlusMinus.processExpandEvent(), which broadcasts expand events to registered listeners:

```
    protected synchronized void processExpandEvent(
                                ItemExpandEvent event) {
        Enumeration e = listeners.elements();
        while(e.hasMoreElements()) {
            ItemExpandListener l = (ItemExpandListener)
                                e.nextElement();
            l.itemExpandStateChanged(event);
        }
    }
```

processExpandEvent() simply cycles through the currently registered listeners and invokes itemExpandStateChanged() for each.

The `PlusMinus` constructor invokes `addMouseListener()` with an inner class version of `MouseAdapter` in order to handle mouse pressed events. Whenever a mouse pressed event occurs, the expansion state of the instance of `PlusMinus` is toggled, and the component is repainted.

```
public PlusMinus() {
  addMouseListener(new MouseAdapter() {
    public void mousePressed(MouseEvent event) {
      if(expanded) contract();
      else         expand  ();
      repaint();
    }
  });
}
```

Example 5-22 shows the implementation of the `PlusMinus` class in its entirety.

Example 5-22 PlusMinus Class

```
import java.util.*;
import java.awt.*;
import java.awt.event.*;

public class PlusMinus extends Component
                       implements ItemExpandable {
  protected boolean  expanded      = false;
  private   Object[] expandedItems = new Object[1];
  private   Vector   listeners     = new Vector();

  public PlusMinus() {
    addMouseListener(new MouseAdapter() {
      public void mousePressed(MouseEvent event) {
        if(expanded) contract();
        else         expand  ();
      }
    });
  }
  public void paint(Graphics g) {
    drawBorder(g);
    drawPlusOrMinus(g);
  }
  public void expand() {
    ItemExpandEvent event =
      new ItemExpandEvent(this, // we are ItemExpandable
                          this, // we are item
                   ItemExpandEvent.EXPANDED);
    expanded = true;
    processExpandEvent(event);
```

```java
      repaint();
   }
   public void contract() {
      ItemExpandEvent event =
         new ItemExpandEvent(this,  // we are event source
                             this, // we are item
                             ItemExpandEvent.CONTRACTED);
      expanded = false;
      processExpandEvent(event);
      repaint();
   }
   public Dimension getPreferredSize() {
      return new Dimension(21,21);
   }
   public Object[] getExpandedItems() {
      if(expanded) {
         expandedItems[0] = this;
         return expandedItems;
      }
      else
         return null;
   }
   public void addExpandListener(ItemExpandListener l) {
      listeners.addElement(l);
   }
   public void removeExpandListener(ItemExpandListener l) {
      listeners.removeElement(l);
   }
   protected synchronized void processExpandEvent(
                                 ItemExpandEvent event) {
      Enumeration e = listeners.elements();
      while(e.hasMoreElements()) {
         ItemExpandListener l = (ItemExpandListener)
                                e.nextElement();
         l.itemExpandStateChanged(event);
      }
   }
   private void drawBorder(Graphics g) {
      Dimension size = getSize();
      g.setColor(Color.darkGray.brighter());
      g.drawRect(0,0,size.width-1,size.height-2);
   }
   private void drawPlusOrMinus(Graphics g) {
      Dimension size = getSize();
      if(expanded) drawMinusSign(g, size, Color.black);
      else         drawPlusSign (g, size, Color.black);
   }
   private void drawMinusSign(Graphics g, Dimension size,
```

```
                        Color color) {
    g.setColor(color);
    g.drawLine(2,size.height/2,size.width-3,size.height/2);
}
private void drawPlusSign(Graphics g, Dimension size,
                        Color color) {
    g.setColor(color);
    g.drawLine(size.width/2,2,size.width/2,size.height-3);
    g.drawLine(2,size.height/2,size.width-3,size.height/2);
}
}
```

Finally, we need an applet with which to test out our custom component. This turns out to be trivial—the applet is shown in action in Figure 5-10. Our applet implements the `ItemExpandListener` interface, creates an instance of `PlusMinus`, and registers itself as being interested in expand events.

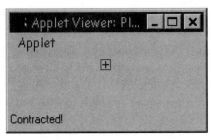 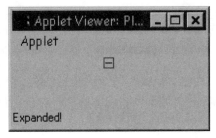

Figure 5-10 PlusMinusTest Applet
The picture on the left shows the PlusMinus custom
component contracted; on the right, it's expanded.

Example 5-23 PlusMinusTest Applet

```
import java.applet.Applet;
import java.awt.*;

public class PlusMinusTest extends     Applet
                        implements ItemExpandListener {
    public void init() {
        PlusMinus pm = new PlusMinus();
        pm.addExpandListener(this);
        add(pm);
    }
    public void itemExpandStateChanged(ItemExpandEvent event) {
        ItemExpandable ie    = event.getItemExpandable();
        Object[]       items = ie.getExpandedItems();

        if(items != null) showStatus("Expanded!");
```

```
      else                    showStatus("Contracted!");
    }
  }
```

Whenever the plus minus component is expanded or contracted, it fires an
`ItemExpandEvent`, which the applet is listening for.

The AWT Event Queue

The 1.1 release of the AWT provides an event queue—`java.awt.EventQueue`,
which provides the methods listed in Table 5-8.

Table 5-8 `java.awt.EventQueue` **Public Methods**

Method	Description
`void postEvent(AWTEvent theEvent)`	Posts an event to a queue.
`AWTEvent getNextEvent() throws InterruptedException`	Returns the next event in a queue. This method removes the event from a queue.
`AWTEvent peekEvent()`	Returns the next event in a queue. This method does not remove the event from a queue.
`AWTEvent peekEvent(int id)`	Returns the next event in the queue of the specified type. This method does not remove the event from the queue.

Obviously, the event queue is useful when you would like to take a look at what's
in the AWT event queue. The AWT's event queue is accessible by invoking
`Toolkit.getEventQueue()`[15].

In order to generate an event that is handled similarly to other AWT events, an
instance of `EventQueue` is instantiated, an event is created, and the event is
posted to the queue via the `EventQueue.postEvent()` method. This technique
is illustrated later on in Graphic Java—see "ExclusiveImageButtonPanel" on
page 705.

Finally, we should note that events posted to either the AWT's event queue or a
local event queue will not be delivered to a component's peer. For instance, if an
action event is created for a button, and the event is posted to an event queue, the
button's action listeners will be notified of the event, but the button will not
depress and pop back up, as it would if the event were generated via user input.

15. Subject to security restrictions.

AWT TIP...

Events Posted To An Event Queue Are Not Delivered To Peers

When an event is posted to an event queue, it is delivered to the component specified as the source of the event. Subsequently, if event listeners have been added to the component in question, the event is delivered to registered listeners. However, events posted to an event queue are not passed on to native peers; in other words, the component will not give any visual feedback that the event has occurred.

Event Handling Design

Although the new event model is much improved over the old model, you may find yourself pining for the simplicity of the old model where you essentially had only one choice for handling events, namely, extending a component and embedding event handling code in the extension[16]. The new model, coupled with inner classes, allows for much more flexibility than the old event model. For instance, when handling events with the delegation-based event model you can:

- Use the old event model.

- Use the inheritance-based mechanism provided with the new model.

- Have components listen to themselves.

- Encapsulate the event handling code in a separate listener class.

In addition to the approaches outlined above, you can also employ inner classes when handling events. In spite of all the choices you face when implementing event handling, deciding which approach to use is actually easier than it appears. As we shall soon discover, in nearly every case, the best approaches are the last two—the first two approaches are rarely (if ever) recommended. Let's take a look at each option and then discuss whether or not to use inner classes.

Using the Old Event Model

This option is viable because the new event model supports the old model. However, at some point in the future the old model will cease to be supported, so it's a good idea to bite the bullet and revamp your event handling code sooner

---

16. Actually, you could manually delegate event handling to another object, but it's a lot of work and is quite error-prone.

than later. Employing the old event model winds up being double work, as you will eventually have to change it. Therefore, using the old event model is not recommended.

Using Inheritance-Based Event Handling

In nearly every case, listening to yourself or delegating to a separate event handling class is preferable to using the inheritance-based mechanism because the inheritance-based mechanism in the new event model suffers from the same deficiencies as the old event model. See "Shortcomings of the Original Event Model" on page 86 for a discussion of the old event model's deficiencies.

Listening to Yourself

You know the age-old question: "Are you crazy if you talk to yourself?" and the age-old reply: "Only if you answer." Perhaps you would be considered merely eccentric if you only listen to yourself. When handling events for a component, having the component register itself as a listener is a valid, and often recommended, approach.

When basic event handling for a component is not likely to change regardless of the manner in which the component is extended, it makes perfect sense to embed the event handling in the component by having the component listen to itself. Components listen to themselves by implementing a particular listener interface (or extending an adapter class), and then adding themselves as a listener:

```
public class SomeComponent extends Canvas
                           implements MouseAdapter{
  public SomeComponent() {
    addMouseListener(this); // listens to its own mouse events
  }
  public void mousePressed(MouseEvent event) {
    // React to mouse pressed
  }
  public void mouseEntered(MouseEvent event) { }
  public void mouseExited (MouseEvent event) { }
  public void mouseClicked(MouseEvent event) { }
  public void mouseReleased(MouseEvent event) { }
}
```

Of course, there are drawbacks to listening to yourself. First, you are almost certain to have to implement no-op event handling methods because you cannot extend an adapter class (components already extend either `Component` or an extension of `Component`). However, as we've seen in "ThreeDButton With Inner Classes for Event Handling" on page 124, we can employ inner classes to eliminate this drawback. In fact, our `SomeComponent` class can be rewritten as:

```
public class SomeComponent extends Canvas
  public SomeComponent() {
    addMouseListener(new MouseAdapter() {
      public void mousePressed(MouseEvent event) {
        // React to mouse pressed
      }
    });
  }
  ...
```

Another drawback to listening to yourself is that it involves hardcoding event handling in the component that fires the events. However, as we saw in "ThreeDButton With Interchangeable Default Event Handling" on page 127, this drawback is easily obviated by providing a mechanism to replace the default listener(s). Also, you can decide whether you'd like to make the overriding mechanism available to all classes, or whether you'd like to restrict such meddling to an extension of the component, by making the appropriate methods either public or protected, respectively.

There are a number of strategies to employ if you'd like to be able to swap default listeners at runtime. In "ThreeDButton With Interchangeable Default Event Handling" on page 127, we provided a constructor that took a listener argument for specifying an alternate listener. However, that approach allows the listener to be set at construction time only. For a more flexible approach, you can provide setters and getters for the suspect listener:

```
public class IHaveADefaultEventHandlerThatIsReplaceable
                extends Component {
  private MouseListener listener;

  public IHaveADefaultEventHandlerThatIsReplaceable() {
    addMouseListener(listener = new MouseAdapter() {
      public void mousePressed(MouseEvent event) {
        // default event handling for mouse pressed
      }
    });
  }
  public void setMouseListener(MouseListener newListener) {
    if(listener != null)
      remove(listener);

    addMouseListener(listener = newListener);
  }
  ...
}
```

Notice that although a default mouse listener is added to the component in its constructor, it can be swapped out at any time by invoking `setMouseListener()`.

In short, basic event handling that is not likely to change (or will rarely change) is a good candidate for listening to yourself. Whether or not you also provide a mechanism for changing the default event handling behavior depends on just how stable you believe the event handling for the component in question happens to be.

Encapsulating Event Handling in a Separate Class

Encapsulating event handling in a separate class is preferable when you have default event handling for a basic component but you are fairly certain that the event handling will be modified, either at runtime or by extensions of the component. Of course, you're probably thinking that that's exactly what we just illustrated in the last section, by employing the "listen to yourself pattern." However, encapsulating the event handling in a separate class is a more flexible approach because, unlike listening to yourself, it provides a top-level base (event handling) class that others may extend to suite their needs.

The drawback to this approach is that you must implement a separate class, and you must somehow associate the event handling class with the component that fires the appropriate events. However, for event handling that is a likely candidate for change, this drawback is a small price to pay.

In general, then, it is a good idea to encapsulate event handling in a separate class when you can envision the event handling in question being modified for your component, especially when the default event handling is a candidate for subclassing. As a matter of fact, we implement a hierarchy of event listeners for the Graphic Java Toolkit's image buttons in "ImageButtons" on page 661.

Employing Inner Classes

Typically, the decision to use inner classes is most pertinent when you are listening to yourself, as we've seen with our `ThreeDButton` event handling discussion. Realize that inner classes are basically syntactic sugar. Syntactic sugar, in spite of the derogatory connotations usually associated with the term, can often be an exceedingly good thing.

We recommend that you use inner classes as long as their use not require you to adopt an approach that is unsatisfactory for the given circumstance. For instance, if you are quite certain that some particular event handling functionality is likely to change for a given component, then using inner classes to fuse the event handling into the component class, without providing a mechanism for modifying the event handling in question, would be a pretty bonehead design decision.

Named Inner Classes vs. Anonymous Inner Classes

Of course, if you are going to use inner classes, then the next thing to consider is whether or not you want to give the class a name. The solution is quite straightforward: if you have components that will share the listener, then give the class a name. If the class has a name, then you can instantiate one listener for multiple components, as the following pseudo-code illustrates:

```
Choice c1, c2, c3;
MyComponentListener listener = new MyComponentListener();
...
c1.add(listener);
c2.add(listener);
c3.add(listener);
...

class MyComponentListener extends ItemListener {
  // handle item state changes for all three choices
}
```

On the other hand, if the event handling is very specific to a particular component, an anonymous inner class is more convenient:

```
Button addButton = new Button("Add ...");
addButton.addActionListener(new ActionListener() {
  public void actionPerformed(ActionEvent event) {
     // Implementation specific to the add button only
  }
});
```

Propagating Events to Containers

We'll conclude our discussion of the new event model by making some observations about propagating events to a component's container. Note that automatic propagation is flat out not possible with the new event model. While some may argue that such a mechanism is indispensable, we'll go out on a limb here by voting for its exclusion in future versions of the AWT. For one thing, as we discuss in "Shortcomings of the Original Event Model" on page 86, mixing automatic propagation with the component hierarchy can result in subtle bugs, at least as it was implemented in the old model. For another thing, we believe that the best approach is to have objects interested in events fired by a particular component to explicitly register interest in those events. Surely, there are cases where one could argue that automatic propagation is a must-have, but such

situations, in our humble opinion, are few and far between. Finally, relying on automatic propagation of events, instead of explicitly expressing interest in a set of events for a given component often obfuscates code to such a degree that the inconvenience of explicitly registering interest is well worth it.

Summary

This chapter has covered the delegation-based event model that supersedes the inheritance-based model that came with the original AWT. Although the original event model was sufficient for applets (and applications) with simple event handling needs, it did not scale well for a number of reasons (see "Shortcomings of the Original Event Model" on page 86). The new event model addresses nearly all of the drawbacks of the original event model, while maintaining compatibility, at least for the time being, with the old model.

We've explored many of the aspects of the new event model in this chapter: events, components, and listeners, along with semantic events, consuming events, firing standard and custom events from custom components, etc.

While the new event model is greatly improved over the original model, the developer is now faced with a number of choices with regards to implementing event handling. We've provided some guidelines for different approaches in "Event Handling Design" on page 141, which will help you move from the old event model to the new.

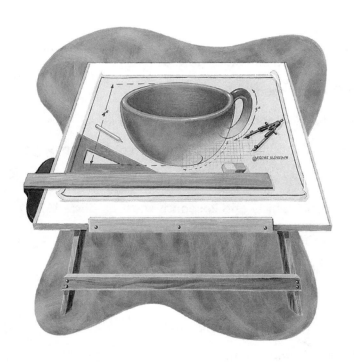

CHAPTER
6

The AWT
Component
Class

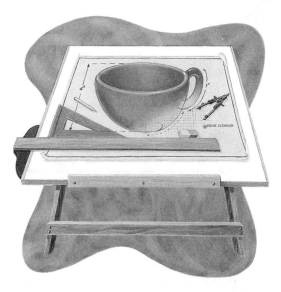

Nearly half of all the classes in the AWT are components that are derived from the `java.awt.Component` class. In this chapter, we introduce the `Component` class and the services it provides for its extensions. In subsequent chapters, we'll discuss specific AWT components, such as buttons, labels, scrollbars, lists, dialogs, etc.

Components

All of the standard AWT components in the 1.1 release of the AWT are heavyweight components, which means that each component is rendered in a native, opaque window. While the 1.1 version of the AWT provides a framework for developing lightweight custom components[1], it does not provide any specific lightweight components. Lightweight versions of all existing heavyweight components will be provided in a subsequent release of the AWT.

All of the standard AWT components have native, platform-dependent peers that do much of the work behind the scenes. Implementing a peer-based design enabled the original designers of the AWT to rapidly develop a user interface toolkit that retained native look and feel across platforms. However, even though most developers do not have to deal directly with peers, the peer approach results in a number of drawbacks when developing user interfaces using the AWT[2]. A

---

1.   See *Lightweight Components* on page 475 for a discussion of lightweights.

subsequent release of the AWT will provide peerless counterparts of the heavyweight AWT components to give developers the option of circumventing the peer-based approach. Table 6-1 repeats the standard AWT components listed in Table 1-2 on page 7.

Table 6-1 AWT Heavyweight Components

Component	Superclass	Description
Button	Component	A textual button for triggering an action.
Canvas	Component	A canvas for painting graphics.
Checkbox	Component	A checkable boolean component.
Choice	Component	Pop-down menu of textual entries.
Dialog	Window	A window that can be modal.
FileDialog	Dialog	A platform-dependent dialog for selecting files.
Frame	Window	Top-level window with titlebar and optional menubar.
Label	Component	Component that displays a string.
List	Component	A scrollable list of textual entries.
Panel	Container	A generic container of components.
Scrollbar	Component	An Adjustable component for scrolling items.
ScrollPane	Container	A scrollable container.
TextArea	TextComponent	A multi-line, scrollable textfield.
TextComponent	Component	Base functionality for TextArea and TextField.
TextField	TextComponent	A single-line component for entering text.
Window	Container	A borderless window with no title.

Note that some components, namely Dialog, FileDialog, Frame, Panel, Window and ScrollPane, are containers that can contain other components.

java.awt.Component

Every AWT component is ultimately an extension of the java.awt.Component class. java.awt.Component is an abstract class that encapsulates the common functionality among AWT components. In fact, so much functionality is

2. See "Peers and Platform Independence" on page 4 and "Components and Peers" on page 157 for discussions of the advantages and disadvantages of peers.

embedded in the `Component` class that it provides a whopping 120 public methods. Instead of discussing each and every method, we'll focus on the basic aspects of components that you are likely to deal with on a regular basis. Note that some aspects of components are discussed in other places in *Graphic Java*, for instance, attaching a popup menu to a component is discussed in "Popup Menus" on page 320, while containers are discussed at length in "Components, Containers, and Layout Managers" on page 373—we will not repeat such discussions in this chapter.

Component Properties

All components share a common set of properties that can be obtained and set after construction; the properties are listed in Table 6-2.

Table 6-2 java.awt.Component Properties Modifiable at Runtime

Property	Set/Get Methods
Background Color	`void setBackground(Color)` `Color getBackground()`

Bounds	`void setBounds(Rectangle)`
	 `void setBounds(int,int,int,int)`
	 `Rectangle getBounds()`

Cursor	`void setCursor(Cursor)` `Cursor getCursor()`
Enabled	`void setEnabled(boolean)` `boolean isEnabled()`
Font	`void setFont(Font)` `Font getFont()`
Foreground Color	`void setForeground(Color)` `Color getForeground()`
Locale	`void setLocale(Locale)` `Locale getLocale()`

Location	`void setLocation(Point)`
	 `void setLocation(int,int)`
	 `Point getLocation()`
	 `Point getLocationOnScreen()`

Name	`void setName()` `String getName()`
Size	`void setSize(Dimension)` `Dimension getSize()`
Visible	`void setVisible(boolean)` `boolean isVisible()`

All of the methods listed in Table 6-2 are `java.awt.Component` methods and therefore can be invoked on any extension of the `Component` class. Foreground and background colors, location, visibility, etc., can all be set for all AWT components.

Deprecated Methods

Table 6-2 purposely leaves out deprecated methods from the original AWT. Many component methods in the original version of the AWT were named inconsistently. For example, to get the font associated with a component you would invoke `getFont()`; however, to get the bounds of a component, you would invoke `bounds()`. As a result, it was difficult to remember which methods were preceded with get/set and which were not. Fortunately, the 1.1 release of the AWT remedies the inconsistent naming, and as a result many of the old methods are now deprecated, meaning they will no longer be supported in subsequent releases of the AWT. In fact, `javac` has been fitted with a new option *-deprecation*, which will issue a warning any time you use a deprecated method.

Deprecated Methods and Compatibility

The new 1.1 methods that replace their deprecated counterparts simply call the deprecated method. For instance, `enable()` is deprecated—the new method to use is `setEnabled()`. The implementation of `Component.setEnabled()` looks like so:

```
public void setEnabled(boolean b) {
  enable(b);
}
```

Invoking `setEnabled()` or the deprecated `enable()` will result in the same code being executed. However, if you override either `setEnabled()` or `enable()`, things aren't quite so simple.

If you override `setEnabled()` in a custom component without overriding `enable()`, then existing client code that calls the deprecated `enable()` will get the wrong enabling behavior. If you override `enable()` without overriding `setEnabled()`, then you will get deprecation warnings when you compile your code. However, if you override *both* methods in the same manner as the Component class, the compiler will not issue a warning, and invoking either method will result in the same code being called:

```
/**
 * @deprecated as of JDK1.1
 */
public void setEnabled() {
```

```
  enable();
}
public void enable() {
  // new behavior ...
}
```

Therefore, if you need to override either a deprecated method, or the method that replaces the deprecated version, you should override both methods, and add a comment that includes the @deprecated tag for the deprecated version. This technique ensures that invoking either method will result in the same code being called, and the code will compile without compiler warnings.

AWT TIP ...

Override Deprecated Methods and Their Replacement Methods

If you need to override a method that replaces a deprecated method, you should override the deprecated version of the method in addition to the new version. The new version should simply invoke the deprecated method, like so:

```
/**
* @deprecated - the deprecated tag will suppress compiler warnings
*/
public Point location() {
// new behavior ...
}
public Point getLocation() {
return location();
}
```

Doing so will ensure that the same code is invoked no matter which method is called and will also avoid compiler warnings about implementing deprecated methods.

NOTE: In the interest of both brevity and clarity, the listings that appear in *Graphic Java* do not adhere to the technique presented in the "Override Deprecated Methods and Their Replacement Methods" AWT Tip.

Finally, to assist you in renaming deprecated AWT methods, Table 6-3 lists the deprecated methods in the 1.1 release of the AWT, and the replacement methods (or alternative technique).

Table 6-3 AWT Deprecated Methods

Class/Interface	Deprecated Method	Replacement Method/Alternative
CheckboxGroup	getCurrent()	getSelectedCheckbox()
	setCurrent()	setSelectedCheckbox()
Choice	countItems()	getItemCount()
Component	action()	use ActionListener
	bounds()	getBounds()
	disable()	setEnabled(false)
	deliverEvent()	dispatchEvent()
	enable()	setEnabled(true)
	getPeer()	NO REPLACEMENT
	gotFocus()	processFocusEvent()
	handleEvent()	processEvent()
	hide()	setVisible(false)
	inside()	contains()
	keyDown()	processKeyEvent()
	keyUp	processKeyEvent()
	layout()	doLayout()
	locate()	getComponentAt()
	location()	getLocation()
	lostFocus()	processFocusEvent()
	minimumSize()	getMinimumSize()
	mouseDown()	processMouseEvent()
	mouseEnter()	processMouseEvent()
	mouseExit()	processMouseEvent()
	mouseMove()	processMouseEvent()
	mouseUp()	processMouseEvent()
	move()	setLocation()
	nextFocus()	transferFocus()
	postEvent()	dispatchEvent()
	preferredSize()	getPreferredSize()
	reshape()	setBounds()
	resize()	setSize()
	size()	getSize()

Table 6-3 AWT Deprecated Methods (Continued)

Class/Interface	Deprecated Method	Replacement Method/Alternative
	show()	setVisible()
Container	countComponents()	getComponentCount()
	deliverEvent()	dispatchEvent()
	insets	getInsets()
	layout()	doLayout()
	locate()	getComponentAt()
	minimumSize()	getMinimumSize()
	nextFocus()	transferFocus()
	preferredSize()	getPreferredSize()
FontMetrics	getMaxDecent()	getMaxDescent()
Frame	getCursorType()	getCursor()
	setCursor(int)	setCursor(Cursor)
Graphics	getClipRect()	getClipBounds()
LayoutManager	addLayoutComponent(String, Component)	addLayoutComponent(Component, Object)
List	allowsMultipleSelection()	isMultipleMode()
	clear()	removeAll()
	countItems()	getItemCount()
	delItems()	NO REPLACEMENT
	isSelected()	isIndexSelected()
	minimumSize()	getMinimumSize()
	preferredSize()	getPreferredSize()
	setMultipleSelections()	setMultipleMode()
Menu	countItems()	getItemCount()
	countMenus()	getMenuCount()
	disable()	setEnabled(false)
	enable()	setEnabled(true)
	getPeer()	NO REPLACEMENT
Polygon	getBoundingBox()	getBounds()
Rectangle	inside()	inside()
	move()	setLocation()
	reshape()	setBounds()

Table 6-3 AWT Deprecated Methods (Continued)

Class/Interface	Deprecated Method	Replacement Method/Alternative
	resize()	setSize()
ScrollPane	layout()	doLayout()
Scrollbar	getLineIncrement()	getUnitIncrement()
	getPageIncrement()	getBlockIncrement()
	getVisible()	getVisibleAmount()
	setLineIncrement()	setUnitIncrement()
	setPageIncrement()	setBlockIncrement()
	setVisible()	setVisibleAmount()
TextArea	appendText()	append()
	insertText()	insert()
	minimumSize()	getMinimumSize()
	preferredSize()	getPreferredSize()
	replaceText()	replaceRange()
TextField	minimumSize()	getMinimumSize()
	preferredSize()	getPreferredSize()
	setEchoCharacter()	setEchoChar()
Window	nextFocus()	transferFocus()
	postEvent()	dispatchEvent()

Component Location, Bounds, and Coordinates

A component's location is relative to the container in which it resides, whereas its bounds represent the actual pixel width and height of the component. If you'd like to find out the actual screen coordinates of a component, the 1.1 version of the AWT introduces a new method:

```
Point java.awt.Component.getLocationOnScreen().
```

Coordinates used in component methods are relative to the upper left-hand corner of the component in question. If you wish to draw a rectangle in a canvas, for example, and you specify the location of the rectangle as (10,10), the upper left-hand corner of the rectangle will be located 10 pixels below and to the right of the upper left-hand corner of the canvas.

Component Preferred, Minimum, and Maximum Sizes

Components can specify their preferred, minimum and maximum sizes, by overriding getPreferredSize(), getMinimumSize() and getMaximumSize(), respectively.

It is important to emphasize, however, that overriding the methods listed above does not guarantee anything about a component's size. The methods are merely guidelines that may well be ignored by the objects that size components—layout managers. We will cover layout managers and preferred component sizes in "Components, Containers, and Layout Managers" on page 373.

Component Visibility and Responsiveness

All components, other than frames, windows, and dialogs[3], are visible by default. The setVisible() method from java.awt.Component may be used to set the visibility of individual components. If you need to toggle the visibility of a set of components, you should consider using the CardLayout layout manager (see "The CardLayout Layout Manager" on page 396) instead of individually managing the visibility of each component.

You can also toggle a component's responsiveness to user input by invoking the setEnabled() method, passing in either true or false to enable or disable, respectively, a component's responsiveness to user input. Components provide platform-dependent visual feedback when they are not enabled.

Components and Peers

As stated previously, most developers do not have to deal directly with peers. However, a handful of Component methods will behave differently if they are invoked before a component's peer has been created—those methods are listed in Table 6-4.

Peers are created in a component's addNotify() method. If you need to invoke one of the methods listed in Table 6-4 before a component's peer has been created, you essentially have two choices. You can either invoke addNotify() directly, which *may* cause the component's peer to be created, or you can override addNotify() and, after invoking super.addNotify()[4], call the methods that depend upon the peer's existence. In general, we recommend the latter approach—invoking addNotify() directly can be risky business because the

---

3. Invoking setVisible(true) on frames, windows and dialogs makes them visible.
4. The call to super.addNotify() is crucial.

AWT may not yet be prepared to create the component's peer[5]. The technique of overriding `addNotify()` is illustrated in "The Font Selection Panel" on page 768.

Table 6-4 java.awt.Component Methods That Depend Upon Peers

Method	Behavior Exhibited Before Peer Creation
`Image createImage(int,int)`	Returns `null`.
`ColorModel getColorModel()`	Returns the toolkit's color model—not the component's.
`Font getFont()`	Returns `null`.
`FontMetrics getFontMetrics()`	Returns the toolkit's font metrics—not the component's.
`Graphics getGraphics()`	Returns `null`.
`Dimension getPreferredSize()`	Returns minimum size, not preferred size.
`Dimension getMinimumSize()`	Returns value of `getSize()`.
`Dimension getSize()`	Returns a `Dimension` of zero width and height unless the component has been explicitly sized, in which case it returns the explicit size.
`Toolkit getToolkit()`	Returns the default toolkit—not the component's.
`boolean isFocusTraversable()`	Returns `false`.
`void requestFocus()`	Does nothing.

AWT TIP...

A Peerless Component May Misbehave

While most Java developers will never have to directly manipulate a component's peer, peers have a way of making themselves known. Some java.awt.Component methods, for instance, depend upon the component's peer having been previously instantiated. If the peer does not exist at the time of the call, the methods behave differently than they would if the peer existed. For example, Component.requestFocus() does nothing, and createImage() returns a null reference if either method is invoked on a peerless component.

---

5. If that is the case, `addNotify()` can lead to a `NullPointerException` being thrown.

The Future of Peers

A subsequent release of the AWT will provide peerless replacements for the current AWT components. It is recommended that you switch to the new peerless components when they become available, unless it is imperative that your applets (and applications) retain native look and feel across platforms. Although the peer approach results in the retention of native look and feel, peers in general can cause more problems than they solve.

Components and Zorder

Previous versions of the AWT made no guarantees about the depth, or *zorder*[6] of components. The 1.1 release of the AWT defines zorder to be the same as the order in which components are added to their containers, from front to back. The first component added to a container is the frontmost component, and the last component added will be displayed behind all other components in the component's container.

The applet shown in Figure 6-1 contains six buttons added to the applet in numerical order, starting with Button 1 and ending with Button 6. Although there is currently no support for setting the zorder of a component once it has been added to a container[7], the AWT does allow components to be added to and removed from a container at a specified position.

Whenever a button in the applet shown in Figure 6-1 is activated, it is removed from the applet, along with the component at position zero (the frontmost component). The buttons are then added back to the container with their zorders switched, so the button clicked on becomes the frontmost component, while the previously frontmost component assumes the zorder of the button selected. The picture on the right shows the applet after button 6 has been activated—Button 6 goes to the front, and Button 1 goes to the back, while the other buttons maintain their current zorder.

6. The term zorder comes from three-dimensional coordinate systems, where the z axis represents the third dimension.
7. This capability will be added in a subsequent release of the AWT.

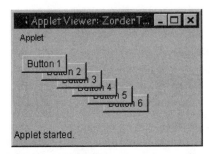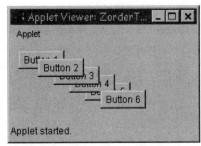

Figure 6-1 An Applet That Changes the Zorder of its Buttons
Clicking on a button brings it to the top and sends the button that
was previously on top to the back. The picture on the left is the
applet in its initial state; the picture on the right is the applet after
Button 6 is activated.

Each button in the applet shares a single action listener that performs the
aforementioned shenanigans, like so:

```
class Listener implements ActionListener {
  public void actionPerformed(ActionEvent event) {
    Button   button = (Button)event.getSource();
    int      zorder = getZorder(button);
    Button   top    = (Button)getComponent(0);

    remove(button);
    remove(top);

    add(button, 0);
    add(top, zorder);
    validate();
  }
  private int getZorder(Button button) {
    for(int i=0; i < getComponentCount(); ++i) {
      Component c = getComponent(i);
      if(c == button)
        return i;
    }
    return -1;
  }
}
```

The java.awt.Container class does not provide a method to obtain the zorder of
a component, so we've implemented one ourselves. The action listener gets the
zorder of the button that fired the action event, and then gets the top component
(whose zorder is zero). Then, after removing both buttons, the buttons are added

back to the container with their zorders switched. Finally, `validate()` is invoked on the applet, which causes it to lay out all of its components. The applet is listed in its entirety in Example 6-1.

Example 6-1 ZorderTest Applet

```java
import java.applet.Applet;
import java.awt.*;
import java.awt.event.*;
import gjt.BulletinLayout;

public class ZorderTest extends Applet {
   Button buttonOne    = new Button("Button 1");
   Button buttonTwo    = new Button("Button 2");
   Button buttonThree  = new Button("Button 3");
   Button buttonFour   = new Button("Button 4");
   Button buttonFive   = new Button("Button 5");
   Button buttonSix    = new Button("Button 6");

   public void init() {
      Listener listener = new Listener();

      setLayout(new BulletinLayout());

      buttonOne.setLocation   (10,10);
      buttonTwo.setLocation   (35,20);
      buttonThree.setLocation (55,30);
      buttonFour.setLocation  (75,40);
      buttonFive.setLocation  (95,50);
      buttonSix.setLocation   (115,60);

      add(buttonOne);
      add(buttonTwo);
      add(buttonThree);
      add(buttonFour);
      add(buttonFive);
      add(buttonSix);

      buttonOne.addActionListener   (listener);
      buttonTwo.addActionListener   (listener);
      buttonThree.addActionListener (listener);
      buttonFour.addActionListener  (listener);
      buttonFive.addActionListener  (listener);
      buttonSix.addActionListener   (listener);
   }
   class Listener implements ActionListener {
      public void actionPerformed(ActionEvent event) {
         Button   button = (Button)event.getSource();
```

```
        int     zorder  = getZorder(button);
        Button  top     = (Button)getComponent(0);

        remove(button);
        remove(top);

        add(button, 0);
        add(top, zorder);
        validate();
    }
    private int getZorder(Button button) {
        for(int i=0; i < getComponentCount(); ++i) {
            Component c = getComponent(i);
                if(c == button)
                    return i;
        }
        return -1;
    }
  }
}
```

One thing to note about our applet is that we set the layout manager to an instance of gjt.BulletinLayout, which lays out components as though they were pinned to a bulletin board, at whatever their location has been set to. If a component has been explicitly resized, then the bulletin layout lays them out at their current size; otherwise, it lays them out according to their preferred size. Using gjt.BulletinLayout is preferable to setting a container's layout manager to null—see "gjt.BulletinLayout" on page 444.

Also, note that removing components and adding them back to a container is a stopgap measure until the AWT supports setting zorder without adding and removing components. If you must implement changing zorder of components, for now you may wish to employ adding and removing components at specified depths, but in the future you will want to change such code to use the forthcoming AWT feature for setting zorder explicitly.

AWT TIP...

Isolate Code That Controls ZOrder

Changing a component's zorder by removing it from a container and adding it at a specific index is a technique that should be used sparingly. It is also code that should be isolated, so that it is relatively easy to change once the AWT supports specifying a component's zorder directly.

Components and Cursors

Another new feature for 1.1 is the ability to set a component's cursor. Previous versions of the AWT supported changing the cursor for a frame, but not for other components. Additionally, instead of representing cursors as integer constants as before, the AWT has added a `Cursor` class—to set the cursor for a component, you pass the component's `setCursor()` method an instance of a `Cursor`. The `Cursor` class comes with a set of predefined cursors, which can be accessed by invoking `Cursor.getPredefinedCursor()`, which expects to be passed one of the integer constants listed in Table 6-5.

Table 6-5 java.awt.Cursor Static Public Constants for Predefined Cursors

Cursor
DEFAULT_CURSOR
CROSSHAIR_CURSOR
TEXT_CURSOR
WAIT_CURSOR
SW_RESIZE_CURSOR
SE_RESIZE_CURSOR
NW_RESIZE_CURSOR
NE_RESIZE_CURSOR
N_RESIZE_CURSOR
S_RESIZE_CURSOR
W_RESIZE_CURSOR
E_RESIZE_CURSOR
HAND_CURSOR
MOVE_CURSOR

Figure 6-2 shows an applet equipped with a choice whose items represent predefined cursors. When a cursor is selected, the applet's cursor is changed to reflect the selection. Changing the cursor for a container, such as our applet, also changes the cursor for all of the container's components—therefore, changing the cursor in the applet shown in Figure 6-2, for example, also changes the cursor for the choice as well.

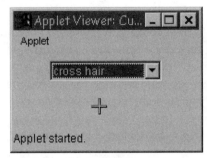

Figure 6-2 An Applet That Changes Its Cursor
When cursors are selected from the choice, the applet's cursor is
changed to the selected cursor. Changing the cursor for a
container changes the cursor for all of the container's
components.

Most of the action takes place in the `CursorChoice` custom component, which
extends `java.awt.Choice`, shown in listing Example 6-2. `CursorChoice`
maintains two arrays—an array of strings displayed in the choice, and a
corresponding array of cursors obtained from calls to
`Cursor.getPredefinedCursor()`.

 Example 6-2 `CursorChoice` **Custom Component**

```
import java.awt.*;

public class CursorChoice extends Choice {
  private String cursorNames[] = {
              "default",          "cross hair",
              "text",             "wait",
              "southwest resize", "southeast resize",
              "northwest resize", "northeast resize",
              "north resize",     "south resize",
              "west resize",      "east resize",
              "hand",             "move" };

  private Cursor cursors[] = {
     Cursor.getPredefinedCursor(Cursor.DEFAULT_CURSOR),
     Cursor.getPredefinedCursor(Cursor.CROSSHAIR_CURSOR),
     Cursor.getPredefinedCursor(Cursor.TEXT_CURSOR),
     Cursor.getPredefinedCursor(Cursor.WAIT_CURSOR),
     Cursor.getPredefinedCursor(Cursor.SW_RESIZE_CURSOR),
     Cursor.getPredefinedCursor(Cursor.SE_RESIZE_CURSOR),
     Cursor.getPredefinedCursor(Cursor.NW_RESIZE_CURSOR),
     Cursor.getPredefinedCursor(Cursor.NE_RESIZE_CURSOR),
```

```
      Cursor.getPredefinedCursor(Cursor.N_RESIZE_CURSOR),
      Cursor.getPredefinedCursor(Cursor.S_RESIZE_CURSOR),
      Cursor.getPredefinedCursor(Cursor.W_RESIZE_CURSOR),
      Cursor.getPredefinedCursor(Cursor.E_RESIZE_CURSOR),
      Cursor.getPredefinedCursor(Cursor.HAND_CURSOR),
      Cursor.getPredefinedCursor(Cursor.MOVE_CURSOR) };

   public CursorChoice() {
      for(int i=0; i < cursors.length; ++i) {
         add(cursorNames[i]);
      }
   }
   public Cursor getSelectedCursor() {
      return Cursor.getPredefinedCursor(getSelectedIndex());
   }
   public void setSelectedCursor(Cursor cursor) {
      for(int i=0; i < cursors.length; ++i) {
         if(cursors[i].equals(cursor)) {
            select(i);
            break;
         }
      }
   }
}
```

Two methods are provided for getting and setting the currently selected cursor: `getSelectedCursor()` and `setSelectedCursor()`, respectively. The former method returns the cursor currently selected in the choice, and the latter allows the cursor selected in the choice to be set programmatically.

As an aside, note that we purposely did not name the methods `getCursor()` and `setCursor()`, because we would have overridden `Component.getCursor()` and `Component.setCursor()`, respectively. In order to allow the cursor for the choice to be set, we would have had to invoke the `Component` methods in each overridden method, but that would mean the cursor for the choice could not vary from the cursor displayed in the choice, so we chose to give the methods different names.

The applet displayed in Figure 6-2 on page 164 is listed in Figure 6-6.

Example 6-3 CursorChoiceTest **Applet**

```
import java.applet.Applet;
import java.awt.*;
import java.awt.event.*;

public class CursorChoiceTest extends Applet {
   private CursorChoice cursorChoice = new CursorChoice();
```

```
public void init() {
    add(cursorChoice);

    cursorChoice.addItemListener(new ItemListener() {
        public void itemStateChanged(ItemEvent event) {
            setCursor(cursorChoice.getSelectedCursor());
        }
    });
}
}
```

The applet contains a lone component—the `CursorChoice`. Whenever an item in the choice is selected, the applet's `setCursor()` method is invoked with the currently selected cursor in the choice.

Components and Serialization

AWT components provide built-in support for serialization. Actually, a more accurate statement is that the Java language provides support for serialization, and AWT components take advantage of that support. The AWT adds additional support for serializing event listeners associated with its components.

We won't discuss Java's support for serialization—that is beyond the scope of this book—however, we will discuss serializing AWT components because the AWT affords you the option of serializing a component's listeners along with the component itself.

Figure 6-3 shows an application initially containing a lone button. When the button is activated, the button's listener serializes the button and writes it to a file. Then, the listener turns around and reads the serialized button from the file, creating a new button that is added to the frame.

 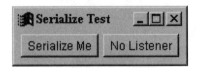

Figure 6-3 Serializing a Button
Activating the "Serialize Me" button serializes the button, writes it out to a file, and then creates a new button by reading the serialized button from the file. The new button is then added to the frame.

As you can probably guess, the application shown in Figure 6-3 writes out only the button itself, and not the button's listener. If you activate the "No Listener" button, no action will be performed. After reading in the serialized button, we changed its label to reflect the fact that the button has no action listener associated with it.

The entire application is listed in Example 6-4.

Example 6-4 SerializeTest **Application**

```java
import java.awt.*;
import java.awt.event.*;
import java.io.*;

public class SerializeTest extends Frame {
  static Frame f;
  Button button;

  static public void main(String args[]) {
     f = new SerializeTest();
     f.pack();
     f.setVisible(true);
  }
  static public Frame getFrame() {
     return f;
  }
  public SerializeTest() {
     super("Serialize Test");
     button.addActionListener(new ButtonListener());

     setLayout(new FlowLayout());
     add(button = new Button("Serialize Me"));

     addWindowListener(new WindowAdapter() {
        public void windowClosing(WindowEvent event) {
           dispose();
           System.exit(0);
        }
     });
  }
}
class ButtonListener implements ActionListener {
  public void actionPerformed(ActionEvent event) {
     try {
        doSerialize((Button)event.getSource());
     }
     catch(Exception e) {
        e.printStackTrace();
```

```
        }
    }
    private void doSerialize(Button button) throws
                                    IOException ,
                                    ClassNotFoundException {
        // Write out button to file ...

        FileOutputStream fo = new FileOutputStream("button");
        ObjectOutputStream so = new ObjectOutputStream(fo);
        so.writeObject(button);
        so.flush();

        // Read button from file ...

        FileInputStream fi = new FileInputStream("button");
        ObjectInputStream si = new ObjectInputStream(fi);
        Button b = (Button)si.readObject();
        b.setLabel("No Listener");

        // Add button to frame ...

        Frame f = SerializeTest.getFrame();
        f.add(b);
        f.pack();
        f.setVisible(false);
        f.setVisible(true);
    }
}
```

The doSerialize() method of the ButtonListener class is where all of the serialization and deserialization takes place. First, the button is written to a file.

```
FileOutputStream fo = new FileOutputStream("button");
ObjectOutputStream so = new ObjectOutputStream(fo);
so.writeObject(button);
so.flush();
```

An ObjectOutputStream is wrapped in a FileOutputStream, and the stream's writeObject() method is invoked and passed a reference to the button, which ultimately causes java.awt.Button.writeObject() to be invoked.

Then the button is read from the file.

```
FileInputStream fi = new FileInputStream("button");
ObjectInputStream si = new ObjectInputStream(fi);
Button b = (Button)si.readObject();
b.setLabel("No Listener");
```

Notice that after the button is read in, its label is changed; otherwise, the label would be the same as the label of the button that was serialized to the file.

Finally, we add the button to the frame, pack the frame, and toggle the frame's visibility, which causes the frame to lay out its contents and resize to encompass the components it contains.

```
Frame f = SerializeTest.getFrame();
f.add(b);
f.pack();
f.setVisible(false);
f.setVisible(true);
```

Notice that we have not invoked any AWT methods whatsoever in order to serialize (and deserialize) the button—all of the serialization support is supplied by the Java language itself.

As we alluded to earlier, the AWT adds the ability to serialize a component's listeners in addition to the component itself. In fact, if our listener had implemented the `java.io.Serializable` interface, it would have been serialized along with the button and read back in, thanks to the fact that `java.awt.Button` has overridden both `readObject()` and `writeObject()` to serialize and deserialize its action listeners. As a result, activating a reconstituted button would cause it to be serialized and deserialized also. Figure 6-4 shows our application after modifying ButtonListener to implement the `Serializable` interface.

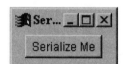 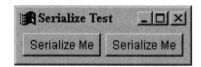

Figure 6-4 Serializing a Button and Its `ActionListener`
The "Serialize Me" button *and* its action listener are serialized and deserialized. Clicking on any of the buttons in the application will cause it to be serialized to a file, read back in, and added to the frame.

Modifying the `ButtonListener` class to implement the `Serializable` interface and removing the line that modified the newly created button's label were the only changes that we made to the original application. As a result, the button's listener is serialized along with the button—therefore, activating the newly created button will result in it too being serialized and reconstituted.

Components and Internationalization

The 1.1 JDK includes support for internationalization; however, complete coverage of internationalization is beyond the scope of *Graphic Java*—none of the internationalization support resides in the `java.awt` package or its subpackages.

On the other hand, all AWT components have a `Locale` associated with them, so we'll take the time to briefly discuss the ramifications of that, and at the same time provide you with an applet that internationalizes an extremely simple graphical user interface (GUI). We will give you enough of an overview of internationalization so that you will be able to effectively internationalize a more complex user interface.

Locales

As you can see from "java.awt.Component Properties Modifiable at Runtime" on page 151, the `Component` class provides `getLocale()` and `setLocale()` methods, so obviously a component may have a `Locale` associated with it.

A locale is an *identifier* that represents a specific geographical, political or cultural region. The `java.util.Locale` class provides a number of public `Locale` instances that save you the trouble of instantiating a `Locale` when the need arises.

The important thing to remember about locales is that they are simply an identifier—nothing more and nothing less. For instance, we can set a textfield's locale to `Locale.French`.

```
TextField field = new TextField();
field.setLocale(Locale.FRENCH);
```

However, doing so does not mean that the textfield will somehow magically display its text in French. All it means is that we've *identified* the textfield as an

AWT component that should render its text in French. It is not the responsibility of the textfield to ensure that its text is in French—that responsibility is left for someone else, namely, you, to take care of. The rest of our discussion on internationalization will center around that responsibility.

Resource Bundles

A resource bundle contains locale-specific data that can be loaded at runtime. For instance, here's a resource bundle containing a single key/value pair.

```
import java.util.*;

public class LabelsBundle_en extends ListResourceBundle {
  static final Object[][] contents = {
    {"Identifier", "English GUI"}
  };
  public Object[][] getContents() {
    return contents;
  }
}
```

All bundles (classes ultimately derived from `java.util.ResourceBundle`) contain key/value pairs, where the key identifies a locale-specific object in the bundle.

The `LabelsBundle_en` class extends `ListResourceBundle`, (from the `java.util` package) and implements the lone abstract method defined by `ListResourceBundle`: `getContents()`. The `getContents()` method returns an array, where each item in the array is a key/value pair—each key must be a string, while the value associated with the key may be any object. In our case, of course, the value is also a string. Additionally, we only have one key/value pair in our bundle, namely the string "English GUI" that is identified by the key "Identifier".

Here's another bundle that we'll put to use, along with `LabelsBundle_en` in just a moment.

```
import java.util.*;

public class LabelsBundle_fr extends ListResourceBundle {
  static final Object[][] contents = {
    {"Identifier", "GUI en Francais"}
  };
  public Object[][] getContents() {
    return contents;
  }
}
```

LabelsBundle_fr is a resource bundle that also contains a string resource: "GUI en Francais" that is identified by the key "Identifier".

The SimpleI18NTest Applet

The internationalized applet shown in Figure 6-5 contains a choice and a label. When an item is selected from the choice, the locale of the label is changed to reflect the currently selected item in the choice. The applet then modifies the text of the label in response to the change in locale.

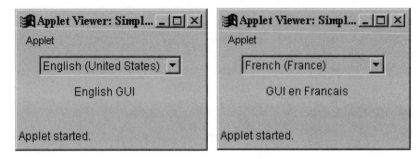

Figure 6-5 SimpleI18NTest Applet
Selecting an item in the choice causes the label's locale to be modified.

The first order of business for the applet is to create its complex GUI.

```
public class SimpleI18NTest extends Applet
                            implements ItemListener {
  private Label  guiLabel = new Label();
  private Choice choice   = new Choice();

  public void init() {
    choice.add(Locale.ENGLISH.getDisplayName());
    choice.add(Locale.FRENCH.getDisplayName());
    choice.addItemListener(this);

    add(choice);
    add(guiLabel);

    guiLabel.setLocale(Locale.ENGLISH);
    internationalize();
  }
```

The strings added to the choice are obtained from two of the public `Locale` objects available from the `Locale` class: `Locale.ENGLISH` and `Locale.FRENCH`. The `Locale.getDisplayName()` method returns the name of the locale in the language of the default locale, which for us is English.

The choice and the label are then added to the applet, and the label's locale is initially set to `Locale.ENGLISH`. Finally, one of the applet's private methods, `internationalize()`, which we'll discuss shortly, is invoked.

The applet is specified as an item listener for the choice.

```
public void itemStateChanged(ItemEvent event) {
   int index = choice.getSelectedIndex();

   if(index == 0) guiLabel.setLocale(Locale.ENGLISH);
   else           guiLabel.setLocale(Locale.FRENCH);

   internationalize();
   validate();
}
```

Whenever an item is selected in the choice, the locale of the `guiLabel` is set appropriately, and then `internationalize()` is once again invoked, followed by a call to `validate()`, which lays out the components contained in the applet.

```
private void internationalize() {
   String s = getIdentifierString(guiLabel.getLocale());

   if(s != null) {
      guiLabel.setText(s);
      guiLabel.invalidate();
   }
}
```

The `internationalize()` method obtains the string for the text of the label by invoking another private method, `getIdentifierString()`, which is passed the locale of the `guiLabel`. If the string returned is non-null, the text of the `guiLabel` is set, and the `guiLabel` is invalidated, so that the call to `validate()` in `itemStateChanged()` results in the applet's components being laid out—see "Forcing a Container to Lay Out Its Components" on page 385).

```
private String getIdentifierString(Locale l) {
   ResourceBundle bundle = null;
   try {
      bundle = ResourceBundle.getBundle("LabelsBundle", l);
   }
   catch(MissingResourceException e) {
```

```
        e.printStackTrace();
    }
    if(bundle == null)
        return null;
    else
        return (String)bundle.getObject("Identifier");
}
```

Finally we come to the interesting part of the applet, as far as internationalization is concerned: obtaining the value of the "Identifier" key from the appropriate resource bundle depending upon the locale of the guiLabel.

ResourceBundle.getBundle() is a static method that returns a ResourceBundle. The getBundle() method is passed a string and a locale, which are used to identify the *class* of the appropriate bundle; a class loader is used to create an instance of the appropriate resource bundle, which is returned.

If the locale passed to getBundle() is Locale.ENGLISH, then ResourceBundle.getBundle() looks for a LabelsBundle_en.class file in the current CLASSPATH. If the locale is Locale.FRENCH, then a LabelsBundle_fr.class file is searched for. If the .class file is found, a class loader instantiates an instance of the class, and returns the bundle. If the .class file is not found, a MissingResourceException is thrown. We should note that we have oversimplified the search mechanism used by getBundle()—see the JDK documentation for a complete description of the search algorithm used.

At any rate, if getBundle() was able to locate the appropriate .class file and instantiate an instance of the resource bundle, we invoke the bundle's getObject() method, which is passed the appropriate key and returns the value associated with the key.

To recap: if getBundle() is passed the locale Locale.ENGLISH, for example, it appends "_en.class" to the string it is passed, and searches for a file of that name in the current CLASSPATH. If the .class file is found, a class loader instantiates an instance of LabelBundles_en and returns it. The getObject() method of LabelBundles_en is passed the "Identifier" string, and returns "English GUI". If the locale is Locale.FRENCH, then LabelBundles_fr.class is searched for, and the getObject() method of LabelBundles_fr returns "GUI en Francais" when passed the key "Identifier".

The SimpleI18NTest applet is shown in Example 6-5 for completeness.

Example 6-5 SimpleI18NTest **Applet**

```java
import java.applet.Applet;
import java.util.*;
import java.awt.*;
import java.awt.event.*;

public class SimpleI18NTest extends Applet
                           implements ItemListener {
  private Label  guiLabel = new Label();
  private Choice choice   = new Choice();

  public void init() {
     choice.add(Locale.ENGLISH.getDisplayName());
     choice.add(Locale.FRENCH.getDisplayName());
     choice.addItemListener(this);

     add(choice);
     add(guiLabel);

     guiLabel.setLocale(Locale.ENGLISH);
     internationalize();
  }
  public void itemStateChanged(ItemEvent event) {
     int index = choice.getSelectedIndex();

     if(index == 0) guiLabel.setLocale(Locale.ENGLISH);
     else           guiLabel.setLocale(Locale.FRENCH);

     internationalize();
     validate();
  }
  private void internationalize() {
     String s = getIdentifierString(guiLabel.getLocale());

     if(s != null) {
        guiLabel.setText(s);
        guiLabel.invalidate();
     }
  }
  private String getIdentifierString(Locale l) {
     ResourceBundle bundle = null;

     try {
        bundle = ResourceBundle.getBundle("LabelsBundle", l);
     }
     catch(MissingResourceException e) {
     e.printStackTrace();
```

```
        }
    if(bundle == null)
        return null;
    else
        return (String)bundle.getObject("Identifier");
    }
}
```

Separating the GUI From Internationalization Code

One final note about internationalization is the fact that, by employing a class loader to instantiate the appropriate type of resource bundle, the internationalization data is totally separated from the GUI code. This allows Java applets and applications to be written once and internationalized externally. In other words, if we wanted to provide an Italian version of our GUI, we would need only to implement a `LabelsBundle_it` class that returned the appropriate Italian version of the identifier string and make sure that the .class file for `LabelsBundle_it` is in our CLASSPATH[8].

Available Locales and Two-Letter Codes

Before we move on to component events, we will leave you with a table of the `Locale` constants provided by the `Locale` class, and the two-letter codes for both countries and languages in Table 6-6. The codes in the table can be found at the following websites:

- Countries: *http://www.chemie.fu-berlin.de/diverse/doc/ISO_3166.html*

- Languages: *http://www.ics.uci.edu/pub/ietf/http/related/iso639.txt*

Table 6-6 Locales and Codes for Countries and Languages

Country/Language	Code
Locale.CANADA	CA
Locale.CANADA_FRENCH	--
Locale.CHINA	CN
Locale.CHINESE	zh
Locale.ENGLISH	en
Locale.FRANCE	FR
Locale.FRENCH	fr
Locale.GERMAN	de

8. Of course, we would also have to add an option to our choice, but that is an implementation detail of how the GUI switches from one language to another that could be generalized in a better fashion.

Table 6-6 Locales and Codes for Countries and Languages (Continued)

Country/Language	Code
Locale.GERMANY	DE
Locale.ITALIAN	it
Locale.ITALY	IT
Locale.JAPAN	JP
Locale.JAPANESE	ja
Locale.KOREA	KP
Locale.KOREAN	ko
Locale.PRC	--
Locale.SIMPLIFIED_CHINESE	--
Locale.TAIWAN	TW
Locale.TRADITIONAL_CHINESE	--
Locale.UK	UK
Locale.US	US

Component Events

If you take a look at "AWT Component Listener Registration Methods" on page 97, you will see that five kinds of event listeners can be attached to any component: ComponentListener, FocusListener, KeyListener, MouseListener and MouseMotionListener—see "Listeners" on page 98). All AWT components are capable of firing component, focus, key, mouse and mouse motion events.

The original AWT was quite inconsistent as far as components firing events. For instance, a Label did not fire any events, which made it impossible, for instance, to extend Label and implement a selectable label by processing mouse events. The new event model that comes with the 1.1 version of the AWT is much more consistent with respect to components firing events. We'd like to test out all component/event combinations on each of the three supported platforms, but unfortunately, the Macintosh 1.1 release is lagging behind the Motif and Windows 95 releases by a few months, and therefore we were unable to test the new event model on the Macintosh. As a result, instead of providing you with an indication of which components consistently fire events on each of the platforms, we've instead opted to provide you with an applet that tests event firing for each of the AWT components (except for those that extend java.awt.Window).

A Component Event Test Applet

What we're after is an applet that contains an instance of each AWT component and that somehow indicates when a component fires events associated with listeners that can be attached to a `java.awt.Component`[9]. Our applet is shown in Figure 6-6.

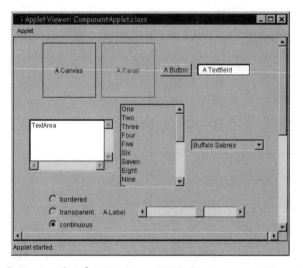

Figure 6-6 An Applet for Testing AWT Component Events
Each of the AWT components is equipped with debugging event listeners that print out events as they occur.

The first order of business is to develop debugging versions of each of the listeners that can be added to an instance of `java.awt.Component`. Since events implement a `toString()` method, this is a simple matter. The implementation of the `DbgKeyListener` class is shown in Example 6-6. Since the rest of the debug listeners are implemented in exactly the same manner, we won't bother to list them here. Of course, you can see their implementations, in addition to running the applet, from the CD that comes with the book if you are so inclined.

Example 6-6 DbgKeyListener Class

```
import java.awt.*;
import java.awt.event.*;

public class DbgFocusListener implements FocusListener {
```

9. Note that we're not testing events fired by specific components, such as action events.

```
public void focusGained(FocusEvent event) {
   System.out.println(event.toString());
}
public void focusLost(FocusEvent event) {
   System.out.println(event.toString());
}
}
```

We also won't bother to list the applet displayed in Figure 6-6 because we have no discussion to accompany the code and the listing is rather lengthy.

In a subsequent version of *Graphic Java* we will provide specific information regarding which components fire which events on the three supported platforms. In the meantime, if you run across a situation where you suspect a component is not firing one of the events associated with the event listeners that can be added to it, you can run the applet shown in Figure 6-6 on page 178 in order to confirm your suspicions.

Summary

The AWT provides 17 extensions of `java.awt.Component`—a collection of basic, useful components for implementing user interfaces. All of the components are currently heavyweight components that have peers and render themselves in their own native, opaque windows. The AWT provides support for implementing lightweight components, but does not provide any specific lightweight components (as of 1.1 final).

`java.awt.Component` provides a great deal of functionality for its extensions, from setting/getting background/foreground colors to tracking location and size, to attaching cursors, to zordering components; the `Component` class covers a fair bit of ground.

Now that we've covered the `Component` class, we will explore the extensions of Component provided by the AWT.

CHAPTER

7

Basic Components: Labels, Buttons, Canvases, and Panels

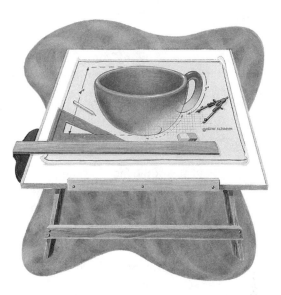

This chapter covers the most basic of the AWT components: labels, buttons, canvases, and panels. Labels and buttons are simple components that display a label. Canvases provide a surface upon which to paint graphics; panels are the most basic container provided by the AWT.

Labels and Buttons

`Label` and `Button` are the simplest AWT components. Labels and buttons both display text—the difference is that buttons typically have a 3D border, and you can activate a button, which should initiate an action of some sort.

java.awt.Label

A `Label` is a simple textual label that doesn't do much; in fact a label doesn't do anything other than display text. You can set the component properties of a label, its foreground and background colors, font, cursor, etc.[1]

Since a label can be resized to be bigger than the text it displays, it comes with the ability to set its alignment—you can display the label's text justified left, right, or centered by specifying an alignment at construction time or after the label is

---

1. This is true, of course, for all extensions of `java.awt.Component`, so we will not mention the fact for any subsequent components we discuss.

constructed by invoking `Label.setAlignment()`. `java.awt.Label` defines three `public static` integer values for its alignment:

- `Label.LEFT`

- `Label.CENTER`

- `Label.RIGHT`

By virtue of the fact that `Label` extends `Component`, labels fire component, mouse, and mouse motion events[2]. As a result, you can find out when a label is moved, resized, shown or hidden. Additionally, you can monitor mouse events that occur in a label if you wish. Since labels are not interested in accepting keyboard focus, they do not, by default, fire focus or key events.

We'll implement a simple extension of `Label` that prints out events and toggles between being selected and deselected when a mouse press occurs in the label, along with an applet that tests it out. You can see our applet in action in Figure 7-1.

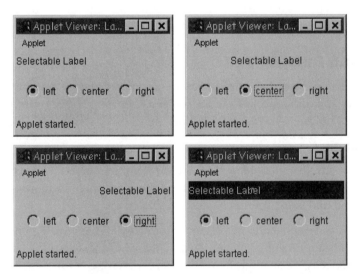

Figure 7-1 A Selectable Label
The `LabelTest` applet allows the alignment of a selectable label to be modified. The picture on the lower right shows the label selected.

---

2. Again, this is true of all extensions of `Component`, so we will not mention it for any components subsequently discussed in this chapter.

Before we show you the entire applet, let's discuss the code that's pertinent to labels.

First of all, our applet implements `ItemListener` because checkboxes fire item events—see "Item Events" on page 112. When a checkbox is checked, we set the alignment of the label accordingly:

```
public void itemStateChanged(ItemEvent event) {
    Checkbox cbox = (Checkbox)event.getSource();
    if(cbox == left)   label.setAlignment(Label.LEFT);
    if(cbox == right)  label.setAlignment(Label.RIGHT);
    if(cbox == center) label.setAlignment(Label.CENTER);
}
```

The default alignment for labels is `Label.LEFT`, which you can see for yourself if you run the applet—we don't specify the alignment until a checkbox is checked, and the label is initially shown aligned to the left.

We also extend `Label` and add instances of debug listeners to listen for component, mouse and mouse motion events. An anonymous inner class implementation[3] of `MouseListener` is added to the label that switches the foreground and background colors when a mouse press occurs, thereby toggling selection of the label:

```
class SelectableLabel extends Label {
  public SelectableLabel(String label) {
    super(label);

    addComponentListener(new DbgComponentListener());
    addMouseListener(new DbgMouseListener());
    addMouseMotionListener(new DbgMouseMotionListener());

    addMouseListener(new MouseAdapter() {
      public void mousePressed(MouseEvent event) {
        Color foreground = getForeground();
        setForeground(getBackground());
        setBackground(foreground);
      }
    });
  }
}
```

The applet, along with the implementation of `SelectableLabel`, is shown in its entirety in Example 7-1.

---

3.   See "Anonymous Inner Classes" on page 125.

Example 7-1 LabelTest Applet

```java
import java.applet.Applet;
import java.awt.*;
import java.awt.event.*;

public class LabelTest extends Applet implements ItemListener {
   CheckboxGroup group  = new CheckboxGroup();
   Checkbox left    = new Checkbox("left",   true,  group);
   Checkbox right   = new Checkbox("right",  false, group);
   Checkbox center  = new Checkbox("center", false, group);
   Label    label   = new SelectableLabel("Selectable Label");

   public void init() {
      Panel checkboxPanel = new Panel();

      left.addItemListener(this);
      right.addItemListener(this);
      center.addItemListener(this);

      checkboxPanel.add(left);
      checkboxPanel.add(center);
      checkboxPanel.add(right);

      setLayout(new BorderLayout(10,10));
      add(label, "North");
      add(checkboxPanel, "Center");
   }
   public void itemStateChanged(ItemEvent event) {
      Checkbox cbox = (Checkbox)event.getSource();
      if(cbox == left)   label.setAlignment(Label.LEFT);
      if(cbox == right)  label.setAlignment(Label.RIGHT);
      if(cbox == center) label.setAlignment(Label.CENTER);
   }
}
class SelectableLabel extends Label {
  public SelectableLabel(String label) {
     super(label);

     addComponentListener(new DbgComponentListener());
     addMouseListener(new DbgMouseListener());
     addMouseMotionListener(new DbgMouseMotionListener());

     addMouseListener(new MouseAdapter() {
        public void mousePressed(MouseEvent event) {
           Color foreground = getForeground();
           setForeground(getBackground());
           setBackground(foreground);
```

```
        }
      });
   }
}
```

Remember that our debug listeners print out events as they occur. If we start the applet, wheel the mouse into the label, click the mouse button, and wheel the mouse back out of the label, we see the following output being printed (we've compressed some of the mouse move events):

```
java.awt.event.MouseEvent[MOUSE_ENTERED,(0,10),mods=0,clickCount=0
] on label1
java.awt.event.MouseEvent[MOUSE_MOVED,(0,10),mods=0,clickCount=0]
on label1
java.awt.event.MouseEvent[MOUSE_PRESSED,(3,10),mods=0,clickCount=1
] on label1
java.awt.event.MouseEvent[MOUSE_RELEASED,(3,10),mods=0,clickCount=
1] on label1
java.awt.event.MouseEvent[MOUSE_CLICKED,(3,10),mods=0,clickCount=1
] on label1
java.awt.event.MouseEvent[MOUSE_MOVED,(0,9),mods=0,clickCount=0] on
label1
java.awt.event.MouseEvent[MOUSE_EXITED,(379,219),mods=0,clickCount
=0] on label1
```

Notice that there are no component events being generated for labels—that's a bug, which may very well be fixed by the time you read this[4].

java.awt.Button

Buttons, like labels, display text. Buttons however, typically have a 3D appearance and trigger some action when they are activated—buttons fire action events when they are activated.

The applet shown in Figure 7-2 contains two panels, each of which contains exactly one button. The North panel uses its default layout—a `FlowLayout`, so the button is sized to its preferred size[5], which is just big enough to hold the text it displays plus a little elbow room. The center panel employs a `BorderLayout` and adds its button as the center component; therefore, the button is stretched to the width and height of the panel. The top button, when activated, toggles the enabled state of the bottom button, and vice versa.

---

4. There are one or more subsequent patch releases due out after 1.1. Our code is based on 1.1, so bugs we encounter may be fixed by the time the book is in your hands.

5. See "The FlowLayout Layout Manager" on page 399.

Figure 7-2 ButtonTest Applet
Two buttons reside in separate panels with different layout
managers—thus, the buttons are shaped differently. The top
button toggles the enabled state of the bottom button, and vice
versa.

Our `ButtonTest` applet is listed in Example 7-2. Notice that the top button
implements an inner class representation of its action listener, and, simply for
illustration, the bottom button opts to add an action listener that is a separate, top-
level class. Whether a button's listener is an inner class representation or a
separate class does not have any behavioral effect—either way, the
`performAction()` method of the listener associated with the button is invoked
when the button is activated.

Buttons, unlike labels, are interested in accepting focus. When the mouse is
pressed in a an enabled button it is given focus (whether or not the mouse is
released inside the button). Since buttons are willing to accept focus, they also fire
key events. When a button has focus, it will fire key events, regardless of the
location of the mouse[6].

Example 7-2 ButtonTest Applet

```
import java.applet.Applet;
import java.awt.*;
import java.awt.event.*;

public class ButtonTest extends Applet {
  Button top    = new Button("Toggle bottom button");
  Button bottom = new Button("Toggle top button");

  public void init() {
    Panel bottomPanel = new Panel();
    Panel topPanel    = new Panel();
```

6.   This is true for all components that accept keyboard focus.

```
bottomPanel.setLayout(new BorderLayout());
bottomPanel.add(bottom, "Center");

topPanel.add(top);

setLayout(new BorderLayout());
add(topPanel, "North");
add(bottomPanel. "Center");

top.addActionListener(new ActionListener() {
    public void actionPerformed(ActionEvent event) {
        if(bottom.isEnabled()) bottom.setEnabled(false);
        else                   bottom.setEnabled(true);
    }
});
    bottom.addActionListener(new BottomActionListener(top));
  }
}
class BottomActionListener implements ActionListener {
  private Button otherButton;

  public BottomActionListener(Button otherButton) {
    this.otherButton = otherButton;
  }
  public void actionPerformed(ActionEvent event) {
    if(otherButton.isEnabled())
        otherButton.setEnabled(false);
    else
        otherButton.setEnabled(true);
  }
}
```

Canvases and Panels

The aptly named canvas provides a surface upon which you can perform graphical operations. A panel is essentially the same as a canvas, except that a panel, unlike a canvas, is also a container that can container other components. Neither Canvas nor Panel, by default, is interested in accepting keyboard focus, and therefore do not fire key or focus events.

Until the advent of lightweight components in the 1.1 release of the AWT, Canvas and Panel were the components of choice to extend when developing custom components[7]. For custom components that did not contain other components,

---

7. The lightweight component framework provides the ability to extend Component and Container directly. See "Lightweight Components" on page 475.

such as an image button, `Canvas` was the logical choice for the component's superclass. On the other hand, a custom component that needed to contain other components, such as a border, would be a likely candidate for extending `Panel`. Now, of course, one must decide whether to implement a lightweight component by extending `Component` instead of `Canvas`, or to implement a lightweight container by extending `Container` instead of `Panel`.

java.awt.Canvas

`Canvas` is a simple component that you can draw into. Although you can create an instance of `Canvas` and draw into it, it is much more common to extend `Canvas` and override its `paint()` method. That way, whenever a canvas is repainted, it redraws its contents correctly.

As you can see in Figure 7-3 and the subsequent listing in Example 7-3, our applet for exercising the `Canvas` class implements an extension of `Canvas` that draws two borders around the canvas: a 3D border inside of a black border, so that we can see the bounds of the canvas. Additionally, we employ the graphics object associated with the canvas to paint some text and graphics inside the canvas.

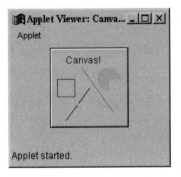

Figure 7-3 `CanvasTest` Applet
A `Canvas` is a component that provides a surface upon which to perform graphical operations, such as drawing text and graphics.

Example 7-3 CanvasTest Applet

```java
import java.applet.Applet;
import java.applet.Applet;
import java.awt.*;
import java.awt.event.*;

public class CanvasTest extends Applet {
  public void init() {
     Canvas canvas = new ExampleCanvas();
     canvas.addComponentListener(new DbgComponentListener());
     add(canvas);
  }
}
class ExampleCanvas extends Canvas {
  public void paint(Graphics g) {
     Dimension size = getSize();
     g.drawRect(0,0,size.width-1,size.height-1);
     g.setColor(Color.lightGray);
     g.draw3DRect(1,1,size.width-3,size.height-3,true);

     g.setColor(Color.blue);
     g.drawString("Canvas!",20,20);

     g.setColor(Color.orange);
     g.fillRect(10,40,20,20);
     g.setColor(Color.red);
     g.drawRect(9,39,22,22);

     g.setColor(Color.gray);
     g.drawLine(40,25,80,80);
     g.setColor(Color.black);
     g.drawLine(50,50,20,90);

     g.setColor(Color.cyan);
     g.fillArc(60,25,30,30,0,270);
  }
  public Dimension getPreferredSize() {
     return new Dimension(100,100);
  }
}
```

Notice that we have overridden getPreferredSize() to return a dimension 100 pixels wide and 100 pixels tall. If the call to getPreferredSize() is commented out, the applet will look like the one pictured in Figure 7-4.

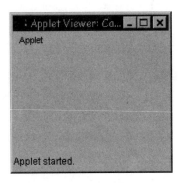

Figure 7-4 A Canvas Extension With (0,0) Size
If an extension of Canvas does not override getPreferredSize(), the canvas may not show up at all, depending upon the layout manager that lays it out and whether it has been explicitly sized.

The reason for the invisible canvas becomes apparent after looking at the output generated by the debug component event listener attached to our canvas:

```
java.awt.event.ComponentEvent[COMPONENT_MOVED (100,5 0x0)] on
canvas0
```

While the canvas has been moved to (100,5), its size is (0,0). The Applet class has a FlowLayout layout manager by default, and FlowLayout lays out components according to their preferred size. As a result, one of the most common mistakes made by developers starting out with the AWT is to create a canvas, paint into it and add it to an applet, only to have the canvas be a no-show. The solution, of course, is to either override getPreferredSize() for the canvas in question.

java.awt.Panel

You can think of a panel as a canvas that can contain other components. As a matter of fact, if you take the `CanvasTest` applet and replace every occurrence of Canvas with Panel, you'll wind up with an applet that looks like the one in Figure 7-5.

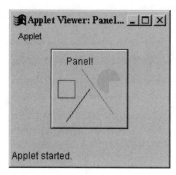

Figure 7-5 `PanelTest` Applet
A Panel can be drawn into in exactly the same manner as a canvas.

Panels, then, are a generic container that you can also paint into. Panels, like other AWT containers, use a layout manager to lay out the components they contain—a panel's default layout manager is a `FlowLayout`.[8]

While the `Panel` class is commonly extended to implement custom components, you are much more likely to simply instantiate a panel for the purpose of adding components. For instance, that is exactly what we did for our `ButtonTest` applet, listed in Example 7-2 on page 186—we created two panels—`topPanel` and `bottomPanel`, each of which contained a single button.

---

8. See "`Container` Default Layout Managers" on page 393.

Since panels are containers and containers can contain other containers, panels are often nested in order to lay out user interface screens. Our `PanelTest2` applet, shown in Figure 7-6, contains an instance of `WorkPanel`, which in turn contains two other panels—one that contains the label and textfield and another that contains the Ok and Cancel buttons.

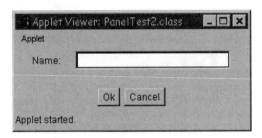

Figure 7-6 `PanelTest2` Applet
The applet contains an instance of `WorkPanel`, which contains two panels—one for the label and textfield and another that contains the buttons.

The `PanelTest2` applet is listed in Example 7-4. The `WorkPanel` class is an extension of `Panel` that might come in handy when implementing custom dialogs, for example. `WorkPanel` sets its layout to a `BorderLayout` and adds a center panel and a south panel. The center panel must be provided at construction time—the contents of the center panel would vary depending upon the user input required. The south panel contains the buttons that would typically be activated when the user was done entering input into the components residing in the center panel.[9]

Example 7-4 PanelTest2 Applet

```
import java.applet.Applet;
import java.awt.*;

public class PanelTest2 extends Applet {
  public void init() {
    Panel      center   = new Panel();
    WorkPanel workPanel = new WorkPanel(center);

    workPanel.addButton("Ok");
    workPanel.addButton("Cancel");
```

9. The GJT provides a similar dialog class. See "gjt.WorkDialog" on page 731.

```
        center.add(new Label("Name:"));
        center.add(new TextField(25));
        setLayout(new BorderLayout());
        add(workPanel);
    }
}
class WorkPanel extends Panel {
  Panel centerPanel;
  Panel buttonPanel = new Panel();

  public WorkPanel(Panel centerPanel) {
      this.centerPanel = centerPanel;

      setLayout(new BorderLayout());
      add("Center", centerPanel);
      add("South",  buttonPanel);
  }
  public void addButton(String label) {
      buttonPanel.add(new Button(label));
  }
}
```

Summary

Labels, buttons, canvases, and panels are the most basic components provided by the AWT. Labels and buttons both display a label; canvases and panels both provide a surface upon which to perform graphical operations. Out of the four components, panels are the only component which also doubles as a container that can contain other components.

CHAPTER
8

Item Selectables: Checkboxes, Choices, and Lists

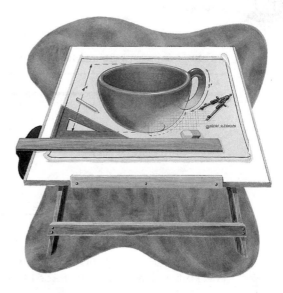

We've grouped checkboxes, choices, and lists together because they are the only AWT components that implement the ItemSelectable interface[1]. Before we discuss each of the three components in detail, we'll briefly discuss the ItemSelectable interface.

The java.awt.ItemSelectable Interface

Classes that implement the ItemSelectable interface have zero or more items that can be selected, or in the case of checkboxes, checked. We've listed the methods defined in the ItemSelectable interface in Table 8-1. As you can probably gather, classes that implement the ItemSelectable interface fire *item* events, thus, the item listener registration methods. The ItemListener interface defines one method: void itemStateChanged(ItemEvent). Whenever an item in an ItemSelectable changes state, an item event is fired to all currently registered item listeners.[2]

---

1. CheckboxMenuItem also implements the ItemSelectable interface but is not a component. See "Checkbox Menu Items" on page 311.
2. See "Item Events" on page 112.

195

Table 8-1 java.awt.ItemSelectable Interface

Method	Intent
`Object[] getSelectedObjects()`	Return an array of the currently selected items.
`void addItemListener(ItemListener)`	Add an item listener, which will be notified whenever an item changes state.
`void removeItemListener(ItemListener)`	Remove an item listener.

java.awt.Checkbox

A checkbox is a component that represents a boolean state. We've already seen checkboxes in action in our `LabelTest` applet shown in "LabelTest Applet" on page 184.

Checkboxes fire item events whenever they are checked or unchecked. In order to react to a checkbox being checked or unchecked, an item listener is added to the checkbox. When the checkbox fires an item event, the item listener's `itemStateChanged()` method is invoked and passed an instance of `ItemEvent`.

Since checkboxes often exist in mutually exclusive groups, they can be added to a `java.awt.CheckboxGroup`, which ensures that only one checkbox in the group is checked at any given time. Note that a `CheckboxGroup` is not a component and therefore cannot be added to a container. As a result, regardless of whether you add checkboxes to a checkbox group or not, you must individually add the checkboxes to the container in which they reside.

Typically, checkboxes are used under one of two circumstances: a group of checkboxes that are not mutually exclusive or a group that is mutually exclusive. Our first applet deals with the former, and our next applet deals with the latter.

Non-Mutually Exclusive Groups of Checkboxes

You can use checkboxes to represent a set of boolean options that are not mutually exclusive. For example, in a print dialog, you might want to let the user select a number of printing options, as shown in Figure 8-1.

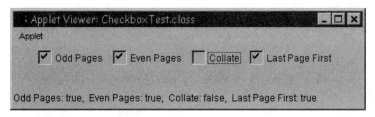

Figure 8-1 `CheckboxTest` Applet
A set of non-mutually exclusive checkboxes for printing options.

Checking or unchecking any of the four checkboxes in the applet updates the applet's status bar to reflect which items are checked and which are not. The applet is listed in Example 8-1.

Example 8-1 CheckboxTest Applet

```java
import java.applet.Applet;
import java.awt.*;
import java.awt.event.*;

public class CheckboxTest extends Applet {
  public void init() {
    setLayout(new BorderLayout());
    add(new PrintOptionsPanel(this), "Center");
  }
}
class PrintOptionsPanel extends Panel {
  Checkbox  oddPages, evenPages, collate, lastFirst;
  Listener  listener = new Listener();
  Applet    applet;

  public PrintOptionsPanel(Applet anApplet) {
    applet    = anApplet;
    oddPages  = new Checkbox("Odd Pages");
    evenPages = new Checkbox("Even Pages");
    collate   = new Checkbox("Collate");
    lastFirst = new Checkbox("Last Page First");

    oddPages.addItemListener (listener);
    evenPages.addItemListener(listener);
    collate.addItemListener  (listener);
    lastFirst.addItemListener(listener);

    add(oddPages);
    add(evenPages);
    add(collate);
```

```
      add(lastFirst);
   }
   class Listener implements ItemListener {
      public void itemStateChanged(ItemEvent event) {
         applet.showStatus(
            "Odd Pages: "        + oddPages.getState()  + ",  " +
            "Even Pages: "       + evenPages.getState() + ",  " +
            "Collate: "          + collate.getState()   + ",  " +
            "Last Page First: " + lastFirst.getState());
      }
   }
}
```

Notice that the `PrintOptionsPanel` contains a named inner class[3] that implements `ItemListener`. One instance of the `Listener` class is instantiated and specified as the listener for each of the checkboxes. As a result, whenever a checkbox is checked or unchecked, the `itemStateChanged()` method in the `Listener` class is invoked. `PrintOptionsPanel.itemStateChanged()` calls the applet's `showStatus()` method, invoking `getState()` for each checkbox. `Checkbox.getState()` returns a boolean value indicating whether the checkbox in question is checked.

Mutually Exclusive Groups of Checkboxes

It is often the case that a group of checkboxes is used to represent a set of mutually exclusive options. Our next applet adds a pair of checkboxes to a checkbox group to facilitate choosing whether to print all the pages of a hypothetical document, or only a specified range of pages. When the Print All checkbox is checked, the labels and textfields associated with range printing are disabled. Likewise, checking the Print Range checkbox enables the labels and textfields, in addition to requesting focus for the starting page textfield.

Figure 8-2 shows two snapshots of the applet, one with the Print All checkbox checked, and another with the Print Range checkbox checked.

Notice that checkboxes under Windows 95 change their appearance when they are part of a checkbox group. Example 8-2 lists the applet in its entirety.

---

3. See "Named Inner Classes" on page 124.

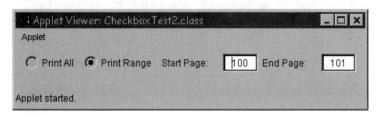

Figure 8-2 CheckboxTest2 Applet
A pair of mutually exclusive checkboxes for specifying which
pages to print. Checking the Print All checkbox disables the
labels and textfields for printing a range of pages. Checking the
Print Range checkbox enables them.

Example 8-2 CheckboxTest2 Applet

```java
import java.applet.Applet;
import java.awt.*;
import java.awt.event.*;

public class CheckboxTest2 extends Applet {
  public void init() {
     add(new PrintRangePanel(100, 101));
  }
}
class PrintRangePanel extends Panel {
  Checkbox   printAll, printRange;
  Label      startPage, endPage;
  TextField startField, endField;

  public PrintRangePanel(int start, int end) {
     CheckboxGroup group= new CheckboxGroup();

     printAll   = new Checkbox("Print All", false, group);
     printRange = new Checkbox("Print Range", true, group);

     startPage = new Label("Start Page:");
     endPage   = new Label("End Page:");
```

```
        startField = new TextField(Integer.toString(start));
        endField   = new TextField(Integer.toString(end));

        add(printAll);  add(printRange);
        add(startPage); add(startField);
        add(endPage);   add(endField);

        printRange.addItemListener(new ItemListener() {
            public void itemStateChanged(ItemEvent event) {
                if(printRange.getState()) {
                    startField.setEnabled(true);
                    endField.setEnabled  (true);
                    startPage.setEnabled (true);
                    endPage.setEnabled   (true);

                    startPage.repaint();
                    endPage.repaint();

                    startField.requestFocus();
                }
            }
        });
        printAll.addItemListener(new ItemListener() {
            public void itemStateChanged(ItemEvent event) {
                if(printAll.getState()) {
                    startField.setEnabled(false);
                    endField.setEnabled  (false);
                    startPage.setEnabled (false);
                    endPage.setEnabled   (false);

                    startPage.repaint();
                    endPage.repaint();
                }
            }
        });
    }
}
```

The first thing to note is that we've invoked a different Checkbox constructor—one that takes a CheckboxGroup argument. The constructor adds the checkbox to the specified checkbox group. Additionally, note that the constructor also takes a boolean variable signifying whether the checkbox is initially checked.

The item listeners for the two checkboxes take care of setting the enabled state of the labels and fields associated with range printing. Also, when the Print Range checkbox is checked, it requests focus for the starting page field. After the starting page field is filled in, a TAB will move the focus to the ending page field—because the ending page field is added to the panel after the starting page field[4].

Choices and Lists

Choices and lists both display a list of strings that can be selected. Whereas a list supports multiple selection, a choice allows only single selection of its items. Lists typically display one or more of their items at all times, while choices display only the selected item until they are activated, at which time a popup list of their items becomes available for making a selection.

Making a Choice: List or Choice?

It is often the case that choices and lists may be used interchangeably. The choice, if you will, whether to use a list or a choice in a given situation often depends upon the following:

- The amount of screen real estate available
- Whether it is desirable to display more than one item at all times
- Whether or not multiple selection is required

If more than one item needs to be displayed at all times or multiple selection is required, a list is the way to go. If screen real estate is tight and only single selection is required, then choices often get the nod.

Another consideration when deciding whether to use a choice or a list is the number of items in the component. Under Windows 95, the popup list for a choice may (automatically) be equipped with a scrollbar, depending upon the number of items in the choice. However, under Motif, the popup list does not provide a scrollbar no matter how many items need to be displayed. Since very long popup lists are unwieldy to manipulate, it often makes sense to use a list instead of a choice when there are a large number of items to choose from.

Figure 8-3 shows two applets, one that employs choices, and another that employs lists for selecting a font.

---

4. Actually, the ending page label is between the two textfields, but labels do not accept focus.

Figure 8-3 Two Applets for Selecting a Font
Both of the applets shown above contain a panel for selecting a
font. The top applet uses choices for font family, style, and size
selection; the bottom applet uses lists for the same purpose.

java.awt.Choice

We'll start our discussion of choices by taking a look at the implementation of the
applet that employs choices shown in Figure 8-3. Since our applet is rather
lengthy, we'll start out by showing you the code pertinent to choices, and then
we'll list the applet in its entirety.

The choices reside in an extension of `Panel`—`FontPanel`:

```
class FontPanel extends Panel {
  private ChoiceTest choiceTest;
  private Choice familyChoice = new Choice(),
               styleChoice = new Choice(),
               sizeChoice = new Choice();

  public FontPanel(ChoiceTest applet) {
    Listener listener = new Listener();

    choiceTest = applet;

    populateFonts();
    populateStyles();
    populateSizes();
```

```
      add(familyChoice);
      add(styleChoice);
      add(sizeChoice);

      familyChoice.addItemListener(listener);
      styleChoice.addItemListener (listener);
      sizeChoice.addItemListener  (listener);
   }
```

After populating the three choices in the `populateFonts()`,
`populateStyles()` and `popuplateSizes()` methods, the `FontPanel`
constructor adds an instance of `Listener` to each choice; `Listener` is a named
inner class that implements `ItemListener`. We'll take a look at
`Listener.itemStateChanged()`, which is invoked when any of the items in
the three choices changes state, after we look at the methods that populate the
choices.

```
   private void populateFonts() {
        String fontNames[] = getToolkit().getFontList();

        for(int i=0; i < fontNames.length; ++i)
          familyChoice.add(fontNames[i]);
   }
   private void populateStyles() {
      styleChoice.add("Plain");
      styleChoice.add("Bold");
      styleChoice.add("Italic");
      styleChoice.add("BoldItalic");
   }
   private void populateSizes() {
      String sizes[] = {"12", "14", "16", "18", "24", "36"};

      for(int i=0; i < sizes.length; ++i)
         sizeChoice.add(sizes[i]);
   }
```

`java.awt.Choice` provides an `add()` method that takes a string for adding
items, which we make liberal use of for adding items to the family, style, and sizes
choices.

The only other method of interest, as far as choices are concerned, is the
`itemStateChanged()` method of the `Listener` class:

```
   public class Listener implements ItemListener {
       public void itemStateChanged(ItemEvent event) {
          choiceTest.updateLabel(getSelectedFont());
       }
   }
```

The `choiceTest` variable is a member of the `FontPanel` class and is a reference to the applet itself. Whenever an item in any of the three choices changes state, the listener attached to each of the choices invokes the applet's `updateLabel()` method and passes the currently selected font. You can see the `ChoiceTest.updateLabel()` method in our complete listing of the applet in Example 8-3.

Example 8-3 ChoiceTest Applet

```java
import java.applet.Applet;
import java.awt.*;
import java.awt.event.*;

public class ChoiceTest extends Applet {
  private FontPanel fontPanel = new FontPanel(this);
  private Label      label     = new Label(" ", Label.CENTER);

  public void init() {
    setLayout(new BorderLayout());
    add(fontPanel, "North");
    add(label, "Center");
  }
  public void start() {
    updateLabel(fontPanel.getSelectedFont());
  }
  public void updateLabel(Font font) {
    label.setText(fullNameOfFont(font));
    label.setFont(font);
  }
  private String fullNameOfFont(Font font) {
    String family = font.getFamily();
    String style  = new String();

    switch(font.getStyle()) {
        case Font.PLAIN:  style = " Plain ";  break;
        case Font.BOLD:   style = " Bold ";   break;
        case Font.ITALIC: style = " Italic "; break;

        case Font.BOLD + Font.ITALIC:
            style = " Bold Italic ";
            break;
    }
    return family + style + Integer.toString(font.getSize());
  }
}
class FontPanel extends Panel {
  private ChoiceTest choiceTest;
```

```java
private Choice familyChoice = new Choice(),
              styleChoice  = new Choice(),
              sizeChoice   = new Choice();

public FontPanel(ChoiceTest applet) {
   Listener listener = new Listener();

   choiceTest = applet;

   populateFonts();
   populateStyles();
   populateSizes();

   add(familyChoice);
   add(styleChoice);
   add(sizeChoice);

   familyChoice.addItemListener(listener);
   styleChoice.addItemListener (listener);
   sizeChoice.addItemListener  (listener);
}
public class Listener implements ItemListener {
   public void itemStateChanged(ItemEvent event) {
       choiceTest.updateLabel(getSelectedFont());
   }
}
public Font getSelectedFont() {
   return new Font(familyChoice.getSelectedItem(),
                   styleChoice.getSelectedIndex(),
                   Integer.parseInt(
                       sizeChoice.getSelectedItem())));
}
private void populateFonts() {
    String fontNames[] = getToolkit().getFontList();

    for(int i=0; i < fontNames.length; ++i)
      familyChoice.add(fontNames[i]);
}
private void populateStyles() {
   styleChoice.add("Plain");
   styleChoice.add("Bold");
   styleChoice.add("Italic");
   styleChoice.add("BoldItalic");
}
private void populateSizes() {
   String sizes[] = {"12", "14", "16", "18", "24", "36"};

   for(int i=0; i < sizes.length; ++i)
```

```
          sizeChoice.add(sizes[i]);
    }
}
```

A major complaint about the `java.awt.Choice` class in the original release of the AWT was the fact that there was no way to delete an item from a choice. Choices that had to represent a dynamic, as opposed to a static, list of strings often had to resort to replacing the original choice with a brand new choice that contained the pertinent items of the moment. Fortunately, the 1.1 release of the AWT fixes that oversight, by providing a number of methods that are variations on deleting items from a choice.

Our next applet provides a mechanism for adding items to, and deleting items from, a choice. As you can see from Figure 8-4, our applet provides a textfield that always contains a string representing the currently selected item in the choice with a remove item button alongside it. Activating the remove item button deletes the currently selected item. The applet also provides a second textfield/button combination for adding items to the choice. The Add Item button adds the string currently displayed in the corresponding textfield to the choice.

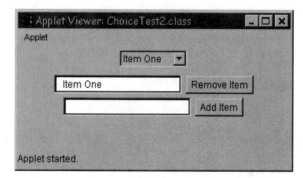

Figure 8-4 An Applet That Programmatically Manipulates a `Choice` Items can be deleted from, and added to, the choice.

All of the action worth discussing takes place in the event handlers for the choice and the two buttons. When an item in the choice is selected, we must set the text in the Remove Item textfield to reflect the currently selected item in the choice, which is a simple task:

```
choice.addItemListener(new ItemListener() {
  public void itemStateChanged(ItemEvent event) {
    removeField.setText(choice.getSelectedItem());
  }
});
```

When an item in the choice is selected, we invoke
`Choice.getSelectedItem()`, that returns the string for the currently selected
item in the choice, which we pass along to the textfield's `setText()` method.
Note that `getSelectedItem()` may return `null` only if the choice contains no
items; if a choice has one or more items, one of the items is always selected.

When the Remove Item button is activated, we delete the item from the choice
with the same string contained in the textfield:

```
removeButton.addActionListener(new ActionListener() {
        public void actionPerformed(ActionEvent event) {
            String fieldStr = removeField.getText();

            if( ! isValidItem(fieldStr)) {
                ChoiceTest2.this.showStatus("That's cheating!");
                removeField.setEnabled(false);
            }
            else if(choice.getItemCount() > 1) {
                choice.remove(removeField.getText());

                Object[] objs = choice.getSelectedObjects();
                removeField.setText((String)objs[0]);
            }
        }
    });
}
boolean isValidItem(String string) {
    int numItems = choice.getItemCount();

    for(int i=0; i < numItems; ++i) {
        if(choice.getItem(i).equals(string))
            return true;
    }
    return false;
}
```

First, we need to check that the text contained in the textfield is a valid item in the
choice, and unfortunately, the `Choice` class does not provide such a method, so
we must take matters into our own hands. The `isValidItem()` method iterates
over the items in the choice until it finds a match for the string it was passed, at
which time it returns `true` to signify that the string passed in is a valid item in the
choice. If no match was found, the method returns `false`. If the string in the
textfield is not a valid item, then we've run across a malicious user, so we disable
the textfield by invoking its `setEnabled()` method with a `false` value.

If the string in the textfield represents a valid item in the choice, and if there is more than one item in the choice[5], we invoke `remove()` on the choice, passing it the string that represents the item to be removed. Once the item has been removed, the remove textfield is now out of synch, so we invoke `Choice.getSelectedObjects()`, which returns an array of, well, of selected objects.

You may find it curious that `Choice` implements a method that returns an array of selected objects, when it can only have strings as its items, and furthermore, only supports single selection. The Choice class implements `getSelectedObjects()` because it implements the `ItemSelectable` interface, which is a more general representation of components that can contain one or more selectable items. For a choice, `getSelectedObjects()` will always return either `null` if there are no selected items (meaning there are no items at all), or it will return an array of strings with the selected item as the first string in the array. Then, we set the remove textfields text to the first string in the selected objects array.

Finally, when the Add Item button is selected, we pass the text in the corresponding textfield to the choice's `add()` method:

```
addButton.addActionListener(new ActionListener() {
  public void actionPerformed(ActionEvent event) {
    choice.add(addField.getText());
  }
```

The applet shown in Figure 8-4 is listed in its entirety in Example 8-4.

Example 8-4 ChoiceTest2 Applet—**Programmatically Manipulating a Choice**

```
import java.applet.Applet;
import java.applet.Applet;
import java.awt.*;
import java.awt.event.*;

public class ChoiceTest2 extends Applet {
  private TextField addField     = new TextField(20);
  private TextField removeField  = new TextField(20);
  private Choice    choice       = new Choice();
  private Button    addButton    = new Button("Add Item");
  private Button    removeButton = new Button("Remove Item");

  public void init() {
```

5. We could have let the number of items in the choice go to zero, but it would have complicated matters.

```
Panel north  = new Panel();
Panel center = new Panel();

north.add(choice);

center.add(removeField);
center.add(removeButton);
center.add(addField);
center.add(addButton);

setLayout(new BorderLayout());
add(north, "North");
add(center, "Center");

choice.add("Item One");
choice.add("Item Two");
choice.add("Item Three");

removeField.setText(choice.getItem(0));

choice.addItemListener(new ItemListener() {
    public void itemStateChanged(ItemEvent event) {
        removeField.setText(choice.getSelectedItem());
    }
});
addButton.addActionListener(new ActionListener() {
    public void actionPerformed(ActionEvent event) {
        choice.add(addField.getText());
    }
});
removeButton.addActionListener(new ActionListener() {
    public void actionPerformed(ActionEvent event) {
        String fieldStr = removeField.getText();

        if( ! isValidItem(fieldStr)) {
            ChoiceTest2.this.showStatus("That's cheating!");
            removeField.setEnabled(false);
        }
        else if(choice.getItemCount() > 1) {
            choice.remove(removeField.getText());

            Object[] objs = choice.getSelectedObjects();
            removeField.setText((String)objs[0]);
        }
    }
});
}
boolean isValidItem(String string) {
```

```
    int numItems = choice.getItemCount();
    for(int i=0; i < numItems; ++i) {
        if(choice.getItem(i).equals(string))
            return true;
    }
    return false;
  }
}
```

java.awt.List

As we mentioned previously, the `List` and `Choice` components have a great deal in common. As a matter of fact, if you take the applet listed in "ChoiceTest Applet" on page 204, and do a global search and replace on every occurrence of *Choice* with `List`, you very nearly wind up with the applet that employs lists shown in "Two Applets for Selecting a Font" on page 202. The only difference to account for is the fact that choices always have (only) one item selected if they have one or more items, while lists do not have any items initially selected.

Recall in the "ChoiceTest Applet" on page 204, that we overrode the applet's start method in order to determine the font that was initially selected:

```
public void start() {
    updateLabel(fontPanel.getSelectedFont());
}
```

The pitfall associated with using this approach with lists, of course, is that lists don't have items initially selected, so in the `FontPanel.getSelectedFont()` method, after our global search and replace mentioned above, we have:

```
public Font getSelectedFont() {
    return new Font(familyList.getSelectedItem(),
                    styleList.getSelectedIndex(),
                    Integer.parseInt(
                        sizeList.getSelectedItem()));
}
```

Since no item is currently selected in any of the lists, the call to `familyList.getSelectedItem()` returns a `null` reference, and the `Font` constructor does not take kindly to being passed a `null` reference for the name of the font. As a result, an exception is thrown.

The simple fix, then is to select an item each of the lists after they are created, which we accomplish by invoking `List.select(0)` for each list, which selects the first item in the list:

```
public FontPanel(ListTest applet) {
  Listener listener = new Listener();
```

```
   listTest = applet;

   populateFonts();
   populateStyles();
   populateSizes();

   add(familyList);
   add(styleList);
   add(sizeList);

   familyList.addItemListener(listener);
   styleList.addItemListener (listener);
   sizeList.addItemListener  (listener);

   familyList.select(0);
   styleList.select(0);
   sizeList.select(0);
}
```

After globally replacing *Choice* with *List* in the `ChoiceTest` applet, and applying the simple fixes shown above, we now have a working applet that allows selection of a font with lists instead of choices. For completeness, we'll list the entire applet in Example 8-5.

Example 8-5 ListTest Applet

```
import java.applet.Applet;
import java.awt.*;
import java.awt.event.*;

public class ListTest extends Applet {
  private FontPanel fontPanel = new FontPanel(this);
  private Label     label     = new Label(" ", Label.CENTER);

  public void init() {
     setLayout(new BorderLayout());
     add(fontPanel, "North");
     add(label, "Center");
  }
  public void start() {
     updateLabel(fontPanel.getSelectedFont());
  }
  public void updateLabel(Font font) {
     label.setText(fullNameOfFont(font));
     label.setFont(font);
  }
  private String fullNameOfFont(Font font) {
     String family = font.getFamily();
```

```
        String style  = new String();

        switch(font.getStyle()) {
            case Font.PLAIN:  style = " Plain ";  break;
            case Font.BOLD:   style = " Bold ";   break;
            case Font.ITALIC: style = " Italic "; break;

            case Font.BOLD + Font.ITALIC:
                style = " Bold Italic ";
                break;
        }
        return family + style + Integer.toString(font.getSize());
    }
}
class FontPanel extends Panel {
  private ListTest listTest;
  private List familyList = new List(),
               styleList  = new List(),
               sizeList   = new List();

    public FontPanel(ListTest applet) {
        Listener listener = new Listener();

        listTest = applet;

        populateFonts();
        populateStyles();
        populateSizes();

        add(familyList);
        add(styleList);
        add(sizeList);

        familyList.addItemListener(listener);
        styleList.addItemListener (listener);
        sizeList.addItemListener  (listener);

        familyList.select(0);
        styleList.select(0);
        sizeList.select(0);
    }
    public class Listener implements ItemListener {
        public void itemStateChanged(ItemEvent event) {
            listTest.updateLabel(getSelectedFont());
        }
    }
    public Font getSelectedFont() {
        return new Font(familyList.getSelectedItem(),
```

```
                     styleList.getSelectedIndex(),
                     Integer.parseInt(
                         sizeList.getSelectedItem())));
   }
   private void populateFonts() {
      String fontNames[] = getToolkit().getFontList();

      for(int i=0; i < fontNames.length; ++i)
         familyList.add(fontNames[i]);
   }
   private void populateStyles() {
      styleList.add("Plain");
      styleList.add("Bold");
      styleList.add("Italic");
      styleList.add("BoldItalic");
   }
  private void populateSizes() {
    String sizes[] = {"12", "14", "16", "18", "24", "36"};

    for(int i=0; i < sizes.length; ++i)
       sizeList.add(sizes[i]);
    }
  }
```

A Double-List Component

Our next applet implements a common user interface component that contains
two lists; items can be moved back and forth between the two lists. We'll name
our component DoubleList[6] and give it an applet to test it out. You can see our
applet in action in Figure 8-5. DoubleList exercises a good percentage of the
public methods provided by the List class.

The buttons in the center of the component work like so:

- > moves selected items from the left list to the right list
- >> moves all items from the left list to the right list
- < moves selected items from the right list to the left list
- << moves all items from the right list to the left list

Additionally, items moved from one side to the other must appear at the top of
the list they are moved to so that they can be seen without scrolling. Also,
selection of items must be preserved when they are moved from one list to
another. Finally, the DoubleList component provides the following accessor
methods:

6.   The Graphic Java Toolkit contains an almost identical custom component.

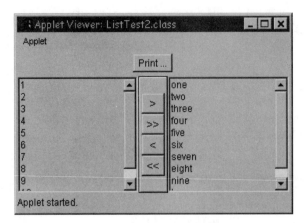

Figure 8-5 A DoubleList Component
Items can be moved back and forth from one list to the other by
activating the buttons in the center panel.

- `String[] getRightSideItems()`

- `String[] getRightSideSelectedItems()`

- `String[] getLeftSideItems()`

- `String[] getLeftSideSelectedItems()`

The applet contains, in addition to the DoubleList component, a Print button to
print out the items and selected items in each list, using the aforementioned
methods. The applet is quite lengthy so we'll digest it in small pieces and restrict
our discussion to the code that is pertinent to lists.

First, let's take a look at the DoubleList implementation. DoubleList
maintains references to the two lists it contains, and a reference to the panel
containing the buttons, referred to as the controlPanel:

```
class DoubleList extends Panel {
  private List left = new List(), right = new List();
  private Panel controlPanel = new ControlPanel(this);

  public DoubleList(String[] leftStrs, String[] rightStrs) {
  ...
    left.setMultipleMode(true);
    right.setMultipleMode(true);

    for(int i=0; i < leftStrs.length; ++i)
      left.add(leftStrs[i]);
```

```
      for(int i=0; i < rightStrs.length; ++i)
         right.add(rightStrs[i]);
   }
```

The omitted code sets the layout manager to an instance of `GridBagLayout`[7], sets constraints for the two lists and control panel, and adds them to the double list (note that `DoubleList` extends `Panel`). `List.setMultipleMode()` is invoked for each list, and is passed `true`, which as you might guess, enables multiple selection mode for the lists. Then, we add strings to the appropriate list by invoking `List.add(String)`, which adds an item to the end of a list.

`DoubleList.moveLeftToRight()` is invoked when the > button is activated, and moves all selected items in the left list to the right list.

```
   private String[] leftStrs = { "1", "2", "3", "4", "5",
                                 "6", "7", "8", "9", "10"};
   private String[] rightStrs = { "one", "two", "three", "four",
                                  "five", "six", "seven",
                                  "eight", "nine", "ten"};
   public void moveLeftToRight() {
      String[] leftSelected = left.getSelectedItems();
      int[]    leftSelectedIndexes = left.getSelectedIndexes();

      for(int i=0; i < leftSelectedIndexes.length; ++i) {
         left.remove(leftSelectedIndexes[i]-i);
      }
      for(int i=0; i < leftSelected.length; ++i) {
         right.add(leftSelected[i], i);
         right.select(i);
      }
   }
```

First, all of the selected items and selected indexes in the left list are obtained by invoking `List.getSelectedItems()`, and `List.getSelectedIndexes()`, respectively.

```
   public void moveLeftToRight() {
      String[] leftSelected = left.getSelectedItems();
      int[]    leftSelectedIndexes = left.getSelectedIndexes();
```

Then, we remove each of the selected items from the left list.

```
   for(int i=0; i < leftSelectedIndexes.length; ++i) {
      left.remove(leftSelectedIndexes[i]-i);
   }
```

---

7. For an in-depth look at `GridBagLayout`, see "The GridBagLayout Layout Manager" on page 403.

At this point you probably have two questions. First, why are we using indices to remove items when the List class provides a remove (String) method? Second, why is the rather curious argument of (leftSelectedIndexes [i] -i) passed to remove (int)?

The answer to the first question is that List.remove (String) removes the *first* item in the list that matches the string passed in. If we had duplicate items in the list, and we removed by string, we could potentially remove the wrong item.

The answer to the second question stems from the fact that we are modifying the list each time through the loop, by removing one item, so we must decrement each index by the number of items that we've deleted.

Finally, we add the items to the right list.

```
for(int i=0; i < leftSelected.length; ++i) {
    right.add(leftSelected[i], i);
    right.select(i);
}
```

Each item is added by invoking List.add (String, int), where the integer argument specifies the position in the list where the item will be added. The positions, of course, start at zero, and increase by one each time through the loop, which means the items are added at the top of the list. Finally, we select each item by invoking List.select (int), because we are retaining selection when moving items, and all of the items that we are moving were originally selected.

DoubleList.moveRightToLeft () is implemented in exactly the same manner as moveLeftToRight (), except that the lists are swapped, so we won't bother to discuss it.

Next, we have the straightforward moveAllRightToLeft (), which moves all the items in the right list (selected or not) to the left list, and retains selection.

```
public void moveAllRightToLeft() {
    int rightCnt = right.getItemCount();

    for(int i=0; i < rightCnt; ++i) {
        left.add(right.getItem(i), i);

        if(right.isIndexSelected(i))
            left.select(i);
    }
    right.removeAll();
}
```

We cycle through all of the items in the right list and add each one to the left list, once again employing `List.add(String, int)` to ensure that the added items show up at the top of the left list. In addition, if the item was selected in the right list, we select it in the left list. When we're all done moving items, we invoke `List.removeAll()`, which removes all of the items in the right list. Once again, `moveAllLeftToRight()` is implemented in exactly the same manner as `moveAllRightToLeft()`, so we won't bother to discuss it.

Finally, we have the accessor methods that return the all of the items and all of the selected items for each list.

```
public String[] getRightSideItems() {
    return right.getItems();
}
public String[] getRightSideSelectedItems() {
    return right.getSelectedItems();
}
public String[] getLeftSideItems() {
    return left.getItems();
}
public String[] getLeftSideSelectedItems() {
    return left.getSelectedItems();
}
```

These methods simply delegate to the appropriate list, invoking either `List.getItems()` or `List.getSelectedItems()`, both of which return an array of strings.

One final note about `DoubleList`. Even though its name implies that it contains lists, `DoubleList` does not provide accessors to its lists, even though it would have been easier to implement `List getLeftList()` and `List getRightList()` methods and let the caller dig out the items and selected items directly from the lists themselves.

In general, it is preferable to implement delegation methods that return pertinent information, rather than expose the implementation of a class by returning references to enclosed objects. Hiding the implementation of a class by not providing accessors to enclosed objects affords a class more leeway in changing its implementation in the future.

In the case of `DoubleList`, you might argue that it really doesn't matter whether the implementation is hidden or not, since it is highly unlikely that `DoubleList` would ever swap out its lists for a different type of object. Consider, however, that the AWT in the future will provide lightweight versions of all its (heavyweight) components, and therefore `DoubleList` might like to swap out its heavyweight lists for a lightweight version, in which case hiding the implementation was good foresight.

Typically, deciding whether to provide accessors to enclosed objects is a trade-off between hiding the implementation of the class and providing clients with the information they need. Another alternative to returning direct references to enclosed objects is to return a reference to an interface that the enclosed object implements, as discussed in the OO Tip "Hide Implementations Of Enclosed Objects By Returning References To Interfaces" on page 110.

Now, without further ado, we present the applet shown in Figure 8-5 on page 214 in its entirety.

Example 8-6 ListTest2 Applet

```java
import java.applet.Applet;
import java.awt.*;
import java.awt.event.*;

public class ListTest2 extends Applet {
  private DoubleList list;
  private Button    printButton = new Button("Print ...");
  private String[] leftStrs = { "1", "2", "3", "4", "5",
                       "6", "7", "8", "9", "10"};
  private String[] rightStrs = { "one", "two", "three", "four",
                         "five", "six", "seven",
                         "eight", "nine", "ten"};
  public void init() {
     Panel controlPanel = new Panel();
     controlPanel.add(printButton);

     setLayout(new BorderLayout());
     add(controlPanel, "North");
     add(list = new DoubleList(leftStrs, rightStrs), "Center");

     printButton.addActionListener(new ActionListener() {
        public void actionPerformed(ActionEvent event) {
            String[] left = list.getLeftSideItems();
            String[] right = list.getRightSideItems();
            String[] sleft = list.getLeftSideSelectedItems();
            String[] sright = list.getRightSideSelectedItems();

            System.out.println("Left Side Items:");
            for(int i=0; i < left.length; ++i)
               System.out.println(left[i]);
            System.out.println();
```

```java
            System.out.println("Right Side Items:");
            for(int i=0; i < right.length; ++i)
                System.out.println(right[i]);
            System.out.println();

            System.out.println("Left Side Selected Items:");
            for(int i=0; i < sleft.length; ++i)
                System.out.println(sleft[i]);
            System.out.println();

            System.out.println("Right Side Selected Items:");
            for(int i=0; i < sright.length; ++i)
                System.out.println(sright[i]);
            System.out.println();
        }
    });
  }
}
class DoubleList extends Panel {
  private List left = new List(), right = new List();
  private Panel controlPanel = new ControlPanel(this);

  public DoubleList(String[] leftStrs, String[] rightStrs) {
    GridBagLayout      gbl = new GridBagLayout();
    GridBagConstraints gbc = new GridBagConstraints();

    setLayout(gbl);

    gbc.fill    = GridBagConstraints.BOTH;
    gbc.weightx = 1.0;
    gbc.weighty = 1.0;
    gbl.setConstraints(left, gbc);

    gbc.fill    = GridBagConstraints.VERTICAL;
    gbc.weightx = 0;
    gbc.weighty = 1.0;
    gbl.setConstraints(controlPanel, gbc);

    gbc.fill    = GridBagConstraints.BOTH;
    gbc.weightx = 1.0;
    gbc.weighty = 1.0;
    gbl.setConstraints(right, gbc);

    add(left);
    add(controlPanel);
    add(right);
```

```
        left.setMultipleMode (true);
        right.setMultipleMode(true);

        for(int i=0; i < leftStrs.length; ++i)
            left.add(leftStrs[i]);

        for(int i=0; i < rightStrs.length; ++i)
            right.add(rightStrs[i]);
    }
    public void moveLeftToRight() {
        String[] leftSelected = left.getSelectedItems();
        int[]    leftSelectedIndexes = left.getSelectedIndexes();

        for(int i=0; i < leftSelectedIndexes.length; ++i) {
            left.remove(leftSelectedIndexes[i]-i);
        }
        for(int i=0; i < leftSelected.length; ++i) {
            right.add(leftSelected[i], i);
            right.select(i);
        }
    }
    public void moveRightToLeft() {
        String[] rightSelected = right.getSelectedItems();
        int[]    rightSelectedIndexes = right.getSelectedIndexes();

        for(int i=0; i < rightSelectedIndexes.length; ++i) {
            right.remove(rightSelectedIndexes[i]-i);
        }
        for(int i=0; i < rightSelected.length; ++i) {
            left.add(rightSelected[i], i);
            left.select(i);
        }
    }
    public void moveAllRightToLeft() {
        int rightCnt = right.getItemCount();

        for(int i=0; i < rightCnt; ++i) {
            left.add(right.getItem(i), i);

            if(right.isIndexSelected(i))
                left.select(i);
        }
        right.removeAll();
    }
    public void moveAllLeftToRight() {
        int leftCnt = left.getItemCount();

        for(int i=0; i < leftCnt; ++i) {
```

```java
            right.add(left.getItem(i), i);

            if(left.isIndexSelected(i))
                right.select(i);
        }
        left.removeAll();
    }
    public String[] getRightSideItems() {
        return right.getItems();
    }
    public String[] getRightSideSelectedItems() {
        return right.getSelectedItems();
    }
    public String[] getLeftSideItems() {
        return left.getItems();
    }
    public String[] getLeftSideSelectedItems() {
        return left.getSelectedItems();
    }
}
class ControlPanel extends Panel {
    private DoubleList   doubleList;
    private Button leftToRight      = new Button(">");
    private Button allLeftToRight  = new Button(">>");
    private Button rightToLeft      = new Button("<");
    private Button allRightToLeft  = new Button("<<");
    private Font    buttonFont       = new Font("TimesRoman",
                                          Font.BOLD, 14);
    public ControlPanel(DoubleList dblList) {
        this.doubleList = dblList;

        GridBagLayout        gbl = new GridBagLayout();
        GridBagConstraints gbc = new GridBagConstraints();

        setLayout(gbl);

        gbc.gridwidth = GridBagConstraints.REMAINDER;
        gbc.fill      = GridBagConstraints.HORIZONTAL;
        gbl.setConstraints(leftToRight,     gbc);
        gbl.setConstraints(allLeftToRight, gbc);
        gbl.setConstraints(rightToLeft,     gbc);
        gbl.setConstraints(allRightToLeft, gbc);

        add(leftToRight);
        add(allLeftToRight);
        add(rightToLeft);
        add(allRightToLeft);
```

```java
        leftToRight.setFont    (buttonFont);
        allLeftToRight.setFont(buttonFont);
        rightToLeft.setFont    (buttonFont);
        allRightToLeft.setFont(buttonFont);

        leftToRight.addActionListener(new ActionListener() {
            public void actionPerformed(ActionEvent event) {
                doubleList.moveLeftToRight();
            }
        });
        allLeftToRight.addActionListener(new ActionListener() {
            public void actionPerformed(ActionEvent event) {
                doubleList.moveAllLeftToRight();
            }
        });
        rightToLeft.addActionListener(new ActionListener() {
            public void actionPerformed(ActionEvent event) {
                doubleList.moveRightToLeft();
            }
        });
        allRightToLeft.addActionListener(new ActionListener() {
            public void actionPerformed(ActionEvent event) {
                doubleList.moveAllRightToLeft();
            }
        });
    }
    public Insets getInsets() {
        return new Insets(4,4,4,4);
    }
    public void paint(Graphics g) {
        Dimension size = getSize();
        g.setColor(Color.black);
        g.drawRect(0,0,size.width-1,size.height-1);
        g.setColor(Color.lightGray);
        g.fill3DRect(1,1,size.width-2,size.height-2,true);
    }
}
```

OO TIP

Hide Enclosed Objects

When a class contains other objects, it is often tempting to provide accessors to the enclosed objects so that clients can obtain information directly from the enclosed objects. However, providing such accessors reveals the implementation of a class, which restricts implementation changes that the class can make in the future. It is often a better design to implement delegation methods that return information pertaining to enclosed objects. In reality, deciding whether to provide accessor methods to enclosed objects is often a trade-off between the likelihood of implementation changes that swap out the enclosed objects with different types of objects vs. the amount of information clients of the class need to access.

Summary

The AWT offers three components that implement the `ItemSelectable` interface: choices, checkboxes, and lists. Item selectables, of course, are components that contain zero or more selectable items. Item selectables are also capable of firing item events whenever an item is selected or deselected.

Choices and lists serve similar purposes; which one to employ in a given situation depends upon the needs of the moment. We have provided some guidelines for deciding whether to use a choice or list depending upon the requirements of the user interface in which they reside.

We've also provided some examples of common user interface components, such as a double list and a font panel for selecting a font. While the intent behind introducing the components was to illustrate particulars of choices and lists, we have also provided similar components in the Graphic Java Toolkit provided on the CD.

CHAPTER
9

Text
Components

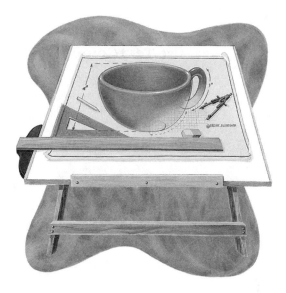

The AWT provides two components for displaying editable text: `TextArea` and `TextField`. The `TextField` component provides a single line of editable text, and the `TextArea` component provides a multi-line textarea that can be thought of as a miniature text editor.

Before we launch into our discussion concerning these two components, we should point out that although the components are useful in their own right, they can be difficult to extend in a meaningful manner because they are peer-based components. While this is true for all of the AWT's heavyweight components, we wish to emphasize the point here; it is not uncommon for newcomers to the AWT to attempt to extend or modify the functionality provided by the textarea to implement a custom text editor. For instance, if you wanted to change the textarea to underline text when selected, instead of displaying the text in reverse video, you'd be out of luck, as that functionality is buried in the textarea's peer and cannot be modified[1].

---

1. Future versions of the AWT will provide peerless versions of existing components.

java.awt.TextComponent

`TextField` and `TextArea` both extend the `TextComponent` class.
`TextComponent`, as a matter of fact, exists solely to provide fundamental text
editing capabilities for `TextArea` and `TextField`.

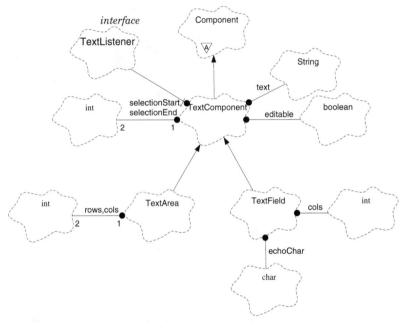

Figure 9-1 `TextComponent` Class Diagram
`TextComponent` maintains text, selection range, and editability
of the component. `TextComponent` cannot be instantiated by
classes outside the java.awt package.

As evidenced by the class diagram in Figure 9-1, `TextComponent` provides the
following functionality:

- Get and set text.

- Get and set selected text.

- Get and set editable mode.

- Position the insertion caret.[2].

2. Since caret manipulation is handled by the peer, there is no evidence of caret
   responsibility in Figure 9-1.

Table 9-1 lists the public methods provided by the `TextComponent` class.

Table 9-1 java.awt.TextComponent Public Methods

Method	Description
`String getText()`	Returns the text currently in the component.
`void setText(String)`	Sets the text.
`String getSelectedText()`	Returns the selected text.
`void select(int, int)`	Sets the selected text. The first `int` is the selection start; the second is the selection end.
`int getSelectionStart()`	Returns the staring position of the selection range.
`void setSelectionStart(int)`	Sets the start of selection range.
`int getSelectionEnd()`	Returns the end position of the selection range.
`void setSelectionEnd(int)`	Sets the end of the selection range.
`void selectAll()`	Selects all of the text in the component.
`int getCaretPosition()`	Returns the caret (insert) position.
`void setCaretPosition(int)`	Sets the caret (insert) position.
`boolean isEditable()`	Returns whether the textarea is editable.
`void setEditable(boolean)`	Sets the ability to edit text in the component.
`void addTextListener(TextListener)`	Adds a text listener.
`void removeTextListener(TextListener)`	Removes a text listener.

`TextComponent` is not available for you to instantiate directly. Even though `TextComponent` is a concrete (meaning not abstract) class, it does not provide any public constructors, and therefore classes outside of the `java.awt` package cannot instantiate a `TextComponent`.

As you can see, all of the necessary get and set methods are provided to either inquire about, or set the value of, the textarea's text, selected text, caret position, and editable mode. In addition, `TextComponent` provides the ability to add text listeners that will be notified whenever its text changes.

Text Selection

As you can see from Table 9-1 on page 227, a `TextComponent` maintains the range of the currently selected text. Figure 9-2 shows an applet with a lone textfield, whose selection range has been set. Although we used a `TextField`, we could have used a `TextArea` and gotten the same result because `TextField` and `TextArea` both inherit their text selection functionality from `TextComponent`.

Figure 9-2 Selection Range for Text Components
Selection range begins at zero. The range includes the low end but stops just short of the top end (the 3 is selected, but the 7 is not).

When figuring selection range, begin counting at zero. The selection range includes the lower end of the range, but not the upper. Notice in Figure 9-2 that the low end of the range (3) is selected, but the top end (7) is not. For the last character in the text to be selected, an index equal to the length of the string must be specified as the end of the selection range. If you're used to C or C++, having the range start at zero makes you feel right at home, but using an index equal to the length of a string might make you think twice. Finally, if there is no selection, `getSelectionStart()` and `getSelectionEnd()` both return the caret position.

TextComponent Listeners

Text components, by default, accept focus, and as a result fire key and focus events in addition to the events fired by all components (see "Components and Internationalization" on page 170). Text components also fire text events and therefore support adding and removing text listeners. The `TextListener`[3] interface defines one abstract method: void

---

3.   See "java.awt.event Listeners" on page 99.

textChangedValue(TextEvent). Text listeners are notified whenever the text they are interested in has been changed. As a result, a text listener can be attached to any extension of TextComponent, for keeping a watchful eye over each and every key entered and/or deleted.

Here's a small dose of pseudo-code for hooking up a text listener to a textfield:

```
public class ATextListener implements TextListener {
  public void textChangedValue(TextEvent event) {
     System.out.println("TextField's text changed value");
  }
}
...
  TextField field = new TextField(20);
  ATextListener listener = new TextListener();

  field.addTextListener(listener);
...
```

java.awt.TextField

Ok, so we know that TextField inherits all of the functionality provided by its superclass, TextComponent. A TextField, as a result, can manage selection, editable mode, and caret positioning. You can also add text listeners to a textfield and watch the text change in the field. So, let's take a look at the additional functionality TextField provides for editing its one line of text. First, take a look at the four constructors provided by the TextField class.

1. TextField()

2. TextField(String text)

3. TextField(int columns)

4. TextField(String text, int columns)

If someone were to put a gun to your head and shout "quick! what's the columns argument for, and you'd better be right!" we're pretty confident that you could calmly reel off the fact that the columns, of course, indicate how many characters fit in the textfield.

If the guy with the gun were really sharp, he might ask if specifying a column width of 9 means that there will always be 9 characters displayed, regardless of font family, style, and point size. The answer, of course, is probably not, because most fonts are not monospaced, so the width of different characters can vary, making one-size-fits-all-for-X-columns an ill-fated pursuit.

AWT TIP ...

Use Monospaced Font For Precise Column Width

Since most fonts are variable width, the sizes of individual characters in the font set can have varying widths, making a field with a certain number of columns an approximation. If a textfield must reflect an exact column width, setting the font for the textfield to monospaced will do. Here's how to change a fields font to a monospaced font:

```
field.setFont(new Font("Monospaced", Font.PLAIN, 12))
```

Table 9-2 lists the interesting public methods provided by `TextField`.

Table 9-2 java.awt.TextField Public Methods

Method	Description
`int getColumns()`	Gets the current number of columns displayed.
`void setColumns(int)`	Sets the number of columns displayed.
`char getEchoChar()`	Gets echo character.
`void setEchoChar(char)`	Sets the echo character.
`boolean echoCharIsSet()`	Is the echo character set?
`void addActionListener(ActionListener listener)`	Registers action listeners to listen for action events generated by typing enter in the textfield.
`void removeActionListener(ActionListener listener)`	Removes an action listener.

`TextField` also provides methods for calculating the preferred, minimum and maximum sizes for itself for a given number of columns.

`TextField` turns out to be a pretty bland, but quite useful, tool in the AWT toolchest. It doesn't bring much to the party though, above and beyond what it gets from `TextComponent`, other than firing action events and providing manipulation for the *echo* character.

The echo character, of course, is what is echoed back into the field when characters are typed into the field. If you have a supersecret textfield with sensitive data, you can make the echo character be something like '*', or some other equally deceptive character.

A `TextField` fires action events when you activate the enter key—see "Semantic Events" on page 105.

We've got two applets concerning textfields coming up for you. Both deal with input validation, which is useful to have at your disposal, and will also help us illustrate some of the finer points of dealing with textfields.

Input Validation

The ugly task of input validation raises its head with amazing regularity. As a result, we'll spend a bit of time talking about two kinds of input validation:

- Exit validation
- On-the-fly validation

The exit mechanism waits until an attempt has been made to exit the textfield, at which time parties guilty of entering invalid data into the textfield are punished accordingly.

The on-the-fly mechanism watches the textfield like a hawk, noting each and every keystroke and quickly assessing whether or not the new addition (or deletion) to the textfield is, in fact, legal. Once again retribution is swift.

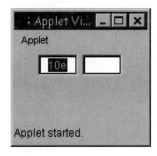

Figure 9-3 Exit Validation
You can never leave the field on the left if you've typed in something that's not an integer.

Exit Validation

Our first applet dealing with input validation contains two textfields. When an attempt is made to leave the left textfield, whether by pressing the TAB key, pressing the enter key, or trying to mouse out, a check is made to make sure that the data entered in the left textfield is a valid integer. If not, focus is politely requested for the left textfield (and always granted), and then all of the text in the field is deservedly selected to admonish the integer challenged. The applet is listed in Example 9-1.

Example 9-1 ExitValidatorTest Applet

```java
import java.applet.Applet;
import java.awt.*;
import java.awt.event.*;

public class ExitValidatorTest extends Applet {
  TextField     fieldOne = new TextField(3);
  TextField     fieldTwo = new TextField(3);
  ExitValidator validator = new ExitValidator();

  public void init() {
    fieldOne.addActionListener(validator);
    fieldOne.addFocusListener (validator);

    add(fieldOne);
    add(fieldTwo);
  }
}
class ExitValidator extends      FocusAdapter
                    implements ActionListener {
  public void actionPerformed(ActionEvent event) {
    validate((TextField)event.getSource());
  }
  public void focusLost(FocusEvent event) {
    validate((TextField)event.getSource());
  }
  private void validate(TextField field) {
    try {
      Integer.parseInt(field.getText());
    }
    catch(NumberFormatException e) {
      field.requestFocus();
      field.selectAll();
    }
  }
}
```

First, we should confess that the textfield on the right exists solely to provide another component to point the focus at—only the left hand textfield has the necessary listeners attached for validation.

`ExitValidator` deals with focus and action events. Focus lost events are generated when you try and leave the textfield. Typing `enter` in a textfield fires an action event, which is deftly handled by `ExitValidator`.

Our validation is pretty simple-minded. We ask the Integer class to parse the string in the left textfield. If the string does not represent a valid integer, `Integer.toString()` throws a `NumberFormatException`, which we catch. Once we've caught the exception, we request focus for the field and select all of the text within the field.

That was exciting enough, we're sure, but wait, there's more! Let's take a quick look at the fascinating world of on-the-fly field validation.

Validating on the Fly

This scenario involves watching keystrokes and not letting illegal characters see the light of day. It's interesting that this approach was not possible under previous releases of the AWT, because try as you might, you couldn't stop an event from being passed on to a component's peer. With the 1.1 version of the AWT, of course, we can `consume()` input events[4], which is exactly what we do in our next applet, shown in Figure 9-4. The applet itself is listed immediately following, in Example 9-2.

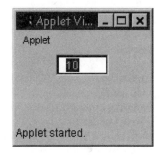

Figure 9-4 On-the-fly Validation
Offending characters are caught and their associated event is consumed before they can get to the textfield's peer, so the characters never show up in the field.

Example 9-2 FlyValidatorTest Applet

```
import java.applet.Applet;
import java.awt.*;
import java.awt.event.*;

public class FlyValidatorTest extends Applet {
  TextField    field = new TextField(5);
  FlyValidator validator = new FlyValidator();
```

---

4.   See "Consuming Events" on page 119.

```
public void init() {
    field.addKeyListener(validator);
    add(field);
  }
}
class FlyValidator extends KeyAdapter {
  public void keyPressed(KeyEvent event) {
    TextField field     = (TextField)event.getSource();
    String    oldstring = field.getText();
    String    newstring = new String();
    int       value     = 0, newValue;

    try {
       if(!oldstring.equals(""))
          value = Integer.parseInt(oldstring);

       newstring += event.getKeyChar();
       newValue  = Integer.parseInt(newstring);
    }
    catch(NumberFormatException e) {
       event.consume();
       field.selectAll();
    }
  }
}
```

This time we attach a key listener to the textfield and watch for key pressed
events. The cool thing about intercepting key presses is that the key press hasn't
been delivered to the textfield's peer yet[5], so if we don't like the key pressed, we
can consume the event and the keystroke never reaches the peer. This, of course,
is exactly what we do if our exception-provoking tomfoolery catches the integer
challenged in command of the keyboard.

Notice that we don't have to be concerned with focus events when validating on
the fly. Since we're validating every keystroke as it comes in and consuming
events associated with illegal characters, the textfield always displays a valid
integer (or an empty string).

As an aside, note that we check the string in the textfield against the empty string:
"". That's because both TextField and TextArea initialize their text to an
empty string if you don't specify what the initial text should be.

---

5.   Event listeners get a crack at input events before their peers.

AWT TIP ...

TextArea.getText() May Return An Empty String

Textfields and textareas devoid of text return an empty string: "". To see whether a textfield or textarea currently has no text, check the string against "", like so:

```
if(field.getText().equals("")) // field is empty
```

java.awt.TextArea

`TextArea` and `TextField` are nearly identical except for one rather obvious difference: a textarea provides more than one row of text, while a textfield provides only a single line of text. `TextArea`, like `TextField` is quite generous about providing ample constructors to choose from.

- `TextArea()`

- `TextArea(String)`

- `TextArea(int rows, int cols)`

- `TextArea(String s, int rows, int cols)`

- `TextArea(String s, int rows, int cols, int scrollbarPolicy)`

Of course, if you really want the textarea to be sized precisely, you should set the textarea's font to monospaced, as we advised for textareas.

The scrollbar policy passed to the last constructor listed must be one of the following:

- `TextArea.SCROLLBARS_NONE`

- `TextArea.SCROLLBARS_BOTH`

- `TextArea.SCROLLBARS_HORIZONTAL_ONLY`

- `TextArea.SCROLLBARS_VERICAL_ONLY`

We'll leave the interpretation of the constants listed above as an exercise for the reader.

Table 9-3 lists the interesting public methods implemented by
`java.awt.TextArea`. As you can see, `TextArea` provides minimal
functionality for text replacement and setting the number of rows and columns.
`TextArea`, like `TextField`, inherits most of its functionality from
`TextComponent`.

Table 9-3 java.awt.TextArea Public Methods

Method	Description
int getColumns()	Returns the number of columns.
void setColumns(int)	Sets the number of columns (characters).
int getRows()	Returns the number of text rows.
void setRows(int)	Sets the number of text rows.
void insert(String,int)	Inserts text at specified location.
void append(String)	Adds text to the end of the component.
void replaceRange(String s int start,int end)	Replaces range starting at start and ending at end with the string s.
int getScrollbarVisibility()	Returns scrollbar visibility policy.

A `TextArea` can contain more than one row of text, whereas a `TextField` is
restricted to one row. Nonetheless, each class implements the same method for
returning the text it contains: `String getText()`. The difference is that the
`TextArea` implementation of `getText()` embeds newline characters in its
string whenever a new row of text begins (excluding the first row).

Search and Replace

Perhaps you noticed that the `TextArea` class provides few methods for text
manipulation: `insert()`, `append()` and `replaceRange()`. That may not
strike you as odd until you realize that `TextField` has no such methods;
`TextField` and its superclass, `TextComponent`, have no text editing
capabilities whatsoever. It would be better for all involved if `TextComponent`
could wrest the text editing mantle from `TextArea`, and then `TextField` could
reap the benefits.

Since `TextArea` is the only text component with editing capabilities, our next
applet, shown in Figure 9-5, is a simple text editor that implements find, change,
and change & find capabilities.[6]

6. The `TextArea` under 1.1 final under Windows 95 (only) had a bug that caused
    the wrong characters to be selected for a find, if the characters were not in the top
    row.

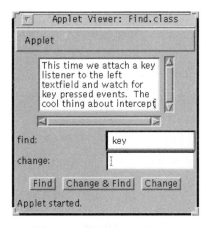

Figure 9-5 Search and Replace in a Text Area
The text editing capabilities of a `TextArea` are used to implement
search and replace functionality.

We'll take a look at the areas of the applet pertaining to text editing in a textarea,
and then we'll list the applet in its entirety. The applet maintains references to all
of the AWT components shown in the applet:

```
TextArea      editor = new TextArea(5,20);
TextField     findField = new TextField(5),
           changeField = new TextField(5);
```

When the Change button is selected, the currently selected text in the textarea, if
any, is replaced with the text contained in the "change:" textfield, by invoking the
applet's `replace()` method.

```
void replace(String change) {
    int start = editor.getSelectionStart(),
        end   = editor.getSelectionEnd();

    if(start != end)
        editor.replaceRange(change,start,end);
}
```

`TextArea` does not provide a method to determine if text is selected, so we check
to see if the starting position of the selection range differs from the end position. If
the start and end positions differ, then the text is selected, and we invoke the
textarea's `replaceRange()` method to replace the text.

Our only other task is to find text in the textarea.

```
void findNext(String find) {
    String edit   = editor.getText();
```

```
int    start  = editor.getSelectionStart(),
       end    = editor.getSelectionEnd(),
       index  =  -1;

index = edit.indexOf(find, start+1);

if(index == -1 && start != 0) {
   index = edit.indexOf(find);
}
if(index != -1) {
   editor.setSelectionStart(index);
   editor.setSelectionEnd(index + find.length());
}
}
```

Once again, we get the start and end positions of the selection range, along with the text in the textfield. If there is selected text (meaning `start != end`), we invoke `String.indexOf()` to search for the index of the next occurrence of the find string, starting at the character after the start of the selection range. If `String.indexOf()` returns -1, then no substring was found.

If no substring was found and `start` is not at the beginning of the string, we call a version of `String.indexOf()` that starts the search at the beginning of the string. This ensures that once we get to the end and there are no further matches, the search starts over at the beginning.

If we've got an index that's something other than -1, we reset the selection range.

The entire applet is listed in Example 9-3.

Example 9-3 Find Applet

```
import java.applet.Applet;
import java.awt.*;
import java.awt.event.*;

public class Find extends Applet {
   TextArea    editor          = new TextArea(5,20);
   Label       findLabel       = new Label("find:"),
               changeLabel     = new Label("change:");

   TextField   findField       = new TextField(5),
               changeField     = new TextField(5);

   Button      findButton      = new Button("Find"),
               changeFindButton = new Button("Change & Find"),
               changeButton    = new Button("Change");
```

```
public void init() {
   Panel north  = new Panel(),
         center = new Panel(),
         south  = new Panel();

   north.add(editor);

   center.setLayout(new GridLayout(2,2));
   center.add(findLabel);
   center.add(findField);
   center.add(changeLabel);
   center.add(changeField);

   south.add(findButton);
   south.add(changeFindButton);
   south.add(changeButton);

   setLayout(new BorderLayout());
   add(north, "North");
   add(center,"Center");
   add(south, "South");

   findButton.addActionListener(new ActionListener() {
      public void actionPerformed(ActionEvent event) {
         findNext(findField.getText());
      }
   });
   changeButton.addActionListener(new ActionListener() {
      public void actionPerformed(ActionEvent event) {
         replace(changeField.getText());
      }
   });
   changeFindButton.addActionListener(new ActionListener() {
      public void actionPerformed(ActionEvent event) {
         int start = editor.getSelectionStart(),
             end   = editor.getSelectionEnd();

         if(start != end)
            replace(changeField.getText());

         findNext(findField.getText());
      }
   });
}
void replace(String change) {
   int start = editor.getSelectionStart(),
       end   = editor.getSelectionEnd();
```

```
            if(start != end)
                editor.replaceRange(change,start,end);
        }
        void findNext(String find) {
            String edit  = editor.getText();
            int    start = editor.getSelectionStart(),
                   end   = editor.getSelectionEnd(),
                   index = -1;

            index = edit.indexOf(find, start+1);

            if(index == -1 && start != 0) {
                index = edit.indexOf(find);
            }
            if(index != -1) {
                editor.setSelectionStart(index);
                editor.setSelectionEnd(index + find.length());
            }
        }
    }
}
```

Summary

This chapter covered the text components provided by the AWT: textfields and textareas. We've discussed not only textfields and textareas but also taken a look at their superclass: TextComponent, which provides a number of services shared by textfields and text areas. Additionally, we've taken a short detour to discuss input validation for textfields, both exit validation and on-the-fly validation.

CHAPTER 10

Scrolling: Scrollbars and Scrollpanes

When developing applets, or any graphical user interface, for that matter, it usually doesn't take long before the need arises to scroll something. In the world of the AWT, that *something* is nearly always a component—usually a container—or an image.

Before the 1.1 version of the AWT, implementing scrolling required you to manually attach scrollbars to a container and then subsequently monitor scrollbar events in order to scroll the contents of the container accordingly, which was a fairly complicated and error-prone process.

The 1.1 release of the AWT still provides a basic scrollbar component, but it also comes with a `ScrollPane` container. `ScrollPane` greatly simplifies the process of scrolling a component—a component is simply added to the scrollpane, and all of the scrolling details are handled without programmer intervention.

java.awt.Scrollbar

Although the advent of scrollpane takes away much of scrollbar's thunder, scrollbars are still useful in their own right; for instance, a scrollbar could be used to implement a quick and dirty slider component—a component, in fact, that we'll use to illustrate the properties and events associated with scrollbars. Our slider contains a scrollbar and a label that displays the scrollbar's current value. For visual effect, we'll wrap the scrollbar and label in a 3D rectangle outlined with a black border. Figure 10-1 shows our slider component in action.

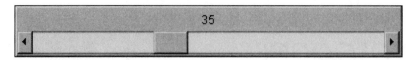

Figure 10-1 A `Slider` Component
A slider consists of a scrollbar and a label that displays the
scrollbar's current value. The scrollbar and label are contained in
a panel with an outlined 3D border.

Instead of embedding the functionality that paints the 3D border and black
outline in the `Slider` class itself, we'll create a separate class, `BorderedPanel`.
By encapsulating the bordering functionality in a separate class, we make it
available for others to use. The `BorderedPanel` class is a simple panel that
overrides `paint()` in order to paint its borders.

Example 10-1 `BorderedPanel` Class

```
import java.awt.*;

public class BorderedPanel extends Panel {
  public Insets getInsets() {
     return new Insets(2,2,2,2);
  }
  public void paint(Graphics g) {
     Dimension size = getSize();

     g.setColor(SystemColor.windowBorder);
     g.drawRect(0,0,size.width-1,size.height-1);

     g.setColor(SystemColor.activeCaptionBorder);
     g.draw3DRect(1,1,size.width-3,size.height-3,true);
  }
}
```

`BorderedPanel` also overrides `getInsets()` so that the components
contained in the panel do not encroach upon the area in which the 3D border and
outline are drawn. If `BorderedPanel` did not override `getInsets()`, the
borders would be drawn underneath the panel's components and therefore
would not be visible. See "Painting a Container's Components" on page 382 for
more information on painting graphics in a container.

The `Slider` class extends `BorderedPanel` and implements the `Adjustable`
interface. It sets its layout to an instance of `BorderLayout` and adds a label as
the north component and a scrollbar as the south component. An anonymous

inner class implementing `AdjustmentListener` is added to the scrollbar so that whenever the scrollbar's value changes, the label's text is set to reflect the current value of the scrollbar.

```
public class Slider extends BorderedPanel implements Adjustable {
  Scrollbar scrollbar;
  Label     valueLabel;

  public Slider(int initialValue, int visible,
                int min, int max) {
    String initialValueStr = Integer.toString(initialValue);

    valueLabel = new Label(initialValueStr, Label.CENTER);
    scrollbar  = new Scrollbar(Scrollbar.HORIZONTAL,
                               initialValue,
                               visible, min, max);
    setLayout(new BorderLayout());
    add(valueLabel, "North");
    add(scrollbar, "Center");

    scrollbar.addAdjustmentListener(new AdjustmentListener() {
        public void adjustmentValueChanged(AdjustmentEvent e) {
            valueLabel.setText(
                Integer.toString(scrollbar.getValue()));
        }
    });
  }
  ...
```

The rest of the implementation for the `Slider` class implements the methods defined in the `Adjustable` interface (see "Adjustment Events" on page 108) by delegating to the enclosed scrollbar.

Note that it would have been much easier to forgo implementing the `Adjustable` interface by providing an accessor to the scrollbar instead, so that clients could directly manipulate the scrollbar itself, but that would have exposed the implementation of the `Slider` class. In this case, the slider's scrollbar is a likely candidate to be replaced with something that more closely resembles a real slider component in the future, and therefore the effort required to keep the slider's implementation hidden is justifiable[1].

Example 10-2 lists the `Slider` class in its entirety.

---

1. See "Hide Enclosed Objects" on page 223.

Example 10-2 Slider Class

```java
import java.awt.*;
import java.awt.event.*;

public class Slider extends BorderedPanel implements Adjustable {
  Scrollbar scrollbar;
  Label     valueLabel;

  public Slider(int initialValue, int visible,
                int min, int max) {
    String initialValueStr = Integer.toString(initialValue);

    valueLabel = new Label(initialValueStr, Label.CENTER);
    scrollbar  = new Scrollbar(Scrollbar.HORIZONTAL,
                               initialValue,
                               visible, min, max);
    setLayout(new BorderLayout());
    add(valueLabel, "North");
    add(scrollbar, "Center");

    scrollbar.addAdjustmentListener(new AdjustmentListener() {
        public void adjustmentValueChanged(AdjustmentEvent e) {
          valueLabel.setText(
              Integer.toString(scrollbar.getValue()));
        }
    });
  }
  public void addAdjustmentListener(AdjustmentListener l) {
    scrollbar.addAdjustmentListener(l);
  }
  public void removeAdjustmentListener(AdjustmentListener l) {
    scrollbar.removeAdjustmentListener(l);
  }
  public int getOrientation() {
    return scrollbar.getOrientation();
  }
  public void setOrientation(int orient) {
    scrollbar.setOrientation(orient);
  }
  public int getValue() {
    return scrollbar.getValue();
  }
  public int getVisibleAmount() {
    return scrollbar.getVisibleAmount();
  }
  public int getMinimum() {
    return scrollbar.getMinimum();
```

```
   }
   public int getMaximum() {
      return scrollbar.getMaximum();
   }
   public int getUnitIncrement() {
      return scrollbar.getUnitIncrement();
   }
   public int getBlockIncrement() {
      return scrollbar.getBlockIncrement();
   }
   public void setValue(int value) {
      scrollbar.setValue(value);
      valueLabel.setText(Integer.toString(value));
   }
   public void setVisibleAmount(int value) {
      scrollbar.setVisibleAmount(value);
   }
   public void setMinimum(int min) {
      scrollbar.setMinimum(min);
   }
   public void setMaximum(int max) {
      scrollbar.setMaximum(max);
   }
   public void setUnitIncrement(int inc) {
      scrollbar.setUnitIncrement(inc);
   }
   public void setBlockIncrement(int inc) {
      scrollbar.setBlockIncrement(inc);
   }
}
```

Adjustable Interface

The `java.awt.Adjustable` interface defines methods for setting and getting
the properties associated with an adjustable object (value, minimum, maximum,
etc.)—see Table 5-6 on page 109 for a complete list of `Adjustable` methods. The
applet shown in Figure 10-2 implements a control panel for dynamically changing
the properties of a slider and exercises all of the methods in the `Adjustable`
interface.

The `SliderTest` applet creates an instance of `ControlPanel` and an instance
of `Slider`, specifying the former as the north component and the latter as the
center component of the applet itself.

```
public class SliderTest extends Applet {
   private Slider      slider       = new Slider(35,10,0,100);
   private ControlPanel controlPanel = new ControlPanel(slider);
```

```
    public void init() {
        setLayout(new BorderLayout(10,10));
        add(controlPanel, "North");
        add(slider, "Center");
    }
}
```

`ControlPanel` employs an instance of `GridBagLayout` to lay out two columns, where the left column consists of labels and the right column consists of controls (mostly textfields). We'll show you the applet in its entirety, but we won't discuss the use of `GridBagLayout` for the `ControlPanel`. "The GridBagLayout Layout Manager" on page 403 provides an in-depth discussion of `GridBagLayout`.

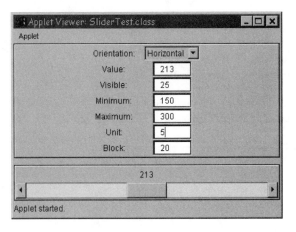

Figure 10-2 `SliderTest` Applet
An applet that allows the properties of a slider (scrollbar) to be modified and tracked.

`ControlPanel` first instantiates its components.

```
class ControlPanel extends    BorderedPanel
                implements AdjustmentListener {
  private Slider slider;

  private Label orientLabel = new Label("Orientation:"),
          valueLabel = new Label("Value:"),
          minLabel    = new Label("Minimum:"),
          maxLabel    = new Label("Maximum:"),
          visibleLabel = new Label("Visible:"),
          unitLabel   = new Label("Unit:"),
          blockLabel  = new Label("Block:");

  private Choice orientChoice = new Choice();
```

```
private TextField valueField = new TextField(5),
                  minField = new TextField(5),
                  maxField    = new TextField(5),
                  visibleField = new TextField(5),
                  unitField   = new TextField(5),
                  blockField  = new TextField(5);
```

The `ControlPanel` constructor takes a reference to the slider it manipulates and adds itself as an *adjustment listener* of the slider. Remember that the slider implements the `Adjustable` interface and delegates `Adjustable` methods to the enclosed scrollbar, so adjustment listeners can be added to the slider, which in turn adds them to the scrollbar itself.

```
public ControlPanel(Slider aSlider) {
  slider = aSlider;
  slider.addAdjustmentListener(this);
  readSliderValues();
  ...
}
```

Whenever the slider's value changes, the control panel's `adjustmentValueChanged()` is invoked, which obtains the current value for the slider and sets the value of the `valueField` textfield appropriately.

```
public void adjustmentValueChanged(AdjustmentEvent e) {
  valueField.setText(Integer.toString(slider.getValue()));
}
```

After adding itself as an adjustment listener for the slider, the control panel reads in the initial values of the slider by invoking `Adjustable` methods implemented by the slider.

```
void readSliderValues() {
  String value  = Integer.toString(slider.getValue()),
         min    = Integer.toString(slider.getMinimum()),
         max    = Integer.toString(slider.getMaximum()),
         vis    = Integer.toString(slider.getVisibleAmount()),
         unit   = Integer.toString(slider.getUnitIncrement()),
         blck   = Integer.toString(slider.getBlockIncrement());

  valueField.setText    (value);
  minField.setText      (min);
  maxField.setText      (max);
  visibleField.setText (vis);
  unitField.setText     (unit);
  blockField.setText    (blck);
}
```

In addition to updating the text displayed in the `valueField` textfield whenever the slider's value changes, we also want the properties of the slider to be updated whenever a value is specified in the control panel. This is accomplished by adding action listeners to all of the textfields in the control panel[2].

```java
valueField.addActionListener(new ActionListener() {
   public void actionPerformed(ActionEvent event) {
      slider.setValue(
         Integer.parseInt(valueField.getText()));
   }
});
visibleField.addActionListener(new ActionListener() {
   public void actionPerformed(ActionEvent event) {
      slider.setVisibleAmount(
         Integer.parseInt(visibleField.getText()));
   }
});
minField.addActionListener(new ActionListener() {
   public void actionPerformed(ActionEvent event) {
      slider.setMinimum(
         Integer.parseInt(minField.getText()));
   }
});
maxField.addActionListener(new ActionListener() {
   public void actionPerformed(ActionEvent event) {
      slider.setMaximum(
         Integer.parseInt(maxField.getText()));
   }
});
unitField.addActionListener(new ActionListener() {
   public void actionPerformed(ActionEvent event) {
      slider.setUnitIncrement(
         Integer.parseInt(unitField.getText()));
   }
});
blockField.addActionListener(new ActionListener() {
   public void actionPerformed(ActionEvent event) {
      slider.setBlockIncrement(
         Integer.parseInt(blockField.getText()));
   }
});
```

2. A textfield fires an action event whenever enter is typed in the textfield. See "Action Events" on page 106.

The action listeners for the textfields all invoke `TextField.getText()` to obtain the string currently displayed in the textfield, which is then passed to `Integer.parseInt()` which returns an integer value[3]. Once we have the integer value in hand, it is passed to the appropriate `Adjustable` method implemented by the slider (which is in turn passed to the scrollbar contained in the slider).

An item listener is added to the choice that controls the orientation of the slider.

```
orientChoice.addItemListener(new ItemListener() {
    public void itemStateChanged(ItemEvent event) {
        int index = orientChoice.getSelectedIndex();

        if(index == 0)
            slider.setOrientation(Scrollbar.HORIZONTAL);
        else
            slider.setOrientation(Scrollbar.VERTICAL);

        readSliderValues();
    }
});
```

There are a couple of points of interest here. First, note that we could take a peek in the `java.awt.Scrollbar` class and discover the following:

```
public class Scrollbar extends Component implements Adjustable {
    public static final intHORIZONTAL = 0;
    public static final intVERTICAL   = 1;
```

Having knowledge of the explicit values for `Scrollbar.HORIZONTAL` and `Scrollbar.VERTICAL`, coupled with the fact that indices for a choice start at zero, we could simplify the implementation of the item listener associated with the `orientChoice`, like so:

```
orientChoice.addItemListener(new ItemListener() {
    public void itemStateChanged(ItemEvent event) {
        slider.setOrientation(orientChoice.getSelectedIndex());
        readSliderValues();
    }
});
```

However, this would be committing one of the cardinal object-oriented sins: relying upon the implementation of a class. If, in the future, the Scrollbar class changed the values of the HORIZONTAL and VERTICAL constants, our not-so-

---

3. Of course, the value typed into the textfield must be a valid integer value, or an exception will be thrown, which we do not bother to catch.

clever shortcut would break. As a result, we opt for a few more lines of code to ensure that our code will continue to work even if the implementation of Scrollbar changes[4].

Second, we invoke readSliderValues() after changing the orientation because we found that some of the scrollbar's values are reset when the orientation of the scrollbar is modified, resulting in our fields being out of synch.

The SliderTest applet is shown in Example 10-3.

Example 10-3 SliderTest Applet

```java
import java.applet.Applet;
import java.awt.*;
import java.awt.event.*;

public class SliderTest extends Applet {
   private Slider        slider          = new Slider(35,10,0,100);
   private ControlPanel controlPanel = new ControlPanel(slider);

   public void init() {
      setLayout(new BorderLayout(10,10));
      add(controlPanel, "North");
      add(slider, "Center");
   }
}
class ControlPanel extends      BorderedPanel
                   implements AdjustmentListener {
   private Slider slider;

   private Label orientLabel = new Label("Orientation:"),
            valueLabel    = new Label("Value:"),
            minLabel      = new Label("Minimum:"),
            maxLabel      = new Label("Maximum:"),
            visibleLabel = new Label("Visible:"),
            unitLabel     = new Label("Unit:"),
            blockLabel    = new Label("Block:");

   private Choice orientChoice = new Choice();

   private TextField valueField = new TextField(5),
                minField = new TextField(5),
                maxField = new TextField(5),
                visibleField = new TextField(5),
                unitField = new TextField(5),
```

4.   Of course, the values for the constants must still be integers, but we can only do so much.

```
                blockField   = new TextField(5);
public void adjustmentValueChanged(AdjustmentEvent e) {
    valueField.setText(Integer.toString(slider.getValue()));
}
public ControlPanel(Slider aSlider) {
    slider = aSlider;
    slider.addAdjustmentListener(this);
    readSliderValues();

    GridBagLayout      gbl = new GridBagLayout();
    GridBagConstraints gbc = new GridBagConstraints();

    orientChoice.add("Horizontal");
    orientChoice.add("Vertical");

    setLayout(gbl);

    gbc.gridwidth = 1;
    gbl.setConstraints(orientLabel, gbc);
    add(orientLabel);

    gbc.gridwidth = GridBagConstraints.REMAINDER;
    gbl.setConstraints(orientChoice, gbc);
    add(orientChoice);

    gbc.gridwidth = 1;
    gbl.setConstraints(valueLabel, gbc);
    add(valueLabel);

    gbc.gridwidth = GridBagConstraints.REMAINDER;
    gbl.setConstraints(valueField, gbc);
    add(valueField);

    gbc.gridwidth = 1;
    gbl.setConstraints(visibleLabel, gbc);
    add(visibleLabel);

    gbc.gridwidth = GridBagConstraints.REMAINDER;
    gbl.setConstraints(visibleField, gbc);
    add(visibleField);

    gbc.gridwidth = 1;
    gbl.setConstraints(minLabel, gbc);
    add(minLabel);

    gbc.gridwidth = GridBagConstraints.REMAINDER;
    gbl.setConstraints(minField, gbc);
```

```
add(minField);

gbc.gridwidth = 1;
gbl.setConstraints(maxLabel, gbc);
add(maxLabel);

gbc.gridwidth = GridBagConstraints.REMAINDER;
gbl.setConstraints(maxField, gbc);
add(maxField);

gbc.gridwidth = 1;
gbl.setConstraints(unitLabel, gbc);
add(unitLabel);

gbc.gridwidth = GridBagConstraints.REMAINDER;
gbl.setConstraints(unitField, gbc);
add(unitField);

gbc.gridwidth = 1;
gbl.setConstraints(blockLabel, gbc);
add(blockLabel);

gbc.gridwidth = GridBagConstraints.REMAINDER;
gbl.setConstraints(blockField, gbc);
add(blockField);

orientChoice.addItemListener(new ItemListener() {
   public void itemStateChanged(ItemEvent event) {
      int index = orientChoice.getSelectedIndex();

      if(index == 0)
         slider.setOrientation(Scrollbar.HORIZONTAL);
      else
         slider.setOrientation(Scrollbar.VERTICAL);

      readSliderValues();
   }
});
valueField.addActionListener(new ActionListener() {
   public void actionPerformed(ActionEvent event) {
      slider.setValue(
         Integer.parseInt(valueField.getText()));
   }
});
visibleField.addActionListener(new ActionListener() {
   public void actionPerformed(ActionEvent event) {
      slider.setVisibleAmount(
         Integer.parseInt(visibleField.getText()));
```

```
            }
        });
        minField.addActionListener(new ActionListener() {
            public void actionPerformed(ActionEvent event) {
                slider.setMinimum(
                Integer.parseInt(minField.getText()));
            }
        });
        maxField.addActionListener(new ActionListener() {
            public void actionPerformed(ActionEvent event) {
                slider.setMaximum(
                    Integer.parseInt(maxField.getText()));
            }
        });
        unitField.addActionListener(new ActionListener() {
            public void actionPerformed(ActionEvent event) {
                slider.setUnitIncrement(
                    Integer.parseInt(unitField.getText()));
            }
        });
        blockField.addActionListener(new ActionListener() {
            public void actionPerformed(ActionEvent event) {
                slider.setBlockIncrement(
                    Integer.parseInt(blockField.getText()));
            }
        });
    }
    void readSliderValues() {
        String value = Integer.toString(slider.getValue()),
            min   = Integer.toString(slider.getMinimum()),
            max   = Integer.toString(slider.getMaximum()),
            vis   = Integer.toString(slider.getVisibleAmount()),
            unit  = Integer.toString(slider.getUnitIncrement()),
            blck  = Integer.toString(slider.getBlockIncrement());

        valueField.setText   (value);
        minField.setText     (min);
        maxField.setText     (max);
        visibleField.setText(vis);
        unitField.setText    (unit);
        blockField.setText   (blck);
    }
}
```

java.awt.ScrollPane

If you've had to manually implement scrolling with the previous versions of the AWT, you'll surely appreciate the `java.awt.ScrollPane` class, which makes its debut in the 1.1 release of the AWT.

`java.awt.ScrollPane` is a container, although it differs from other AWT containers by virtue of the fact that it can only contain one component at a time. As a matter of fact, the `ScrollPane` class overrides `Container.addImpl()`[5] to ensure that the scrollpane always contains only one component. Therefore, if you invoke any of the `add()` methods provided by the `Container` class on a scrollpane, the existing component contained in the scrollpane will be removed and the component added will be the only component contained in the scrollpane. Of course, the component contained in a scrollpane may be a container, so a scrollpane can scroll more than one component at a time.

`ScrollPane` also allows a scrollbar display policy to be set at construction time only. The valid constants for the scrollbar display policy are:

- `ScrollPane.SCROLLBARS_AS_NEEDED` (Default)
- `ScrollPane.SCROLLBARS_ALWAYS`
- `ScrollPane.SCROLLBARS_NEVER`

As you can probably guess, setting the display policy to `SCROLLBARS_AS_NEEDED` results in scrollbars being displayed only if the component being scrolled is larger than the scrollpane itself, whereas setting the display policy `SCROLLBARS_ALWAYS` or `SCROLLBARS_NEVER` results in scrollbars being displayed all the time or never, respectively. `SCROLLBARS_AS_NEEDED` is the default display policy if you construct an instance of `ScrollPane` without specifying a policy. You may wonder why the third option is provided at all—what good is a scrollpane if the contents cannot be scrolled? The answer is that a scrollpane can still be scrolled programmatically even if no scrollbars are displayed. We'll discuss programmatic scrolling a little later on.

Scrolling Components

Our first applet, shown in Figure 10-3, scrolls components and provides a button that toggles the component currently contained in the scrollpane. We are using two panels from the GJT unit tests, `ImageStore` and `ImageButtonTestPanel` as the components to be scrolled by the scrollpane. The contents of the panels and,

---

5. `Container.addImpl()` is a new protected method for 1.1 that is invoked by the overloaded `add()` methods in the `Container` class.

therefore, their implementations, have no bearing on our discussion; we simply wanted to scroll something more interesting than a simple container that contained indiscriminate components. So, we'll list the code for the applet, but we won't list the code for the panels that are being scrolled.

As you can see from Figure 10-3, one of the panels is large enough to require both horizontal and vertical scrollbars, whereas the other panel does not require any scrollbars (when the size of the scrollpane is the same as that specified in the applet tag in the html file).

 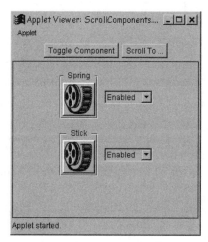

Figure 10-3 `ScrollComponent` Applet
A scrollpane that toggles the container that it scrolls.

A scrollpane is quite simple to use. For instance, our applet initially creates the two panels that will be displayed in the scrollpane, the scrollpane itself, and then the image store panel is added to the scrollpane. Notice that since the image buttons used in the image store panel may take a few seconds to load, we set the cursor for the applet to the wait cursor in the `init()` method and then set it back to the default cursor in the `start()` method[6].

```
public class ScrollComponents extends Applet {
    private ScrollPane           scroller;
    private ImageStore           imageStore;
    private ImageButtonTestPanel ibPanel;

    public void init() {
        setCursor(Cursor.getPredefinedCursor(Cursor.WAIT_CURSOR));
```

6. Which is not a bad idea in general. See "Components and Cursors" on page 163.

```
      imageStore = new ImageStore(this);
      ibPanel    = new ImageButtonTestPanel(this);
      scroller   = new ScrollPane();

      scroller.add(imageStore);
      setLayout(new BorderLayout());
      add(new TogglePanel(scroller, imageStore, ibPanel), "North");
      add(scroller, "Center");
   }
   public void start() {
      setCursor(
      Cursor.getPredefinedCursor(Cursor.DEFAULT_CURSOR));
   }
}
```

In fact, since scrolling is handled automatically by the scrollpane, the rest of our applet consists only of the implementation of the toggle panel that contains a button for toggling the component being scrolled, and another button for programmatically scrolling the component. Since we'll discuss programmatic scrolling later, we won't repeat that discussion here; instead, we'll show you the code pertinent to toggling the component currently displayed in the scrollpane.

```
toggleButton.addActionListener(new ActionListener() {
    public void actionPerformed(ActionEvent event) {
        if(scroller.getComponent(0) == imageStore)
            scroller.add(ibPanel);
        else
            scroller.add(imageStore);

        scroller.getParent().validate();
    }
});
```

We obtain a reference to the first (and only) component contained in the scrollpane by invoking `Container.getComponent()`, passing an index of zero, which returns the first (and only) component in the scrollpane. If the component currently being scrolled is the image store, then the image button panel is added to the scrollpane, and vice versa. Note that after we add the component to the scrollpane, we invoke `validate()` on the scrollpane's container in order to force the scrollpane to be laid out, which updates the scrollbars (if any) associated with the scrollpane. Also, note that we do not remove the current component before adding a component, because, as we mentioned previously, that is taken care of automatically.

The entire applet is listed in Example 10-4.

Example 10-4 ScrollComponents Applet

```java
import java.applet.Applet;
import java.awt.*;
import java.awt.event.*;

public class ScrollComponents extends Applet {
   private ScrollPane           scroller;
   private ImageStore           imageStore;
   private ImageButtonTestPanel ibPanel;

   public void init() {
      setCursor(Cursor.getPredefinedCursor(Cursor.WAIT_CURSOR));

      imageStore = new ImageStore(this);
      ibPanel    = new ImageButtonTestPanel(this);
      scroller   = new ScrollPane();

      scroller.add(imageStore);

      setLayout(new BorderLayout());
      add(new TogglePanel(scroller, imageStore, ibPanel), "North");
      add(scroller, "Center");
   }
   public void start() {
      setCursor(
         Cursor.getPredefinedCursor(Cursor.DEFAULT_CURSOR));
   }
}
class TogglePanel extends Panel {
   Button  toggleButton = new Button("Toggle Component");
   Button  scrollButton = new Button("Scroll To ...");
   ScrollDialog         dialog;
   ScrollPane           scroller;
   ImageButtonTestPanel ibPanel;
   ImageStore           imageStore;

   public TogglePanel(ScrollPane           scrollpane,
                 ImageStore           store,
                 ImageButtonTestPanel panel) {
      this.imageStore = store;
      this.ibPanel    = panel;
      this.scroller   = scrollpane;

      add(toggleButton);
      add(scrollButton);

      scrollButton.addActionListener(new ActionListener() {
```

```
    public void actionPerformed(ActionEvent event) {
        Point loc = TogglePanel.this.getLocationOnScreen();

        if(dialog == null) {
            dialog = new ScrollDialog(scroller);
        }
        dialog.setLocation(loc.x, loc.y);
        dialog.show();
    }
});
toggleButton.addActionListener(new ActionListener() {
    public void actionPerformed(ActionEvent event) {
        if(scroller.getComponent(0) == imageStore)
            scroller.add(ibPanel);
        else
            scroller.add(imageStore);

        scroller.getParent().validate();
    }
});
  }
}
```

Scrolling Images

So far we've seen how to scroll a component, but what if you need to scroll an image? Images are not components, and therefore an image cannot be added to a scrollpane. The answer, of course, is to stick the image in a container and then add the container to the scrollpane, which is just what our next applet, shown in Figure 10-4 does.

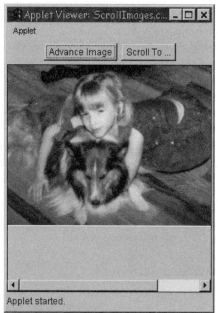

Figure 10-4 `ScrollImage` Applet
A scrollpane that cycles through an array of pictures. The
Advance Image button advances the image to the next one in the
array.

The first order of business, therefore, is to implement a container that contains an image[7].

```
class ImageCanvas extends Canvas {
  private Image image;

  public ImageCanvas(Image image) {
    MediaTracker mt = new MediaTracker(this);

    mt.addImage(image, 0);
    try              { mt.waitForID(0);      }
    catch(Exception e) { e.printStackTrace(); }

    this.image = image;
  }
  public void paint(Graphics g) {
    g.drawImage(image, 0, 0, this);
  }
  public void update(Graphics g) {
    paint(g);
  }
  public Dimension getPreferredSize() {
    return new Dimension(image.getWidth(this),
                         image.getHeight(this));
  }
}
```

The `ImageCanvas` constructor waits for the image it was passed to load; the image is drawn in the `ImageCanvas.paint()` method. Notice that we've also overridden `update()` to invoke `paint()` directly; otherwise, the canvas will be cleared each time `update()` is called. Also, we've overridden `getPreferredSize()` to return the width and height of the image.

The applet itself creates a scrollpane and loads up an array of images, in addition to creating a control panel that will contain the advance image and scroll buttons. The control panel is added to the applet as the north component, and the scrollpane is added as the center component.

```
public class ScrollImages extends Applet {
  private ScrollPane  scroller = new ScrollPane();
  private Image[]     images   = new Image[3];

  public void init() {
    loadImages(getCodeBase());
```

7.   The GJT provides a similar, more feature-filled `ImageCanvas` component.

```
scroller = new ScrollPane();
scroller.add(new ImageCanvas(images[0]));

setLayout(new BorderLayout());
add(new ControlPanel(scroller, images), "North");
add(scroller, "Center");
}
private void loadImages(URL base) {
    images[0] = getImage(base, "gifs/ashleyAndRoy.gif");
    images[1] = getImage(base, "gifs/ashleyAndSabre.gif");
    images[2] = getImage(base, "gifs/anjinAndMariko.gif");
}
}
```

As with our previous applet, the only point of interest left to discuss is the advancing of the images, which is done by the Advance Image button in the control panel.

```
advanceButton.addActionListener(new ActionListener() {
  public void actionPerformed(ActionEvent event) {
    Container container = scroller.getParent();

    container.setCursor(Cursor.getPredefinedCursor(
                        Cursor.WAIT_CURSOR));

    curImage = (curImage == images.length - 1) ? 0 : curImage + 1;

    scroller.add(new ImageCanvas(images[curImage]));

    container.validate();

    container.setCursor(Cursor.getPredefinedCursor(
                        Cursor.DEFAULT_CURSOR));
  }
});
```

Since the image may take a perceptible amount of time to load, we set the scrollpane container's cursor to the wait cursor before creating a new instance of image canvas, and then reset to the default cursor after we're done creating and adding the new image canvas to the scrollpane. Note that as before, we invoke `validate()` on the scrollpane's container to force the scrollpane to be laid out.

The entire applet is listed in Figure 10-4.

Example 10-5 ScrollImages Applet

```java
import java.applet.Applet;
import java.net.URL;
import java.awt.*;
import java.awt.event.*;

public class ScrollImages extends Applet {
  private ScrollPane  scroller = new ScrollPane();
  private Image[]     images = new Image[3];

  public void init() {
     loadImages(getCodeBase());

     scroller = new ScrollPane();
     scroller.add(new ImageCanvas(images[0]));

     setLayout(new BorderLayout());
     add(new ControlPanel(scroller, images), "North");
     add(scroller, "Center");
  }
  private void loadImages(URL base) {
     images[0] = getImage(base, "gifs/ashleyAndRoy.gif");
     images[1] = getImage(base, "gifs/ashleyAndSabre.gif");
     images[2] = getImage(base, "gifs/anjinAndMariko.gif");
  }
}
class ControlPanel extends Panel {
  ScrollPane   scroller;
  ScrollDialog dialog;
  Button       advanceButton = new Button("Advance Image");
  Button       scrollButton  = new Button("Scroll To ...");
  Image[]      images;
  int          curImage = 0;

  public ControlPanel(ScrollPane scrollpane, Image[] pics) {
     scroller = scrollpane;
     images   = pics;

     advanceButton.addActionListener(new ActionListener() {
        public void actionPerformed(ActionEvent event) {
           Container container = scroller.getParent();

           container.setCursor(Cursor.getPredefinedCursor(
                     Cursor.WAIT_CURSOR));

           curImage = (curImage == images.length - 1) ?
                  0 : curImage + 1;
```

```
            scroller.add(new ImageCanvas(images[curImage]));
            container.validate();

            container.setCursor(Cursor.getPredefinedCursor(
                           Cursor.DEFAULT_CURSOR));
        }
    });
    scrollButton.addActionListener(new ActionListener() {
        public void actionPerformed(ActionEvent event) {
            Point loc = ControlPanel.this.getLocationOnScreen();

            if(dialog == null) {
                dialog = new ScrollDialog(scroller);
            }
            dialog.setLocation(loc.x, loc.y);
            dialog.show();
        }
    });
    add(advanceButton);
    add(scrollButton);
  }
}
class ImageCanvas extends Canvas {
  private Image image;

  public ImageCanvas(Image image) {
    MediaTracker mt = new MediaTracker(this);
    mt.addImage(image, 0);

    try { mt.waitForID(0); }
    catch(Exception e) { e.printStackTrace(); }

    this.image = image;
  }
  public void paint(Graphics g) {
    g.drawImage(image, 0, 0, this);
  }
  public void update(Graphics g) {
    paint(g);
  }
  public Dimension getPreferredSize() {
    return new Dimension(image.getWidth(this),
                         image.getHeight(this));
  }
}
```

Programmatic Scrolling

Scrollpanes also support programmatic scrolling by providing an overloaded `setScrollPosition()` method; one version of the method takes two integer values, and the other takes a point. In order for the `setScrollPosition()` methods to work, the scrollpane must contain a component and the point specified must be valid. A valid point lies within the following boundary:

- X: 0
- Y: 0
- Width: Width of component - width of viewport
- Height: Height of component - height of viewport

The size of the component, of course, can be obtained by invoking `Component.getSize()`, and the size of the viewport can be obtained by invoking `ScrollPane.getViewportSize()`. The size of the viewport is the size of the scrollpane minus the scrollpane's insets. The insets account for the width or height of the vertical or horizontal scrollbars, respectively, and any borders drawn by the scrollpane's peer.

The applets discussed previously for scrolling components and images both contain a provision for programmatic scrolling. Each applet contains a Scroll To button that brings up a dialog for setting the x and y values to scroll to. The applet and dialog are shown in Figure 10-5.

The Scroll To buttons have an action listener that shows the dialog—the dialog is created if necessary, and its position is set to the upper left-hand corner of the panel containing the Scroll To button. The code below is from the `ScrollImages` applet:

```
scrollButton.addActionListener(new ActionListener() {
    public void actionPerformed(ActionEvent event) {
        Point loc = ControlPanel.this.getLocationOnScreen();
        if(dialog == null) {
            dialog = new ScrollDialog(scroller);
        }
        dialog.setLocation(loc.x, loc.y);
        dialog.setVisible(true);
    }
});
```

`Component.getLocationOnScreen()` is used to get the position of the control panel, which is then used to set the dialog's location. Notice that the dialog is passed the scrollpane when it is constructed.

Figure 10-5 Programmatically Scrolling a `ScrollPane`
A dialog allows the scrollpane in the applet to be scrolled
programmatically.

The dialog contains two buttons—a Scroll button and a Done button. The action
listener for the scroll button invokes the dialog's `scroll()` method, which
extracts the values from the textfields and invokes `setScrollPosition()` on
the scrollpane passed to the dialog's constructor.

```
scrollButton.addActionListener(new ActionListener() {
   public void actionPerformed(ActionEvent event) {
      scroll ();
   }
});
...
void scroll() {
  scroller.setScrollPosition(Integer.parseInt(xField.getText()),
                       Integer.parseInt(yField.getText()));
}
```

The Done button's action listener checks to see if the current scroll position of the
scrollpane is different from the values in the textfields, and if so, it also invokes
`scroll()` before disposing of the dialog[8].

```
doneButton.addActionListener(new ActionListener() {
    public void actionPerformed(ActionEvent event) {
        Point pos = scroller.getScrollPosition();
        int   x   = Integer.parseInt(xField.getText());
        int   y   = Integer.parseInt(yField.getText());

        if(pos.x != x || pos.y != y)
            scroll ();

        dispose();
    }
});
```

Finally, we've also added an instance of `FieldListener`, a named inner class of `ScrollDialog`, to the two textfields so that an `enter` typed into the textfield will also invoke the `scroll()` method.

```
  ...
  xField.addActionListener(listener);
  yField.addActionListener(listener);
  ...
class FieldListener implements ActionListener {
  public void actionPerformed(ActionEvent event) {
     scroll();
  }
}
```

We should point out that our simple example performs no error checking, so, for instance, typing a value into the `xField` textfield and subsequently typing `enter` without typing a value into the `yField` textfield will result in an exception being thrown.

`ScrollPane` is a welcome addition to the AWT, and is really an essential component for an industrial-strength user interface toolkit. The code for the `ScrollDialog` class is listed in Example 10-6.

Example 10-6 `ScrollDialog` Class

```
import java.awt.*;
import java.awt.event.*;

public class ScrollDialog extends Dialog {
  private ScrollPane scroller;
  private Panel  buttonPanel  = new Panel();
```

8.   See "Window.dispose() Disposes of the Window's Resources, Not the AWT Component" on page 283.

```java
private Panel  controlPanel = new Panel();
private Button doneButton   = new Button("Done");
private Button scrollButton = new Button("Scroll");

private Label xLabel = new Label("X:"),
             yLabel = new Label("Y:");

private TextField xField = new TextField(3),
                  yField = new TextField(3);

public ScrollDialog(ScrollPane scrollpane) {
    super(getFrame(scrollpane), "Scroll To");
    FieldListener listener = new FieldListener();
    this.scroller = scrollpane;

    GridBagLayout       gbl = new GridBagLayout();
    GridBagConstraints gbc = new GridBagConstraints();

    controlPanel.setLayout(gbl);

    gbl.setConstraints(xLabel, gbc);
    controlPanel.add(xLabel);

    gbc.gridwidth = GridBagConstraints.REMAINDER;
    gbl.setConstraints(xField, gbc);
    controlPanel.add(xField);

    gbc.gridwidth = 1;
    gbl.setConstraints(yLabel, gbc);
    controlPanel.add(yLabel);

    gbc.gridwidth = GridBagConstraints.REMAINDER;
    gbl.setConstraints(yField, gbc);
    controlPanel.add(yField);

    buttonPanel.add(doneButton);
    buttonPanel.add(scrollButton);

    setLayout(new BorderLayout());
    add(controlPanel, "Center");
    add(buttonPanel, "South");

    xField.addActionListener(listener);
    yField.addActionListener(listener);

    scrollButton.addActionListener(new ActionListener() {
        public void actionPerformed(ActionEvent event) {
            scroll ();
```

```
            }
        });
        doneButton.addActionListener(new ActionListener() {
            public void actionPerformed(ActionEvent event) {
                Point pos = scroller.getScrollPosition();
                int   x   = Integer.parseInt(xField.getText());
                int   y   = Integer.parseInt(yField.getText());

                if(pos.x != x || pos.y != y)
                    scroll ();

                dispose();
            }
        });
    }
    class FieldListener implements ActionListener {
        public void actionPerformed(ActionEvent event) {
            scroll();
        }
    }
    public void show() {
        pack();
        xField.requestFocus();
        super.show();
    }
    void scroll() {
        scroller.setScrollPosition(
            Integer.parseInt(xField.getText()),
            Integer.parseInt(yField.getText()));
    }
    static Frame getFrame(Component c) {
        Frame       frame = null;

        while((c = c.getParent()) != null) {
            if(c instanceof Frame)
                frame = (Frame)c;
        }
        return frame;
    }
}
```

Summary

The 1.1 version of the AWT introduces the `ScrollPane` class, which makes scrolling a component a snap. Additionally, the AWT also provides a scrollbar class, in the event that you wish to take scrolling into your own hands.

In this chapter we've discussed scrollbars and scrollpanes at length and provided applets that scroll both components and images.

Although a scrollpane is sufficient for scrolling components perhaps 90 percent of the time, there are times when scrolling a single container is not convenient (or even possible, depending upon the size of the container). As a result, the Graphic Java Toolkit provides a scrolling framework that is written entirely in Java, as opposed to a scrollpane, which delegates to a native peer. "Scrollers" on page 781 discusses the GJT scrolling framework in detail.

CHAPTER 11

Windows, Frames, and Dialogs

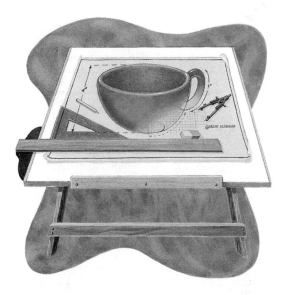

The AWT provides three basic components that display a window on screen: `Window`, `Frame`, and `Dialog`[1]. While all three components are windows, the differences between the three are not always readily apparent, and therefore it can sometimes be difficult to decide which component to use in a given situation. As a result, we have summarized the properties of the three components in Table 11-1.

Table 11-1 Window, Frame and Dialog Properties[1,2]

Property	Window	Frame	Dialog
Modal	No	No	No/CSG
Resizable	No	Yes/SG	Yes/SG
TitleBar	No	Yes	Yes
Border	No	Yes	Yes
Title	No	Yes/CSG	Yes/CSG
Menubar	No	Yes/SG	No
Focus Manager	Yes	Yes	Yes

1. There's also `FileDialog`, which we will discuss later on.

Table 11-1 Window, Frame and Dialog Properties (Continued)[1],[2]

Property	Window	Frame	Dialog
Warning String	Yes/G	Yes/G	Yes/G
Icon Image[3]	No	Yes/SG	No
Anchored To A Frame	Yes	No	Yes

1. Yes/No refers to default status of the property.
2. C = settable at construction time, S = setter method available,
   G = getter method available (either get...() or is...()).
3. Not all platforms support iconizing windows.

java.awt.Window is the most basic component of the three and, in fact, is the superclass of both Frame and Dialog. Windows have no border, titlebar or menubar and cannot be resized. Windows are best suited for displaying something in a borderless rectangular region that needs to float on top of other components, such as a splash screen for displaying product information, or bubble help for a component, both of which we will take the time to explore shortly.

java.awt.Frame is an extension of Window that comes with a border and a titlebar and is resizable. Additionally, you can attach a menubar to a frame, as we have discussed at length in "Menus" on page 297. Frames are the component of choice when an application window is required that needs to be iconized, and/or fitted with a menubar.

java.awt.Dialog is also an extension of Window that, like a frame, comes with a border and titlebar and is resizable. Unlike a frame, a dialog cannot support a menubar, and dialogs can be modal, whereas frames and windows cannot. Dialogs are the window of choice when a temporary window is required to capture user input. The AWT also provides a lone extension of java.awt.Dialog—FileDialog, for selecting a filename to load or save.

Another thing to note is that windows and dialogs must be anchored to a frame, meaning that a frame must be passed to the Window and Dialog constructors. While this may seem somewhat limiting, it should be noted that the frame does not have to be visible, an important loophole that we'll take advantage of when discussing splash screens, for instance.

java.awt.Window

java.awt.Window is the superclass for both Frame and Dialog, and provides a good deal of functionality for both of its extensions. Table 11-2 lists the public methods provided by java.awt.Window (we've omitted some overridden Component methods, such as addNotify()).

Table 11-2 java.awt.Window Public Methods

Method	Description
void pack()	Sets the size of the window to the minimum size that will display all contained components.
void show()	Makes the window visible. If the window is already visible, it is brought to the front of all other windows.
void dispose()	Hides the window and disposes of the platform-dependent resources used by the window.
void toFront()	Places the window in front of all other windows.
void toBack()	Places the window behind all other windows.
String getWarningString()	Returns the warning string.
void addWindowListener(WindowListener)	Adds a WindowListener to the window.
void removeWindowListener(WindowListener)	Removes a WindowListener from the window.
Component getFocusOwner()	Returns the component that currently has keyboard focus.

As you can see from Table 11-2, windows fire window events by virtue of the fact that window listeners can be added and removed to and from a window. See Table 5-2 on page 99 for a list of the methods defined by the WindowListener interface, and Table 5-3 on page 100 for a list of the methods defined by the WindowEvent class.

Windows can also provide a reference to the component they contain that currently has keyboard focus. Each Window keeps a FocusMgr around that tracks the focus among the window's components. Window.getFocusOwner() asks the focus manager for a reference to the currently selected component and then passes it back. See "Standard AWT Components and Keyboard Traversal" on page 536 for more information on keyboard traversal.

Splash Screen

In addition to providing basic windowing functionality for frames and dialogs, the `java.awt.Window` class is useful in its own right. We'll start off with a Java application that displays a splash screen—a window that typically displays product information while an application loads. Our splash screen will display an image for ten seconds and then exit. The splash screen is shown in Figure 11-1.

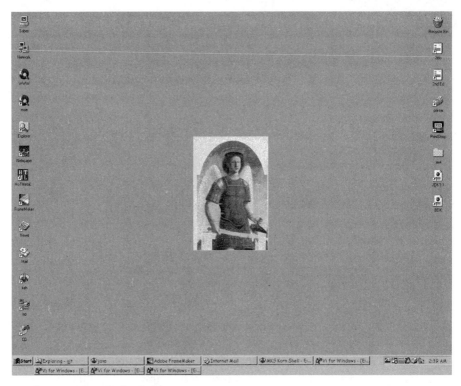

Figure 11-1 Splash Screen
A Java application displays a splash screen centered on the desktop when it starts up. The splash screen is implemented with a `java.awt.Window`.

The application creates a window that contains an image canvas that in turn displays the image. After the window and the image canvas are created, the location of the splash screen is calculated, using `Toolkit.getScreenSize()`, which returns the size in pixels of the desktop. Subsequently the window is shown, and placed in front of all other windows.

```java
public class SplashTest extends Frame {
  Toolkit toolkit = Toolkit.getDefaultToolkit();
  Window  window;
  Image   image;

  static public void main(String[] args) {
     Frame frame = new SplashTest();
  }
  public SplashTest() {
     ImageCanvas canvas;
     window  = new Window(this);
     image   = toolkit.getImage("gifs/saint.gif");
     canvas  = new ImageCanvas(image);

     window.add(canvas, "Center");

     Dimension scrnSize  = toolkit.getScreenSize();
     int       imgWidth  = image.getWidth(this),
               imgHeight = image.getHeight(this);

     window.setLocation(scrnSize.width/2  - (imgWidth/2),
                        scrnSize.height/2 - (imgHeight/2));

     window.setSize(imgWidth,imgHeight);
     window.show();
     window.toFront();

     try { Thread.currentThread().sleep(10000); }
     catch(Exception e) { e.printStackTrace(); }

     window.dispose();
     System.exit(0);
  }
}
```

There are few points to note about the `SplashTest` class. First, note that we've explicitly resized the window instead of invoking `pack()` because `pack()` was not up to the task under Solaris. `Window.pack()` resizes (and lays out) the window so that it is just big enough to hold all of the components it contains. Under Windows 95, `pack()` worked just fine.

Second, we have invoked `toFront()` immediately after the call to `show()`. While you might expect `show()` to bring the window being shown to the front, that is not necessarily the case on all platforms, so if you want the window to come to the front when it is shown, you should call `toFront()` after invoking `show()`. Note that `show()` is guaranteed to bring the window to the front if the window is already visible, but the window will not necessarily be brought to the front if it is not already visible.

Third, before we exit the application, we invoke `Window.dispose()`, which hides the window and frees the resources associated with the *native* window.

The entire application is listed in Example 11-1.

AWT TIP...

Invoke toFront() After show() for Windows That Are Not Visible

Window.show() is guaranteed to bring the window being shown to the front only if the window is currently visible. If the window is not visible, show() makes no such guarantee. Therefore, to ensure that a window being shown will wind up in front of all other windows, invoke toFront() after calling show().

Example 11-1 SplashTest Application

```java
import java.awt.*;
import java.awt.event.*;

public class SplashTest extends Frame {
  Toolkit toolkit = Toolkit.getDefaultToolkit();
  Window  window;
  Image   image;

  static public void main(String[] args) {
    Frame frame = new SplashTest();
  }
  public SplashTest() {
    ImageCanvas canvas;

    window  = new Window(this);
    image   = toolkit.getImage("gifs/saint.gif");
    canvas  = new ImageCanvas(image);

    window.add(canvas, "Center");

    Dimension scrnSize  = toolkit.getScreenSize();
    int       imgWidth  = image.getWidth(this),
              imgHeight = image.getHeight(this);
```

```java
        window.setLocation(scrnSize.width/2  - (imgWidth/2),
                            scrnSize.height/2 - (imgHeight/2));

        window.setSize(imgWidth,imgHeight);
        window.show();
        window.toFront();

        try { Thread.currentThread().sleep(10000); }
        catch(Exception e) { e.printStackTrace(); }
        window.dispose();
        System.exit(0);
    }
}
class ImageCanvas extends Canvas {
    private Image image;

    public ImageCanvas(Image image) {
        MediaTracker mt = new MediaTracker(this);
        mt.addImage(image, 0);

        try                { mt.waitForID(0);        }
        catch(Exception e) { e.printStackTrace(); }

        this.image = image;
    }
    public void paint(Graphics g) {
        g.drawImage(image, 0, 0, this);
    }
    public void update(Graphics g) {
        paint(g);
    }
    public Dimension preferredSize() {
        return new Dimension(image.getWidth(this),
                             image.getHeight(this));
    }
}
```

Bubble Help

One popular windowing system feature not supported by the 1.1 version of the AWT is bubble help (aka tool tips). Bubble help consists of a small textual window that is typically displayed when the cursor rests over a component, such as an image button in a toolbar. Although the AWT does not explicitly support bubble help, it is nonetheless quite simple to implement, graphically speaking[2].

---

2.   See "ImageButtons and Bubble Help" on page 676 for more on bubble help.

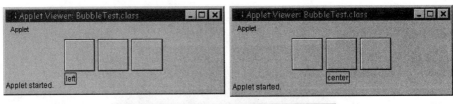

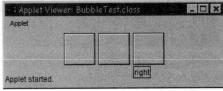

Figure 11-2 BubbleTest Applet
Three panels are equipped with a bubble—a popup window that
displays a string.

Figure 11-2 shows an applet that displays three makeshift canvases whose
paint() method paints a 3D border. Each panel is equipped with a Bubble—an
extension of Window that paints a rectangle with an enclosed string.

Example 11-2 Bubble Class

```java
import java.awt.*;
import java.awt.event.*;

public class Bubble extends Window {
  private String text;

  public Bubble(Component comp, String text) {
     super(getFrame(comp));
     this.text = text;
     setForeground(SystemColor.textText);
  }
  public Dimension getPreferredSize() {
     Graphics    g = getGraphics();
     FontMetrics fm = g.getFontMetrics();

     return new Dimension(fm.stringWidth(text)+4,
                   fm.getHeight()+4);
  }
  public void paint(Graphics g) {
     Dimension   size = getSize();
     FontMetrics fm   = g.getFontMetrics();
```

```
      g.drawRect(0,0,size.width-1,size.height-1);
      g.drawString(text,2,fm.getAscent()+2);
   }
   public void show() {
      pack();
      super.show();
   }
   static Frame getFrame(Component c) {
      Frame frame = null;

      while((c = c.getParent()) != null)
         if(c instanceof Frame)
            frame = (Frame)c;

      return frame;
   }
}
```

`Bubble` has a lone constructor that takes a component (any component will do) and a string. The component is used to obtain a reference to a frame, which is then passed to the `Window` constructor. Additionally, the constructor sets its foreground color to `SystemColor.textText`, which simply represents text color—see "System Colors" on page 534. Bubble overrides `paint()` to paint a border around the window, and the string passed to the constructor centered in the window. `show()` is overridden to invoke `pack()` and then call `super.show()`, which is a common technique when extending java.awt.`Window`.

The `BubbleTest` applet shown in Figure 11-2 is listed in Example 11-3.

Example 11-3 `BubbleTest` Applet

```
import java.applet.Applet;
import java.awt.*;
import java.awt.event.*;

public class BubbleTest extends Applet {
   public void init() {
      BubblePanel left   = new BubblePanel("left");
      BubblePanel center = new BubblePanel("center");
      BubblePanel right  = new BubblePanel("right");

      add(left);
      add(center);
      add(right);
   }
}
```

```
class BubblePanel extends BorderedPanel {
  Bubble bubble;
  String bubbleText;

  public BubblePanel(String string) {
    bubbleText = string;

    addMouseListener(new MouseAdapter() {
      public void mouseEntered(MouseEvent event) {
        BubblePanel canvas  = BubblePanel.this;
        Point         scrnLoc = canvas.getLocationOnScreen();
        Dimension     size    = getSize();

        if(bubble == null)
          bubble = new Bubble(canvas, bubbleText);

        bubble.setLocation(scrnLoc.x,
                  scrnLoc.y + size.height + 2);
        bubble.show();
      }
      public void mouseExited(MouseEvent event) {
        if(bubble != null && bubble.isShowing())
          bubble.dispose();
      }
    });
  }
  public Dimension getPreferredSize() {
    return new Dimension(50,50);
  }
}
```

BubblePanel is an extension of BorderedPanel (see [3] that has a bubble. When the mouse enters the bubble panel, the bubble associated with the bubble panel is constructed if it has not already been created, and after its location is set, is shown. When the mouse exits the bubble canvas, the bubble is disposed of.

Notice that a bubble panel may potentially call dispose() on its bubble many times, whereas the bubble itself is only created once. It is important to realize that dispose() does not dispose of the bubble object, but merely releases the system resources associated with the window that the bubble represents. Therefore, we can dispose of and show a bubble repeatedly without having to construct a new bubble instance after every call to dispose(). Another important point to

3. See "BorderedPanel Class" on page 244.

remember is that dispose() invokes hide() on the window, so not only does it release the system resources associated with the window, but it also hides the window.

AWT TIP ...

Window.dispose() Disposes of the Window's Resources, Not the AWT Component

Window.dispose() disposes of the native resources associated with a window. It does not dispose of the AWT component representing the window. As a result, a java.awt.Window object may be disposed of repeatedly without the AWT component requiring reconstruction. Additionally, Window.dispose() also hides the window, so when you need to hide a window, a single call to dispose() will do the job, and you can turn around and show() the window without having to reconstruct the AWT window component.

---

java.awt.Frame

If the Window class represents the base model of AWT window components, Frame is the fully loaded model. Features included with the Frame class are a border, titlebar, and an optional menubar. Frames can also be resized and fitted with an icon image, which will be displayed when the frame is iconified[4]. The downside of frames is that they are tagged with a string warning potential users that your frame may be *untrustworthy*. Browsers are in charge of the warning string enforcement policy[5]—trusted applets that show a frame should not have the warning string displayed. And before you ask, the AWT provides no mechanism for modifying or removing the warning string, although a getWarningString() is provided by the Frame class in case the string is hard to read on screen.

One benefit of the Frame class is that you don't have to dig around for a frame to pass to the constructor, as you do when constructing a Window or a Dialog. Frames are standalone windows, whereas windows and dialogs must be anchored by a frame supplied at construction time.

---

4. We found setting the icon image to be problematic with JDK1.1 final.
5. Browsers typically have their own security manager and also decide the contents of the warning string.

"Menus" on page 297 has many examples of frames and menubars, so we won't bother to explore creating menubars and menus in this chapter. In addition, since frames are straightforward to use, we'll present a simple applet that creates and displays a frame with a lone button. The lone button is used to dispose of the frame. You can see our applet and its resultant frame in Figure 11-3.

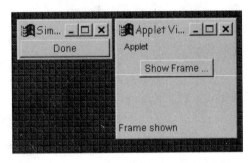

Figure 11-3 SimpleFrameTest Applet
An applet creates and shows a frame. The frame (on the left) has a full complement of system buttons in its titlebar: iconify, maximize, and close buttons, along with an image for when it is iconified. Contrast this to the dialog's titlebar in the similar-looking applet in Figure 11-4 on page 287.

The applet is fairly short-winded and easy to digest, so we'll list the entire applet in Example 11-4, and then have a short discussion.

Example 11-4 SimpleFrameTest Applet

```
import java.applet.Applet;
import java.awt.*;
import java.awt.event.*;

public class SimpleFrameTest extends Applet {
  Button launchButton = new Button("Show Frame ...");
  Frame  frame        = new Frame ("Simple Frame");

  public void init() {
    add(launchButton);

    launchButton.addActionListener(new ActionListener() {
        public void actionPerformed(ActionEvent event) {
          Frame myFrame = getFrame(SimpleFrameTest.this);
          Point scrnLoc = myFrame.getLocationOnScreen();
          Dimension frameSize = frame.getSize();
```

```
                frame.setLocation(scrnLoc.x - frameSize.width - 2,
                            scrnLoc.y);
                showStatus(null);
                frame.show();
                showStatus("Frame shown");
            }
        });
    }
    public void start() {
        Button doneButton = new Button("Done");

        frame.add (doneButton);
        frame.pack();

        doneButton.addActionListener(new ActionListener() {
            public void actionPerformed(ActionEvent event) {
                frame.dispose();
                showStatus(null);
            }
        });
        frame.addWindowListener(new WindowAdapter() {
            public void windowClosing(WindowEvent event) {
                System.out.println("Window Closing");
                frame.dispose();
            }
            public void windowClosed(WindowEvent event) {
                showStatus("Window Closed");
            }
        });
    }
    static Frame getFrame(Component c) {
        Frame frame = null;
        while((c = c.getParent()) != null) {
            if(c instanceof Frame)
                frame = (Frame)c;
        }
        return frame;
    }
}
```

The applet's `init()` method creates the complex user interface employed by the applet and then adds an action listener to the launch button. When activated, the location of the applet's frame is obtained in order to locate the frame created by the applet.

The `start()` method adds a button to the frame and then packs the frame. When the Done button is activated, the frame is disposed of. Our frame also listens for window closing and window closed events. `WindowListener.windowClosing()` is called when the window is closed through a system mechanism—using the close box or the window's system menu to close the window. If you don't call `dispose()` in the `windowClosing()` method of one of the frame's window listeners[6], then the window will not be closed.

Notice that we call the applet's `showStatus()` method immediately after showing the frame. You can see the status line doing its thing in Figure 11-3 on page 284. The reason for updating the status line is to convince you that frames are not modal—they do not block thread execution while the frame is showing, nor do they block input to other windows. In other words, when the frame is shown, the status line of the applet is immediately updated. We'll experiment with modality in our next section on dialogs, but modality is one of the few options not available with the `Frame` class.

AWT TIP ...

Frames Don't Close By Default

Frames, by default, will not close when their close box is activated or *Quit* is selected from the system menu (or whatever equivalent mechanisms the operating system provides). If you want the user to be able to close the frame through system means, you must listen for the window closing event to be fired by the frame. windowClosing() should invoke dispose() on the frame in order to go through with the closing of the window. Once the window is closed, a window closed event is generated and sent to all of the window's window listeners.

---

java.awt.Dialog

From an evolutionary perspective, dialogs lie between windows and frames. Dialogs share many of the amenities found in frames, but they lack the frame's status as being a fully operational application window. Dialogs cannot support menubars or be iconified, two essentials of application window functionality.

However, dialogs do have something that windows and frames do not—modality. Dialogs can be either modal or non-modal, and before we go any further, let's define what that means. Being modal means blocking two things:

---

6.   It is highly advisable to call `dispose()` for a frame only once between calls to `show()`. A frame can have more than one window listener. Beware.

- thread execution

- input to other windows

When a modal dialog is shown, input is blocked to all other windows in the dialog's ancestry[7]. Also, execution of the thread that showed the dialog is blocked until the dialog is closed. Notice from Table 11-1 on page 273 that dialogs are not modal by default, and that modality can be set at construction time or at your leisure. The `Dialog` class also provides an accessor that will tell you the dialog's current modality setting in case you lose track.

Another noteworthy item concerning dialogs is that the AWT, compared to most user interface toolkits, is currently quite thin in the dialog department, with only one offering as far as `Dialog` extensions go: the `FileDialog`. In "Dialogs" on page 715, we examine extending the `Dialog` class to provide a number of useful `Dialog` extensions, such as message, question, yes/no and progress dialogs. If you want to explore dialogs in more detail, *page 715* is the place to go. For now, we'll look at an applet, `SimpleDialogTest`, which is similar to our `SimpleFrameTest`.

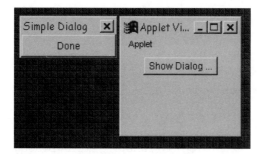

Figure 11-4 `SimpleDialogTest` Applet
An applet creates and shows a dialog. Notice the stripped-down titlebar for the dialog—no iconified image, iconify, or maximize buttons. Contrast the dialog's titlebar with that of the frame displayed in Figure 11-3 on page 284.

7. You didn't think we were passing frames to dialog constructors for nothing, did you?

Example 11-5 SimpleDialogTest Applet

```java
import java.applet.Applet;
import java.awt.*;
import java.awt.event.*;

public class SimpleDialogTest extends Applet {
  Button launchButton = new Button("Show Dialog ...");
  Dialog dialog;
  Frame myFrame;

  public void init() {
     add(launchButton);

     launchButton.addActionListener(new ActionListener() {
        public void actionPerformed(ActionEvent event) {
           Point scrnLoc = myFrame.getLocationOnScreen();
           Dimension dialogSize = dialog.getSize();

           dialog.setLocation(scrnLoc.x - dialogSize.width - 2,
                              scrnLoc.y);
           showStatus(null);
           dialog.show();
           showStatus("Dialog shown");
        }
     });
  }
  public void start() {
     Button doneButton = new Button("Done");

     myFrame = getFrame(SimpleDialogTest.this);
     dialog  = new Dialog(myFrame, "Simple Dialog", true);

     dialog.add(doneButton);
     dialog.pack();
     dialog.setResizable(false);

     doneButton.addActionListener(new ActionListener() {
        public void actionPerformed(ActionEvent event) {
           dialog.dispose();
           showStatus(null);
        }
     });
     dialog.addWindowListener(new WindowAdapter() {
        public void windowClosing(WindowEvent event) {
           System.out.println("Window Closing");
           dialog.dispose();
        }
```

```
            public void windowClosed(WindowEvent event) {
                System.out.println("Window Closed");
            }
        });
    }
    static Frame getFrame(Component c) {
        Frame frame = null;
        while((c = c.getParent()) != null) {
            if(c instanceof Frame)
                frame = (Frame)c;
        }
          return frame;
    }
}
```

Like the "`SimpleFrameTest Applet`" on page 284, we have the paraphernalia associated with listening for action and window events, with the same results.

Notice that the applet's status bar does not show "Dialog Shown" until the dialog is closed. That's because our dialog is modal and, therefore, when it is shown, suspends execution of the thread that showed the dialog, so that the call below to `showStatus()` does not occur until the dialog is closed.

```
public void actionPerformed(ActionEvent event) {
    Point scrnLoc = myFrame.getLocationOnScreen();
    Dimension dialogSize = dialog.getSize();

    dialog.setLocation(scrnLoc.x - dialogSize.width - 2,
                       scrnLoc.y);
    showStatus(null);
    dialog.show();
    showStatus("Dialog shown");
}
```

The applet's `start()` method packs the dialog and sets its resizable property to `false`. Repeated attempts to size the dialog were consistently thwarted.

AWT TIP...

The AWT's Meaning of Modality

Modal dialogs block input to all other windows in the dialog's ancestry. Modal dialogs also block execution of the thread that was responsible for showing the dialog. As a result, a line of code immediately following a call to setVisible(true) will not be invoked until a modal dialog has been dismissed:

```
Dialog d = new Dialog(frame, true); // true signifies modal
...
d.setVisible(true);
// This line of code is not executed until dialog is dismissed.
```

java.awt.FileDialog

The AWT provides a peer-based file dialog that in reality is the native file dialog for whatever platform you are running on. The file dialog—no surprises here—provides a mechanism for selecting a filename. The file dialog also allows for entries in the dialog to be filtered by specifying a filename filter. You can see the file dialogs for Solaris and Windows 95 in Figure 11-5.

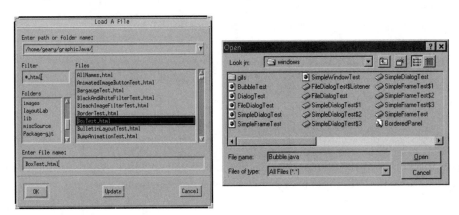

Figure 11-5 Solaris and Windows95 File Dialogs

It's a snap to put up a file dialog and decipher the filename selected, which is just what our applet shown in Figure 11-6 and listed in Example 11-6 does.

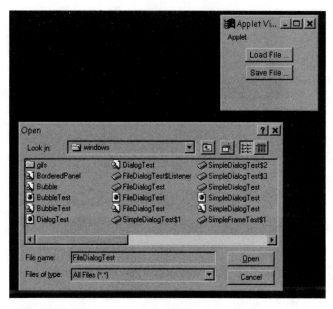

Figure 11-6 FileDialogTest Applet
The applet can open the file dialog in either load or save mode.
The file dialog displayed above is the loading version.

Example 11-6 FileDialogTest Applet

```
import java.applet.Applet;
import java.awt.*;
import java.awt.event.*;

public class FileDialogTest extends Applet {
  Button     loadButton = new Button("Load File ...");
  Button     saveButton = new Button("Save File ...");
  Listener   listener   = new Listener();
  FileDialog dialog;
  String     filename;

  public void init() {
    add(loadButton);
    add(saveButton);
    loadButton.addActionListener(listener);
    saveButton.addActionListener(listener);
  }
  class Listener implements ActionListener {
    public void actionPerformed(ActionEvent event) {
      Button button = ((Button)event.getSource());
      Frame myFrame = getFrame(button);
```

```
            showStatus(null);

            if(button == loadButton)
               dialog = new FileDialog(myFrame, "Load A File");
            else
               dialog = new FileDialog(myFrame, "Save A File",
                                          FileDialog.SAVE);
            dialog.show();

            if((filename = dialog.getFile()) != null) {
               showStatus(filename);
            }
            else {
               showStatus("FileDialog Cancelled");
            }
         }
      }
   static Frame getFrame(Component c) {
      Frame frame = null;
      while((c = c.getParent()) != null) {
         if(c instanceof Frame)
            frame = (Frame)c;
      }
      return frame;
   }
}
```

If the load button is activated, a file dialog is opened in its default mode, which is
`FileDialog.LOAD`. If the save button is activated, the file dialog is set to
`FileDialog.SAVE` mode. Whether you choose load or save, your motivation
doesn't change: you want to show the file dialog and subsequently obtain the
filename that was selected. Once you have the filename, it's up to you to do the
actual saving or loading—the file dialog doesn't save or load anything on its own.
You can see a file dialog in both LOAD and SAVE modes under Windows 95 in
Figure 11-7.

What it means to specify LOAD or SAVE mode is platform dependent—usually
it's a cosmetic change in the file dialog. The Windows 95 file dialog will confirm
file overwrites when in SAVE mode; the Solaris dialog allows selection of an
existing filename in SAVE mode, figuring that you'll handle the overwrite
dilemma yourself.

`FileDialog.getFile()` either returns a string representing the filename or
returns `null` if the dialog was canceled.

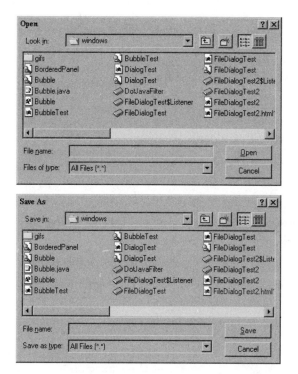

Figure 11-7 `FileDialog` in LOAD and SAVE Modes
The top picture shows a file dialog in LOAD mode, while the
bottom picture shows a file dialog in SAVE mode, both under
Windows95.

Let's take a look at one more applet that specifies a filename filter for the file
dialog. Although the applet listed in Example 11-7 correctly specifies a filename
filter of *.java, the filter did not work correctly under the 1.1 final version of the
AWT.

Example 11-7 `FileDialogTest2` Applet

```java
import java.applet.Applet;
import java.awt.*;
import java.awt.event.*;
import java.io.*;

class DotJavaFilter implements FilenameFilter {
  public boolean accept(File dir, String name) {
     return name.endsWith(".java");
  }
}
```

```java
public class FileDialogTest2 extends Applet {
    Button      loadButton = new Button("Load File ...");
    Button      saveButton = new Button("Save File ...");
    Listener    listener   = new Listener();
    FileDialog dialog;
    String      filename;

    public void init() {
        add(loadButton);
        add(saveButton);
        loadButton.addActionListener(listener);
        saveButton.addActionListener(listener);
    }
    class Listener implements ActionListener {
        public void actionPerformed(ActionEvent event) {
            Button button = ((Button)event.getSource());
            Frame myFrame = getFrame(button);

            showStatus(null);

            if(button == loadButton)
                dialog = new FileDialog(myFrame, "Load A File");
            else
                dialog = new FileDialog(myFrame, "Save A File",
                                        FileDialog.SAVE);
            dialog.setFilenameFilter(new DotJavaFilter());
            dialog.show();

            if((filename = dialog.getFile()) != null) {
                showStatus(filename);
            }
            else {
                showStatus("FileDialog Cancelled");
            }
        }
    }
    static Frame getFrame(Component c) {
        Frame frame = null;
        while((c = c.getParent()) != null) {
            if(c instanceof Frame)
                frame = (Frame)c;
        }
        return frame;
    }
}
```

Summary

The AWT provides three basic components that create a top-level window: `Window`, `Frame`, and `Dialog`.

Windows are the superclass of both frames and dialogs and are also the only component of the three that can be displayed without a border or titlebar. As a result, windows are used when a basic, borderless rectangular region is required, as is the case for either a splash screen or bubble help.

Frames are the component of choice when more than one application window is needed. Frames are the only AWT component that can be iconified or have a menubar attached—both of which are characteristics of a top-level application window.

Finally, dialogs are the only component that can be modal. Modal dialogs not only block input to other windows in their container ancestry but also block execution of the thread that makes the dialogs visible. The AWT provides a lone extension of the basic `java.awt.Dialog` class: `FileDialog`, for selecting a filename.

CHAPTER 12

Menus

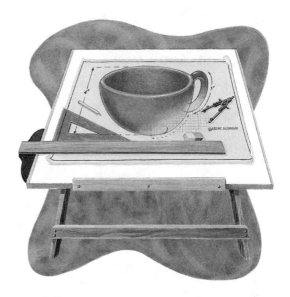

The original release of the AWT supported only one type of menu: ones that reside in a menubar. Furthermore, AWT menus were not components, so it was not possible to draw into a menu (or menuitem). As a result, menus could only contain textual information.

The 1.1 release of the AWT provides a `PopupMenu` class; however, menus are still not extensions of java.awt.Component[1], so it is still not possible to implement owner-drawn menus, which are a common feature under many windowing systems. The 1.1 release of the AWT also provides support for a basic menu feature that was lacking in the original AWT—menu shortcuts, which are discussed in "Menu Shortcuts" on page 546.

Note that, with the exception of the section covering popup menus, all of the examples in this chapter are applications and therefore must be run through the `java` interpreter directly instead of employing `appletviewer` or a browser to invoke the `java` interpreter for you. For instance, to run the `FileMenuTest` application, which we'll discuss shortly, you would execute the following command:

```
java FileMenuTest
```

---

1. This will be remedied in a future release of the AWT.

The Menu Classes

Figure 12-1 shows the relationships between the AWT's menu classes.

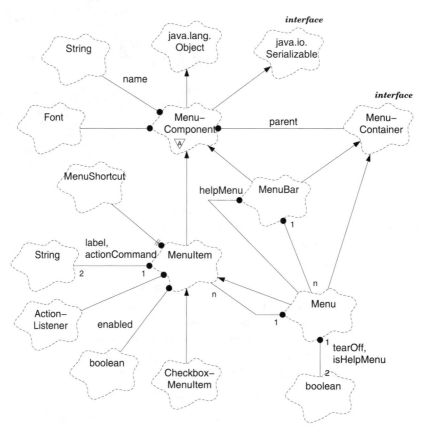

Figure 12-1 AWT Menu Classes Diagram

We will be concerned with four classes when dealing with menus: MenuBar, Menu, MenuItem, and PopupMenu. The first thing to note from the class diagram is that each of these classes extends MenuComponent; a MenuComponent is simply something that can be displayed in a menu. Second, notice that Menu and Menubar both implement MenuContainer, meaning they may both contain instances of MenuComponent. Finally, note that Menu extends MenuItem; this enables us to create cascading menus, as we shall soon discover.

It is worth repeating that none of the menu classes extends `java.awt.Component`. Although this may seem insignificant, consider that since menu items are not components, we may not paint or draw strings inside of a menu. This makes it impossible to render owner-drawn menus (a menu into which graphics may be drawn) in the current AWT.

A File Menu

Let's start off our discussion of menus residing in menubars with a simple example that creates the file menu in Figure 12-2.

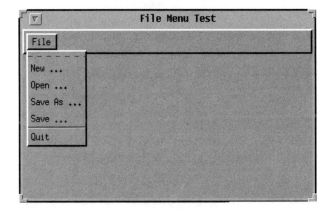

Figure 12-2 A File Menu

Most applications that provide a menubar have a file menu as the leftmost menu in their menubar, and most provide the menu items we have added to our example. Implementing such a menu is straightforward, as illustrated in Example 12-1.

Example 12-1 `FileMenuTest` **Class Source Code**

```
import java.awt.*;
import java.awt.event.*;

public class FileMenuTest extends Frame {
  private MenuBar mbar;

  public static void main(String args[]) {
      FileMenuTest test = new FileMenuTest("File Menu Test");
      test.setBounds(300,300,300,100);
      test.show();
  }
  public FileMenuTest(String s) {
```

```
        super(s);
        MenuBar mbar    = new MenuBar();
        Menu    fileMenu = new Menu("File", true);

        fileMenu.add("New ...");
        fileMenu.add("Open ...");
        fileMenu.add("Save As ...");
        fileMenu.add("Save ...");
        fileMenu.addSeparator();
        fileMenu.add("Quit");

        mbar.add(fileMenu);
        setMenuBar (mbar);

        addWindowListener(new WindowAdapter() {
            public void windowClosing(WindowEvent event) {
                dispose();
                System.exit(0);
            }
        });
    }
}
```

This version of the FileMenuTest class extends Frame and provides a main() method, signifying that we are developing an application, not an applet. (See *Applets and Applications* on page 13 for a discussion of developing applets versus applications.) The FileMenuTest constructor takes a string, which is immediately passed to the superclass' (Frame) constructor. The string passed to the Frame constructor will be used as the title of the window.

The FileMenuTest constructor creates a MenuBar and a Menu. The string passed to the Menu constructor is the menu's title and will be displayed in the menubar.

Adding menu items to a menu is accomplished by invoking the Menu.add() method and passing in a string that will be displayed in the menu item.

After creating the menubar and the menu, FileMenuTest adds the menu to the menubar and then calls Frame.setMenuBar() to set the frame's menubar.

The only event handling our application implements is detecting a window closing event, triggered when the window is closed via a system menu (or close box). See "java.awt.Frame" on page 283, for more information on handling window closing events.

Handling Menu Events

Menubars and menus take care of displaying themselves, but attaching behavior to menu items is something you must handle yourself. Example 12-2 expands `FileMenuTest` to print the label of the item selected and to quit the application when the "Quit" item is selected.

Since menu items fire action events when they are selected, we implement an extension of `ActionListener` that obtains a reference to the menu item that generated the even, and prints out the label associated with the menu item. If the menu item is the Quit menu item, we exit the application, being careful to dispose of the frame before exiting—see "java.awt.Frame" on page 283. In order for our `MenuItemListener` to do its thing, we add it as the action listener for every menu item created.

Example 12-2 Expanded `FileMenuTest` **Class Source Code**

```
import java.awt.*;
import java.awt.event.*;

public class FileMenuTest extends Frame {
  private MenuBar mbar;
  private MenuItem newItem, openItem,
                   saveAsItem, saveItem, quitItem;
  private MenuItemListener menuItemListener =
                           new MenuItemListener();

  public static void main(String args[]) {
      FileMenuTest test = new FileMenuTest("File Menu Test");
      test.setBounds(300,300,300,100);
      test.show();
  }
  public FileMenuTest(String s) {
    super(s);

    MenuBar mbar     = new MenuBar();
    Menu    fileMenu = new Menu("File", true);

    fileMenu.add(newItem = new MenuItem("New ..."));
    fileMenu.add(openItem = new MenuItem("Open ..."));
    fileMenu.add(saveAsItem = new MenuItem("Save As ..."));
    fileMenu.add(saveItem = new MenuItem("Save ..."));
    fileMenu.addSeparator();
    fileMenu.add(quitItem = new MenuItem("Quit"));
```

```
        mbar.add(fileMenu);
        setMenuBar (mbar);

        newItem.addActionListener(menuItemListener);
        openItem.addActionListener(menuItemListener);
        saveAsItem.addActionListener(menuItemListener);
        saveItem.addActionListener(menuItemListener);
        quitItem.addActionListener(menuItemListener);

        addWindowListener(new WindowAdapter() {
            public void windowClosing(WindowEvent event) {
                dispose();
                System.exit(0);
            }
        });
    }
    class MenuItemListener implements ActionListener {
        public void actionPerformed(ActionEvent event) {
            MenuItem item = (MenuItem)event.getSource();
            System.out.println(item.getLabel());

            if(item == quitItem) {
                dispose();
                System.exit(0);
            }
        }
    }
}
```

Since we need a reference to each menu item in order to add a listener to them, we invoke a different Menu constructor—one that takes a MenuItem.

Tear-off Menus

Tear-off menus are implemented under Motif and are menus that, as their name indicates, can be torn off and placed aside for quick access. Tear-off menus have a perforated line at the top of the menu. Once torn off, they are placed in their own window, as illustrated in Figure 12-3.

The Menu class provides a constructor that allows you to specify whether you want the menu being constructed to be a tear-off menu. We invoke this constructor in Example 12-2, passing true as the second argument. Doing so indicates that the menu should be of the tear-off variety.

Windows 95 does not support tear-off menus, so passing true as a second argument to the Menu constructor will have no effect under Windows 95.

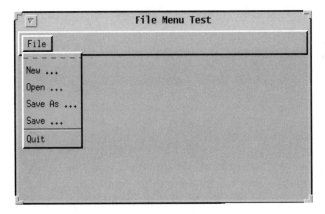

Figure 12-3 A Tear-off Menu
The left picture shows the perforated tear-off menu. The right picture shows the menu after being *torn off.*

A MenuBar Printer

In order to illustrate the relationships between menus, menubars, and menu items, we'll present a simple class in Example 12-3 that walks you through all the menus in a menubar and prints information about each item.

Example 12-3 `MenuBarPrinter` **Class Source Code**

```
import java.awt.Menu;
import java.awt.MenuItem;
import java.awt.MenuBar;

public class MenuBarPrinter {
  static public void print(MenuBar menubar) {
      int       numMenus = menubar.getMenuCount();
      Menu      nextMenu;
      MenuItem nextItem;

      System.out.println();
      System.out.println("MenuBar has "         +
                        menubar.getMenuCount() +
                        " menus");
      System.out.println();

      for(int i=0; i < numMenus; ++i) {
          nextMenu = menubar.getMenu(i);
          System.out.println(nextMenu);
```

```
        int numItems = nextMenu.getItemCount();

        for(int j=0; j < numItems; ++j) {
            nextItem = nextMenu.getItem(j);
            System.out.println(nextItem);
        }
        System.out.println();
      }
   }
}
```

The `MenuBarPrinter` class contains a lone static method, which is passed a `MenuBar` and prints information about each menu in the menubar. Notice that we use `MenuBar.countMenus()`, `MenuBar.getMenu()`, `Menu.countItems()`, and `Menu.getItem()` to traverse through all of the menu items contained in each menu in the menubar.

A FrameWithMenuBar Class

Applications containing a menubar typically do the following things:

1.   Create a menubar

2.   Add menus to the menubar

3.   Set the frame's menubar

In good object-oriented fashion, we will encapsulate these tasks in a base class illustrated in Example 12-4. You can extend this class whenever you need a frame with a menubar.

OO TIP

Encapsulate Common Functionality in Base Classes

Encapsulating common functionality in a base class is one of the tenets of object-oriented development; it increases reuse and reduces reimplementing similar functionality in more than one class. Often, such code is not identified until two or more classes have reimplemented the same functionality. In such cases, it is well worth your while to *refactor* the code in question and push the similar functionality up into a base class.

Example 12-4 FrameWithMenuBar Class Source Code

```java
import java.awt.*;
import java.awt.event.*;

public abstract class FrameWithMenuBar extends Frame {
  private MenuBar       mbar    = new MenuBar();
  private MenuBarPrinter printer;

  abstract protected void createMenus(MenuBar menuBar);

  public FrameWithMenuBar(String s) {
     super(s);

     createMenus(mbar);
     setMenuBar (mbar);

     addWindowListener(new WindowAdapter() {
        public void windowClosing(WindowEvent event) {
           quit();
        }
     });
  }
  protected void quit() {
     if(aboutToBeDestroyed())
        quitNoConfirm();
  }
  protected void quitNoConfirm() {
     System.exit(0);
  }
  public void printMenus() {
      if(printer == null)
         printer = new MenuBarPrinter();

      printer.print(mbar);
  }
  protected boolean aboutToBeDestroyed() {
     return true;
  }
}
```

Each `FrameWithMenuBar` comes complete with a `MenuBar` and `MenuBarPrinter` reference. `FrameWithMenuBar` leaves one abstract method for extensions to implement:

```
void createMenus(MenuBar)
```

Extensions simply create the menus they wish to attach to the menubar and then add them to the menubar passed in to `createMenus()`.

`FrameWithMenuBar` also takes care of the details of handling a window closing event. Before exiting the application, the `aboutToBeDestroyed()` method is invoked. Classes that extend `FrameWithMenuBar` may override `aboutToBeDestroyed()` if they have unfinished business to take care of before the application is exited. Returning `false` from `aboutToBeDestroyed()` will abort the closing of the window.

Note that `aboutToBeDestroyed()` is a protected method. We chose to make `aboutToBeDestroyed()` protected instead of public to ensure that no hooligan developers run around directly invoking `aboutToBeDestroyed()`. Limiting the access of `aboutToBeDestroyed()` to extensions of `FrameWithMenuBar` ensures that the method will only be invoked when the frame is actually about to be destroyed.[2]

Finally, each `FrameWithMenuBar` comes with a `printMenus()` method that prints information about all of the menus in the menubar. Notice that we use a technique known in object-oriented circles as *lazy instantiation* for creating the `MenuBarPrinter`. The `printMenus()` method checks to see if the `MenuBarPrinter` instance is `null`. If so, it creates the `MenuBarPrinter`. This technique ensures that the `MenuBarPrinter` only gets created the first time it is needed.

OO TIP

Employ Lazy Instantiation for Rarely Used Class Members

FrameWithMenuBar can print out the label for each menu in its menubar. While this capability may at times be beneficial, in all honesty it will probably be used sparingly. As a result, it is a good idea to employ lazy instantiation, where an object is not created until it is needed for the first time.

---

2. Actually, the `aboutToBeDestroyed()` method is accessible by extensions of `FrameWithMenuBar` *and* other classes in the same package.

FrameWithMenuBar In Action

To illustrate extending `FrameWithMenuBar`, we present a `FileEditMenuTest`
application in Example 12-5. This extension of `FrameWithMenuBar` attaches
both a file and an edit menu to its menubar.

Example 12-5 `FileEditMenuTest` **Class Source Code**

```
import java.awt.*;
import java.awt.event.*;

public class FileEditMenuTest extends FrameWithMenuBar {
  private MenuItem quitItem;

  public static void main(String args[]) {
    FileEditMenuTest test =
                    new FileEditMenuTest("FileEdit Menu Test");
    test.setBounds(300,300,300,100);
    test.show();
  }
  public FileEditMenuTest(String s) {
    super(s);
  }
  public void createMenus(MenuBar mbar) {
    mbar.add(createFileMenu());
    mbar.add(createEditMenu());
  }
  private Menu createFileMenu() {
    Menu fileMenu = new Menu("File");
    fileMenu.add("New ...");
    fileMenu.add("Open ...");
    fileMenu.add("Save As ...");
    fileMenu.add("Save ...");
    fileMenu.addSeparator();
    fileMenu.add(quitItem = new MenuItem("Quit"));

    quitItem.addActionListener(new ActionListener() {
        public void actionPerformed(ActionEvent event) {
          MenuItem item = (MenuItem)event.getSource();
          if(item == quitItem) {
            dispose();
            System.exit(0);
          }
        }
      }
```

```
        });
        return fileMenu;
    }
    private Menu createEditMenu() {
        Menu editMenu = new Menu("Edit");
        editMenu.add("Cut");
        editMenu.add("Copy");
        editMenu.add("Paste");
        return editMenu;
    }
}
```

We override the required `createMenus()` method in order to add a file menu and an edit menu to the menubar passed in. Note that `FrameWithMenuBar` takes care of creating the menubar and attaching it to the frame, leaving us to take care of business specific to `FileEditMenuTest`, namely, creation of the file and edit menus and adding them to the menubar.

In the remaining examples in this chapter, we will subclass `FrameWithMenuBar` when creating and using AWT menus.

Help Menus

The AWT provides support for a help menu. A help menu is created and added to a menubar just like any other menu. Help menus, however, need to be identified by invoking `MenuBar.setHelpMenu()`, which ensures that the help menu is the rightmost menu in the menubar, regardless of when it was added to the menubar.

Help menus under Motif are right-justified in the menubar itself, while help menus under Windows 95 are simply placed to the right of the other menus in the menubar, as illustrated in Figure 12-4.

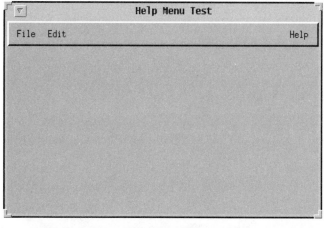

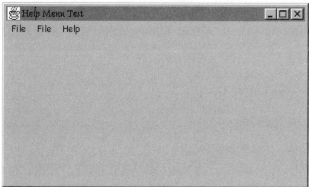

Figure 12-4 Motif and Windows 95 Help Menus
Motif help menus are right-justified in the menubar itself, as in
the top picture. Windows 95 help menus are placed to the right of
the other menus, as in the bottom picture.

Example 12-6 lists an implementation of a help menu.

Example 12-6 HelpMenuTest **Class Source Code**

```java
import java.awt.*;
import java.awt.event.*;
import java.util.Vector;

public class HelpTest extends FrameWithMenuBar {
  private MenuItem quitItem;

  public static void main(String args[]) {
    HelpTest frame = new HelpTest("Help Menu Test");
    frame.setBounds(300,300,300,100);
    frame.show();
  }
  public HelpTest(String s) {
    super(s);
  }
  public void createMenus(MenuBar mbar) {
    Menu helpMenu = createHelpMenu();

    mbar.add(createFileMenu());
    mbar.add(createEditMenu());
    mbar.add(helpMenu);

    mbar.setHelpMenu(helpMenu);
  }
  private Menu createFileMenu() {
    Menu fileMenu = new Menu("File");
    fileMenu.add(quitItem = new MenuItem("Quit"));

    quitItem.addActionListener(new ActionListener() {
        public void actionPerformed(ActionEvent event) {
            MenuItem item = (MenuItem)event.getSource();
            if(item == quitItem) {
                dispose();
                System.exit(0);
            }
        }
    });
      return fileMenu;
  }
  private Menu createEditMenu() {
    Menu editMenu = new Menu("Edit");

    editMenu.add("Cut");
    editMenu.add("Copy");
    editMenu.add("Paste");
```

```
      return editMenu;
   }
   private Menu createHelpMenu() {
      Menu helpMenu = new Menu("Help");

      helpMenu.add("Overview ...");
      helpMenu.add("Topics ...");
      helpMenu.add("About ...");

      return helpMenu;
   }
}
```

Once again, thanks to `FrameWithMenuBar`, we are only concerned with creating menus, adding them to the menubar, and reacting to menu events.

Checkbox Menu Items

The AWT provides a `CheckboxMenuItem` class. A `CheckboxMenuItem` is a menu item that toggles between checked and unchecked when activated. Figure 12-5 shows a `CheckboxMenuItem` at work.

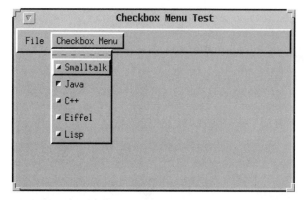

Figure 12-5 A Checkbox Menu Item
Activated menu items toggle between checked or unchecked.

A `CheckboxMenuItem` is often used in a menu that exhibits radio button behavior. That is, when one of the menu items is checked, the other items in the menu are all unchecked, so that only one checkbox menu item is checked at a time.

It is a simple matter to extend `Menu` and provide a `RadioMenu` class that adds `CheckboxMenuItem` items (only) and implements the mutually exclusive selection behavior. Example 5-8 shows the `RadioMenu` implementation.

Example 12-7 `RadioMenu` **Class Source Code**

```
import gjt.Assert;

import java.awt.Menu;
import java.awt.MenuItem;
import java.awt.CheckboxMenuItem;

public class RadioMenu extends Menu {
  public RadioMenu(String s, boolean tearOff) {
     super(s, tearOff);
  }
  public void add(String s) {
     add(new CheckboxMenuItem(s));
  }
  public MenuItem add(MenuItem item) {
     Assert.notFalse(item instanceof CheckboxMenuItem);
     return super.add(item);
  }
  public void selectItem(MenuItem item) {
     CheckboxMenuItem nextItem;
     int              numItems = getItemCount();

     for(int i=0; i < numItems; ++i) {
        if(item != getItem(i)) {
           nextItem = (CheckboxMenuItem)getItem(i);
           nextItem.setState(false);
        }
     }
  }
}
```

`RadioMenu` implements `add(String)` to ensure that the item being added to it is a `CheckboxMenuItem`. Additionally, `RadioMenu` overrides `add(MenuItem)` where it asserts that the item passed in is a `CheckboxMenuItem`. (We discuss the Graphic Java Toolkit's `Assert` class in "Assertions" on page 566.)

`RadioMenu.selectItem()` goes through each of its menu items and sets its state to `false` (unchecked), except for the item that was activated. This ensures that only one item at a time is checked.

`RadioMenuTest` in Example 12-8 illustrates the use of `RadioMenu`.

Example 12-8 RadioMenuTest Class Source Code

```java
import java.awt.*;
import java.awt.event.*;

public class RadioMenuTest extends FrameWithMenuBar {
   private RadioMenu        radioMenu;
   private MenuItem         quitItem;
   private CheckboxMenuItem stItem, javaItem, cppItem,
                            eiffelItem, lispItem;
   public static void main(String args[]) {
      RadioMenuTest test =
                  new RadioMenuTest("FileEdit Menu Test");
      test.setBounds(300,300,300,100);
      test.show();
   }
   public RadioMenuTest(String s) {
      super(s);
   }
   public void createMenus(MenuBar mbar) {
      mbar.add(createFileMenu());
      mbar.add(createRadioMenu());
   }
   private Menu createFileMenu() {
      Menu fileMenu = new Menu("File");
      fileMenu.add(quitItem = new MenuItem("Quit"));

      quitItem.addActionListener(new ActionListener() {
         public void actionPerformed(ActionEvent event) {
            dispose();
            System.exit(0);
         }
      });
      return fileMenu;
   }
   private Menu createRadioMenu() {
      CheckboxItemListener checkboxItemListener =
                           new CheckboxItemListener();
      radioMenu = new RadioMenu("Radio Menu", true);
      stItem = new CheckboxMenuItem("Smalltalk");
      javaItem = new CheckboxMenuItem("Java");
      cppItem = new CheckboxMenuItem("C++");
      eiffelItem = new CheckboxMenuItem("Eiffel");
      lispItem = new CheckboxMenuItem("Lisp");

      radioMenu.add(stItem);
      radioMenu.add(javaItem);
      radioMenu.add(cppItem);
```

```
        radioMenu.add(eiffelItem);
        radioMenu.add(lispItem);

        stItem.addItemListener(checkboxItemListener);
        javaItem.addItemListener(checkboxItemListener);
        cppItem.addItemListener(checkboxItemListener);
        eiffelItem.addItemListener(checkboxItemListener);
        lispItem.addItemListener(checkboxItemListener);

        return radioMenu;
    }
    class CheckboxItemListener implements ItemListener {
        public void itemStateChanged(ItemEvent event) {
            dispose();
            System.exit(0);
        }
    }
}
```

Notice that `RadioMenuTest` calls `RadioMenu.selectItem()` to ensure the mutually exclusive behavior of the menu. Also, notice that checkbox menu items fire item events when activated, and menu items fire action events, as you can see from the manner in which events are handled for the `quitItem` and the checkbox menu items.

Cascading Menus

As previously alluded to, cascading menus are possible with the AWT by virtue of the fact that `Menu` extends `MenuItem`. As we have seen, `Menu.add(MenuItem)` adds a menu item to a menu. Since a `Menu` is a `MenuItem`, the `Menu.add(MenuItem)` method is perfectly happy to take a `Menu` as an argument, which it dutifully adds to itself.

Figure 12-6 shows the cascading menu created by Example 12-9.

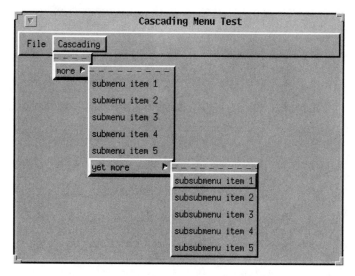

Figure 12-6 A Cascading Menu

Example 12-9 CascadingTest **Class Source Code**

```
import java.awt.*;
import java.awt.event.*;

public class CascadingTest extends FrameWithMenuBar {
  private MenuItem quitItem;

  public static void main(String args[]) {
    CascadingTest test =
        new CascadingTest("Cascading Menu Test");

    test.setBounds(300,300,300,100);
    test.show();
  }
  public CascadingTest(String s) {
    super(s);
  }
  public void createMenus(MenuBar mbar) {
    mbar.add(createFileMenu());
    mbar.add(createCascadingMenu());
  }
  private Menu createFileMenu() {
    Menu fileMenu = new Menu("File");
    fileMenu.add(quitItem = new MenuItem("Quit"));

    quitMenu.addActionListener(new ActionListener() {
```

```
            public void actionPerformed(ActionEvent event) {
                dispose();
                System.exit(0);
            }
        });
        return fileMenu;
    }
    private Menu createCascadingMenu() {
        Menu cascading  = new Menu("Cascading", true);
        Menu submenu    = new Menu("more", true);
        Menu subsubmenu = new Menu("yet more", true);

        submenu.add("submenu item 1");
        submenu.add("submenu item 2");
        submenu.add("submenu item 3");
        submenu.add("submenu item 4");
        submenu.add("submenu item 5");

        subsubmenu.add("subsubmenu item 1");
        subsubmenu.add("subsubmenu item 2");
        subsubmenu.add("subsubmenu item 3");
        subsubmenu.add("subsubmenu item 4");
        subsubmenu.add("subsubmenu item 5");

        submenu.add(subsubmenu);
        cascading.add(submenu);

        return cascading;
    }
}
```

The createCascadingMenu() method creates three menus:

- cascading

- submenu

- subsubmenu

subsubmenu is added to submenu, and submenu is added to cascading.
Notice that a Menu "knows" that we are adding a Menu instead of a MenuItem,
and it does the right thing, which in this case is to create a MenuItem with a pull-
right arrow on the far right edge of the menu item that represents the added
menu.

Dynamically Modifying Menus

So far, we have modified menus before they are created, by adding items to them. Sometimes it is necessary to modify a menu after it is created, which is supported by the AWT.

The `SelfModifyingMenu` illustrated in Figure 12-7 contains an item that is either enabled and disabled by an item above it. `SelfModifyingMenu` also contains two menu items for adding an item and removing the last item added to the menu.

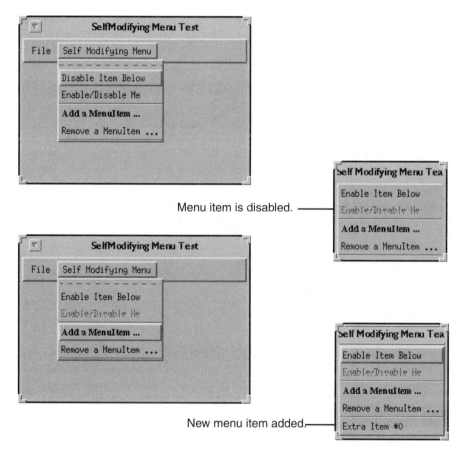

Menu item is disabled.

New menu item added.

Figure 12-7 A Self-Modifying Menu
The top pair of pictures show the "Enable/Disable Me" item grayed-out. The bottom pair of pictures show a menu item added to the menu. Tear-off menus are used to show the different states of the self-modifying menu.

Example 12-10 lists the SelfModifyingMenu class.

Example 12-10 SelfModifyingMenu **Class Source Code**

```java
class SelfModifyingMenu extends Menu {
  private Vector    newItems = new Vector();
  private MenuItemListener menuItemListener =
                              new MenuItemListener();
  private MenuItem toggleItem, enablerItem,
                   addItem, removeItem;

  public SelfModifyingMenu() {
    super("Self Modifying Menu", true);

    add(enablerItem = new MenuItem("Disable Item Below"));
    add(toggleItem  = new MenuItem("Enable/Disable Me"));
    addSeparator();

    add(addItem    = new MenuItem("Add a MenuItem ..."));
    add(removeItem = new MenuItem("Remove a MenuItem ..."));
    addItem.setFont(new Font("TimesRoman", Font.BOLD, 12));
    addSeparator();

    enablerItem.addActionListener(menuItemListener);
    toggleItem.addActionListener(menuItemListener);
    addItem.addActionListener(menuItemListener);
    removeItem.addActionListener(menuItemListener);
  }
  public void addItem() {
    MenuItem newItem =
        new MenuItem("Extra Item #" + newItems.size());

    add(newItem);
    newItems.addElement(newItem);
  }
  public void removeLastItem() {
    if(newItems.size() == 0)
       System.out.println("Hey, nothing to remove!");
    else {
       MenuItem removeMe = (MenuItem)newItems.lastElement();

       remove(removeMe);
       newItems.removeElement(removeMe);
    }
  }
  public void toggleItem() {
     if(toggleItem.isEnabled()) toggleItem.setEnabled(false);
     else                       toggleItem.setEnabled(true);
  }
  class MenuItemListener implements ActionListener {
     public void actionPerformed(ActionEvent event) {
```

```
        MenuItem item = (MenuItem)event.getSource();

        if(item == enablerItem) {
            toggleItem();

            if(toggleItem.isEnabled())
                enablerItem.setLabel("Disable Item Below");
            else
                enablerItem.setLabel("Enable Item Below");
        }
        else if(item == addItem)      addItem();
        else if(item == removeItem) removeLastItem();
    }
  }
}
```

`MenuItemListener.actionPerformed()` is where all the interesting action takes place. If the menu item activated is the `enablerItem`, the `toggleItem()` method is invoked, which toggles the enabled state of the `toggleItem`. After the state of `toggleItem` is toggled, the label for the `enablerItem` is modified to reflect the current enabled state of `toggleItem`.

If the menu item activated is the `addItem`, the `addItem()` method is invoked, which creates a new menu item and adds it to the `newItems` menu:

```
public void addItem() {
  MenuItem newItem =
     new MenuItem("Extra Item #" + newItems.size());

  add(newItem);
  newItems.addElement(newItem);
}
```

If the menu item activated is the `removeItem`, `removeLastItem()` is invoked, which makes sure there is a menu item available for removal by invoking `MenuItem.size()`. After confirming that there is a menu item to remove, `Menu.lastElement()` is invoked to obtain a reference to the last menu item in the menu, and then `Menu.removeElement()` is invoked to remove the last menu item:

```
public void removeLastItem() {
  if(newItems.size() == 0)
     System.out.println("Hey, nothing to remove!");
  else {
     MenuItem removeMe = (MenuItem)newItems.lastElement();

     remove(removeMe);
     newItems.removeElement(removeMe);
  }
}
```

Example 12-11 lists an application that tests out the SelfModifyingMenu class.

Example 12-11 SelfModifyingTest **Class Source Code**

```
import java.awt.*;
import java.awt.event.*;
import java.util.Vector;

public class SelfModifyingTest extends FrameWithMenuBar {
  private SelfModifyingMenu selfModifyingMenu;
  private MenuItem quitItem;

  public static void main(String args[]) {
    Frame frame =
                new SelfModifyingTest("SelfModifying Menu Test");
    frame.setBounds(100,100,300,100);
    frame.show();
  }
  public SelfModifyingTest(String s) {
    super(s);
  }
  public void createMenus(MenuBar mbar) {
    mbar.add(createFileMenu());
    mbar.add(selfModifyingMenu = new SelfModifyingMenu());
  }
  private Menu createFileMenu() {
    Menu fileMenu = new Menu("File");
    fileMenu.add(quitItem = new MenuItem("Quit"));

    quitItem.addActionListener(new ActionListener() {
        public void actionPerformed(ActionEvent event) {
          dispose();
          System.exit(0);
        }
    });
    return fileMenu;
  }
}
```

Popup Menus

Incredible as it may seem, popup menus were nowhere to be found in the original AWT. As a result, many developers implemented their own popups, but since such popups were drawn entirely in Java code and not implemented by a peer, the native look and feel was lost. Fortunately, this deficiency has been remedied in the 1.1 version of the AWT with the introduction of a peer-based popup menu.

Popup menus are extremely easy to use. In this section we'll discuss creating popups, displaying them, and handling the events they generate.

Popups and Components

Popup menus must be attached to an AWT component. In fact, in the 1.1 release of the AWT, `java.awt.Component` has been fitted with two new methods for attaching and removing popup menus:

- `add(PopupMenu popup)`

- `remove(MenuComponent popup)`

Creating a popup menu, attaching it to a component, and displaying it are trivial. The following applet creates a popup menu, adds it to an applet, and then adds four items to the popup menu. When the time is right (bear with us, we'll explain in a moment), the popup menu is shown at the location of the cursor:

Example 12-12 PopupTest Applet

```
import java.applet.Applet;
import java.awt.*;
import java.awt.event.*;

public class PopupTest extends Applet {
  private PopupMenu popup = new PopupMenu();

  public void init() {
    add(popup);

    popup.add(new MenuItem("item one"));
    popup.add(new MenuItem("item two"));
    popup.add(new MenuItem("item three"));
    popup.add(new MenuItem("item four"));

    addMouseListener(new MouseAdapter() {
      public void mousePressed (MouseEvent e) {
        showPopup(e);
      }
      public void mouseClicked (MouseEvent e) {
        showPopup(e);
      }
      public void mouseReleased(MouseEvent e) {
        showPopup(e);
      }
    });
  }
  void showPopup(MouseEvent e) {
    if(e.isPopupTrigger())
      popup.show(this, e.getX(), e.getY());
  }
}
```

Our popup menu can be seen in action in Figure 12-8.

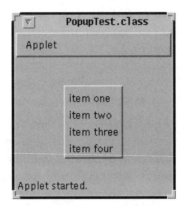

Figure 12-8 Popup Menu
Popup menus should be shown when
`MouseEvent.isPopupTrigger()` method returns `true`.

There are a number of things to note concerning our simple applet.

First of all, we add the popup to the applet. Note that the `add()` method invoked in the first line of `init()` is not the familiar `Container.add()` method that adds a component to a container, but the `Component.add()` method that adds a popup menu to a component.

Second, note that menu items are added to a popup menu in exactly the same manner as items are added to a menu because the `PopupMenu` class extends `Menu`.

Third, we have added a mouse listener to the applet in the form of an inner class extending `MouseAdapter`, which overrides `mousePressed()`, `mouseClicked()` and `mouseReleased()`, all of which invoke the `showPopup()` method.

`showPopup()` checks the event it is passed to see whether the event is a popup trigger; if so, it shows the popup.

Two questions remain unanswered concerning our applet. First, why do we have to override the three mouse event handling methods, and second, why are we passing a reference to the applet to `PopupMenu.show()`?

The answer to the first question lies in the fact that popups are shown in response to a sequence of events, commonly known as the popup *trigger*. The popup trigger varies between platforms, for instance:

- **Motif Popup Trigger:** On a mouse button 3 DOWN, the popup is displayed and stays up if the button is held down or released within a short period of time. A subsequent mouse down, either outside of the popup or in one of the popup's items brings the popup down.

- **Windows 95 Popup Trigger:** The popup is displayed on a mouse button 2 UP. A subsequent mouse button 1 or mouse button 2 down either over an item in the popup, or outside of the popup menu brings the popup down.

Since the algorithm for popup triggers varies between platforms, the AWT must provide a unified mechanism for detecting when the popup trigger has been pulled, so to speak. Since the popup trigger is activated on all platforms as the result of a mouse event, the `MouseEvent` class comes equipped with an `isPopupTrigger()` method that returns `true` if the trigger has been pulled, and `false` if it has not.

Out of all the mouse events that can occur in the AWT, mouse pressed, mouse clicked and mouse released are the only ones that can cause the trigger to be pulled, so we must override them all to check for the trigger.

Note that this is a somewhat awkward way to have to detect the popup trigger. A better solution might have been to implement a popup trigger event that is fired by components equipped with popups. That way, we could register a popup trigger listener with components and not have to deal with generic mouse events. Not only would this be more convenient, but it would be much more in line with the 1.1 delegation-based event model.

The answer to the second question is that popups are shown at an offset to a component. Of course, you must be wondering why we have to pass the same component that the popup is attached to; the answer is that the popup can come up relative to any component contained in the container hierarchy of the component to which the popup is attached. That way, a popup can be attached to, say, a frame, but can be shown relative to any component contained in the frame.

Handling Popup Events

As we saw in "Semantic Events" on page 105, menu items fire action events when they are selected. Example 12-13 lists an applet that handles the action events fired by a popup menu.

Example 12-13 PopupActionTest Applet

```java
import java.applet.Applet;
import java.awt.*;
import java.awt.event.*;

public class PopupActionTest extends Applet {
  private PopupMenu popup = new PopupMenu();
  private MenuItem  itemOne, itemTwo, itemThree, itemFour;
  private PopupActionListener actionListener;

  public void init() {
    add(popup);

    popup.add(itemOne   = new MenuItem("item one"));
    popup.add(itemTwo   = new MenuItem("item two"));
    popup.add(itemThree = new MenuItem("item three"));
    popup.add(itemFour  = new MenuItem("item four"));

    actionListener = new PopupActionListener();

    itemOne.addActionListener   (actionListener);
    itemTwo.addActionListener   (actionListener);
    itemThree.addActionListener(actionListener);
    itemFour.addActionListener  (actionListener);

    addMouseListener(new MouseAdapter() {
      public void mousePressed (MouseEvent e) {
        showPopup(e);
      }
      public void mouseClicked (MouseEvent e) {
        showPopup(e);
      }
      public void mouseReleased(MouseEvent e) {
        showPopup(e);
      }
    });
  }
  void showPopup(MouseEvent e) {
    if(e.isPopupTrigger())
      popup.show(this, e.getX(), e.getY());
  }
  class PopupActionListener implements ActionListener {
    public void actionPerformed(ActionEvent event) {
      MenuItem mi = (MenuItem)event.getSource();
      showStatus(mi.getLabel());
    }
  }
}
```

The `PopupActionTest` applet is essentially the same as the previous applet, except that we've added event handling in order to detect when an item in the popup has been selected[3]. We maintain references to each item in the popup, so that we can add a single instance of `ActionListener` to each menu item. When an item is selected from the popup, our action listener calls `Applet.showStatus()` to display the label of the item selected in the status bar of the applet.

Showing Popups Relative To Components

As we noted earlier, `PopupMenu.show()` takes three arguments—a component and an x,y location. The location specifies an offset from the upper left-hand corner of the component. The component can be any component in the container hierarchy associated with the component to which the popup is attached. Our final popup applet, shown in Figure 12-9 illustrates showing a popup over different components in the applet's containment hierarchy.

The applet contains three `ColoredCanvas` instances, along with a `Choice` for selecting which colored canvas the popup will be shown relative to. When a selection is made from the choice, the popup is shown 5 pixels below and 5 pixels to the right of the colored canvas selected in the choice. Note that although the popup is attached to the applet, we don't detect the firing of the applet's popup trigger, and therefore the only mechanism we provide for showing the popup is by making a selection from the choice. Once again, we'd like to point out that the call to `add(popup)` invokes `Component.add(PopupMenu)`, while the other calls to `add()` invoke `Container.add(Component)`, as we've indicated with comments as you can see in Example 12-14, which lists the source for the applet.

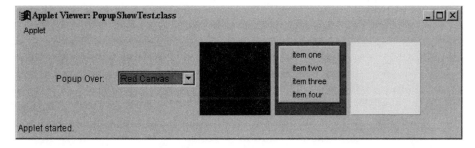

Figure 12-9 Popups Are Shown Relative to Specific Components
Popups can be shown relative to any component in the container hierarchy of the component to which the popup is attached.

---

3. Note that we're using inner classes here. See "Named Inner Classes" on page 124.

Example 12-14 `PopupShowTest` Applet

```java
import java.applet.Applet;
import java.awt.*;
import java.awt.event.*;

public class PopupShowTest extends Applet {
  Choice        choice = new Choice();
  PopupMenu     popup  = new PopupMenu();

  ColoredCanvas popupRelativeToMe;
  ColoredCanvas blueCanvas, redCanvas, yellowCanvas;

  public void init() {
    blueCanvas        = new ColoredCanvas(Color.blue);
    redCanvas         = new ColoredCanvas(Color.red);
    yellowCanvas      = new ColoredCanvas(Color.yellow);
    popupRelativeToMe = blueCanvas;

    popup.add(new MenuItem("item one"));
    popup.add(new MenuItem("item two"));
    popup.add(new MenuItem("item three"));
    popup.add(new MenuItem("item four"));

    add(popup);                         // Component.add(PopupMenu)
    add(new Label("Popup Over:"));// Container.add(Component)
    add(choice);
    add(blueCanvas);                    // Container.add(Component)
    add(redCanvas);                     // Container.add(Component)
    add(yellowCanvas);                  // Container.add(Component)

    choice.add("Blue Canvas");
    choice.add("Yellow Canvas");
    choice.add("Red Canvas");

    choice.addItemListener(new ItemListener() {
       public void itemStateChanged(ItemEvent event) {
          Choice c     = (Choice)event.getSource();
          String label = c.getSelectedItem();

          if(label.equals("Blue Canvas"))
             popupRelativeToMe = blueCanvas;
          else if(label.equals("Red Canvas"))
             popupRelativeToMe = redCanvas;
             else if(label.equals("Yellow Canvas"))
                popupRelativeToMe = yellowCanvas;

          popup.show(popupRelativeToMe, 5, 5);
       }
    });
  }
}
class ColoredCanvas extends Canvas {
  private Color color;
```

```
    public ColoredCanvas(Color color) {
       this.color = color;
    }
    public void paint(Graphics g) {
       Dimension size = getSize();
       g.setColor  (color);
       g.fill3DRect(0,0,size.width-1,size.height-1,true);
    }
    public Dimension getPreferredSize() {
       return new Dimension(100,100);
    }
}
```

Summary

The 1.0.2 version of the AWT supports menus that reside in menubars only; subsequent versions of the AWT will include popup menus that can be displayed over any component. The AWT menu classes do not extend java.awt.Component and therefore cannot be drawn into. This means that it is currently impossible to create owner-drawn menus with the AWT.

Menubars and menus are easy to create and display in the AWT; however, there is a certain amount of drudgery that every application with a menubar must implement. We have encapsulated that drudgery in a FrameWithMenuBar class that is extended by most of the example applications in this chapter. We have also presented a general-utility class, MenuBarPrinter, that prints each menu and menu item contained in a menubar.

Tear-off menus are supported by the AWT. A menu is designated as a tear-off menu at construction time by passing an additional boolean argument to a Menu constructor; a true value indicates that the menu is to be a tear-off; a false value indicates that the menu is not a tear-off. Tear-off menus are not supported under Windows 95.

 The AWT supports help menus, which are like ordinary menus in every respect except that they are always the rightmost menu in the menubar. Under Motif, the help menu is right-justified in the menubar itself. Under Windows 95, the menu is simply the rightmost menu in the menubar.

The AWT also supports checkbox menu items, and we have presented a general-purpose class—RadioMenu—which provides checkbox menu items that are mutually exclusive, ensuring that only one of its items is checked at any given time.

We have also explored implementing cascading menus and menus that can be modified dynamically. Since Menu extends MenuItem, a Menu can be added as an item to another menu. Menus can have their items enabled or disabled after their creation, and items can be added to or removed from a menu after construction.

Currently, setting a menu item's font does not work under Windows 95, and setting a menu item's label after construction does not work under either Motif or Windows 95.

CHAPTER 13

Images

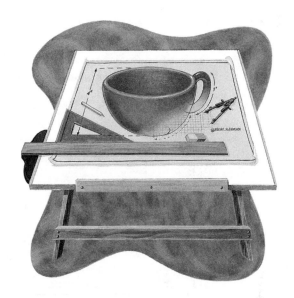

There are two major topics of discussion concerning images and the AWT: obtaining and displaying images, and image manipulation. We will discuss each topic in this chapter, and we will subsequently encounter a good deal of real-life use of images in the chapters that describe the Graphic Java Toolkit custom components.

We'll begin by introducing some applets and applications that show various display characteristics and nuances of displaying images. Then we'll introduce a couple of GJT custom components that illustrate how to filter images.

In order to make the most of this chapter, you will want to run the applets discussed. Some paint images a line at time, some paint all at once, some have an annoying flash, and some are nice and smooth—all characteristics we can't really capture in static screen snapshots.

The Image Class and the Image Package

The AWT provides a `java.awt.Image` class. References to `java.awt.Image` are passed to methods of other AWT objects for displaying and manipulating images. For instance, images can be displayed in a component by invoking `Graphics.drawImage(Image, int, int, ImageObserver)`.

329

`java.awt.Image` is an abstract class that simply defines methods that provide information about an image. Table 13-1 lists the abstract methods that `java.awt.Image` defines.

Table 13-1 `java.awt.Image` **Methods**

Method
`public abstract int getWidth(ImageObserver observer);`
`public abstract int getHeight(ImageObserver observer);`
`public abstract ImageProducer getSource();`
`public abstract Graphics getGraphics();`
`public abstract Object getProperty(String name,` `                                    ImageObserver observer);`
`public abstract void flush();`

Nearly all of the infrastructure for creating and manipulating images resides in the `java.awt.image` *package* (not to be confused with the `java.awt.Image` *class*). The `java.awt.image` package defines interfaces for producing and obtaining an image, along with classes for filtering and manipulating images. The `java.awt.Image` class provides a reference to an image, but it is actually the `java.awt.image` package that undertakes all of the grunt work associated with obtaining and manipulating images.

Image Producers and Image Observers

If you've ever visited a website containing a number of images, you're aware that it takes some time to download those images, especially over a network. As a result, much of the image-related work in the AWT, such as loading and drawing an image is handled asynchronously—even obtaining the width and height of an image is an asynchronous activity. The sender and receiver of asynchronous image transactions are defined by two AWT interfaces: `java.awt.image.ImageProducer` and `java.awt.image.ImageObserver`.

An `ImageProducer` is responsible for producing the bits of an image and for passing them along to an `ImageObserver`. An `ImageProducer` notifies an `ImageObserver` of its progress by invoking the only method defined by the `ImageObserver` interface: `imageUpdate()`.

Implementors of `ImageObserver` are ubiquitous in the AWT, mainly because `Component` implements `ImageObserver`. Every component, therefore, is an `ImageObserver` that can choose to be updated on the progress a given `ImageProducer` is making when undertaking an asynchronous operation.

Understanding that image-related tasks happen asynchronously and understanding the relationship between `ImageProducer` and `ImageObserver` are key to understanding image manipulation in the AWT. In the rest of this chapter, we illustrate these concepts through a number of applets.

AWT TIP ...

All Components Are Image Observers

A number of asynchronous methods related to image manipulation in the AWT require an ImageObserver argument. For instance, obtaining the width of an image is accomplished by invoking Image.getWidth(ImageObserver). As a result, newcomers to the AWT often wonder where to get a reference to an ImageObserver to pass to asynchronous methods such as getWidth(). The answer is that every component in the AWT is an ImageObserver because java.awt.Component implements the ImageObserver interface. Therefore, any component can be passed to a method that takes an ImageObserver argument.

Obtaining and Displaying Images

Let's begin by taking a look at a very simple applet, shown in Figure 13-1 and listed in Example 13-1, that obtains an image and displays it in a canvas.

Figure 13-1 A Simple Applet That Displays an Image

Notice that we do a couple things in this applet solely for the sake of illustration; we print the codebase—the URL defining the location of the applet—and we print the width and height of the image in the showImageSize() method.

Example 13-1 Simple Applet That Displays an Image

```
import java.net.URL;
import java.applet.Applet;
import java.awt.Graphics;
import java.awt.Image;

public class ImageTestAppletSimple extends Applet {
  private Image im;

  public void init() {
     URL codebase = getCodeBase();
     System.out.println(codebase);
     im = getImage(codebase, "saint.gif");
     showImageSize();
  }
  public void paint(Graphics g) {
     g.drawImage(im,0,0,this);
  }
  private void showImageSize() {
     System.out.print  ("Image width=" + im.getWidth(this));
     System.out.println(" height=" + im.getHeight(this));
  }
}
```

The method we're most interested in is the Applet.getImage() method called in the init() method, which returns a reference to an Image. To illustrate the asynchronous behavior of loading an image, we call showImageSize() immediately after the call to getImage() returns. If you run the applet, you'll see that showImageSize() prints the following for the width and height of the image:

```
Image width=-1 height=-1
```

Although your first thought may be that this is an extremely small image, the rather odd-looking values for width and height indicate that although getImage() has returned an Image, the bits that define the image are not yet loaded. Image.getWidth() and Image.getHeight() return -1 until the image is fully loaded.

When you run the applet, you can see the image being loaded chunks of pixels at time, from top to bottom, depending upon the speed of your processor. That's because the `Graphics.drawImage()` method (invoked in the `paint()` method) also runs asynchronously. Let's take a closer look at that call:

```
g.drawImage(im,0,0,this);
```

`Graphics.drawImage()` is passed an:

- `Image` (`im`)
- x,y coordinate (`0,0`) (the upper left-hand corner of the graphics)
- `ImageObserver` object (`this`)

We're most interested in the last argument: `this`, of course, is the applet itself. If we trace its lineage, we see that `Applet` extends `Component` and `Component` implements `ImageObserver`. Classes like `Applet` that need to deal with images asynchronously implement the `ImageObserver` interface, and, as we pointed out previously[1], all components in the AWT are image observers. The `ImageObserver` interface defines a collection of constants and one method, `imageUpdate()`. `ImageObserver.imageUpdate()` is defined as:

```
public boolean imageUpdate(Image img, int infoflags,
    int x, int y, int width, int height);
```

All asynchronous methods dealing with images take an `ImageObserver` as an argument. Table 13-2 lists these methods.

Table 13-2 Methods That Are Passed an `ImageObserver`

Method
`boolean Component.prepareImage(Image image,` `                          ImageObserver observer)`
`boolean Component.prepareImage(Image image, int width, int height,` `                          ImageObserver observer)`
`int Component.checkImage(Image image, ImageObserver observer)`
`int Component.checkImage(Image image, int width, int height,` `                          ImageObserver observer)`
`boolean Graphics.drawImage(Image img, int x, int y,` `                          ImageObserver observer);`

`boolean Graphics.drawImage(Image img, int x, int y,`
`                          int width, int height,`
`                          ImageObserver observer);`

---

1. See "All Components Are Image Observers" on page 331.

Table 13-2 Methods That Are Passed an `ImageObserver` **(Continued)**

Method
```public boolean Graphics.drawImage(Image img, int x, int y,``` ```Color bgcolor,``` ```ImageObserver observer);```
```public boolean Graphics.drawImage(Image img, int x, int y,``` ```int width, int height,``` ```Color bgcolor,``` ```ImageObserver observer);```
```public int Image.getWidth(ImageObserver observer);```
```public int Image.getHeight(ImageObserver observer);```
```public boolean Toolkit.prepareImage(Image image, int width,``` ```int height,``` ```ImageObserver observer);```
```public int Toolkit.checkImage(Image image, int width, int height,``` ```ImageObserver observer);```
```public Image Toolkit.createImage(ImageProducer producer);```

Differences Between Applets and Applications

Applets provide built-in support for obtaining images: namely, the
`Applet.getImage()` method. A Java application, however, does not extend
`Applet`, so you need to write an application that is going to incorporate images a
little differently than you do an applet. Example 13-2 illustrates how an
application obtains and displays an image.

Example 13-2 Application With an Image

```
import java.applet.Applet;
import java.awt.*;
import java.awt.event.*;

public class ImageTestApplication extends Frame {
  Image im;

  static public void main(String args[]) {
    ImageTestApplication app = new ImageTestApplication();
    app.show();
  }
  public ImageTestApplication() {
    super("Image Test");
    im = Toolkit.getDefaultToolkit().getImage("saint.gif");
    setBounds(100, 100, 220, 330);
```

```
    addWindowListener(new WindowAdapter() {
        public void windowClosing(WindowEvent event) {
            dispose();
            System.exit(0);
        }
    });
  }
  public void paint(Graphics g) {
    g.drawImage(im,0,0,this);
  }
}
```

The application obtains an `Image` in the `ImageTestApplication` constructor. Instead of calling `Applet.getImage()`, the application calls the `getImage()` method from the `Toolkit` class. We first call the static `getDefaultToolkit()`, which returns the default toolkit for the platform the application is running on, and then we invoke the toolkit's `getImage()` method. Note that the `Toolkit.getImage()` method is overloaded to take either a `URL` or a `String` as an argument.

Waiting for an Image to Load

As we noted above, both the applet and application we have presented so far load their image in chunks, from the top of the image to the bottom, because of the asynchronous nature of image loading. A more aesthetically pleasing approach is to wait for the image to load completely before displaying it. There are a number of ways in which to accomplish this; one way is to implement `imageUpdate()`, which keeps us informed as to the progress of the loading of the image in question.

The applet in Example 13-3 is almost exactly like the one in Example 13-1 on page 332, except that it implements `ImageObserver.imageUpdate()`.

Example 13-3 Image Loading All at Once

```
import java.net.URL;
import java.applet.Applet;
import java.awt.Graphics;
import java.awt.Image;

public class ImageTestAppletWithUpdate extends Applet {
  private Image im;

  public void init() {
      URL codebase = getCodeBase();
      System.out.println(codebase);
```

```
        im = getImage(codebase, "saint.gif");
        showImageSize();
    }
    public void paint(Graphics g) {
      g.drawImage(im,0,0,this);
    }
    public boolean imageUpdate(Image image, int flags,
                               int x, int y, int w, int h)
    {
        System.out.println("imageUpdate(): x=" + x + ", y=" +
                            y + "  w=" + w + ",h=" + h);
        if((flags & ALLBITS) != 0)
            repaint();

        return true;
    }
    private void showImageSize() {
        System.out.print  ("Image width=" + im.getWidth(this));
        System.out.println(" height=" + im.getHeight(this));
    }
}
```

Our implementation of imageUpdate() prints the x, y, width, and height of each row of pixels as they are passed in. If you run the applet, you'll see printed output something like this:

```
Image width=-1 height=-1
imageUpdate():   x=0,  y=0   w=217,h=321
imageUpdate():   x=0,  y=0   w=217,h=1
imageUpdate():   x=0,  y=1   w=217,h=1
imageUpdate():   x=0,  y=2   w=217,h=1
imageUpdate():   x=0,  y=3   w=217,h=1
imageUpdate():   x=0,  y=4   w=217,h=1
```

As we previously pointed out, as soon as the image is returned by getImage(), showImageSize() is invoked, and prints:

```
Image width=-1 height=-1
```

Of course, the mystery associated with this applet is who is invoking our applet's imageUpdate() method. Every Image has an associated ImageProducer, which, as we've alluded to before, provides the actual bits for the image[2]. As soon as the call to getImage() is made, the ImageProducer for the Image im begins to load the image, and our applet goes on to bigger and better things (namely, invoking showImageSize()). As the image is being loaded, the

---

2.   See "Image Producers and Image Observers" on page 330.

ImageProducer associated with im calls our applet's imageUpdate() method every time it obtains a new scanline. As is usually the case, we are not actually interested in doing anything with each scanline as it is handed to us, other than to print out some statistics that illustrate the asynchronous nature of image loading.

Note that our applet's implementation of imageUpdate() uses the ImageObserver constant ALLBITS to determine when the Image is completely loaded. Once the flags ANDed with ALLBITS are non-zero, we know that all the bits for the image have been loaded. Once the image has been completely loaded, we call repaint(), and this time, since the image is ready and waiting to be displayed, it is blasted into the applet in one fell swoop.

The ImageObserver interface defines several constants besides ALLBITS, as shown in Table 13-3.

Table 13-3 ImageObserver **Constants**

Constant	Indicates...
ABORT	the imageUpdate() was aborted.
ALLBITS	all bits have been loaded into the Image.
ERROR	an error occurred during an imageUpdate().
FRAMEBITS	another complete frame of a multiframe Image is available.
HEIGHT	the height of the Image is available.
PROPERTIES	the Image's properties are available.
SOMEBITS	more pixels are available for a scaled variation of the Image.
WIDTH	the width of the Image is available.

Although the applet above displays its image all at once, it takes some time for the image to load (especially with us printing out statistics from imageUpdate()). Additionally, the larger the image is, the longer it will take for the image to load. If you have a web page, for instance, with a number of large images, the delay incurred by waiting for each image to load may be unacceptable. In such a case, you may wish to paint each scanline of the image as it becomes available. Painting a scanline at a time does not reduce the time required to load the image, but it does at least provide feedback that the image is being fetched. Our next applet does exactly that.

Painting Images a Scanline at a Time

Example 13-4, lists an applet that is a variation of the one we just looked at. Instead of calling `repaint()` after all the bits have been loaded into the `Image` object, this applet calls `repaint()` every time `imageUpdate()` is called.

Example 13-4 Image Loading With Dynamic Updates

```java
import java.net.URL;
import java.applet.Applet;
import java.awt.Graphics;
import java.awt.Image;

public class ImageTestAppletWithDynamicUpdate extends Applet {
  private Image im;

  public void init() {
      URL codebase = getCodeBase();
      System.out.println(codebase);
      im = getImage(codebase, "saint.gif");
      showImageSize();
  }
  public void paint(Graphics g) {
    g.drawImage(im,0,0,this);
  }
  public boolean imageUpdate(Image image, int flags,
                             int x, int y, int w, int h)
  {
      System.out.println("imageUpdate():  x=" + x + ", y=" +
                         y + "  w=" + w + ",h=" + h);
      repaint();
      return true;
  }
  private void showImageSize() {
      System.out.print  ("Image width=" + im.getWidth(this));
      System.out.println(" height=" + im.getHeight(this));
  }
}
```

This applet, as advertised, paints each scanline as it becomes available. However, we have incurred a horrible penalty for keeping users informed as to the progress of our image loading: the image flashes as it is being drawn. Our next applet employs a simple mechanism to smoothly display each scanline without any flashing.

Eliminating the Flash

The culprit of the annoying flashing is the applet's `update()` method. Recall from our *Applets and Applications* chapter that a call to a component's `repaint()` method results in the component's `update()` method being called as soon as possible. Therefore, when we called `repaint()` in Example 13-4, a call to `update()` was scheduled. The default implementation of `Component.update()` is to erase the entire background of the component and invoke the component's `paint()` method. Therefore, each time a scanline is available, we invoke `repaint()`, resulting in a call to `update()`, which erases the background and then invokes `paint()`. Our implementation of `paint()` draws as much of the image as is currently available. All of this erasing and repainting results in the flashing which we seek to eliminate.

The simple solution, illustrated by Example 13-5, is to override `update()` to call `paint()` directly. This eliminates the constant erasure of the applet's background and results in the image being displayed in a smooth fashion.

Example 13-5 Image Loading Without Flashing

```
import java.net.URL;
import java.applet.Applet;
import java.awt.Graphics;
import java.awt.Image;

public class ImageTestAppletWithSmoothDynamicUpdate
                              extends Applet {
  private Image im;

  public void init() {
      URL codebase = getCodeBase();
      System.out.println(codebase);
      im = getImage(codebase, "saint.gif");
      showImageSize();
  }
  public void paint(Graphics g) {
    g.drawImage(im,0,0,this);
  }
  public boolean imageUpdate(Image image, int flags,
                      int x, int y, int w, int h)
  {
      System.out.println("imageUpdate():  x=" + x + ", y=" +
                      y + "  w=" + w + ",h=" + h);
      repaint();
      return true;
  }
  public void update(Graphics g) {
```

```
        paint(g);
    }
    private void showImageSize() {
        System.out.print  ("Image width=" + im.getWidth(this));
        System.out.println(" height=" + im.getHeight(this));
    }
}
```

Of course, it still takes awhile for the image to paint, mostly because we are still doggedly printing out statistics for each scanline. You may wish to modify the applet so that it does not print out statistics each time a scanline is available; you will notice a considerable increase in speed by doing so.

AWT TIP ...

update() Clears the Background Before Invoking paint()

Component.update(), which is invoked whenever repaint() is called, first clears the background of the component and then calls paint(). While this is a desirable default behavior, it causes the component to flash because the component is cleared before it is painted. In order to eliminate the flash, override update() to call paint() directly.

Using MediaTracker

The MediaTracker class provides a more convenient way than we've illustrated thus far to manage the asynchronous loading of an Image object. Essentially, a MediaTracker object can *track* or monitor the loading of an image. Let's look at the applet in Example 13-6.

Example 13-6 Image Loading With the MediaTracker Class

```
import java.net.URL;
import java.applet.Applet;
import java.awt.Graphics;
import java.awt.Image;
import java.awt.MediaTracker;

public class ImageTestAppletWithMediaTracker extends Applet {
    private Image im;

    public void init() {
        URL codebase = getCodeBase();
        System.out.println(codebase);

❶       MediaTracker tracker = new MediaTracker(this);

        im = getImage(codebase, "saint.gif");
```

```
❷        tracker.addImage(im, 0);
❸        try { tracker.waitForID(0); }
         catch(InterruptedException e) { }

         showImageSize();
     }
   public void paint(Graphics g) {
     g.drawImage(im,0,0,this);
   }
   private void showImageSize() {
       System.out.print  ("Image width=" + im.getWidth(this));
       System.out.println(" height=" + im.getHeight(this));
   }
 }
```

Using `MediaTracker` is a simple, three-step process:

1. Create an instance of it, as we've done in line ❶.

2. Use `MediaTracker.addImage()` to specify the image that needs to be tracked, as we've done in line ❷.

3. Create a `try/catch` block as we do in line ❸. The `try` block waits for the image associated with ID to fully load. The `MediaTracker waitForID()` method may throw an `InterruptedException`, so it's necessary to implement a `catch` block. In our case, we catch it but don't do anything with it, which is typically the case in practice.

If you wish to wait for images to load entirely before displaying them, employing an instance of `MediaTracker` is probably the way to go. Using `MediaTracker` means that you need not override `imageUpdate()` and go through the trouble of ANDing the correct constant with the `flags` variable passed in.

However, using `MediaTracker` requires you to implement the three steps outlined above. The Graphic Java Toolkit encapsulates the steps involved in using `MediaTracker` in the (static) `gjt.Util.waitForImage()` method. This reduces waiting for an image to one simple statement—no overriding methods or fooling around with ANDing bits, or implementing `try/catch` blocks. Example 13-7 illustrates use of `gjt.Util.waitForImage()`.

Example 13-7 Image Loading With the `gjt.Util` Class

```
import java.net.URL;
import java.applet.Applet;
import java.awt.Graphics;
import java.awt.Image;
```

```
import gjt.Util;

public class ImageTestAppletWithGJTUtil extends Applet {
  private Image im;

  public void init() {
      URL codebase = getCodeBase();
      System.out.println(codebase);

      im = getImage(codebase, "saint.gif");
      Util.waitForImage(this, im);
      showImageSize();
  }
  public void paint(Graphics g) {
    g.drawImage(im,0,0,this);
  }
  private void showImageSize() {
      System.out.print  ("Image width=" + im.getWidth(this));
      System.out.println(" height=" + im.getHeight(this));
  }
}
```

The implementation of the Graphic Java Toolkit `Util.waitForImage()` method is straightforward:

```
public static void waitForImage(Component component,
                                Image image){
  MediaTracker tracker = new MediaTracker(component);
  try {
     tracker.addImage(image, 0);
     tracker.waitForID(0);
  }
  catch(InterruptedException e) { e.printStackTrace(); }
}
```

As you can see, `gjt.Util.waitForImage()` simply encapsulates the steps involved in using `MediaTracker`, which we would otherwise have to reimplement for each image we wish to load in this fashion.

Filtering Images

Thus far, we've shown you how to obtain and display images and highlighted some features of the AWT (and the GJT) along the way. There will be times, however, when you will need to manipulate images in a more sophisticated fashion. The `java.awt.image` package provides the infrastructure for filtering images. Furthermore, the GJT provides four image filters:

- `gjt.image.BlackAndWhiteFilter`

- `gjt.image.BleachImageFilter`
- `gjt.image.DissolveFilter`
- `gjt.image.NegativeFilter`

The `BlackAndWhiteFilter` produces a black-and-white version of a color image, and the `BleachImageFilter` produces a brighter version of an image. The `DissolveFilter` creates a more transparent version of an image, whereas the `NegativeFilter` creates a negative version of an image (like a negative of a photograph). The class diagram in Figure 13-2 illustrates the `java.awt.image` classes involved in filtering images and also shows where the GJT filters fit in.

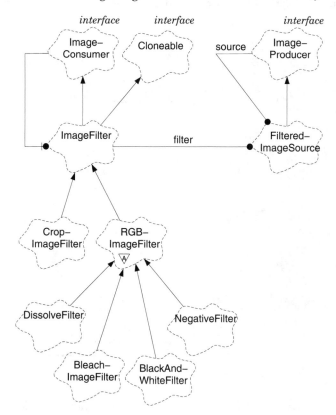

Figure 13-2 Image Filter Class Diagram
A `FilteredImageSource` is an `ImageProducer` that runs the bits of an image supplied by another `ImageProducer` through an `ImageFilter`, producing a filtered version of the original image. All of the extensions of `RGBImageFilter` shown above are from the `gjt.image` package.

All of the GJT filters listed above extend RGBImageFilter—an abstract filter that leaves the actual filtering of pixels to extensions but provides the infrastructure for delivering one pixel at a time from an image. We'll first take a look at how the gjt.image.BleachImageFilter is used and implemented, along with the implementations of gjt.image.BlackAndWhiteFilter and gjt.image.NegativeFilter, and then we'll take a look at the gjt.image.DissolveImageFilter.

To begin, look at Figure 13-3. It shows the effect of running an image through the gjt.image.BleachImageFilter. The image on the left is the original image; the image on the right is the image produced after the original image is run through the gjt.image.BleachImageFilter.

Figure 13-3 Bleaching Images

To illustrate the gjt.image.BleachImageFilter in action, we'll look at Example 13-8, which is the unit test for the bleach filter.

After you've looked through Example 13-8, we'll highlight some of the dynamics of passing an image through a filter. Then we'll look specifically at the inner workings of the gjt.image.BleachImageFilter.

Example 13-8 Bleaching an Image With a Filter

```java
package gjt.test;

import java.applet.Applet;
import java.awt.*;
import java.awt.event.*;
❶ import java.awt.image.FilteredImageSource;

import gjt.*;
import gjt.image.BleachImageFilter;

public class BleachImageFilterTest extends UnitTest {
  public String title() {
      return "BleachImageFilter Test " +
              "(Click picture to Bleach/Unbleach Picture)";
  }
  public Panel centerPanel() {
      return new BleachImageFilterTestPanel(this);
  }
}
class BleachImageFilterTestPanel extends Panel {
  BleachImageFilterTestCanvas canvas;

  public BleachImageFilterTestPanel(Applet applet) {
     add(canvas = new BleachImageFilterTestCanvas(applet));
     canvas.addMouseListener(new MouseAdapter() {
        public void mousePressed(MouseEvent event) {
            canvas.toggleBleaching();
            canvas.repaint();
        }
     });
  }
}
  class BleachImageFilterTestCanvas extends Canvas {
❷   private Image    im;
❸   private Image    bleached;
    private boolean showingBleached = false;

    public BleachImageFilterTestCanvas(Applet applet) {
      int    bp;
      String bleachPercent =
                 applet.getParameter("bleachPercent");
      if(bleachPercent != null)
         bp = new Integer(bleachPercent).intValue();
      else
         bp = 50;
```

```
        im = applet.getImage(applet.getCodeBase(),
                             "gifs/saint.gif");
        Util.waitForImage(this, im);

❹      FilteredImageSource source =
            new FilteredImageSource(im.getSource(),
                                    new BleachImageFilter(bp));
❺      bleached = createImage(source);
❻      Util.waitForImage(this, bleached);

        showImageSize();
    }
    public Dimension getPreferredSize() {
        return new Dimension(im.getWidth(this),
                             im.getHeight(this));
    }
❼   public void paint(Graphics g) {
        if(showingBleached) g.drawImage(bleached,0,0,this);
        else                g.drawImage(im,       0,0,this);
    }
    public void toggleBleaching() {
        showingBleached = showingBleached ? false : true;
    }
    private void showImageSize() {
        System.out.print("Image width=" + im.getWidth(this));
        System.out.println(" height=" + im.getHeight(this));
    }
}
```

The first thing to note about this applet is that in line ❶, we import
FilteredImageSource from the java.awt.image package. The
FilteredImageSource class implements the ImageProducer interface. As
you can see in line ❹, a FilteredImageSource is constructed with an
ImageProducer and an ImageFilter.

Line ❷ declares im, which is the original, unbleached image, while in line ❸ we
declare bleached, which is the bleached version of the original image.

Line ❹ creates a new instance of FilteredImageSource, which is used to filter
the original image and produce a bleached version of the image.

FilteredImageSource is an ImageProducer that produces a filtered version
of an image. A FilteredImageSource is constructed with an ImageProducer,
which supplies the bits of the original image, and an ImageFilter, which not
surprisingly, filters the image supplied by the ImageProducer. Note that in this
particular case, we obtain the ImageProducer from the original image by
invoking Image.getSource(). Remember that each image has an

`ImageProducer` that can produce the bits for its associated image. `FilteredImageSource` prods the image producer it was passed in its constructor to cough up the bits of the original image and then runs those bits through the image filter that was also supplied to its constructor. Finally, since `FilteredImageSource` is an image producer itself, it can be passed to `Component.createImage(ImageProducer)`—as is done on line ❺—to produce the filtered version of the original image.

The `Component.createImage()` method takes an `ImageProducer` for an argument. The `createImage()` method knows how to obtain the bits of an image from the specified `ImageProducer` argument. Figure 13-4 sketches how this transaction of events takes place.

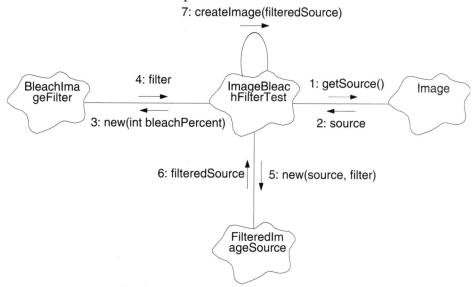

Figure 13-4 Image Filtering Process
The `ImageBleachFilterTest` applet obtains the `ImageProducer` for the original image, creates a `BleachImageFilter`, and then uses the `ImageProducer` and the `BleachImageFilter` to construct a `FilteredImageSource`. Finally, the `FilteredImageSource` is passed to `Applet.createImage()`, which returns a filtered version of the original image.

Of course, all of this happens asynchronously, so in line ❻ we use the `waitForImage()` method from the `gjt.Util` class, to wait for the bleached version of the original image to be fully loaded.

In line ❼, we override the `paint()` method to enable toggling between the standard and bleached images.

gjt.image.BleachImageFilter

Now that we've seen how a FilteredImageSource is used to produce a filtered version of an image, we will reveal the implementation of BleachImageFilter. There are a couple of important items to note about gjt.image.BleachImageFilter as you look through its implementation. For example, notice that it extends RGBImageFilter; it is standard AWT practice to extend RGBImageFilter for filtering images. Doing so requires overriding the only abstract method defined by RGBImageFilter: filterRGB(), which is passed one pixel at a time for filtering.

Also, note the use of canFilterIndexColorModel (a boolean instance variable of RGBImageFilter) in the gjt.image.BleachImageFilter constructor. When canFilterIndexColorModel is set to false, the filterRGB() method is called to filter every pixel in an image. (The default behavior of an RGBImageFilter is to convert each pixel in the image, one at a time.) If canFilterIndexColorModel is set to true, as in gjt.image.BleachImageFilter, the filterRGB() method is passed one pixel for each *color* in the ColorModel. Setting canFilterIndexColorModel to true allows the BleachImageFilter to filter by color and avoids the overhead of calling filterRGB() for every pixel in an image. Before we look at the implementation of gjt.image.BleachImageFilter, take a look at Table 13-4, which lists the responsibilities (public methods) of the gjt.image.BleachImageFilter class.

Table 13-4 gjt.image.BleachImageFilter **Responsibilities**

Methods	Description
int percent()	Defines the extent to which an image will be bleached.
void percent(int percent)	Sets bleaching percent.
int filterRGB(int x, int y, int rgb)	Brightens each color in the image.

Example 13-9 lists the gjt.image.BleachImageFilter implementation.

Example 13-9 `gjt.image.BleachImageFilter` **Class Source Code**

```
package gjt.image;

import java.awt.image.*;
import gjt.Assert;

public class BleachImageFilter extends RGBImageFilter {
  private int percent;

  public BleachImageFilter(int percent) {
      Assert.notFalse(percent >= 0 && percent <= 100);
      this.percent = percent;
      canFilterIndexColorModel = true;
  }
  public int  percent()            { return percent;    }
  public void percent(int percent) { percent = percent; }

  public int filterRGB(int x, int y, int rgb) {
      DirectColorModel cm =
          (DirectColorModel)ColorModel.getRGBdefault();

      int    alpha = cm.getAlpha(rgb);
      int    red   = cm.getRed(rgb);
      int    green = cm.getGreen(rgb);
      int    blue  = cm.getBlue (rgb);
      double percentMultiplier = (double)percent/100;

      red   = Math.min((int)
                 (red + (red * percentMultiplier)), 255);
      green = Math.min((int)
                 (green + (green * percentMultiplier)), 255);
      blue  = Math.min((int)
                 (blue  + (blue  * percentMultiplier)), 255);

      alpha = alpha << 24;
      red   = red   << 16;
      green = green << 8;

      return alpha | red | green | blue;
  }
}
```

The `BleachImageFilter` constructor sets `canFilterIndexColorModel` to true. As we mentioned previously, this means that `BleachImageFilter.filterRGB()` will only be called as many times as there are colors in the `ColorModel`, instead of for every pixel in the image. Filters that modify colors independently of the position of pixels in the image should do likewise to avoid a great deal of unnecessary overhead.

Of course, `filterRGB()` is where all of the action takes place. On line ❶, we obtain the default RGB color model, which we put to work on line ❷ to extract the alpha, red, green, and blue components of the pixel (`rgb`) passed in, which is a color model's only raison d'etre. The red, green, blue, and alpha values for a pixel always fall between 0 and 255; the higher the number, the brighter the color.

Starting on line ❸, we set each value to the minimum of (original value + original value * percent/100) and 255. For instance, if the original value of the red component was 150 and our `percent` was 50, we would set the red component to 150 + (150 * 50/100), which turns out to be 225. However, if the red component was 250, we would set the red component to 255, because 250 + (250 * 50/250) turns out to be 300, which is greater than the maximum allowed value of 255.

Finally, on line ❹, we shift the alpha, red, and green bits in order to place them in the correct location bitwise. The alpha component of a color occupies bits 25–32, the red component occupies bits 17–24, and the green component occupies bits 9–16. The blue component of a pixel occupies bits 1–8, so there is no need to shift the blue component.

On line ❺, we reconstruct a pixel value from the shifted components, by ORing them. The reconstructed pixel value is then returned from the `filterRGB()` method. Remember, the job of `filterRGB()` is to take a pixel value, convert it however it sees fit, and then return the modified pixel value. Since `BleachImageFiliter.filterRGB()` gets invoked for every color in the image's color model, each color is brightened by the percentage specified by the percent member of the `BleachImageFilter`.

Notice that `BleachImageFilter` does not modify the alpha component of the pixel value; the alpha component controls the transparency (or opacity, depending upon your point of view) of a pixel. The `gjt.image.DissolveFilter`, which we will discuss shortly, controls the transparency of an image and thus manipulates the alpha value of each pixel in the color model. This leaves the red, blue, and green components untouched. But we are getting ahead of ourselves.

gjt.image.BlackAndWhiteFilter

The GJT also comes with a filter that produces a black-and-white version of a color image. Since our book is in black and white, we won't show you the unit test for `gjt.image.BlackAndWhiteFilter`, but we thought you should see the implementation of the filter, which is shown in Example 13-10.

Example 13-10 `gjt.image.BlackAndWhiteFilter` **Class Source Code**

```
package gjt.image;

import java.awt.image.*;
import gjt.Assert;

public class BlackAndWhiteFilter extends RGBImageFilter {
  public BlackAndWhiteFilter() {
    canFilterIndexColorModel = true;
  }
  public int filterRGB(int x, int y, int rgb) {
    DirectColorModel cm =
        (DirectColorModel)ColorModel.getRGBdefault();
    int    alpha = cm.getAlpha(rgb);
    int    red   = cm.getRed  (rgb);
    int    green = cm.getGreen(rgb);
    int    blue  = cm.getBlue (rgb);
    int    mixed = (red + green + blue) / 3;

    red   = blue = green = mixed;
    alpha = alpha << 24;
    red   = red   << 16;
    green = green << 8;
    return alpha | red | green | blue;
  }
}
```

Just like `BleachImageFilter`, `BlackAndWhiteFilter` extends `RGBImageFilter` and sets `canFilterIndexColorModel` to `true` in order to filter each color in the colormap instead of filtering each pixel in the image. Also, like `BleachImageFilter`, we use the color model to obtain references to the red, green, blue, and alpha components of each color in the colormap.

The values for the red, green and blue components of each color are averaged, and that average is used as the replacement color, which effectively drains the image of its color.

gjt.image.NegativeFilter

By now, you may have realized that implementing an image filter is a fairly simple task: you simply extend `RGBImageFilter`, choose whether you want to filter by color or by each pixel in the image, and implement `filterRGB()`. In fact, the most difficult aspect of developing image filters usually involves coding the algorithm in `filterRGB()` for filtering the pixels (or colors) of an image. A little later on, in "PixelGrabber and MemoryImageSource" on page 363, we'll look

at filtering images that can potentially change size, which requires a different
approach, but in the meantime, we'll show you another filter that produces a
negative of an image—you can see the effect in Figure 13-5.

Figure 13-5 gjt.image.NegativeFilter
The gjt.image.NegativeFilter produces a negative of an
image.

Example 13-11 lists the implementation of gjt.image.NegativeFilter.

Example 13-11 gjt.image.NegativeFilter **Class Source Code**

```
package gjt.image;

import java.awt.image.*;

public class NegativeFilter extends RGBImageFilter {
  public NegativeFilter() {
      canFilterIndexColorModel = true;
  }
  public int filterRGB(int x, int y, int rgb) {
    DirectColorModel cm =
        (DirectColorModel)ColorModel.getRGBdefault();
```

```
int    alpha = cm.getAlpha(rgb);
  int    red   = cm.getRed  (rgb);
  int    green = cm.getGreen(rgb);
  int    blue  = cm.getBlue (rgb);

red   = Math.abs(255 - red);
green = Math.abs(255 - green);
blue  = Math.abs(255 - blue );

alpha = alpha << 24;
red   = red   << 16;
green = green << 8;

  return alpha | red | green | blue;
  }
}
```

As you can see, we are once again singing the familiar refrain of extending
`RGBImageFilter`, setting `canFilterIndexColorModel` to `true` in order to
filter by color, and employing the color model to obtain the red, green, blue, and
alpha components of each pixel. Then, we simply subtract each component from
255 to obtain the inverse color, and return the new pixel value.

Example 13-12 shows the implementation of the unit test for
`gjt.image.NegativeFilter`.

Example 13-12 `gjt.test.NegativeFilterTest` **Class Source Code**

```
package gjt.test;

import java.applet.Applet;
import java.awt.*;
import java.awt.event.*;
import java.awt.image.FilteredImageSource;
import gjt.Util;
import gjt.image.NegativeFilter;

public class NegativeFilterTest extends UnitTest {
  public String title() {
      return "NegativeFilter Test " +
             "(Click below to toggle Negative)";
  }
  public Panel centerPanel() {
      return new NegativeFilterTestPanel(this);
  }
}
class NegativeFilterTestPanel extends Panel {
  NegativeFilterTestCanvas canvas;
```

```
    public NegativeFilterTestPanel(Applet applet) {
       add(canvas = new NegativeFilterTestCanvas(applet));

       canvas.addMouseListener(new MouseAdapter() {
          public void mousePressed(MouseEvent event) {
             canvas.toggleNegative();
             canvas.repaint();
          }
       });
    }
 }
 class NegativeFilterTestCanvas extends Canvas {
   private Image    im;
   private Image    negative;
   private boolean showingNegative = false;

   public NegativeFilterTestCanvas(Applet applet) {
      im = applet.getImage(applet.getCodeBase(), "gifs/saint.gif");
       Util.waitForImage(this, im);

       FilteredImageSource source =
           new FilteredImageSource(im.getSource(),
                                   new NegativeFilter());

       negative = createImage(source);
      Util.waitForImage(this, negative);
   }
   public Dimension getPreferredSize() {
      return new Dimension(im.getWidth(this),
                           im.getHeight(this));
   }
   public void paint(Graphics g) {
       if(showingNegative) g.drawImage(negative,0,0,this);
       else                g.drawImage(im,     0,0,this);
   }
   public void toggleNegative() {
      showingNegative = showingNegative ? false : true;
   }
 }
```

The Color Model and the Alpha Value of a Pixel

In case our brief discussion of the ColorModel class and the alpha value of a pixel left you wanting more, we will cover both in a bit more detail before diving into the gjt.image.DissolveFilter.

Each pixel in an image has an RGB color value. The alpha, red, green, and blue components of a pixel can be accessed by the invoking the methods defined by awt.image.ColorModel, which are described in Table 13-5.

Table 13-5 awt.image.ColorModel **Public Abstract Instance Methods**

Abstract Methods	Description
int getAlpha(int pixel)	Returns the opacity for a color in a pixel.
int getRed(int pixel)	Returns the integer value for red.
int getBlue(int pixel)	Returns the integer value for blue.
int getGreen(int pixel)	Returns the integer value for green.
int getPixelSize()	Returns pixel size.
int getRGB(int pixel)	Returns the integer RGB value.

Besides having a red, green, and blue value, each pixel value also includes an *alpha* value. The alpha value represents the transparency of a color and, like its red, green, and blue counterparts, is an integer whose value is always between 0 and 255. An alpha value of 0 means the color is completely transparent, and an alpha value of 255 means the color is completely opaque. You can see the effect of modifying an image's alpha value in Figure 13-6.

Figure 13-6 Dissolving Images
The gjt.image.ImageDissolver in action.

gjt.image.DissolveFilter

The gjt.image.DissolveFilter sets the level of transparency for each color in an image. Table 13-6 lists the DissolveFilter public instance methods, followed by the implementation of gjt.image.DissolveFilter in Example 13-13.

Table 13-6 gjt.image.DissolveFilter **Responsibilities**

Methods	Description
void setOpacity(int opacity)	Sets the opacity for a color.
int filterRGB(int x, int y, int rgb)	Returns the RGB value.

Example 13-13 gjt.image.DissolveFilter **Class Source Code**

```
package gjt.image;

import java.awt.image.*
import gjt.Assert;

public class DissolveFilter extends RGBImageFilter {
 private int opacity;

  public DissolveFilter() {
      this(0);
  }
  public DissolveFilter(int opacity) {
      canFilterIndexColorModel = true;
      setOpacity(opacity);
  }
  public void setOpacity(int opacity) {
      Assert.notFalse(opacity >= 0 && opacity <= 255);
      this.opacity = opacity;
  }
  public int filterRGB(int x, int y, int rgb) {
      DirectColorModel cm =
          (DirectColorModel)ColorModel.getRGBdefault();
      int alpha = cm.getAlpha(rgb);
      int red   = cm.getRed  (rgb);
      int green = cm.getGreen(rgb);
      int blue  = cm.getBlue (rgb);

      alpha = opacity;
      return alpha << 24 | red << 16 | green << 8 | blue;
  }
}
```

The the image filters discussed so far manipulate the red, green, and blue components of each pixel passed into `filterRGB()` and leave the alpha component untouched. `DissolveFilter` does the inverse, letting the red, green, and blue components pass through untouched, modifying only the alpha value. `DissolveFilter` sets the alpha value for each color in the image to its `opacity`.

gjt.image.ImageDissolver

Now that we've seen how `gjt.image.DissolveFilter` manipulates the alpha value of each color in an image, let's look at `gjt.image.ImageDissolver`, which uses `DissolveFilter` for the practical purpose of fading an image in or out.

Table 13-7 lists the `ImageDissolver` responsibilities.

Table 13-7 `gjt.image.ImageDissolver` **Responsibilities**

Methods	Description
`void fadeIn(int x, int y)`	Fades in the image.
`void fadeOut(int x, int y)`	Fades out the image.

`gjt.image.ImageDissolver` creates an array of images of varying transparency, from totally translucent to totally opaque, with the assistance of a `gjt.image.DissolveFilter`. The `fadeIn()` and `fadeOut()` methods cycle through the array of images and display each image in a `Component` that is passed to the `ImageDissolver` constructor. `fadeIn()` cycles through the array from the totally transparent image to the totally opaque image, and `fadeOut()` cycles through the array in reverse order.

Example 13-14 on page 361 shows the `gjt.image.ImageDissolver` class in its entirety. However, it is a fairly complicated class, so we'll guide you through some of the highlights before showing you the entire class.

One of the first things to point out is that the `ImageDissolver` contains two `Image` objects: one for the image to be drawn on screen and one for the image to be drawn off screen. This is our first exposure to double buffering, which warrants a short introduction[3].

Double buffering is a technique for smoothly drawing a series of images. Each image is first drawn in an off-screen buffer and then copied, or *blitted*[4], to an area on screen. Double buffering eliminates the flicker associated with drawing a

---

3. We explore double buffering in detail in *Lightweight Components* on page 475.

series of images and is discussed in more detail in "DoubleBufferedContainer" on page 489. `ImageDissolver` employs double buffering for a flicker-free fading effect.

After declaring the on-screen and off-screen images, we declare an array of images to hold the images created by `gjt.image.DissolveFilter`:

```
Image      image, offscreen;
Image[]    dissolvedImages;
```

`ImageDissolver` has two constructors:

```
    public ImageDissolver(Component comp, Image image) {
        this(comp, image, _defaultNumImages, _defaultPause);
    }
    public ImageDissolver(Component comp, Image im,
❶                         int numImages, int pause) {
        this.image      = im;
        this.comp       = comp;
        this.numImages  = numImages;
     pauseInterval      = pause;

❷      Util.waitForImage(comp, im);
❸      dissolvedImages = createImages(image, numImages, comp);
    }
```

Note that both constructors take a `Component`, which is the component into which the images will be drawn. Also, the second constructor in line ❶ takes a `pause` value, which is used to control the rate at which the images are faded in and out. Line ❷ makes use of the `waitForImage()` method from the `gjt.Util` class to ensure that the image passed in is fully loaded. (Recall from *Using MediaTracker* on page 340 that this method encapsulates the `MediaTracker` capability for waiting for the asynchronous loading of an image to complete.)

On line ❸, the constructor calls `createImages()`. This is where `gjt.image.ImageDissolver` creates an array of images with varying degrees of transparency:

```
    static public Image[] createImages(Image image,
                                        int numImages,
                                        Component component) {
        Image         images[] = new Image[numImages];
        MediaTracker  tracker  = new MediaTracker(component);
```

4. *Blit* is a term derived from the phrase bit block transfer. A block transfer is sometimes referred to as a BLT (not to be confused with the sandwich), so *blit* is short for a Bit BLT.

```
DissolveFilter        filter;
FilteredImageSource fis;

for(int i=0; i < numImages; ++i) {
    filter = new DissolveFilter((255/(numImages-1))*i);
    fis    = new FilteredImageSource(image.getSource(),
                                        filter);

     images[i] = component.createImage(fis);
    tracker.addImage(images[i], i);
}
try { tracker.waitForAll(); }
catch(InterruptedException e) { }

return images;
}
```

CreateImages() is passed the original image, the number of images to be produced, and component into which the images will be drawn. A DissolveFilter is created with a specified opacity. Notice that when i is 0, the opacity passed to the filter's constructor is (255/ (numImages-1)) * i, which turns out to be zero, no matter what numImages is. When i is equal to numImages-1, the opacity turns out to be (255 / (numImages-1)) * (numImages-1), or 255. Therefore, createImages() creates an array of numImages images whose transparency varies from totally transparent (alpha value of 0) to totally opaque (alpha value of 255). The images in between have varying degrees of transparency.

We add each image created to an instance of MediaTracker (tracker), and we have tracker wait for all the images in the array to be fully loaded. Finally, we return the array of images created.

Next, let's look at the gjt.image.ImageDissolver public fadeIn() method:

```
public void fadeIn(int x, int y) {
    if(offscreen == null)
        offscreen = comp.createImage(image.getWidth(comp),
                                        image.getHeight(comp));

    Graphics offg  = offscreen.getGraphics();
    Graphics compg = comp.getGraphics();

    if(offg != null && compg != null) {
        clearComponent(compg, x, y);
        for(int i=0; i < numImages; ++i) {
            blitImage(compg, offg, x, y, i);
            pause    ();
```

```
        }
        blitOpaqueImage(compg, offg, x, y);
        offg.dispose();
        compg.dispose();
    }
}
```

`createImage()` creates the off-screen image, if it has not been created previously, that has the same width and height as each image in the array of images to be displayed.

The `Graphics` object for the off-screen and on-screen images is obtained via calls to `getGraphics()`. Then the work of fading in an array of images begins. The first order of business for `fadeIn()` is to erase the region of the component into which the images will be drawn, which is exactly what `clearComponent()` does. Then, `fadeIn()` cycles through the array of images, blitting each image into the component at the specified location. Each pass through the loop is accompanied by a call to `pause()`, which pauses for the amount of time in milliseconds specified by the `pauseInterval` member. Note that we are careful to dispose of any `Graphics` obtained by a call to `Component.getGraphics()`—see "Disposing of a Graphics Object" on page 29.

The `blitImage()` method first draws an image from the array into the off-screen buffer and then copies the image into the component at the specified offset.

```
    private void blitImage(Graphics compg, Graphics offg,
                           int x, int y, int index) {
        offg.drawImage (dissolvedImages[index], 0, 0, comp);
        compg.drawImage(offscreen,              x, y, comp);
    }
```

We use the `Graphics` object of the off-screen image to draw an image from the `Image` array into the off-screen image, and then the image is blitted from the off-screen image into the component.

Now we are ready to present the `gjt.image.ImageDissolver` class in its entirety in Example 13-14. You might pay special attention to the `pause()` method, which simply causes the current thread to sleep for the time specified in `pauseInterval` (in milliseconds).

Example 13-14 `gjt.image.ImageDissolver` **Class Source Code**

```
package gjt.image;

import java.awt.*;
import java.awt.image.*;
import gjt.Util;

public class ImageDissolver {
  private static int _defaultNumImages = 10,
                     _defaultPause = 50;
  Component comp;
  int       numImages, pauseInterval;
  Image     image, offscreen;
  Image[]   dissolvedImages;

  static public Image[] createImages(Image image,
                                     int numImages,
                                     Component component) {
     Image        images[] = new Image[numImages];
     MediaTracker tracker  = new MediaTracker(component);

     DissolveFilter      filter;
     FilteredImageSource fis;

     for(int i=0; i < numImages; ++i) {
         filter = new DissolveFilter((255/(numImages-1))*i);
         fis    = new FilteredImageSource(image.getSource(),
                                          filter);

         images[i] = component.createImage(fis);
         tracker.addImage(images[i], i);
     }
     try { tracker.waitForAll(); }
     catch(InterruptedException e) { }

     return images;
  }
  public ImageDissolver(Component comp, Image image) {
     this(comp, image, _defaultNumImages, _defaultPause);
  }
```

```java
public ImageDissolver(Component comp, Image im,
                      int numImages, int pause) {
    this.image = im;
    this.comp = comp;
    this.numImages = numImages;
    pauseInterval = pause;

    Util.waitForImage(comp, im);
    dissolvedImages = createImages(image, numImages, comp);
}
public void fadeIn(int x, int y) {
    if(offscreen == null)
        offscreen = comp.createImage(image.getWidth(comp),
                                     image.getHeight(comp));

    Graphics offg  = offscreen.getGraphics();
    Graphics compg = comp.getGraphics();

    if(offg != null && compg != null) {
        clearComponent(compg, x, y);
        for(int i=0; i < numImages; ++i) {
            blitImage(compg, offg, x, y, i);
            pause     ();
        }
        blitOpaqueImage(compg, offg, x, y);
        offg.dispose();
        compg.dispose();
    }
}
public void fadeOut(int x, int y) {
    if(offscreen == null)
        offscreen = comp.createImage(image.getWidth(comp),
                                     image.getHeight(comp));

    Graphics offg  = offscreen.getGraphics();
    Graphics compg = comp.getGraphics();

    if(offg != null && compg != null) {
        blitOpaqueImage(compg, offg, x, y);
        for(int i=numImages-1; i >= 0; --i) {
            clearOffscreen();
            blitImage      (compg, offg, x, y, i);
            pause          ();
        }
        offg.dispose();
        compg.dispose();
    }
}
```

```
  private void blitImage(Graphics compg, Graphics offg,
                         int x, int y, int index) {
      offg.drawImage (dissolvedImages[index], 0, 0, comp);
      compg.drawImage(offscreen,                x, y, comp);
  }
  private void blitOpaqueImage(Graphics compg, Graphics offg,
                               int x, int y) {
      offg.drawImage(image, 0, 0, comp);
      compg.drawImage(offscreen, x, y, comp);
  }
  private void clearComponent(Graphics compg, int x, int y) {
      clearOffscreen();
      compg.drawImage(offscreen, x, y, comp);
  }
  private void clearOffscreen() {
      Graphics offg = offscreen.getGraphics();

      offg.setColor(comp.getBackground());
      offg.fillRect(0, 0,
              image.getWidth(comp), image.getHeight(comp));
      offg.dispose();
  }
  private void pause() {
      try { Thread.currentThread().sleep(pauseInterval); }
      catch(InterruptedException e) { }
  }
}
```

PixelGrabber and MemoryImageSource

The `java.awt.image` package provides two classes for converting an image to an array of pixels, and back into an image again. `PixelGrabber` grabs pixels from a `java.awt.Image` and produces an array of bits representing the image. `MemoryImageSource` is used to do the inverse, taking an array of bits representing an image and producing a `java.awt.Image`. We'll take a look at both classes and provide a utility that allows an image to be embedded in a class.

Embedding Images in a Class

Reading images from files is the manner in which nearly all Java applets (and applications) obtain images to display. Such an approach, however, has a number of drawbacks:

- Reading images from a file takes time.
- Image files must be in a specific location.
- The name of the image file must match what is in the code.

Whether you can afford the time it takes to read an image from a file varies from one applet to another. Even though image loading is an asynchronous activity, reading images from a file still takes time. Some applets that need to display a large number of images in a hurry may find the overhead involved in reading images from a file to be unacceptable.

Additionally, image files must be in a specific location. If an image file gets moved to a different directory or renamed, the image file will not be found at runtime, and the image will not be displayed.

Lastly, note that the name of the image file is hardwired into the source code. This creates a dependency between the code and the name of the image file. Creating dependencies between classes is one thing, but creating a dependency between a class and an external resource is asking for trouble. How then, does one dispense with reading images from a file and still display images in an applet or application? The solution is to embed the definition of the image, in the form of an array, into a class. An instance of `java.awt.image.MemoryImageSource` can then be used to construct the image, given the array definition. The trick, of course, is to come up with the array in the first place, given an image —of course, that's the purview of the `PixelGrabber` class.

Before we proceed, we should mention that the `Java` language produces an executable statement for each constant it runs across in an array. As a result, embedding an image in a class can result in the size of the .class file increasing dramatically, and therefore the performance benefits gained from embedding an image in a class can be negated if the .class file has to be downloaded. As a result, we recommend that you use the technique of embedding images in a class only for small images, or in classes that will not be downloaded over the net.

AWT TIP ...

Be Careful About Embedding Images in a Class

Since an executable statement is generated for every constant found in a Java array, embedding images in a class can dramatically increase the size of the associated .class file. As a result, we recommend that you only embed small images in a class, or restrict embedding images to classes that will not be downloaded over the net.

java.awt.MemoryImageSource

As we mentioned previously, an instance of `MemoryImageSource` can be used to produce an image, given an array of bits that represent the image. Figure 13-7 shows an applet that displays an image that was originally an array of bits, and was transformed into an image by employing an instance of `MemoryImageSource`.

Figure 13-7 An Image Constructed by `MemoryImageSource`

The listing for the applet shown in Figure 13-7 is shown in Example 13-15.

Example 13-15 `DisplayImageFromArray` **Class Source Code**

```java
import java.applet.Applet;
import java.awt.*;
import java.awt.image.*;

public class DisplayImageFromArray extends Applet {
  private Image im;

  public void init() {
    MemoryImageSource mis = new MemoryImageSource(diskWidth,
                                                  diskHeight,
                                                  disk, 0,
                                                  diskWidth);
    im = createImage(mis);
  }
  public void paint(Graphics g) {
    g.drawImage(im, 0, 0, this);
  }
  private int diskWidth=29;
  private int diskHeight=29;
  private int disk[] = { ... };
}
```

Notice that we've omitted the guts of the disk array. If we had included the actual array definition for our small image, the listing would have grown to 5 pages!

The `MemoryImageSource` class from the `java.awt.image` package is an implementation of the `ImageProducer` interface whose sole purpose is to produce an image, given an array representing the bits of the image.

The first thing our applet does is create an instance of `MemoryImageSource`:

```
MemoryImageSource mis = new MemoryImageSource(diskWidth,
                                              diskHeight,
                                              disk, 0,
                                              diskWidth);
```

The first two arguments to the constructor specify the width and height of the image. The third argument is the array itself, and the last two arguments specify the offset into the array of the first pixel and the number of pixels in the array per line, respectively.

After the `MemoryImageSource` is created, `Applet.createImage()` is invoked, which creates an instance of `java.awt.Image`, given the `MemoryImageSource` (`ImageProducer`) instance:

```
im = createImage(mis);
```

Then, of course, the image created by the call to `createImage()` is drawn in the applet's `paint()` method.

Now that we've seen how to use an instance of `MemoryImageSource` to produce an image given an array representing the bytes of the image, the only thing left to do is to come up with the array in the first place.

java.awt.PixelGrabber

We need a utility that can read an image from a file, grab the pixels associated with the image, and spit out a file containing an array definition of the image—a job tailor made for `PixelGrabber`. Once we have the array definition, we can embed it in a class and use the `MemoryImageSource` class to produce the image, as outlined above.

Since the listing for the utility is rather lengthy, we'll discuss the important parts of it first and then show you the entire listing. The utility must perform the following steps:

- Ensure that the application is invoked properly.
- Read the image file.

- Grab the pixels associated with the image
- Write out the array definition to a file.

Since applets have restrictions placed upon them when it comes to reading and writing files, our utility will be an application, which is free to read and write files.

Each of the steps outlined above is encapsulated in a method of the ImageToArray class. The code germane to our discussion, of course, is converting the image into an array of bits, which is accomplished by the grabPixels() method:

```
private boolean grabPixels() {
    boolean success = true;
    pixels = new int[width * height];
    PixelGrabber pg = new PixelGrabber(im, 0, 0, width, height,
                                       pixels, 0, width);
    try {
        pg.grabPixels();
    }
    catch(InterruptedException e) {
        System.err.println("Grabbing Interrupted");
        e.printStackTrace();
        success = false;
    }
    return success;
}
```

An instance of PixelGrabber is instantiated, which grabs the pixels associated with the image. PixelGrabber grabs a rectangular section of pixels associated with an image—the rectangular region is specified in the PixelGrabber constructor.

The call to the PixelGrabber constructor above tells it to grab pixels associated with the image im, with (0,0) being the coordinate of the upper left corner of the rectangle. We also pass along the width and height of the image, along with a preallocated array for holding the pixels. The last two arguments to the PixelGrabber constructor specify the offset into the array for the first pixel (zero), and the scansize, which is the distance from the start of one row to the next row of pixels in the image.

Note that PixelGrabber.grabPixels() may throw an InterruptedException, which we are required to catch. If the grabbing of pixels is interrupted, we print out an error message and then have the exception print out a stack trace. If we encounter such an exception, grabPixels() returns false, indicating that the operation was a failure; otherwise, true is returned.

After `PixelGrabber` has stuffed the integer values representing the bytes of the image into an array, the array definition, along with variables representing the width and height of the array are written to a file.

The complete listing for the ImageToArray class is shown in Example 13-16.

Example 13-16 `ImageToArray` **Class Source Code**

```java
import java.io.*;
import java.applet.Applet;
import java.awt.*;
import java.awt.image.*;

public class ImageToArray extends Frame {
  private PrintStream ps;
  private Image      im;
  private int[]      pixels;
  private int        width, height, intsPerRow=8;
  private boolean    usageValid = true;
  private String     arrayName, imageFilename, arrayFilename;
  private String     arrayAccess = "private";

  static public void main(String args[]) {
    ImageToArray app = new ImageToArray(args);
    System.exit(0);
  }
  public ImageToArray(String args[]) {
    checkArgs(args);

    if(usageValid) {
      try {
        readImage();

        if(grabPixels())
          writeArrayToFile();
      }
      catch(IOException e) {
        System.err.println("Can't open output file");
        e.printStackTrace();
      }
      return;
    }
  }
  private boolean checkArgs(String args[]) {
    if((args.length != 3)) {
      System.err.println(
          "Wrong number of command line arguments");
      showUsage();
```

```
      }
      else if( ! (new File(args[0])).exists()) {
         System.err.println("Cannot find image file");
         showUsage();
      }
      if(usageValid) {
         imageFilename = args[0];
         arrayFilename = args[1];
         arrayName     = args[2];
      }
      return usageValid;
   }
   private void showUsage() {
      System.err.println("Usage:  java " + getClass().getName() +
                       " [image file] [array file] [array name]");
      usageValid = false;
   }
   private void readImage() {
      MediaTracker tracker = new MediaTracker(this);

      im = Toolkit.getDefaultToolkit().getImage(imageFilename);

      try {
         tracker.addImage(im, 0);
         tracker.waitForID(0);
      }
      catch(InterruptedException e) {
         System.err.println("MediaTracker Interrupted");
         e.printStackTrace();
      }
      width  = im.getWidth(this);
      height = im.getHeight(this);
   }
   private boolean grabPixels() {
      boolean success = true;

      pixels = new int[width * height];

      PixelGrabber pg = new PixelGrabber(im, 0, 0, width, height,
                                         pixels, 0, width);
      try {
         pg.grabPixels();
      }
      catch(InterruptedException e) {
         System.err.println("Grabbing Interrupted");
         e.printStackTrace();
         success = false;
      }
```

```
        return success;
    }
    private void writeArrayToFile() throws IOException {
        ps = new PrintStream(new FileOutputStream(arrayFilename));

        ps.println(arrayAccess + " int " + arrayName +
                            "Width=" + width  + ";");
        ps.println(arrayAccess + " int " + arrayName +
                            "Height=" + height + ";");
        ps.println();
        ps.println(arrayAccess + " int " + arrayName + "[] = { ");

        for(int h=0, r=0; h < width*height; ++h) {
            ps.print(pixels[h] + ",");

            if(r == intsPerRow-1) {
                ps.println();
                System.err.print(".");
                System.err.flush();
            }
            r = r == intsPerRow-1 ? 0 : r+1;
        }
        ps.println("};");
        ps.close();
        System.err.println();
    }
}
```

Summary

There are two major areas of concern when incorporating images into applets.
One is the basic task of obtaining and displaying images. The other is the task of
manipulating images.

This chapter has covered the basics of obtaining and displaying images, including
the distinction between ImageProducer and ImageObserver, and loading
images a scanline at a time or all at once. We have also discussed elimination of
flashing when painting an image a scanline at a time, along with the use of
MediaTracker for waiting for images to load. Additionally, we have introduced
image filtering and double buffering and presented two GJT image filters:
gjt.image.BleachImageFilter and gjt.image.DissolveFilter. We
have also presented a GJT custom component that can be used to fade an image in
or out of a java.awt.Component.

We've also taken a look at `PixelGrabber` and `MemoryImageSource`, and presented a utility that writes out an array of bits, given an image. The utility can be used to embed images directly into a class as an alternative to reading in an image from a file, but embedding images should be only be used for small images or for classes that will not be downloaded over the net.

CHAPTER
14

Components, Containers, and Layout Managers

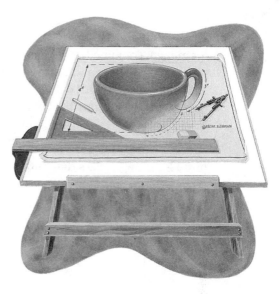

Perhaps the most fundamental relationship in the entire AWT is the relationship between components, containers, and layout managers. Understanding how the three relate to one another is paramount to developing nontrivial applets and applications using the AWT. As a result, we will spend a good deal of effort to illustrate not only the relationships between components, containers, and layout managers, but also the standard AWT layout managers and the implementation of custom layout managers.

No matter how thorough we are in this chapter, we realize that readers are not going to become layout manager gurus without significant exposure to using and implementing layout managers in the real world. When we cover custom components from the Graphic Java Toolkit in "Extending the AWT—The Graphic Java Toolkit" on page 557, we'll be dealing with a different layout situation in nearly every chapter, which will lead us to a number of insights concerning layout managers and their relationships with components and containers.

The Big Three of the AWT

To really get your teeth into the AWT, you're going to have to deal with components, containers, and layout managers in a fairly sophisticated fashion. This means you're going to have to be sensitive to the nuances of their relationship to one another. Primarily, you need to know where one stops working for you and where another starts.

A component contained in a container is quite likely to be subjected to a life of stretching, squashing, and being moved about. Although you might suspect the component's container of dishing out such punishment, containers are spatially challenged; they delegate the laying out[1] of their components to a layout manager. A container's layout manager is the sole force behind positioning and shaping the components contained in its associated container.

Figure 14-2 shows a class diagram for `java.awt.Container`.

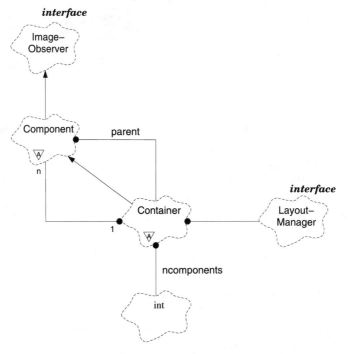

Figure 14-1 `Container` Class Diagram
Every container maintains a reference to a layout manager that positions and shapes the components contained in the container.

Containers are simply components that can contain other components. They don't actually *do* anything with the components they contain; they just keep track of them.

---

1.   Laying out a component involves setting the component's location and size.

The AWT provides a handful of classes that extend `Container`, as illustrated in Figure 14-2.

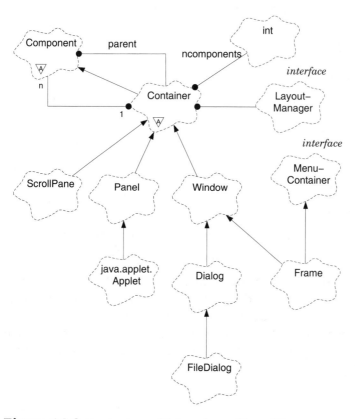

Figure 14-2 `Container` Extensions Class Diagram
The AWT provides a number of `Container` extensions. All containers maintain a reference to a layout manager.

Every container has access to a `LayoutManager` that is responsible for positioning and shaping the components contained in the container. When an event occurs that causes a container to lay out its components (such as resizing a window), the container's layout manager is called upon to lay out the components that reside in the container.

Layout Management and the Strategy Pattern

Essentially, then, containers farm out the job of laying out their components to a layout manager. Different layout managers implement different algorithms for laying out components, and containers are free to choose the layout algorithm of their choice by employing the appropriate layout manager. This technique of defining a family of algorithms and encapsulating each one in a class is known as the *strategy pattern*.[2] The delegation-based event handling model provided by the AWT is also an example of the strategy pattern—components delegate their event handling to a listener—see "Delegation-Based Event Model (AWT 1.1 and Beyond)" on page 93.

LayoutManagers

`LayoutManager` is an interface that defines the following methods:

```
void       addLayoutComponent (String name, Component comp);
void       removeLayoutComponent(String name, Component comp);
Dimension  preferredLayoutSize (Container parent);
Dimension  minimumLayoutSize  (Container parent);
void       layoutContainer  (Container parent);
```

Layout managers are responsible for:

- Calculating the preferred and minimum sizes for a container
- Laying out the components contained in a container

It's important to note that while each container has exactly one layout manager, a single layout manager may wind up working for more than container. Therefore, when a layout manager has to perform some work for a container, it must be passed a reference to the container requesting its services. In fact, if you look at `Panel.java`, you will see that a `java.awt.Panel`, by default, shares a single and presumably overworked `FlowLayout`:

```
public class Panel extends Container {
   final static LayoutManager panelLayout = new FlowLayout();
      .
      .
      .
   public Panel() {
      setLayout(panelLayout);
   }
```

Since `panelLayout` is a static member, there is only one `panelLayout` for all instances of `Panel`. When a `Panel` equipped with its default layout manager is laid out, a reference to the `Panel` is passed to the `layoutContainer(Container)` method of the `static panelLayout` instance, which obliges by laying out the components in yet another `Panel`.

2. See Gamma, Helm, Johnson, Vlissides. *Design Patterns*, p. 315. Addison-Wesley, 1994.

Two Types of Layout Managers

All layout managers lay out (position and size) components for one or more containers. However, some layout managers attach information (constraints) to each component that determines how the component is to be laid out. For instance, BorderLayout attaches compass points to its components in order to determine where the component is to be placed within the border—"North", "South", "East", "West", and "Center". Other layout managers do not attach any constraints to individual components, for instance, FlowLayout, which simply lays out components from left to right and top to bottom, as they fit within their container.

The 1.1 version of the AWT adds a new interface for layout managers that associate constraints with their components. The new interface is uninspiringly named LayoutManager2—with such a descriptive name, our discussion to follow is probably not necessary, but we'll press ahead anyhow.

LayoutManager2 extends the LayoutManager interface and adds the following methods:

```
voidaddLayoutComponent(Component c, Object constraints);
DimensionmaximumLayoutSize(Container);
floatgetLayoutAlignmentX (Container);
floatgetLayoutAlignmentY(Container);
voidinvalidateLayout(Container);
```

addLayoutComponent() allows a component to be added to a layout manager with constraints attached. The type of object that composes a constraint is up to the implementor of the LayoutManager2 interface. For instance, the constraint for a GridBagLayout must be a GridBagConstraints reference, whereas a BorderLayout requires the constraint to be a String. See Table 14-1 for a list of the constraints for each layout manager.

maximumLayoutSize() returns the maximum size for a container, given the current constraints of the component. The getLayoutAlignment...() methods are for future use and are not currently used in the AWT.

invalidateLayout() signifies that the layout manager should discard any information it has cached concerning the constraints of its objects.

Table 14-1 lists the layout manager interfaces implemented by the standard AWT layout managers. For layout managers that implement the `LayoutManager2` interface and therefore attach constraints to the components they lay out, the constraints are also listed.

Table 14-1 Interfaces Implemented by Standard AWT Layout Managers.

Layout Manager	Implements	Component Constraints
BorderLayout	LayoutManager2	String specifying compass point.
CardLayout	LayoutManager2	String specifying name.
GridBagLayout	LayoutManager2	GridBagConstraints specifying grid constraints.
FlowLayout	LayoutManager	NONE.
GridLayout	LayoutManager	NONE.

Layout Managers and Container Insets

Every container has a set of *insets* associated with it. Insets specify the container's top, bottom, left, and right inside margins, defined in pixels, as illustrated in Figure 14-3.

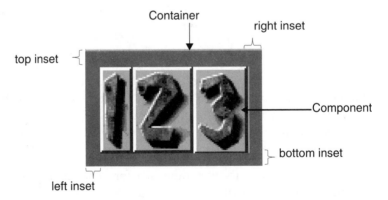

Figure 14-3 Container With Insets

Layout managers are careful not to lay out components inside a container's insets; however, graphics may still be drawn in the insets region.

A container's insets values are important because layout managers are careful not to place components anywhere inside a container's insets[3], although containers themselves can override `paint()` and paint into their insets area if they desire, which is how the border was painted in the container shown in Figure 14-3.

`java.awt.Container` defines the following `getInsets()`[4] method that provides access to a container's insets:

```
Insets Container.getInsets()
```

`Container`, however, does not define a separate method for setting its insets. If you want to set a container's insets, you must extend a class derived from `Container` and overwrite the `getInsets()` method, like so:

```
public Insets getInsets() {
   return new Insets(10,10,10,10);
}
```

Notice that `Container.getInsets()` is a little off-kilter with the rest of the AWT; most parameters of AWT classes have both a get and a set method, meaning you can query and/or change the parameter at runtime without having to extend a class to change a parameter. This is not the case with a container's insets; a container must override `getInsets()` in order to change its insets. This relegates setting a container's insets to a per-class basis instead of a per-object basis.

AWT TIP ....

Frame Insets Are Unique

The insets for a Frame, by default, include the height of the menu bar, if the frame is so equipped. This knowledge comes in handy if you accidentally draw into a frame underneath its menu bar. While layout managers will not place components inside a container's insets, there is nothing to stop you from performing graphical operations inside a containers insets.

Peers and Insets

You might be curious to know what the default insets are for each extension of `java.awt.Container`[5]. Let's track this down by looking at `Insets Container.getInsets()`:

---

3.   We speak only for the standard AWT layout managers. It is up to implementors of custom layout managers to respect the insets of a container.
4.   `getInsets()` replaces the deprecated `getInsets()` for the 1.1 release of the AWT.
5.   See "Components and Peers" on page 157 for a more in-depth look at peers.

```
public Insets getInsets() {
  return getInsets();
}
public Insets getInsets() {
  ContainerPeer peer = (ContainerPeer)this.peer;
  return (peer != null) ? peer.getInsets() : new Insets(0, 0, 0,
0);
}
```

getInsets() returns the insets provided by the deprecated getInsets() method.

If a container does not override getInsets(), then its peer supplies the value. If the container does not yet have a peer, an Insets with zero for all margins is returned. Now, if we look at ContainerPeer.java to find out the value a container's peer returns for insets, we see this:

```
public interface ContainerPeer extends ComponentPeer {
  Insets getInsets();
}
```

Now we've hit a dead end, as is always the case when trying to track down peer behavior, because all peers are defined in terms of interfaces.

The reason we cannot find out a default value for insets is because there isn't one. Each container's peer is given leeway to return whatever insets make sense for the platform on which the peer resides, and therefore there is no cross-platform default for the insets of a Container. The peer approach—using native peer components—retains look-and-feel across platforms, and this is one of the trade-offs with which we must deal as a consequence.

We'll explore in more depth exactly how layout managers deal with a container's insets when we discuss developing custom layout managers later on in this chapter.

Layout Managers and Component Preferred Sizes

Components implement two very important methods that affect their interactions with layout managers:

```
// Component methods
public  Dimension getPreferredSize();
public  Dimension getMinimumSize();
```

As their names suggest, getPreferredSize() returns the preferred size of the component, and getMinimumSize() returns the minimum size a component can tolerate.

Layout managers are tasked with calculating the preferred and minimum sizes for a container by implementing the following methods from the `LayoutManager` interface:

```
// LayoutManager methods
Dimension preferredLayoutSize(Container)
Dimension minimumLayoutSize  (Container)
```

Such methods typically cycle through all of the container's components and fashion preferred and minimum sizes for the container by taking into account each component's preferred and minimum sizes.

Layout managers, of course, are also responsible for laying out their container's components. They do this by implementing the `layoutContainer()` method:

```
void layoutContainer(Container)
```

While some layout managers completely ignore the preferred size of the components they lay out, others are infinitely receptive to each and every component's plea to be shaped according to their preferred size. Still other layout managers will pay attention to only half of a component's preferred size. `BorderLayout`, for instance, will respect a north component's preferred height, but stretches the component to fill its container horizontally, thereby ignoring the component's preferred width. Table 14-2 shows a list of the standard AWT layout managers and their attitudes toward a component's preferred and minimum sizes.

Table 14-2 Layout Managers and Preferred Sizes

Layout Manager	Respects Component's Preferred Size Like This...
`BorderLayout`	North and south components: Respects height, ignores width. East and west components: Respects width, ignores height. Center component: Ignores both preferred width and height.
`FlowLayout`	Respects preferred width and height if component has not been explicitly sized.
`CardLayout`	Ignores preferred width and height.
`GridLayout`	Ignores preferred width and height.
`GridBagLayout`	Varies depending on `GridBagConstraints` for the component. (See *GridBagLayout and GridBagConstraints* on page 404)

Override getPreferredSize() and getMinimumSize() When Extending Canvas

When you create custom components that extend Canvas, always override getPreferredSize() and getMinimumSize(). By default, the preferred size for a Canvas is (0,0). If your Canvas resides in a container whose layout manager honors preferred width and preferred height, you'll never see the Canvas displayed if you neglect to override getPreferredSize(). Failing to override these methods may lead you on a long debugging session in order to figure out why your component is not appearing on the screen.

Painting a Container's Components

Containers do not have to explicitly paint the heavyweight components they contain; a container's components are painted (or drawn, if you will) automatically. Custom components that extend `Container` only need to override their `paint(Graphics)` method if they need to perform graphical operations above and beyond painting the components they contain or if they contain lightweight components.[6]

TenPixelBorder

It's about time that we presented some code that illustrates the concepts we've discussed up to this point. We'll start with the `TenPixelBorder` class, which illustrates many of the topics we have covered so far. `TenPixelBorder` is a simple class, so we'll show you the code in Example 14-1 and then highlight the essentials of how it works.

Example 14-1 `TenPixelBorder` **Class Source Code**

```
import java.awt.*;

public class TenPixelBorder extends Panel {
  public TenPixelBorder(Component borderMe) {
      setLayout(new BorderLayout());
      add(borderMe, "Center");
  }
  public Insets getInsets() {
      return new Insets(10,10,10,10);
  }
  public void paint(Graphics g) {
      Dimension mySize  = getSize();
```

6.   Lightweights are explicitly drawn in `Container.paint()`. See "Remember to Invoke super.paint() When Overriding Container.paint()" on page 480..

```
Insets    myInsets = getInsets();

g.setColor(Color.gray);

// Top Inset area
g.fillRect(0,0,mySize.width,myInsets.top);

// Left Inset area
g.fillRect(0,0,myInsets.left,mySize.height);

// Right Inset area
g.fillRect(mySize.width - myInsets.right,0,
           myInsets.right,mySize.height);

// Bottom Inset area
g.fillRect(0,mySize.height - myInsets.bottom,
           mySize.width,mySize.height);
    }
  }
```

TenPixelBorder extends Panel, thereby inheriting the ability to contain components. An instance of TenPixelBorder must be constructed with a Component (borderMe), which it adds to itself. Notice that TenPixelBorder sets its layout manager to an instance of BorderLayout and adds borderMe as the center component. The result is that borderMe is reshaped to fill the entire space taken up by TenPixelBorder, minus the space taken up by the insets specified by the overridden TenPixelBorder.getInsets() method [7].

Finally, TenPixelBorder overrides paint() and fills the insets area with a gray color. Remember that the components contained by TenPixelBorder, namely, borderMe, will be painted automatically, so the overridden TenPixelBorder.paint(Graphics) is only concerned with painting the border. Additionally, while the BorderLayout layout manager will ensure that borderMe does not encroach upon the area specified by TenPixelBorder.getInsets(), TenPixelBorder (like any container) is free to draw into its insets area. Figure 14-4 shows a simple applet that exercises an instance of TenPixelBorder.

---

7. Center components fill the available space that is not occupied by the north, south, east, and west components laid out by a BorderLayout. Since borderMe is the only component within TenPixelBorder, it fills the entire area of the panel minus insets.

Figure 14-4 `TenPixelBorderTestApplet` in Action
Components do not encroach on a container's insets; however,
the insets can still be drawn into. The panel in the applet shown
above has insets of 10 pixels all around.

Example 14-2 lists the `TenPixelBorderTestApplet`.

Example 14-2 `TenPixelBorderTestApplet` **Class Source Code**

```
import java.applet.Applet;
import java.awt.*;
import gjt.ImageButton;

public class TenPixelBorderTestApplet extends Applet {
  public void init() {
      Image image = getImage(getCodeBase(),"gifs/center.gif");

      ImageButton     button = new ImageButton    (image);
      TenPixelBorder border = new TenPixelBorder(button);

      setLayout(new BorderLayout());
      add(border, "Center");
  }
}
```

The `TenPixelBorderTestApplet` passes a `gjt.ImageButton` to the
`TenPixelBorder` constructor. Although we have not yet discussed GJT image
buttons, they significantly spruce up our examples throughout this chapter, and

their use is simple enough to be easily understood. For now, it is enough to know that a `gjt.ImageButton` is a custom component that can be added to a `Container`, just like any other component.

Also, note that `TenPixelBorderTestApplet` centers an instance of `TenPixelBorder`. Since the applet itself has not defined any insets, the instance of `TenPixelBorder` fills all the available space in the applet.

Forcing a Container to Lay Out Its Components

It is not uncommon for situations to arise where it is necessary to force a container to lay out its components. Since the recipe for programmatically forcing a layout is not readily apparent, we'll take some time to explore the issue here.

Figure 14-5 shows an applet containing a panel with a textfield and two buttons for adjusting the textfield's font size—the applet itself is listed in Example 14-3.

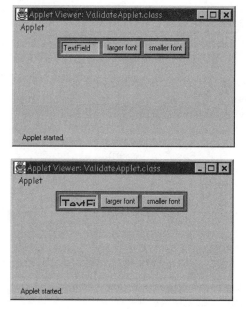

Figure 14-5 `ValidateApplet`
The buttons adjust the size of the textfield's font. After the font size is adjusted, the applet needs to be laid out in order for the textfield and its container to resize to accommodate the new font size.

Example 14-3 `ValidateApplet` **Class Source Code**

```java
import java.applet.Applet;
import java.awt.*;
import java.awt.event.*;

public class ValidateApplet extends Applet {
  private GrayPanel grayPanel = new GrayPanel();
  public void init() {
     add(grayPanel);
  }
}
class GrayPanel extends Panel implements ActionListener {
  private TextField  field    = new TextField("TextField");
  private Button     lgButton = new Button    ("larger font");
  private Button     smButton = new Button    ("smaller font");

  public GrayPanel() {
     lgButton.addActionListener(this);
     smButton.addActionListener(this);

     add(field);
     add(lgButton);
     add(smButton);

     setBackground(Color.gray);
  }
  public void actionPerformed(ActionEvent event) {
     Button button  = (Button)event.getSource();
     Font   curFont = field.getFont();
     int    newSize = curFont.getSize();

     if(button == lgButton) newSize += 3;
     if(button == smButton) newSize -= 3;
     field.setFont(new Font(curFont.getFamily(),
                          curFont.getStyle(), newSize));
  }
  public void paint(Graphics g) {
     g.setColor(Color.black);
     g.drawRect(0,0,getSize().width-1,getSize().height-1);
  }
}
```

The applet contains an instance of `GrayPanel`—a panel with a gray background containing the textfield and buttons.

Changing the font size results in an immediate update in the textfield's font, but the textfield and its container do not grow or shrink to accommodate the text displayed in the textfield. In order for the textfield and its container to resize to accommodate the textfield's new font size, the applet needs to lay out its components. In other words, when the textfield's font is modified, we'd like to force a layout of the applet.

All components, at any given time are either *valid* or *invalid*. Invalid components need to be laid out, while valid components do not. Calling `validate()` on a container that is invalid (and whose peer has been created) results in a call to the container's `layout()` method. So our job is relatively easy—after setting the size of the field's font, we invalidate the field, and then invoke `validate()` on the parent (container) of the `GrayPanel`, which happens to be the applet.

```
public void actionPerformed(ActionEvent event) {
  Button button  = (Button)event.getSource();
  Font   curFont = field.getFont();
  int    newSize = curFont.getSize();

  if(button == lgButton) newSize += 3;
  if(button == smButton) newSize -= 3;

  field.setFont(new Font(curFont.getFamily(),
                      curFont.getStyle(), newSize));
  field.invalidate();
  getParent().validate();
}
```

However, realize that we never explicitly invalidated the applet itself, although we did explicitly validate it[8]. Remember that a call to `validate()` for a container will only result in a call to `layout()` if the container itself is invalid (and the container has a peer). How then, did the applet get invalidated?

Invalidating an AWT component invalidates not only the component itself, but also the container in which it resides. Note that since a container is also a component it behaves in exactly the same manner[9]—invalidating itself and then invalidating its container. Thus, an `invalidate()` call on a component can actually walk up the container hierarchy and invalidate all of the containers in its container hierarchy[10]. As a result, the call to `field.invalidate()` invalidated

---

8. We could have called `invalidate()` on the applet instead of the textfield, but that would have eliminated our segue into propagation of invalidation for a component.
9. `java.awt.Container` does not override `invalidate()`.

not only the field, but the `GrayPanel` and the applet itself. Subsequently calling validate on the applet forces the applet to be laid out, which results in the `GrayPanel` and textfield being resized to accommodate the new font size.

Invalidation of a component occurs naturally as a side effect to a number of `java.awt.Component` and `java.awt.Container` methods, as you can see from Table 14-3. Since a call to `Component.setFont()` does not invalidate the component, we are left to manually invalidate the textfield by calling `invalidate()` directly. If we had also invoked one of the methods listed in Table 14-3 in addition to setting the font, the call to `invalidate()` would not have been required.

Table 14-3 `Component` and `Container` **Methods That Invalidate the Component.**

Method
`void Component.addNotify()`
`void Component.show()`
`void Component.hide()`
`void Component.setSize(int width,int height)`
`void Component.setBounds(int x,int y,int width,int height)`
`void Component.setLayout(LayoutManager)`
`void Container.add(Component)`
`void Container.remove(Component)`
`void Container.removeAll()`

Another fairly common task is to resize a window or dialog when its components change size. Example 14-4 introduces two new classes to our `ValidateApplet` (which is now `ValidateApplet2`): `ValidateDialog`, which contains an instance of `GrayPanel` and `LaunchPanel`, an extension of `GrayPanel` that adds a button for launching a `ValidateDialog`.

10. We say *can* because an extension of container could override its `invalidate()` method to behave differently.

Example 14-4 `ValidateApplet` **Class Source Code**

```java
import java.applet.Applet;
import java.awt.*;
import java.awt.event.*;

public class ValidateApplet2 extends Applet {
  private LaunchPanel launchPanel = new LaunchPanel();
  public void init() {
    add(launchPanel);
  }
}
class GrayPanel extends Panel implements ActionListener {
  private TextField  field    = new TextField("TextField");
  private Button      lgButton = new Button  ("larger font");
  private Button      smButton = new Button  ("smaller font");

  public GrayPanel() {
    lgButton.addActionListener(this);
    smButton.addActionListener(this);

    add(field);
    add(lgButton);
    add(smButton);

    setBackground(Color.gray);
  }
  public void paint(Graphics g) {
    g.setColor(Color.black);
    g.drawRect(0,0,getSize().width-1,getSize().height-1);
  }
  public void actionPerformed(ActionEvent event) {
    Button button  = (Button)event.getSource();
    Font    curFont = field.getFont();
    int     newSize = curFont.getSize();

    if(event.target == lgButton) newSize += 3;
    if(event.target == smButton) newSize -= 3;

    field.setFont(new Font(curFont.getFamily(),
                      curFont.getStyle(),
                      newSize));
    field.invalidate();
    getParent().validate();
  }
}
class LaunchPanel extends GrayPanel implements ActionListener {
  private Button launchButton = new Button("launch ...");
```

```
        private ValidateDialog validateDialog;

        public LaunchPanel() {
           add(launchButton);
           launchButton.addActionListener(this);
        }
        public void actionPerformed(ActionEvent event) {
           if(validateDialog == null) {
              validateDialog =
                 new ValidateDialog(gjt.Util.getFrame(this),
                                "Validate Dialog",
                                true);
           }
           validateDialog.show();
        }
    }
    class ValidateDialog extends Dialog {
      public ValidateDialog(Frame frame, String title,
                              boolean modal) {
        super(frame, title, true);
        add("Center", new GrayPanel());
        pack();

        addWindowListener(new WindowAdapter() {
           public void windowClosing(WindowEvent event) {
              dispose();
           }
        });
      }
      public void validate() {
        super.validate();
        setSize(getPreferredSize().width,
                getPreferredSize().height);
      }
    }
```

Since `GrayPanel` calls `validate()` on its container, which is now a
`ValidateDialog`, we override the dialog's `validate()` method, where we
resize the dialog to accommodate the preferred size of the dialog's `GrayPanel`.
Figure 14-6 shows the dialog before and after the font size of the textfield has been
changed.

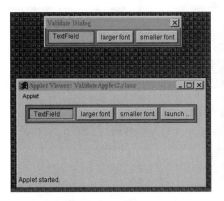 

Figure 14-6 `ValidateApplet2`
The dialog resizes when the font in its textfield is modified.

AWT TIP ...

Forcing a Container to Lay Out Its Components

Invoking Container.validate() forces the container to lay out its components.
However, the layout will only occur if the container is invalid. Containers are
invalidated implicitly by the methods listed in "`Component` and `Container`
Methods That Invalidate the Component." on page 388. If none of the methods
listed in Table 14-3 has been invoked for one of the container's components,
then invalidate() must be called directly for the container before invoking vali-
date().

Standard AWT Layout Managers

The AWT comes with five standard layout managers, as shown in Table 14-4.

Table 14-4 The AWT's Default Layout Manager Classes

Layout Manager	Description
BorderLayout	Lays out components around the sides and in the center of the container in north, east, west, south, and center positions. Gaps between components can be specified. BorderLayout is the default layout manager for Window, Dialog and Frame containers.
CardLayout	Displays one component at a time from a *deck* of components. Components can be swapped in and out.
FlowLayout	Displays components left to right, top to bottom. FlowLayout is the default layout manager for panels and applets.
GridBagLayout	Arranges components in a grid, using an elaborate set of grid constraints.
GridLayout	Lays out components in a grid, with each component stretched to fill its grid cell. Horizontal and vertical gaps between components can be specified.

The designers of the AWT hit a home run with the implementation of layout management and event handling by employing the strategy pattern for each[11]. Containers are not responsible for laying out their own components; they delegate that responsibility to a layout manager. By encapsulating the algorithm for laying out components in a separate class, the layout functionality is available for others to use (and extend), while containers may be fitted with different layout managers at runtime. The same benefits apply for the delegation-based event model. The AWT designers also did a decent job of providing a set of default layout managers, which are sufficient to handle probably 90 percent of all your layout needs.

The five layout managers in Table 14-4 provide a range of capabilities, from BorderLayout, a simple layout manager that is useful in an infinite variety of layouts, to the behemoth GridBagLayout, a very complex layout manager that can lay out nearly anything you can imagine.

---

11. See "Layout Management and the Strategy Pattern" on page 375.

The AWT classes that extend `Container` each have a default layout manager. `BorderLayout` is by far the AWT's most frequently used layout manager. As Table 14-5 shows, it is the default layout manager for most of the AWT containers. Note that `java.awt.Container` has a `null` layout manager.

Table 14-5 `Container` **Default Layout Managers**

Container Class	Default Layout Manager
Container	null
Panel	FlowLayout
Window	BorderLayout
Dialog	BorderLayout
Frame	BorderLayout

Which Layout Manager to Use?

Programmers new to the AWT may be confused about which of the AWT's standard layout managers to employ in a given situation. In fact, that's largely the result of practice, trial, and error. However, Table 14-6 presents some high-level guidelines that you might find useful.

Table 14-6 Layout Manager Decision Table

Layout Manager	Use When...	An Example Is...
BorderLayout	A container divides its components into regions: north and south, or east and west. A single component needs to fill the entire area of the container it resides in.	gjt.UnitTest, TenPixelBorder.
CardLayout	You want to control the visibility of sets of components under different circumstances.	A set of panels that presents itself as a stack of tabbed folders.
FlowLayout	A container's components fill the container from left to right, top to bottom.	A container that places components one immediately following another.

Table 14-6 Layout Manager Decision Table (Continued)

Layout Manager	Use When...	An Example Is...
GridLayout	A container divides its components into a grid.	A calendar or spreadsheet.
GridBagLayout	A container has complicated layout needs.	Input forms, such as a container that has components for name, address, zip code, etc.

The BorderLayout Layout Manager

Once you've worked on a few nested layouts, you'll come to appreciate the neat ability of BorderLayout to lay out components into regions. Nearly every nested layout has a BorderLayout lurking somewhere inside.

BorderLayout, like CardLayout and GridBagLayout, implements the LayoutManager2 interface, meaning it attaches constraints to the components it lays out. The constraints for a component laid out by an instance of BorderLayout are strings, which are passed to the container's add(Container, Object) method. The object (string) specifies the location of the component—either "North", "South", "East", "West" or "Center".

Figure 14-7 shows an applet that uses an instance of BorderLayout.

Example 14-5 shows the implementation of the BorderLayoutApplet class. BorderLayoutApplet is very similar to TenPixelBorderTestApplet, except that it adds five image buttons, one for each of the compass points and center.

BorderLayout stretches the north and south components horizontally so that the components span the entire width of the container in which they reside, while sizing them vertically according to their preferred height. The east and west components are stretched vertically so that they span the entire height of the container in which they reside minus the combined heights of the north and south components; they are sized horizontally according to their preferred width. The Center component gets whatever space is left over, regardless of its preferred size.

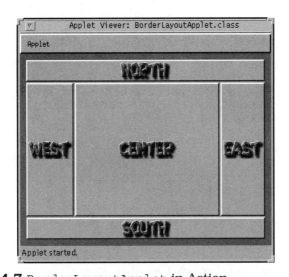

Figure 14-7 `BorderLayoutApplet` in Action
`BorderLayout` lays out at most five components. North and
south components span the width of the container, and east and
west components span the height of the container minus the
combined heights of the north and south components. The center
component gets whatever real estate is left over. Component
position is specified by the string (Object) passed to
`Container.addComponent(Component, Object)`.

Example 14-5 `BorderLayoutApplet` **Class Source Code**

```
import java.net.URL;
import java.applet.Applet;
import java.awt.*;
import gjt.ImageButton;

public class BorderLayoutApplet extends Applet {
  private ImageButton north, south, east, west, center;

  public void init() {
      URL cb = getCodeBase();
      Panel buttonPanel = new Panel();
      TenPixelBorder border = new TenPixelBorder(buttonPanel);
```

```
north  = new ImageButton(getImage(cb,"gifs/north.gif"));
east   = new ImageButton(getImage(cb,"gifs/east.gif"));
west   = new ImageButton(getImage(cb,"gifs/west.gif"));
center = new ImageButton(getImage(cb,"gifs/center.gif"));
south  = new ImageButton(getImage(cb,"gifs/south.gif"));

buttonPanel.setLayout(new BorderLayout(2,2));
buttonPanel.add(north,  "North");
buttonPanel.add(south,  "South");
buttonPanel.add(east,   "East");
buttonPanel.add(west,   "West");
buttonPanel.add(center, "Center");

setLayout(new BorderLayout());
add(border, "Center");
   }
}
```

Notice that we've specified horizontal and vertical gaps between components of 2 pixels each when we created the BorderLayout instance. BorderLayout also provides set/get methods for specifying and obtaining the horizontal and vertical gaps.

The CardLayout Layout Manager

CardLayout keeps track of a deck, if you will, of components. From this deck, it can display or *deal* any one container at a time. Although it is nowhere near as versatile as the other AWT layout managers, it is nonetheless quite useful for components such as a tabbed panel. CardLayout implements the LayoutManager2 interface; component constraints are strings representing a name for the component.

Figure 14-8 shows an applet that uses a CardLayout to display four components in succession.

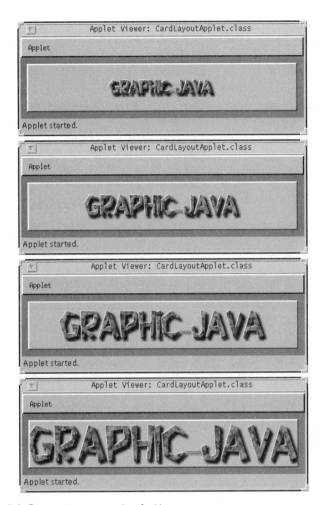

Figure 14-8 CardLayout in Action
The applet above employs a CardLayoutApplet to cycle through
four panels. Each panel displays a different image.

Table 14-7 lists the methods implemented by CardLayout (in addition to those
defined in LayoutManager and LayoutManager2) that allow clients to control
which component is currently displayed. Notice that the show() method takes a
string specifying the name of the component to be displayed. The show()
method is the rationale behind CardLayout implementing LayoutManager2,
thus requiring constraints to be placed upon the components it lays out; the
constraints are names of the components.

Table 14-7 `CardLayout` **Stacking Methods**

Method	Description
`void first(Container)`	Displays the first component added to the container.
`void last(Container)`	Displays the last component added to the container.
`void next(Container)`	Displays the component added to the container after the currently displayed component. If the current component is the last, then the first component is displayed.
`void previous(Container)`	Displays the component added to the container before the currently displayed component. If the current component is the first, then the last component is displayed.
`void show(Container, String)`	Shows the component whose name matches the string passed in. If no components match the name, the method does nothing.

Example 14-6 lists the `CardLayoutApplet` code. Notice as you look through the code that `CardLayout` is unique among layout managers in that it has methods you can call directly to control which component is displayed. In the overridden `mouseUp()` method, we invoke one of those methods: `CardLayout.next(Component)`.

Example 14-6 `CardLayoutApplet` **Class Source Code**

```
import java.applet.Applet;
import java.net.URL;
import java.awt.*;
import java.awt.event.*;
import gjt.ImageButton;

public class CardLayoutApplet extends Applet {
  private ImageButton tiny, small, med, lrg;
  private Panel cardPanel = new Panel(),
                tinyPanel = new Panel(),
                smallPanel = new Panel(),
                MediumPanel = new Panel(),
                LargePanel = new Panel();
  private CardLayout  card = new CardLayout();

  public void init() {
    TenPixelBorder border   = new TenPixelBorder(cardPanel);
    URL             cb = getCodeBase();
```

```
      ButtonListener buttonListener = new ButtonListener();

      cardPanel.setLayout(card);

      tinyPanel.setLayout  (new BorderLayout());
      smallPanel.setLayout (new BorderLayout());
      MediumPanel.setLayout(new BorderLayout());
      LargePanel.setLayout (new BorderLayout());

      tiny  = new ImageButton(getImage(cb,"gifs/gjTiny.gif"));
      small = new ImageButton(getImage(cb,"gifs/gjSmall.gif"));
      med   = new ImageButton(getImage(cb,"gifs/gjMedium.gif"));
      lrg   = new ImageButton(getImage(cb,"gifs/gjLarge.gif"));

      tiny.addActionListener(buttonListener);
      small.addActionListener(buttonListener);
      med.addActionListener(buttonListener);
      lrg.addActionListener(buttonListener);

      tinyPanel.add  (tiny, "Center");
      smallPanel.add (small,"Center");
      MediumPanel.add(med,  "Center");
      LargePanel.add (lrg,  "Center");

      cardPanel.add("tiny",  tinyPanel);
      cardPanel.add("small", smallPanel);
      cardPanel.add("med",   MediumPanel);
      cardPanel.add("lrg",   LargePanel);

      setLayout(new BorderLayout());
      add(border, "Center");
   }
   class ButtonListener implements ActionListener {
      public void actionPerformed(ActionEvent event) {
         card.next(cardPanel);
      }
   }
}
```

The FlowLayout Layout Manager

FlowLayout simply shoves in components, left to right, top to bottom. Like BorderLayout, it is a basic layout that is handy in a variety of layout situations. Unlike BorderLayout, FlowLayout does not implement the LayoutManager2 interface and does not require constraints to be placed upon components it lays out.

Figure 14-9 shows how `FlowLayout` positions components when a window has been resized.

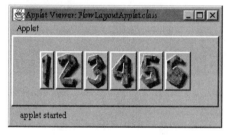

Figure 14-9 `FlowLayout` in Action
FlowLayout lays out components from left to right, top to bottom.

Example 14-7 shows the `FlowLayoutApplet` code.

Example 14-7 `FlowLayoutApplet` **Class Source Code**

```
import java.net.URL;
import java.applet.Applet;
import java.awt.*;
import gjt.ImageButton;

public class FlowLayoutApplet extends Applet {
    private ImageButton one, two, three, four, five, six;

    public void init() {
        URL            cb = getCodeBase();
        Panel          panel = new Panel();
        TenPixelBorder border = new TenPixelBorder(panel);
```

```
one     = new ImageButton(getImage(cb, "gifs/one.gif"));
two     = new ImageButton(getImage(cb, "gifs/two.gif"));
three   = new ImageButton(getImage(cb, "gifs/three.gif"));
four    = new ImageButton(getImage(cb, "gifs/four.gif"));
five    = new ImageButton(getImage(cb, "gifs/five.gif"));
six     = new ImageButton(getImage(cb, "gifs/six.gif"));

panel.setLayout(new FlowLayout());
panel.add(one);
panel.add(five);
panel.add(two);
panel.add(three);
panel.add(four);
panel.add(five);
panel.add(six);

setLayout(new BorderLayout());
add(border, "Center");
    }
}
```

FlowLayout is handy when you have a fixed-size component and you wish to lay out components in either a row or a column.

FlowLayout is also the only AWT layout manager that sizes components according to their preferred widths and heights. See "Layout Managers and Component Preferred Sizes" on page 380.

The GridLayout Layout Manager

GridLayout, as you might guess, lays out components in a grid; clients can set the gap between components and the number of rows and columns either at construction time or after the GridLayout is constructed[12]. GridLayout is obviously useful when you want to lay out components in applets such as spreadsheets or calendars. Figure 14-10 shows output from an applet with ImageButton components positioned by GridLayout.

12. Setting rows/columns/gaps after construction is a new feature in the 1.1 AWT.

Figure 14-10 GridLayout in Action

GridLayout lays out components in a grid, where every grid cell contains one component. The grid cells are all the same size.

Example 14-8 shows the GridLayoutApplet code. Notice that the applet explicitly sets the number of rows and columns in the call to the GridLayout constructor. The applet also sets the horizontal and vertical gaps between the components (image buttons) to ten pixels.

Example 14-8 GridLayoutApplet **Class Source Code**

```
import java.net.URL;
import java.applet.Applet;
import java.awt.*;
import gjt.ImageButton;
import gjt.StickyImageButtonController;

public class GridLayoutApplet extends Applet {
  private ImageButton one, two, three, four, five, six,
                      seven, eight, nine, ten;

  public void init() {
    URL             cb = getCodeBase();
    Panel           buttonPanel = new Panel();
    TenPixelBorder  border = new TenPixelBorder(buttonPanel);

    one   = new ImageButton(getImage(cb, "gifs/one.gif"));
    two   = new ImageButton(getImage(cb, "gifs/two.gif"));
    three = new ImageButton(getImage(cb, "gifs/three.gif"));
    four  = new ImageButton(getImage(cb, "gifs/four.gif"));
    five  = new ImageButton(getImage(cb, "gifs/five.gif"));
```

```
six   = new ImageButton(getImage(cb, "gifs/six.gif"));
seven = new ImageButton(getImage(cb, "gifs/seven.gif"));
eight = new ImageButton(getImage(cb, "gifs/eight.gif"));
nine  = new ImageButton(getImage(cb, "gifs/nine.gif"));
ten   = new ImageButton(getImage(cb, "gifs/ten.gif"));

buttonPanel.setLayout(new GridLayout(3,2,10,10));
buttonPanel.add(one);
buttonPanel.add(two);
buttonPanel.add(three);
buttonPanel.add(four);
buttonPanel.add(five);
buttonPanel.add(six);
buttonPanel.add(seven);
buttonPanel.add(eight);
buttonPanel.add(nine);
buttonPanel.add(ten);

setLayout(new BorderLayout());
add(border, "Center");
  }
}
```

Components laid out by a `GridLayout` completely fill the grid cell they occupy. Additionally, you cannot control any constraints concerning grid cell properties for a component. For instance, you cannot specify how many grid cells a component occupies because each component always occupies exactly one grid cell. `GridBagLayout`, on the other hand, allows grid cell constraints to be attached to each component that specify how much of the grid cell the component occupies, and how many grid cells the component spans, in addition to a number of other constraints.

The GridBagLayout Layout Manager

Like `GridLayout`, `GridBagLayout` positions components in a grid. Unlike `GridLayout`, in which you explicitly specify the number of rows and columns in the grid, `GridBagLayout` determines the number of rows and columns from constraints placed upon the components it lays out. Also, unlike `GridLayout`, `GridBagLayout` allows components to span more than one grid cell— components may also overlap, as we shall soon discover.

`GridBagLayout` is capable of handling nearly any layout situation; however, it is one of the most complex and difficult classes in the AWT to use. Developers are often put off by its complexity, but it's an extremely useful layout manager. For that reason, we will apply a three-pronged approach to covering `GridBagLayout`.

First, we'll discuss the GridBagConstraints that are associated with components laid out by GridBagLayout, which is typically the most confusing aspect of the most maligned of layout managers.

Second, we've provided an applet on the CD that allows you to modify the GridBagConstraints associated with a grid of image buttons; we believe you will find the applet indispensable in furthering your understanding of how GridBagLayout works.

Third, we've included a section that covers laying out user input forms, which is a common task for GridBagLayout. We also use GridBagLayout in a number of Graphic Java Toolkit components, which are covered in the second part of the book; in addition to our coverage here, the real world examples from the GJT should serve to further illustrate how to make good use of GridBagLayout.

GridBagLayout and GridBagConstraints

GridBagLayout extends the LayoutManager2 interface and therefore attaches constraints to every component it lays out (see "Two Types of Layout Managers" on page 377). The constraints associated with a component are specified by a GridBagConstraints object. GridBagLayout supplies a setConstraints() method for setting the constraints of a component, which is used as follows:

```
// In a method of a hypothetical java.awt.Container extension
...
GridBagLayout gbl = new GridBagLayout();
GridBagConstraints gbc = new GridBagConstraints();
...
setLayout(gbl);
...
// set variables contained in gbc, for example:
// gbc.anchor = GridBagConstraints.NORTH;
...
gbl.setConstraints(component, gbc);
add(component);
...
// modify variables contained in gbc, for example:
// gbc.anchor = GridBagConstraints.WEST;
...
gbl.setConstraints(anotherComponent, gbc);
add(anotherComponent);
...
```

Before a component can be added to a container equipped with a GridBagLayout, the component in question must first have a set of constraints associated with it, which is where GridBagLayout.setConstraints() enters the picture.

As you can see from the pseudocode above, instances of GridBagLayout and GridBagConstraints are instantiated, and the container's layout manager is set to the instance of GridBagLayout. Constraints for each component are specified by setting variables in the GridBagConstraints instance, and subsequently invoking GridBagLayout setConstraints(), which is passed a Component and a reference to the GridBagConstraints object. The GridBagLayout.setConstraints() method copies the constraints it is passed, so the same instance of GridBagConstraints can be used for multiple components.

GridBagLayout is unique among the AWT layout managers because it is the only layout manager to attach constraints that are not strings to a component. BorderLayout and CardLayout, both of which also attach constraints to components[13], use strings to specify component positions and component names, respectively.

The GridBagConstraints class provides a variety of instance variables and constants that control parameters associated with a component. Components laid out by a GridBagLayout can span multiple grid cells, can fill their grid cells wholly or partially, and the grid cells themselves can consume a certain percentage of extra space over and above the preferred size of the component they contain.

Table 14-8 lists the variables and constants provided by the GridBagConstraints class.

---

13. See "Interfaces Implemented by Standard AWT Layout Managers." on page 378.

Table 14-8 `GridBagConstraints` **Instance Variables and Valid Values**

Instance Variable	Default Value	Valid Values	Specifies...
`anchor`	CENTER	CENTER EAST NORTH NORTHEAST NORTHWEST SOUTH SOUTHEAST SOUTHWEST WEST	Where to anchor a component within its grid cells.
`fill`	NONE	BOTH HORIZONTAL VERTICAL NONE	The manner in which the component fills the grid cells it occupies.
`gridx` `gridy`	RELATIVE	RELATIVE or integer values representing an x,y position in the grid.	The position of the component's upper left-hand grid cell.
`gridwidth` `gridheight`	1 1	RELATIVE REMAINDER or integer values representing the width and height in grid cells.	The number of grid cells in both horizontal and vertical directions allotted for the component. Whether or not a component fills its grid cells depends upon the `fill` attribute.
`ipadx` `ipady`	0 0	Integer values representing number of pixels.	Internal padding that increases the component's preferred size. Negative values are allowed, which reduces the component's preferred size.

Table 14-8 `GridBagConstraints` **Instance Variables and Valid Values (Continued)**

Instance Variable	Default Value	Valid Values	Specifies...
`insets`	(0,0,0,0)	An `Insets` object.	External padding between the edges of the component and edges of its grid cells. Negative values are allowed, which cause the component to extend outside of its grid cells.
`weightx` `weighty`	0.0 0.0	`double` values representing weighting given to a component's grid cells relative to other components in the same row or column.	How extra space is consumed by the component's grid cells. Whether or not a component fills its grid cells depends upon the `fill` attribute. Values must be positive.

The mechanics of fitting a container with an instance of `GridBagLayout` and setting constraints for the components in the container is straightforward, as we've already discovered. The difficulty associated with using `GridBagLayout` comes from understanding exactly what each of the constraints listed in Table 14-8 means, and how they interact.

Grid Cells and Display Area

Since a component may be allotted more than one grid cell in both the horizontal and vertical directions (by specifying `gridwidth` and `gridheight` constraints), we'll refer to the combined area of a component's grid cells as its *display area*. When we reference a component's grid cell, we'll be referring to the grid cell defined by the `gridx` and `gridy` constraints, which is the component's upper left hand grid cell.

Display Area vs. Component

One of the biggest obstacles to becoming proficient at using `GridBagLayout` is understanding the distinction between a component's display area and the component itself. Some of the constraints associated with a component apply to the component's display area, other constraints apply to the component itself, and yet other constraints apply to both. Table 14-9 lists the `GridBagConstraints` variables and whether they apply to the component, the component's display area, or both.

Table 14-9 GridBagConstraints **and Components**

Constraint	Applies to
anchor	Component.
fill	Component.
gridx, gridy	Component.
gridwidth, gridheight	Display area, but may affect component size depending upon fill constraint.
weightx, weighty	Display area, but may affect component size depending upon fill constraint.
insets	Both
ipadx, ipady	Both

The anchor constraint specifies the anchor position of a component within its display area. The fill constraint specifies the manner in which a component expands to fill its display area. The anchor and fill constraints have no effect on the component's display area—no matter how you specify the two constraints, the size of component's display area is unaffected.

The gridx and gridy constraints determine the upper left-hand grid cell for the component's display area and does not affect the size of the display area itself.

On the other hand, gridwidth and gridheight specify the size of the component's display area (how many grid cells the component is allotted in the horizontal and vertical directions, respectively). The weightx and weighty constraints specify how much extra space over and above the component's preferred size is occupied by the component's display area. Both the weights and size constraints apply only to the component's display area; however, the size of the component itself may also be affected depending upon the fill constraint associated with the component.

The insets constraint defines *external* padding between the edges of the component and the edges of component's display area. Setting the insets to a non-zero value can affect both the size of the component and the size of the component's display area.

The *internal* padding (specified by the ipadx and ipady) modifies the component's preferred size, and may also modify the size of the component's display area, when the display area is equal to the preferred size of the component.

AWT TIP ...

Components and Their Display Areas

Components laid out by a GridBagLayout are displayed in a grid of cells, collectively referred to as their display area. Some grid bag constraints placed upon components apply to the component itself, while others apply to the component's display area. Understanding this distinction is key to mastering the use of GridBagLayout.

Now let's take a look at each of the constraints used by GridBagLayout to lay out its components.

GridBagConstraints.anchor

The `GridBagConstraints.anchor` variable specifies where a component is anchored in its display area.

It's important to note that setting the `anchor` constraint may seemingly have no effect if the component's `fill` constraint is set to anything other than `GridBagConstraints.NONE`, due to the fact that the component will expand to fill a portion of its display area.

Although it is probably evident from the constants themselves, Table 14-10 lists the positions associated with the `GridBagConstraints.anchor` variables.

Table 14-10 `GridBagConstraints` **Anchor Points**

Anchor Point	Results in the Component Being Positioned at ...
NORTHWEST	Upper left-hand corner of the display area.
NORTH	Top of the display area–centered horizontally.
NORTHEAST	Upper right-hand corner of the display area.
EAST	Right side of the display area–centered vertically.
CENTER	Center, both horizontal and vertical, of the display area.
WEST	Left side of the display area–centered vertically.
SOUTHWEST	Lower left-hand corner of the display area.
SOUTH	Bottom of the display are–centered horizontally.
SOUTHEAST	Lower right-hand corner of the display area.

Figure 14-11 shows an image button laid out by a `GridBagLayout` at various anchor points within its display area.

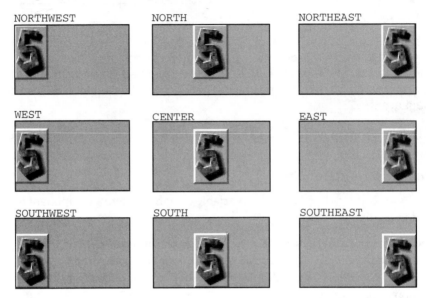

Figure 14-11 `GridBagConstraints` Anchors
The `anchor` constraint determines the position at which a component is anchored in its display area.

Realize that the `anchor` constraint does not necessarily equate to a compass point in a *single* grid cell because the anchor position is relative to the component's display area, not its (upper left) grid cell.

In Figure 14-12, image button #2 has a display area that is 2 grid cells wide, 2 grid cells high, and an `anchor` constraint of CENTER. As a result, the image button is centered in its display area, which causes it to overlap image buttons #5 and #6.

Although the anchor constraint is relative to a component's display area, it does not affect the display area itself—only the placement of the component within the display area is affected.

Figure 14-12 Anchor Constraint Is Relative to Display Area
Image button #2 has a display area 2 grid cells wide and 2 grid
cells high, and is anchored in the center of its display area.

GridBagConstraints.fill

The `fill` constraint specifies how much of a component's display area is filled by
the component.

Table 14-11 lists valid constants for the `GridBagConstraints.fill` variable,
along with the meaning associated with each constant. Note that setting the `fill`
constraint to `GridBagConstraints.NONE` will cause the component to be sized
according to its preferred width and height.

Table 14-11 `GridBagConstraints` **Fill Constants**

When `fill` Constant is ...	The Component ...
NONE	is sized according to its preferred size.
HORIZONTAL	fills its display area horizontally—height is preferred height.
VERTICAL	fills its display area vertically—width is preferred width.
BOTH	fills its display area both horizontally and vertically.

Figure 14-13 shows ten image buttons, all of which have their `fill` constraint set
to `GridBagConstraints.BOTH`, except for image buttons #1 and #7.

Image button #1 has a display area 1 grid cell wide, 2 grid cells high, a fill constraint of VERTICAL, and an anchor constraint of CENTER. The image button's width is sized to its preferred width.

Image button #7 has a display area 3 grid cells wide, 1 grid cell high, a fill constraint of HORIZONTAL, and an anchor of CENTER. The image button's height is its preferred height.

Image button #10 has a display area 2 grid cells wide and 1 grid cell high, a fill constraint of NONE, and an anchor of CENTER.

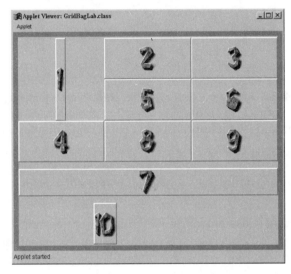

Figure 14-13 GridBagConstraints Fill
The GridBagConstraints.fill variable determines how much of its display area a component fills.

GridBagConstraints.gridx and GridBagConstraints.gridy

The gridx and gridy constraints specify the upper left-hand grid cell of a component's display area. Grid locations are zero-based, and therefore a grid cell in the upper left-hand corner of a container always has a (gridx,gridy) of (0,0).

In addition to specifying a numerical grid position, both gridx and gridy may be assigned GridBagConstraints.RELATIVE. A RELATIVE setting for gridx means that the component will be placed to the right of the last component added to the container. A RELATIVE setting for gridy means that the component will be placed in the row below the last component added to the container.

Table 14-12 enumerates the difference between specifying numerical values for `gridx` and `gridy` versus specifying `GridBagConstraints.REMAINDER`.

Table 14-12 `GridBagConstraints` `gridx` **and** `gridy`

gridx/gridy Values	Description
`Integer`	Specifies the position of a component's upper left-hand grid cell in its display area.
`RELATIVE`	`gridx`: component is placed to the right of the last component added to container.
	`gridy`: component is placed in the row below the last component added to the container.

The applet shown in Figure 14-14 contains ten image buttons laid out by an instance of `GridBagLayout`. Image button #1, of course, has a grid position of (0,0), while the grid position for image button #10, for instance, is (0,3).

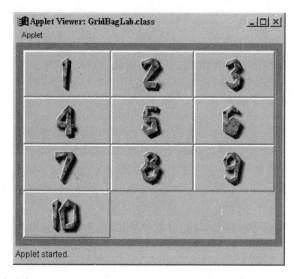

Figure 14-14 `GridBagConstraints` `gridx` and `gridy` Grid locations are zero-based—image button #1 has a (gridx,gridy) of (0,0); image button #8, for instance, is at position (1,2).

When the image buttons in Figure 14-14 were added to their container, they were added in numerical order, starting with image button #1 and ending with image button #10. As a result, the `gridx` constraint for image buttons 2, 3, 5, 6, 8 and 9 could have been specified as `GridBagConstraints.RELATIVE`, which would place them to the right of image buttons 1, 2, 4, 5, 7, and 8, respectively. Likewise, the `gridy` constraint for image buttons 4, 7, and 10 could have been specified as `GridBagConstraints.RELATIVE`, placing them in rows 1, 2 and 3, respectively.

`GridBagLayout` is capable of anchoring more than one component in the same grid cell. If two components share the same grid cell, the component displayed on top is controlled by the component's zorder (see "Components and Zorder" on page 159).

Figure 14-15 shows the same applet displayed in Figure 14-14, with the constraints modified for image button #2, such that its grid position is (0,0), and therefore is anchored in the same grid cell as image button #1.

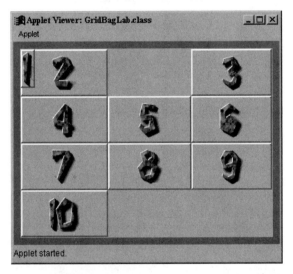

Figure 14-15 Two Components Anchored in the Same Grid Cell
Image button #1 and image button #2 are both anchored in the (0,0) grid cell. When two components share a grid cell, component zorder determines which component is on top.

Since zorder determines which overlapping component is displayed on top, and since image button #1 was added to the container before image button #2[14], image button #1 is always displayed on top of image button #2. Therefore, in order for image button #2 to be visible, we had to modify some constraints for image button #1, namely, `fill: GridBagConstraints.NONE`, and anchor: `GridBagConstraints.NORTHWEST`.

14. The order in which components are added to their container determines zorder.

GridBagConstraints.gridwidth and *GridBagConstraints.gridheight*

The `gridwidth` and `gridheight` constraints determine the size of a component's *display area*, not necessarily the size of the component itself.

In addition to integer values for `gridwidth` and `gridheight`, the values `GridBagConstraints.RELATIVE` and `GridBagConstraints.REMAINDER` may also be specified. `RELATIVE` means that the component will be the next to last component in its row (for `gridwidth`) or the next to last component in its column (for `gridheight`). A value of `REMAINDER` results in the component being the last component in its row (`gridwidth`) or column (`gridheight`). Specifying `REMAINDER` will cause the component's display area to expand in order to span as many grid cells as required to be the last component in its respective row or column.

Table 14-13 summarizes the values that may be specified for `gridwidth` and `gridheight`.

Table 14-13 `GridBagConstraints` `gridwidth` **and** `gridheight`

gridwidth/gridheight Values	Description
`Integer`	The size of the component's display area in grid cells.
`RELATIVE`	`gridwidth`: component is the next to last in its row.
	`gridheight`: component is the next to last in its column.
`REMAINDER`	`gridwidth`: component is the last in its row.
	`gridheight`: component is the last in its column.

Figure 14-16 shows our applet with 10 image buttons, where two of the image buttons have had their `gridwidth` and `gridheight` values modified from the default values of 1, as follows: image button #2 has a `gridwidth` of 2 and a `gridheight` of 1; image button #9 has a `gridwidth` and a `gridheight` of `GridBagConstraints.REMAINDER`, which causes its display area to expand in order to become the last component in its respective row and column. Note that the image button itself also expands to fill its entire display area because its `fill` constraint has been set to `GridBagConstraints.BOTH`.

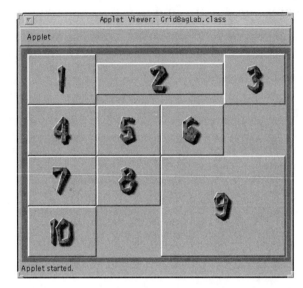

Figure 14-16 GridBagConstraints gridwidth and gridheight
The values assigned to gridwidth and gridheight determine the
size of a component's display area in the horizontal and vertical
directions, respectively. Image button #2 has a gridwidth of 2 and
a gridheight of 1, and image button #9 has a gridwidth and a
gridheight of GridBagConstraints.REMAINDER.

One of the subtleties of using GridBagLayout is the fact that a component's
constraints interact to produce a desired (or undesired) effect. For instance, if we
set the fill constraint for image button #9 in Figure 14-16 to NONE, the image
button itself will not expand out to the edges of the container, however its display
area will.

GridBagConstraints.weightx and GridBagConstraints.weighty

If a container is larger than the combined preferred sizes of its components, then a
component's weightx and weighty constraints determine how much of the
extra space a component's *display area* consumes. The weightx and weighty
constraints apply strictly to the component's display area, and not the component
itself, although components can be coaxed into filling their display areas in a
number of different ways, by setting the fill variable.

GridBagConstraints.weightx and GridBagConstraints.weighty are
the only constraints that are specified as double values. Additionally, both
weightx and weighty must be positive. Typically, weightx and weighty are
specified as a number between 0.0 and 1.0, although numbers greater than 1.0
may be specified. The weighting of each component in a given row or column is

relative to the weights of the other components that reside in the same row or column, so you can stick with numbers between 0.0 and 1.0, or use larger numbers if desired.

Up until now, the weights of every image button in the `GridBagLab` applet shown in the preceding figures have been (1.0, 1.0), and therefore each image button's display area received an equal share of the extra space available in the container. If we modify the weight constraints to (0.0, 0.0) for each image button, then none of the image buttons is allotted any extra space, as you can see from Figure 14-17

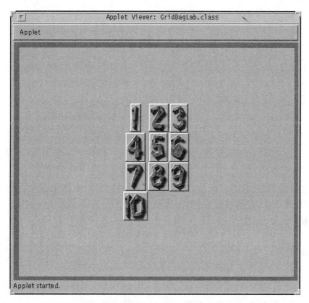

Figure 14-17 `GridBagLayout` Weight Constraints
`weightx` and `weighty` constraints determine how much extra space a component's display area takes up. The image buttons displayed above all have weights of (0,0), and therefore none of them get any extra space.

The image buttons in Figure 14-17 have also had their fill constraint set to NONE— in the previous figures they were all set to BOTH.

Setting all of the component's weights to (0.0, 0.0) causes the components to be clumped together in the middle of the container— `GridBagLayout` puts all of the extra space between the outside of the grid of components and the inside of the container when none of the components have a weighting greater than 0.0.

In order to shed some light on exactly how weighting works, let's change the `weightx` to 1.0 for image button #1 and leave all the other constraints as they were. You can see the results of our tinkering in Figure 14-18.

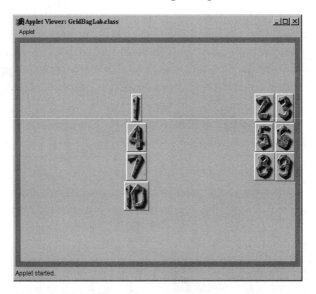

Figure 14-18 Weight Constraints Are Applied Per Row or Column
Image button #1 has a weight of (1.0, 0.0). All of the other image
buttons have weights of (0.0, 0.0).

Since image button #1 has a `weightx` of 1.0 and the other image buttons in its row have a `weightx` of 0.0, the display area for image button #1 takes up 100 percent of the extra space in the horizontal direction. Note that the image button itself does not take up the extra space, although it would if its `fill` constraint were set to either BOTH or HORIZONTAL.

Another point of interest is the fact that all of the image buttons in the same column as image button #1 have also had their display areas expanded to take up the extra space in their respective rows, even though their `weightx` constraint is still set to 0.0. This is a necessity if a grid is to be maintained.

This leads us to an interesting conclusion: weighting is applied on a column/row basis and not per component. For instance, in Figure 14-18 the `weightx` value for each *column* is 1.0, 0.0, and 0.0. Therefore, the left-hand column is given all of the extra space in the horizontal direction.

AWT TIP

Weighting Is Applied on a Row/Column Basis

GridBagLayout maintains a *grid* of components. Each row and column is given a weighting, which is determined from the weights of the row or column's components. The weighting of a row or column is equal to the weighting of the component with the highest weighting in the row or column.

A component's weighting affects not only how much extra space the component's display area is given, but also potentially affects the display areas of components residing in the same row *and* the same column. Setting image button #1's `weightx` constraint in Figure 14-18 caused the display areas of the components in the same column (#4, #7 and #10) to grow in the horizontal direction. If the image buttons in the same row (#2 and #3) had non-zero `weightx` constraints, their display areas may also have been affected by modifying image button #1's `weightx` constraint. All of this is due to the fact that horizontal weighting is relative to components in the same row, and vertical weighting is relative to components in the same column.

The `weightx` and `weighty` constraints are unique by virtue of the fact that their values may affect not only the size of their own display area, but also the size of *other* component's display areas.

If we set the `weightx` constraint for both image button #1 and image button #2 to 0.5, then the respective columns will each take up half of the extra space in the horizontal direction, as you can see from Figure 14-19.

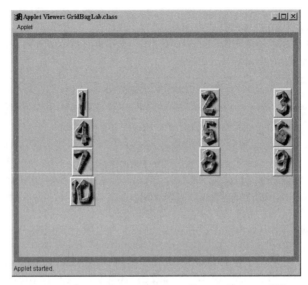

Figure 14-19 Weighting Determines Extra Space Allotment.
Image button #1 and image button #2 both have a `weightx` of 0.5.
All other image buttons have weights of (0,0).

If you have a sharp eye (or a ruler handy), you may take exception to our claim that columns 1 and 2 each get half of the extra space. However, realize that this does not mean that columns 1 and 2 have the exact same width—in fact they do not.

Columns 1 and 2 are not the same width because image button #1 and image button #2 do not have the same preferred widths. Let's suppose that the container is 100 pixels wide, and the preferred sizes of image buttons 1, 2, and 3 are 5, 10, and 7 pixels, respectively. When `GridBagLayout` sees that image buttons #1 and #2 are evenly dividing the extra space in their row, it first calculates the extra space available, which is 100 - (5 + 10 + 7) = 78 pixels. Therefore, columns 1 and 2 each get 39 pixels added to their widths, which means column 1 is 39 + 5 = 44 pixels, while column 2 is 39 + 10 = 49 pixels. The display area size for components of equal weighting will only be the same if the preferred sizes of the components in question are identical.

AWT TIP...

Equal Weighting Does Not Necessarily Equate to Equal Display Area Sizes

If two components in the same row or column have equal weighting, that does not necessarily mean that their display areas will be the same size. Only if the preferred sizes of the two components are identical will their display areas wind up being the same size.

Weighting works the same in both the horizontal and vertical directions. Figure 14-20 takes our applet one step further, by specifying weights for image buttons 4, 7, and 10 as 0.25, 0.50, and 0.25, respectively.

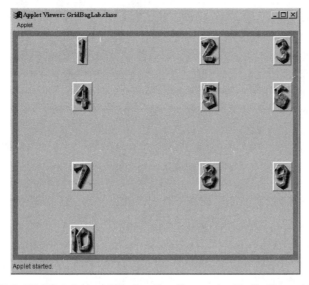

Figure 14-20 Weighting Works the Same in Both Directions Image buttons 4, 7, and 10 have `weighty` constraints of 0.25, 0.50, 0.25, respectively. All other image buttons have `weighty` constraints of 0.0.

GridBagConstraints.insets

Just like insets can be specified for a container, they can also be specified for a component's display area with an `Insets` object. Figure 14-21 shows our `GridBagLab` applet, where image button #5 has an insets value of (10,5,10,0). All of the other image buttons have the default insets of (0,0,0,0).

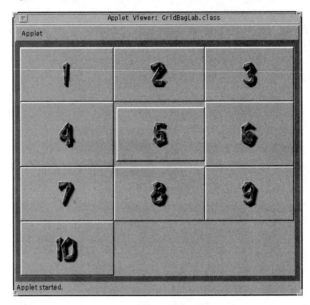

Figure 14-21 `GridBagConstraints.insets` Constraint

Notice that the display area for image button #5 is reduced as a result of setting the insets constraints, in much the same manner as setting the insets for a container reduces the available real estate for laying out components—see "Layout Managers and Container Insets" on page 378.

Insets can also be specified as negative, resulting in a component overstepping the bounds of its display area. Figure 14-22 shows image button #5 fitted with an insets of (-10,-10,-10,-10).

Figure 14-22 A Negative Insets Value
Image button #5 has an insets constraint of (-10,-10,-10,-10). A
negative insets constraint causes a component to overstep the
boundaries of its display area.

As you can see, image button #5 does indeed overstep the boundaries of its
display area. Realize that zordering results in image button #5 being partially
covered by image buttons 2, 3 and 4, as they were added to the container prior to
image button #5 and therefore have a higher zorder (see "Components and
Zorder" on page 159).

GridBagConstraints.ipadx and GridBagConstraints.ipady

While the `insets` constraint specifies an *external* padding between the edges of a
component and its display area, `ipadx` and `ipady` specify an *internal* padding
applied to the component (not the display area).

The rarely used `ipadx` and `ipady` constraints result in a component's preferred
and minimum sizes increasing (for positive values) and decreasing (for negative
values).

We're not sure exactly where you would want to use the padding constraints, but
being the kitchen sink of layout managers, GridBagLayout supports this rarely
used feature.

In Figure 14-22, our `GridBagLab` applet has `ipadx` and `ipady` values of (20,20) for image button #5 and (-5,-5) for image button #10.

Figure 14-23 `ipadx` and `ipady` Constraints
Image button #5 has `ipadx` and `ipady` constraints of (20,20), and image button #10 has `ipadx` and `ipady` constraints of (-5,-5). Positive padding increases the size of the component; negative padding decreases the component's size.

GridBagLab

Although our coverage of `GridBagLayout` should be sufficient to communicate the basic principles, we have found it most beneficial to run the `GridBagLab` applet in order to achieve a deeper understanding of how `GridBagLayout` works. On the CD, under the `partOneSource/layout` directory, you will find the `GridBagLab` applet used to produce the figures that we've used to illustrate `GridBagLayout`.

Figure 14-24 shows `GridBagLab` in action.

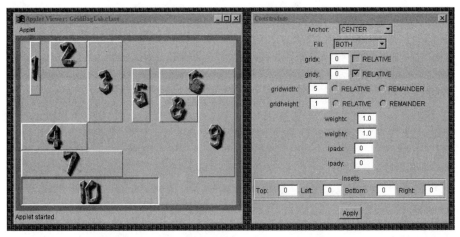

Figure 14-24 `GridBagLab` Applet
The `GridBagLab` applet provided on the CD allows grid bag
constraints to be set for the 10 image buttons displayed in the
applet's window.

`GridBagLab` is provided as a convenience for you to explore setting constraints
on components laid out by `GridBagLayout`. It should not be construed as
exemplary GUI and/or object-oriented design.

It is our hope that `GridBagLab`, combined with the extensive coverage of
`GridBagLayout` in *Graphic Java* will empower you to use this complicated, but
extremely useful, layout manager with confidence.

Our discussion of `GridBagLayout` will conclude by taking a look at a specialty
of `GridBagLayout`: laying out input forms.

GridBagLayout and Input Forms

One of the most common uses of `GridBagLayout` is to lay out input forms such
as the one depicted in Figure 14-25. As a result, we'll take a short detour to discuss
creating input forms with `GridBagLayout`.

Figure 14-25 Using `GridBagLayout` to Lay Out an Input Form
`GridBagLayout` is often used to lay out input forms like the one
pictured above.

We use the `PurchaseApplet` shown in Figure 14-25 to discuss keyboard
traversal in "Standard AWT Components and Keyboard Traversal" on page 536;
however, we do not discuss the applet's use of `GridBagLayout` there, so we will
cover that ground here[15].

The applet contains an instance of `ThreeDPanel`, which in turn contains an
instance of `ButtonPurchaseForm`:

```
public class PurchaseApplet extends Applet {
    public void init() {
        ThreeDPanel p = new ThreeDPanel();
        p.add(new ButtonPurchaseForm());
        add(p);
    }
}
class ThreeDPanel extends Panel {
    public void paint(Graphics g) {
        g.setColor(Color.lightGray);
        g.draw3DRect(0,0,getSize().width-1,
                        getSize().height-1,true);
    }
}
```

15. You can find `PurchaseApplet` in the
    `partOneSource/desktop/mouseless/keytraverse` directory on the CD.

`ThreeDPanel` simply draws a 3D rectangle in order to give our input form a little panache. The interesting code, from the standpoint of `GridBagLayout`, resides in `ButtonPurchaseForm`, which extends `Panel` and instantiates all of the components used in the input form:

```
class ButtonPurchaseForm extends Panel {
  Separator sep = new Separator();
  Label title   = new Label("Purchase Something Now");
  Label name    = new Label("Name:");
  Label address = new Label("Address:");
  Label payment = new Label("Purchase Method:");
  Label phone   = new Label("Phone:");
  Label city    = new Label("City:");
  Label state   = new Label("State:");

  TextField nameField    = new TextField(25);
  TextField addressField = new TextField(25);
  TextField cityField    = new TextField(15);
  TextField stateField   = new TextField(2);

  Choice    paymentChoice = new Choice();
  Button    paymentButton = new Button("Purchase");
  Button    cancelButton = new Button("Cancel");
  ...
```

A `gjt.Separator` is used to separate the title from the rest of the components in the panel. The use of the `Separator` class has no bearing here, other than the fact that it is laid out by `GridBagLayout` just like the rest of the components used in the panel.

The `ButtonPurchaseForm` constructor contains all of the code that sets constraints for the components and adds them to the panel. The first order of business, of course, is to create instances of `GridBagLayout` and `GridBagConstraints` and then set the container's layout manager to the instance of `GridBagLayout`. In addition, we add the three payment options to the `paymentChoice` and set the font of the title.

```
public ButtonPurchaseForm() {
    GridBagLayout      gbl = new GridBagLayout();
    GridBagConstraints gbc = new GridBagConstraints();

    setLayout(gbl);

    paymentChoice.add("Visa");
    paymentChoice.add("MasterCard");
    paymentChoice.add("COD");
```

```
title.setFont(new Font("Times-Roman",
              Font.BOLD + Font.ITALIC, 16));
```

Now we are ready to set the constraints for the components to be laid out in the panel. First, constraints are set for the title (a Label), which is added to the container.

```
gbc.anchor    = GridBagConstraints.NORTH;
gbc.gridwidth = GridBagConstraints.REMAINDER;
gbl.setConstraints(title, gbc);
add(title);
```

We specify the anchor point for the title as NORTH, so the title is centered at the top of the form. The gridwidth is set to REMAINDER, so that the title is the last (and only) component in its row. Next, we set the constraints for the separator.

```
gbc.fill      = GridBagConstraints.HORIZONTAL;
gbc.insets    = new Insets(0,0,10,0);
gbl.setConstraints(sep, gbc);
add(sep);
```

Notice that we are using the same instance of GridBagConstraints to specify the constraints for all of the components in the form. As we stated earlier, GridBagLayout.setConstraints() makes a copy of the constraints it is passed, and therefore the same instance of GridBagConstraints can be used for multiple components with different constraints.

The fill constraint for the separator is set to HORIZONTAL, so that the separator spans the width of the panel. Insets are also specified for the separator as (0,0,10,0). The integer values passed to an Insets constructor specify, in order, top, left, bottom, and right insets. As a result, a bottom insets of ten pixels is specified for the separator, which provides some breathing room between the bottom of the separator and the top of the next components to be added to the panel, namely, a label and an associated textfield for entering a name.

Next, the name label and textfield are added to the panel.

```
gbc.anchor    = GridBagConstraints.WEST;
gbc.gridwidth = 1;
gbc.insets    = new Insets(0,0,0,0);
gbl.setConstraints(name, gbc);
add(name);

gbc.gridwidth = GridBagConstraints.REMAINDER;
gbl.setConstraints(nameField, gbc);
add(nameField);
```

The `anchor` constraint for the `name` label is set to `WEST`, and the `gridwidth` is set to 1. Even though the default value for `gridwidth` is 1 (see "GridBagConstraints Instance Variables and Valid Values" on page 406), we must explicitly set it here because we previously set it to `REMAINDER` in order for the title and separator to be the last (and only) components in their row. The insets constraint is set, only this time, we specify zeros all the way around. Once again, we are setting a constraint's values to the default values for the constraint because we previously set it to a nondefault value.

For `nameField`, we leave all the constraints as they were for the `name` label, except that we set the `gridwidth` to `REMAINDER`, which causes the textfield to be the last component in its row. Remember that previously we set the `fill` constraint to be `HORIZONTAL`, and therefore the textfield, like the label[16], will fill its display area in the horizontal direction. Additionally, we previously set the `anchor` constraint to be `WEST`, so both the label and textfield are left-justified in their respective display areas.

The constraints for the address label and textfield are set in a similar manner to the constraints for the name label and textfield.

```
gbc.gridwidth = 1;
gbl.setConstraints(address, gbc);
add(address);

gbc.gridwidth = GridBagConstraints.REMAINDER;
gbl.setConstraints(addressField, gbc);
add(addressField);
```

Next, the constraints are set for the city label and textfield.

```
gbc.gridwidth = 1;
gbl.setConstraints(city, gbc);
add(city);

gbl.setConstraints(cityField, gbc);
add(cityField);
```

Notice that we did not set the `gridwidth` for the textfield to `REMAINDER`, because the textfield is not the last component in its row—we still have the state label and field to add to the row.

```
gbl.setConstraints(state, gbc);
add(state);
```

---

16. `nameLabel` is left-justified, as that is the default justification for a `java.awt.Label`. See "java.awt.Label" on page 181.

```
gbc.gridwidth = GridBagConstraints.REMAINDER;
gbl.setConstraints(stateField, gbc);
add(stateField);
```

The stateField, however, is the last component in the row, so we set its gridwidth constraint to REMAINDER.

Next, the payment label and choice have their constraints set and are added to the container.

```
gbc.gridwidth = 1;
gbl.setConstraints(payment, gbc);
gbc.insets = new Insets(5,0,5,0);
add(payment);

gbc.gridwidth = GridBagConstraints.REMAINDER;
gbc.fill      = GridBagConstraints.NONE;
gbl.setConstraints(paymentChoice, gbc);
add(paymentChoice);
```

The insets constraint for both the payment label and choice is set to five pixels both top and bottom to provide a little separation for the payment components.

Finally, another GJT component is added to the panel—a gjt.ButtonPanel, which is simply a panel that contains a horizontal separator and buttons that are centered in the panel[17]. Two buttons are added to the button panel, which in turn has its constraints set and is added to the panel.

```
ButtonPanel buttonPanel = new ButtonPanel();
buttonPanel.add(paymentButton);
buttonPanel.add(cancelButton);

gbc.anchor     = GridBagConstraints.SOUTH;
gbc.insets     = new Insets(5,0,0,0);
gbc.fill       = GridBagConstraints.HORIZONTAL;
gbc.gridwidth = 4;
gbl.setConstraints(buttonPanel, gbc);
add(buttonPanel);
}
```

Notice that the gridwidth constraint for the button panel is set to 4. Since the row containing the city and state labels and fields consists of 4 grid cells, the button panel must have a gridwidth of 4 if its display area is to span the entire width of the form, as you can see from Figure 14-26. Similarly, of course, we could have set the gridwidth to GridBagConstraints.REMAINDER[18].

---

17. See "gjt.ButtonPanel" on page 734.

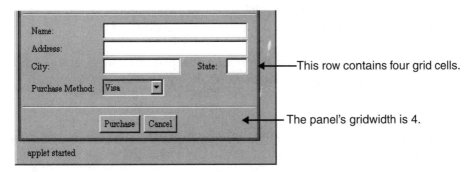

This row contains four grid cells.

The panel's gridwidth is 4.

Figure 14-26 Specifying `GridBagConstraints.gridwidth`
The panel containing the separator and the buttons has its
gridwidth set to 4 so that it spans the width of the container.

Additionally, the `fill` constraint for the `buttonPanel` is set to `HORIZONTAL` to
ensure that the button panel itself, in addition to its display area, spans the entire
width of the form.

Finally, an `insets` constraint is specified for the button panel, which gives the
panel a top inset of 5 pixels. Notice that the pixel distance between the bottom of
the purchase components and the top of the separator contained in the button
panel is actually 10 pixels, because the purchase components also have a bottom
inset of 5 pixels.

Laying Out Components in Nested Panels

A `Container` can contain components, and, fortunately for all involved, the
AWT designers chose to make `Container` an extension of `Component`. What
that means, of course, is that containers can contain not only components, but also
other containers, since a `Container` is a `Component`. (This is an implementation
of a design pattern known as *composite*. [19])

This crucial ability—to nest containers inside of one another—is a necessity if we
are to design screens of much complexity for use in applets. Attempting to lay out
a complicated screenful of containers with a single layout manager can turn out to
be exercise in futility, no matter which layout manager you choose for the job.

18. See "GridBagConstraints.gridwidth and GridBagConstraints.gridheight" on
    page 415.
19. See.Gamma, Helm, Johnson, Vlissides. *Design Patterns*, p. 163. Addison-Wesley,
    1995.[add year]

Although we can give you some guidelines to follow, designing nested panels is something that is best learned by experimenting with different layout managers and layout situations. In *Extending the AWT—The Graphic Java Toolkit*, we will explore designing nested panels in nearly every chapter; for now we'll take a look at a single contrived example—an applet that allows you to vary the settings of a GridLayout.

GridLabApplet displays a grid comprising instances of gjt.ImageButton. The applet includes controls for setting the number of rows and columns and for setting the horizontal and vertical gaps between the image buttons. Figure 14-27 shows a picture of GridLabApplet in action.

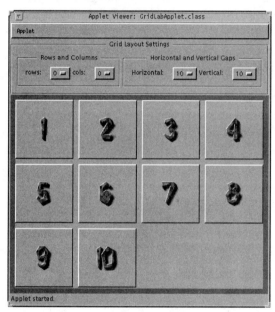

Figure 14-27 Nested Panels in an Applet
The GridLabApplet includes several layers of panels.

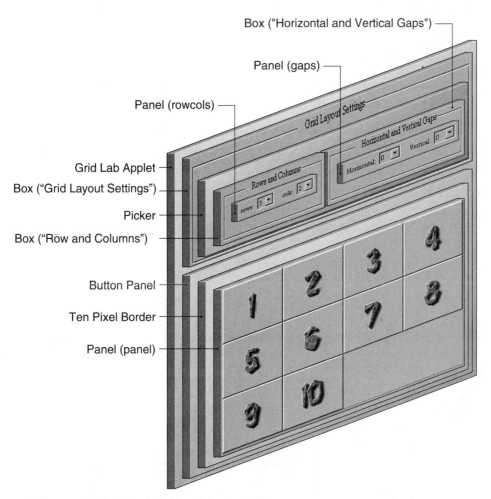

Figure 14-28 Nested Panel Layout Diagram

This applet is layered a little bit like an onion with its multiple layers, so we'll refer both to the diagram above and to appropriate sections of the GridLabApplet code to describe how the applet is assembled.

GridLabApplet sets its layout manager to an instance of BorderLayout. The north component is a gjt.Box from the Graphic Java Toolkit. In the code, the north component is set like this:

```
add("North",  new Box(picker, "Grid Layout Settings"));
```

The gjt.Box component surrounds a Panel named Picker. The constructor for the Picker class creates two more instances of Panel, one for the Row/Column and one for the Horizontal/Vertical gaps.

```
public Picker(ButtonPanel buttonPanel) {
  Panel rowCols = new Panel();
  Panel gaps    = new Panel();

    •
    •
    •

  add(new Box(rowCols,  "Rows and Columns"));
  add(new Box(gaps,     "Horizontal and Vertical Gaps"));
```

The rowCols and gaps panels are added to the Picker panel, but first they're wrapped in boxes. (gjt.Box *surrounds* a component and draws a border and title around the component.)

All of this results in the components in the "Grid Layout Settings" Box being laid out like so:

Now, in the center of the `GridLabApplet`, we add a `Button Panel`:

```
add("Center", buttonPanel);
```

The `ButtonPanel` class creates an instance of `Panel` and an instance of `TenPixelBorder`:

```
private Panel          panel  = new Panel();
private TenPixelBorder border = new TenPixelBorder(panel);
```

As we have discussed previously, `TenPixelBorder` employs a `BorderLayout` to center the component it is passed and draws a gray border ten pixels thick around the component—see "TenPixelBorder" on page 382.

The `panel` passed to the `border` is the one that holds the buttons that will be positioned in a grid. First, several `gjt.ImageButton` variables are declared:

```
private ImageButton    one, two, three, four, five,
                       six, seven, eight, nine, ten;
```

The `ButtonPanel` constructor then creates instances of `gjt.ImageButton`, adds them to the `panel`, and sets the layout manager for the `panel` to an instance of `GridLayout`:

```
public ButtonPanel(Applet applet) {
    URL cb = applet.getCodeBase();

    one   = new ImageButton(applet.getImage(
                            cb, "gifs/one.gif"));
    two   = new ImageButton(applet.getImage(
                            cb, "gifs/two.gif"));
    three = new ImageButton(applet.getImage(
                            cb, "gifs/three.gif"));
        .
        .
        .
    panel.setLayout(new GridLayout(3,2));
    panel.add(one);   panel.add(two);   panel.add(three);
    panel.add(four);  panel.add(five);  panel.add(six);
    panel.add(seven); panel.add(eight); panel.add(nine);
    panel.add(ten);

    setLayout(new BorderLayout());
    add       (border, "Center");
}
```

Notice that at the end of this constructor we add `border`, which is our
`TenPixelBorder` instance, to the center of the `ButtonPanel`. The
`ButtonPanel` is centered beneath the north component and looks like this:

Communication Among Nested Panels

In applets with multiple nested panels, actions that occur in one panel may
require a layout manager to reposition and resize components in other panels.
That's certainly true in our `GridLabApplet`. When a user selects from the "Rows
and Columns" or "Gaps" `Choice` components, the `ButtonPanel` needs to
update accordingly. For example, look at the buttons in Figure 14-29.

To force `ButtonPanel` to lay out its components after a selection has been made
in a choice, we have to do a few things. First of all, we have to make sure that if a
choice is selected, the `Picker` panel has access to the `ButtonPanel`. To
accomplish that, we pass in an instance of `ButtonPanel` in the `Picker`
constructor:

```
public Picker(ButtonPanel buttonPanel) {
```

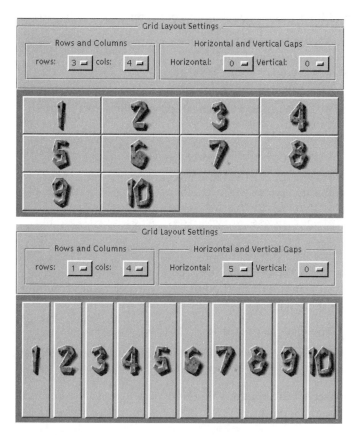

Figure 14-29 Nested Panel Updates

The `ButtonPanel` updates when selections are made in the `Picker` panel. In this case, the bottom picture shows the `ButtonPanel` updated with one row specified and a horizontal gap of 5. (Note that when the number of rows has been set, the columns button value does not update because `GridLayout.getColumns()` returns the value last assigned via `setColumns()`, not the actual number of columns displayed.)

Second, we add the `Picker` panel as an item listener for each `Choice`.

```
hchoice.addItemListener(this);
vchoice.addItemListener(this);
rowChoice.addItemListener(this);
colChoice.addItemListener(this);
```

`Picker.itemStateChanged()` makes sense of the selection made:

```
public boolean itemStateChanged(ItemEvent event) {
  int rows, cols, hgap, vgap;

  rows = Integer.parseInt(rowChoice.getSelectedItem());
  cols = Integer.parseInt(colChoice.getSelectedItem());
  hgap = Integer.parseInt(hchoice.getSelectedItem());
  vgap = Integer.parseInt(vchoice.getSelectedItem());

  buttonPanel.updateLayout(rows, cols, hgap, vgap);
}
```

The `itemStateChanged()` method extracts integer values from the four `Choice` objects it contains, like so:

```
numRows = Integer.parseInt(rowChoice.getSelectedItem());
```

`Integer.parseInt()` is a `static` method that parses a `String` and returns a `int` value.

Once we've extracted the integer values, we pass them to the `ButtonPanel` `updateLayout()` method:

```
public void updateLayout(int rows, int cols,
                         int hgap, int vgap) {
    try {
      gridLayout.setRows(rows);
      gridLayout.setCols(cols);
      gridLayout.setHgap(hgap);
      gridLayout.setVgap(vgap);

      panel.invalidate();
      border.validate();
    }
    catch(IllegalArgumentException e) {
      MessageDialog d = MessageDialog.getMessageDialog(
          Util.getFrame(this),
          (DialogClient)this,
          "Error",
          "Row: 0  Col: 0 is an illegal combination");
```

```
        d.pack();
        d.show();
    }
  }
```

The appropriate values for row, column and gaps are set for the `gridLayout`[20].

Recall that invoking `setLayout()` (line) invalidates the panel[21]. A panel is considered invalid anytime it has been changed and needs to be laid out again.

In line Σ, we call the `validate()` method for the `border`, which is the parent container of `panel`. The `Container.validate()` method checks whether the components contained in the container are valid or invalid. If any of them are invalid, their `layout()` method is invoked.

By calling `setLayout()`, we implicitly invalidate `panel`. By invoking `validate()` for the border (which is the `panel` container), we force `panel` to be laid out. Doing so reshapes and redisplays all of the components it contains—see "`Component` and `Container` Methods That Invalidate the Component." on page 388.

GridLabApplet Implementation

Now let's look through the entire code for the `GridLabApplet` in Example 14-9. Although the main focus in this applet is how it's composed of nested panels and how it employs layout managers in the respective panels, also note that it uses a few of the custom components from the Graphic Java Toolkit, including the `gjt.Box`, `gjt.MessageDialog`, `gjt.DialogClient`, `gjt.ImageButton`, and the `gjt.Util` classes. As you look through the code, refer to Figure 14-27 on page 432 and the two primary panels. One is called `Picker`; it is the north component of the applet and contains `gjt.Box`, `Panel`, `Label`, and `Choice` components. The other is called `ButtonPanel`; it is centered beneath `Picker` and contains a `TenPixelBorder` which (ultimately) contains the image buttons displayed in a grid.

---

20. The methods `setRows()`, `setColumns()`, `setHgap()` and `setVgap()` are new for 1.1.
21. See "`Component` and `Container` Methods That Invalidate the Component." on page 388.

Example 14-9 `GridLabApplet` **Class Source Code**

```java
import java.applet.Applet;
import java.net.URL;
import java.awt.*;
import java.awt.event.*;
import gjt.Box;
import gjt.DialogClient;
import gjt.ImageButton;
import gjt.MessageDialog;
import gjt.Util;

public class GridLabApplet extends Applet {
  public void init() {
    ImageButtonPanel buttonPanel = new ImageButtonPanel(this);
    Picker        picker       = new Picker(buttonPanel);

    setLayout(new BorderLayout());
    add(new Box(picker, "Grid Layout Settings"), "North");
    add(buttonPanel, "Center");
  }
}

class ImageButtonPanel extends Panel implements DialogClient {
  private ImageButton one, two, three, four, five,
                      six, seven, eight, nine, ten;

  private Panel            panel  = new Panel();
  private TenPixelBorder border = new TenPixelBorder(panel);
  private GridLayout       gridLayout;

  public ImageButtonPanel(Applet applet) {
    URL cb = applet.getCodeBase();

    one   =
      new ImageButton(applet.getImage(cb, "gifs/one.gif"));
    two   =
      new ImageButton(applet.getImage(cb, "gifs/two.gif"));
    three =
      new ImageButton(applet.getImage(cb,"gifs/three.gif"));
    four  =
      new ImageButton(applet.getImage(cb, "gifs/four.gif"));
    five  =
      new ImageButton(applet.getImage(cb, "gifs/five.gif"));
    six   =
      new ImageButton(applet.getImage(cb, "gifs/six.gif"));
    seven =
      new ImageButton(applet.getImage(cb, "gifs/seven.gif"));
```

```java
  eight =
     new ImageButton(applet.getImage(cb, "gifs/eight.gif"));
  nine  =
     new ImageButton(applet.getImage(cb, "gifs/nine.gif"));
  ten   =
     new ImageButton(applet.getImage(cb, "gifs/ten.gif"));

  panel.setLayout(gridLayout = new GridLayout(3,2));
  panel.add(one);    panel.add(two);    panel.add(three);
  panel.add(four);   panel.add(five);   panel.add(six);
  panel.add(seven);  panel.add(eight);  panel.add(nine);
  panel.add(ten);

  setLayout(new BorderLayout());
  add        (border, "Center");
}
public void updateLayout(int rows, int cols,
                         int hgap, int vgap) {
  try {
     gridLayout.setRows(rows);
     gridLayout.setColumns(cols);
     gridLayout.setHgap(hgap);
     gridLayout.setVgap(vgap);

     panel.invalidate();
     border.validate();
  }
  catch(IllegalArgumentException e) {
     MessageDialog d = new MessageDialog(
           Util.getFrame(this),
              (DialogClient)this,
              "Error",
              "Row: 0  Col: 0 is an illegal combination", null);

        d.pack();
        d.show();
     }
  }
  public void dialogDismissed(Dialog d) { }
  public void dialogCancelled(Dialog d) { }
}

class Picker extends Panel implements ItemListener {
  private Label  hgapLabel = new Label("Horizontal:");
  private Label  vgapLabel = new Label("Vertical:");
  private Label  rowLabel  = new Label("rows:");
  private Label  colLabel  = new Label("cols:");
```

```
private Choice hchoice   = new Choice();
private Choice vchoice   = new Choice();
private Choice rowChoice = new Choice();
private Choice colChoice = new Choice();

private ImageButtonPanel buttonPanel;

public Picker(ImageButtonPanel buttonPanel) {
    Panel rowCols = new Panel();
    Panel gaps    = new Panel();

    this.buttonPanel = buttonPanel;
    hchoice.addItem("0");
    hchoice.addItem("5");
    hchoice.addItem("10");
    hchoice.addItem("15");
    hchoice.addItem("20");

    vchoice.addItem("0");
    vchoice.addItem("5");
    vchoice.addItem("10");
    vchoice.addItem("15");
    vchoice.addItem("20");

    rowChoice.addItem("0");
    rowChoice.addItem("1");
    rowChoice.addItem("2");
    rowChoice.addItem("3");
    rowChoice.addItem("4");
    rowChoice.addItem("5");
    rowChoice.select (3);

    colChoice.addItem("0");
    colChoice.addItem("1");
    colChoice.addItem("2");
    colChoice.addItem("3");
    colChoice.addItem("4");
    colChoice.addItem("5");
    colChoice.select (2);

    rowCols.add(rowLabel);
    rowCols.add(rowChoice);
    rowCols.add(colLabel);
    rowCols.add(colChoice);

    gaps.add(hgapLabel);
    gaps.add(hchoice);
    gaps.add(vgapLabel);
```

```
        gaps.add(vchoice);

        hchoice.addItemListener(this);
        vchoice.addItemListener(this);
        rowChoice.addItemListener(this);
        colChoice.addItemListener(this);

        add(new Box(rowCols, "Rows and Columns"));
        add(new Box(gaps,    "Horizontal and Vertical Gaps"));
    }
    public void itemStateChanged(ItemEvent event) {
        int rows, cols, hgap, vgap;

        rows = Integer.parseInt(rowChoice.getSelectedItem());
        cols = Integer.parseInt(colChoice.getSelectedItem());
        hgap = Integer.parseInt(hchoice.getSelectedItem());
        vgap = Integer.parseInt(vchoice.getSelectedItem());

        buttonPanel.updateLayout(rows, cols, hgap, vgap);
    }
}
```

Custom Layout Managers

Although the AWT's standard layout managers are well equipped to handle most layout situations, there comes a time when they just won't do. You will also find that for certain types of layouts, it is simpler to use a custom layout manager that deals with an exact type of layout than it is to use one of the AWT's layout managers, even though one of them may suffice.

A custom layout manager involves implementing the LayoutManager interface, which is defined as:

```
void        addLayoutComponent (String name, Component comp);
void        removeLayoutComponent(String name, Component comp);
Dimension   preferredLayoutSize (Container parent);
Dimension   minimumLayoutSize  (Container parent);
void        layoutContainer  (Container parent);
```

We've discussed each of these methods in detail earlier in this chapter, so instead of rehashing the responsibilities of each method, let's take a look at some custom layout managers that implement them.

gjt.BulletinLayout

Upon hearing of layout managers, newcomers to the AWT often have an overwhelming compulsion to simply set their container's layout manager to null and explicitly position and size the components displayed in their container.

Almost without exception, such a strategy is ill-fated. A container with a null layout manager will not be able to cope with resize events. As soon as this discovery is made, the next step is to override setSize() to reposition and reshape the components laid out in the container. Once things have degenerated to this point, all of the benefits of the strategy pattern (see the "Layout Management and the Strategy Pattern" on page 375 for more discussion of the strategy pattern) go down the tubes. The algorithm for laying out components becomes hardcoded in the container, and therefore the container cannot easily change its layout strategy. Furthermore, once the layout strategy is hardcoded in the container, it is not available for others to use.

Usually, such object-oriented backsliding is prompted by the need for a simple layout strategy that merely moves components to their specified location and shapes them to their actual or preferred size. The Graphic Java Toolkit encapsulates such a strategy in a simple layout manager: the gjt.BulletinLayout, which lays out components as though they were on a bulletin board. Components are positioned according to their location and shaped according to either their size or, if the component has not been explicitly sized, their preferred size.

gjt.BulletinLayout will serve as our first foray into implementing custom layout managers. Example 14-10 lists its implementation. Notice that BulletinLayout implements addLayoutComponent() and removeLayoutComponent() as no-ops, which indicates that it does not keep track of a finite set of components to lay out. Instead, it lays out all the components it finds in the container it is currently laying out.

Also note that BulletinLayout implements preferredLayoutSize() and minimumLayoutSize() to simply return the union of all the preferred and minimum sizes for all the visible components. These two methods invoke a number of container methods, such as getInsets(), countComponents(), and getComponent(), that are routinely used by layout managers.

BulletinLayout implements the required layoutContainer(), which operates on all visible components and reshapes them so that they reside at their specified location and are resized according to their (explicit or preferred) sizes.

Example 14-10 `gjt.BulletinLayout` **Class Source Code**

```
package gjt;

import java.awt.*;
import java.util.Hashtable;

public class BulletinLayout implements LayoutManager {
  private Hashtable hash = new Hashtable();

  public void addLayoutComponent(String s, Component comp) {
  }
  public void removeLayoutComponent(Component comp) {
  }
  public Dimension preferredLayoutSize(Container target) {
     Insets     insets     = target.getInsets();
     Dimension dim         = new Dimension(0,0);
     int        ncomponents = target.getComponentCount();
     Component comp;
     Dimension d;
     Rectangle size = new Rectangle(0,0);
     Rectangle compSize;

     for (int i = 0; i < ncomponents; i++) {
        comp = target.getComponent(i);

        if(comp.isVisible()) {
           d = comp.getSize();
           compSize = new Rectangle(comp.getLocation());
           compSize.width  = d.width;
           compSize.height = d.height;

           size = size.union(compSize);
        }
     }
     dim.width  += size.width + insets.right;
     dim.height += size.height + insets.bottom;

     return dim;
  }
  public Dimension minimumLayoutSize(Container target) {
     Insets     insets     = target.getInsets();
     Dimension dim         = new Dimension(0,0);
     int        ncomponents = target.getComponentCount();
     Component comp;
     Dimension d;
     Rectangle minBounds = new Rectangle(0,0);
     Rectangle compMinBounds;
```

```
        for (int i = 0; i < ncomponents; i++) {
            comp = target.getComponent(i);

            if(comp.isVisible()) {
                d = comp.getMinimumSize();
                compMinBounds = new Rectangle(comp.getLocation());
                    compMinBounds.setSize(d.width, d.height);
                    minBounds = minBounds.union(compMinBounds);
            }
        }
        dim.width  += minBounds.width  + insets.right;
        dim.height += minBounds.height + insets.bottom;

        return dim;
    }
    public void layoutContainer(Container target) {
        Insets     insets      = target.getInsets();
        int        ncomponents = target.getComponentCount();
        Component comp;
        Dimension sz, ps;
        Point loc;

        for (int i = 0; i < ncomponents; i++) {
            comp = target.getComponent(i);

            if(comp.isVisible()) {
                sz   = comp.getSize();
                ps   = comp.getPreferredSize();
                    loc  = getComponentLocation(comp);

                if(sz.width < ps.width || sz.height < ps.height)
                    sz = ps;

                comp.setBounds(loc.x, loc.y, sz.width, sz.height);
            }
        }
    }
    private Point getComponentLocation(Component comp) {
        Insets insets = comp.getParent().getInsets();
        Point  loc    = comp.getLocation();

        if( ! hash.containsKey(comp)) {
            addComponentToHashtable(comp);
        }
        else {
            Point oldLocation = (Point)hash.get(comp);

            if(oldLocation.x != loc.x || oldLocation.y != loc.y) {
                addComponentToHashtable(comp);
```

```
        }
    }
    return comp.getLocation();
  }
  private void addComponentToHashtable(Component comp) {
    Insets insets = comp.getParent().getInsets();
    Point  loc    = comp.getLocation();

    comp.setLocation(loc.x + insets.left, loc.y + insets.top);
    hash.put(comp, comp.getLocation());
  }
}
```

Notice that `BulletinLayout` maintains a hash table of components and their locations. This is done because we only want to add the top and left insets to the position of a component the first time it is laid out or if its location changes after it is laid out the first time.

Exercising the BulletinLayout Custom Layout Manager

`BulletinLayout` comes with a unit test that lays out a few random components at specific locations, as you can see from Figure 14-30.

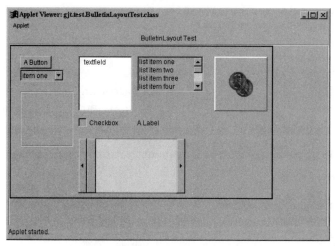

Figure 14-30 `BulletinLayout`
BulletinLayout positions components at their location, and shapes them according to either explicit or preferred size of the component.

A blue border is drawn around the preferred size of the container that contains all of the components in the applet. The status line of the applet displays the minimum and preferred sizes of the container.

The unit test for `BulletinLayout` is rather lengthy, but much of the code is taken up with creating and setting parameters for the components displayed in the applet.

Locations for all of the components are explicitly set, whereas only five of the components have their sizes explicitly set; the rest will be sized to their preferred size by `BulletinLayout`.

```
button.setLocation(10,10);
choice.setLocation(10,35);
label.setLocation(230, 120);
checkbox.setLocation(120, 120);

borderAroundCanvas.setLocation(10, 75);
borderAroundCanvas.setSize(100,100);

textfield.setLocation(120,10);
textfield.setSize(100,100);

scrollbar.setLocation(120, 160);
scrollbar.setSize(200,100);

imageButton.setLocation(375, 10);
imageButton.setSize(100,100);

list.setLocation(230, 10);
list.setSize(100,100);
```

The button, choice, label and checkbox are sized according to their preferred sizes since their size was not explicitly set. The `gjt.test.BulletinLayoutTest` listing is shown in Example 14-11.

Example 14-11 `gjt.test.BulletinLayoutTest` **Class Source Code**

```
package gjt.test;

import java.applet.Applet;
import java.awt.*;
import gjt.*;

public class BulletinLayoutTest extends UnitTest {
  public String title() { return "BulletinLayout Test"; }
  public Panel centerPanel() {
     return new BulletinLayoutTestPanel(this);
  }
}

class BulletinLayoutTestPanel extends Panel {
  private Applet        applet;
```

```
private Button          button;
private Choice          choice;
private TextField       textfield;
private Checkbox        checkbox;
private List            list;
private Label           label;
private Scrollbar       scrollbar;
private Border          borderAroundCanvas;
private ImageButton     imageButton;
private DrawnRectangle dr;

public BulletinLayoutTestPanel(Applet applet) {
   this.applet = applet;

   createComponents();
   setLayout(new BulletinLayout());

   add(button);              add(choice);
   add(borderAroundCanvas); add(textfield);
   add(checkbox);            add(scrollbar);
   add(list);                add(label);
   add(imageButton);

   button.setLocation(10,10);
   choice.setLocation(10,35);
   label.setLocation(230, 120);
   checkbox.setLocation(120, 120);

   borderAroundCanvas.setLocation(10, 75);
   borderAroundCanvas.setSize(100,100);

   textfield.setLocation(120,10);
   textfield.setSize(100,100);

   scrollbar.setLocation(120, 160);
   scrollbar.setSize(200,100);

   imageButton.setLocation(375, 10);
   imageButton.setSize(100,100);

   list.setLocation(230, 10);
   list.setSize(100,100);
}
public Insets getInsets() {
   return new Insets(10,10,10,10);
}
public void paint(Graphics g) {
   Dimension ps = getPreferredSize();
   Dimension ms = getMinimumSize();

   paintPreferredSizeBorder(ps);
```

```
        super.paint(g);
        applet.showStatus("Minimum Size:   " + ms.width + ","
                      + ms.height + "    " +
                      "Preferred Size:   " + ps.width + ","
                      + ps.height);
    }
    private void paintPreferredSizeBorder(Dimension ps) {
        dr.setSize(ps.width, ps.height);
        dr.paint();
    }
    private void createComponents() {
        button           = new Button("A Button");
        choice           = new Choice();
        textfield        = new TextField("textfield");
        checkbox         = new Checkbox("Checkbox");
        list             = new List();
        label            = new Label("A Label");
        scrollbar        = new Scrollbar(Scrollbar.HORIZONTAL);
        borderAroundCanvas = new EtchedBorder(new Canvas());
        imageButton = new ImageButton(
                        applet.getImage(applet.getCodeBase(),
                            "gifs/two_cents.gif"));
        dr = new DrawnRectangle(this);
        dr.setLocation(0,0);
        dr.setThickness(2);
        dr.setLineColor(Color.blue);

        choice.add("item one");
        choice.add("item two");
        choice.add("item three");
        choice.add("item four");

        list.add("list item one");
        list.add("list item two");
        list.add("list item three");
        list.add("list item four");
        list.add("list item five");
        list.add("list item six");
        list.add("list item seven");
        list.add("list item eight");
        list.add("list item nine");

        scrollbar.setValues(0,100,0,1000);
    }
}
```

gjt.RowLayout

You might wonder why we need custom layout managers at all. After all, we've
shown that the standard AWT layout managers are fairly comprehensive in what
they can do and that the GridBagLayout layout manager is powerful enough to

lay out almost anything. However, there are occasions when it's simpler and more straightforward to encapsulate some layout functionality in a custom layout manager than it is to commit to memory the constraints necessary to manipulate `GridBagLayout`. In fact, our `GridLabApplet` offers a case in point. Look at Figure 14-31 and notice what happens to the `Picker` when the applet is resized horizontally to about half its starting size.

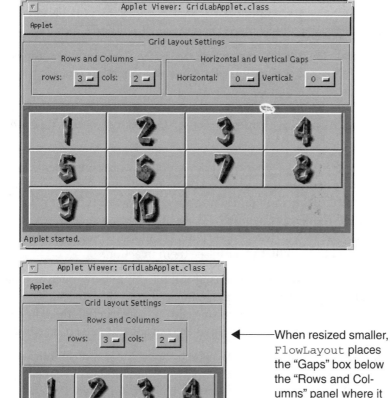

When resized smaller, `FlowLayout` places the "Gaps" box below the "Rows and Columns" panel where it is no longer visible.

Figure 14-31 `FlowLayout` Resize Behavior
FlowLayout moves components to the next row if they don't fit in the current row.

The `Picker` panel does not have a layout manager explicitly set, so it is using the default layout manager for `Panel`, which is `FlowLayout`. From the output in Figure 14-31, it appears that `FlowLayout` is unable to position the "Gaps" box appropriately. Actually, `FlowLayout` has positioned it, but you can't see it. When the applet is resized small enough that there's no longer enough room to place another component to the right of the previous one, `FlowLayout` places the next component in the next row. In `GridLabApplet`, this is causing the "Gaps" box to be hidden, because `FlowLayout` doesn't care if the `Picker` panel is tall enough to display the "Gaps" box it has placed below the "Rows and Columns" box.

We want the buttons in the boxes centered, even if both boxes don't entirely fit in the panel, so here's a case where the default layout manager is insufficient for the behavior we want. And although we could probably use `GridBagLayout` to accomplish the desired behavior, we want a more general-purpose solution that won't require us to deal with a variety of constraints each and every time we want to employ it.

Additionally, there are times when you just want to lay out components in a row or column and be guaranteed that the components will stay aligned in their row or column, no matter what kind of resizing adversity comes their way. The Graphic Java Toolkit provides two such layout managers: `gjt.RowLayout` and `gjt.ColumnLayout`. We'll discuss their implementations and show their accompanying unit tests so that you can see them in action.

The `gjt.RowLayout` layout manager is useful for components such as toolbars that might contain image buttons displayed in a row. As its name suggests, `gjt.RowLayout` lays out components in a row. At construction time, horizontal and vertical orientations and the gap between components can be specified.

To start with, take a look at Table 14-14, which shows the responsibilities of the `gjt.RowLayout` class. You'll notice that these are the standard five methods that must be defined by any class that implements `LayoutManager`.

`RowLayout` implements `addLayoutComponent()` and `removeLayoutComponent()` as no-ops—`RowLayout` does not keep track of individual components but instead lays out all of the components in containers it is called upon to lay out.

`gjt.RowLayout` is a fairly involved layout manager, so before looking at the entire source code for it, we'll highlight some details about its implementation. As described in Table 14-14, the `gjt.RowLayout` `addLayoutComponent()` and

Table 14-14 gjt.RowLayout **Responsibilities**

Methods	Description
void addLayoutComponent(String name, Component comp)	Is a *no-op* implementation.
void removeLayoutComponent(Component comp)	Is a *no-op* implementation.
Dimension preferredLayoutSize(Container targert)	Returns the preferred container height and width for the layout manager.
Dimension minimumLayoutSize(Container targert)	Returns the minimum container height and width for the layout manager.
void layoutContainer(Container target)	Positions components in a container.

removeLayoutComponent() are no-op methods, so the implementations of the other methods from the LayoutManager interface reveal exactly how gjt.RowLayout works. We'll start with preferredLayoutSize():

```
public Dimension preferredLayoutSize(Container target) {
   Insets      insets      = target.getInsets();
   Dimension dim           = new Dimension(0,0);
   int         ncomponents = target.countComponents();
   Component comp;
   Dimension d;
```

preferredLayoutSize() returns the preferred width and height of the container passed in. The insets for the container that gjt.RowLayout is going to lay out are obtained, and the preferredLayoutSize() return value is initialized to 0,0. The Component comp is a reference to the next component to be positioned and sized in the container. The Dimension d is used to hold the preferred size of each component in the container.

Next, preferredLayoutSize() loops through the components in the container and calculates the preferred size of the container.

```
    for (int i = 0; i < ncomponents; i++) {
      comp = target.getComponent(i);

      if(comp.isVisible()) {
❶        d = comp.getPreferredSize();

❷        dim.width  += d.width;
❸        dim.height  = Math.max(d.height, dim.height);

❹        if(i > 0) dim.width += gap;
      }
```

```
    }
❺   dim.width  += insets.left + insets.right;
❻   dim.height += insets.top + insets.bottom;

    return dim;
  }
```

The `for` loop cycles through every component in the container. If the `component` is visible, then the component's `getPreferredSize()` is assigned to d in line ❶. As the method loops through each component in the container, the component's preferred width is added to `dim.width` in line ❷. The preferred width of the container will be equal to the sum of the widths of all visible components plus the gaps between them.

The `dim.height` calculated in line ❸ is going to end up being the height of the tallest component in the row.

Line ❹ accounts for the gap between components. i is 0 the first time through the loop, so the gap is not added until the second time through the loop.

Line ❺ adds the left and right insets of the container to the preferred width, and line ❻ adds the top and bottom insets of the container to the preferred height. This results in the final preferred width and height for a container whose layout manager is an instance of `gjt.RowLayout`.

The `minimumLayoutSize()` implementation is calculated exactly like the `preferredLayoutSize()` except that `Dimension d` holds the minimum size of each component in the container instead of the preferred size:

```
    d = comp.getMinimumSize();
```

Note that this method of looping through the container's components is typically the way `preferredLayoutSize()` and `minimumLayoutSize()` are implemented. The algorithms for each method are often mirror images of each other, with the exception of gathering either the preferred or minimum size of the component, respectively.

(Rather than duplicate the algorithm for `preferredLayoutSize()` and `minimumLayoutSize()`, we could have coded the algorithm in a third method and passed a `boolean` value to determine whether we were calculating the preferred or minimum size. However, for the sake of illustration and because custom layout managers are often implemented with two distinct, but very similar methods, we've chosen to be a little redundant.)

The `layoutContainer()` method implementation defines exactly how components in a container are going to be positioned and sized. It calculates the positions where the container starts positioning its components. Here's how it works:

```
public void layoutContainer(Container target) {
   Insets     insets       = target.getInsets();
   int        ncomponents  = target.countComponents();
   int        top          = 0;
   int        left         = insets.left;
   Dimension  tps          = target.getPreferredSize();
   Dimension  targetSize   = target.getSize();
   Component  comp;
   Dimension  ps;

   if(horizontalOrientation == Orientation.CENTER)
      left = left + (targetSize.width/2) - (tps.width/2);
   if(horizontalOrientation == Orientation.RIGHT)
      left = left + targetSize.width - tps.width;

   for (int i = 0; i < ncomponents; i++) {
      comp = target.getComponent(i);

   if(comp.isVisible()) {
      ps  = comp.getPreferredSize();

   if(verticalOrientation == Orientation.CENTER)
      top = (targetSize.height/2) - (ps.height/2);
   else if(verticalOrientation == Orientation.TOP)
      top = insets.top;
   else if(verticalOrientation == Orientation.BOTTOM)
      top = targetSize.height - ps.height - insets.bottom;

      comp.setSize(left,top,ps.width,ps.height);
      left += ps.width + gap;
   }
 }
```

❶ and ❷ mark the two `if(horizontalOrientation ...)` lines.
❸, ❹, ❺ mark the three `verticalOrientation` lines.
❻ marks `comp.setSize(...)`.
❼ marks `left += ps.width + gap;`.

Lines ❶ and ❷ set the left edge according to the horizontal orientation. If the orientation is CENTER, the left edge is set to half of the container's width, minus half of the container's preferred size. Remember that the preferred size of the container, calculated in the `preferredLayoutSize()` is just large enough to hold all the components. If the horizontal orientation is RIGHT, then the left edge is set to the width of the container minus the preferred width of the container.

Then, `layoutContainer()` cycles through all of the components in the container and assesses the vertical orientation in lines ❸, ❹, and ❺.

Note that the `setSize()` call in line ❻ uses the left and top we've just calculated and also uses the component's preferred height and width. As a result, `RowLayout` will not stretch or shrink any component to any size other than the component's preferred height and width.

Line ❼ modifies the `left` value, placing it at the left edge of the next component so the loop can cycle through and position it appropriately.

Now, let's take a look at the `gjt.RowLayout` code in Example 14-12. Notice that a `gjt.RowLayout` has four constructors that take a variety of orientation and gap settings. As is our practice, the first three constructors call the fourth one, which does the work:

Example 14-12 `gjt.RowLayout` **Class Source Code**

```
package gjt;

import java.awt.*;

public class RowLayout implements LayoutManager {
  static private int _defaultGap = 5;

  private int gap;
  private Orientation verticalOrientation;
  private Orientation horizontalOrientation;

  public RowLayout() {
      this(Orientation.CENTER,
          Orientation.CENTER, _defaultGap);
  }
  public RowLayout(int gap) {
      this(Orientation.CENTER, Orientation.CENTER, gap);
  }
  public RowLayout(Orientation horizontalOrient,
                  Orientation verticalOrient) {
      this(horizontalOrient, verticalOrient, _defaultGap);
  }
  public RowLayout(Orientation horizontalOrient,
                  Orientation verticalOrient, int gap) {
      Assert.notFalse(gap >= 0);
      Assert.notFalse(
          horizontalOrient == Orientation.LEFT   ||
          horizontalOrient == Orientation.CENTER ||
          horizontalOrient == Orientation.RIGHT);
      Assert.notFalse(
          verticalOrient   == Orientation.TOP    ||
          verticalOrient   == Orientation.CENTER ||
```

```
        verticalOrient   == Orientation.BOTTOM);

    this.gap                 = gap;
    this.verticalOrientation   = verticalOrient;
    this.horizontalOrientation = horizontalOrient;
}
public void addLayoutComponent(String name, Component comp) {
}
public void removeLayoutComponent(Component comp) {
}
public Dimension preferredLayoutSize(Container target) {
    Insets     insets     = target.getInsets();
    Dimension dim        = new Dimension(0,0);
    int        ncomponents = target.countComponents();
    Component comp;
    Dimension d;

    for (int i = 0; i < ncomponents; i++) {
        comp = target.getComponent(i);

        if(comp.isVisible()) {
            d = comp.getPreferredSize();

            dim.width  += d.width;
            dim.height  = Math.max(d.height, dim.height);

            if(i > 0) dim.width += gap;
        }
    }
    dim.width  += insets.left + insets.right;
    dim.height += insets.top + insets.bottom;

    return dim;
}
public Dimension minimumLayoutSize(Container target) {
    Insets     insets     = target.getInsets();
    Dimension dim        = new Dimension(0,0);
    int        ncomponents = target.countComponents();
    Component comp;
    Dimension d;

    for (int i = 0; i < ncomponents; i++) {
        comp = target.getComponent(i);

        if(comp.isVisible()) {
            d = comp.getMinimumSize();

            dim.width  += d.width;
```

```
                    dim.height  = Math.max(d.height, dim.height);

                    if(i > 0) dim.width += gap;
             }
         }
         dim.width  += insets.left + insets.right;
         dim.height += insets.top + insets.bottom;

         return dim;
    }
    public void layoutContainer(Container target) {
        Insets    insets      = target.getInsets();
        int       ncomponents = target.countComponents();
        int       top         = 0;
        int       left        = insets.left;
        Dimension tps         = target.getPreferredSize();
        Dimension targetSize  = target.getSize();
        Component comp;
        Dimension ps;

        if(horizontalOrientation == Orientation.CENTER)
            left = left + (targetSize.width/2) - (tps.width/2);
        if(horizontalOrientation == Orientation.RIGHT)
            left = left + targetSize.width - tps.width;

        for (int i = 0; i < ncomponents; i++) {
            comp = target.getComponent(i);

            if(comp.isVisible()) {
                ps  = comp.getPreferredSize();

                if(verticalOrientation == Orientation.CENTER)
                    top = (targetSize.height/2) - (ps.height/2);
                else if(verticalOrientation == Orientation.TOP)
                    top = insets.top;
                else if(
                    verticalOrientation == Orientation.BOTTOM)
                    top = targetSize.height -
                            ps.height - insets.bottom;

                comp.setSize(left,top,ps.width,ps.height);
                left += ps.width + gap;
            }
        }
    }
}
```

Exercising the RowLayout Custom Layout Manager

Now that we've seen the implementation of the `gjt.RowLayout`, let's see it in action. For an idea of how `gjt.RowLayout` works, take a look at Figure 14-32, which shows the `RowLayoutApplet`.

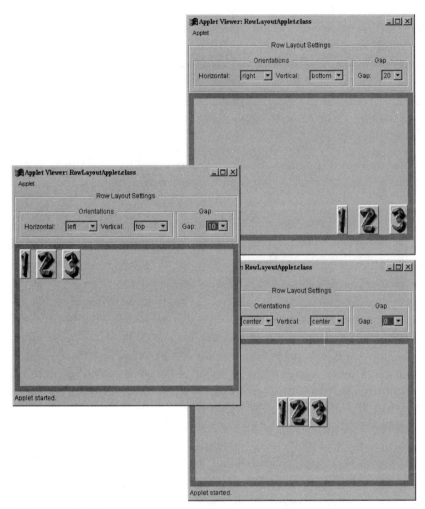

Figure 14-32 `RowLayout` at Work
This sequence of pictures shows `RowLayout` positioning image buttons in a row, with various orientation and gap settings.

You may have noticed that there are several parallels between
RowLayoutApplet and GridLabApplet, which we explored earlier in this
chapter. If you followed that discussion, then you'll quickly see what's going on
in RowLayoutApplet. Table 14-15 summarizes the similarities between the two
applets.

Table 14-15 GridLabApplet **and** RowLayoutApplet **Comparison**

GridLabApplet **Panels**	RowLayoutApplet **Panels**	**Position**
ButtonPanel	RowButtonPanel	North
Picker	RowPicker	Center

Besides the panel construction and layout, also notice that just as
GridLabApplet has itemStateChanged() and updateLayout() methods
to communicate among panels, RowLayout has itemStateChanged() and
updateOrientations() to communicate among panels. Also, just as
GridLabApplet has a ButtonPanel and Picker Panel, RowLayoutApplet
has RowButtonPanel and RowPicker.

To illustrate how panels are layered in the RowLayoutApplet, take a look at
Figure 14-33 before we go through the code.

Now, let's take a look at some of the unique characteristics of
RowLayoutApplet, starting with its init() method, where two panels are
positioned with an instance of BorderLayout. One panel is in the north and one
is in the center:

```
public void init() {
  setLayout(new BorderLayout());
  add(buttonPanel = new RowButtonPanel(this), "Center");
  add(new Box(new RowPicker(buttonPanel),
                "Row Layout Settings"), "North");
}
```

The RowPicker is a bit more complex than the RowButtonPanel, so we'll look
at it first.

```
class RowPicker extends Panel implements ItemListener {
  private Label   horientLabel = new Label("Horizontal:");
  private Label   vorientLabel = new Label("Vertical:");
  private Label   gapLabel     = new Label("Gap:");

  private Choice hchoice   = new Choice();
  private Choice vchoice   = new Choice();
  private Choice gapChoice = new Choice();
```

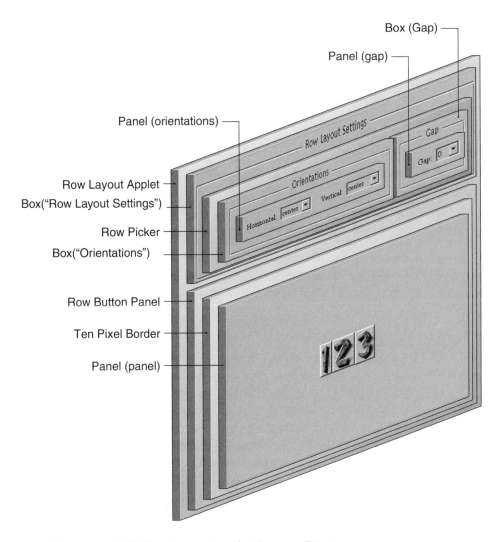

Figure 14-33 RowLayoutApplet Layout Diagram

```
private RowButtonPanel buttonPanel;

public RowPicker(RowButtonPanel buttonPanel) {
   Panel orientations = new Panel();
   Panel gap         = new Panel();

   this.buttonPanel = buttonPanel;
   hchoice.addItemListener(this);
   hchoice.addItem("left");
   hchoice.addItem("center");
```

```
hchoice.addItem("right");
hchoice.select(1);

vchoice.addItemListener(this);
vchoice.addItem("top");
vchoice.addItem("center");
vchoice.addItem("bottom");
vchoice.select(1);

gapChoice.addItemListener(this);
gapChoice.addItem("0");
gapChoice.addItem("5");
gapChoice.addItem("10");
gapChoice.addItem("15");
gapChoice.addItem("20");

orientations.add(horientLabel);
orientations.add(hchoice);
orientations.add(vorientLabel);
orientations.add(vchoice);

gap.add(gapLabel);
gap.add(gapChoice);

add(new Box(orientations,  "Orientations"));
add(new Box(gap,           "Gap"));
}
```

The first order of business is to create the Label and Choice components. The RowPicker constructor takes a buttonPanel. RowPicker maintains a reference to the RowButtonPanel instance in order to update it when the choice values are modified.

Two panels are created to hold the Label and Choice components. These panels will each be enclosed in a gjt.Box.

Next, let's look at RowButtonPanel. The RowButtonPanel is the center component in Figure 14-33 on page 461.

```
class RowButtonPanel extends Panel implements DialogClient {
   private ImageButton    one, two, three;
   private Panel          panel  = new Panel();
   private TenPixelBorder border = new TenPixelBorder(panel);

   public RowButtonPanel(Applet applet) {
      URL cb = applet.getCodeBase();

      one    = new ImageButton(applet.getImage(codeBase,
```

```
                                       "gifs/one.gif"));
        two    = new ImageButton(applet.getImage(cb,
                                       "gifs/two.gif"));
        three = new ImageButton(applet.getImage(cb,
                                       "gifs/three.gif"));

        panel.setLayout(new RowLayout(0));
        panel.add(one);
        panel.add(two);
        panel.add(three);

        setLayout(new BorderLayout());
        add        (border, "Center");
    }
}
```

Note that `panel` is passed to the `TenPixelBorder` constructor. Instances of `gjt.ImageButton` are created, and we set the layout manager of the `panel` to an instance of `gjt.RowLayout`. The `setLayout()` call sets the layout manager for the `RowButtonPanel` to be an instance of `BorderLayout`, which will center the border. So what we have here is three instance s of `ImageButton` being laid out by `RowLayout` inside a panel inside a border being laid out by `BorderLayout`. Clear as mud? Refer back to Figure 14-33 on page 461 and that should help.

We haven't mentioned it yet, but `RowLayoutApplet` provides for specifying both the horizontal and vertical orientations in the `Choice` components. `RowPicker.itemStateChanged()` and `ButtonPanel.updateOrientations()` methods manage this in `RowLayoutApplet`. The `itemStateChanged()` method is invoked whenever a selection is made in one of the choices.

```
  public void itemStateChanged(ItemEvent event) {
    String horient, vorient;
    int     gap;

    horient = hchoice.getSelectedItem();
    vorient = vchoice.getSelectedItem();
    gap     = Integer.parseInt(gapChoice.getSelectedItem());

    buttonPanel.updateOrientations(
                Orientation.fromString(horient),
                Orientation.fromString(vorient), gap);
  }
```

The selected string in the gap choice is converted into an integer value. Then we invoke the fromString() method from the gjt.Orientation class in order to convert the string selected in the choice to a gjt.Orientation constant. gjt.Orientation.fromString() returns an appropriate Orientation constant, given a string representing the constant. The orientation constants are then passed along to the updateOrientations() method.

The updateOrientations() method uses the orientation values to create and set a new instance of RowLayout:

```
public void updateOrientations(Orientation horient,
                                Orientation vorient,
                                int gap) {
    panel.setLayout(new RowLayout(horient, vorient, gap));
    border.validate();
}
```

Remember that the call to setLayout() invalidates the panel and its container (border), and therefore the call to border.validate() results in the panel being laid out.

RowLayoutApplet Implementation

Now let's look through the RowLayoutApplet class in Example 14-13. As you look through the code, particularly note the use of RowButtonPanel and RowPicker. You may also want to refer to the 3-D layout diagram in Figure 14-33 on page 461.

Example 14-13 RowLayoutApplet **Class Source Code**

```
import java.applet.Applet;
import java.net.URL;
import java.awt.*;
import java.awt.event.*;
import gjt.*;

public class RowLayoutApplet extends Applet {
  private RowButtonPanel buttonPanel;

  public void init() {
    setLayout(new BorderLayout());
    add(buttonPanel = new RowButtonPanel(this), "Center");
    add(new Box(new RowPicker(buttonPanel),
                     "Row Layout Settings"), "North");
  }
}
class RowButtonPanel extends Panel implements DialogClient {
  private ImageButton    one, two, three;
  private Panel          panel  = new Panel();
```

```
   private TenPixelBorder border = new TenPixelBorder(panel);

   public RowButtonPanel(Applet applet) {
      URL cb = applet.getCodeBase();

      one   = new ImageButton(applet.getImage(cb,
                              "gifs/one.gif"));
      two   = new ImageButton(applet.getImage(cb,
                              "gifs/two.gif"));
      three = new ImageButton(applet.getImage(cb,
                              "gifs/three.gif"));

      panel.setLayout(new RowLayout(0));
      panel.add(one);
      panel.add(two);
      panel.add(three);

      setLayout(new BorderLayout());
      add       (border, "Center");
   }
   public void updateOrientations(Orientation horient,
                                  Orientation vorient,
                                  int gap) {
      panel.setLayout(new RowLayout(horient, vorient, gap));
      border.validate();
   }
   public void dialogDismissed(Dialog d) { }
}
class RowPicker extends Panel implements ItemListener {
   private Label  horientLabel = new Label("Horizontal:");
   private Label  vorientLabel = new Label("Vertical:");
   private Label  gapLabel     = new Label("Gap:");

   private Choice hchoice   = new Choice();
   private Choice vchoice   = new Choice();
   private Choice gapChoice = new Choice();

   private RowButtonPanel buttonPanel;

   public RowPicker(RowButtonPanel buttonPanel) {
      Panel orientations = new Panel();
      Panel gap          = new Panel();

      this.buttonPanel = buttonPanel;

      hchoice.addItemListener(this);
      hchoice.addItem("left");
      hchoice.addItem("center");
      hchoice.addItem("right");
      hchoice.select(1);
```

```
        vchoice.addItemListener(this);
        vchoice.addItem("top");
        vchoice.addItem("center");
        vchoice.addItem("bottom");
        vchoice.select(1);

        gapChoice.addItemListener(this);
        gapChoice.addItem("0");
        gapChoice.addItem("5");
        gapChoice.addItem("10");
        gapChoice.addItem("15");
        gapChoice.addItem("20");

        orientations.add(horientLabel);
        orientations.add(hchoice);
        orientations.add(vorientLabel);
        orientations.add(vchoice);

        gap.add(gapLabel);
        gap.add(gapChoice);

        add(new Box(orientations, "Orientations"));
        add(new Box(gap,          "Gap"));
    }
    public void itemStateChanged(ItemEvent event) {
        String horient, vorient;
        int    gap;

        horient = hchoice.getSelectedItem();
        vorient = vchoice.getSelectedItem();
        gap     = Integer.parseInt(gapChoice.getSelectedItem());

        buttonPanel.updateOrientations(
                Orientation.fromString(horient),
                Orientation.fromString(vorient), gap);
    }
}
```

gjt.ColumnLayout

The ColumnLayout layout manager is another custom layout manager provided by the Graphic Java Toolkit. It is very similar in design and capability to the RowLayout layout manager, except that it positions components in columns instead of rows. You'll notice in Table 14-16 that, like all custom layout managers, ColumnLayout implements the standard LayoutManager methods.

Since the ColumnLayout implementation is so close to the RowLayout custom layout manager, we won't discuss it. We include it here for completeness. Example 14-14 shows the ColumnLayout code.

Table 14-16 `gjt.ColumnLayout` **Responsibilities**

Methods	Description
`void addLayoutComponent(` `   String name, Component comp)`	Is a no-op implementation.
`void removedLayoutComponent(` `   Component comp)`	Is a no-op implementation.
`Dimension preferredLayoutSize(` `   Container targert)`	Returns the preferred container height and width for the layout manager.
`Dimension minimumLayoutSize(` `   Container targert)`	Returns the minimum container height and width for the layout manager.
`void layoutContainer(` `   Container target)`	Positions components in a container.

Example 14-14 `gjt.ColumnLayout` **Class Source Code**

```
package gjt;

import java.awt.*;

public class ColumnLayout implements LayoutManager {
   static private int _defaultGap = 5;

   private int        gap;
   private Orientation horizontalOrientation;
   private Orientation verticalOrientation;

   public ColumnLayout() {
      this(Orientation.CENTER,
          Orientation.CENTER, _defaultGap);
   }
   public ColumnLayout(int gap) {
      this(Orientation.CENTER, Orientation.CENTER, gap);
   }
   public ColumnLayout(Orientation horizontalOrient,
                       Orientation verticalOrient) {
      this(horizontalOrient, verticalOrient, _defaultGap);
   }
   public ColumnLayout(Orientation horizontalOrient,
                       Orientation verticalOrient, int gap) {
      Assert.notFalse(gap >= 0);
      Assert.notFalse(
         horizontalOrient == Orientation.LEFT   ||
         horizontalOrient == Orientation.CENTER ||
         horizontalOrient == Orientation.RIGHT);
      Assert.notFalse(
         verticalOrient   == Orientation.TOP    ||
```

```
                verticalOrient    == Orientation.CENTER ||
                verticalOrient    == Orientation.BOTTOM);

        this.gap                   = gap;
        this.verticalOrientation   = verticalOrient;
        this.horizontalOrientation = horizontalOrient;
    }
    public void addLayoutComponent(String name,
                                    Component comp) {

    }
    public void removeLayoutComponent(Component comp) {
    }

    public Dimension preferredLayoutSize(Container target) {
        Insets    insets      = target.getInsets();
        Dimension dim         = new Dimension(0,0);
        int       ncomponents = target.countComponents();
        Component comp;
        Dimension d;

        for (int i = 0; i < ncomponents; i++) {
            comp = target.getComponent(i);

            if(comp.isVisible()) {
                d = comp.getPreferredSize();
                if(i > 0)
                    dim.height += gap;

                dim.height += d.height;
                dim.width   = Math.max(d.width, dim.width);
            }
        }
        dim.width  += insets.left + insets.right;
        dim.height += insets.top  + insets.bottom;
        return dim;
    }
    public Dimension minimumLayoutSize(Container target) {
        Insets    insets      = target.getInsets();
        Dimension dim         = new Dimension(0,0);
        int       ncomponents = target.countComponents();
        Component comp;
        Dimension d;

        for (int i = 0; i < ncomponents; i++) {
            comp = target.getComponent(i);

            if(comp.isVisible()) {
                d = comp.getMinimumSize();
```

```
                dim.width   = Math.max(d.width, dim.width);
                dim.height += d.height;

                if(i > 0) dim.height += gap;
            }
        }
        dim.width  += insets.left + insets.right;
        dim.height += insets.top  + insets.bottom;

        return dim;
    }
    public void layoutContainer(Container target) {
        Insets    insets           = target.getInsets();
        int       top              = insets.top;
        int       left             = 0;
        int       ncomponents      = target.countComponents();
        Dimension getPreferredSize = target.getPreferredSize();
        Dimension targetSize       = target.getSize();
        Component comp;
        Dimension ps;

        if(verticalOrientation == Orientation.CENTER)
            top += (targetSize.height/2) -
                    (getPreferredSize.height/2);
        else if(verticalOrientation == Orientation.BOTTOM)
            top = targetSize.height - getPreferredSize.height +
                    insets.top;

        for (int i = 0; i < ncomponents; i++) {
            comp = target.getComponent(i);
            left = insets.left;

            if(comp.isVisible()) {
                ps = comp.getPreferredSize();

                if(horizontalOrientation == Orientation.CENTER)
                    left = (targetSize.width/2) - (ps.width/2);
                else if(
                  horizontalOrientation == Orientation.RIGHT) {
                    left = targetSize.width - ps.width -
                            insets.right;
                }
                comp.setSize(left,top,ps.width,ps.height);
                top += ps.height + gap;
            }
        }
    }
}
```

Exercising the ColumnLayout Custom Layout Manager

Figure 14-34 shows the `ColumnLayoutApplet`. As you can see, the `ColumnLayout` layout manager positions components in column format according to the orientations specified in the `Choice` selections in the top panel of the applet.

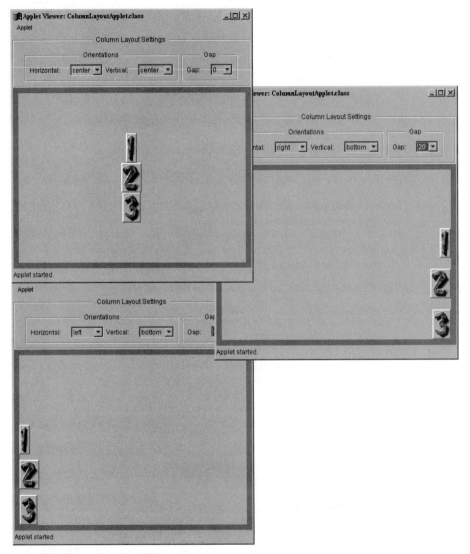

Figure 14-34 ColumnLayout at Work
This sequence of pictures shows ColumnLayout positioning image buttons in their container.

Example 14-15 shows the `ColumnLayoutApplet` code, so you can see how it employs the `ColumnLayout` layout manager. Again, since `ColumnLayoutApplet` is very similar to `RowLayoutApplet`, we will not bother to discuss the code.

Example 14-15 `ColumnLayoutApplet` **Class Source Code**

```
import java.applet.Applet;
import java.net.URL;
import java.awt.*;
import java.awt.event.*;
import gjt.*;

public class ColumnLayoutApplet extends Applet {
  private ColumnButtonPanel buttonPanel;

  public void init() {
     setLayout(new BorderLayout());
     add(buttonPanel = new ColumnButtonPanel(this), "Center");
     add(new Box(new ColumnPicker(buttonPanel),
                     "Column Layout Settings"), "North");
  }
}
class ColumnButtonPanel extends Panel implements DialogClient {
  private ImageButton     one, two, three;
  private Panel           panel  = new Panel();
  private TenPixelBorder border = new TenPixelBorder(panel);

  public ColumnButtonPanel(Applet applet) {
     URL cb = applet.getCodeBase();

     one   = new ImageButton(applet.getImage(cb,
                          "gifs/one.gif"));
     two   = new ImageButton(applet.getImage(cb,
                          "gifs/two.gif"));
     three = new ImageButton(applet.getImage(cb,
                          "gifs/three.gif"));

     panel.setLayout(new ColumnLayout(0));
     panel.add(one);
     panel.add(two);
     panel.add(three);

     setLayout(new BorderLayout());
     add       (border, "Center");
  }
  public void updateOrientations(Orientation horient,
                               Orientation vorient,
```

```
                              int gap) {
      panel.setLayout(new ColumnLayout(horient, vorient, gap));
      border.validate();
   }
   public void dialogDismissed(Dialog d) { }
}
class ColumnPicker extends Panel implements ItemListener {
   private Label   horientLabel = new Label("Horizontal:");
   private Label   vorientLabel = new Label("Vertical:");
   private Label   gapLabel     = new Label("Gap:");

   private Choice hchoice   = new Choice();
   private Choice vchoice   = new Choice();
   private Choice gapChoice = new Choice();

   private ColumnButtonPanel buttonPanel;

   public ColumnPicker(ColumnButtonPanel buttonPanel) {
      Panel orientations = new Panel();
      Panel gap          = new Panel();

      this.buttonPanel = buttonPanel;

      hchoice.addItemListener(this);
      hchoice.addItem("left");
      hchoice.addItem("center");
      hchoice.addItem("right");
      hchoice.select(1);

      vchoice.addItemListener(this);
      vchoice.addItem("top");
      vchoice.addItem("center");
      vchoice.addItem("bottom");
      vchoice.select(1);

      gapChoice.addItemListener(this);
      gapChoice.addItem("0");
      gapChoice.addItem("5");
      gapChoice.addItem("10");
      gapChoice.addItem("15");
      gapChoice.addItem("20");

      orientations.add(horientLabel);
      orientations.add(hchoice);
      orientations.add(vorientLabel);
      orientations.add(vchoice);

      gap.add(gapLabel);
```

```
    gap.add(gapChoice);

    add(new Box(orientations, "Orientations"));
    add(new Box(gap,          "Gap"));
  }
  public void itemStateChanged(ItemEvent event) {
    String horient, vorient;
    int    gap;

    horient = hchoice.getSelectedItem();
    vorient = vchoice.getSelectedItem();
    gap     = Integer.parseInt(gapChoice.getSelectedItem());

    buttonPanel.updateOrientations(
        Orientation.fromString(horient),
        Orientation.fromString(vorient), gap);
  }
}
```

Summary

Containers in the AWT delegate positioning and shaping the components they contain to a layout manager. The AWT provides a set of five layout managers that are sufficient for most layout needs.

The tricky part about using the standard AWT layout managers is knowing when to use which one, but there are a few tips (see *Standard AWT Layout Managers* on page 392) that can help you until you've gained enough practice and experience that the decision is second nature.

The standard layout managers are fairly comprehensive in terms of the number of ways they can arrange components in a display. However, for those occasions when they just don't provide the desired behavior, you can implement your own implementation of the LayoutManager (or LayoutManager2) interface and create your own custom layout manager. This is as simple as defining the five methods in the LayoutManager interface, as we've shown in the Graphic Java Toolkit's BulletinLayout, RowLayout, and ColumnLayout custom layout managers.

CHAPTER 15

Lightweight Components

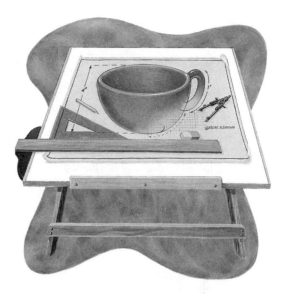

AWT components are heavyweight, meaning they have a native peer and are rendered in an opaque window of their own. Since a heavyweight component is rendered in its own opaque window, it must always be rectangular in shape; if you want a see-through component, a heavyweight won't cut the mustard. Also, as you might suspect, a 1/1 ratio of native window per AWT component is not exactly ideal from a performance perspective.

Lightweight components do not require a native window because they are rendered in their container's graphics. As a result, lightweight components require less resources than heavyweight components, and their backgrounds are transparent. Having transparent backgrounds means that lightweight components can appear to be non-rectangular, even though the bounding box of a lightweight component (obtained by invoking `Component.getBounds()`) is rectangular.

Lightweight Components

Developing custom components under previous versions of the AWT typically involved extending either `java.awt.Canvas` or `java.awt.Panel`—the latter was extended when a custom component had to function as a container.

Lightweight custom components are implemented simply by extending either `java.awt.Component` or `java.awt.Container`. With previous versions of the AWT, `Component` and `Container` could only be extended by classes residing in the `java.awt package`, because their constructors had package scope. This restriction has been removed in 1.1—classes outside of the `java.awt` package may now extend either `Component` or `Container`.

The AWT: A Heavyweight World

In principle, creating a lightweight component (or container) is a simple matter: extend either Component or Container, and you have a lightweight component or container, respectively.

In the guts of the AWT code, however, things are not so simple. For quite some time now, AWT code has been accustomed to being passed components that have their own native windows, and that come complete with a native peer. Suddenly, the same code is being asked to deal with a different breed of component. As a result, as of 1.1.1, lightweight components suffered from a number of bugs. For instance, lightweight components did not receive focus like their heavyweight counterparts, and lightweight containers did not properly lay out heavyweight components. We expect many of the bugs to be fixed in the near future, perhaps by the time you read this. A patch release of the AWT (1.1.2), with expected lightweight bug fixes, was scheduled to be released shortly after we went to press.

Lightweights vs. Heavyweights

Lightweights are lightweight by virtue of the fact that they do not require their own native window in which to be rendered. Instead, they are painted into their container's window. This has serious repercussions in the AWT code because code that used to rely on components having their own window—and therefore coordinate system—now has to watch for lightweights and translate them into the parent container's coordinate system.

Another distinction to enumerate is that lightweight components do not have a peer, as their heavyweight counterparts do[1].

Our point here is that heavyweight components are peer-based components that are rendered in their own native window, whereas lightweights are peerless and are drawn into the windows of their container.

---

1. Actually, the 1.1 version of the AWT provides a lightweight peer, but it is merely a placeholder that will be deprecated in subsequent releases of the AWT.

A Simple Lightweight Component

As you might have deduced by the preceding introduction, lightweight components are extremely simple to implement—a lightweight component is lightweight by virtue of the fact that it extends either `Component` or `Container`. Since lightweights are components, we can manipulate lightweights in exactly the same manner as we do their heavyweight counterparts; that is, we can set their locations, paint them, add them to containers, and so on.

A Simple Heavyweight Component

Let's start out by implementing a simple *heavyweight* component that extends `Panel` and paints an image. Then, in order to illustrate the ease of implementing lightweight components (and to point out a potential pitfall), we'll turn our heavyweight component into a lightweight—you can see the implementation of our simple heavyweight component in Example 15-1.

Example 15-1 A Simple Heavyweight Component That Paints an Image

```
import java.applet.Applet;
import java.awt.*;

public class SimpleHeavyweight extends Applet {
  private Image dining, paper;

  public void init() {
     dining = getImage(getCodeBase(),"../gifs/Dining.gif");
     paper  = getImage(getCodeBase(),"../gifs/paper.gif");
     add(new Heavyweight(dining));
  }
  public void paint(Graphics g) {
     gjt.Util.wallPaper(this, g, paper);
  }
}
class Heavyweight extends Panel {
  private Image    image;

  public Heavyweight(Image image) {
     this.image = image;
     gjt.Util.waitForImage(this, image);
  }
  public void paint(Graphics g) {
     g.drawImage(image, 0, 0, this);
  }
  public Dimension getPreferredSize() {
     return new Dimension(image.getWidth(this),
                          image.getHeight(this));
  }
}
```

There are a couple of things to note about our simple heavyweight component and the applet that exercises it. First, note that we use two methods from the gjt.Util[2] class—one to wait for an image to load and another to wallpaper the background of the applet with an image. Second, as you can see from Figure 15-1, our heavyweight component is indeed drawn in its own opaque window.

Figure 15-1 A Simple *Heavyweight* Component
Note the opaque background of the component, which signifies that the component is painted within its own opaque window.

From Heavyweight to Lightweight

In order to turn our heavyweight component into a lightweight, we simply change its superclass to Component instead of Panel, as we've done in Example 15-2.

Example 15-2 A Simple Lightweight Component That Paints an Image

```
import java.applet.Applet;
import java.awt.*;

public class SimpleLightweight extends Applet {
  private Image dining, paper;
    public void init() {
        dining = getImage(getCodeBase(),"../gifs/Dining.gif");
        paper  = getImage(getCodeBase(),"../gifs/paper.gif");
        add(new Lightweight(dining));
  }
  public void paint(Graphics g) {
    gjt.Util.wallPaper(this, g, paper);
  }
}
class Lightweight extends Component {
```

2.   We introduced the gjt.Util class in "Using MediaTracker" on page 340.

```
   private Image    image;

   public Lightweight(Image image) {
      this.image = image;
      gjt.Util.waitForImage(this, image);
   }
   public void paint(Graphics g) {
      g.drawImage(image, 0, 0, this);
   }
   public Dimension getPreferredSize() {
      return new Dimension(image.getWidth(this),
                           image.getHeight(this));
   }
}
```

However, if you compile and run the `SimpleLightweight` applet, you may be surprised to find that the applet displays no components whatsoever! Although we have indeed turned our heavyweight component into a lightweight simply by changing its superclass to `Component`, the lightweight component is a no-show because we have overridden `Container.paint()`[3] in our applet class. Taking a look at the implementation of `Container.paint()` in Example 15-3 will shed some light on why our lightweight component is not showing up in our applet.

Example 15-3 `Container.paint()` Implementation

```
public void paint(Graphics g) {
   int ncomponents = this.ncomponents;
   Rectangle clip = g.getClipBounds();

   for (int i = 0; i < ncomponents; i++) {
      Component comp = component[i];

      if (comp != null && comp.peer instanceof
                           java.awt.peer.LightweightPeer) {
         Rectangle cr = comp.getBounds();

         if (cr.intersects(clip)) {
            Graphics cg = g.create(cr.x, cr.y,
                                   cr.width, cr.height);
            comp.paint(cg);
         }
      }
   }
}
```

3. `Container.paint()` was added in 1.1 for the express purpose of painting light-weights—there was no `Container.paint()` method in the 1.02 version of the AWT.

`Container.paint()` is responsible for painting all of the lightweight components contained in the container, as long as they intersect the bounds of the clip rectangle associated with the container's graphics. Since our container (the applet) has overridden `Container.paint()`, none of the lightweight components are painted. The fix for our broken applet, then, is to invoke `super.paint()` to ensure that the lightweight components get painted, as shown below.

```
public void paint(Graphics g) {
    gjt.Util.wallPaper(this, g, paper);
    super.paint(g);
}
```

Now our lightweight component is painted in the applet, as you can see in Figure 15-2. Notice that there is no opaque border around the image—our lightweight component is painted in its container's graphics, not in an opaque window of its own.

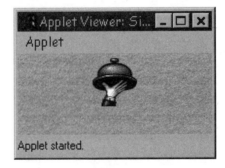

Figure 15-2 Serving Up a Simple Lightweight Component
Note that the lightweight is painted in its container's graphics, not in its own opaque window.

AWT TIP...

Remember to Invoke super.paint() When Overriding Container.paint()

In order to ensure that a container paints the lightweight components it contains, it is imperative that you invoke super.paint() in overridden paint() methods for your containers. Even if your container contains only heavyweight components, it is still a good idea to call super.paint(). Invoking super.paint() for a container with no lightweight components will resolve to a no-op, and you may very well decide to add lightweight components to the container in the future.

Lightweight Containers

Lightweight *components* extend `java.awt.Component`, and lightweight *containers* extend `java.awt.Container`. In Example 15-4, we've added a lightweight container to the previous applet. Just like any other container, we can add components to a lightweight container, which we've done by adding an instance of `Lightweight` to our lightweight container.

Example 15-4 A Lightweight Container

```
import java.applet.Applet;
import java.awt.*;

public class SimpleLightweightContainer extends Applet {
  private Image dining, paper;

  public void init() {
     dining = getImage(getCodeBase(),"../gifs/Dining.gif");
     paper  = getImage(getCodeBase(),"../gifs/paper.gif");

     Container container = new LightweightContainer(paper);
     container.add(new Lightweight(dining));
     setLayout(new BorderLayout());
     add(container, "Center");
  }
}
class LightweightContainer extends Container {
  private Image wallpaperImage;

  public LightweightContainer(Image wallpaperImage) {
     this.wallpaperImage = wallpaperImage;
  }
  public void paint(Graphics g) {
     gjt.Util.wallPaper(this, g, wallpaperImage);
     super.paint(g);
  }
}
class Lightweight extends Component {
  private Image    image;

  public Lightweight(Image image) {
     this.image = image;
     gjt.Util.waitForImage(this, image);
  }
  public void paint(Graphics g) {
     g.drawImage(image, 0, 0, this);
  }
  public Dimension getPreferredSize() {
```

```
          return new Dimension(image.getWidth(this),
                               image.getHeight(this));
    }
  }
```

Note that we've followed our own advice and invoked `super.paint()` in the lightweight container's overridden `paint()` method to ensure that the lightweight components get painted. However, once again, much to our chagrin, our lightweight component is nowhere to be found. This time the catch is this: `Container`, unlike all other AWT containers, has no default layout manager, and therefore our lightweight component never gets laid out. The solution, of course, is to fit our lightweight container with a layout manager:

```
public LightweightContainer(Image wallpaperImage) {
  this.wallpaperImage = wallpaperImage;
  setLayout(new FlowLayout());
}
```

Once we've fitted our lightweight container with a layout manager, the container's components get laid out, and our applet once again looks like the applet in Figure 15-2.

AWT TIP ...

Lightweight Containers Must Be Fitted With a Layout Manager

Lightweight containers, by default, have a null layout manager. If you want a lightweight container's components (regardless of whether they are lightweight or heavyweight components) to be painted, you must fit the lightweight container with a layout manager of some sort. Alternatively, you can manually set the locations of each component in the container, but the preferred approach is to fit the container with a layout manager.

DoubleBuffering

Double buffering is an essential tool for smoothly painting and dragging lightweight components (not to mention smooth animations). As we saw in "gjt.image.ImageDissolver" on page 357, double buffering involves painting images into an offscreen buffer, then, after everything has been rendered in the offscreen buffer, blitting the contents (partial or whole) of the offscreen buffer to the onscreen graphics. In fact, if you take a look at the documentation for lightweight components (see http://www.javasoft.com/products/JDK/1.1/docs/guide/awt/designspec/lig

htweights.html) you will find a simplistic example of double buffering—the
`DoubleBufferPanel` shown in Example 15-5—that can be used to smoothly
paint lightweight components.

Example 15-5 `DoubleBufferPanel`—A Simplistic Double Buffering Example

```java
import java.awt.*;

public class DoubleBufferPanel extends Panel {
  Image offscreen;
  /**
  * null out the offscreen buffer as part of invalidation
  */
  public void invalidate() {
    super.invalidate();
    offscreen = null;
  }
  /**
  * override update to *not* erase the background before painting
  */
  public void update(Graphics g) {
    paint(g);
  }
  /**
  * paint children into an offscreen buffer, then blast entire
  * image
  * at once.
  */
  public void paint(Graphics g) {
    if(offscreen == null) {
      offscreen = createImage(getSize().width, getSize().height);
    }
    Graphics og = offscreen.getGraphics();
    og.setClip(0,0,getSize().width, getSize().height);
    super.paint(og);
    g.drawImage(offscreen, 0, 0, null);
    og.dispose();
  }
}
```

While `DoubleBufferPanel` does a good job of illustrating the basic technique
of double buffering, it is impractical for real-world usage because:

- Painting, erasing or moving a single component is not supported.
- Painting a background into the panel is not supported.
- The entire offscreen buffer is blitted to the screen even if only part of the
  buffer needs to be updated.

In the pages that follow, we'll implement a double buffered container that remedies all of the above maladies and provides some extra bells and whistles in the process. Our double buffered container relies on two other classes:

- `gjt.Util`—as we've seen, provides some handy utility methods.
- `OffscreenBuffer`—encapsulates the grunt work of manipulating offscreen buffers.

gjt.Util

`gjt.Util` is a simple utility class that, among other things, includes support for handling three rather mundane tasks: waiting for an image to load, wallpapering (tiling) the background of a component with an image, and stretching an image over the background of a component. We've used `gjt.Util` previously and we felt that it was time to show you the implementation of some of the methods we've been using[4]. The relevant methods from `gjt.Util` are shown in Example 15-6.

Example 15-6 `gjt.Util` Graphics Utility Methods

```
public class Util {
...
  public static void waitForImage(Component component,
                                  Image image) {
    MediaTracker tracker = new MediaTracker(component);
    try {
        tracker.addImage(image, 0);
        tracker.waitForID(0);
    }
    catch(InterruptedException e) { e.printStackTrace(); }
  }
  public static void wallPaper(Component component,
                               Graphics  g,
                               Image      image) {
    Dimension compsize = component.getSize();

    waitForImage(component, image);

    int patchW = image.getWidth(component);
    int patchH = image.getHeight(component);

    Assert.notFalse(patchW != -1 && patchH != -1);

    for(int r=0; r < compsize.width; r += patchW) {
```

4. We did show the implementation of `gjt.Util.waitForImage()` in "Using MediaTracker" on page 340.

```
            for(int c=0; c < compsize.height; c += patchH)
                g.drawImage(image, r, c, component);
        }
    }
    public static void stretchImage(Component component,
                                    Graphics  g,
                                    Image     image) {
        Dimension sz = component.getSize();
        waitForImage(component, image);
        g.drawImage(image, 0, 0, sz.width, sz.height, component);
    }
    ...
}
```

OffscreenBuffer

Since a great deal of the implementation for a double buffered container involves managing offscreen buffers, we've encapsulated that functionality in a class of its own: OffscreenBuffer, shown in Example 15-7. OffscreenBuffer actually maintains two offscreen buffers: a background buffer that contains nothing but the background, and a workplace buffer, into which we render images before blitting them to the screen. OffscreenBuffer is a fairly simple-minded class— as you can see, it maintains two offscreen buffers and keeps track of the DoubleBufferedContainer on whose behalf it is manipulating the buffers, along with the current size of the offscreen buffer:

```
public class OffscreenBuffer {
    private DoubleBufferedContainer container;
    private Image wpBuffer,   // workplace  buffer
                  bgBuffer;   // background buffer
    private Dimension offscreenSize;

    public OffscreenBuffer(DoubleBufferedContainer container) {
        this.container = container;
    }
    ...
```

Note that DoubleBufferedContainer and OffscreenBuffer are tightly coupled; in fact, OffscreenBuffer cannot exist without an instance of DoubleBufferedContainer. As a result, implementing OffscreenBuffer as an inner class of DoubleBufferedContainer[5] is a recommended approach; however, we felt the clarity of the code would benefit from implementing OffscreenBuffer as a top-level class.

The responsibilities of OffscreenBuffer fall into three categories:

5. We have done exactly that in the GJT version of DoubleBufferedContainer.

1.   Getters for buffers (Images) and Graphics:

```java
public Image getWorkplaceBuffer () { return wpBuffer; }
public Image getBackgroundBuffer() { return bgBuffer; }

public Graphics getWorkplaceGraphics () {
    return wpBuffer.getGraphics();
}
public Graphics getBackgroundGraphics() {
    return bgBuffer.getGraphics();
}
```

2.   Blitting methods for blitting all or parts of one buffer to another (or to the screen). OffscreenBuffer provides two variations of its blitting methods: one, taking no arguments, that blits an entire buffer to another buffer (or the screen), and another that takes a clipping rectangle, for clipping the blitting to the specified rectangle:

```java
public void blitWorkplaceToScreen() {
    blitWorkplaceToScreen(null);
}
public void blitBackgroundToWorkplace() {
    blitBackgroundToWorkplace(null);
}
public void blitWorkplaceToScreen(Rectangle clip) {
    Graphics screenGraphics = container.getGraphics();
    if(clip != null) {
        screenGraphics.setClip(clip);
    }
    screenGraphics.drawImage(wpBuffer, 0, 0, container);
    screenGraphics.dispose();
}
public void blitBackgroundToWorkplace(Rectangle clip) {
    Graphics wpg = getWorkplaceGraphics();
    if(clip != null) {
        wpg.setClip(clip);
    }
    wpg.drawImage(bgBuffer, 0, 0, container);
    wpg.dispose();
}
```

3.   The creation and updating of the buffers themselves:

```java
void update() {
    if(needNewOffscreenBuffer()) {
        createBuffers();
    }
}
```

```
      private boolean needNewOffscreenBuffer() {
          Dimension size = container.getSize();
          return (wpBuffer == null ||
                  size.width  != offscreenSize.width ||
                  size.height != offscreenSize.height);
      }
      private void createBuffers() {
          offscreenSize = container.getSize();
          wpBuffer      = createOffscreenImage(offscreenSize);
          bgBuffer      = createOffscreenImage(offscreenSize);
      }
      private Image createOffscreenImage(Dimension size) {
          Image image = container.createImage(size.width,
                                              size.height);
          Graphics g  = image.getGraphics();
          gjt.Util.waitForImage(container, image);
          g.dispose();

          return image;
      }
  }
```

OffscreenBuffer is shown in its entirety in Example 15-7.

Example 15-7 Class OffscreenBuffer

```
  import java.awt.*;

  public class OffscreenBuffer {
    private DoubleBufferedContainer container;
    private Image wpBuffer,  // workplace  buffer
                 bgBuffer;  // background buffer
    private Dimension offscreenSize;

    public OffscreenBuffer(DoubleBufferedContainer container) {
       this.container = container;
    }
    public Image getWorkplaceBuffer () { return wpBuffer; }
    public Image getBackgroundBuffer() { return bgBuffer; }

    public Graphics getWorkplaceGraphics() {
       return wpBuffer.getGraphics();
    }
    public Graphics getBackgroundGraphics() {
       return bgBuffer.getGraphics();
    }
    public void blitWorkplaceToScreen() {
       blitWorkplaceToScreen(null);
    }
```

```
public void blitBackgroundToWorkplace() {
   blitBackgroundToWorkplace(null);
}
public void blitWorkplaceToScreen(Rectangle clip) {
   Graphics screenGraphics = container.getGraphics();
   if(clip != null) {
      screenGraphics.setClip(clip);
   }
   screenGraphics.drawImage(wpBuffer, 0, 0, container);
   screenGraphics.dispose();
}
public void blitBackgroundToWorkplace(Rectangle clip) {
   Graphics wpg = getWorkplaceGraphics();
   if(clip != null) {
      wpg.setClip(clip);
   }
   wpg.drawImage(bgBuffer, 0, 0, container);
   wpg.dispose();
}
void update() {
   if(needNewOffscreenBuffer()) {
      createBuffers();
   }
}
private boolean needNewOffscreenBuffer() {
   Dimension size = container.getSize();
   return (wpBuffer == null ||
           size.width  != offscreenSize.width ||
           size.height != offscreenSize.height);
}
private void createBuffers() {
   offscreenSize = container.getSize();
   wpBuffer      = createOffscreenImage(offscreenSize);
   bgBuffer      = createOffscreenImage(offscreenSize);
}
private Image createOffscreenImage(Dimension size) {
   Image image = container.createImage(size.width,
                                       size.height);
   Graphics g  = image.getGraphics();
   gjt.Util.waitForImage(container, image);
   g.dispose();
   return image;
}
}
```

It's worth pointing out that we could have gotten away with only one offscreen buffer (the workplace buffer) and dispensed with the background buffer—the background buffer, at first glance, may seem to be a somewhat wasteful luxury.

Without a background buffer, when we need to blit a *piece* of the background into a particular region, we could repaint the entire background with clipping set to the region we need to blit into, thus obviating the need for a separate background buffer. However, such a technique means that no matter how small the region is that we're blitting a piece of the background into, the entire background still gets redrawn. When the background is tiled from a relatively small image, the time required for blitting a piece of the background into a region is proportional to the size of the background. With a small background, for instance, dragging a lightweight component or animating a sprite is quite snappy, but the performance degrades considerably if the background covers a fair bit of ground. As a result, we chose to be somewhat wasteful with our memory usage, in exchange for excellent performance when blitting pieces of the background into a particular region—an operation, that, as it turns out, is quite common, especially when dragging lightweight components.

AWT TIP ...

Display Lightweight Components In a Double-Buffered Container

Lightweight containers, instead of being drawn by native peers (as heavyweight components are) are drawn entirely in Java code. Therefore, in order to eliminate flashing when lightweights are painted, it is advisable to place lightweights in a double-buffered container. The Graphic Java Toolkit comes with just such a container: gjt.DoubleBufferedContainer, which is very similar to the double buffered container discussed in this chapter.

DoubleBufferedContainer

Finally, we come to the implementation of `DoubleBufferedContainer` itself, shown in Example 15-8. `DoubleBufferedContainer` creates an instance of `OffscreenBuffer`, and provides a constructor that takes an image which is used to wallpaper the background of the container. The same constructor also adds a component listener, which is defined inline as an inner class[6]. When `DoubleBufferedContainer` is resized, it will update its buffers and repaint in order to ensure that the offscreen buffers are always in synch with the size of the `DoubleBufferedContainer`:

```
public class DoubleBufferedContainer extends Container {
   private    Image           wallpaperImage;
   protected OffscreenBuffer buffers =
                          new OffscreenBuffer(this);
```

---

6. See "Anonymous Inner Classes" on page 125 for a discussion of inner classes and event handling.

```
public DoubleBufferedContainer() {
   this(null);
}
public DoubleBufferedContainer(Image wallpaperImage) {
   if(wallpaperImage != null)
      setWallpaperImage(wallpaperImage);

   addComponentListener(new ComponentAdapter() {
      public void componentResized(ComponentEvent event) {
         buffers.update();
         repaint();
      }
   });
}
```

The `DoubleBufferedContainer.paint()` method first checks to see if the window in which the container resides has been damaged[7]; if so, it blits the workplace buffer to the screen, clipped to the damaged area of the window, thus repainting only the damaged area.

```
public void paint(Graphics g) {
   if(windowDamaged(g)) {
      buffers.blitWorkplaceToScreen(g.getClipBounds());
   }
   else {
      Graphics  wpg  = buffers.getWorkplaceGraphics();
      Dimension size = getSize();

      paintBackground();
      wpg.setClip(0,0,size.width,size.height);
      super.paint(wpg);
      buffers.blitWorkplaceToScreen();
      wpg.dispose();
   }
}
protected boolean windowDamaged(Graphics g) {
   Rectangle clip = g.getClipBounds();
   Dimension size = getSize();
   return ((clip.x != 0 || clip.y != 0) ||
           (clip.width  < size.width    ||
           clip.height < size.height));
}
```

7. If the clip rectangle associated with the Graphics passed to paint() is not equal to the size of the container, then the window in which the container resides has been damaged.

If the window has not been damaged, the entire container is painted. First `paintBackground()` is called, which in turn calls `paintBackground(Rectangle)` with a null value for the clipping rectangle, indicating that the entire background needs repainting. `paintBackground(Graphics)` uses the `gjt.Util.wallPaper` method to wallpaper the background of the workplace buffer if the image is non-null. Notice that extensions of `DoubleBufferedContainer` can override `paintBackground(Graphics)` if they wish to provide an alternate method of painting the background. Regardless, the point is that `paintBackground(Graphics)` paints the background into the workplace buffer and not to the screen.

After the background is painted into the workplace buffer, `paint()` sets the clipping rectangle of the workplace buffer's graphics to the size of the container[8] and invokes `super.paint(wpg)`. `Container.paint()`, as we saw in Example 15-3 on page 479, iterates over any lightweight components it contains and paints each lightweight component that intersects the clipping rectangle of the graphics object it is passed. Notice that up until now, all of the action has taken place in either the background buffer or the workplace buffer—nothing has been painted onscreen. Finally, the `paint()` method blits the entire workplace to the screen, providing flicker-free painting of the lightweight components in the container:

```
protected void paintBackground() {
  paintBackground((Rectangle)null);
}
protected void paintBackground(Rectangle clip) {
  Graphics g = buffers.getBackgroundGraphics();
  if(clip != null) {
    g.setClip(clip);
  }
  paintBackground(g);
  buffers.blitBackgroundToWorkplace();
  g.dispose();
}
protected void paintBackground(Graphics g) {
  if(wallpaperImage != null) {
    gjt.Util.wallPaper(this, g, wallpaperImage);
  }
}
```

8. This is a new feature in 1.1. In the 1.02 version of the AWT, clipping rectangles could only be made smaller than the current clipping rectangle.

DoubleBufferedContainer also provides methods for painting, erasing, and moving a single lightweight component. paintComponent() and eraseComponent() are overloaded: one version of the methods takes a lone argument—the component to be painted/erased—and another method takes an additional boolean argument that indicates whether the onscreen representation of the component should be updated. moveComponent() calls the latter versions of eraseComponent() and paintComponent(), passing a false value to indicate that the onscreen representation of the component should not be updated. After the component has been erased, moved, and repainted in the workplace buffer, moveComponent() blits the workplace buffer to the screen, clipped by the union of the component's original and new bounds:

```
public void paintComponent(Component comp) {
  paintComponent(comp, true);
}
public void eraseComponent(Component comp) {
  eraseComponent(comp, true);
}
public void paintComponent(Component comp, boolean update) {
  Graphics  wpg     = buffers.getWorkplaceGraphics();
  Rectangle bounds = comp.getBounds();
  Graphics  compGraphics;

  compGraphics = wpg.create(bounds.x,       bounds.y,
                            bounds.width,  bounds.height);
  comp.paint(compGraphics);
  if(update)
     buffers.blitWorkplaceToScreen(bounds);

  wpg.dispose();
}
public void eraseComponent(Component comp, boolean update) {
  Rectangle bounds = comp.getBounds();

  buffers.blitBackgroundToWorkplace(bounds);
  paintOverlappingComponents(comp);

  if(update)
     buffers.blitWorkplaceToScreen(bounds);
}
public void moveComponent(Component comp, Point newLoc) {
  Rectangle oldBounds = comp.getBounds();

  eraseComponent(comp, false);  // erase - no screen update
  comp.setLocation(newLoc);     // move component
  paintComponent(comp, false);  // paint comp - no update
```

```
buffers.blitWorkplaceToScreen(
   oldBounds.union(comp.getBounds()));
}
```

DoubleBufferedContainer also provides a method for painting all of the
components that overlap a given component, which is invoked in the
`eraseComponent(Component, boolean)` method.
`paintOverlappingComponents()` sets the clipping rectangle for the
workplace buffer to the bounds of the component in question, sets the visibility of
the component to false, so that the component itself is not drawn[9]; then,
`Container.paint()` is invoked, which paints each component that intersects
the clipping rectangle of the component. Finally, the visibility of the component is
set to `true`, so that it will subsequently be drawn when calls to
`Container.paint()` are made:

```
protected void paintOverlappingComponents(Component comp) {
    Graphics  wpg    = buffers.getWorkplaceGraphics();
    Rectangle bounds = comp.getBounds();

    wpg.setClip    (bounds);      // set offscreen clip to bounds
    comp.setVisible(false);       // so comp won't be drawn below
    super.paint    (wpg);         // draw all but comp
    comp.setVisible(true);        // reset comp visibility
    wpg.dispose();
}
```

The complete listing for `DoubleBufferedContainer` is shown in
Example 15-8.

Example 15-8 `DoubleBufferedContainer`

```
import java.awt.*;
import java.awt.event.*;

public class DoubleBufferedContainer extends Container {
    private   Image             wallpaperImage;
    protected OffscreenBuffer buffers =
                              new OffscreenBuffer(this);

    public DoubleBufferedContainer() {
        this(null);
    }
```

---

9. Actually, `Container.paint()` paints all lightweights, whether they are visible
    or not. As a result, the lightweight's `paint()` method should only paint the light-
    weight if it is visible.

```java
public DoubleBufferedContainer(Image wallpaperImage) {
   if(wallpaperImage != null)
      setWallpaperImage(wallpaperImage);

      addComponentListener(new ComponentAdapter() {
         public void componentResized(ComponentEvent event) {
            buffers.update();
            repaint();
         }
      });
}
public void setWallpaperImage(Image wallpaperImage) {
   this.wallpaperImage = wallpaperImage;
   gjt.Util.waitForImage(this, wallpaperImage);
}
public void update(Graphics g) {
   paint(g);
}
public void paint(Graphics g) {
   if(windowDamaged(g)) {
     buffers.blitWorkplaceToScreen(g.getClipBounds());
   }
   else {
      Graphics  wpg  = buffers.getWorkplaceGraphics();
      Dimension size = getSize();

      paintBackground();
      wpg.setClip(0,0,size.width,size.height);
      super.paint(wpg);
      buffers.blitWorkplaceToScreen();
      wpg.dispose();
   }
}
public void paintComponent(Component comp) {
   paintComponent(comp, true);
}
public void eraseComponent(Component comp) {
   eraseComponent(comp, true);
}
public void paintComponent(Component comp, boolean update) {
   Graphics  wpg    = buffers.getWorkplaceGraphics();
   Rectangle bounds = comp.getBounds();
   Graphics  compGraphics;

   compGraphics = wpg.create(bounds.x,      bounds.y,
                              bounds.width, bounds.height);
   comp.paint(compGraphics);
   if(update)
```

```
         buffers.blitWorkplaceToScreen(bounds);

      wpg.dispose();
   }
   public void eraseComponent(Component comp, boolean update) {
      Rectangle bounds = comp.getBounds();

      buffers.blitBackgroundToWorkplace(bounds);
      paintOverlappingComponents(comp);

      if(update)
         buffers.blitWorkplaceToScreen(bounds);
   }
   public void moveComponent(Component comp, Point newLoc) {
      Rectangle oldBounds = comp.getBounds();

      eraseComponent(comp, false);   // erase - no screen update
      comp.setLocation(newLoc);      // move component
      paintComponent(comp, false);   // paint comp - no update

      buffers.blitWorkplaceToScreen(
               oldBounds.union(comp.getBounds()));
   }
   protected boolean windowDamaged(Graphics g) {
      Rectangle clip = g.getClipBounds();
      Dimension size = getSize();
      return ((clip.x != 0 || clip.y != 0) ||
              (clip.width  < size.width   ||
               clip.height < size.height));
   }
   protected void paintOverlappingComponents(Component comp) {
      Graphics  wpg     = buffers.getWorkplaceGraphics();
      Rectangle bounds = comp.getBounds();

      wpg.setClip     (bounds); // set offscreen clip to bounds
      comp.setVisible(false);   // so comp won't be drawn below
      super.paint     (wpg);    // draw all but comp
      comp.setVisible(true);    // reset comp visibility
      wpg.dispose();
   }
   protected void paintBackground() {
      paintBackground((Rectangle)null);
   }
   protected void paintBackground(Rectangle clip) {
      Graphics g = buffers.getBackgroundGraphics();
      if(clip != null) {
         g.setClip(clip);
      }
```

```
            paintBackground(g);
            buffers.blitBackgroundToWorkplace();
            g.dispose();
        }
        protected void paintBackground(Graphics g) {
            if(wallpaperImage != null) {
                gjt.Util.wallPaper(this, g, wallpaperImage);
            }
        }
    }
```

Dragging Lightweight Components

Now that we've got an industrial-strength, double buffered container in which to place our lightweight components, let's give it a spin and drag some lightweights around on it.

Lightweight And LightweightDragger

First, we need a lightweight component that knows how to drag itself over our double buffered container. Example 15-9 shows a new version of `Lightweight` that employs an instance of `LightweightDragger` as its mouse and mouse motion listeners.

Example 15-9 `Lightweight` and `LightweightDragger` Classes

```
    import java.awt.*;
    import java.awt.event.*;

    class Lightweight extends Component {
      private Image                image;
      private LightweightDragger dragger;

      public Lightweight(Image image) {
         this.image = image;
         gjt.Util.waitForImage(this, image);

         dragger = new LightweightDragger(this);
         addMouseListener       (dragger);
         addMouseMotionListener(dragger);
      }
      public void paint(Graphics g) {
         if(isVisible()) {
             g.drawImage(image, 0, 0, this);
         }
      }
      public Dimension getPreferredSize() {
         return new Dimension(image.getWidth(this),
```

```
                       image.getHeight(this));
  }
}
class LightweightDragger extends      MouseAdapter
                       implements MouseMotionListener {
  private Component component;
  private Point      press;
  private boolean dragging = false;

  public LightweightDragger(Component component) {
     this.component = component;
  }
  public void mousePressed(MouseEvent event) {
     press    = new Point(event.getX(), event.getY());
     dragging = true;
  }
  public void mouseReleased(MouseEvent event) {
     dragging = false;
  }
  public void mouseClicked(MouseEvent event) {
     dragging = false;
  }
  public void mouseMoved(MouseEvent event) {
  }
  public void mouseDragged(MouseEvent event) {
     if(dragging) {
         DoubleBufferedContainer c;
         Point loc = component.getLocation();
         Point pt  = new Point();

         pt.x = event.getX() + loc.x - press.x;
         pt.y = event.getY() + loc.y - press.y;

         c = (DoubleBufferedContainer)component.getParent();
         c.moveComponent(component, pt);
     }
  }
}
```

Notice that our `Lightweight` class is unchanged from the previous version in Example 15-4 on page 481, except that it creates a `LightweightDragger` and assigns it to listen for mouse and mouse motion events.

`LightweightDragger` maintains an association with the component it is responsible for dragging. When a mouse press occurs in the lightweight component, the lightweight dragger stores the location of the mouse press for future reference and sets `dragging` to `true`. When the mouse is clicked or released, `dragging` is set to `false`. All of the interesting action takes place in `LightweightDragger.mouseDragged()`, which simply calls on the double buffered container in which the lightweight resides to move the component. Note that the location to which the component is moved is not the same as the location at which the drag occurred; we must adjust the location, based on the distance between the initial mouse press and the upper left-hand corner of the component.

Exercising Lightweight and LightweightDragger

Now all that's left is to implement an applet that creates a double buffered container and adds some lightweights to it. Example 15-10 shows just such an applet.

Example 15-10 DBCTest

```
import java.net.URL;
import java.applet.Applet;
import java.awt.*;
import java.awt.event.*;

public class DBCTest extends Applet {
  public void init() {
    setLayout(new BorderLayout());
      add(new DBCTestPanel(this), "Center");
  }
}
class DBCTestPanel extends Panel {
  private DoubleBufferedContainer container;

  public DBCTestPanel(Applet applet) {
    URL    b = applet.getCodeBase();

    Image mandrill = applet.getImage(b, "../gifs/mandrill.jpg");
    Image paper    = applet.getImage(b, "../gifs/paper.gif");
    Image gj       = applet.getImage(b, "../gifs/gjMedium.gif");
    Image skelly   = applet.getImage(b, "../gifs/skelly.gif");

    container = new DoubleBufferedContainer();
    container.setWallpaperImage(paper);

    container.add(new Lightweight(mandrill));
    container.add(new Lightweight(skelly));
    container.add(new Lightweight(gj));

    setLayout(new BorderLayout());
    add(container, "Center");
  }
  public void update(Graphics g) {
```

```
        paint(g);
    }
}
```

Figure 15-3 shows our applet as it appears initially.
`DoubleBufferedContainer` sets its layout manager to a `FlowLayout` by default, so we needn't concern ourselves with setting the layout manager for the double buffered container.

Figure 15-3 `DoubleBufferedContainer` with Lightweight Components Laid Out

Of course, in a static medium such as a book, we cannot show you the components being dragged about on our double buffered container—the best we can do is to show you an updated screen-shot of our applet after we've dragged our lightweights around. Of course, we've provided the source code (and associated class/html files) on the CD that accompanies the book, so you can try it out for yourself. Figure 15-4 shows the applet after we've dragged the lightweights around. Note that thanks to the `paintOverlappingComponents()` method in `DoubleBufferedContainer`, our lightweights can not only be dragged over the background of the container but also can be dragged over each other.

Finally, note that our `DoubleBufferedContainer` is quite versatile. In fact, in "Sprite Animation" on page 809, we develop another lightweight component— sprites, which are easily animated on a double buffered container.

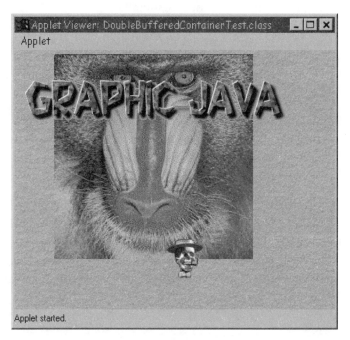

Figure 15-4 Lightweight Components After Being Dragged. `DoubleBufferedContainer` is implemented so that lightweights can be dragged over each other in addition to being dragged over the background.

Summary

Lightweight components are a new addition to the AWT with the advent of the 1.1 release of the JDK. Lightweight components, unlike their heavyweight counterparts, do not require a native, opaque window in which to render themselves and, therefore, have transparent backgrounds. As a result, lightweight components can appear to be nonrectangular, although their bounding boxes are in fact rectangular.

Lightweight components are extremely simple to implement; they merely need to extend `java.awt.Component` (for lightweight components) or `java.awt.Container` (for lightweight containers).

There are a couple of pitfalls to be aware of when developing lightweight components and lightweight containers. First, custom containers that contain lightweight components and override paint() must be sure to invoke super.paint(), or the lightweight components will not be painted. Second, java.awt.Container is equipped with a null layout manager, so if you expect components residing in a lightweight container to be laid out, you must manually set the container's layout manager.

Lightweight components, unlike heavyweight components, are rendered entirely in Java[10], and therefore require a double buffered container in which to render themselves. We've expended a fair bit of energy in this chapter to provide you with a versatile double buffered container that can be used not only for painting lightweight components but that also provides support for dragging lightweights, in addition to double buffered sprite animation, as you can see in "Sprite Animation" on page 809. For your convenience, the Graphic Java Toolkit comes with a DoubleBufferedContainer that is nearly identical to the one we discussed in this chapter.

Lightweight components (and containers) are a welcome and necessary addition to the AWT. Although the peer approach taken by the original designers of the AWT had a certain number of benefits, it also suffers from a number of drawbacks, not the least of which stem from the fact that AWT components are heavyweight; that is, they require native, opaque windows. The lightweight component framework provides an alternative to the peer approach and at the same time enables developers to develop transparent components that are not nearly as resource intensive as their heavyweight counterparts. Finally, subsequent versions of the AWT will provide lightweight implementations of the heavyweight components, such as buttons and choices, currently supplied by the AWT.

---

10. Heavyweight components are rendered by their native peers.

CHAPTER
16

Clipboard and Data Transfer

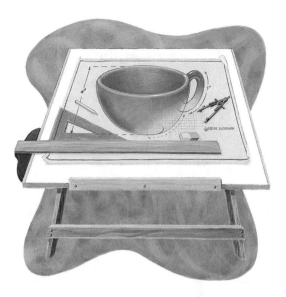

Nearly every modern windowing system includes support for a clipboard—a rendezvous point for data of various kinds; data can be transferred to and retrieved from the clipboard.

While previous versions of the AWT did not explicitly support clipboard and data transfer, version 1.1 of the AWT comes complete with data transfer and clipboard support. In fact, the AWT provides access to two kinds of clipboards: the *system* clipboard, and *local* clipboards. As you might suspect, manipulation of the system clipboard actually manipulates the native windowing system clipboard. We mention this because copying data onto the system clipboard in a Java applet or application makes it available to other programs, not just to other AWT components. Alternatively, applets can also create, for their own internal use, local clipboards that do not involve the native windowing clipboard.

In this chapter we'll take a look at the fundamental concepts behind data transfer and the clipboard, followed by examples that place data on both the system clipboard and local clipboards and retrieve data from the clipboards in some fashion. As of this writing, the `java.awt.datatransfer` package only provides explicit support for placing Java strings onto the clipboard, but we'll take a look at the steps involved in placing other kinds of data, such as images and custom AWT components, on the clipboard.

The java.awt.datatransfer Package

The clipboard and data transfer mechanism are implemented with a handful of classes and interfaces, all of which reside in the `java.awt.datatransfer` package. The classes and interfaces from `java.awt.datatransfer` are listed in Table 16-1.

Table 16-1 java.awt.datatransfer Classes and Interfaces

Class/Interface	Class or Interface	Purpose
Clipboard	Class	`Transferables` can be copied to and retrieved from the clipboard.
ClipboardOwner	Interface	An interface for classes that copy data to the clipboard.
DataFlavor	Class	Data flavors (formats) supported by a `Transferable`.
StringSelection	Class	A `Transferable` that encapsulates textual data.
Transferable	Interface	Interface for items that can be placed on the clipboard.
UnsupportedFlavorException	Class	Thrown by a `Transferable` when a requested data flavor is not supported.

The concepts behind the clipboard and the data transfer mechanism are quite simple. First of all, only a `ClipboardOwner` can copy data onto the clipboard. By copying data onto the clipboard, the clipboard owner becomes the current owner of the data on the clipboard. Furthermore, only one type of object can be copied to or retrieved from the clipboard—a *transferable* object. Transferables encapsulate data of some sort and are able to provide their data in one or more different *data flavors*. For instance, a transferable that contains an image may choose to provide the image in two different flavors—either as a reference to an instance of `java.awt.Image` or as an array of pixels.

The Clipboard Class

`java.awt.datatransfer.Clipboard` is an extremely simple class. There are only three things you can do to a clipboard, other than construct one, as you can see from Table 16-2: get the name of the clipboard, set the contents of the clipboard, and retrieve the current contents of the clipboard. Notice that there is no setName() method—setting the name of the clipboard is done at construction time. Furthermore, you can either create a local clipboard via the Clipboard constructor or you can obtain a reference to the system clipboard by invoking Toolkit.getSystemClipboard().

Table 16-2 Methods Defined By the java.awt.datatransfer.Clipboard Class

Method	Description
String getName()	Returns the name of the clipboard.
void setContents(Transferable, ClipboardOwner)	Sets the contents of the clipboard to the transferable passed in. Also sets the owner of the clipboard.
Transferable getContents(Object)	Returns the contents of the clipboard. The Object parameter is the requestor of the clipboard contents.

Copying Data to and Retrieving Data from a Clipboard

Before we launch into our first example, let's enumerate the steps involved in copying data to a clipboard and subsequently retrieving it.

To Copy Data to a Clipboard:

- Either instantiate a clipboard or obtain a reference to an existing clipboard.
- Wrap the data in a transferable object (which could involve implementing an extension of Transferable).
- Copy the transferable to the clipboard, specifying both the transferable and the owner of the clipboard.

To Retrieve Data From the Clipboard:

- Obtain a reference to the clipboard that contains the data you are interested in.
- (Optional.) Determine if the clipboard contents (a transferable) provides its data in a palatable flavor.
- If the transferable currently on the clipboard provides its data in a flavor acceptable to you, ask the transferable to produce its data in the flavor in question.

The ClipboardOwner Class

Depending upon the native facilities available for data transfer, the contents of the clipboard may not actually be copied to the clipboard until the data is requested from the clipboard. Such a scenario is known as a *lazy data mode*, and is the reason for the ClipboardOwner interface. The clipboard owner is the object that puts the data on the clipboard, and it must make sure that the data placed on the clipboard is accessible up until the time its lostOwnership() method is invoked. lostOwnership() is the only method defined by the ClipboardOwner interface, and is invoked when another object places data on the clipboard. If, for some reason, a clipboard owner needs to release the resources associated with an item it placed on the clipboard, it is only safe to do so after the lostOwnership() method is invoked. In practice, the lostOwnership() method is almost always implemented as a no-op.

Ok, enough discussion about data transfer concepts and the steps involved in using the clipboard. Let's get on with some examples.

The System Clipboard

As you can see in Figure 16-1, our first applet contains a textfield, a textarea, and two buttons. After text is typed into the textfield, activating the Copy To System Clipboard button places the textfield's text onto the system clipboard. Subsequently, activating the Paste From System Clipboard button retrieves the text currently on the clipboard and places it in the textarea.

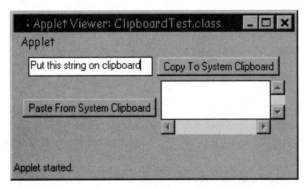

Figure 16-1 Copying a String to the System Clipboard
Activating the Copy To System Clipboard button copies the text from the textfield and places it on the system clipboard.

Before we show you the applet in its entirety, let's take a look at the code that implements the steps outlined previously for placing data on and retrieving data from a clipboard.

First, we obtain a reference to the system clipboard:

```
public class ClipboardTest extends      Applet
                            implements ClipboardOwner {
private Clipboard clipboard;
private TextField copyFrom;
private TextArea  copyTo;
private Button    copy, paste;

public void init() {
  // Obtain a reference to the system clipboard
  clipboard = getToolkit().getSystemClipboard();
...
```

As we noted earlier, a reference to the system clipboard is obtained by invoking the getSystemClipboard()[1] static method supplied by the Toolkit class. Next, we wrap the text contained in the textfield in a transferable and place the transferable on the system clipboard:

```
class CopyListener implements ActionListener {
  public void actionPerformed(ActionEvent event) {

    // Wrap the data in a transferable object
    StringSelection contents =
            new StringSelection(copyFrom.getText());

    // Place the transferable onto the clipboard
    clipboard.setContents(contents, ClipboardTest.this);
  }
}
```

CopyListener, as you might suspect, is the action listener for the "Copy To System Clipboard" button. Note that the transferable is an instance of StringSelection, which is provided by the AWT for wrapping textual data.

Finally, we retrieve the text from the system clipboard when the Paste From System Clipboard button is activated:

```
class PasteListener implements ActionListener {
  public void actionPerformed(ActionEvent event) {
    Transferable contents = clipboard.getContents(this);

    // Determine if data is available in string flavor
    if(contents != null &&
       contents.isDataFlavorSupported(
                DataFlavor.stringFlavor)) {
```

---

1.   Note that Toolkit.getSystemClipboard() is subject to security restrictions.

```
try {
    String string;
    // Have contents cough up string
    string = (String) contents.getTransferData(
                    DataFlavor.stringFlavor);
    copyTo.append(string);
}
catch(Exception e) {
    e.printStackTrace();
}
        }
    }
}
```

`PasteListener` is the action listener for the Paste From System Clipboard button, and the first thing its `actionPerformed()` method does is to obtain the contents of the clipboard via the clipboard's `getContents()` method.

`Clipboard.getContents()` requires us to pass a reference to the object that is requesting the data (the `PasteListener`). Once we have a reference to the transferable currently on the clipboard, we ask the transferable if the data it contains is available in the particular data flavor we are interested in. If there was indeed a transferable on the clipboard and it supports `DataFlavor.stringFlavor`, then we invoke the clipboard's `getTransferData()`, telling the transferable the type of data flavor we'd like returned. Finally, we append the string obtained from the transferable to the text area.

The fruits of our labor can be seen in Figure 16-2, and the listing for the entire applet can be seen in Example 16-1.

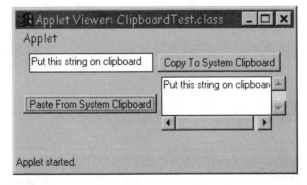

Figure 16-2 Retrieving a String From the System Clipboard
Activating the Paste From System Clipboard button retrieves the text from the system clipboard and appends it to the textarea.

Example 16-1 ClipboardTest

```java
import java.applet.Applet;
import java.awt.*;
import java.awt.event.*;
import java.awt.datatransfer.*;

public class ClipboardTest extends     Applet
                         implements ClipboardOwner {
  private Clipboard clipboard;
  private TextField copyFrom;
  private TextArea  copyTo;
  private Button    copy, paste;

  public void init() {
      // Obtain a reference to the system clipboard
      clipboard = getToolkit().getSystemClipboard();

      copyFrom = new TextField(20);
      copyTo   = new TextArea(3, 20);
      copy     = new Button("Copy To System Clipboard");
      paste    = new Button("Paste From System Clipboard");

      add(copyFrom);
      add(copy);
      add(paste);
      add(copyTo);

      copy.addActionListener (new CopyListener());
      paste.addActionListener(new PasteListener());
  }
  class CopyListener implements ActionListener {
      public void actionPerformed(ActionEvent event) {
          // Wrap the data in a transferable object
          StringSelection contents =
                      new StringSelection(copyFrom.getText());

          // Place the transferable onto the clipboard
          clipboard.setContents(contents, ClipboardTest.this);
      }
  }
  class PasteListener implements ActionListener {
      public void actionPerformed(ActionEvent event) {
          Transferable contents = clipboard.getContents(this);

          // Determine if data is available in string flavor
          if(contents != null &&
             contents.isDataFlavorSupported(
```

```
                        DataFlavor.stringFlavor)) {
        try {
            String string;

            // Have contents cough up string
            string = (String) contents.getTransferData(
                            DataFlavor.stringFlavor);
            copyTo.append(string);
        }
        catch(Exception e) {
            e.printStackTrace();
        }
      }
    }
  }
}
  public void lostOwnership(Clipboard    clip,
                    Transferable transferable) {
    System.out.println("Lost ownership");
  }
}
```

Pasting From the System Clipboard to Other Applications

As we alluded to earlier, copying data to the system clipboard makes it available
to other programs in addition to other AWT components. After we copied the text
onto the system clipboard, we opened a document in FrameMaker® and did a
paste operation. The result can be seen in Figure 16-3.

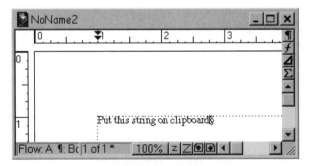

Figure 16-3 Pasting Clipboard Contents Into Another Application
Text placed on the clipboard from an applet is pasted into a
FrameMaker document.

Local Clipboards

In Example 16-1 on page 509, we manipulated the system clipboard. You can also create local clipboards, by invoking the lone `Clipboard` constructor that takes a string as an argument. The string specifies the name of the clipboard, so that you can keep track of several clipboards if need be. As we saw in Table 16-2 on page 505, the `Clipboard` class comes with a `getName()` method so that you can determine which clipboard you currently have in hand.

Data Transfer Mechanism

Now that we've introduced the basics of data transfer and manipulating a clipboard and provided a simple example of cutting and pasting text to/from the system clipboard, let's take a closer look at the data transfer mechanism.

Data Flavors

No, you cannot taste data; flavor, in this case, can be thought of as a synonym for format. One data flavor for an image, for instance, might be a `java.awt.Image`; another flavor for an image might be an array of pixels representing the image in question.

Data flavors fall into two general categories:

- A Java class
- MIME (Multipurpose Internet Mail Extensions) Type Representation[2]

All this means is that you can either construct a `DataFlavor` by specifying the particular Java class that the data flavor represents, or you can construct a data flavor by specifying a string that represents a data type. If you choose to construct a data flavor with a string representing the data type, the string should conform to a standard MIME type. If you construct a `DataFlavor` by specifying a Java class, it will be assigned the MIME type "application/x-javaserializedobject". For instance, if you look at the source for `java.awt.datatransfer.DataFlavor`, you will see that the `DataFlavor` class provides two constructors:

```
public DataFlavor(Class representationClass,
                  String humanPresentableName)

public DataFlavor(String mimeType, String humanPresentableName)
```

---

2. If you want to read the gory details concerning MIME types, check out http://206.21.31.20/notes/rfcs1/30ee_1e2.htm.

Regardless of which constructor you use, you must provide a human presentable name for your particular data flavor, but you probably figured that out on your own!

The `DataFlavor` class contains two static public instances of `DataFlavor`, each representing a different flavor of text. One flavor is represented by `java.lang.String`; the other is represented by a MIME type for plain text:

```
static { // This is from the DataFlavor class
  try {
    stringFlavor =
        new DataFlavor(Class.forName("java.lang.String"),
                    "Unicode String");
    plainTextFlavor =
        new DataFlavor("text/plain; charset=unicode",
                    "Plain Text");
  ...
```

So, don't get hung up on MIME types. MIME types are simply a standard way to describe certain flavors of data, and since there is already a standard established, it makes perfect sense to use it instead of defining another standard. Table 16-3 lists the public methods provided by the `DataFlavor` class.

Table 16-3 java.awt.datatransfer.DataFlavor Public Methods

Method	Description
String getMimeType()	Returns MIME type for data flavor.
Class getRepresentationClass()	Returns the Java class the data flavor represents.
String getHumanPresentableName()	Returns the human presentable name of the data flavor.
void setHumanPresentableName(String)	Sets the human presentable name of the data flavor.
boolean equals(DataFlavor)	Determines if another data flavor is equal to the data flavor on whose behalf the method is called.
boolean isMimeTypeEqual(String)	Determines if the data flavor has a MIME type equivalent to the `String` passed in.
boolean isMimeTypeEqual(DataFlavor)	Convenience method implemented as: `return isMimeTypeEqual(flavor.getMimeType())`

Transferables and Data Flavors

As we mentioned previously, there's only one type of object that can be placed on or retrieved from a clipboard—a `Transferable`, which is an interface that defines the three methods listed in Table 16-4.

Table 16-4 Methods Defined By the java.awt.datatransfer.Transferable Interface

Method	Intent
`DataFlavor[] getTransferDataFlavors()`	Provides an array of data flavors supported by the transferable.
`boolean isDataFlavorSupported(DataFlavor)`	Determine if a particular data flavor is supported by the transferable.
`Object getTransferData(DataFlavor) throws UnsupportedFlavorException, IOException;`	Returns an `Object` representing the specified flavor.

A transferable then, is simply a wrapper around some piece of data. Since a given type of data may be packaged in different flavors, a transferable is a data wrapper that manages the flavors of the particular type of data it encapsulates.

Notice that `getTransferData()` can throw either an `UnsupportedFlavorException` if the requested data flavor is not supported, or an `IOException` if an object representing the given data flavor cannot be created. Of course, you can avoid having an `UnsupportedFlavorException` thrown by calling `isDataFlavorSupported()` to find out if a particular data flavor is supported before invoking `getTransferData()`, as we did in Example 16-1.

StringSelection

The `java.awt.datatransfer` package comes with one implementation of `Transferable` that encapsulates text: `StringSelection`. `StringSelection` can cough up its string in one of two different flavors: as a `java.lang.String`, or as plain text. As you might guess, `StringSelection` uses the two (public) static instances of `DataFlavor` provided by the `DataFlavor` class for representing its string (see "Data Flavors" on page 511).

In Example 16-1, we asked an instance of `StringSelection` obtained from the clipboard for its text in the form of a `java.lang.String`:

```
if(contents != null &&
    contents.isDataFlavorSupported(DataFlavor.stringFlavor)) {
```

```
try {
    String string;

    // Have contents cough up string
    string = (String) contents.getTransferData(
                       DataFlavor.stringFlavor);
...
```

We could also have asked the `StringSelection` object for its text represented as plain text:

```
if(contents != null &&
   contents.isDataFlavorSupported(DataFlavor.plainTextFlavor)) {
    try {
        int i;
        StringReader s = (StringReader)
            contents.getTransferData(DataFlavor.plainTextFlavor);

        while((i = s.read()) != -1) {
            System.out.println((char)i);
        }
    }
...
```

Copying Images to a Clipboard

As we have seen, manipulating clipboards is relatively straightforward. Perhaps the most difficult aspect of the clipboard/data transfer mechanism is copying data other than text to a clipboard, and even that is not rocket science, especially once you've got the hang of it.

ImageSelection—A Transferable for Encapsulating Images

The first order of business is to develop a class that implements `Transferable` and encapsulates an image. Our first version of such a class will offer a lone data flavor for representing the image—`java.awt.Image`. A little later on we'll add another data flavor for good measure.

We'll follow the naming convention established by `StringSelection`, and name our class `ImageSelection`. Additionally, like `StringSelection`, we'll also implement the `ClipboardOwner` interface[3] as a convenience, so that the contents and the owner of the clipboard can be specified as the same object when setting the contents of the clipboard.

```
public class ImageSelection implements Transferable,
                                ClipboardOwner {
    static public DataFlavor ImageFlavor;
```

---

3.   See The ClipboardOwner Class on page 506. It is often the case that classes implementing `Transferable` also implement the `ClipboardOwner` interface.

```
private DataFlavor[] flavors = {ImageFlavor};
private Image image;
```

ImageSelection contains a static public instance of DataFlavor that clients
can use to specify the data flavor in which they'd like the image to be produced.
Since ImageSelection only has one data flavor for its image, it maintains an
array of data flavors that has only one entry. The array, of course, will be returned
from the getTransferDataFlavors() method. Finally, ImageSelection
maintains a reference to the image that it currently represents.

ImageSelection implements a static block that creates the ImageFlavor
instance:

```
static {
    try {
        ImageFlavor = new DataFlavor(
            Class.forName("java.awt.Image"),"AWT Image");
    }
    catch(ClassNotFoundException e) {
        e.printStackTrace();
    }
}
```

Notice that our data flavor is constructed with a Java class instead of a MIME
type, and with a human presentable name of "AWT Image".

ImageSelection provides a lone constructor that takes a reference to an image,
and implements the three methods required by the Transferable interface:

```
public ImageSelection(Image image) {
  this.image = image;
}
public synchronized DataFlavor[] getTransferDataFlavors() {
  return flavors;
}
public boolean isDataFlavorSupported(DataFlavor flavor) {
  return flavor.equals(ImageFlavor);
}
public synchronized Object getTransferData(DataFlavor flavor)
                throws UnsupportedFlavorException, IOException {
  if(flavor.equals(ImageFlavor)) {
    return image;
  }
  else {
    throw new UnsupportedFlavorException(flavor);
  }
}
public void lostOwnership(Clipboard c, Transferable t) {
}
```

If the data flavor requested in `getTransferData()` is equal to the `ImageFlavor` instance, the image is returned; otherwise, an `UnsupportedFlavorException` is thrown. Also, as is typically the case, since `ImageSelection` never releases the resources associated with the image it encapsulates, its `lostOwnership()` method is implemented as a no-op.

That's all there is to implementing a transferable that encapsulates an image. For completeness, `ImageSelection` is shown in its entirety in Example 16-2.

Example 16-2 ImageSelection Class

```
import java.awt.*;
import java.awt.datatransfer.*;
import java.io.*;

public class ImageSelection implements Transferable,
                              ClipboardOwner {
  static public DataFlavor ImageFlavor;

  private DataFlavor[] flavors = {ImageFlavor};
  private Image image;

  static {
    try {
       ImageFlavor = new DataFlavor(
          Class.forName("java.awt.Image"), "AWT Image");
    }
    catch(ClassNotFoundException e) {
       e.printStackTrace();
    }
  }
  public ImageSelection(Image image) {
     this.image = image;
  }
  public synchronized DataFlavor[] getTransferDataFlavors() {
     return flavors;
  }
  public boolean isDataFlavorSupported(DataFlavor flavor) {
     return flavor.equals(ImageFlavor);
  }
  public synchronized Object getTransferData(DataFlavor flavor)
     throws UnsupportedFlavorException, IOException {
     if(flavor.equals(ImageFlavor)) {
        return image;
     }
     else {
        throw new UnsupportedFlavorException(flavor);
     }
```

```
    }
    public void lostOwnership(Clipboard c, Transferable t) {
    }
}
```

Now let's put our `ImageSelection` class to use by copying an image to a local clipboard and subsequently retrieving it.

Using the ImageSelection Class

As you can see from Figure 16-4, our applet contains two image canvases, one of which initially contains an image, along with a copy button and a paste button. The Copy button, of course, copies the image to a clipboard—this time, we'll copy the image to a local clipboard instead of the system clipboard. Activating the Paste button retrieves the image from the local clipboard and puts it into the right-hand image canvas.

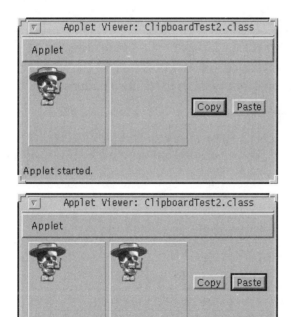

Figure 16-4 Copying And Retrieving an Image to/from a Clipboard
The top picture shows the applet in its initial state. After activating the copy and paste buttons, the applet looks like the bottom picture—the image has been copied to a clipboard, and then pasted from the clipboard into the right-hand image canvas.

Our applet creates a local clipboard, with the name "image clipboard," along with the various AWT components used in the applet:

```java
public class ClipboardTest2 extends      Applet
                           implements ClipboardOwner {
   private Clipboard   clipboard;
   private ImageCanvas copyFrom = new ImageCanvas();
   private ImageCanvas copyTo   = new ImageCanvas();
   private Button copy  = new Button("Copy");
   private Button paste = new Button("Paste");

   public void init() {
      clipboard = new Clipboard("image clipboard");

      copyFrom.setImage(getImage(getCodeBase(),"skelly.gif"));
      add(copyFrom);
      add(copyTo);
      add(copy);
      add(paste);
      copy.addActionListener (new CopyListener());
      paste.addActionListener(new PasteListener());
   }
```

Next, we implement event listeners for the two buttons:

```java
class CopyListener implements ActionListener {
  public void actionPerformed(ActionEvent event) {
    ImageSelection contents =
            new ImageSelection(copyFrom.getImage());

    clipboard.setContents(contents, ClipboardTest2.this);
  }
}
class PasteListener implements ActionListener {
  public void actionPerformed(ActionEvent event) {
    Transferable contents = clipboard.getContents(this);

    if(contents != null &&
       contents.isDataFlavorSupported(
          ImageSelection.ImageFlavor)) {
       try {
          Image image;
          image = (Image) contents.getTransferData(
                  ImageSelection.ImageFlavor);
          copyTo.setImage(image);
       }
       catch(Exception e) {
          e.printStackTrace();
       }
```

```
        }
    }
}
```

`CopyListener.actionPerformed()` creates an instance of
`ImageSelection`, which it places on the clipboard. Notice that the clipboard
owner (the second argument to `setContents()`) is specified as
`ClipboardTest2.this` because `CopyListener` is an inner class of
`ClipboardTest2` and it is `ClipboardTest2`, not `CopyListener`, that
implements the `ClipboardOwner` interface.

`PasteListener.actionPerformed()`, after obtaining the contents of the
clipboard, checks to see if the transferable currently on the clipboard supports the
`ImageSelection.ImageFlavor` data flavor. Obviously, we are engaging in a
bit of paranoia here—we know who put the data on the clipboard, and so we
know that `ImageSelection.ImageFlavor` is supported, but such tight
coupling between the object that places data on the clipboard and objects that
retrieve the data is not always the case, so we make the check for the sake of
illustration. Finally, we retrieve the image from the transferable and place it in the
right-hand image canvas.

The entire applet is shown in Example 16-3. Note that the implementation of
`ImageCanvas` has no bearing on the concepts we are stressing but is included for
completeness.

Example 16-3 ClipboardTest2

```java
import java.applet.Applet;
import java.awt.*;
import java.awt.event.*;
import java.awt.datatransfer.*;

public class ClipboardTest2 extends      Applet
                        implements ClipboardOwner {
    private Clipboard   clipboard;
    private ImageCanvas copyFrom = new ImageCanvas();
    private ImageCanvas copyTo   = new ImageCanvas();
    private Button copy  = new Button("Copy");
    private Button paste = new Button("Paste");

    public void init() {
        clipboard = new Clipboard("image clipboard");

        copyFrom.setImage(getImage(getCodeBase(),"skelly.gif"));
        add(copyFrom);
        add(copyTo);
```

```
        add(copy);
        add(paste);

        copy.addActionListener (new CopyListener());
        paste.addActionListener(new PasteListener());
    }
    class CopyListener implements ActionListener {
        public void actionPerformed(ActionEvent event) {
            ImageSelection contents =
                    new ImageSelection(copyFrom.getImage());

            clipboard.setContents(contents, ClipboardTest2.this);
        }
    }
    class PasteListener implements ActionListener {
        public void actionPerformed(ActionEvent event) {
            Transferable contents = clipboard.getContents(this);
            if(contents != null &&
                contents.isDataFlavorSupported(
                    ImageSelection.ImageFlavor)) {
                try {
                    Image image;
                    image = (Image) contents.getTransferData(
                            ImageSelection.ImageFlavor);
                    copyTo.setImage(image);
                }
                catch(Exception e) {
                    e.printStackTrace();
                }
            }
        }
    }
  public void lostOwnership(Clipboard    clip,
                            Transferable transferable) {
     System.out.println("Lost ownership");
  }
}
class ImageCanvas extends Panel {
  private Image image;

  public ImageCanvas() {
     this(null);
  }
  public ImageCanvas(Image image) {
     if(image != null)
        setImage(image);
  }
  public void paint(Graphics g) {
```

```
    g.setColor(Color.lightGray);
    g.draw3DRect(0,0,getSize().width-1,
                    getSize().height-1,true);
    if(image != null) {
        g.drawImage(image, 1, 1, this);
    }
}
public void update(Graphics g) {
    paint(g);
}
public void setImage(Image image) {
    this.image = image;
    try {
        MediaTracker tracker = new MediaTracker(this);
        tracker.addImage(image, 0);
        tracker.waitForID(0);
    }
    catch(Exception e) { e.printStackTrace(); }

    if(isShowing()) {
        repaint();
    }
}
public Image getImage() {
    return image;
}
public Dimension getPreferredSize() {
    return new Dimension(100,100);
}
}
```

Adding an Additional Flavor

Now we'll take our `ImageSelection` class and add support for another data flavor[4]. Our additional flavor will take the form of an array of bits that represents the image. The `ImageSelection2` class contains two `static public` `DataFlavor` objects, which are placed in the `flavors` array. Additionally, the static block now constructs both flavors:

```
public class ImageSelection2 implements Transferable,
                                    ClipboardOwner {
  static public DataFlavor ImageFlavor;
  static public DataFlavor ImageArrayFlavor;
  private DataFlavor[] flavors = {ImageFlavor,
                              ImageArrayFlavor};
  private Image image;
```

---

4. Note that we have resisted bad jokes about Baskin and Robbins.

```
    private int   width, height;

    static {
       try {
          ImageFlavor = new DataFlavor(
             Class.forName("java.awt.Image"), "AWT Image");

          ImageArrayFlavor = new DataFlavor("image/gif",
                                            "GIF Image");
       }
       catch(ClassNotFoundException e) {
          e.printStackTrace();
       }
    }
```

Notice that the `ImageSelection2` constructor is passed the width and height of
the image, which are needed in order to return an array of pixels representing the
image. Once again, we implement the methods defined in the `Transferable`
interface.

```
public ImageSelection2(Image image, int width, int height) {
   this.image  = image;
   this.width  = width;
   this.height = height;
}
public synchronized DataFlavor[] getTransferDataFlavors() {
   return flavors;
}
public boolean isDataFlavorSupported(DataFlavor flavor) {
   return flavor.equals(ImageFlavor) ||
          flavor.equals(ImageArrayFlavor);
}
public synchronized Object getTransferData(
                                   DataFlavor flavor)
   throws UnsupportedFlavorException, IOException {
   if(flavor.equals(ImageFlavor)) {
      return image;
   }
   else if(flavor.equals(ImageArrayFlavor)) {
      return imageToArray();
   }
   else
      throw new UnsupportedFlavorException(flavor);
}
```

By now the methods listed above should need little commentary. Notice that
`ImageSelection2.getTransferData()` returns the image as either a
`java.awt.Image` or an array of pixels, depending upon the requested data

flavor. Of course, the only mystery left to uncover involves the inner workings of the `imageToArray()` method, which employs an instance of `PixelGrabber` for obtaining the pixels associated with the image[5]:

```
private int[] imageToArray() {
  int[] pixels = new int[width*height];
  PixelGrabber pg = new PixelGrabber(image,0,0,
                     width,height,pixels,0,width);
  try { pg.grabPixels(); }
  catch(InterruptedException e) { e.printStackTrace(); }
  return pixels;
}
```

`ImageSelection2` is listed in Example 16-4.

Example 16-4 ImageSelection2

```
import java.awt.*;
import java.awt.image.*;
import java.awt.datatransfer.*;
import java.io.*;

public class ImageSelection2 implements Transferable,
                                ClipboardOwner {
  static public DataFlavor ImageFlavor;
  static public DataFlavor ImageArrayFlavor;

  private DataFlavor[] flavors = {ImageFlavor,
                         ImageArrayFlavor};
  private Image image;
  private int   width, height;

  static {
    try {
      ImageFlavor = new DataFlavor(
        Class.forName("java.awt.Image"), "AWT Image");

      ImageArrayFlavor = new DataFlavor("image/gif",
                             "GIF Image");
    }
    catch(ClassNotFoundException e) {
      e.printStackTrace();
    }
  }
  public ImageSelection2(Image image, int width, int height) {
```

5. See "PixelGrabber and MemoryImageSource" on page 363 for more information on `PixelGrabber` and image manipulation.

```
      this.image  = image;
      this.width  = width;
      this.height = height;
   }
   public synchronized DataFlavor[] getTransferDataFlavors() {
      return flavors;
   }
   public boolean isDataFlavorSupported(DataFlavor flavor) {
      return flavor.equals(ImageFlavor) ||
          flavor.equals(ImageArrayFlavor);
   }
   public synchronized Object getTransferData(
                               DataFlavor flavor)
          throws UnsupportedFlavorException, IOException {
      if(flavor.equals(ImageFlavor)) {
         return image;
      }
      else if(flavor.equals(ImageArrayFlavor)) {
         return imageToArray();
      }
      else
         throw new UnsupportedFlavorException(flavor);
   }
   public void lostOwnership(Clipboard c, Transferable t) {
   }
   private int[] imageToArray() {
      int[] pixels = new int[width*height];
      PixelGrabber pg = new PixelGrabber(image,0,0,
                         width,height,pixels,0,width);
      try { pg.grabPixels(); }
      catch(InterruptedException e) { e.printStackTrace(); }
      return pixels;
   }
}
```

All that's left is to modify our applet to ask for the new data flavor when retrieving the image from the clipboard:

```
class PasteListener implements ActionListener {
   public void actionPerformed(ActionEvent event) {
      Transferable contents = clipboard.getContents(this);

      if(contents != null) {
         try {
            int[] array = (int[])
                  contents.getTransferData(
                    ImageSelection2.ImageArrayFlavor);
```

```
        copyTo.setImage(
            waveThis(array,width,height));
    }
    catch(Exception e) {
        e.printStackTrace();
    }
  }
 }
}
```

We obtain the array of bits from our `ImageSelection2` instance by asking for the `ImageArrayFlavor`, and then we pass the array to the `waveThis()` method, which, purely for entertainment purposes, runs the array through a sine wave filter and returns a new image, which we set as the image for the right-hand image canvas. You can see the results of our shenanigans in Figure 16-5. Since the `waveThis()` method has no bearing on clipboard and data transfer, we won't bother to list it; the code, of course, is on the CD in the back of the book.

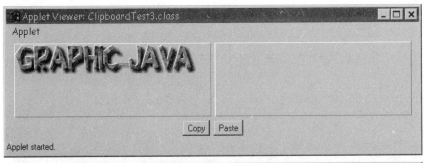

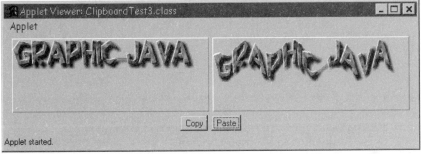

Figure 16-5 Retrieving an Image off the Clipboard as an Array of Bits
The picture on the left is copied to the clipboard and retrieved as an array of bits. The array of bits is run through a sine wave function, the result of which is displayed in the right-hand image canvas.

Transferring Custom AWT Components

Our final example, at the risk of beating data transfer to death, is to implement a transferable that encapsulates a custom component[6].

Note: there is a bug under the 1.1.1 release of the AWT that causes the following applet to throw an exception under Windows 95 (it works fine under Solaris).

A Transferable for Encapsulating a Custom Component

Our custom component will be a very simplistic image button[7], whose implementation we won't bother to discuss. Instead, we will simply show the implementation of `ImageButtonSelection` and the applet that exercises it. The complete implementation of `ImageButtonSelection` is listed in Example 16-5.

Example 16-5 ImageButtonSelection

```
import java.awt.*;
import java.awt.datatransfer.*;
import java.io.*;

public class ImageButtonSelection implements Transferable,
                                   ClipboardOwner {
  public static DataFlavor ImageButtonFlavor;
  private DataFlavor[] flavors = {ImageButtonFlavor};
  private ImageButton imageButton;

  static {
      try {
          ImageButtonFlavor = new DataFlavor(
              Class.forName("ImageButton"),
              "ImageButton");
      }
      catch(ClassNotFoundException e) {
          e.printStackTrace();
      }
  }
  public ImageButtonSelection(ImageButton imageButton) {
      this.imageButton = imageButton;
  }
  public synchronized DataFlavor[] getTransferDataFlavors() {
      return flavors;
  }
```

6. To be fair, this should be a very common requirement, so we feel justified including it.
7. The GJT comes with a much more complete `ImageButton` class.

```
public boolean isDataFlavorSupported(DataFlavor flavor) {
    return flavor.equals(ImageButtonFlavor);
}
public synchronized Object getTransferData(DataFlavor flavor)
    throws UnsupportedFlavorException, IOException {
    if(flavor.equals(ImageButtonFlavor)) {
        return imageButton;
    }
    else
        throw new UnsupportedFlavorException(flavor);
}
public void lostOwnership(Clipboard c, Transferable t) {
}
}
```

We have but one lone data flavor—`ImageButtonFlavor`. By now, the implementation of `ImageButtonSelection` should require no explanation, so without further ado, we'll move on to an applet that copies image buttons to and from a clipboard.

ImageButton Transfer Applet

First, let's take a look at the applet, both in its initial state and after we've copied a single image button three times from the clipboard, in Figure 16-6.

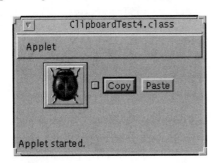

Figure 16-6 Copying and Retrieving an ImageButton to/from a Clipboard
The picture on the left shows the applet in its initial state. After activating the Copy button once and the Paste button three times, the applet looks like the picture on the right.

Rather than bore you with the details of the inner workings of the applet, we'll have a brief discussion and show you the code. The applet is composed of four components: two instances of `ImageButtonCanvas` and two instances of `java.awt.Button`. An `ImageButtonCanvas` draws a 3D rectangle inside of a black rectangle and contains image buttons. `ImageButtonCanvas`, when it is laid out, expands to accommodate the image buttons it currently contains; thus, the original canvas on the left is just big enough to hold the single image button, while the image canvas on the right is initially at its minimum size.

Copying and retrieving image buttons to/from the clipboard is accomplished with the following (by now familiar) code:

```
class CopyListener implements ActionListener {
    public void actionPerformed(ActionEvent event) {
        ImageButton button = copyFrom.getImageButton();
        ImageButtonSelection contents =
                    new ImageButtonSelection(button);

        clipboard.setContents(contents, ClipboardTest4.this);
    }
}
class PasteListener implements ActionListener {
    public void actionPerformed(ActionEvent event) {
    Transferable contents = clipboard.getContents(this);

    if(contents != null) {
        try {
            ImageButton imageButton =
                (ImageButton) contents.getTransferData(
                        ImageButtonSelection.ImageButtonFlavor);

            copyTo.setImageButton(imageButton);
            copyTo.invalidate();
            validate();
        }
        catch(Exception e) {
            e.printStackTrace();
        }
    }
  }
 }
}
```

Notice that we invalidate the `copyTo ImageButtonCanvas` and then invoke `validate()` on its container (the applet) in order to force the image button canvas to be laid out whenever an image button is pasted to it. The entire applet is shown in Example 16-6.

Example 16-6 ClipboardTest4

```java
import java.applet.Applet;
import java.awt.*;
import java.awt.event.*;
import java.awt.datatransfer.*;

public class ClipboardTest4 extends      Applet
                          implements ClipboardOwner {
  private Clipboard clipboard;
  private ImageButtonCanvas copyFrom = new ImageButtonCanvas();
  private ImageButtonCanvas copyTo   = new ImageButtonCanvas();
  private Button copy  = new Button("Copy");
  private Button paste = new Button("Paste");

  public void init() {
     clipboard = getToolkit().getSystemClipboard();

     copyFrom.setImageButton(
        new ImageButton(getImage(getCodeBase(),
                    "ladybug.gif")));
     add(copyFrom);
     add(copyTo);
     add(copy);
     add(paste);

     copy.addActionListener (new CopyListener());
     paste.addActionListener(new PasteListener());
  }
  class CopyListener implements ActionListener {
     public void actionPerformed(ActionEvent event) {
        ImageButton button = copyFrom.getImageButton();
        ImageButtonSelection contents =
                new ImageButtonSelection(button);

        clipboard.setContents(contents, ClipboardTest4.this);
     }
  }
  class PasteListener implements ActionListener {
     public void actionPerformed(ActionEvent event) {
        Transferable contents = clipboard.getContents(this);

        if(contents != null) {
           try {
              ImageButton imageButton =
                  (ImageButton) contents.getTransferData(
                       ImageButtonSelection.ImageButtonFlavor);
```

```
                copyTo.setImageButton(imageButton);
                copyTo.invalidate();
                validate();
            }
            catch(Exception e) {
                e.printStackTrace();
            }
        }
    }
}
    public void lostOwnership(Clipboard    clip,
                             Transferable transferable) {
        System.out.println("Lost ownership");
    }
}
class ImageButtonCanvas extends Panel {
    private ImageButton imageButton;

    public ImageButtonCanvas() {
        this(null);
    }
    public ImageButtonCanvas(ImageButton imageButton) {
        if(imageButton != null)
            setImageButton(imageButton);
    }
    public void paint(Graphics g) {
        g.setColor   (Color.black);
        g.drawRect   (0,0,getSize().width-1,getSize().height-1);
        g.setColor   (Color.lightGray);
        g.draw3DRect(1,1,getSize().width-3,
                    getSize().height-3,true);
    }
    public void setImageButton(ImageButton button) {
        imageButton = button;
        add(new ImageButton(imageButton.getImage()));
        if(isShowing()) {
            repaint();
        }
    }
    public ImageButton getImageButton() {
        return imageButton;
    }
}
```

Summary

The 1.1 version of the AWT introduces support for clipboards, both local clipboards and access to the system clipboard. Copying data to the system clipboard makes the data available to other programs in addition to other AWT components.

The AWT's data transfer mechanism consists of transferables and data flavors. Transferables encapsulate data and can provide access to their data in one or more data flavors.

Transferring textual data is supported by the `java.awt.datatransfer` package; however, you are on your own when transferring data of other types. We've demonstrated how to transfer both images and AWT custom components to and from clipboards, in order to illustrate transferring nontextual data types.

CHAPTER 17

System Colors, Mouseless Operation, and Printing

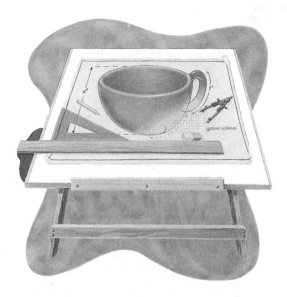

This chapter explores three new features of the 1.1 version of the AWT: system colors, mouseless operation, and printing.

Most windowing systems provide symbolic representations of colors for standard features of components. The 1.1 release of the AWT provides a set of symbolic colors that you should use instead of hardcoding colors for such things as the background color for controls (user interface components), window borders, and shadows, among other things. Support for system colors comes in the form of a `java.awt.SystemColor` class, which we'll take the time to briefly explore.

The original AWT lacked explicit support for mouseless operation. With the advent of 1.1, the AWT supports mouseless operation on two fronts: tabbing between components and menu shortcuts. We'll explore both mechanisms in this chapter.

Finally, a major impediment to developing industrial-strength user interfaces with the AWT has been overcome in 1.1—the AWT now includes support for printing. Printing support has been seamlessly integrated into the existing AWT graphics model; as a result, it is intuitive and simple to use. The flip side of this, however, is that implementing platform-independent support for printing is notoriously tricky to nail down, so there were still some outstanding bugs concerning printing. However, we expect these to be smoothed out in the near future, perhaps by the time you read this.

System Colors

One of the newcomers to the AWT for 1.1 is the `java.awt.SystemColor` class.
`SystemColor` extends `java.awt.Color` so you may use an instance of
`SystemColor` exactly as you would use an instance of `java.awt.Color`. The
`SystemColor` class offers a set of public static instances for representing a wide
range of colors, all of which are listed in Table 17-1.

Table 17-1 AWT SystemColor Instances and Default Values

Instance Name	Represents ...	Default Value
`activeCaption`	Active caption background	Color(0,0,128)
`activeCaptionBorder`	Active caption border	lightGray
`activeCaptionText`	Active caption text	white
`control`	Control background	lightGray
`controlDkShadow`	Control dark shadow	black
`controlHighlight`	Control highlight	white
`controlLtHighlight`	Control light highlight	Color(224,224,224)
`controlShadow`	Control shadow	gray
`controlText`	Control text	black
`desktop`	Desktop background	Color(0,92,92)
`inactiveCaption`	Inactive caption background	gray
`inactiveCaptionBorder`	Inactive caption border	lightGray
`inactiveCaptionText`	Inactive caption text	lightGray
`info`	Info background	Color(224,224,0)
`infoText`	Info text	black
`menu`	Menu background	lightGray
`menuText`	Menu text	black
`scrollbar`	Scrollbar background	Color(224,224,224)
`text`	Text background	lightGray
`textHighlight`	Text highlight	Color(0,0,128)
`textHighlightText`	Text highlight text	white
`textInactiveText`	Inactive text	gray
`textText`	Text	black
`window`	Window background	white
`windowBorder`	Window border	black
`windowText`	Window text	black

System colors fall into two general categories: those with which you must concern yourself, and those that are automatically handled by the AWT. For instance, the AWT will ensure that windows it creates have a border color of `SystemColor.windowBorder`. Developers, on the other hand, should ensure that any custom components they create have a background color of `SystemColor.control`. Note that the default values in Table 17-1 are used in case there is no appropriate value for a particular platform.

All that's required to use a system color is to access the appropriate static instance of `SystemColor`. For instance, in a custom component's `paint()` method, you could paint the background of the component and draw some text in the following manner:

```
public void paint(Graphics g) {
  Dimension size = getSize();

  g.setColor(SystemColor.control);
  g.clearRect(0,0,size.width-1,size.height-1);
  g.setColor(SystemColor.controlText);
  g.drawString("CustomComponent", x, y);
}
```

AWT TIP ...

Custom Components Should Use System Colors Whenever Applicable

While standard AWT components use system colors automatically, developers are responsible for ensuring that any custom components they create use system colors where appropriate. Custom components developed under previous versions of the AWT that hardcoded colors should be refactored to use system colors instead.

Mouseless Operation

Support for mouseless operation encompasses two mechanisms: keyboard traversal and menu shortcuts, both of which are quite simple to implement[1]. We'll start off with keyboard traversal and then move on to menu shortcuts.

Keyboard Traversal

GUI users today expect to be able to navigate user interface components either by using the mouse or the keyboard. Although all components could be activated using the mouse in the original AWT, explicit support for keyboard traversal was

---

1. Support for mouseless operation will be expanded in future versions of the AWT.

only available if it was supported by the native windowing system. As a result, the mechanism for keyboard traversal was inconsistent between platforms and was not supported in the underlying AWT code.

The 1.1 release of the AWT provides a unified mechanism across platforms for moving the focus from one component to another:

- TAB moves focus forward to the next component.
- SHIFT-TAB moves focus backwards to the previous component.

The order of traversal, i.e., which component is in front o, or behind another component, is defined by the order in which components are added to their containers[2]. If the first component added to a container has focus, a TAB will move the focus to the second component added to the container, whereas a subsequent SHIFT-TAB moves the focus back to the first component. There is one catch, however: not all components are willing to accept focus on every platform. For instance, buttons are willing to accept focus under Windows 95 and Motif, but not on the Macintosh. The `java.awt.Component` class, as a result, comes equipped with an `isFocusTraversable()` method, which returns `true` if the component supports accepting focus and `false` if it does not.

Standard AWT Components and Keyboard Traversal

The 1.1 version of `java.awt.Window` maintains an association with an instance of `java.awt.FocusManager`. The `FocusManager` class keeps track of which component currently has focus and manages moving the focus forward and backwards in response to a TAB or SHIFT-TAB, respectively. If you are only dealing with standard AWT components, you don't have to give keyboard traversal a second thought, apart from ensuring that you add components to a container in the order desired for keyboard traversal. Our first applet illustrates keyboard traversal in a container that might be used to make a purchase of some sort, shown in Figure 17-1.

Keyboard traversal for the standard AWT components in our applet is handled by the window's focus manager—our rather long-winded applet is shown in Example 17-1. Note that we use two GJT custom components: `gjt.Separator` and `gjt.ButtonPanel`, but they have little bearing on the concepts we are stressing here. The separator serves to visually spruce up the applet to a small degree, and the button panel simplifies the layout of the Purchase and Cancel buttons.

2. This also defines the zorder of components—See "Components and Zorder" on page 159.

Figure 17-1 Keyboard Traversal With Standard AWT Components
Keyboard traversal is handled automatically for standard AWT
components. Order of traversal is defined by the order in which
components are added to their containers.

One thing worth noting about the GJT components used in the applet, however, is
that neither of them is interested in accepting focus. Custom components, unlike
the standard AWT components, must provide explicit support for keyboard
traversal, as we shall see in our next applet. Also, our applet employs an instance
of GridBagLayout to lay out the components in an aesthetically pleasing
manner; however, that is more the purview of "Components, Containers, and
Layout Managers" on page 373. The intention of the PurchaseApplet is to
illustrate that keyboard traversal is handled automatically for standard AWT
components and that the order of traversal is defined by the order in which
components are added to their containers.

Example 17-1 PurchaseApplet

```
import java.applet.Applet;
import java.awt.*;
import gjt.Separator;
import gjt.ButtonPanel;

public class PurchaseApplet extends Applet {
  public void init() {
    ThreeDPanel p = new ThreeDPanel();
    p.add(new ButtonPurchaseForm());
    add(p);
  }
}
class ThreeDPanel extends Panel {
```

```java
    public void paint(Graphics g) {
       g.setColor(Color.lightGray);
       g.draw3DRect(0,0,getSize().width-1,getSize().height-1,true);
    }
}
class ButtonPurchaseForm extends Panel {
  Separator sep = new Separator();
  Label title   = new Label("Purchase Something Now");
  Label name    = new Label("Name:");
  Label address = new Label("Address:");
  Label payment = new Label("Purchase Method:");
  Label phone   = new Label("Phone:");
  Label city    = new Label("City:");
  Label state   = new Label("State:");

  TextField nameField    = new TextField(25);
  TextField addressField = new TextField(25);
  TextField cityField    = new TextField(15);
  TextField stateField   = new TextField(2);

  Choice    paymentChoice = new Choice();
  Button    paymentButton = new Button("Purchase");
  Button    cancelButton = new Button("Cancel");

  public ButtonPurchaseForm() {
     GridBagLayout      gbl = new GridBagLayout();
     GridBagConstraints gbc = new GridBagConstraints();

     setLayout(gbl);

     paymentChoice.add("Visa");
     paymentChoice.add("MasterCard");
     paymentChoice.add("COD");

     title.setFont(new Font("Times-Roman",
                 Font.BOLD + Font.ITALIC, 16));

     gbc.anchor    = GridBagConstraints.NORTH;
     gbc.gridwidth = GridBagConstraints.REMAINDER;
     gbl.setConstraints(title, gbc);
     add(title);

     gbc.fill      = GridBagConstraints.HORIZONTAL;
     gbc.insets    = new Insets(0,0,10,0);
     gbl.setConstraints(sep, gbc);
     add(sep);

     gbc.anchor    = GridBagConstraints.WEST;
```

```
gbc.gridwidth = 1;
gbc.insets    = new Insets(0,0,0,0);
gbl.setConstraints(name, gbc);
add(name);

gbc.gridwidth = GridBagConstraints.REMAINDER;
gbl.setConstraints(nameField, gbc);
add(nameField);

gbc.gridwidth = 1;
gbl.setConstraints(address, gbc);
add(address);

gbc.gridwidth = GridBagConstraints.REMAINDER;
gbl.setConstraints(addressField, gbc);
add(addressField);

gbc.gridwidth = 1;
gbl.setConstraints(city, gbc);
add(city);

gbl.setConstraints(cityField, gbc);
add(cityField);
gbl.setConstraints(state, gbc);
add(state);

gbc.gridwidth = GridBagConstraints.REMAINDER;
gbl.setConstraints(stateField, gbc);
add(stateField);

gbc.gridwidth = 1;
gbl.setConstraints(payment, gbc);
gbc.insets = new Insets(5,0,5,0);
add(payment);

gbc.gridwidth = GridBagConstraints.REMAINDER;
gbc.fill      = GridBagConstraints.NONE;
gbl.setConstraints(paymentChoice, gbc);
add(paymentChoice);

ButtonPanel buttonPanel = new ButtonPanel();
buttonPanel.add(paymentButton);
buttonPanel.add(cancelButton);

gbc.anchor    = GridBagConstraints.SOUTH;
gbc.insets    = new Insets(5,0,0,0);
gbc.fill      = GridBagConstraints.HORIZONTAL;
gbc.gridwidth = 4;
```

```
    gbl.setConstraints(buttonPanel, gbc);
    add(buttonPanel);
  }
}
```

Once again, the order in which we've added the components to their container defines the order in which keyboard focus is traversed. Obviously, our representation of the applet in Figure 17-1 cannot convey keyboard traversal, so you may wish to run the applet from the CD in order to verify that we have indeed been telling the truth.

Custom Components and Keyboard Traversal

While keyboard traversal is handled automatically for the standard AWT components, you are pretty much on your own if you are developing a custom component. Fortunately, implementing keyboard traversal support for custom components is very straightforward. We will start out by enumerating the steps involved followed by an example, which should serve to set you well on your way to implementing support for keyboard traversal in your own custom components.

The first order of business when considering keyboard traversal is to decide whether or not your particular custom component is interested in accepting keyboard focus. For instance, in the previous applet, we used an instance of gjt.Separator, which has no interest whatsoever in accepting focus. If your component is interested in accepting focus, then you should adhere to the following:

1.   Override isFocusTraversable() to return true[3].

2.   Implement a FocusListener that responds appropriately to gaining/losing focus. Typically, this involves some type of visual feedback.

3.   Implement a MouseListener that invokes requestFocus() in the appropriate mouse handler method.

4.   Add the focus listener and mouse listener implemented in steps 2 and 3 to the component.

That's all there is to supporting keyboard traversal in custom components. Let's take a look at a simple custom component whose only purpose is to illustrate implementing keyboard traversal.

---

3.   By default, it is up to a component's peer to provide the return value from isFocusTraversable().

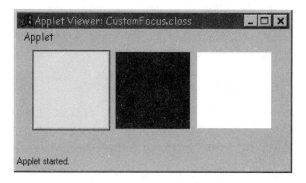

Figure 17-2 Keyboard Traversal With Custom Components
It is up to the developer to provide keyboard traversal support for
custom components. The component on the left currently has
focus.

Our custom component is simply a blotch of color that is interested in receiving
keyboard focus. Since the implementation of ColoredCanvas is relatively short,
we'll show you the code for the entire component in Example 17-2 and then
discuss the code pertinent to supporting keyboard traversal.

Example 17-2 ColoredCanvas Class—ColoredCanvas Tracking Focus

```
class ColoredCanvas extends Canvas {
  Color   color;
  boolean hasFocus = false;

  public ColoredCanvas(Color color) {
    this.color = color;

    addMouseListener(new MouseAdapter() {
      public void mousePressed(MouseEvent event) {
        requestFocus();
      }
    });
    addFocusListener(new FocusListener() {
      public void focusGained(FocusEvent e) {
        hasFocus = true;
        repaint();
      }
      public void focusLost(FocusEvent event) {
        hasFocus = false;
        repaint();
      }
    });
  }
```

```
public boolean isFocusTraversable() {
   return true;
}
public void paint(Graphics g) {
   Dimension size = getSize();

   g.setColor  (color);
   g.fill3DRect(2,2,size.width-4,size.height-4,true);

   if(hasFocus) {
       g.setColor(Color.black);
       g.drawRect(0,0,size.width-1,size.height-1);
   }
}
public Dimension getPreferredSize() {
   return new Dimension(100,100);
}
}
```

As required, ColoredCanvas implements isFocusTraversable() to return
true. We have also implemented a FocusListener that responds appropriately
to gaining/losing focus and added it to the component in one fell swoop, through
the magic of inner classes[4]. In addition, we've implemented a MouseListener
that requests focus whenever a mouse press occurs and added it to the
component.

We've also implemented one additional step not listed above—we've tracked
whether or not the component has focus. If the component has focus, then its
paint() method draws a black border around the component; if the component
does not have focus, no border is drawn. This provides visual feedback when the
component has focus and ensures that any subsequent repainting of the
component will provide the correct visual feedback.

However, we have done a little more work than we need to in order to track
whether or not the component currently has focus, for there is another object that
is already doing that for us—the focus manager associated with the window in
which the component resides. Example 17-3 lists a new and improved version of
ColoredCanvas that asks the frame in which it resides whether or not it is the
focus owner.

---

4. See "Anonymous Inner Classes" on page 125 for a discussion of inner classes and
   event handling.

Example 17-3 ColoredCanvas Class—FocusManager Tracking Focus

```
class ColoredCanvas extends Canvas {
  Color color;

  public ColoredCanvas(Color color) {
     this.color = color;
     addMouseListener(new MouseAdapter() {
        public void mousePressed(MouseEvent event) {
           requestFocus();
        }
     });
     addFocusListener(new FocusListener() {
        public void focusGained(FocusEvent e) {
           repaint();
        }
        public void focusLost(FocusEvent event) {
           repaint();
        }
     });
  }
  public boolean isFocusTraversable() {
     return true;
  }
  public void paint(Graphics g) {
     Dimension size = getSize();

     g.setColor  (color);
     g.fill3DRect(2,2,size.width-4,size.height-4,true);

❶    if(getFrame().getFocusOwner() == this) {
        g.setColor(Color.black);
        g.drawRect(0,0,size.width-1,size.height-1);
     }
  }
  public Dimension getPreferredSize() {
     return new Dimension(100,100);
  }
  public Frame getFrame() {
     Component c = this;
       while((c = c.getParent()) != null) {
          if(c instanceof Frame)
              return (Frame)c;
       }
       return null;
  }
}
```

Notice that this version of `ColoredCanvas` no longer explicitly keeps track of whether it currently has the keyboard focus. On line ❶ we invoke `Frame.getFocusOwner()` to determine if the component currently has the keyboard focus.

You may take issue with the fact that our new version of `ColoredCanvas` has traded tracking whether it has focus with having to implement a method that returns the frame in which the canvas resides. However, such functionality is better placed in a utility class, such as `gjt.Util`, that all classes have access to. Regardless of whether the component itself keeps track of whether it currently has the keyboard focus,—we recommend that you let the focus manager handle that responsibility— `ColoredCanvas` is now able to accept keyboard focus, either by tabbing or pressing the mouse, and provides visual feedback indicating whether or not it currently has focus.

Finally, the entire applet in Example 17-4.

Example 17-4 CustomFocus Applet

```java
import java.applet.Applet;
import java.awt.*;
import java.awt.event.*;

public class CustomFocus extends Applet {
  ColoredCanvas yellowCanvas = new ColoredCanvas(Color.yellow);
  ColoredCanvas blueCanvas   = new ColoredCanvas(Color.blue);
  ColoredCanvas whiteCanvas  = new ColoredCanvas(Color.white);

  public void init() {
    add(yellowCanvas);
    add(blueCanvas);
    add(whiteCanvas);
    yellowCanvas.requestFocus();
  }
}
class ColoredCanvas extends Canvas {
  Color color;

  public ColoredCanvas(Color color) {
    this.color = color;

    addMouseListener(new MouseAdapter() {
      public void mousePressed(MouseEvent event) {
        requestFocus();
      }
    });
    addFocusListener(new FocusListener() {
```

```
      public void focusGained(FocusEvent e) {
         repaint();
      }
      public void focusLost(FocusEvent event) {
         repaint();
      }
   });
}
public boolean isFocusTraversable() {
   return true;
}
public void paint(Graphics g) {
   Dimension size = getSize();

   g.setColor  (color);
   g.fill3DRect(2,2,size.width-4,size.height-4,true);

   if(getFrame().getFocusOwner() == this) {
      g.setColor(Color.black);
      g.drawRect(0,0,size.width-1,size.height-1);
   }
}
public Dimension getPreferredSize() {
   return new Dimension(100,100);
}
public Frame getFrame() { // See gjt.Util for similar method
   Component c = this;

   while((c = c.getParent()) != null) {
       if(c instanceof Frame)
      return (Frame)c;
    }
    return null;
 }
}
```

AWT TIP ...

Let the Window's Focus Manager Track Focus For Custom Components

Every AWT window comes with an instance of FocusManager that is responsible for tracking which component in the window currently has keyboard focus. Windows also come with a method,: getFocusOwner(), that returns a reference to the component that currently has focus. Custom components should use the Window.getFocusOwner() method to determine if they currently have keyboard focus.

Menu Shortcuts

Menu shortcuts provide the ability to activate a menu item by using the keyboard. Menu shortcuts are also known as menu accelerators or keyboard equivalents. Shortcuts have a key modifier that varies between platforms:

- Macintosh: <Command>
- Windows 95: <Control>
- Motif: <Control>

The `java.awt.Toolkit` class in 1.1 has been fitted with a method that returns the appropriate modifier: `Toolkit.getMenuShortcutKeyMask()`, should you ever have the need to programmatically determine the modifier key on a particular platform.

Menu items must provide some kind of visual indication that a shortcut may be used to activate the menu item, when applicable. Such visual indication varies between platforms, and is handled in a platform-dependent manner by the AWT.

Menu Classes and Shortcuts

Menu shortcuts are attached to menu items by instantiating an instance of `MenuShortcut`, which is passed either to a menu item's constructor or to a menu item's `setShortcut()` method. Table 17-2 shows the public methods of the `java.awt.MenuShortcut` class.

Table 17-2 java.awt.MenuShortcut Public Methods

Method	Description
`int getKey()`	Returns raw key code, e.g.: 'c', 't', etc.
`boolean usesShiftModifier()`	Returns true if SHIFT modifier is used.
`boolean equals(MenuShortcut)`	If keycode and shift modifiers are the same, two shortcuts are equal.
`String toString()`	Description of the shortcut.

Table 17-3 shows the methods that have been added to the `java.awt.MenuItem` class to accommodate menu shortcuts.

Table 17-3 java.awt.MenuItem Methods Dealing With Menu Shortcuts

Method	Description
`MenuItem(String, MenuShortcut)`	Constructs with menu shortcut.
`MenuShortcut getShortcut()`	Returns shortcut for item.
`void setShortcut(MenuShortcut)`	Sets shortcut for item.
`void deleteShortcut()`	Deletes an item's shortcut.

Note that the first method in Table 17-3 is a `MenuItem` constructor; menu items can have their shortcut specified either at construction time or after construction. Additionally, `java.awt.MenuItem` provides methods for obtaining an item's shortcut and removing a shortcut from a menu item.

Finally, `java.awt.MenuBar` has some additional methods to deal with menu shortcuts, as you can see from Table 17-4.

Table 17-4 java.awt.MenuBar Methods Dealing With Menu Shortcuts

Method	Description
`MenuItem getShorcutMenuItem(` `MenuShortcut)`	Returns menu item with specified short-cut.
`Enumeration shortcuts()`	Returns an enumeration of all shortcuts in the menu items contained in the menubar's menus.
`boolean handleShortcut(KeyEvent)`	Process shortcut key event.
`void deleteShortcut(` `MenuShortcut)`	Deletes shortcut from appropriate menu item.

A Menu Shortcuts Example

Table 17-4 shows a Java application that has a menubar with an Edit menu that has shortcuts for the cut, copy and paste menu items.

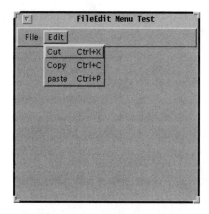

Figure 17-3 Menu Shortcuts Displayed in a MenuItem
Menu shortcuts are attached to the cut, copy and paste menu items in a Motif window. Visual indication of shortcuts in menu items varies between platforms.

Our application simply creates a menu shortcut for the cut, copy and paste menu items and then constructs the menu items by passing in the appropriate shortcut. The applet is listed in its entirety in Example 17-5.

Example 17-5 ShorcutTest Application

```java
import java.awt.*;
import java.awt.event.*;

public class ShortcutTest extends Frame {
  MenuItem quitItem;
  MenuBar mbar = new MenuBar();

  public static void main(String args[]) {
    ShortcutTest test = new ShortcutTest("FileEdit Menu Test");

    test.setBounds(300,300,300,300);
    test.show();
  }
  public ShortcutTest(String s) {
    super(s);

    mbar.add(createFileMenu());
    mbar.add(createEditMenu());
    setMenuBar(mbar);

    quitItem.addActionListener(new ActionListener() {
      public void actionPerformed(ActionEvent event) {
        dispose();
        System.exit(0);
      }
    });
  }
  private Menu createFileMenu() {
    Menu fileMenu = new Menu("File");
    fileMenu.add(quitItem = new MenuItem("Quit"));
    return fileMenu;
  }
  private Menu createEditMenu() {
    Menu editMenu = new Menu("Edit");

    MenuShortcut copyShortcut  = new MenuShortcut('c');
    MenuShortcut cutShortcut   = new MenuShortcut('x');
    MenuShortcut pasteShortcut = new MenuShortcut('p');

    MenuItemListener itemListener = new MenuItemListener();

    MenuItem cutItem  = new MenuItem("Cut",    cutShortcut),
```

```
            copyItem = new MenuItem("Copy",  copyShortcut),
            pasteItem = new MenuItem("paste", pasteShortcut);

     cutItem.addActionListener  (itemListener);
     copyItem.addActionListener (itemListener);
     pasteItem.addActionListener(itemListener);

     editMenu.add(cutItem);
     editMenu.add(copyItem);
     editMenu.add(pasteItem);

     return editMenu;
   }
 }
 class MenuItemListener implements ActionListener {
   public void actionPerformed(ActionEvent event) {
     MenuItem item = (MenuItem)event.getSource();
       System.out.println(item.getLabel());
   }
 }
```

The `createEditMenu()` method is where all of the action takes place as far as menu shortcuts are concerned. Three shortcuts are created, each of which is passed to the appropriate `MenuItem` constructor. That's all there is to attaching shortcuts to menu items—from here on out the AWT will process the appropriate keystrokes to activate the menu item associated with a shortcut.

Printing

With the 1.1 release of the AWT you can print a `Graphics` object—but not just any Graphics object; you can only print a `PrintGraphics` object. You can either manually draw into the graphics or have a component draw into it; either way, after you are done painting into the graphics, you can turn around and print it. If a component prints into the graphics object, and the component is a container, you can choose to print all of the components contained within the container's containment hierarchy.

Obtaining a Reference to a PrintGraphics

Whether you want to paint a (hierarchy of) component(s) or you just want to paint into a graphics object and then print it, you must first obtain a reference to a special extension of the `Graphics` class—a `PrintGraphics`. This is a four-step process, outlined below:

1. Obtain a reference to a frame.

2. Obtain a reference to the default toolkit.

3. Invoke the toolkit's `getPrintJob()` method, passing in the frame obtained in step 2, which returns a reference to a `PrintJob`.

4. Invoke the print job's `getGraphics()` method which returns a reference to a `PrintGraphics`.

Once you have a reference to a `PrintGraphics` object, you can either pass it to a component's `print()` or `printAll()` methods, or you can paint into it as you would any graphics object. Printing the graphics merely requires you to invoke the graphics's `dispose()` method, which flushes it to the printer. When you are done printing, you should invoke `end()` on the print job obtained in step 3 above.

> **AWT TIP**
>
> *Use the gjt.Util.printComponent() Method for Printing AWT Components*
>
> Perhaps the most common printing requirement is to print out an AWT component. The Graphic Java Toolkit comes with a printComponent() method in the gjt.Util class that encapsulates recursively printing all of the components contained in a container (or just printing the component if it is not a container). When you just want to print out a component, it is much more convenient to use the utility method provided by the GJT Util class instead of coding the steps necessary to print the component by hand.

An Applet That Prints Itself

Let's start out with a simple applet that prints itself[5], shown in Figure 17-4.

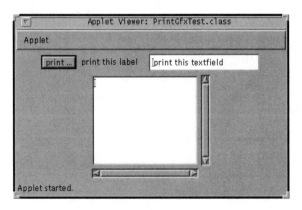

Figure 17-4 An Applet That Prints Itself
The print button prints out all of the components contained in the applet.

The listing for our applet is shown in Example 17-6.

Example 17-6 PrintApplet

```
import java.applet.Applet;
import java.awt.*;
import java.awt.event.*;
import java.util.Properties;

public class PrintApplet extends Applet {
  Button printButton = new Button("print ...");

  public void init() {
     add(printButton);
     add(new Label("print this label"));
     add(new TextField("print this textfield"));
     add(new TextArea(10,20));

     printButton.addActionListener(new ActionListener() {
        public void actionPerformed(ActionEvent event) {
           printComponents(PrintApplet.this);
        }
     });
  }
  static Frame getFrame(Component c) {
     while((c = c.getParent()) != null) {
        if(c instanceof Frame)
           return (Frame)c;
     }
     return null;
  }
  static void printComponents(Component c) {
     Frame    frame = getFrame(c);
     Toolkit tk     = Toolkit.getDefaultToolkit();

     if(tk != null) {
        String   name = c.getName() + " print job";
        PrintJob pj   = tk.getPrintJob(frame,name,
                                        (Properties)null);
        if(pj != null) {
           Graphics pg = pj.getGraphics();

           if(pg != null) {
              c.printAll(pg);
              pg.dispose();
```

❶
❷
❸
❹

5. All applets are capable of printing themselves in 1.1—see appletviewer's Applet
    menu.

```
            }
            pj.end();
          }
        }
      }
    }
```

The most interesting method in our applet, of course, is the `static` `printComponents()` method. By the way, If `printComponents()` were placed in a utility class[6], it would be available to print any component. The bullets alongside the code correspond to the steps outlined previously for obtaining a reference to a print graphics. After obtaining the reference to the print graphics, we pass it to the component's (the component is the applet in this case) `printAll()` method, and then invoke its `dispose()` method, which flushes it to the printer. Optionally, once we had the reference to the print graphics, we could have drawn directly into it and then printed it out:

```
if(pg != null) {
  pg.drawLine(10,10,50,50);
  pg.dispose();
}
```

The Print Dialog and Its Properties

One thing that we've glossed over is the fact that `Toolkit.getPrintJob()` shows a platform-dependent print dialog. The Motif version of the print dialog is shown in Figure 17-5.

If the print button in the dialog is activated, `Toolkit.getPrintJob()` returns a non-null reference to a `PrintJob`. If the cancel button is activated, then a null reference is returned. As a result, you always need to check the return value of `Toolkit.getPrintJob()` to find out whether the job was cancelled.

6.   As you can probably guess, the `gjt.Util` class comes with a similar method.

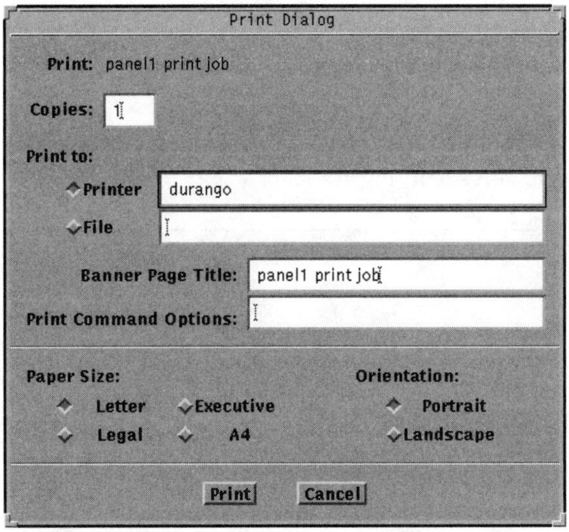

Figure 17-5 Motif Print Dialog
`Toolkit.getPrintJob()` shows a platform-dependent print dialog.

Another point we need to expand upon is that `Toolkit.getPrintJob()` takes two arguments in addition to a frame: the name of the print job and a `Properties` object. The properties passed in specifies any platform-dependent printing properties, for instance, you could specify that "awt.print.printer" is "durango", and "awt.print.numCopies" is "2":

```
static void printComponents(Component c) {
   Toolkit     tk    = Toolkit.getDefaultToolkit();
   Frame       frame = getFrame(c);
   Properties props = new Properties();

   props.put("awt.print.printer",   "durango");
   props.put("awt.print.numCopies", "2");

   if(tk != null) {
      String    name = c.getName() + " print job";
      PrintJob pj    = tk.getPrintJob(frame, name, props);

      if(pj != null) {
         Graphics pg = pj.getGraphics();

         if(pg != null) {
            c.printAll(pg);
            pg.dispose();
         }
```

```
        pj.end();
    }
    System.out.println(props);
...
```

Specifying the two properties above results in those properties being set in the print dialog, as you can see in Figure 17-6.

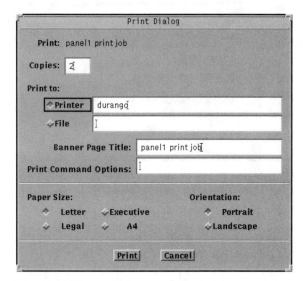

Figure 17-6 Motif Print Dialog With Preset Properties
The number of copies and printer name were specified with the
properties object passed to `Toolkit.getPrintJob()`

Another nifty feature of `Toolkit.getPrintJob()` is that it modifies the properties it is passed so that the values match whatever the user entered in the print dialog. In the code snippet above, we print out the properties object after the call to `getPrintJob()` returns. In the print dialog, we changed the number of copies to 1 and changed the printer to sabre. As you can see from the output, those changes were stored in the properties object we passed in:

```
{awt.print.numCopies=1, awt.print.printer=sabre,
 awt.print.paperSize=letter, awt.print.destination=printer,
 awt.print.orientation=portrait}
```

Pagination

You're on your own as far as pagination is concerned[7]. Each print graphics will print out a single page, so it's up to you to organize your print graphics when printing multiple pages. However, the `PrintJob` class will lend a hand by providing two methods concerning pagination:

- `Dimension getPageDimension()`
- `int getPageResolution()`

The former method returns the page dimension in pixels; the latter returns the page resolution in pixels per inch. It's up to you to do the math.

Summary

The 1.1 version of the AWT provides three features that are essential to developing anything but the most trivial of applications: access to system colors, mouseless operation, and printing. For the most part, each feature is straightforward to use and fits well with the existing AWT infrastructure.

Access to system colors is provided so that developers can develop custom components that adhere to platform-dependent colors for everything from the background color of controls to the highlight color for text. Developers should use system colors wherever appropriate instead of hardcoding colors in their custom components. It should also be noted that the AWT uses system colors to provide a unified look and feel with other applications on the desktop.

Mouseless operation is an expected feature for graphical user interfaces that was conspicuous in its absence in the original AWT. The AWT has laid the foundation for mouseless operation by providing two basic features: keyboard traversal and menu shortcuts. More support for mouseless operation will be added in future versions of the AWT.

Finally, the AWT has provided access to platform-dependent printing. The model used for printing is in line with the AWT's graphics model and is intuitive and easy to use. A major chunk of functionality is wrapped up in the toolkit's `getPrintJob()` method, which posts a platform-dependent print dialog and provides a mechanism for getting and setting the properties in the dialog.

---

7. You didn't expect `Toolkit.getPrintJob()` to do *everything*, did you?

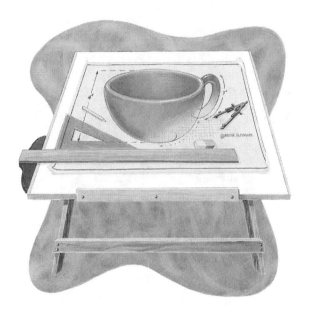

CHAPTER

18

Introducing the Graphic Java Toolkit

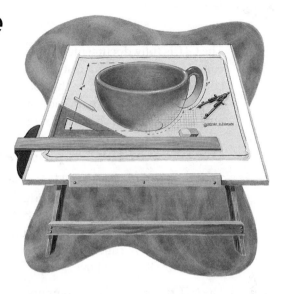

Graphic Java comes with a toolkit of high-level custom components built on top of the AWT. While the AWT provides low-level components such as buttons, scrollbars, and checkboxes, the Graphic Java Toolkit (GJT) provides high-level custom components such as image buttons, component and image scrollers, bargauges, convenience dialogs, and more. The GJT also provides packages for double buffered sprite animation, rubberbanding, and image filters.

The intent of the Graphic Java Toolkit is threefold:

- To provide a comprehensive set of high-level custom components built on top of the AWT that you can incorporate into your Java applets and applications
- To provide a vehicle for exploring the AWT in depth
- To illustrate techniques and good practices for developing your own custom components

Each of the chapters that follow examines one or more custom components from the GJT. In these chapters, we will burrow deeper into the AWT than we have thus far. Custom components will subclass `Component`, `Container`, `Canvas`, and `Panel`, use the AWT's layout managers, further explore `Font` and `FontMetrics`, show techniques for double buffered sprite animation, and, perhaps most importantly, illustrate how to develop both heavyweight and lightweight [1]custom components.

The GJT is fully documented, and nearly every custom component in the GJT comes with its own unit test applet. We suggest that you use your favorite Java-enabled browser to peruse the documentation on each custom component and use `appletviewer` to run each unit test as we work our way through the GJT and the AWT in the chapters to come.

Overview of the Graphic Java Toolkit

The Graphic Java Toolkit (GJT) is a set of Java packages that extend the capabilities of the AWT, by providing more than 45 custom components. The GJT is not a replacement for the AWT, but augments the functionality the AWT provides. The packages include a suite of custom components, double buffered sprite animation, rubberbanding, image filters, and a comprehensive set of test applets for all of the above.

The GJT provides custom components in the following functional areas:

Table 18-1 Graphic Java Toolkit Components

Functional Area	Components
Rectangles/Borders And Boxes	Etched, 3D, and flat rectangles & borders drawn into a component. Boxes and borders are containers.
Rubberbanding	Linear, elliptical, and rectangular rubberbands can be attached to any component.
Dialogs	Message, question, yes/no, progress, work, and font dialogs.
Lightweight Components	Double buffered container, image button, toolbar, label canvas, image canvas, bargauge, separator, playfield.
Custom Layouts	Bulletin, row, column, tree, scroller.
Image Filters	B&W, bleach, negative, wave, dissolve.
Scrollers	Image scroller and scroller base class.
Sprite Animation	Sprite, playfield, collision detectors.
Miscellaneous Components	Selectable container, box, bubble, toolbox, splash screen, cursor and color choices, double list, state button, button panel, drawing panel, assertions, stopwatch, utility class.

---

1. See "Lightweight Components" on page 475.

The GJT Packages

Table 18-2 shows the packages that compose the GJT.

Table 18-2 Graphic Java Toolkit Packages

Package Name	Contents
gjt	High-level custom components for developing user interfaces, including separators, borders, dialogs, image buttons, toolbars, scrollers, and more. The gjt package also includes utility classes and a set of custom layout managers.
gjt.animation	A set of classes for double buffered sprite animation. Animation takes place on a Playfield, where sprites are animated by cycling through a sequence of images. Collision detectors detect collisions between sprites, and between sprites and the edges of the playfield.
gjt.image	A set of classes that support image manipulation, such as the bleaching, fading in, and fading out of images.
gjt.rubberband	A collection of classes that provide the infrastructure for rubberbanding. Included are classes for rubberbanding lines, rectangles, and ellipses, along with a RubberbandPanel, which is a Panel that can be fitted with any rubberband; user interaction for rubberbanding is automatically handled.
gjt.test	A comprehensive set of unit tests for all of the custom components in the other GJT packages. In addition to unit tests, all classes in the GJT are fully documented. HTML files for the entire GJT are provided on the CD that accompanies this book.

The GJT Classes

The next set of tables lists the classes available in each of the GJT packages. Table 18-3 shows the classes that compose the gjt package. Classes in **bold** are lightweight components.

Table 18-3 gjt **Package Classes**

Classes (bold == lightweight components)	Use
Utility Classes	
Assert	Assertion checking.
BorderFactory	Instantiates a border given a border style.
BorderStyle	Defines styles for borders – raised, inset, etched, etc.
Etching	Defines styles of etching – either etched-in or etched-out.
Orientation	Defines orientations and alignments.
RectangleFactory	Instantiates a drawn rectangle (or extension) given a border style.
Stopwatch	A thread masquerading as a stopwatch.
Util	A collection of static utility methods.
Custom Components	
Bargauge	A 3-D rectangle filled with a specified color.
Border	A border drawn around a Component.
Box	An etched border and title around a Component.
Bubble	A window that displays a string - used for bubble help.
ButtonPanel	A separator above a row of buttons that can be placed in a container.
ChoiceCardPanel	A Choice controls display of any number of Panels.
ColorChoice	A Choice for selecting a color.
CursorChoice	A Choice for selecting a cursor.
DoubleBufferedContainer	For displaying and animating lightweight components and sprites.
DoubleList	Two list - items can be moved back and forth.
DrawingPanel	The basis for a paint program.
DrawnRectangle	A rectangle drawn with varying degrees of thickness and shades of color.
EtchedBorder	A Border that draws either etched-in or etched-out.
EtchedRectangle	A DrawnRectangle that draws either etched-in or etched-out.

Table 18-3 `gjt` **Package Classes** (Continued)

Classes (bold == lightweight components)	Use
`ExclusiveImageButtonPanel`	Only one `ImageButton` selected at a time.
`FontDialog`	A `Dialog` for selecting a font.
`FrameWithMenuBar`	A frame with a menubar that provides an alternative to extending `Frame`.
`GJTDialog`	Base class for GJT dialogs.
`IconCardPanel`	A set of image buttons controls display of any number of panels.
`ImageButton`	A button that displays an image.
`ImageButtonPanel`	A `Panel` containing image buttons.
`ImageCanvas`	A `Canvas` that displays an `Image`.
`ImageScroller`	A scroller that enables smooth scrolling of an `Image`.
`LabelCanvas`	A `Canvas` simulating a selectable label.
`MessageDialog`	A `Dialog` that displays a `String`.
`Postcard`	A panel with an image on one side and a component on the other.
`ProgressDialog`	A `Dialog` with a `Bargauge` that monitors activity.
`QuestionDialog`	A `Dialog` that asks for user input.
`RadioMenu`	A menu with mutually exclusive checkbox menu items.
`Scroller`	Base class for `ImageScroller`.
`SelectableContainer`	A container that implements `ItemSelectable` that can fire item events.
`Separator`	Etched lines used to separate logical compartments of user interface widgets.
`SplashScreen`	A borderless window that displays an image.
`StateButton`	An `ImageButton` that cycles images.
`ThreeDBorder`	A `Border` that draws either raised or inset.
`ThreeDRectangle`	A `DrawnRectangle` that draws either raised or inset.
`Toolbar`	A row of image buttons.
`Toolbox`	A window that contains a column of image buttons.

Table 18-3 gjt Package Classes (Continued)

Classes (bold == lightweight components)	Use
YesNoDialog	A Dialog that asks a question and provides Yes/No buttons for a response.
WorkDialog	A dialog that contains a button panel and a work area.
Custom Layout Managers	
BulletinLayout	Positions components in a bulletin-board style.
ColumnLayout	Positions components in a column.
RowLayout	Positions components in a row.
ScrollerLayout	Lays out two scrollbars and a viewport for a scroller.

Table 18-4 shows the classes that compose the gjt.animation package.

Table 18-4 gjt.animation **Package Classes**

Classes (bold == lightweight component)	Use
EdgeCollisionDetector	Detects collisions between sprites and playfield boundaries.
Playfield	Canvas on which sprites are animated.
Sequence	A sequence of images.
Sprite	Animated objects on a Playfield.
SpriteCollisionDetector	Detects collisions between sprites.

Table 18-5 shows the classes that compose the gjt.rubberband package.

Table 18-5 gjt.rubberband **Package Classes**

Classes	Use
Rubberband	Base class for GJT rubberbands.
RubberbandEllipses	Rubberband that does ellipses.
RubberbandPanel	Panel that can be fitted with a rubberband.
RubberbandLine	Rubberband that does lines.
RubberbandRectangle	Rubberband that does rectangles.

Table 18-6 shows the classes that compose the `gjt.test` package.

Table 18-6 `gjt.test` **Package Classes**

Classes	Use
TitledPanel	Panel with a title and horizontal separator.
UnitTest	Applet extension for unit testing components.

Table 18-7 shows the classes that compose the `gjt.image` package.

Table 18-7 `gjt.image` **Package Classes**

Classes	Use
BleachImageFilter	Filter that creates a bleached version of an image.
BlackAndWhiteFilter	Turns a color image into black and white.
DissolveFilter	Filter that creates an image of varying degrees of opacity/transparency.
ImageDissolver	Fades images in or out of a component.
NegativeFilter	Turns an image into its negative.

Custom Components in the Graphic Java Toolkit

Each custom component in the GJT is composed of a set of classes that are designed to work together to provide a useful tool for developing user interfaces.

All of the classes in each custom component have been documented and run through the `javadoc` program; you can find the HTML files for all of the classes in the GJT in the `graphicJava` directory on the CD.

AWT TIP ...

Packaging Custom Components

Nearly all of the GJT custom components come with a unit test—an applet that exercises the components. Unit tests serve three very important purposes: They exercise the custom component, they guard against bugs that might be introduced when the component is extended or reworked in the future, and they provide example code for potential clients. The best unit tests offer a balance between putting their custom components through every imaginable scenario and being simple enough to be understood by the curious developer. Additionally, all custom components in this book come with Booch class diagrams. These show the static relationships between classes, such as which classes extend or implement other classes (or interfaces) and how classes are associated with one another. Such diagrams do wonders for quickly providing an overview of how collaborating classes are associated and enhance understanding of your custom components.

The GJT Utility Classes

The Graphic Java Toolkit comes with a number of utility classes that are used by many of the other classes in the GJT. The utility classes fall into three categories: assertions, type-safe constants, and utility. We will discuss each briefly.

Assertions

In his excellent book *Object-Oriented Software Construction*, Bertand Meyer discusses the concept of programming by contract [2]. Essentially, the relationship between a class and its clients is viewed as a formal agreement—a contract of sorts. The methods of a class should guarantee that they will hold up their end of the contract by reliably performing their intended function. However, the caller of such methods has to hold up its end of the contract by invoking the method with arguments that are correct. As a result, methods of a class should ensure that arguments they are passed are correct—only then can they fulfill their end of the contract.

For instance, consider the `gjt.Bargauge` class, which provides a method for setting the fill percent of the bargauge: `setFillPercent(double)`. Obviously, the `Bargauge` class should *assert* that the value passed into its `setFillPercent()` method lies between 0 and 100. If this check is not made, and a `Bargauge` is passed a bogus percentage, it will not fulfill its end of the

---

2. See Meyer, Bertrand. *Object-Oriented Software Construction*, Chapter 7. Prentice Hall, 1984.

contract and will work unreliably. Java provides an exception for use in asserting the validity of arguments, the aptly named `IllegalArgumentException`. Such an exception would be used like this:

```
public setFillPercent(double percent) {
  if(percent < 0 || percent > 100)
    throw new IllegalArgumentException("Bargauge: bad percent");
  .
  .
  .
}
```

If `Bargauge.setFillPercent()` is passed a value that does not lie between 0 and 100, it will throw an `IllegalArgumentException`. However, littering one's code with conditional checks followed by a `throw` statement is often more overhead than many developers are willing to bear. As a result, the GJT provides an assertion class that provides a shorthand notation for asserting arguments. The same method written with the `gjt.Assert` class looks like this:

```
public setFillPercent(double percent) {
  Assert.notFalse(percent > 0 && percent < 100);
  .
  .
  .
}
```

The `gjt.Assert` class provides a number of convenience methods for asserting arguments, as listed in Table 18-8. The last two methods are passed a string, which is forwarded to the `IllegalArgumentException` constructor.

Table 18-8 `gjt.Assert` **Methods**

Methods
`isTrue(boolean)`
`isTrue(boolean, String)`
`isFalse(boolean)`
`isFalse(boolean, String)`
`notFalse(boolean)`
`notFalse(boolean,String)`
`notNull(Object)`
`notNull(Object,String)`

Type-Checked Constants

It is common practice in the AWT to designate constants by declaring `public static final` members of the class to which the constants pertain. For instance, `java.awt.Label` defines a set of integers used to specify its justification:

```
public static final int LEFT = 0;
public static final int CENTER = 1;
public static final int RIGHT = 2;
```

The `Label` class provides a constructor that allows you to specify the string the `Label` displays and its orientation:

```
public Label(String label, int alignment)
```

After our discussion concerning programming by contract, you would expect the `Label` constructor to assert that the `alignment` passed in is a valid value, either 0, 1, or 2. And sure enough, the `Label` constructor will throw an `IllegalArgumentException` if you attempt to slip it something other than 0, 1, or 2 [3].

Such a strategy for coding constants, however, puts the responsibility for checking arguments such as `alignment` squarely on the shoulders of the class that has declared the constants—in this case the `Label` class. In addition, other classes that need to specify `LEFT`, `RIGHT`, and `CENTER` must declare their own constants and perform the same checking when they are passed integer values for representing the constants.

The Graphic Java Toolkit approach is to provide classes that act as *type-checked* constants. For instance, the `gjt.BorderStyle` class defines constants representing raised and inset borders:

```
public class BorderStyle {
   public static final BorderStyle NONE   = new BorderStyle();
   public static final BorderStyle RAISED = new BorderStyle();
   public static final BorderStyle INSET  = new BorderStyle();
   public static final BorderStyle ETCHED = new BorderStyle();
   public static final BorderStyle SOLID  = new BorderStyle();

   public String toString() {
      String s = new String();

      if(this == BorderStyle.NONE)
         s = getClass().getName() + "=NONE";
      else if(this == BorderStyle.RAISED)
```

3.   Other AWT classes are not so disciplined at checking arguments representing constants and will simply misbehave when passed a invalid value.

```
        s = getClass().getName() + "=RAISED";
    else if(this == BorderStyle.INSET)
        s = getClass().getName() + "=INSET";
    else if(this == BorderStyle.ETCHED)
        s = getClass().getName() + "=ETCHED";
    else if(this == BorderStyle.SOLID)
        s = getClass().getName() + "=SOLID";

    return s;
  }
  private BorderStyle() { }   // defeat instantiation
}
```

The `gjt.ThreeDRectangle` class takes an instance of `ThreeDBorderStyle` as an argument to one of its constructors:

```
public ThreeDRectangle(Component drawInto,
                       BorderStyle state,
                       int thickness, int x, int y,
                       int w, int h)
```

Clients constructing a `ThreeDRectangle` pass the constructor one of the two `public static final BorderStyle` *objects*:

```
rect = new ThreeDRectangle(c, BorderStyle.RAISED, ...);
```

Since an object is being passed to the `ThreeDRectangle` constructor for specifying the border style, it is the compiler that does the checking for us, thus the name type-checked constants. Any method that takes a `ThreeDBorderStyle` object as an argument is guaranteed that the object will be either `ThreeDBorderStyle.RAISED` or `ThreeDBorderStyle.INSET`, for these are the only two instances of `ThreeDBorderStyle` in existence [4].

The type-checked constant approach has other benefits as well. For instance, since the constants are defined within the confines of their own class, we can provide a `toString()` method for printing out the values of the constants, as we have done for `gjt.ThreeDBorderStyle`. To print a `ThreeDBorderStyle` object, you can simply do the following:

```
void someFictitiousMethod(BorderStyle style) {
  System.out.println(style);
}
```

The `System.out.println()` call results in the invocation of `BorderStyle.toString()`, which prints one of the following:

4. The private default constructor in `ThreeDBorderStyle` ensures that no other objects of type `ThreeDBorderStyle` can ever be instantiated.

- `BorderStyle=RAISED`
- `BorderStyle=INSET`
- `BorderStyle=ETCHED`
- `BorderStyle=SOLID`

Conversely, printing an integer representing a constant requires the method doing the printing to match up the string representation with the integer value, like this:

```
void anotherFictitiousMethod(int leftCenterOrRight) {
  if(leftCenterOrRight == LEFT)
    System.out.println("LEFT");
  else if(leftCenterOrRight == CENTER)
    System.out.println("CENTER");
  else if(leftCenterOrRight == RIGHT)
    System.out.println("RIGHT");
}
```

The gjt.Util Class

The Graphic Java Toolkit provides a `Util` class which, as its name suggests, provides a number of utility methods. All of the methods are `static` and can therefore be invoked by `Util.`*name*`()`, where *name* is the name of the method. The utility methods provided by `gjt.Util` are summarized in Table 18-9.

Table 18-9 `gjt.Util` Methods

Methods	Action
`Applet getApplet(Component)`	Returns applet in which component resides.
`Dialog getDialog(Component)`	Returns dialog in which component resides, or null if component does not reside in a dialog.
`Frame getFrame(Component)`	Returns frame in which component resides.
`void setCursor(int, Component)`	Sets cursor for component.
`void stretchImage(Component, Graphics, Image)`	Stretches an image over a component's background.
`void waitForImage(Component, Image)`	Waits for an image to load.
`void wallPaper(Component, Graphics, Image)`	Wallpapers component with image.

The GJT test Package

Each custom component comes with an applet that serves as a unit test for the component. All of the unit test applets reside in the gjt.test package and consist of .java, .class, and .html files. The HTML files are meant to be run with appletviewer or, alternatively, in a Java-enabled browser.

The gjt.test package includes two simple classes that provide some infrastructure for the unit tests: TitledPanel and UnitTest.

TitledPanel is simply a Panel that is fitted with a BorderLayout, with a centered Label:

```
public class TitledPanel extends Panel {
  public TitledPanel(String title) {
      setLayout(new BorderLayout());
      add(new Label(title, Label.CENTER), "Center");
  }
}
```

UnitTest is an abstract class that extends Applet and that is fitted with a BorderLayout. UnitTest places a TitledPanel in the north and a Panel created by derived classes wrapped in a gjt.EtchedBorder in the center:

```
abstract public class UnitTest extends Applet {
  abstract public String title();
  abstract public Panel  centerPanel();
  private Panel center;

  public void init() {
     Util.setCursor(Cursor.WAIT_CURSOR, this);
     Panel titledPanel = new TitledPanel(title());
     setLayout(new BorderLayout());
     add(titledPanel, "North");
     add(new EtchedBorder(center = centerPanel()), "Center");
  }
  public void start() {
     Util.setCursor(Cursor.DEFAULT_CURSOR, this);
  }
}
```

Note that classes derived from UnitTest must provide a title for the unit test and they must supply a Panel that is placed below the TitledPanel. Figure 18-1 shows the layout of UnitTest.

Another feature of UnitTest is that it sets the cursor to WAIT_CURSOR in init() and subsequently changes the cursor back to DEFAULT_CURSOR in start(). Since some applets take awhile to load, it's nice to provide some feedback to the user that the applet is truly being loaded and not just stuck in limbo.

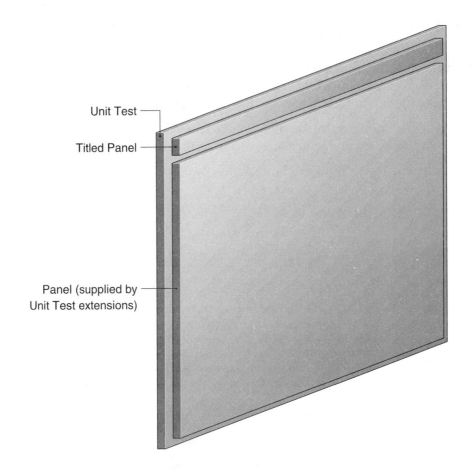

Unit Test

Titled Panel

Panel (supplied by
Unit Test extensions)

Figure 18-1 Unit Test Layout Diagram

Summary

The GJT is a collection of approximately 45 custom components built directly on top of the AWT. The GJT is not a replacement for the AWT; instead, it provides more components that you can use alongside AWT components.

Each GJT custom component comes with a unit test—a simple applet that tests the functionality of the applet. Unit tests make great example code for illustrating the usage of the GJT components and also ensure high quality of the components. Each component's unit test is run after changes are made to the component to make sure new bugs have not been introduced by recent modifications.

On the CD, you will find tar and zip files of the Graphic Java Toolkit. Untarring (or unzipping) grfxjava.tar[zip] will produce a graphicJava_1.1 directory. The directory structure for the GJT source, class files and javadoc documentation is shown in Figure 18-2.

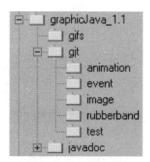

Figure 18-2 GJT Directory Structure
The GJT has a directory for each of its packages, along with a javadoc directory that contains javadoc-generated documentation. Point your browser at /graphicJava_11/gjt/javadoc/packages.html.

Each custom component in the GJT consists of the following:

- A set of collaborating classes
- A set of class diagrams
- A unit test that exercises the custom component

As a general rule, we suggest that custom components you develop on your own also include these items.

All custom components obviously must consist of the first item: a set of collaborating classes, although sometimes the number of classes is simply one (for example, refer to the Box component).

Class diagrams are excellent for portraying the static relationships between classes; they also communicate a great deal of information that is not easily gleaned from verbiage alone. If you have access to a tool that produces class diagrams, we highly recommend that you include class diagrams as part of your own custom components.

The third item serves three essential purposes: it exercises the custom component, it guards against bugs that might be introduced when the component is extended or reworked in the future, and it provides example code for potential clients interested in using the custom component.

CHAPTER 19

Separators and Bargauges

This chapter covers two GJT custom components: `Separator` and `Bargauge`. Both of the components are lightweight components[1], so this chapter will serve to augment "Lightweight Components" on page 475 by providing real world examples of lightweight components. Also, in our quest to demystify `GridBagLayout`, the separator unit test provides yet another example of `GridBaglayout` in action.

gjt.Separator

Nearly every modern-day user-interface toolkit comes with something akin to a separator: etched lines used to separate logical compartments of user interface widgets.

`gjt.Separator` is one of the simplest custom components the GJT provides. Its simplicity merits it the distinction of being the one of the first custom components we present.

---

1. Lightweight components extend `java.awt.Component`. See "Lightweight Components" on page 475.

Separator Associations and Responsibilities

gjt.Separator is a lightweight component, meaning it is an extension of java.awt.Component. Remember, the main difference between lightweight and heavyweight components is that heavyweight components are drawn in their own native (opaque) window, whereas lightweights are drawn in their container's graphics. Since a separator contains no other components, Component is the logical superclass to use. Figure 19-1 shows the class diagram for gjt.Separator.

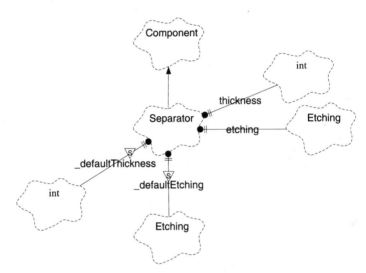

Figure 19-1 gjt.Separator Class Diagram

As you can see, gjt.Separator is a simple custom component that keeps track of the state of its etching and its thickness. The Etching object associated with the Separator is either Etching.IN or Etching.OUT (see "Type-Checked Constants" on page 568).

To highlight the responsibilities of gjt.Separator, Table 19-1 lists its public methods.

Table 19-1 gjt.Separator **Responsibilities**

Methods	Description
void paint(Graphics g)	Overrides Component paint(). Paints either a horizontal or vertical separator.
Dimension getMinimumSize()	Overrides Component minimumSize(). Returns the preferredSize().
Dimension getPreferredSize()	Overrides Component preferredSize(). Sets preferredSize to something other than 0,0.
String paramString()	Returns a string describing the parameters of a separator.

Table 19-2 lists the associations maintained by a Separator.

Table 19-2 gjt.Separator **Associations**

Variables	Description
Etching etching	Defines the etching style used by the separator.
int thickness	Defines the thickness of the separator.

A Separator also has two static private variables that define the default etching style and etching thickness:

```
static private Etching _defaultEtching   = Etching.IN;
static private int     _defaultThickness = 2;
```

These define the default etching and thickness for all instances of Separator.

Before looking through the code in Example 19-1 on page 580, we'll point out several items of particular interest. First, you'll notice when you look through the source that Separator overrides getPreferredSize() in order to return thickness for both width and height:

```
public Dimension getPreferredSize() {
  return new Dimension(thickness, thickness);
}
```

Using the default Separator constructor results in a separator two pixels wide and two pixels tall—a separator that's barely visible. Setting them both to thickness essentially gives the layout manager something to work with. For example, if a separator were positioned and sized with BorderLayout and the separator were positioned in the north or south, BorderLayout would respect the preferred height of the separator but would ignore its preferred width. The height would be the default thickness, two pixels, and the width would be the width of the container in which the separator resides.

The Separator class counts on a layout manager to size the separator in one dimension. The unaffected dimension typically ends up being the default thickness, depending upon the layout manager[2].

AWT TIP ...

Avoid Hardcoding Orientation

Notice that the Graphic Java Toolkit does not have separate classes for horizontal and vertical separators. In some cases, changing the size of a container may change the orientation of a custom component from horizontal to vertical, or vice versa. Because of this, it is best if your custom components can cope with either orientation, as does gjt.Separator. Note that if a gjt.Separator starts out as a horizontal separator and is laid out such that its orientation changes to vertical, it is able to cope and repaints itself correctly.

The Separator. paint() method sets brighter to SystemColor.controlLtHighlight and darker to SystemColor.controlShadow. Notice that the separator is painted differently, depending upon its orientation.

```
public void paint(Graphics g) {
  Dimension size = getSize();
  Color brighter = SystemColor.controlLtHighlight;
  Color darker   = SystemColor.controlShadow;

  if(etching == Etching.IN) {
    if(size.width > size.height)
       paintHorizontal(g, size, darker, brighter);
    else
       paintVertical(g, size, darker, brighter);
  }
  else {
    if(size.width > size.height)
       paintHorizontal(g, size, brighter, darker);
    else
       paintVertical(g, size, brighter, darker);
  }
}
```

---

2. See "Layout Managers and Component Preferred Sizes" on page 380.

AWT TIP ...

Avoid Hardcoding Colors Used for Shading

Notice that Separator uses the SystemColor[1] class to derive the bright and dark shades that it uses to create an etched effect. We could have taken a different approach and specified Color.white and Color.darkGray (or some other explicit combination) for our etching color shades. However, using the SystemColor class ensures that our separator will be colored similarly to other native user interface components.

1. See "System Colors" on page 534.

The paint() method also calls either paintHorizontal() or paintVertical(). Each of these methods takes the Graphics object passed to the paint() method and repeatedly draws lines to represent the etched-in or etched-out lines of the separator:

```
private void paintHorizontal(Graphics g, Dimension size,
                             Color top, Color bottom) {
   g.setColor(top);
   int y = (size.height/2) - (thickness/2);

   while(y < (size.height/2)) {
      g.drawLine(0, y, size.width, y);
      ++y;
   }
   g.setColor(bottom);
   y = size.height/2;

   while(y < ((size.height/2) + (thickness/2))) {
      g.drawLine(0, y, size.width, y);
      ++y;
   }
}
private void paintVertical(Graphics g, Dimension size,
                           Color left, Color right) {
   g.setColor(left);
   int i = (size.width/2) - (thickness/2);

   while(i < (size.width/2)) {
      g.drawLine(i, 0, i, size.height);
      ++i;
   }
   g.setColor(right);
   i = size.width/2;
```

```
  while(i < ((size.width/2) + (thickness/2))) {
     g.drawLine(i, 0, i, size.height);
     ++i;
  }
}
```

Notice that to achieve the etched appearance, these methods draw two sets of lines, one with a control light highlight color, and the other with a control shadow color. Also notice that a `Separator` may have its thickness set to any desired value; however, values greater than 4 pixels tend to loose the etching effect.

With these relationships and responsibilities as a backdrop, let's take a look at the code for the `Separator` class in Example 19-1. You'll notice that, as is the custom in GJT components, there are a number of constructors, all of which call the final constructor. A `Separator` can be constructed with either thickness or etching specified, with both specified, or with neither specified, in which case the default values are used. Separators are most often constructed with the default constructor, which relies on the default values for etching and thickness, but it is a nice touch to provide clients with a wide range of choices when constructing custom components.

Example 19-1 `gjt.Separator` **Class Source Code**

```
package gjt;

import java.awt.*;

public class Separator extends Component {
   static private Etching _defaultEtching   = Etching.IN;
   static private int     _defaultThickness = 2;

   private Etching etching;
   private int     thickness;

   public Separator() {
      this(_defaultThickness, _defaultEtching);
   }
   public Separator(int thickness) {
      this(thickness, _defaultEtching);
   }
   public Separator(Etching etching) {
      this(_defaultThickness, etching);
   }
   public Separator(int thickness, Etching etching) {
      this.etching   = etching;
      this.thickness = thickness;
      setSize(thickness, thickness);
   }
   public Dimension getMinimumSize() {
```

```java
      return getPreferredSize();
}
public Dimension getPreferredSize() {
   return new Dimension(thickness, thickness);
}
public void paint(Graphics g) {
   Dimension size = getSize();
   Color brighter = SystemColor.controlLtHighlight;
   Color darker   = SystemColor.controlShadow;

   if(etching == Etching.IN) {
      if(size.width > size.height)
         paintHorizontal(g, size, darker, brighter);
      else
         paintVertical(g, size, darker, brighter);
   }
   else {
      if(size.width > size.height)
         paintHorizontal(g, size, brighter, darker);
      else
         paintVertical(g, size, brighter, darker);
   }
}
public String paramString() {
   Dimension   size = getSize();
   Orientation orient = size.width > size.height ?
                        Orientation.HORIZONTAL :
                        Orientation.VERTICAL;
   return super.paramString() + "thickness=" +
          thickness + "," + etching + "," + orient;
}
private void paintHorizontal(Graphics g, Dimension size,
                             Color top, Color bottom) {
   g.setColor(top);
   int y = (size.height/2) - (thickness/2);

   while(y < (size.height/2)) {
      g.drawLine(0, y, size.width, y);
      ++y;
   }
   g.setColor(bottom);
   y = size.height/2;

   while(y < ((size.height/2) + (thickness/2))) {
      g.drawLine(0, y, size.width, y);
      ++y;
   }
}
private void paintVertical(Graphics g, Dimension size,
                           Color left, Color right) {
    g.setColor(left);
```

```
        int i = (size.width/2) - (thickness/2);

        while(i < (size.width/2)) {
            g.drawLine(i, 0, i, size.height);
            ++i;
        }
        g.setColor(right);
        i = size.width/2;

        while(i < ((size.width/2) + (thickness/2))) {
            g.drawLine(i, 0, i, size.height);
            ++i;
        }
    }
}
```

Exercising the Separator

When putting gjt.Separator to the fire in our unit test, SeparatorTest draws two separators, as shown in Figure 19-2.

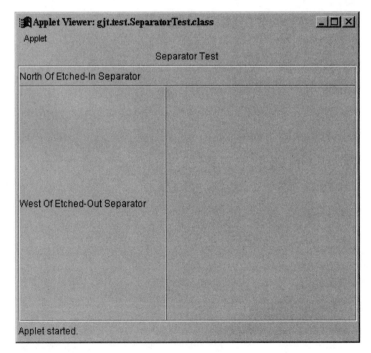

Figure 19-2 gjt.Separator Unit Test

As you can see from Figure 19-2, the unit test draws one horizontal and one vertical separator. The horizontal separator is etched in, the vertical separator is etched out, and each separator has an accompanying label. To see exactly how this set of components and containers is laid out in three dimensions, look at Figure 19-3.

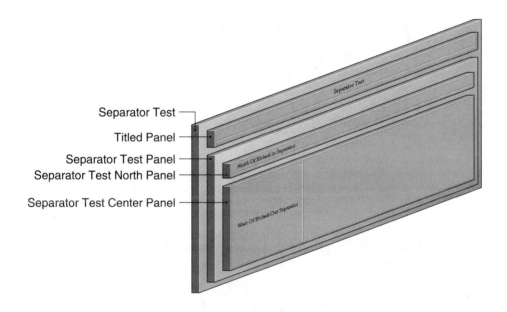

Separator Test
Titled Panel
Separator Test Panel
Separator Test North Panel
Separator Test Center Panel

Separator Test
North Of Etched-In Separator
West Of Etched-Out Separator

FIG. ST

Figure 19-3 `SeparatorTest` Layout Diagram

You'll want to refer to Figure 19-3 as you look through the `Separator` unit test in Example 19-2. Pay attention to the layering of components within containers. Also, note the use of different layout managers in different containers and the way they position components in the display. We'll spend some time describing exactly how `GridBagLayout` is being used after you've read through the code.

Example 19-2 `gjt.test.SeparatorTest` **Class Source Code**

```java
package gjt;

import java.awt.*;
import gjt.Etching;
import gjt.Separator;

public class SeparatorTest extends UnitTest {
  public String title      () { return "Separator Test"; }
  public Panel  centerPanel() {
     return new SeparatorTestPanel();
  }
}

class SeparatorTestPanel extends Panel {
  public SeparatorTestPanel() {
     setLayout(new BorderLayout());
     add(new SeparatorTestNorthPanel (), "North");
     add(new SeparatorTestCenterPanel(), "Center");
  }
}

class SeparatorTestNorthPanel extends Panel {
  Separator separator = new Separator();

  public SeparatorTestNorthPanel() {
     setLayout(new BorderLayout());
     add(new Label("North Of Etched-In Separator"), "North");
     add(separator, "South");
  }
}

class SeparatorTestCenterPanel extends Panel {
  Separator separator = new Separator(Etching.OUT);

  public SeparatorTestCenterPanel() {
     GridBagConstraints gbc = new GridBagConstraints();
     GridBagLayout      gbl = new GridBagLayout();
     Label label = new Label("West Of Etched-Out Separator");

     setLayout(gbl);
     gbc.anchor  = GridBagConstraints.WEST;
     gbc.insets  = new Insets(0,0,0,10);
     gbl.setConstraints(label, gbc);
     add(label);

     gbc.insets  = new Insets(0,0,0,0);
```

```
       gbc.weightx = 1.0;
       gbc.weighty = 1.0;
       gbc.fill    = GridBagConstraints.VERTICAL;
       gbl.setConstraints(separator, gbc);
       add(separator);
    }
  }
```

First, note that the horizontal separator and its associated label are laid out by a BorderLayout, with the label in the north and the separator in the south. The vertical separator and its associated label are laid out by a GridBagLayout, in the SeparatorTestCenterPanel:

```
  class SeparatorTestCenterPanel extends Panel {
❶    Separator separator = new Separator(Etching.OUT);

     public SeparatorTestCenterPanel() {
        GridBagConstraints gbc = new GridBagConstraints();
        GridBagLayout      gbl = new GridBagLayout();
        Label label = new Label("West Of Etched-Out Separator");

        setLayout(gbl);
❷       gbc.anchor  = GridBagConstraints.WEST;
❸       gbc.insets  = new Insets(0,0,0,10);
        gbl.setConstraints(label, gbc);
        add(label);

        gbc.insets  = new Insets(0,0,0,0);
        gbc.weightx = 1.0;
        gbc.weighty = 1.0;
❹       gbc.fill    = GridBagConstraints.VERTICAL;
        gbl.setConstraints(separator, gbc);
        add(separator);
    }
  }
```

The separator is constructed in line ❶, with its etching specified as Etching.OUT. After the Label is constructed, the GridBagConstraints anchor and insets are set (lines ❷ and ❸) for the label. Note that the insets are set so as to provide some space between the label and the vertical separator. Otherwise, the separator would butt up against the right edge of the label.

The same GridBagConstraints instance is used for both the label and the separator, so the anchor constraint is still WEST for the Separator. However, we override the previous insets and set the weightx, weighty, and fill constraints. The weighty constraint is set to 1 to ensure that the grid cell in which the Separator resides stretches in the vertical direction (refer to

"GridBagConstraints.weightx and GridBagConstraints.weighty" on page 416). The `weightx` value of 1 causes the cell in which the vertical separator resides to take up the remaining space to the right of the vertical separator. Specifying the `fill` constraint to `GridBagConstraints.VERTICAL` in line ❹ ensures that the separator itself fills its display area (and thus the entire container) in the vertical direction.

gjt.Bargauge

The Graphic Java Toolkit provides a `Bargauge` class that draws a 3-D border that can be filled with a color. Clients of `gjt.Bargauge` can specify both the fill color and the percentage of the bargauge that will be filled on the next call to `Bargauge.fill()`.

A bargauge's fill color is specified at construction time, but clients can specify both fill percentage and fill color after construction.

Bargauge Associations and Responsibilities

To see how `Bargauge` relates to the AWT and the GJT, look at Figure 19-4.

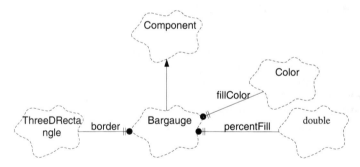

Figure 19-4 `gjt.Bargauge` Class Diagram

As you can see, `gjt.Bargauge` is another simple, lightweight custom component that extends `Canvas`. A bargauge maintains an association with a `ThreeDRectangle`, which it uses to paint a 3-D border around itself. `Bargauge` also maintains a fill color and a percentage of the bargauge that will be filled upon the next call to `Bargauge.fill()`.

Table 19-3 shows the responsibilities of a `gjt.Bargauge`.

Table 19-3 `gjt.Bargauge` **Responsibilities**

Methods	Description
`void fill()`	Fills the bargauge rectangle.
`Dimension getMinimumSize()`	Overrides `Component minimumSize()`. Returns the `preferredSize()`.
`void paint(Graphics g)`	Overrides `Component paint()`. Redraws the border and fills a rectangle.
`Dimension getPreferredSize()`	Overrides `Component preferredSize()`. Sets `preferredSize` to something other than 0,0.
`void setSize(int w, int h)`	Overrides `Component resize()`.
`void setBounds(int x, int y, int w, int h)`	Overrides `Component reshape()`. Resizes the border by calling `ThreeDRectangle resize()`
`void setFillColor( Color fillColor)`	Sets the color for filling the bargauge.
`void setFillPercent( double percentage)`	Sets the percentage of the bargauge to be filled. Default is 0, so it must be explicitly set.

Table 19-4 shows the associations of a `gjt.Bargauge`.

Table 19-4 `gjt.Bargauge` **Associations**

Variables	Description
`ThreeDRectangle border`	Draws a 3-D border around the bargauge.
`Color fillColor`	The color to be used for filling the bargauge.
`double fillPercent`	The percent of the bargauge to be filled.

We'll focus our discussion less on how `Bargauge` works and more on those things we've done peculiar to developing a custom component. For instance, when you look through the implementation of `gjt.Bargauge` in Example 19-3 on page 590, you'll notice that it overrides `setSize()` and `setBounds()`:

```
public void setSize(int w, int h) {
    setBounds(getLocation().x, getLocation().y, w, h);
}
public void setBounds(int x, int y, int w, int h) {
    super.setBounds(x,y,w,h);
    border.setSize(w,h);
}
```

Notice how `setSize()` calls `setBounds()`, using the
`Component.getLocation()` method to determine the upper left-hand corner
of the bargauge. `setBounds()` passes those coordinates, along with the width
and height, to `super.setBounds()`. Then, we resize the border, ensuring that it
sizes proportionately to the bargauge.

AWT TIP

Call super.setBounds() When Overriding setBounds()

It is often necessary when developing custom components to override set-
Bounds(). For instance, gjt.Bargauge overrides setBounds() so that it can
reshape its border. One thing that is easily forgotten and can lead to a frustrat-
ing debugging session is the fact that when overriding setBounds(), you must
remember to call super.setBounds() or the component will not reshape correctly.

Let's also take a closer look at how `gjt.Bargauge` overrides the
`getPreferredSize()` method:

```
public Dimension getPreferredSize() {
    int w = border.getThickness() * 3;
    return new Dimension(w, w*4);
}
```

`gjt.Bargauge` specifies its preferred width as three times the border thickness,
and its height as four times the width. The height calculation is somewhat
arbitrary. The width, however, is important because we want to ensure that when
a bargauge is filled, we can see the color. If the width were less than three times
the border thickness, there would not be enough room inside the border to
display the color. As it is, we provide room for the border on the left, the border
on the right, and the width of the border in the middle for the fill color.

You'll notice that `gjt.Bargauge` overrides the `paint()` method in order to raise and paint the border and to fill the bargauge by invoking the `fill()` method. The `fill()` method clears the interior of the bargauge and, depending on its orientation, fills it accordingly:

```
public void fill() {
  Graphics g = getGraphics();

  if((g != null) && (percentFill > 0)) {
    Rectangle b        = border.getInnerBounds();
    int        fillw   = b.width;
    int        fillh   = b.height;

    if(b.width > b.height) fillw *= percentFill/100;
    else                   fillh *= percentFill/100;

    g.setColor(fillColor);
    border.clearInterior();

    if(b.width > b.height)
       g.fillRect(b.x, b.y, fillw, b.height);
    else
       g.fillRect(b.x, b.y + b.height - fillh,
                  b.width, fillh);

    g.dispose();
  }
}
```

Notice that the `fill()` method is careful to dispose of the `Graphics` it obtains from `Component.getGraphics()`—see "`Disposing of a Graphics Object`" on page 29). Now let's take a look at the code for the `gjt.Bargauge` class in its entirety in Example 19-3.

Notice while you look through the code that the `gjt.Bargauge` constructor does not provide a default color. We assume that clients of `Bargauge` will want to specify a color that has some relevance rather than an arbitrary color, so we require them to specify a color at the time of construction.

Example 19-3 gjt.Bargauge **Class Source Code**

```java
package gjt;

import java.awt.*;

public class Bargauge extends Component {
  private double            percentFill = 0;
  private ThreeDRectangle border = new ThreeDRectangle(this);
  private Color            fillColor;

  public Bargauge(Color fillColor) {
    setFillColor(fillColor);
  }
  public void setFillColor(Color fillColor) {
    this.fillColor = fillColor;
  }
  public void setFillPercent(double percentage) {
    Assert.notFalse(percentage >= 0 && percentage <= 100);
    percentFill = percentage;
  }
  public void setSize(int w, int h) {
    setBounds(getLocation().x, getLocation().y, w, h);
  }
  public void setBounds(int x, int y, int w, int h) {
    super.setBounds(x,y,w,h);
    border.setSize(w,h);
  }
  public Dimension getMinimumSize() { return
    getPreferredSize();
  }
  public Dimension getPreferredSize() {
    int w = border.getThickness() * 3;
    return new Dimension(w, w*4);
  }
  public void paint(Graphics g) {
    border.raise();
    border.paint();
    fill();
  }
  public void fill() {
    Graphics g = getGraphics();

    if((g != null) && (percentFill > 0)) {
      Rectangle b     = border.getInnerBounds();
      int       fillw = b.width;
      int       fillh = b.height;
```

```
         if(b.width > b.height) fillw *= percentFill/100;
         else                    fillh *= percentFill/100;

         g.setColor(fillColor);
         border.clearInterior();

         if(b.width > b.height)
            g.fillRect(b.x, b.y, fillw, b.height-1);
         else
            g.fillRect(b.x, b.y + b.height - fillh,
                       b.width-1, fillh);
         g.dispose();
      }
   }
   protected String paramString() {
      Dimension size = getSize();
      Orientation orient = size.width > size.height ?
                           Orientation.HORIZONTAL :
                           Orientation.VERTICAL;
      String    str  = "fill percent=" + percentFill + "," +
                       "orientation=" + orient     + "," +
                       "color"        + fillColor;
      return str;
   }
}
```

You've probably noticed that we've used paramString() in several
components already described, but it's worth noting here because it leads us to
one of our AWT Tips.

AWT TIP

Implement paramString() for Custom Components

If you've done any significant AWT development without a debugger, you've
come to appreciate the fact that you can invoke toString() on any of the standard AWT components and obtain some meaningful information about the
component. Custom components should also provide the same service by
implementing paramString(). Note that the Component class implements a
toString() method, which invokes Component.paramString(). Overriding
paramString() to supply a string representing the parameters of your custom
component is a nice touch that clients of your custom components will be
grateful for.

Exercising the Bargauge

We've provided a couple of test applets to show gjt.Bargauge in action. The first one, called SimpleBargaugeTest in Example 19-4, illustrates how the applet can be resized to the point that it changes the bargauge's orientation from vertical to horizontal, and the bargauge continues to function normally. Figure 19-5 shows a picture of the simple bargauge test.

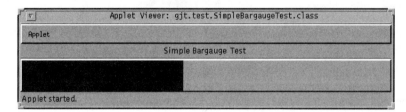

Figure 19-5 gjt.Bargauge Class Simple Test
The bargauge continues to operate properly, even when it is resized and changes orientation from horizontal to vertical.

This simple test creates a single, animated Bargauge. (Run this test with the appletviewer, so that the window can be resized such that the bargauge changes its orientation.)

Example 19-4 `gjt.test.SimpleBargaugeTest` **Class Source Code**

```java
package gjt.test;

import java.awt.*;
import java.awt.event.*;
import gjt.Bargauge;

public class SimpleBargaugeTest extends UnitTest {
  public String title() {
    return "Simple Bargauge Test";
  }
  public Panel centerPanel() {
    return new SimpleBargaugeTestPanel();
  }
}
class SimpleBargaugeTestPanel extends Panel implements Runnable {
  private Bargauge gauge = new Bargauge(Color.blue);
  private boolean  running = true;
  private Thread   t;

  public SimpleBargaugeTestPanel() {
    setLayout(new BorderLayout());
    add(gauge, "Center");

    t = new Thread(this);
    t.start();

    addMouseListener(new MouseAdapter() {
      public void mousePressed(MouseEvent event) {
        if(running) { t.suspend(); running = false; }
        else        { t.resume (); running = true;  }
      }
    });
  }
  public boolean isRunning() {
    return running;
  }
```

```
public Thread getThread() {
   return t;
}
public void run() {
   while(true) {
       try { Thread.currentThread().sleep(500,0); }
       catch(InterruptedException e) { }

       gauge.setFillPercent(Math.random() * 100);
       gauge.fill();
   }
 }
}
```

The full-blown unit test for gjt.Bargauge creates a set of vertical or horizontal gauges filled with random colors, as in Figure 19-6.

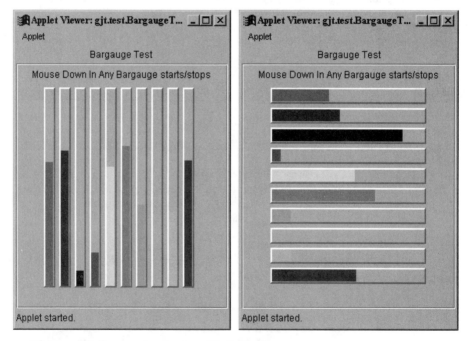

Figure 19-6 gjt.Bargauge Unit Test
The orientation of the bargauges is passed as a parameter to the applet.

As you can see, the `gjt.Bargauge` unit test creates an array of vertical (or horizontal) animated bargauges. The orientation of the bargauges is based on the orientation parameter passed to the applet. Figure 19-7 shows a layout diagram of the bargauge unit test.

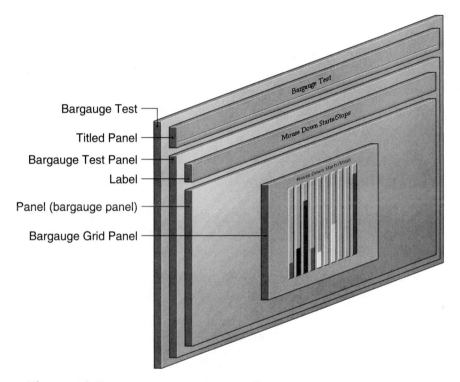

Figure 19-7 `BargaugeTest` Layout Diagram

Example 19-5 shows how this unit test uses the `Bargauge` class. You'll want to reference Figure 19-7 as you look through the `BargaugeTest` unit test.

One specific topic of interest in this unit test is the use of layout managers, particularly in the `BargaugeTestPanel` class:

```
class BargaugeTestPanel extends Panel {
   public BargaugeTestPanel(Bargauge[] gauges, String orient,
                         MouseListener listener) {
      Panel bargaugePanel = new Panel();

      setLayout(new BorderLayout());

      add("North",new Label(
            "Mouse Down In Any Bargauge starts/stops",
```

```
                    Label.CENTER));

         add(bargaugePanel, "Center");

         bargaugePanel.add(new BargaugeGridPanel(
                        gauges,orient,listener));
      }
   }
```

A panel (bargaugePanel) is centered in BargaugeTestPanel (see Figure 19-7), which has a BorderLayout layout manager, and a label is specified as the north component. Then, a BargaugeGridPanel is added to bargaugePanel, which by default uses a FlowLayout layout manager. This ensures that the BargaugeGridPanel is always centered in the bargaugePanel. (You can see this in the unit test output in Figure 19-6 on page 594. Whenever the applet is resized, BargaugeGridPanel remains centered in the horizontal direction.)

Example 19-5 lists the unit test in its entirety.

Example 19-5 gjt.test.BargaugeTest **Class Source Code**

```
package gjt.test;

import java.awt.*;
import java.awt.event.*;
import java.applet.*;
import gjt.*;

public class BargaugeTest extends UnitTest {
   private Bargauge[] gauges = new Bargauge[10];
   private Thread     animatorThread;
   private boolean    running;

   public String title() {
      return "Bargauge Test";
   }
   public Panel  centerPanel() {
      return new BargaugeTestPanel(gauges,
         getParameter("orientation"),
         new MouseAdapter() {
            public void mousePressed(MouseEvent event) {
               if(running == true) {
                  animatorThread.suspend();
                  running = false;
               }
               else {
                  animatorThread.resume ();
                  running = true;
```

```
                  }
               }
         });
   }
   public void start() {
      super.start();
      animatorThread = new BargaugeAnimator(gauges);
      animatorThread.start();
      running = true;
   }
   public void stop() {
      super.stop();
      animatorThread.suspend();
      running = false;
   }
}
class BargaugeTestPanel extends Panel {
   public BargaugeTestPanel(Bargauge[] gauges, String orient,
                            MouseListener listener) {
      Panel bargaugePanel = new Panel();

      setLayout(new BorderLayout());

      add("North",new Label(
            "Mouse Down In Any Bargauge starts/stops",
            Label.CENTER));

      add(bargaugePanel, "Center");
      bargaugePanel.add(new BargaugeGridPanel(
                        gauges,orient,listener));
   }
}
class BargaugeGridPanel extends Panel {
   private Dimension  preferredSize = new Dimension(200, 250);

   public BargaugeGridPanel(Bargauge[] gauges, String orient,
                            MouseListener listener) {
      Bargauge nextGauge;
      Color    color = Color.gray;

      if("horizontal".equals(orient))
         setLayout(new GridLayout(gauges.length,0,5,5));
      else
         setLayout(new GridLayout(0,gauges.length,5,5));

      for(int i=0; i < gauges.length; ++i) {
         switch(i) {
            case 1:  color = Color.darkGray;    break;
```

```
         case 2:   color = Color.blue;        break;
         case 3:   color = Color.magenta;     break;
         case 4:   color = Color.yellow;      break;
         case 5:   color = Color.green;       break;
         case 6:   color = Color.cyan;        break;
         case 7:   color = Color.orange;      break;
         case 8:   color = Color.pink;        break;
         case 9:   color = Color.red;         break;
         case 10:  color = Color.yellow;      break;
      }
      nextGauge = new Bargauge(color);
      gauges[i] = nextGauge;
      gauges[i].addMouseListener(listener);
      add(nextGauge);
    }
  }
  public Dimension getPreferredSize() { return preferredSize; }
  public Dimension getMinimumSize  () { return preferredSize; }
}
class BargaugeAnimator extends Thread {
  private Bargauge[] gauges;
  private boolean    firstAnimation = true;

  public BargaugeAnimator(Bargauge[] gauges) {
    this.gauges = gauges;
  }
  public void run() {
    int count = gauges.length;

    while(true) {
        try { Thread.currentThread().sleep(500,0); }
        catch(InterruptedException e) { }

        for(int i=0; i < count; ++i) {
           gauges[i].setFillPercent(Math.random() * 100);
           gauges[i].fill();

           if(firstAnimation)
              System.out.println(gauges[i].toString());
        }
        firstAnimation = false;
    }
  }
}
```

Summary

In this chapter, we've explored the `gjt.Separator` and `gjt.Bargauge` custom components from the Graphic Java Toolkit and described their implementations and unit tests. Presenting these custom components has prompted a few guidelines you can use in creating your own custom components. For example, when overriding `setBounds()`, it's imperative that you call `super.setBounds()` or else the component will not reshaped correctly. (The peer will never be given a chance to reshape.) Also, it's a useful practice when implementing custom components to override `paramString()`. By so doing, you supply clients of your component with a string representing parameters in the custom component.

CHAPTER
20

Boxes and Borders

This chapter discusses four GJT custom containers: `Box`, `Border`, `EtchedBorder` and `ThreeDBorder`, all of which extend `java.awt.Panel`. Each custom container discussed in this chapter contains exactly one component and visually enhances the component by drawing a border of sorts around the outside of the component—because of this, we have lumped them all together in one chapter.

gjt.Box

User interface toolkits frequently provide something akin to the `gjt.Box` class to group a logical collection of components that perform a related function. (Various windowing systems refer to classes that serve this function by other names. For instance, Motif calls this a Frame.) Figure 20-1 shows three instances of `gjt.Box` in action. As you can see, a box consists of a border, drawn either etched in or etched out, and a title, which can be either left, center, or right-justified.

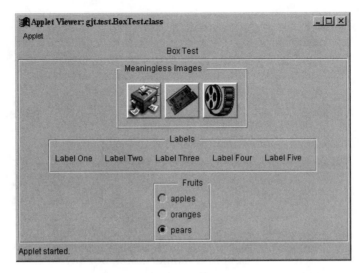

Figure 20-1 `gjt.Box` in Action
Boxes draw a border (etched in or etched out) around
components, along with a title at the top of the border (left, right,
or center-justified).

`gjt.Box` is a simple container that overrides `paint()` to draw its border.
Figure 20-2 shows the class diagram for gjt.Box.

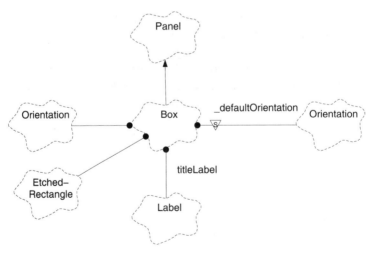

Figure 20-2 `gjt.Box` Class Diagram

A box employs an etched rectangle to draw the border of the box. A box also keeps track of the label it displays and the orientation of the components it contains.

Table 20-1 lists the responsibilities (public methods) for the `Box` class.

Table 20-1 `gjt.Box` **Responsibilities**

Methods	Description
void etchedIn()	Sets the etching value to `Etching.IN`[1].
void etchedOut()	Sets the etching value to `Etching.OUT`.
void paint(Graphics g)	Paints the etched border.
void setSize(int w, int h)	Resizes the box according to the new dimensions.
void setBounds(int x, int y, int w, int h)	Positions the box and reshapes it according to the new size and location.

1. `Etching` is a GJT class.

Table 20-2 lists the associations (class members) for the `Box` class. Note that the `Box` class does not keep track of the component it contains—that is left to the `Panel` class that `Box` extends. A box is concerned only with painting the border, as the painting of the components contained in a container is handled automatically.

Table 20-2 `gjt.Box` **Associations**

Variables	Description
EtchedRectangle box	The etched rectangle drawn around the component.
Label title	The title displayed at the top of the box.
Orientation orient	The orientation of the title string.

The painting of the border is handled by the instance of `EtchedRectangle`[1], which greatly simplifies the implementation of `Box.paint()`:

```
public void paint(Graphics g) {
   box.paint();
   super.paint(g); // ensure that lightweight components
                   // are painted
}
```

1. See "Drawing an Etched Rectangle" on page 35.

The `Box.paint()` method is careful to invoke `super.paint()` in order to ensure that any contained lightweight components are properly rendered[2].

The `Box` class also must ensure that the top of the box (`EtchedRectangle`) is drawn through the middle of the title. This is accomplished by overriding the `setBounds()` method, which is invoked any time the container is resized.

```
public void setBounds(int x, int y, int w, int h) {
  super.setBounds(x,y,w,h);

  FontMetrics fm    = titleLabel.getFontMetrics(
                            titleLabel.getFont());
  int          top  = getInsets().top + fm.getAscent();
  Dimension    size = getSize();

  box.setBounds(0, top, size.width-1, size.height-top-1);
}
```

After invoking `super.setBounds()`, the top of the etched rectangle is calculated by adding the font ascent for the title label to the top inset of the container. See "Manipulating Fonts" on page 50 for more information about fonts and font metrics.

Most of the rest of the implementation of the `Box` class resides in a constructor, and involves the use of `GridBagLayout` to position the title of the box and the component around which the border is drawn.

The `Box` class implements four constructors in order to allow flexibility for specifying the component, title, and orientation of the title. The first three constructors all invoke the fourth constructor.

```
public Box(Component surrounded, String title) {
  this(surrounded,
       new Label(title, Label.CENTER),
       _defaultOrientation);
}
public Box(Component   surrounded,
           String      title,
           Orientation orient) {
  this(surrounded, new Label(title, Label.CENTER), orient);
}
public Box(Component surrounded, Label label) {
  this(surrounded, label, _defaultOrientation);
}
```

2. See "Remember to Invoke super.paint() When Overriding Container.paint()" on page 480.

Notice that the Box class allows the title to be specified either as a string or as a label. Additionally, the orientation may be specified at construction time, or left unspecified, in which case it defaults to being center-justified.

The fourth constructor has the code pertinent to GridBagLayout.

```
    public Box(Component    surrounded,
                 Label        label,
                 Orientation orient) {
      Assert.notNull(surrounded);
      Assert.notNull(label);

      titleLabel  = label;
      this.orient = orient;

❶    GridBagLayout       gbl = new GridBagLayout();
❷    GridBagConstraints gbc = new GridBagConstraints();

❸    setLayout(gbl);
      gbc.gridwidth = GridBagConstraints.REMAINDER;

      if(orient == Orientation.CENTER)
         gbc.anchor = GridBagConstraints.NORTH;
      else if(orient == Orientation.RIGHT) {
         gbc.anchor = GridBagConstraints.NORTHEAST;
         gbc.insets = new Insets(0,0,0,5);
      }
      else if(orient == Orientation.LEFT) {
         gbc.anchor = GridBagConstraints.NORTHWEST;
         gbc.insets = new Insets(0,5,0,0);
      }

      gbl.setConstraints(titleLabel, gbc);
      add(titleLabel);

      gbc.insets  = new Insets(0,5,5,5);
      gbc.anchor  = GridBagConstraints.NORTHWEST;
      gbc.weighty = 1.0;
      gbc.weightx = 1.0;
      gbc.fill    = GridBagConstraints.BOTH;
      gbl.setConstraints(surrounded,gbc);
      add(surrounded);
    }
```

In lines ❶ and ❷, instances of GridBagLayout and GridBagConstraints, are created, respectively. The setLayout() call in line ❸ then sets the GridBagLayout as the layout manager for the Box. The remaining lines set

GridBagConstraints instance variables for the layout manager to use. We'll talk about each of the remaining lines in this constructor in smaller units to more completely illustrate how they work.

First, let's look at the line that sets the gridwidth to be used in laying out the Label component:

```
gbc.gridwidth = GridBagConstraints.REMAINDER;
```

gridwidth is often specified as REMAINDER. This specification means that the component owns the remainder of the space available in the row, which means that the component will be the last in its row [3]. The next component added to the container will be positioned in the next row. Setting gridwidth to REMAINDER ensures that the next component added is positioned in the row below the titleLabel.

The next setting specifies the anchor location of the titleLabel, and is dependent upon the desired orientation for the title—either NORTH, NORTHEAST, or NORTHWEST[4].

This ensures that when a box is resized, the titleLabel component stays positioned at the top of the box. Notice that an insets constraint is also specified if the title is left- or right-justified to ensure that the corners of the box are not obliterated by the titleLabel.

Next, we set the constraints and add titleLabel to the container. The call to setConstraints() is where GridBagLayout is passed the GridBagConstraints values we've set.

```
gbl.setConstraints(titleLabel, c);
add(titleLabel);
```

So far, here's what we've set with GridBagConstraints:

- gridwidth to REMAINDER, ensuring the next component will be positioned below the title label

- anchor position to NORTH, NORTHEAST, or NORTHWEST, depending upon orientation specified for the title

---

3. Similarly, a value of REMAINDER for gridheight indicates that the component is the last component in its *column*. See "GridBagConstraints.gridwidth and Grid-BagConstraints.gridheight" on page 415.

4. See "GridBagConstraints.anchor" on page 409.

The call to `setConstraints()` makes those constraints available to the layout manager. This results in the `titleLabel` being positioned at the top of the container:

The Label component may be positioned in the NORTH of the box and is the last component in its row (taking up the REMAINDER of the row.)

The next set of `GridBagConstraints` values establishes constraints for the component around which the border will be drawn. First, the `GridBagConstraint.insets` member is set to the newly created `Insets`. The integer arguments to the `Insets()` method specify the top, left, bottom, and right insets, in that order.

```
gbc.insets  = new Insets(0,5,5,5);
```

Next, the `anchor` position is set to NORTHWEST. Note that up to this point, `gridwidth` is still set to REMAINDER and `anchor` is still set to the previous value for the `titleLabel`:

```
gbc.anchor = GridBagConstraints.NORTHWEST;
```

The `weight.x` and `weight.y` values are set to 1.0, meaning that the component's display area will consume 100 percent of the available space when the container is enlarged:

```
gbc.weighty = 1.0;
gbc.weightx = 1.0;
```

The constructor then sets the `fill` variable to BOTH:

```
gbc.fill = GridBagConstraints.BOTH;
```

This setting indicates that the component will fill the box in both directions. If the box is enlarged, the component will fill the entire box horizontally and vertically, minus the area specified by the insets. No matter what the size of the box, the component inside the box always has a margin between it and the inside border of the container. The component is always 10 pixels less in width than the box and 5 pixels less in height than the box. Any component placed in a box will always have these inset margins, which look like so:

Insets(0,5,5,5)

5 pixel inset on the left.

0 pixel inset for the top.

5 pixel inset on the bottom.

5 pixel inset on the right.

The constraint values are set for the component by virtue of the call to `setConstraints()`:

```
gbl.setConstraints(surrounded,c);
add(surrounded);
```

Notice that the same instance of `GridBagConstraints` used previously is being used for the component. For every call to `setConstraints()`, `GridBagLayout` makes copies of the `GridBagConstraints` variable values; therefore, we can reuse the same `GridBagConstraints` to specify constraints for multiple components. We can continue modifying variables in the same `GridBagConstraints` object without affecting the `titleLabel` positioning we've already established.

The code for the gjt.Box class is shown in its entirety in Example 20-1.

Example 20-1 `gjt.Box` **Class Source Code**

```
package gjt;
import java.awt.*;

public class Box extends Panel {
  static private Orientation _defaultOrientation =
  Orientation.CENTER;
  private EtchedRectangle box = new EtchedRectangle(this);
  private Label          titleLabel;
  private Orientation    orient;

  public Box(Component surrounded, String title) {
    this(surrounded,
```

```
                new Label(title, Label.CENTER),
                _defaultOrientation);
}
public Box(Component    surrounded,
                String        title,
                Orientation orient) {
    this(surrounded, new Label(title, Label.CENTER), orient);
}
public Box(Component surrounded, Label label) {
    this(surrounded, label, _defaultOrientation);
}
public Box(Component    surrounded,
                Label        label,
                Orientation orient) {
    Assert.notNull(surrounded);
    Assert.notNull(label);

    titleLabel  = label;
    this.orient = orient;

    GridBagLayout      gbl = new GridBagLayout();
    GridBagConstraints gbc = new GridBagConstraints();

    setLayout(gbl);
    gbc.gridwidth = GridBagConstraints.REMAINDER;

    if(orient == Orientation.CENTER)
        gbc.anchor = GridBagConstraints.NORTH;
    else if(orient == Orientation.RIGHT) {
        gbc.anchor = GridBagConstraints.NORTHEAST;
        gbc.insets = new Insets(0,0,0,5);
    }
    else if(orient == Orientation.LEFT) {
        gbc.anchor = GridBagConstraints.NORTHWEST;
        gbc.insets = new Insets(0,5,0,0);
    }

    gbl.setConstraints(titleLabel, gbc);
    add(titleLabel);

    gbc.insets  = new Insets(0,5,5,5);
    gbc.anchor  = GridBagConstraints.NORTHWEST;
    gbc.weighty = 1.0;
    gbc.weightx = 1.0;
    gbc.fill    = GridBagConstraints.BOTH;
    gbl.setConstraints(surrounded,gbc);
    add(surrounded);
}
```

```
public void etchedIn ()              { box.etchedIn (); }
public void etchedOut()              { box.etchedOut(); }

public void paint(Graphics g) {
box.paint();
   super.paint(g);   // ensure that lightweight components
                  // are painted
}
public void setSize(int w, int h) {
   setBounds(getLocation().x, getLocation().y, w, h);
}
public void setBounds(int x, int y, int w, int h) {
   super.setBounds(x,y,w,h);

   FontMetrics fm    = titleLabel.getFontMetrics(
                           titleLabel.getFont());
   int         top   = getInsets().top + fm.getAscent();
   Dimension   size = getSize();

   box.setBounds(0, top, size.width-1, size.height-top-1);
}
protected String paramString() {
   return super.paramString() + ",etching=" +
          (box.isEtchedIn() ? Etching.IN : Etching.OUT) +
          ",title=" + titleLabel;
}
}
```

gjt.Box Unit Test

We've already seen the unit test that exercises the gjt.Box class on page 602. It just so happens that the gjt.test.BoxTest applet also uses GridBagLayout in order to position three boxes (named iconbox, labelbox, and checkboxbox) in the container. Figure 20-3 shows how the three boxes are positioned and sized when the applet is resized.

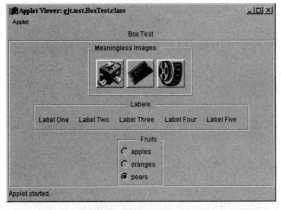

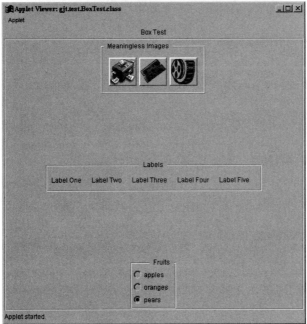

Figure 20-3 gjt.BoxTest Applet Resized
Boxes maintain their respective positioning when the applet is
resized.

When the applet is resized, the three boxes remain centered horizontally and hold their respective anchor positions vertically. No matter how the applet is resized, the three boxes are always centered horizontally. In the vertical direction, the iconbox stays in the north, the checkboxbox stays in the south, and the labelbox stays centered. Using GridBagLayout, we achieve this layout effect in only a few lines of code (which emphasizes the power of this most-maligned of the AWT layout managers). Here's the set of GridBagConstraints parameters that defines this behavior:

```
GridBagLayout        gbl = new GridBagLayout();
GridBagConstraints gbc = new GridBagConstraints();
...
setLayout(gbl);
gbc.anchor     = GridBagConstraints.NORTH;
❶  gbc.gridwidth = GridBagConstraints.REMAINDER;
❷  gbc.weighty    = 0.50;
gbl.setConstraints(iconbox,   gbc);
add(iconbox);
gbl.setConstraints(labelbox,  gbc);
add(labelbox);

❸  gbc.anchor     = GridBagConstraints.SOUTH;
❹  gbc.weighty    = 0;
gbl.setConstraints(checkboxbox, gbc);
add(checkboxbox);
```

Notice that just like the Box component, gjt.test.BoxTest creates an instance of GridBagLayout and an instance of GridBagConstraints. It also sets a series of constraints and calls setConstraints() for each component so that GridBagLayout has access to those constraint values.

Both iconbox and labelbox use exactly the same constraints. Setting their gridwidth to REMAINDER in line ❶ ensures that the labelbox is positioned below the iconbox and that the checboxbox is positioned below the labelbox.

Again, note that GridBagLayout copies constraints, so the same constraints object can be used for more than one component.

The weighty 0.50 setting in line ❷ controls vertical space taken up by the display area when the container is resized—it causes the *display area* of the component to take up half of the extra space in the vertical direction[5]. Note that the boxes themselves do not take up half of the extra space, but the display areas in which they reside are allotted the extra space.

5.   See "GridBagConstraints.weightx and GridBagConstraints.weighty" on page 416.

Don't Confuse Resizing the Grid Cell With Resizing the Component

There's a common misconception that when GridBagLayout repositions components after the container has been resized, the component is resized to fill available space, as set in the weightx and weighty constraints. The components
themselves do not resize to consume that extra space; the grid cells in which
the components reside do. (You can see this behavior by running the BoxTest
applet and resizing it.) To cause the component itself to consume the extra
space, set GridBagConstraints.fill to BOTH.

Lines ❸ and ❹ set the constraints for the checkboxbox. It is anchored in the
south and its weighty is 0.0, so it will always reside at the bottom of the
container and there will never be any extra space beneath it.

Now that we've covered the specific layout portion of the gjt.test.BoxTest,
let's look at the entire class in Example 20-2. Notice that this class uses two other
classes from the Graphic Java Toolkit: gjt.ExclusiveImageButtonPanel and
gjt.Orientation. You'll also notice that gjt.test.BoxTest extends our
standard UnitTest class, which provides a steady framework for printing a title
at the top and displaying a component in the Panel below the title.

Example 20-2 gjt.test.BoxTest **Class Source Code**

```
package gjt.test;

import java.applet.Applet;
import java.awt.*;
import gjt.*;

public class BoxTest extends UnitTest {
  public String title() {
    return "Box Test";
  }
  public Panel centerPanel() {
    return new BoxTestPanel(this);
  }
}
class BoxTestPanel extends Panel {
  private Applet applet;
  private Box    iconbox, labelbox, checkboxbox;
  private Panel  panelInLabelbox    = new Panel();
  private Panel  panelInCheckboxbox = new Panel();
  private ExclusiveImageButtonPanel panelInIconbox;
```

```java
public BoxTestPanel(Applet applet) {
    GridBagLayout      gbl = new GridBagLayout();
    GridBagConstraints gbc = new GridBagConstraints();

    this.applet    = applet;
    panelInIconbox = new ExclusiveImageButtonPanel(
                               Orientation.HORIZONTAL);

    populateIconPanel    ();
    populateLabelPanel    ();
    populateCheckboxPanel();

    iconbox      = new Box(panelInIconbox,
                           "Meaningless Images",
                           Orientation.LEFT);
    labelbox     = new Box(panelInLabelbox,
                           "Labels",
                           Orientation.CENTER);
    checkboxbox = new Box(panelInCheckboxbox,
                           "Fruits",
                           Orientation.RIGHT);
    iconbox.etchedOut();

    setLayout(gbl);
    gbc.anchor    = GridBagConstraints.NORTH;
    gbc.gridwidth = GridBagConstraints.REMAINDER;
    gbc.weighty   = 0.50;
    gbl.setConstraints(iconbox,  gbc);
    add(iconbox);
    gbl.setConstraints(labelbox, gbc);
    add(labelbox);

    gbc.anchor    = GridBagConstraints.SOUTH;
    gbc.weighty   = 0;
    gbl.setConstraints(checkboxbox, gbc);
    add(checkboxbox);
}
private void populateIconPanel() {
    Image ballot, film, ticket;

    ballot  = applet.getImage(applet.getCodeBase(),
                              "gifs/ballot_box.gif");
    ticket  = applet.getImage(applet.getCodeBase(),
                              "gifs/movie_ticket.gif");
    film    = applet.getImage(applet.getCodeBase(),
                              "gifs/filmstrip.gif");

    panelInIconbox.add(ballot);
```

```
      panelInIconbox.add(ticket);
      panelInIconbox.add(film);
  }
  private void populateLabelPanel() {
      panelInLabelbox.add(new Label("Label One"));
      panelInLabelbox.add(new Label("Label Two"));
      panelInLabelbox.add(new Label("Label Three"));
      panelInLabelbox.add(new Label("Label Four"));
      panelInLabelbox.add(new Label("Label Five"));
  }
  private void populateCheckboxPanel() {
      CheckboxGroup group = new CheckboxGroup();

      panelInCheckboxbox.setLayout(new GridLayout(3,0));
      panelInCheckboxbox.add(new Checkbox("apples",
                            group, false));
      panelInCheckboxbox.add(new Checkbox("oranges",
                            group, false));
      panelInCheckboxbox.add(new Checkbox("pears",
                            group, true));
  }
}
```

Borders

For a variety of reasons, it is sometimes useful to draw a border around a component. Perhaps you'd like to use a flat border around a custom component to signify focus[6], or maybe you'd like to jazz up your components by drawing a 3-D or etched border around them.

The Graphic Java Toolkit provides three classes for wrapping a border around a component: `Border`, `EtchedBorder`, and `ThreeDBorder`. The job of the border classes is to contain a component and to draw a border around it with a specified gap between the inside of the border and the outside of the component.

Discussing the border classes will afford us an opportunity to focus on overriding `Panel` and redefining insets.

gjt.Border

The `gjt.Border` class extends `Panel` and tracks the thickness of the border, along with the gap between the border and the component it contains. Additionally, `Border` employs a `DrawnRectangle` to draw a flat border around the component, as illustrated in Figure 20-4.

---

6.   See "Custom Components and Keyboard Traversal" on page 540.

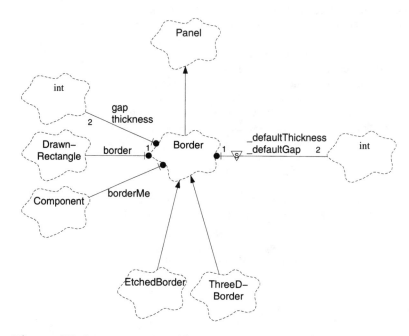

Figure 20-4 gjt.Border Class Diagram

The responsibilities and associations of gjt.Border are listed in Table 20-3 and Table 20-4, respectively.

Table 20-3 gjt.Border **Responsibilities**

Methods	Description
void paint(Graphics g)	Overrides Component paint(). Paints the border.
Dimension getMinimumSize()	Overrides Component getMinimumSize(). Returns getPreferredSize().
void setSize(int w, int h)	Overrides Component setSize(). This is a precautionary measure.
void setBounds(int x, int y, int w, int h)	Overrides Component setBounds(). Reshapes the border.
Insets getInsets()	Overrides Component getInsets(). Returns insets equal to the border thickness plus the gap.

Table 20-3 `gjt.Border` **Responsibilities (Continued)**

Methods	Description
`Rectangle getInnerBounds()`	Returns the inner bounds of the border—the area inside the border.
`Component getComponent()`	Returns the component that the border is drawn around.
`void setLineColor(Color c)`	Sets the line color for the border.
`Color getLineColor()`	Returns the current line color for the border.
`String paramString()`	Returns parameters pertaining to the border.

Table 20-4 `gjt.Border` **Associations**

Variables	Description
`int gap`	Sets the gap between inside of border and outside of component.
`int thickness`	Sets the thickness of the border.
`DrawnRectangle border`	Paints the border.
`Component borderMe`	The component the border is drawn around.

As we've established, a `Border` is a `Panel` containing a single `Component`, around which a border is drawn. Now that we've got a good idea about what a `Border` is, let's look at the actual class code in Example 20-3.

AWT TIP ...

Canvas or Panel?

A Canvas, as its name implies, is a surface on which you can paint. What may be surprising is that you can also paint on a Panel.

The difference between a Canvas and a Panel is that a Panel is a Container, whereas a Canvas is a mere Component. Think of a Panel as a Canvas that can contain components.

Example 20-3 gjt.Border **Class Source Code**

```java
package gjt;

import java.awt.*;

public class Border extends Panel {
   protected int              thickness;
   protected int              gap;
   protected DrawnRectangle border;
   protected Component        borderMe;

   protected static int _defaultThickness = 2;
   protected static int _defaultGap        = 0;

   public Border(Component borderMe) {
      this(borderMe, _defaultThickness, _defaultGap);
   }
   public Border(Component borderMe, int thickness) {
      this(borderMe, thickness, _defaultGap);
   }
   public Border(Component borderMe, int thickness, int gap) {
      this.borderMe  = borderMe;
      this.thickness = thickness;
      this.gap       = gap;

      setLayout(new BorderLayout());
      add(borderMe, "Center");
   }
   public Component getComponent() {
      return borderMe;
   }
   public Insets getInsets() {
      return new Insets(thickness+gap, thickness+gap,
                        thickness+gap, thickness+gap);
   }
   public Rectangle getInnerBounds() {
      return border().getInnerBounds();
   }
   public void setLineColor(Color c) {
      border().setLineColor(c);
   }
   public Color getLineColor() {
      return border().getLineColor();
   }
   public void paint(Graphics g) {
      border().paint();
      super.paint(g);  // ensures lightweight comps get drawn
```

```
    }
    public void setSize(int w, int h) {
        Point location = getLocation();
        setBounds(location.x, location.y, w, h);
    }
    public void setBounds(int x, int y, int w, int h) {
        super.setBounds(x, y, w, h);
        border().setSize(w, h);
    }
    protected String paramString() {
        return super.paramString() + ",border=" +
                border().toString() + ",thickness=" + thickness
                + ",gap=" + gap;
    }
    protected DrawnRectangle border() {
        if(border == null)
            border = new DrawnRectangle(this, thickness);
        return border;
    }
}
```

The component to be bordered, the thickness of the border, and the gap between the component and the border can all be specified at construction time. Only the component *must* be specified at construction time. If the thickness and gap are not specified, they default to values of 2 and 0 pixels, respectively.

Border provides three constructors—one that takes a Component, one that takes a Component and a thickness, and one that takes a Component, thickness and gap. The first two constructors both invoke the third constructor. Appropriate defaults are assigned to thickness and gap if they are not specified.

```
public Border(Component borderMe) {
    this(borderMe, _defaultThickness, _defaultGap);
}
public Border(Component borderMe, int thickness) {
    this(borderMe, thickness, _defaultGap);
}
public Border(Component borderMe, int thickness, int gap) {
    this.borderMe  = borderMe;
    this.thickness = thickness;
    this.gap       = gap;

    setLayout(new BorderLayout());
    add(borderMe, "Center");
}
```

`Border` uses an instance of `BorderLayout` to center the component within itself. Since the centered component is the only component laid out by the `BorderLayout`, the component expands to fill all available space within the border, minus the insets of the border[7]. The `getInsets()` method, which defines the border's insets, returns insets whose thickness is equal to the thickness of the border plus the gap.

```
public Insets getInsets() {
  return new Insets(thickness+gap, thickness+gap,
                    thickness+gap, thickness+gap);
}
```

`gjt.Border` employs a `gjt.DrawnRectangle` to actually paint the border. The drawn rectangle is obtained by invoking the `border()` method.

```
public void paint(Graphics g) {
  border().paint();
  super.paint(g);  // ensures lightweight comps get drawn
}
protected DrawnRectangle border() {
  if(border == null)
    border = new DrawnRectangle(this, thickness);
  return border;
}
```

Derived classes are free to override `DrawnRectangle border()`[8] in order to use an extension of `DrawnRectangle` for drawing their border. Also, notice that the overridden `paint()` method invokes `super.paint(g)` in order to ensure that any lightweight components contained in the border are painted. See "Remember to Invoke super.paint() When Overriding Container.paint()" on page 480.

Notice that although only one component is contained in the border, the component may very well be a container, so a border can actually contain any number of components.

gjt.ThreeDBorder

The `gjt.ThreeDBorder` class extends `Border` and, as its name indicates, draws a 3-D border. Notice as you look through Example 20-4 that the border can be drawn either raised, which is the default, or inset.

---

7. See "The BorderLayout Layout Manager" on page 394.
8. As we shall soon see, that is exactly what `EtchedBorder` and `ThreeDBorder` do.

Example 20-4 `gjt.ThreeDBorder` **Class Source Code**

```
package gjt;

import java.awt.*;

public class ThreeDBorder extends Border {
  public ThreeDBorder(Component borderMe) {
    this(borderMe, _defaultThickness, _defaultGap);
  }
  public ThreeDBorder(Component borderMe,
                      int borderThickness) {
    this(borderMe, borderThickness, _defaultGap);
  }
  public ThreeDBorder(Component borderMe,
                      int borderThickness, int gap) {
    super(borderMe, borderThickness, gap);
  }
  public void inset() { ((ThreeDRectangle)border()).inset(); }
  public void raise() { ((ThreeDRectangle)border()).raise(); }

  public void paintRaised() {
    ((ThreeDRectangle)border()).paintRaised();
  }
  public void paintInset() {
    ((ThreeDRectangle)border()).paintInset ();
  }
  public boolean isRaised() {
    return ((ThreeDRectangle)border()).isRaised();
  }
  protected DrawnRectangle border() {
    if(border == null)
      border = new ThreeDRectangle(this, thickness);
    return border;
  }
}
```

`ThreeDBorder` overrides the `border()` method to return an instance of `ThreeDRectangle`, which is used to paint the border (remember, the border is actually drawn by `Border.paint()`).

Notice that the drawing style used by `paint()` is controlled by `raise()` and `inset()`. Those methods do not cause any painting to be done—they just set the state for the next call to `paint()`. Using the `paintRaised()` and `paintInset()` methods provides the means to set the state and paint in one operation.

gjt.EtchedBorder

gjt.EtchedBorder is a Border that does just what it suggests; it draws an etched border. An EtchedBorder can be drawn either etched in (the default) or etched out. Example 20-5 shows the EtchedBorder class in its entirety.

Just like ThreeDBorder, EtchedBorder overrides the border() method. EtchedBorder.border() returns an EtchedRectangle, which is used to paint the border.

Notice as you look through the code that the drawing style used by paint() is controlled by the etchedIn() and etchedOut() methods. Like the raise() and inset() methods of ThreeDBorder, etchedIn() and etchedOut() do not result in anything being painted but only set the state for the next call to paint(). Using the paintEtchedIn() and paintEtchedOut() methods provides the means to set the state and to paint in one operation.

Example 20-5 gjt.EtchedBorder **Class Source Code**

```
package gjt;

import java.awt.*;

public class EtchedBorder extends Border {
  public EtchedBorder(Component borderMe) {
    this(borderMe, _defaultThickness, _defaultGap);
  }
  public EtchedBorder(Component borderMe,
                      int borderThickness) {
    this(borderMe, borderThickness, _defaultGap);
  }
  public EtchedBorder(Component borderMe,
                      int borderThickness, int gap) {
    super(borderMe, borderThickness, gap);
  }
  public void etchedIn() {
    ((EtchedRectangle)border()).etchedIn();
  }
  public void etchedOut() {
    ((EtchedRectangle)border()).etchedOut();
  }
  public void paintEtchedIn() {
    ((EtchedRectangle)border()).paintEtchedIn ();
  }
  public void paintEtchedOut() {
    ((EtchedRectangle)border()).paintEtchedOut();
  }
```

```
public boolean isEtchedIn() {
    return ((EtchedRectangle)border()).isEtchedIn();
}
protected String paramString() {
    return super.paramString() + (EtchedRectangle)border();
}
protected DrawnRectangle border() {
    if(border == null)
        border = new EtchedRectangle(this, thickness);
    return border;
}
}
```

gjt.test.BorderTest

When we put the Border class to use in our very busy unit test, it looks like the applet in Figure 20-5.

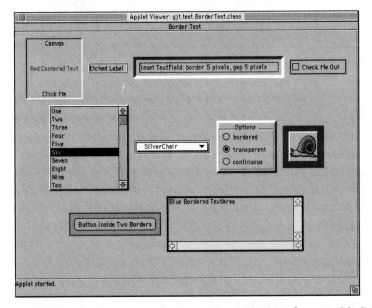

Figure 20-5 gjt.Border Unit Test (screenshot from 1.02 GJT on Mac)

Figure 20-6 illustrates in three dimensions how the unit test is constructed.

Border Test ——

Titled Panel ——

Border Test Panel ——

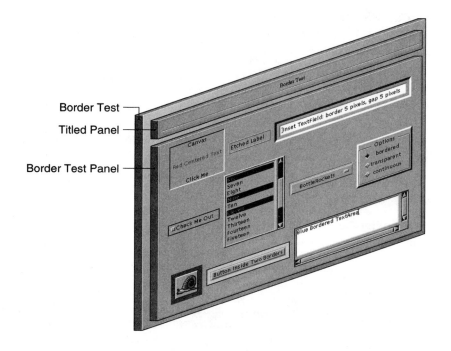

Figure 20-6 `BorderTest` Layout Diagram

You may want to refer to Figure 20-5 and Figure 20-6 as you look through the unit test listing in Example 20-6 on page 630. As you can see, the layout for the `Border` unit test is quite simple. As with all unit tests, the applet lays out a `TitledPanel` in the north, for which we provide the title string—we also provide the `Panel` to be laid out in the center of the applet [9]:

```
public class BorderTest extends UnitTest {
   public String title() {
      return "Border Test";
   }
   public Panel  centerPanel() {
      return new BorderTestPanel(this);
   }
}
```

---

9. See *The GJT test Package* on page 571 for a discussion of the `UnitTest` and `TitledPanel` classes.

Our `BorderTestPanel`, which is laid out in the center of the applet, uses a `FlowLayout` with a centered alignment and horizontal and vertical gaps between components of ten pixels[10]. From there on out, we add ten borders, all of which are constructed by private `BorderTestPanel` methods:

```
public BorderTestPanel(Applet applet) {
    setLayout(new FlowLayout(FlowLayout.CENTER, 10, 10));

    add(new BorderedCanvas());
    add(etchedLabel = new EtchedBorder(new Label("Etched Label")));
    add(threeDBorder = new ThreeDBorder(tf, 5, 5));
    add(new Border(new Checkbox("Check Me Out")));
    add(makeThreeDBorderedList         ());
    add(makeEtchedBorderedChoice       ());
    add(makeThreeDBorderedCheckboxes());
    add(makeBorderedImageButton        (applet));
    add(makeBorderedAWTButton          ());
    add(makeBorderedTextArea           ());

    threeDBorder.inset();
    etchedLabel.etchedOut();
}
```

The important thing to note here is that each of the private methods returns a `Border`. Therefore, each `add()` call in the `BorderTestPanel` constructor is adding a `Border` to itself.

Each private method creates a component and a border. The component is passed to the `Border` constructor, and the border is returned to be added to the `BorderTestPanel`. For instance, the `makeBorderedTextArea()` method looks like this:

```
private Border makeBorderedTextArea() {
    Border border;
    border = new Border(
                new TextArea("Blue Bordered TextArea", 5, 30));
    border.setLineColor(Color.blue);
    return border;
}
```

10. See "The FlowLayout Layout Manager" on page 399.

We pass the `Border` constructor a newly constructed `TextArea`, set the `border` line color to blue, and return the `border`.

Remember that a `Border` can contain multiple components simply by passing its constructor a `Container` —recall that Container is an extension of Component. The `makeThreeDBorderedCheckboxes()` method creates a `Panel`, to which it adds three checkboxes. Then, a `Box` is constructed, which is passed the `panel` and the string "Options". Finally, a `ThreeDBorder` is constructed by passing it the box. The result is that the bordered checkboxes you see in the unit test are actually a `ThreeDBorder` containing a `Box` that contains the three checkboxes:

Through the magic of inheritance, we are able to return a `ThreeDBorder` from a method that returns a `Border`:

```
private Border makeThreeDBorderedCheckboxes() {
   Panel         panel = new Panel();
   Box           box   = new Box(panel, "Options");
   CheckboxGroup group = new CheckboxGroup();

   panel.setLayout(new GridLayout(3,0));
   panel.add(new Checkbox("bordered",    group, false));
   panel.add(new Checkbox("transparent", group, false));
   panel.add(new Checkbox("continuous",  group, true));

   return new ThreeDBorder(box, 4);
}
```

The `CheckBoxGroup` ensures that only one of the checkboxes in the `group` is checked at any given time[11]. The checkboxes are added to the `group` by passing `group` to their constructor.

---

11. See "java.awt.Checkbox" on page 196.

Since a `Border` is a `Panel` to which a component may be added, it is perfectly acceptable to add a border to another border, thus wrapping a component in multiple borders. This is done in the `makeBorderedAWTButton()` method:

```
private Border makeBorderedAWTButton() {
  Button button;
  Border cyanBorder, blackBorder;

  button = new Button("Button Inside Two Borders");
  cyanBorder = new Border(button, 7);
  cyanBorder.setLineColor(Color.cyan);

  blackBorder = new Border(cyanBorder);

  return blackBorder;
}
```

`makeBorderedAWTButton()` places a `java.awt.Button` in the `cyanBorder`. (Refer to the color inserts to see the cyan in the cyan border.) The thickness of the `cyanBorder`, specified at construction time, is seven pixels, and the line color of the `cyanBorder` is set to cyan. The `cyanBorder` is subsequently placed inside the `blackBorder`, and it is the `blackBorder` that is returned and added to the `BorderTestPanel`. The result is a button bordered by a seven-pixel-thick cyan border, bordered by a black border. (The black border that surrounds the button itself is a focus indicator):

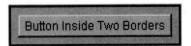

The last thing to note about the `Border` unit test is that we add an instance of `BorderedCanvas`, which is an extension of `ThreeDBorder`:

```
class BorderedCanvas extends ThreeDBorder {
  public BorderedCanvas() {
    super(new TestCanvas());

    getComponent().addMouseListener(new MouseAdapter() {
        public void mousePressed(MouseEvent event) {
          TestCanvas testCanvas = (TestCanvas)event.getSource();
          testCanvas.toggleTextOn();

          if(isRaised()) {
              paintInset ();
              testCanvas.drawCenteredString();
          }
          else {
```

```
                paintRaised();
                testCanvas.repaint();
            }
        }
    });
    }
}
```

The rationale for extending `ThreeDBorder` is that we wish to react to mouse pressed events, which we accomplish by implementing an anonymous inner class[12], and overriding `mousePressed()`. If the border is raised, a mouse pressed event results in painting the border inset. If the border is inset, a mouse pressed results in painting the border raised. The result of all this is that the border is toggled between raised and inset every time a mouse pressed occurs in the canvas.

Notice that the `BorderedCanvas` constructor passes an instance of `TestCanvas` to the `ThreeDBorder` constructor. `TestCanvas` displays two strings, one centered at the top of the canvas ("Canvas") and one centered at the bottom of the canvas ("Click Me"). Additionally, every time a mouse clicked event occurs in the `TestCanvas`, a string ("Red Centered Text") is drawn or erased from the center of the canvas. If the canvas is raised, the string is erased. If the canvas is inset, the string is drawn. The centering of the strings is accomplished by using the size of the canvas and the border's `FontMetrics` [13].

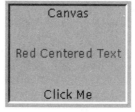

---

12. See "Anonymous Inner Classes" on page 125.
13. See *Graphics, Colors, and Fonts* for more information on use of `FontMetrics`.

```
class TestCanvas extends Canvas {
  private String  centered = new String ("Red Centered Text");
  private boolean textOn  = false;

  public void paint(Graphics g) {
      String       canvas = "Canvas";
      Dimension   size   = getSize();
      FontMetrics fm     = g.getFontMetrics();
      String      click  = "Click Me";

      g.drawString(canvas, (size.width/2) -
                  (fm.stringWidth(canvas)/2),
                  fm.getHeight() - fm.getDescent());
      g.drawString(click, (size.width/2) -
                  (fm.stringWidth(click)/2),
                  size.height - fm.getHeight() +
                  fm.getAscent());
  }
  public void toggleTextOn() {
      textOn = textOn ? false : true;
  }
  public void setTextOn(boolean textOn) {
      this.textOn = textOn;
  }
  public boolean getTextOn() {
      return textOn;
  }
  public Dimension getPreferredSize() {
      Graphics g = getGraphics();
      FontMetrics fm = g.getFontMetrics();

      g.dispose();
      return new Dimension(fm.stringWidth(centered)+10, 100);
  }
  protected void drawCenteredString() {
      Dimension   size = getSize();
      Graphics    g    = getGraphics();
      FontMetrics fm   = g.getFontMetrics();

      g.setColor(Color.red);
      g.drawString(centered,
                  size.width/2-(fm.stringWidth(centered)/2),
                  size.height/2 - (fm.getHeight()/2) +
                  fm.getAscent());
      g.dispose();
  }
}
```

Example 20-6 lists `gjt.test.BorderTest` in its entirety.

Example 20-6 `gjt.test.BorderTest` **Class Source Code**

```java
package gjt.test;

import java.applet.Applet;
import java.awt.*;
import java.awt.event.*;
import gjt.*;

public class BorderTest extends UnitTest {
  public String title() {
     return "Border Test";
  }
  public Panel   centerPanel() {
     return new BorderTestPanel(this);
  }
}

class BorderTestPanel extends Panel {
  TextField tf = new TextField(
               "Inset TextField: border 5 pixels, gap 5 pixels ");
  ThreeDBorder threeDBorder;
  EtchedBorder etchedLabel;
  Border       border;

  public BorderTestPanel(Applet applet) {
     setLayout(new FlowLayout(FlowLayout.CENTER, 10, 10));

     add(new BorderedCanvas());
     add(etchedLabel =
          new EtchedBorder(new Label("Etched Label")));
     add(threeDBorder = new ThreeDBorder(tf, 5, 5));
     add(new Border(new Checkbox("Check Me Out")));
     add(makeThreeDBorderedList       ());
     add(makeEtchedBorderedChoice      ());
     add(makeThreeDBorderedCheckboxes());
     add(makeBorderedImageButton       (applet));
     add(makeBorderedAWTButton         ());
     add(makeBorderedTextArea          ());
```

```java
        threeDBorder.inset();
        etchedLabel.etchedOut();
    }
    private Border makeThreeDBorderedList() {
        List list = new List(10, true);

        list.add("One");
        list.add("Two");
        list.add("Three");
        list.add("Four");
        list.add("Five");
        list.add("Six");
        list.add("Seven");
        list.add("Eight");
        list.add("Nine");
        list.add("Ten");
        list.add("Eleven");
        list.add("Twelve");
        list.add("Thirteen");
        list.add("Fourteen");
        list.add("Fiveteen");
        list.add("Sixteen");
        list.add("Seventeen");
        list.add("Eightteen");
        list.add("Nineteen");
        list.add("Twenty");

        return new ThreeDBorder(list);
    }
    private Border makeEtchedBorderedChoice() {
        Choice choice = new Choice();

        choice.add("Toadies");
        choice.add("SilverChair");
        choice.add("Rug Burns");
        choice.add("Cracker");
        choice.add("Seven Mary Three");
        choice.add("Dishwalla");
        choice.add("Blues Traveler");
        choice.add("BottleRockets");
        choice.add("SpaceHog");
```

```
         return new EtchedBorder(choice);
      }
      private Border makeBorderedImageButton(Applet applet) {
         Image  snail;
         Border border;

         snail = applet.getImage(applet.getCodeBase(),
                              "gifs/snail.gif");
         border  = new Border(new ImageButton(snail), 10);
         border.setLineColor(Color.red);

         return border;
      }
      private Border makeBorderedAWTButton() {
         Button button;
         Border cyanBorder, blackBorder;

         button = new Button("Button Inside Two Borders");
         cyanBorder = new Border(button, 7);
         cyanBorder.setLineColor(Color.cyan);

         blackBorder = new Border(cyanBorder);
         blackBorder.setLineColor(Color.black);

         return blackBorder;
      }
      private Border makeThreeDBorderedCheckboxes() {
         Panel          panel = new Panel();
         Box            box   = new Box(panel, "Options");
         CheckboxGroup group = new CheckboxGroup();

         panel.setLayout(new GridLayout(3,0));
         panel.add(new Checkbox("bordered",    group, false));
         panel.add(new Checkbox("transparent", group, false));
         panel.add(new Checkbox("continuous",  group, true));

         return new ThreeDBorder(box, 4);
      }
      private Border makeBorderedTextArea() {
         Border border;
```

```
      border = new Border(
      new TextArea("Blue Bordered TextArea", 5, 30));
      border.setLineColor(Color.blue);

      return border;
   }
}

class BorderedCanvas extends ThreeDBorder {
  public BorderedCanvas() {
     super(new TestCanvas());

     getComponent().addMouseListener(new MouseAdapter() {
        public void mousePressed(MouseEvent event) {
           TestCanvas testCanvas = (TestCanvas)event.getSource();

           testCanvas.toggleTextOn();
           if(isRaised()) {
              paintInset ();
              testCanvas.drawCenteredString();
           }
           else {
              paintRaised();
              testCanvas.repaint();
           }
        }
     });
  }
}
class TestCanvas extends Canvas {
  private String  centered = new String ("Red Centered Text");
  private boolean textOn   = false;

  public void paint(Graphics g) {
     String       canvas = "Canvas";
     Dimension    size   = getSize();
     FontMetrics  fm     = g.getFontMetrics();
     String       click  = "Click Me";
```

```java
      g.drawString(canvas, (size.width/2) -
                (fm.stringWidth(canvas)/2),
                fm.getHeight() - fm.getDescent());

      g.drawString(click, (size.width/2) -
                (fm.stringWidth(click)/2),
                size.height - fm.getHeight() +
                fm.getAscent());
   }
   public void toggleTextOn() {
      textOn = textOn ? false : true;
   }
   public void setTextOn(boolean textOn) {
      this.textOn = textOn;
   }
   public boolean getTextOn() {
      return textOn;
   }
   public Dimension getPreferredSize() {
      Graphics g = getGraphics();
      FontMetrics fm = g.getFontMetrics();
      g.dispose();
      return new Dimension(fm.stringWidth(centered)+10, 100);
   }
   protected void drawCenteredString() {
      Dimension    size = getSize();
      Graphics     g    = getGraphics();
      FontMetrics  fm   = g.getFontMetrics();

      g.setColor(Color.red);
      g.drawString(centered,
      size.width/2-(fm.stringWidth(centered)/2),
      size.height/2 - (fm.getHeight()/2) +
                fm.getAscent());

      g.dispose();
   }
}
```

Summary

This chapter has introduced four custom containers from the Graphic Java Toolkit: `gjt.Box`, `gjt.Border`, `gjt.EtchedBorder` and `gjt.ThreeDBorder`.

Boxes are used to group logically related groups of components together. The `gjt.Box` class draws a border around a component and places a title at the top of the container. `gjt.Box` and its unit test, `gjt.test.BoxTest`, are studies in the use of `GridBagLayout`.

Note that if you simply want to group components together and give the group a title, `gjt.Box` is more suitable for your needs. Borders are useful in a number of situations and can be used to spruce up components displayed in an applet. The GJT provides three types of borders: `Border`, which draws a flat border, `EtchedBorder`, which draws a border either etched in or etched out, and `ThreeDBorder`, which draws a 3-D border either raised or inset.

Borders extend `Panel` and must be supplied with a component at construction time. The component supplied at construction time is centered in the border by an instance of `BorderLayout`. A border can contain multiple components by being passed a `Container` at construction time. Finally, since a GJT border is a `Panel` and a `Panel` is a `Container`, we can pass a border to another border's constructor, thereby surrounding a component with multiple borders.

CHAPTER 21

Rubberbanding

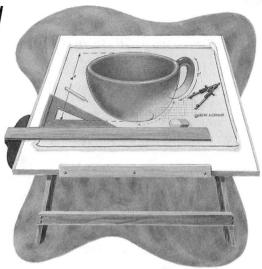

Rubberbanding is an essential tool in the applet developer's toolkit. Rubberbands are useful in a number of different contexts; for instance, one method for selecting multiple items is to stretch a rubberband rectangle around the items to be selected. Drawing programs typically employ rubberbands that enable users to *rubberband* the shape they wish to draw before it is actually drawn on screen.

Rubberbanding involves dynamically updating a geometric shape whose boundary changes as the mouse is dragged. A rubberband must be careful not to disturb any existing graphics beneath it, which is accomplished by painting in XOR mode, as we shall see shortly.

This chapter presents a handful of classes for rubberbanding, including a RubberbandPanel, an extension of Panel that can be fitted with a rubberband. The chapter culminates with a simple drawing program that illustrates the use of rubberbands.

The Graphic Java Toolkit Rubberband Package

The Graphic Java Toolkit includes a separate package for rubberbanding:
gjt.rubberband. Figure 21-1 shows the class diagram for the gjt.rubberband
package.

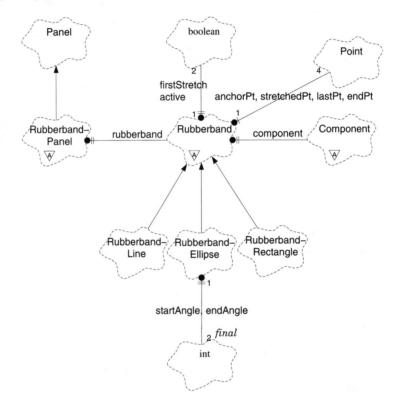

Figure 21-1 gjt.rubberband Package Diagram

The Rubberband Base Class

Before looking at the code for the Rubberband base class, let's briefly outline the
steps involved in rubberbanding a shape on screen:

1. A mouse pressed event occurs in a Component equipped with a Rubber-
    band.

2. The mouse is dragged inside the Component where the mouse pressed
    event occurred.

3. A mouse released event occurs in the same Component.

Step one defines the *anchor* point for the rubberband. The anchor point remains constant throughout the remaining steps. Step two involves dynamically updating the *stretch* point for the rubberband; the stretch point is kept in synch with the last mouse drag location. Step three defines the *end* point for the rubberband. After a rubberbanding operation is complete, a rubberband needs to be able to report the anchor point and the end point of the last rubberbanding operation that occurred, so that the rubberband client can determine the boundary of the rubberbanding operation and take whatever action is appropriate.

The `Rubberband` base class encapsulates the steps outlined above. Extensions of `Rubberband`, namely, `RubberbandLine`, `RubberbandRectangle`, and `RubberbandEllipse`, simply implement the actual drawing of the rubberband.

Rubberband Associations and Responsibilities

Table 21-1 and Table 21-2 summarize the responsibilities and associations of the `Rubberband` class. Note the two abstract methods in Table 21-1. Subclasses of `Rubberband` must implement `drawLast()` and `drawNext()` if they are to be concrete classes.

Table 21-1 `gjt.rubberband.Rubberband` **Responsibilities**

Methods	Description
`void drawLast(Graphics g)`	**Abstract** method that draws the appropriate geometric shape at the *last* rubberband location.
`void drawNext(Graphics g)`	**Abstract** method that draws the appropriate geometric shape at the *next* rubberband location.
`void setComponent(Component c)`	Sets the component the rubberband is drawn in.
`void setActive(boolean b)`	Sets the state of the rubberband to either active or inactive.
`boolean isActive()`	Indicates whether the rubberband is active or inactive.
`Point getAnchor()`	Returns the point of origin of a rubberband operation.
`Point getStretched()`	Returns the current stretched location for a rubberband operation.
`Point getLast()`	Returns the last point in a rubberband operation.

Table 21-1 gjt.rubberband.Rubberband **Responsibilities (Continued)**

Methods	Description
Point getEnd()	Returns the final point in a rubberband operation.
void anchor(Point p)	Sets the anchor point for a rubberband operation.
void stretch(Point p)	Sets the stretched location for a rubberband operation.
void end(Point p)	Sets the end point in a rubberband operation.
Rectangle getBounds()	Returns the current boundary of the rubberband.
Rectangle lastBounds()	Returns the last boundary of the rubberband.

Table 21-2 gjt.rubberband.Rubberband **Associations**

Variables	Description
Point anchorPt	The point of origin for a rubberband operation.
Point stretchedPt	The current point in a rubberband operation.
Point lastPt	The last point in a rubberband operation.
Point endPt	The end point in a rubberband operation.
boolean firstStretch	Indicates whether the rubberband has been stretched.
Component component	The component where rubberbanding will take place.

The Rubberband class provides two constructors—a default constructor and a constructor that takes a reference to a Component. A rubberband's component can be set after construction by invoking setComponent().

Additionally, each rubberband registers itself as both a mouse listener and a mouse motion listener for the component in which it resides. Since a component can potentially have more than one rubberband associated with it, rubberbands can be designated as active or inactive. Only active rubberbands react to mouse events that occur in the rubberband's component.

```
public Rubberband(Component component) {
}
public Rubberband(Component component) {
  setComponent(component)
}
public void setComponent(Component c) {
  this.component = c;

  component.addMouseListener(new MouseAdapter() {
    public void mousePressed(MouseEvent event) {
      if(isActive())
        anchor(event.getPoint());
    }
    public void mouseClicked(MouseEvent event) {
      if(isActive())
        end(event.getPoint());
    }
    public void mouseReleased(MouseEvent event) {
      if(isActive())
        end(event.getPoint());
    }
  });
  component.addMouseMotionListener(new MouseMotionAdapter() {
    public void mouseDragged(MouseEvent event) {
      if(isActive())
        stretch(event.getPoint());
    }
  });
}
}
```

When a mouse pressed occurs in a component equipped with an active rubberband, the rubberband invokes its anchor() method.

```
public void anchor(Point p) {
  firstStretch = true;
  anchorPt.x = p.x;
  anchorPt.y = p.y;

  stretchedPt.x = lastPt.x = anchorPt.x;
  stretchedPt.y = lastPt.y = anchorPt.y;
}
```

`Rubberband.anchor()` is passed the point where the mouse pressed event occurred. The `anchor()` method sets the `anchor`, `stretched`, and `last` points to the point passed in, and `firstStretch` is set to `true`.

Subsequent mouse dragged events in a component equipped with an active rubberband result in the rubberband's `stretch()` method being invoked. When a mouse released event occurs in the component, the active rubberband's `end()` method is invoked.

Painting in XOR Mode

As we've pointed out, `Rubberband` is an abstract class that leaves two methods for extensions to implement:

```
abstract public void drawLast(Graphics g);
abstract public void drawNext(Graphics g);
```

Both of these methods are invoked from within `Rubberband` `stretch()` and `end()` methods. The `stretch()` method is called when a mouse dragged event occurs.

```
public void stretch(Point p) {
  lastPt.x = stretchedPt.x;
  lastPt.y = stretchedPt.y;
  stretchedPt.x = p.x;
  stretchedPt.y = p.y;

  Graphics g = component.getGraphics();
  if(g != null) {
    g.setXORMode(component.getBackground());

    if(firstStretch == true) firstStretch = false;
    else                     drawLast(g);

    drawNext(g);
    g.dispose();
  }
}
```

The first order of business for `stretch()` is to update both the stretched and last points. Next, the `Graphics` object associated with the component upon which rubberbanding is taking place is set to XOR mode. Setting XOR mode with the background color results in the following for all subsequent graphical operations using the `Graphics` object:

- Existing pixels with the current `Graphics` color are changed to the background color, and vice versa.

- Existing pixels that are not in the current color are changed unpredictably but reversibly—drawing the same color over the same pixel twice returns the pixel to its original color.

In essence, the call to `setXORMode()` effectively lets us paint on top of existing pixels without disturbing them.

If it is not the first time the rubberband has been stretched, `drawLast()` is invoked, which draws the rubberband at its last location. Since XOR mode has been set, the call to `drawLast()` will effectively erase the rubberband at its last location. Note that the first time the rubberband is stretched, no erasing is necessary, thus the check against the `firstStretch` variable.

Finally, `drawNext()` is invoked, which draws the rubberband at the next location, and the `Graphics` object is disposed of, which is required anytime we obtain a `Graphics` object via a call to `Component.getGraphics()`—see "Disposing of a Graphics Object" on page 29.

When a mouse released event occurs, an active rubberband invokes its `end()` method.

```
public void end(Point p) {
  lastPt.x = endPt.x = p.x;
  lastPt.y = endPt.y = p.y;

  Graphics g = component.getGraphics();
  if(g != null) {
    g.setXORMode(component.getBackground());
    drawLast(g);
    g.dispose();
  }
}
```

After updating the last and end points, XOR mode is once again set for the `Graphics` object obtained from `Component.getGraphics()`, and `drawLast()` is invoked, which erases the rubberband one final time. Once again, we are careful to dispose of the `Graphics` object obtained from `Component.getGraphics()`.

The `Rubberband` class is listed in its entirety in Example 21-1.

Example 21-1 `gjt.rubberband.Rubberband` **Class Source Code**

```java
package gjt.rubberband;

import java.awt.*;
import java.awt.event.*;

abstract public class Rubberband {
   protected Point anchorPt    = new Point(0,0);
   protected Point stretchedPt = new Point(0,0);
   protected Point lastPt      = new Point(0,0);
   protected Point endPt       = new Point(0,0);

   private Component component;
   private boolean   firstStretch = true;
   private boolean   active = false;

   abstract public void drawLast(Graphics g);
   abstract public void drawNext(Graphics g);
   public Rubberband() {
   }
   public Rubberband(Component c) {
      setComponent(c);
   }
   public void setComponent(Component c) {
      component = c;

      component.addMouseListener(new MouseAdapter() {
         public void mousePressed(MouseEvent event) {
            if(isActive())
               anchor(event.getPoint());
         }
         public void mouseClicked(MouseEvent event) {
            if(isActive())
               end(event.getPoint());
         }
         public void mouseReleased(MouseEvent event) {
            if(isActive())
               end(event.getPoint());
         }
      });
      component.addMouseMotionListener(new MouseMotionAdapter() {
         public void mouseDragged(MouseEvent event) {
            if(isActive())
               stretch(event.getPoint());
         }
      });
   }
   public void setActive(boolean b) {
```

```
      active = b;
   }
   public boolean isActive    () { return active; }
   public Point   getAnchor   () { return anchorPt; }
   public Point   getStretched() { return stretchedPt; }
   public Point   getLast     () { return lastPt; }
   public Point   getEnd      () { return endPt; }

   public void anchor(Point p) {
      firstStretch = true;
      anchorPt.x = p.x;
      anchorPt.y = p.y;

      stretchedPt.x = lastPt.x = anchorPt.x;
      stretchedPt.y = lastPt.y = anchorPt.y;
   }
   public void stretch(Point p) {
      lastPt.x        = stretchedPt.x;
      lastPt.y        = stretchedPt.y;
      stretchedPt.x = p.x;
      stretchedPt.y = p.y;

      Graphics g = component.getGraphics();
      if(g != null) {
         g.setXORMode(component.getBackground());

         if(firstStretch == true) firstStretch = false;
         else                     drawLast(g);

         drawNext(g);
         g.dispose();
      }
   }
   public void end(Point p) {
      lastPt.x = endPt.x = p.x;
      lastPt.y = endPt.y = p.y;

      Graphics g = component.getGraphics();

      if(g != null) {
         g.setXORMode(component.getBackground());
         drawLast(g);
         g.dispose();
      }
   }
   public Rectangle getBounds() {
      return new Rectangle(stretchedPt.x < anchorPt.x ?
               stretchedPt.x : anchorPt.x,
               stretchedPt.y < anchorPt.y ?
```

```
                        stretchedPt.y : anchorPt.y,
                        Math.abs(stretchedPt.x - anchorPt.x),
                        Math.abs(stretchedPt.y - anchorPt.y));
    }

    public Rectangle lastBounds() {
        return new Rectangle(
                        lastPt.x < anchorPt.x ? lastPt.x : anchorPt.x,
                        lastPt.y < anchorPt.y ? lastPt.y : anchorPt.y,
                        Math.abs(lastPt.x - anchorPt.x),
                        Math.abs(lastPt.y - anchorPt.y));
    }
}
```

Drawing Rubberband Lines

As the astute reader will probably figure out, the `RubberbandLine` class
rubberbands lines. Example 21-2 shows the `RubberbandLine` class source code.

Example 21-2 `gjt.rubberband.RubberbandLine` **Class Source Code**

```
package gjt.rubberband;

import java.awt.Component;
import java.awt.Graphics;

public class RubberbandLine extends Rubberband {
    public RubberbandLine() {
    }
    public RubberbandLine(Component component) {
        super(component);
    }
    public void drawLast(Graphics graphics) {
        graphics.drawLine(anchorPt.x, anchorPt.y,
                          lastPt.x,   lastPt.y);
    }
    public void drawNext(Graphics graphics) {
        graphics.drawLine(anchorPt.x,     anchorPt.y,
                          stretchedPt.x, stretchedPt.y);
    }
}
```

Like all extensions of `Rubberband`, `RubberbandLine` can either be constructed
with no arguments or with a component that it passes along to its superclass
constructor.

RubberbandLine.drawLast() draws a line from the anchor point to the last point, and drawNext() draws a line from the anchor point to the stretch point. drawNext() and drawLast() both use the anchorPt, stretchedPt, and lastPt points from the Rubberband class.

Note that RubberbandLine does not concern itself with drawing in XOR mode or tracking the anchor, stretched, or end points of the rubberbanding operation; all of that infrastructure is provided by its superclass, Rubberband.

Drawing Rubberband Rectangles and Ellipses

RubberbandRectangle and RubberbandEllipse work exactly the same as RubberbandLine except that they draw rectangles and ellipses, as you can see in Example 21-3 and Example 21-4, respectively.

Example 21-3 gjt.rubberband.RubberbandRectangle **Class Source Code**

```
package gjt.rubberband;

import java.awt.Component;
import java.awt.Graphics;
import java.awt.Rectangle;

public class RubberbandRectangle extends Rubberband {
  public RubberbandRectangle() {
  }
  public RubberbandRectangle(Component component) {
     super(component);
  }
  public void drawLast(Graphics graphics) {
     Rectangle rect = lastBounds();
     graphics.drawRect(rect.x, rect.y,
                       rect.width, rect.height);
  }
  public void drawNext(Graphics graphics) {
     Rectangle rect = getBounds();
     graphics.drawRect(rect.x, rect.y,
     rect.width, rect.height);
  }
}
```

Example 21-4 `gjt.rubberband.RubberbandEllipse` **Class Source Code**

```
package gjt.rubberband;

import java.awt.Component;
import java.awt.Graphics;
import java.awt.Rectangle;

public class RubberbandEllipse extends Rubberband {
  private final int startAngle = 0;
  private final int endAngle   = 360;

  public RubberbandEllipse() {
  }
  public RubberbandEllipse(Component component) {
     super(component);
  }
  public void drawLast(Graphics graphics) {
     Rectangle r = lastBounds();
     graphics.drawArc(r.x, r.y,
                        r.width, r.height, startAngle, endAngle);
  }
  public void drawNext(Graphics graphics) {
     Rectangle r = getBounds();
     graphics.drawArc(r.x, r.y,
                        r.width, r.height, startAngle, endAngle);
  }
}
```

Note that both `RubberbandRectangle` and `RubberbandEllipse` invoke the `Rubberband.lastBounds()` and `Rubberband.getBounds()` methods to access the last and next boundaries of the rubberband, respectively.

`RubberbandRectangle` invokes the `Graphics.drawRect()` method to draw its rectangles; `RubberbandEllipse` invokes the `Graphics.drawEllipse()` method to draw its ellipses.

A Rubberband Panel

`gjt.rubberband.RubberbandPanel` is an abstract extension of `Panel` that maintains an association with an instance of `Rubberband`.

`RubberbandPanel` implements no constructors, so a default constructor (with no arguments) is generated for it.

RubberbandPanel provides a setRubberband() method for associating a
rubberband with the panel. If a rubberband was previously associated with the
panel, it is made inactive. Next, if the rubberband passed to setRubberband()
is non-null, it is made active, and the rubberband's component is set to the
rubberband panel.

```
public void setRubberband(Rubberband rb) {
   if(rubberband != null) {
      rubberband.setActive(false);
   }
   rubberband = rb;

   if(rubberband != null) {
      rubberband.setActive(true);
      rubberband.setComponent(this);
   }
}
```

RubberbandPanel defines one abstract method.

```
abstract public void rubberbandEnded(Rubberband rb);
```

rubberbandEnded() is invoked by an overridden processMouseEvent()
method if the event is a mouse released event and the rubberband associated with
the RubberbandPanel is non-null.

```
public void processMouseEvent(MouseEvent event) {
   super.processMouseEvent(event);   // fire to listeners

   if(rubberband != null &&
      event.getID() == MouseEvent.MOUSE_RELEASED)
      rubberbandEnded(rubberband);
   }
}
```

If you recall, we previously urged you to avoid the inheritance-based mechanism
provided by the delegation event model—see "Inheritance-Based Mechanism" on
page 115—and here we are, going against our own advice. RubberbandPanel
uses the inheritance-based mechanism because there is no guarantee as to the
order in which event listeners are notified of an event—see "Notification Order
For Multiple Listeners Is Undefined" on page 98. Let us explain.

If RubberbandPanel were not an abstract class and did not override
processMouseEvent(), how would a mouse release, and therefore the end of a
rubberbanding operation get handled? The answer, of course, would be to add a
mouse listener to the RubberbandPanel and have the listener implement
mouseReleased(). Realize that in such a scenario, there are at least two mouse
listeners attached to the RubberbandPanel: one that is listening for a mouse

released event in order to determine when the rubberbanding operation is complete, and any active rubberbands associated with the RubberbandPanel, which react to a mouse released event by erasing the last rubberbanding shape drawn.

Now consider that the delegation event model makes no guarantees as to the order in which multiple listeners attached to a component are notified of an event. Furthermore, consider a drawing program that draws the shape that was rubberbanded after the rubberbanding operation is complete—the rubberband erases the shape when a mouse released event occurs, whereas the drawing program draws the shape. If the rubberband is notified of the mouse released event first, everything is fine, but if the drawing program is notified first, the rubberband will wind up erasing the shape drawn by the drawing program[1].

The last piece to our puzzle is the fact that Component.processMouseEvent() causes all listeners to be notified of the mouse event in question. To ensure that the rubberband erases the shape before extensions of RubberbandPanel are notified of the end of the rubberbanding operation, RubberbandPanel.processMouseEvent() invokes super.mouseEvent(event) before invoking the abstract rubberbandEnded() method. Doing so ensures that mouse listeners are notified of the event before the RubberbandPanel derived class, which implements the rubberbandEnded() method. As a result, our not-so-hypothetical drawing program works as expected.

The RubberbandPanel class is listed in its entirety in Example 21-5.

Example 21-5 gjt.rubberband.RubberbandPanel **Class Source Code**

```
package gjt.rubberband;

import java.awt.*;
import java.awt.event.*;

abstract public class RubberbandPanel extends Panel {
  private Rubberband rubberband;

  abstract public void rubberbandEnded(Rubberband rb);

  public void setRubberband(Rubberband rb) {
    if(rubberband != null) {
      rubberband.setActive(false);
    }
```

1. We must confess that we learned this the hard way.

```
     rubberband = rb;

     if(rubberband != null) {
         rubberband.setActive(true);
         rubberband.setComponent(this);
     }
  }
  public Rubberband getRubberband() {
     return rubberband;
  }
  public void processMouseEvent(MouseEvent event) {
     super.processMouseEvent(event);  // fire to listeners

     if(rubberband != null &&
        event.getID() == MouseEvent.MOUSE_RELEASED)
        rubberbandEnded(rubberband);
     }
  }
}
```

The gjt.DrawingPanel Class

The Graphic Java Toolkit provides a `DrawingPanel` class, that comes standard
with three rubberbands: one each for rubberbanding lines, rectangles and ellipses.
When a rubberbanding operation is complete, `DrawingPanel` draws the shape
that was rubberbanded. Optionally, the shape drawn may be filled.

DrawingPanel extends `RubberbandPanel` and creates rubberbands in its only
constructor.

```
public class DrawingPanel extends RubberbandPanel {
  private Rubberband rbLine, rbRect, rbEllipse;
  private Color    color;
  private boolean fill;

  public DrawingPanel() {
     rbLine   = new RubberbandLine     ();
     rbRect   = new RubberbandRectangle();
     rbEllipse = new RubberbandEllipse  ();
     setRubberband(rbLine);
  }
```

Of course, DrawingPanel implements `rubberbandEnded()` in order to qualify
as a concrete class. `rubberbandEnded()` invokes `drawShape()`, passing along
the rubberband involved in the rubberbanding operation.
DrawingPanel.`drawShape()` determines which of its rubberbands was
responsible for the rubberbanding operation and draws the appropriate shape.

```
public void rubberbandEnded(Rubberband rubberband) {
  drawShape(rubberband);
}
protected void drawShape(Rubberband rb) {
  Graphics g  = getGraphics();
  if(g != null) {
    g.setColor(color);

    if     (rb == rbLine)    drawLine      (rb, g);
    else if(rb == rbRect)    drawRectangle(rb, g);
    else if(rb == rbEllipse) drawEllipse  (rb, g);
    g.dispose();
  }
}
```

drawLine(), drawRectangle() and drawEllipse() obtain the appropriate information from the rubberband they are passed, and do the actual drawing of the shape. Note that extensions of RubberbandPanel may override the protected drawShape() in the event that they have more rubberbands than the three provided by RubberbandPanel.

Finally, the drawLine(), drawRectangle() and drawEllipse() methods do the actual drawing of the appropriate shape.

```
protected void drawLine(Rubberband rb, Graphics g) {
  Point anchor = rb.getAnchor(), end = rb.getEnd();
  g.drawLine(anchor.x, anchor.y, end.x, end.y);
}
protected void drawRectangle(Rubberband rb, Graphics g) {
  Rectangle r = rb.getBounds();
  if(fill)
    g.fillRect(r.x+1, r.y+1, r.width-1, r.height-1);
  else
    g.drawRect(r.x, r.y, r.width, r.height);
}
protected void drawEllipse(Rubberband rb, Graphics g) {
  Rectangle r = rb.getBounds();
  if(fill)
    g.fillArc(r.x+1, r.y+1, r.width-1, r.height-1, 0, 360);
  else
    g.drawArc(r.x, r.y, r.width, r.height, 0, 360);
}
```

The DrawingPanel class is listed in its entirety in Example 21-6.

Example 21-6 gjt.DrawingPanel **Class Source Code**

```java
package gjt;

import java.awt.*;
import java.awt.event.*;
import gjt.rubberband.*;

public class DrawingPanel extends RubberbandPanel {
  private Rubberband rbLine, rbRect, rbEllipse;
  private Color    color;
  private boolean fill;

  public DrawingPanel() {
     rbLine    = new RubberbandLine     ();
     rbRect    = new RubberbandRectangle();
     rbEllipse = new RubberbandEllipse  ();

     setRubberband(rbLine);
  }
  public void rubberbandEnded(Rubberband rubberband) {
     drawShape(rubberband);
  }
  public void drawLines      () { setRubberband(rbLine);    }
  public void drawRectangles() { setRubberband(rbRect);     }
  public void drawEllipses  () { setRubberband(rbEllipse); }

  public void  setColor(Color color) { this.color = color; }
  public Color getColor()                { return color;        }

  public void    setFill(boolean b) { fill = b;    }
  public boolean getFill()            { return fill; }

  protected void drawShape(Rubberband rb) {
     Graphics   g  = getGraphics();

     if(g != null) {
        g.setColor(color);

        if     (rb == rbLine)    drawLine     (rb, g);
        else if(rb == rbRect)    drawRectangle(rb, g);
        else if(rb == rbEllipse) drawEllipse  (rb, g);
        g.dispose();
     }
  }
  protected void drawLine(Rubberband rb, Graphics g) {
     Point anchor = rb.getAnchor(), end = rb.getEnd();
     g.drawLine(anchor.x, anchor.y, end.x, end.y);
  }
  protected void drawRectangle(Rubberband rb, Graphics g) {
     Rectangle r = rb.getBounds();
```

```
    if(fill)
        g.fillRect(r.x+1, r.y+1, r.width-1, r.height-1);
    else
        g.drawRect(r.x, r.y, r.width, r.height);
}
protected void drawEllipse(Rubberband rb, Graphics g) {
    Rectangle r = rb.getBounds();

    if(fill)
        g.fillArc(r.x+1, r.y+1, r.width-1, r.height-1, 0, 360);
    else
        g.drawArc(r.x, r.y, r.width, r.height, 0, 360);
}
}
```

Exercising the Rubberband Package

Figure 21-2 shows the gjt.rubberband package in action. As usual, feel free to run the unit test applet by invoking appletviewer on the RubberbandTest.html file provided on the CD. Doing so should help you to better understand the discussion of the unit test.

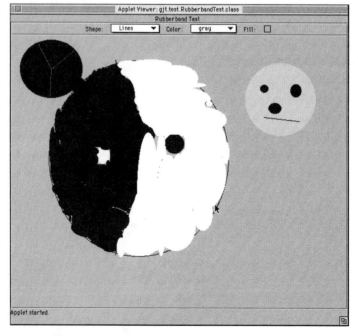

Figure 21-2 gjt.rubberband.Rubberband Unit Test
(screenshot from 1.02 GJT on Mac)

To see exactly how RubberbandTest is laid out in three dimensions, look at Figure 21-3.

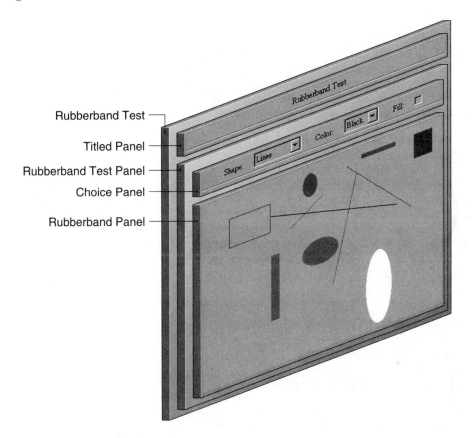

Figure 21-3 RubberbandTest Layout Diagram

As you may have gathered from looking at the unit test, RubberbandTest exercises an instance of DrawingPanel that not only tests the rubberbanding functionality provided in the gjt.rubberband package but also tests the DrawingPanel class.

gjt.test.RubberbandTest is listed in Example 21-7.

Example 21-7 `gjt.test.RubberbandTest` **Class Source Code**

```
package gjt.test;

import java.awt.Panel;

public class RubberbandTest extends UnitTest {
  public String title() {
    return "Rubberband Test";
  }
  public Panel centerPanel() {
    return new RubberbandTestPanel();
  }
}
```

RubberbandTest returns an instance of RubberbandTestPanel as the panel displayed in the center of the applet. RubberbandTestPanel is where all of the action takes place and is listed in Example 21-8[2].

Example 21-8 `gjt.test.RubberbandTestPanel` **Class Source Code**

```
package gjt.test;

import java.awt.*;
import java.awt.event.*;
import gjt.ColorChoice;
import gjt.DrawingPanel;
import gjt.Separator;
import gjt.RowLayout;
import gjt.rubberband.*;

public class RubberbandTestPanel extends Panel {
  private DrawingPanel drawingPanel;
  private ChoicePanel  choicePanel;

  public RubberbandTestPanel() {
    drawingPanel = new DrawingPanel();
    choicePanel  = new ChoicePanel(drawingPanel);

    setLayout(new BorderLayout());
    add(choicePanel, "North");
    add(drawingPanel, "Center");
  }
  public Dimension getPreferredSize() {
    return new Dimension(
```

2.   RubberbandTestPanel is broken out into its own file so that it can be used by other unit tests.

```
                    choicePanel.getPreferredSize().width, 500);
    }
}
class ChoicePanel extends Panel implements ItemListener {
    private DrawingPanel drawingPanel;
    private ColorChoice  colorChoice  = new ColorChoice();
    private Checkbox      fillCheckbox = new Checkbox();

    public ChoicePanel(DrawingPanel drawingPanel) {
        Panel  choicePanel     = new Panel();
        Choice geometricChoice = new Choice();

        this.drawingPanel = drawingPanel;

        geometricChoice.add("Lines");
        geometricChoice.add("Rectangles");
        geometricChoice.add("Ellipses");

        geometricChoice.addItemListener(this);
        colorChoice.addItemListener(this);
        fillCheckbox.addItemListener(this);

        choicePanel.setLayout(new RowLayout(10));
        choicePanel.add(new Label("Shape:"));
        choicePanel.add(geometricChoice);
        choicePanel.add(new Label("Color:"));
        choicePanel.add(colorChoice);
        choicePanel.add(new Label("Fill:"));
        choicePanel.add(fillCheckbox);

        setLayout(new BorderLayout());
        add(choicePanel, "Center");
        add(new Separator(), "South");
    }
    public void itemStateChanged(ItemEvent event) {
        Object target = event.getSource();

        if(target instanceof Checkbox) {
            drawingPanel.setFill(fillCheckbox.getState());
        }
        else if(target instanceof Choice) {
            Choice choice = (Choice)target;

            if(choice.getSelectedItem().equals("Lines")) {
                drawingPanel.drawLines();
            }
            else if(choice.getSelectedItem().equals("Rectangles")) {
                drawingPanel.drawRectangles();
```

```
        }
        else
            if(choice.getSelectedItem().equals("Ellipses")) {
            drawingPanel.drawEllipses  ();
        }
        drawingPanel.setColor(colorChoice.getColor());
    }
  }
  public Insets getInsets() { return new Insets(5,0,5,0); }
}
```

Refactoring the Unit Test

As an aside, we should mention that the gjt.DrawingPanel class was born out
of a first attempt at a RubberbandTest applet, in the manner described below.

The object-oriented design process is an iterative one[3]. Classes are written, and as
other classes are added to a system, insights are gained which often result in
existing classes being *refactored*, meaning their implementations are modified to
some degree according to a number of criterion. One of the mainstays of
refactoring is to identify basic abstractions that may be shared among a number of
different classes in the midst of specialized pieces of functionality. When such
code is identified, it is separated from the specialized code and packaged into its
own class or classes. The specialized code is then refactored to use the newly
created class or classes.

For instance, the original unit test for rubberbanding contained an extension of
RubberbandPanel that was very similar to gjt.DrawingPanel. After the unit
test (a specialized piece of functionality) was implemented, it was observed that
the unit test contained a basic abstraction that was much better placed in a class
that could be made available for all to take advantage of. That abstraction, of
course, was a drawing panel—a panel equipped with a set of rubberbands that
could be used to draw geometric shapes. As a result, the unit test was refactored,
meaning that gjt.DrawingPanel was implemented, and the unit test was

---

3.   See Booch, Grady. *Object-Oriented Analysis And Design*, section 6.1. Ben-
      jamin/Cummings, 1991.

reworked to use an instance of `gjt.DrawingPanel`. Not only did the refactoring produce a general-purpose class for drawing shapes, but it also considerably simplified the implementation of the unit tests—a win all the way around.

OO TIP

Refactor Classes To Extract Basic Abstractions

Object-oriented development involves refactoring classes when it is determined that specialized pieces of functionality contain basic abstractions that are better off placed in their own class or set of classes. In addition to refactoring specialized functionality, it is often the case that one or more classes may contain redundant code that implements similar functionality. In such a case, a base class that implements the redundant functionality is often created, and the classes in question are refactored to extend the newly created base class.

Refactoring involves repeatedly iterating over the implementation of classes and is one of the mainstays of object-oriented development.

Summary

The `gjt.rubberband` package serves as a good reminder that all graphical activities in the AWT occur in a `Component`. All the work is accomplished by the use of a component's `Graphics` object.

We have discussed one of the cornerstones of object-oriented software development—refactoring existing code. One of the principal activities of refactoring is to identify basic abstractions that have been implemented in specialized code. Once the basic abstractions have been identified, they are extracted from the specialized code and placed in a class (or classes) of their own, and the original specialized code is refactored to use the newly created classes.

CHAPTER
22

ImageButtons

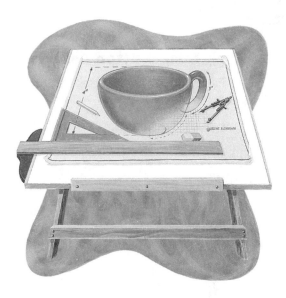

Of all the components missing from the AWT in the initial release of Java, probably the most asked-for is an image button. For this and a number of other reasons, we've included an image button in the Graphic Java Toolkit.

gjt.Image Button

Image buttons are similar to an `java.awt.Button`, except that they display an image instead of text. The Graphic Java Toolkit's version of image button comes with a hierarchy of image button listener classes. As we discussed in "Encapsulating Event Handling in a Separate Listener Class" on page 121, having a hierarchy of classes for handling events affords a great deal of flexibility as far as defining event handling behavior for custom components. Additionally, a hierarchy of listeners eases the development of new event handling classes by providing a pool of classes whose behavior can be extended.

To begin our discussion of the `gjt.ImageButton`, let's look at its associations and responsibilities.

gjt.ImageButton Associations and Responsibilities

Figure 22-1 shows the class diagram for the `gjt.ImageButton` class.

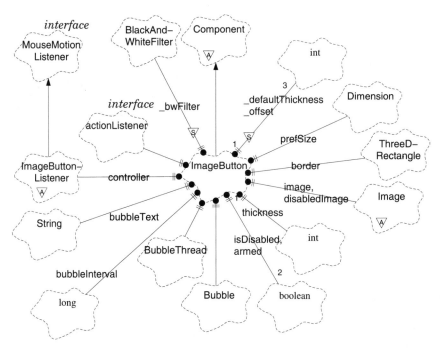

Figure 22-1 `gjt.ImageButton` Class Diagram

As you can see in Figure 22-1, `gjt.ImageButton` extends `Component` and therefore qualifies as a lightweight component—see "Lightweight Components" on page 475. An image button needs to be a `Component` so that it can be laid out and displayed just like any other component, and it also needs to display an `Image`. Since an image button does not contain any components, it does not need to be a container, and therefore we have chosen to extend `java.awt.Component`[1]. `ImageButton` employs a `ThreeDRectangle` for drawing a 3-D border around the `Image` it displays.

An `ImageButton` can be enabled and disabled. By default, every `ImageButton` is enabled; calling `setEnabled(false)` causes the image button's image to be drained of its color by running it through the `BlackAndWhiteFilter` provided by the GJT's image package. (Refer to "gjt.image.BlackAndWhiteFilter" on

---

1. An earlier version of `gjt.ImageButton` extended `java.awt.Canvas`, prior to the days of lightweight components.

page 350 for a discussion of `gjt.image.BlackAndWhiteFilter`). Disabled image buttons ignore mouse events—invoking `setEnabled(true)` on a disabled `ImageButton` restores the original image and causes the `ImageButton` to once again respond to mouse events.

One instance of `gjt.image.BlackAndWhiteFilter` is shared by all instances of `ImageButton`, the `static _bwFilter` member, which creates a black and white version of the original image the first time an image button is disabled.

Each image button maintains an association with a single `ImageButtonListener`, which handles mouse and mouse motion events for its image button. By default, an `ImageButton` is fitted with a `SpringyImageButtonListener`, which implements the same behavior with respect to reacting to mouse events as a `java.awt.Button` does. After constructing an image button, clients are free to change its listener by invoking `ImageButton.setListenerer(ImageButtonListener)`. This allows clients to fit an `ImageButton` with a different derivation of `ImageButtonListener` if the default listener does not fit the bill.

The Graphic Java Toolkit comes with three derivations of `ImageButtonListener`:

- `SpringyImageButtonListener`—Causes its associated `ImageButton` to behave exactly as a `java.awt.Button` with respect to mouse events.
- `StickyImageButtonListener`—Causes the associated `ImageButton` to stick instead of springing back when activated.
- `StateButtonListener`— Is associated with a `StateButton` (an extension of `ImageButton`) that cycles through a set of images when activated.

Image buttons can also be fitted with bubble help. Bubble help consists of a window that displays some text, and is commonly found in image buttons in toolbars. We introduced an implementation of bubble help in "Bubble Help" on page 279.

Image buttons, like their `java.awt.Button` counterparts, fire action events when they are activated. We've already seen how to equip a custom component to fire events in "Firing AWT Events From Custom Components" on page 128, and image buttons will give us another opportunity to see the technique in action in a real-world component.

Table 22-1 lists the responsibilities of a `gjt.ImageButton`. Pay special attention to the `Component` methods `gjt.ImageButton` is overriding and the rationale for doing so.

Table 22-1 gjt.ImageButton **Responsibilities**

Methods	Description
setBubbleHelp(String)	Sets the bubble help displayed beneath the button. The string is null by default.
setBubbleInterval(long)	The delay, in milliseconds, between the time the mouse enters the button and bubble help is displayed. The default is 1000, or one second.
void activate()	Programmatically activates the button.
void arm()	Programmatically arms the button.
disarm()	Programmatically disarms the button.
void setArmed()	Sets the state of the button to armed.
boolean isArmed()	Returns whether the button is armed.
void setThickness()	Sets the thickness of the 3D border.
boolean isRaised()	Returns true if border is raised.
void setRaised()	Sets the border to raised.
boolean isInset()	Returns true if border is inset.
void setInset()	Sets the border to raised.
boolean isDisabled()	Returns enabled state of the button.
void setEnabled(boolean)	Overridden Component method that enables or disables the button depending upon the boolean argument.
void setListener(ImageButtonListener listener)	Specifies a listener for handling mouse and mouse motion events.
ImageButtonListener getListener()	Returns the listener currently in use.
void paint(Graphics g)	Overrides Component.paint(). Paints the border and the image.
void paintInset()	Paints the border inset.
void paintRaised()	Paints the border raised.
Dimension getMinimumSize()	Overrides Component getMinimumSize(). Returns the value returned by getPreferredSize().
Dimension getPreferredSize()	Overrides Component getPreferredSize(). Sets preferred size to the image size plus the border thickness.
void setSize(int x, int y)	Overrides Component setSize().

Table 22-1 gjt.ImageButton **Responsibilities (Continued)**

Methods	Description
void setBounds(int x, int y, int w, int h)	Overrides Component setBounds(). Reshapes the border.
void setImage(Image image)	Sets the image to be displayed.
void processActionEvent()	Fires an action event to listeners.
void addActionListener()	Adds an action listener.
void removeActionListener()	Removes an action listener.

Table 22-2 lists the associations (class members) of the gjt.ImageButton class.

Table 22-2 gjt.ImageButton **Associations**

Variables	Description
static BlackAndWhiteFilter _bwFilter	Creates a bleached version of the image the first time the image button is disabled.
static int _offset	The pixel amount image recesses when image button is painted inset.
static int _defaultThickness	The default border thickness.
ThreeDRectangle border	Paints a 3-D border around an image.
boolean isDisabled	Tracks whether button is currently enabled or disabled.
Dimension prefSize	Specifies the preferred size of the button.
int thickness	Specifies the thickness of the button.
ImageButtonListener listener	Implements the algorithm for reacting to mouse events.
ActionListener actionListener	ActionListener used to fire action events.
Bubble bubble	Bubble for displaying bubble help.
String bubbleText	Text for bubble help.
BubbleThread	Thread for bubble help.
long bubbleInterval	Interval in milliseconds for bubble help delay.
Image image	The image displayed when enabled.
Image disabledImage	The image displayed when disabled.

gjt.ImageButton is one of the most complex classes in the Graphic Java Toolkit, so set's look at a few specific areas of interest before looking at the entire class listing. Like many of the GJT custom components, ImageButton provides a number of constructors, all of which invoke the constructor with the most arguments.

```
public ImageButton() {
  this(null);
}
public ImageButton(Image image) {
  this(image, _defaultThickness);
}
public ImageButton(Image image, int thickness) {
  this(image, thickness, null);
}
public ImageButton(Image image, int thickness,
                   ImageButtonListener listener) {
  setThickness(thickness);

  if(image != null)
     setImage(image);

  if(listener != null)
     setListener(listener);
  else
     setListener(new SpringyImageButtonListener());
  ...
}
```

The image displayed in the image button, the thickness of the image button's border, and the image button's listener can all be specified when an image button is constructed. The image and listener can be specified as null, and the thickness can be left unspecified. If left unspecified, the thickness defaults to a value of 2 pixels, the listener defaults to a springy image button listener, and the image defaults to null. If a null image is specified at the time of construction, it is expected that the image will be set by invoking setImage() before the image button is painted for the first time.

The image, thickness, and listener can be specified after construction.

```
public void setThickness(int thickness) {
  Assert.notFalse(thickness > 0);
  this.thickness = thickness;
  border.setThickness(this.thickness = thickness);

  if(isShowing()) {
     invalidate();
```

```
        getParent().validate();
    }
}
public void setImage(Image image) {
    Assert.notNull(image);
    Util.waitForImage(this, this.image = image);

    if(isShowing()) {
        invalidate();
        getParent().validate();
    }
}
public void setListener(ImageButtonListener l) {
    if(listener != null) {
        removeMouseListener(listener);
        removeMouseMotionListener(listener);
    }
    listener = l;
    addMouseListener(listener);
    addMouseMotionListener(listener);
}
```

Notice that setting the image or thickness affects the appearance of the button, so if the button is showing, it is invalidated, and then its parent is validated, which forces a layout of the image button's container[2].

If the image button's listener is set after construction and the image button already has a listener, the current listener is removed, and the new listener is specified as a mouse and mouse motion listener for the button. We'll discuss the image button listeners in more detail shortly.

ImageButton overrides getPreferredSize(); the preferred size is set to the size of the image plus twice the thickness of the border.

```
public Dimension getPreferredSize() {
    Util.waitForImage(this, image);
    prefSize.width  = image.getWidth (this) + (2*thickness);
    prefSize.height = image.getHeight(this) + (2*thickness);
    return prefSize;
}
```

The gjt.ImageButton paint() method determines whether the image button is raised or inset and calls the appropriate helper method to do the actual painting:

```
public void paint(Graphics g) {
```

2. See "Forcing a Container to Lay Out Its Components" on page 385.

```
   if(isRaised()) paintRaised();
   else           paintInset ();
}
```

As we stated earlier, image buttons fire action events and allow the registration of action listeners via the `processActionEvent()`, `addActionListener()` and `removeActionListener()` methods.

```
public void processActionEvent() {
  if(actionListener != null) {
    actionListener.actionPerformed(
       new ActionEvent(this,
                       ActionEvent.ACTION_PERFORMED,
                       "ImageButton Action"));
  }
  setArmed(false);
}
public synchronized void addActionListener(
                         ActionListener listener) {
  actionListener =
    AWTEventMulticaster.add(actionListener, listener);
}
public synchronized void removeActionListener(
                         ActionListener listener) {
  actionListener =
    AWTEventMulticaster.remove(actionListener, listener);
}
```

See "Firing AWT Events From Custom Components" on page 128 for an in-depth discussion of how the three methods listed above are used to fire events and register event listeners.

Now that we've covered the highlights of the `ImageButton` implementation, let's look at the `gjt.ImageButton` code in Example 22-1. As you're looking, notice how `createDisabledImage()` is called by `setEnabled()` such that a black-and-white (i.e., *disabled*) image is created and used only when necessary. Most image buttons will most likely live their entire lives without ever being disabled—as a result, it would be wasteful to create a black-and-white version of every image button's image when the image button is instantiated. This is another example of employing lazy instantiation, which we've seen previously in our "Employ Lazy Instantiation for Rarely Used Class Members" on page 306.

Example 22-1 gjt.ImageButton **Class Source Code**

```java
package gjt;

import java.awt.*;
import java.awt.image.FilteredImageSource;
import java.awt.event.*;
import java.util.Vector;
import gjt.image.*;

public class ImageButton extends Component {
  private static BlackAndWhiteFilter _bwFilter;
  private static int              _offset          = 1;
  private static int              _defaultThickness = 2;

  private ThreeDRectangle border  = new ThreeDRectangle(this);
  private boolean              isDisabled = false;
  private boolean              armed      = false;
  private Dimension            prefSize   = new Dimension(0,0);
  private int                  thickness;
  private Image                image, disabledImage;
  private ImageButtonListener  listener;
  private ActionListener       actionListener;
  private Bubble               bubble;
  private String               bubbleText;
  private BubbleThread         thread;
  private long                 bubbleInterval = 1000;

  public static void setDefaultThickness(int defThickness) {
     _defaultThickness = defThickness;
  }
  public static int getDefaultThickness() {
     return _defaultThickness;
  }
  public ImageButton() {
     this(null);
  }
  public ImageButton(Image image) {
     this(image, _defaultThickness);
  }
  public ImageButton(Image image, int thickness) {
     this(image, thickness, null);
  }
  public ImageButton(Image image, int thickness,
                     ImageButtonListener listener) {
     setThickness(thickness);

     if(image != null)
```

```java
        setImage(image);

    if(listener != null)
        setListener(listener);
    else
        setListener(new SpringyImageButtonListener());

    addMouseListener(new MouseAdapter() {
        public void mouseEntered(MouseEvent event) {
            if(bubbleText != null) {
                if(bubbleInterval == 0) {
                    showBubbleHelp();
                }
                else {
                    thread = new BubbleThread(ImageButton.this);
                    thread.start();
                }
            }
        }
        public void mousePressed(MouseEvent event) {
            if(bubble != null && bubble.isShowing()) {
                bubble.dispose();
            }
            if(thread != null && thread.isAlive())
                thread.stop();
        }
        public void mouseExited(MouseEvent event) {
            if(bubble != null && bubble.isShowing()) {
                bubble.dispose();
            }
            if(thread != null && thread.isAlive())
                thread.stop();
        }
    });
}
void showBubbleHelp() {
    if(bubbleText != null) {
        Dimension   size  = getSize();
        ImageButton button = ImageButton.this;
        Point scrnLoc = button.getLocationOnScreen();

        if(bubble == null)
            bubble = new Bubble(button, bubbleText);

        bubble.setLocation(scrnLoc.x,
                      scrnLoc.y + size.height + 2);
        bubble.setVisible(true);
    }
```

```
}
public void setBubbleHelp(String bubbleText) {
   this.bubbleText = bubbleText;
}
public void setBubbleInterval(long interval) {
   bubbleInterval = interval;
}
public long getBubbleInterval() {
   return bubbleInterval;
}
// Provision for programmatically manipulating image
// buttons. All functionality is delegated to listener,
// because the listener defines what it means to be armed
// or active.
public void activate  () { listener.activate(this);  }
public void arm       () { listener.arm(this);       }
public void disarm    () { listener.disarm(this);    }

public void setThickness(int thickness) {
   Assert.notFalse(thickness > 0);
   this.thickness = thickness;
   border.setThickness(this.thickness = thickness);
   if(isShowing()) {
      invalidate();
      getParent().validate();
      repaint();
   }
}
public void setArmed(boolean armed) {
   this.armed = armed;
}
public boolean isArmed() {
   return armed;
}
public void setImage(Image image) {
   Assert.notNull(image);
   Util.waitForImage(this, this.image = image);
   if(isShowing()) {
      invalidate();
      getParent().validate();
      repaint();
   }
}
public ImageButtonListener getListener() {
   return listener;
}
public void setListener(ImageButtonListener l) {
   if(listener != null) {
```

```
            removeMouseListener(listener);
            removeMouseMotionListener(listener);
      }
      listener = l;
      addMouseListener(listener);
      addMouseMotionListener(listener);
   }
   public Dimension getMinimumSize() {
      return prefSize;
   }
   public Dimension getPreferredSize() {
      Util.waitForImage(this, image);
      prefSize.width  = image.getWidth (this) + (2*thickness);
      prefSize.height = image.getHeight(this) + (2*thickness);
      return prefSize;
   }
   public boolean isRaised() {
      return border.isRaised();
   }
   public void setRaised() {
      border.raise();
      if(isShowing()) repaint();
   }
   public boolean isInset() {
      return ! border.isRaised();
   }
   public void setInset() {
      border.inset();
      if(isShowing()) repaint();
   }
   public boolean isDisabled() {
      return isDisabled;
   }
   public void setEnabled(boolean enable) {
      if(enable) {
         isDisabled = false;
         if(isShowing()) repaint();
      }
      else {
         isDisabled = true;

         if(disabledImage == null)
            createDisabledImage();

         if(isShowing()) repaint();
      }
   }
   public void setSize(int w, int h) {
```

```
      setBounds(getLocation().x, getLocation().y, w, h);
}
public void setBounds(int x, int y, int w, int h) {
   super.setBounds(x,y,w,h);
   border.setSize(w,h);
}
public void paint(Graphics g) {
   if(isRaised()) paintRaised();
   else            paintInset ();
}
public void paintInset() {
   Point      upperLeft = findUpperLeft();
   Graphics   g         = getGraphics();
   Image      image     = isDisabled() ?
                           disabledImage : this.image;
   Dimension size      = getSize();

   Assert.notNull(image);

   if(g != null) {
      border.clearInterior();
      g.drawImage(image,
                  upperLeft.x + thickness + _offset,
                  upperLeft.y + thickness + _offset,this);

      g.setColor(getBackground().darker());
      for(int i=0; i < _offset; ++i) {
         g.drawLine(thickness+i,thickness+i,
                    size.width-thickness-i,thickness+i);
         g.drawLine(thickness+i,thickness+i,
                    thickness+i,size.height-thickness-i);
      }
      border.paintInset();
      g.dispose();
   }
}
public void paintRaised() {
   Point      upperLeft = findUpperLeft();
   Graphics  g = getGraphics();
   Image     image = isDisabled() ? disabledImage : this.image;

   Assert.notNull(image);

   if(g != null) {
      border.clearInterior();
      g.drawImage(image, upperLeft.x + thickness,
                      upperLeft.y + thickness, this);
      border.paintRaised();
```

```
            g.dispose();
        }
    }
    public void processActionEvent() {
        if(actionListener != null) {
            actionListener.actionPerformed(
                new ActionEvent(this,
                                ActionEvent.ACTION_PERFORMED,
                                "ImageButton Action"));
        }
        setArmed(false);
    }
    public synchronized void addActionListener(
                        ActionListener listener) {
        actionListener =
            AWTEventMulticaster.add(actionListener, listener);
    }
    public synchronized void removeActionListener(
                        ActionListener listener) {
        actionListener =
            AWTEventMulticaster.remove(actionListener, listener);
    }
    private void createDisabledImage() {
        Assert.notNull(image);

        if(_bwFilter == null)
            _bwFilter = new BlackAndWhiteFilter();

        FilteredImageSource fis =
                new FilteredImageSource(image.getSource(),_bwFilter);
        Util.waitForImage(this, disabledImage=createImage(fis));
    }
    private Point findUpperLeft() {
        Dimension size = getSize();
        return new Point((size.width/2) -
                        (prefSize.width/2),
                        (size.height/2) -
                        (prefSize.height/2));
    }
}
class BubbleThread extends Thread {
    ImageButton button;
    public BubbleThread(ImageButton button) {
        this.button = button;
    }
    public void run() {
        long    start = System.currentTimeMillis();
        boolean done = false;
```

```
    while(!done) {
        long delta = System.currentTimeMillis() - start;
        if(delta > button.getBubbleInterval()) {
            button.showBubbleHelp();
            done = true;
        }
    }
  }
}
```

Bubble Help

An image button can be equipped with bubble help by invoking
`ImageButton.setBubbleHelp()`, which is passed a string to be displayed
when the image button's bubble help is shown. Figure 22-2 shows image buttons
in a toolbar[3] that are fitted with bubble help—the print button's bubble help is
currently shown.

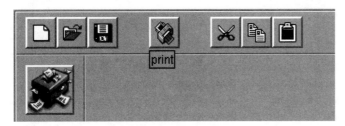

Figure 22-2 Bubble Help for Image Buttons

gjt.Bubble

Implementing bubble help was covered in "Bubble Help" on page 279. The GJT
provides a `Bubble` class that is nearly identical to the class covered on *page 280*,
so we won't bother to discuss the GJT version here. However, we will show you
the listing of the class in Example 22-2.

Example 22-2 `gjt.Bubble` **Class Source Code**

```
package gjt;

import java.awt.*;
import java.awt.event.*;

public class Bubble extends Window {
  private BubblePanel panel;
```

---

3.   See "Toolbars" on page 697 for a discussion of the `Toolbar` class.

```
   public Bubble(Component comp, String text) {
      super(Util.getFrame(comp));
      add(new BubblePanel(text), "Center");
   }
   public void setVisible(boolean b) {
      pack();
      super.setVisible(b);
   }
}
class BubblePanel extends Panel {
   String text;

   public BubblePanel(String text) {
      this.text = text;
      setForeground(Color.black);
   }
   public void paint(Graphics g) {
      Dimension    size = getSize();
      FontMetrics fm    = g.getFontMetrics();

      g.drawRect(0,0,size.width-1,size.height-1);
      g.drawString(text,2,fm.getAscent()+2);
   }
   public Dimension getPreferredSize() {
      Graphics    g  = getGraphics();
      FontMetrics fm = g.getFontMetrics();

      return new Dimension(fm.stringWidth(text)+4,
                           fm.getHeight()+4);
   }
}
```

ImageButtons and Bubble Help

Our focus on bubble help in this chapter is not on how the Bubble class is implemented, but instead on how image buttons go about displaying their bubbles. It would be very distracting if an image button displayed its bubble whenever the cursor entered the button, so a delay is incurred between the time the cursor enters the button and the time the bubble is displayed.

The string displayed in the bubble and the delay are both settable after construction by the setBubbleText() and setBubbleInterval() methods.

```
   public void setBubbleHelp(String bubbleText) {
      this.bubbleText = bubbleText;
   }
   public void setBubbleInterval(long interval) {
```

```
      bubbleInterval = interval;
   }
```

The delay is specified in milliseconds, and the default value is 1000, or one second.

`ImageButton.showBubbleHelp()` is the method that creates and displays the bubble.

```
   void showBubbleHelp() {
     if(bubbleText != null) {
        Dimension size = getSize();
        Point scrnLoc = getLocationOnScreen();

        if(bubble == null)
           bubble = new Bubble(this, bubbleText);

        bubble.setLocation(scrnLoc.x,
                           scrnLoc.y + size.height + 2);

        bubble.setVisible(true);
     }
   }
```

Once again, lazy instantiation is employed to ensure that an instance of `Bubble` is only created as needed. After obtaining the on-screen location of the image button, the bubble is created if necessary, and the bubble's location is set just below the image button. Then the bubble is displayed by invoking its `setVisible()` method.

The tricky part is implementing the delay, which is accomplished by an extension of the `Thread` class.

```
   class BubbleThread extends Thread {
     ImageButton button;

     public BubbleThread(ImageButton button) {
        this.button = button;
     }
     public void run() {
        long    start = System.currentTimeMillis();
        boolean done = false;

        while(!done) {
           long delta = System.currentTimeMillis() - start;

           if(delta > button.getBubbleInterval()) {
              button.showBubbleHelp();
```

```
                done = true;
            }
        }
    }
}
```

A `BubbleThread` must be created with a reference to the image button on whose behalf it is tracking the delay. The `run()` method, invoked whenever the thread is started, logs the start time, and spins its wheels until the current time minus the start time is greater than the image button's bubble interval, at which time it prods the image button to display its bubble help.

The last piece of the puzzle is how the image button creates and manages an instance of `BubbleThread`.

```
public ImageButton(Image image, int thickness,
                   ImageButtonListener listener) {
  ...
  aaddMouseListener(new MouseAdapter() {
    public void mouseEntered(MouseEvent event) {
        if(bubbleText != null) {
            if(bubbleInterval == 0) {
                showBubbleHelp();
            }
            else {
                thread = new BubbleThread(ImageButton.this);
                thread.start();
            }
        }
    }
    public void mousePressed(MouseEvent event) {
        if(bubble != null && bubble.isShowing()) {
            bubble.dispose();
        }
        if(thread != null && thread.isAlive())
            thread.stop();
    }
    public void mouseExited(MouseEvent event) {
        if(bubble != null && bubble.isShowing()) {
            bubble.dispose();
        }
        if(thread != null && thread.isAlive())
            thread.stop();
    }
  });
}
```

The image button's constructor adds a mouse listener to the button that handles mouse entered, pressed, and exited events.

When the mouse enters the image button, an instance of BubbleThread is created, and the thread is started if the button's bubbleText is non-null and the bubble interval is non-zero.

When a mouse press occurs, the bubble is disposed of if it is currently showing. Otherwise, if the thread is still running it is stopped. Stopping the thread ensures that the bubble will not be shown after the button is activated.

Like a mouse pressed event, when the mouse exits the button, the bubble is disposed of if it is currently showing. If the thread is still running, that means that the mouse entered and exited the button before the delay was incurred, and therefore the thread is once again stopped to ensure that the bubble is not shown after the mouse exits the button.

Image Button Listeners

As we discussed in "Encapsulating Event Handling in a Separate Listener Class" on page 121, if a component's event handling is a likely candidate for change, it is sometimes beneficial to separate event handling in a separate class. Doing so provides a base class for event handling that can be extended, and a hierarchy of event handling classes can then be developed.

We can envision a number of scenarios whereby event handling for image buttons is likely to be modified from the default behavior that mimics the event handling for a java.awt.Button. For instance, if image buttons are used to select an operation in a drawing program, the image buttons should stay depressed (or *stick*) when they are activated in order to indicate the current operation. On the other hand, if an image button is used as a +/- button in a tree control, the button should toggle the image it displays every time it is activated.

As a result, we have separated event handling in a separate class and provided a hierarchy of event listeners for image buttons. An image button's event listener may be specified when the image button is constructed, or after construction by invoking the setListener() method, as we have already seen.

Hierarchies of Image Button Listeners

The Graphic Java Toolkit provides a small hierarchy of image button listeners. Hierarchies of image button listeners take advantage of existing listeners to provide specialized behavior, as illustrated in Figure 22-3.

SpringyImageButtonListener encapsulates the algorithm for event handling similar that used for the java.awt.Button class.

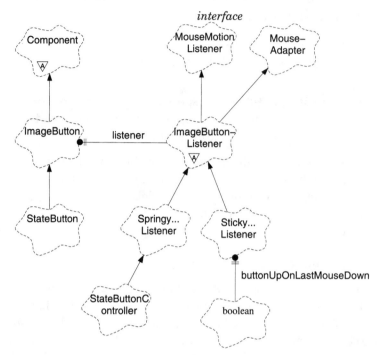

Figure 22-3 `gjt.ImageButtonListener` Class Diagram

`StickyImageButtonListener` implements an algorithm that causes the image button to *stick* after it is activated, in a manner similar to our hypothetical image buttons in a drawing program, as described above.

Finally, the `StateButtonListener` toggles the image displayed in the image button every time the image button is activated, in a manner similar to the hypothetical tree control discussed previously.

The ImageButtonListener Interface

Image button listeners extend a very simple class: `ImageButtonListener`:

```
abstract public class ImageButtonListener
              extends MouseAdapter
              implements MouseMotionListener {

  public void mouseMoved(MouseEvent event) { }
  public void mouseDragged(MouseEvent event) { }

  abstract public void activate  (ImageButton button);
  abstract public void arm       (ImageButton button);
  abstract public void disarm    (ImageButton button);
}
```

`ImageButtonListener` is a class instead of an interface because we want to extend `MouseAdapter` so that extensions do not have to implement all of the methods defined by the `MouseListener` interface. Also, notice that we provide no-op default behavior for mouse moved and dragged events—of course, extensions may give meaningful implementations to the methods if desired[4].

Image button listeners, as a result of the `ImageButtonListener` class, are both mouse and mouse motion listeners. Additionally, it is the image button listeners, not the image buttons themselves, that define what it means for the image button to be activated, armed, and disarmed.

gjt.SpringyImageButtonListener

The `SpringyImageButtonListener` class reacts to mouse and mouse motion events in a manner similar to a `java.awt.Button`.

`SpringyImageButtonListener` defines what it means for its image button to be activated, armed, and disarmed.

```
public void activate(ImageButton ib) {
   ib.processActionEvent();
   if( ! ib.isRaised()) ib.paintRaised();
   ib.setArmed(false);
}
```

When activated, the image button fires action events, which is accomplished by invoking the image button's `processActionEvent()` method. Subsequently, if the image button is not currently drawn raised, its `paintRaised()` method is invoked. Then its state is set to disarmed.

```
public void arm(ImageButton ib) {
   if( ! ib.isInset()) ib.paintInset();
   ib.setArmed(true);
}
```

When armed, the image button is painted inset if it is not already drawn inset, and its state is set to armed.

```
public void disarm(ImageButton ib) {
   if( ! ib.isRaised()) ib.paintRaised();
   ib.setArmed(false);
}
```

Disarming an image button equipped with a springy listener results in the image button being painted raised, and its state being set to disarmed.

---

4. Most image button listeners will not be concerned with mouse moved events, so implementing a no-op default saves them from having to do so.

SpringyImageButtonListener is listed in Example 22-3.

Example 22-3 gjt.SpringyImageButtonListener **Class Source Code**

```java
public class SpringyImageButtonListener extends
                                    ImageButtonListener {
   public void activate(ImageButton ib) {
      ib.processActionEvent();
      if( ! ib.isRaised()) ib.paintRaised();
      ib.setArmed(false);
   }
   public void arm(ImageButton ib) {
      if( ! ib.isInset()) ib.paintInset();
      ib.setArmed(true);
   }
   public void disarm(ImageButton ib) {
      if( ! ib.isRaised()) ib.paintRaised();
      ib.setArmed(false);
   }
   public void mousePressed(MouseEvent me) {
      ImageButton ib = (ImageButton)me.getComponent();

      if(! ib.isDisabled())
         arm(ib);
   }
   public void mouseClicked(MouseEvent me) {
      ImageButton ib = (ImageButton)me.getComponent();

      if(! ib.isDisabled() && ib.isArmed()) {
         activate(ib);
      }
   }
   public void mouseReleased(MouseEvent me) {
      ImageButton ib = (ImageButton)me.getComponent();

      if(ib.contains(me.getPoint().x, me.getPoint().y))
         mouseClicked(me);
   }
   public void mouseDragged(MouseEvent me) {
      ImageButton ib = (ImageButton)me.getComponent();

      if(! ib.isDisabled()) {
         int x = me.getPoint().x;
         int y = me.getPoint().y;

         if(ib.contains(x,y)) arm    (ib);
         else                 disarm(ib);
      }
   }
}
```

A mouse press arms the button if the button is enabled, and a mouse click activates the button if it is enabled and not currently armed. A mouse released event exhibits the same behavior as a mouse clicked event. Finally, a mouse dragged event checks to see if the drag occurred in the image button. If so, the image button is armed; if not, the image button is disarmed.

gjt.StickyImageButtonListener

StickyImageButtonListener also defines what it means to activate, arm and disarm its image button.

```
public void activate(ImageButton ib) {
  ib.processActionEvent();
  ib.setArmed(false);
}
public void arm(ImageButton ib) {
  ib.setArmed(true);
}
public void disarm(ImageButton ib) {
  ib.setArmed(false);
}
```

Activating an image button associated with a sticky image button results in the image button firing action events and disarming itself. Notice that while a springy listener ensures that an activated image button is painted raised, a sticky listener allows an activated button to be painted either raised or inset.

Arming an image button associated with a sticky listener simply sets the state of the button to armed. Whereas a springy listener paints its armed image button inset, a sticky listener does not define whether an armed button is painted raised or inset.

Finally, disarming an image button associated with a sticky listener results in the state of the image button being set to disarmed. Once again, a sticky listener is not concerned with how the button looks when it is disarmed.

StickyImageButtonListener is listed in Example 22-3.

Example 22-4 gjt.StickyImageButtonListener **Class Source Code**

```
public class StickyImageButtonListener extends
                          ImageButtonListener {
  private boolean buttonUpOnLastMouseDown = true;

  public void activate(ImageButton ib) {
    ib.processActionEvent();
    ib.setArmed(false);
  }
```

```java
public void arm(ImageButton ib) {
   ib.setArmed(true);
}
public void disarm(ImageButton ib) {
   ib.setArmed(false);
}
public void mousePressed(MouseEvent event) {
   ImageButton ib = (ImageButton)event.getSource();

   if(! ib.isDisabled()) {
      if(ib.isRaised()) ib.paintInset();
      else              ib.paintRaised();

      buttonUpOnLastMouseDown = ib.isRaised();
      arm(ib);
   }
}
public void mouseClicked(MouseEvent event) {
   ImageButton ib = (ImageButton)event.getSource();

   if(! ib.isDisabled() && ib.isArmed())
      activate(ib);
}
public void mouseReleased(MouseEvent event) {
   ImageButton ib = (ImageButton)event.getSource();
   Point      pt = event.getPoint();

   if(ib.contains(pt.x, pt.y))
      mouseClicked(event);
}
public void mouseDragged(MouseEvent event) {
   ImageButton ib = (ImageButton)event.getSource();

   if(! ib.isDisabled()) {
      Point loc = event.getPoint();

      if(ib.contains(loc.x,loc.y)) {
         if(buttonUpOnLastMouseDown) {
            if( ! ib.isRaised())
               ib.paintRaised();
```

```
            }
            else
            if(ib.isRaised())
                ib.paintInset();
        }
        else {
            if(buttonUpOnLastMouseDown) {
                if(ib.isRaised())
                    ib.paintInset();
            }
            else
                if( ! ib.isRaised())
                    ib.paintRaised();
        }
    }
  }
}
```

A mouse pressed event results in the image button being toggled between raised and inset. Additionally, `mousepressed()` arms the button.

A mouse clicked event activates the button, which results in the button firing an action event.

Most of the complexity resides in the `mouseDragged()` method. (Although we describe the algorithm implemented in `mouseDrag()`, it is much easier to see the behavior by running the `ImageButton` unit test and experimenting with the sticky image button). After a mouse drag is initiated inside the image button, dragging the mouse outside of the image button restores it to the state it was in before the mouse down occurred. Subsequently, dragging the mouse back into the image button toggles its state between inset and raised. Dragging the mouse out of the image button disarms the button; dragging the mouse back into the image button arms the button.

Exercising the Image Button and Its Listeners

Now that we've seen all the `gjt.ImageButton` code and the listeners that manage its mouse events—everything that's under the hood, so to speak—let's put this vehicle in motion and test drive it. To begin with, look at the `ImageButton` unit test in Figure 22-5.

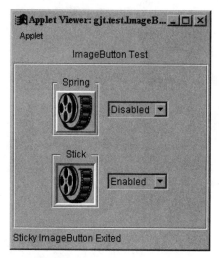

Figure 22-4 `gjt.ImageButton` Unit Test
The top image button is disabled and, therefore, drawn in black
and white. The applet's status line is updated whenever the
buttons are activated or the mouse enters or exits the buttons.

Before diving into the unit test code, let's take a brief look at how
`ImageButtonTest` employs `GridBagLayout`.

```
❶   gbc.anchor    = GridBagConstraints.NORTH;
    springyBox    = new Box(springyButton, "Spring");
❷   gbc.insets    = new Insets(10,0,0,0);
    gbl.setConstraints(springyBox, gbc);
    add(springyBox);

❸   gbc.gridwidth = GridBagConstraints.REMAINDER;
❹   gbc.insets    = new Insets(45,10,0,0);
    gbl.setConstraints(springyChoice, gbc);
    add(springyChoice);

❺   gbc.anchor    = GridBagConstraints.NORTH;
❻   gbc.gridwidth = 1;
    stickyBox     = new Box(stickyButton, "Stick");
    gbc.insets    = new Insets(10,0,0,0);
❼   gbc.weighty   = 1.0;
    gbl.setConstraints(stickyBox, gbc);
    add(stickyBox);

❽   gbc.gridwidth = GridBagConstraints.REMAINDER;
    gbc.insets    = new Insets(45,10,0,0);
    gbl.setConstraints(stickyChoice, gbc);
    add(stickyChoice);
```

In this unit test, `GridBagLayout` has four components to lay out: a `springyButton` and its enable/disable choice, and a `stickyButton` and its enable/disable choice. We set up the `GridBagConstraints` such that each pair of buttons resides in its own grid cell, like this:

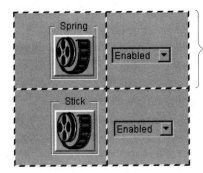

The springy and sticky buttons and their corresponding enable/disable buttons each reside in one grid cell. This is achieved by setting the anchor constraints to NORTH for the sticky and springy buttons (lines ❶ and ❺) and setting the gridwidth constraints to REMAINDER for the enable/disable choices (lines ❸ and ❽). Using REMAINDER for gridwidth ensures that the next component will be positioned underneath the previous component. Note that the anchor set in line ❺ is really unnecessary since the anchor has already been set in line ❶ for this instance of GridBagConstraints. However, we've left it in to draw attention to the sticky button positioning.

Notice that the insets are set for the top of the `springyButton` in lines Σ and the top and left for the enable/disable choice in line ❹. (The `stickyButton` and its enable/disable choice are set up the same way.) We've hardcoded the top insets for the enable/disable choices to 45 pixels in order to center them next to the springy and sticky buttons. We could have calculated this location, but we've hardcoded these insets to keep the code simple.

You might wonder why `gridwidth` in line œ and `weighty` in line – are set for the `stickyButton`. The `gridwidth` is set to override the previous `gridwidth` setting (line ❸), ensuring that the `stickyButton` is allotted one grid cell. The `weighty` constraint is somewhat conspicuous by its presence. We set `weighty` because when the window is resized, we want the sticky button and its enable/disable choice to retain their relative position below the springy button and its enable/disable choice. The `weighty` setting ensures the bottom button grid cells consume any extra space in the vertical direction, as in the next illustration:

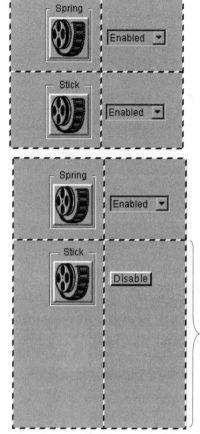

The `weighty` constraints are set to 1 for the bottom buttons. This ensures that these grid cells consume any extra space in the vertical direction when the window is stretched taller. The result is that the bottom-row buttons maintain their relative position below the top row of buttons.

Note that the buttons themselves do not resize to fit the space; only the grid cells change size.

Notice as you look through the code that `ImageButtonTest` class creates an instance of `StickyImageButtonListener` rather than using the default listener. The `stickyButton` is associated with a new instance of `StickyImageButtonListener`:[5]

```
stickyButton.setListener(
        new StickyImageButtonListener(stickyButton));
```

We have also separated the `ImageButtonTestPanel` out into its own file so that it can be used in other GJT unit tests.

---

5.   Note that we do not *have* to call `setListener()` for the `stickyButton`—
merely creating the listener will associate it with the image button.

Example 22-5 gjt.test.ImageButtonTest **Class Source Code**

```java
package gjt.test;
import java.applet.Applet;
import java.awt.*;

public class ImageButtonTest extends UnitTest {
  public String title() {
      return "ImageButton Test";
  }
  public Panel centerPanel() {
      return new ImageButtonTestPanel(this);
  }
}
```

Example 22-6 gjt.test.ImageButtonTestPanel **Class Source Code**

```java
package gjt.test;
import java.applet.Applet;
import java.awt.*;
import java.awt.event.*;
import gjt.*;

public class ImageButtonTestPanel extends Panel
                                 implements ActionListener,
                                 ItemListener {
  private Applet        applet;
  private ImageButton springyButton, stickyButton;
  private Choice        springyChoice, stickyChoice;

  public ImageButtonTestPanel(Applet applet) {
    Image                 image;
    Box                   springyBox, stickyBox;

    this.applet = applet;

    GridBagLayout       gbl = new GridBagLayout();
    GridBagConstraints gbc = new GridBagConstraints();
    image = applet.getImage(applet.getCodeBase(),
                       "gifs/filmstrip.gif");
    springyButton = new ImageButton();
    springyChoice = new Choice      ();
    stickyButton  = new ImageButton(image);
    stickyChoice  = new Choice      ();
    springyChoice.add("Enabled");
    springyChoice.add("Disabled");
    stickyChoice.add("Enabled");
    stickyChoice.add("Disabled");
```

```
            image = applet.getImage(applet.getCodeBase(),
                                 "gifs/filmstrip.gif");
        springyButton.setImage(image);
        stickyButton.addActionListener(this);
        springyButton.addActionListener(this);
        springyChoice.addItemListener(this);
        stickyChoice.addItemListener(this);
        springyButton.setBubbleHelp("Springy Button");
        stickyButton.setBubbleHelp("Sticky Button");
        springyButton.setBubbleInterval(5000);
        stickyButton.setBubbleInterval(500);

        IBTPMouseListener ml =
            new IBTPMouseListener(applet, springyButton,
                                    stickyButton);
        springyButton.addMouseListener(ml);
        stickyButton.addMouseListener(ml);
        stickyButton.setListener(new StickyImageButtonListener());

        setLayout(gbl);
        gbc.anchor     = GridBagConstraints.NORTH;
        springyBox     = new Box(springyButton, "Spring");
        gbc.insets     = new Insets(10,0,0,0);
        gbl.setConstraints(springyBox, gbc);
        add(springyBox);

        gbc.gridwidth = GridBagConstraints.REMAINDER;
        gbc.insets    = new Insets(45,10,0,0);
        gbl.setConstraints(springyChoice, gbc);
        add(springyChoice);

        gbc.anchor    = GridBagConstraints.NORTH;
        gbc.gridwidth = 1;
        stickyBox     = new Box(stickyButton, "Stick");
        gbc.insets    = new Insets(10,0,0,0);
        gbc.weighty   = 1.0;
        gbl.setConstraints(stickyBox, gbc);
        add(stickyBox);

        gbc.gridwidth = GridBagConstraints.REMAINDER;
        gbc.insets    = new Insets(45,10,0,0);
        gbl.setConstraints(stickyChoice, gbc);
        add(stickyChoice);
    }
    public void itemStateChanged(ItemEvent event) {
        String     s      = null;
        Choice     choice = (Choice)event.getSource();
        int        index  = choice.getSelectedIndex();
```

```
      ImageButton button = choice == stickyChoice ?
                        stickyButton : springyButton;

      if(button == stickyButton) s = "Sticky Button ";
      else                       s = "Springy Button ";
      if(index == 0) {
         button.setEnabled(true);
         s += "Enabled";
      }
      else {
         button.setEnabled(false);
         s += "Disabled";
      }
      applet.showStatus(s);
   }
   public void actionPerformed(ActionEvent event) {
      String status = new String();
      Object o = event.getSource();

      if(o == stickyButton)        status = "Sticky Fired";
      else if(o == springyButton) status = "Springy Fired";
      applet.showStatus(status);
   }
}
class IBTPMouseListener extends MouseAdapter {
   private Applet        applet;
   private ImageButton springy, sticky;
      public IBTPMouseListener(Applet applet,
                               ImageButton springy,
                               ImageButton sticky) {
      this.applet  = applet;
      this.springy = springy;
      this.sticky  = sticky;
   }
   public void mouseEntered(MouseEvent event) {
      String s = getButtonType(event.getSource());
      applet.showStatus(s + " ImageButton Entered");
   }
   public void mouseExited(MouseEvent event) {
      String s = getButtonType(event.getSource());
      applet.showStatus(s + " ImageButton Exited");
   }
   private String getButtonType(Object button) {
      if(button == springy) return "Springy";
      else                  return "Sticky";
   }
}
```

gjt.StateButton

Next we'll take a look at an `ImageButton` extension: `gjt.StateButton`.
`StateButton`, in conjunction with its listener (`StateButtonListener`), cycles
through a series of images; the next image in the series is displayed after the state
button has been activated. As you can see in Example 22-7, a `gjt.StateButton`
has a very modest implementation, mostly because its event handling has been
encapsulated in a different class.

Example 22-7 `gjt.StateButton` **Class Source Code**

```
package gjt;

import java.awt.Image;

public class StateButton extends ImageButton {
  private Image[] images;
  private int     state = 0;
  private int     numStates;

  public StateButton(Image[] images) {
    this(images, ImageButton.getDefaultThickness());
  }
  public StateButton(Image[] images, int thickness) {
    super(images[0], thickness, new StateButtonListener());
    this.images = images;
    numStates   = images.length;
    waitForImages();
  }
  public void advanceImage() {
    setImage(nextImage());
  }
  public Image nextImage() {
    if(state + 1 < numStates) state++;
    else                      state = 0;
    return images[state];
  }
  public int state() {
    return state;
  }
  private void waitForImages() {
    for(int i=0; i < images.length; ++i)
      Util.waitForImage(this, images[i]);
  }
}
```

`StateButton` explicitly sets its listener to an instance of
`StateButtonListener`.

Notice also that by virtue of the `gjt.Util.waitForImage()` method, which encapsulates a standard implementation of `MediaTracker`, a `StateButton` waits for all of its images to load before displaying any of them.

All instances of `StateButton`, of course, are fitted by default with a `StateButtonListener`. It is the listener that actually cycles the state button through the next image when the state button is activated. `StateButtonListener` also has a simple implementation, as illustrated in Example 22-8.

Example 22-8 `gjt.StateButtonListener` **Class Source Code**

```
package gjt;

import java.awt.Event;

class StateButtonListener extends SpringyImageButtonListener {
   public void activate(ImageButton ib) {
      ((StateButton)ib).advanceImage();
      super.activate(ib);
   }
}
```

Notice particularly the simplicity and readability of `StateButtonListener`. It's only six lines of code, yet it serves its associated `StateButton` by cycling through a series of images; each time a mouse up is detected in the `StateButton`, the button's image is set to the next image in the array. In addition, `SpringyImageButtonListener`, which is the superclass of `StateButtonListener`, takes care of arming, disarming, and activating the image button.

Exercising the StateButton and Its Listeners

Figure 22-5 shows sample output from the unit test implementation of the `gjt.StateButton` class.

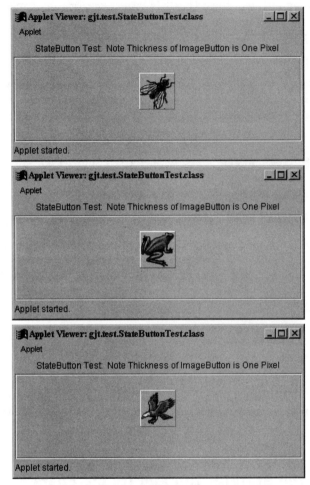

Figure 22-5 gjt.StateButton Unit Test
The series of three pictures results from three consecutive mouse clicks.

Now let's look at the StateButtonTest class in Example 22-9. As you look through the code, notice how gjt.test.StateButtonTest obtains three images and passes in an array to the StateButton constructor. StateButton waits for all the images to be loaded, so the unit test does not concern itself with this. Also pay attention to the use of FlowLayout, which centers the state button with a horizontal gap of 20 and a vertical gap of 20.

Finally, note that we have set the thickness of the image button to one pixel.

Example 22-9 `gjt.test.StateButtonTest` **Class Source Code**

```
package gjt.test;
import java.applet.Applet;
import java.awt.*;
import java.net.URL;
import gjt.StateButton;

public class StateButtonTest extends UnitTest {
  public String title() {
     return "StateButton Test:  Note Thickness of " +
            "ImageButton is One Pixel";
  }
  public Panel  centerPanel() {
     return new StateButtonTestPanel(this);
  }
}
class StateButtonTestPanel extends Panel {
  private URL          codeBase;
  private Image[]      images;
  private StateButton button;

  public StateButtonTestPanel(Applet applet) {
     codeBase  = applet.getCodeBase();
     images    = new Image[3];
     images[0] = applet.getImage(codeBase, "gifs/fly.gif");
     images[1] = applet.getImage(codeBase, "gifs/frog.gif");
     images[2] = applet.getImage(codeBase, "gifs/eagle.gif");

     button    = new StateButton(images, 1);
     setLayout(new FlowLayout(FlowLayout.CENTER, 20, 20));
     add       (button);
  }
}
```

Summary

In the course of developing the GJT `ImageButton` and `StateButton` classes, we've tried to highlight the benefits of separating event handling from the custom component itself. This leads to more modular and maintainable code that can be easily extended and utilized for a range of purposes.

We've also once again looked `GridBagLayout` in use, showing yet another example of it in action.

CHAPTER
23

Toolbars

Most graphical user interfaces today include a toolbar—a row of image buttons at the top of a window. The image buttons contained in a toolbar are typically used as shortcuts to the most common tasks the software in question provides. The Graphic Java Toolkit provides a `Toolbar` class, which we explore in this chapter.

Overview of Toolbar

It is important to realize that there is an underlying abstraction present in the concept of a toolbar: a row of image buttons. The GJT also provides a class that encapsulates that abstraction: an `ImageButtonPanel`, which is a `Panel` containing image buttons that can be oriented either horizontally or vertically. Our discussion of `gjt.Toolbar` encompasses the `ImageButtonPanel`, its mouse event controllers, as well as the `Toolbar` class itself.

We'll start by looking at Figure 23-1, which shows the relationships maintained by `gjt.Toolbar`.

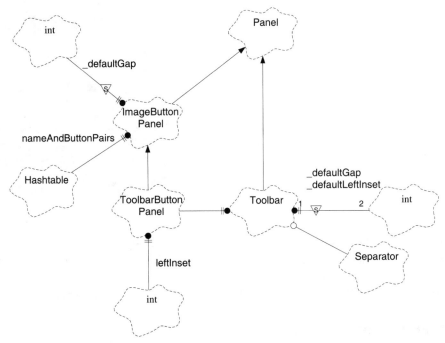

Figure 23-1 gjt.Toolbar Class Diagram

`gjt.Toolbar` is an extension of `Container`, which qualifies it as a lightweight container[1]. `Toolbar` sets its layout manager to an instance of `BorderLayout` and lays out a `ToolbarButtonPanel` (an extension of `ImageButtonPanel`) as its north component and a separator as its south component, as illustrated in Figure 23-2. Note that `Toolbar` does not maintain a reference to the `Separator`, so the class diagram depicts the relationship between a toolbar and separator as a *uses* relationship, not a *has* relationship. `Toolbar` does, however, maintain a reference to an instance of `ToolbarButtonPanel`, and therefore that relationship is depicted as a *has* relationship.

Figure 23-2 A Toolbar
The `Toolbar` has a `ToolbarButtonPanel` as its north component and a separator as its south component.

---

1.   See "Lightweight Components" on page 475.

gjt.Toolbar itself is a very simple custom component that delegates most of its work to the ToolBarButtonPanel it contains. In fact, if you look at Figure 23-1, it is really the ImageButtonPanel (superclass of ToolbarButtonPanel) that we need to investigate first. ToolbarButtonPanel extends ImageButtonPanel but adds very little to it. Therefore, before we look at the Toolbar class implementation, we'll cover ImageButtonPanel in some detail.

gjt.ImageButtonPanel

As is evident from its name, ImageButtonPanel is an extension of Panel that contains image buttons. An ImageButtonPanel can be oriented either horizontally or vertically; as a result, an ImageButtonPanel sets its layout manager to an instance of gjt.RowLayout or gjt.ColumnLayout, depending upon its orientation[2].

ImageButtonPanel Associations and Responsibilities

Table 23-1 lists the responsibilities of an ImageButtonPanel.

Table 23-1 gjt.ImageButtonPanel **Responsibilities**

Methods	Description

void setController(
  ImageButtonPanelController
  controller)
	Sets the controller type.

Insets getInsets()	Sets insets.
ImageButton add(Image image, String name)	Creates an image button, adds it to a panel, and returns a reference to the newly created image button.
ImageButton add(Image image)	Creates an image button with a default name, adds it to a panel, and returns a reference to the newly created image button.
void add(ImageButton button)	Adds an existing image button.
void add(ImageButton button, String name)	Adds an existing image button with a specific name.

2. See *Components, Containers, and Layout Managers* on page 373 for a discussion of gjt.RowLayout and gjt.ColumnLayout.

Table 23-1 `gjt.ImageButtonPanel` **Responsibilities (Continued)**

Methods	Description
`ImageButton getButtonByName(` `String name)`	Returns an `ImageButton` by name.
`String getImageButtonName(` `ImageButton button)`	
`void addSpacer(` `int sizeInPixels)`	Adds space between buttons.

Also look at Table 23-2, which shows the associations of an `ImageButtonPanel`.

Table 23-2 `gjt.ImageButtonPanel` **Associations**

Variables	Description
`static int _defaultGap`	Specifies the default gap between image buttons as 5 pixels.
`Hashtable nameAndButtonPairs`	Keeps track of image buttons by name.

A gap of five pixels is used by default between image buttons in an `ImageButtonPanel`. If a different gap is desired, clients can specify a gap at construction time. An `ImageButtonPanel` also keeps track of its buttons by name; when clients add an image button to an `ImageButtonPanel`, they can optionally specify a name for the image button. An `ImageButtonPanel` is equipped to return the appropriate image button, given its name, or to return a name, given an image button.

You'll notice that `ImageButtonPanel` provides three constructors, offering a range of settings at construction time. The last of the constructors sets the appropriate layout manager, as determined by the orientation of the `ImageButtonPanel`:

```
public ImageButtonPanel(Orientation orient, Orientation horient,
                        Orientation vorient, int gap) {
   Assert.notFalse    (orient == Orientation.HORIZONTAL ||
                        orient == Orientation.VERTICAL);

   if(orient == Orientation.VERTICAL)
      setLayout(new ColumnLayout(horient, vorient, gap));
   else
      setLayout(new RowLayout(horient, vorient, gap));
}
```

The three orientations specified in this constructor are:

- `Orientation orient` – orientation of `ImageButtonPanel`

- `Orientation horient` – horizontal orientation of image buttons within panel
- `Orientation vorient` – vertical orientation of image buttons within panel

`ImageButtonPanel` arbitrarily sets its insets to (10, 10, 10, 10). If different insets are desired, `ImageButtonPanel` must be subclassed.[3]

The `add()` methods enable clients to add an image button to an `ImageButtonPanel`:

```
public ImageButton add(Image image, String name) {
  ImageButton button = new ImageButton(image);
  add(button);
  nameAndButtonPairs.put(name, button);
  return button;
}
```

In this case, the image button panel creates an image button using the image, adds the image button to itself, and then returns the image button to the caller. Clients can add image buttons with or without a name. If they do provide a name, `getButtonByName(String)` and `getButtonName(ImageButton)` can be called to return the appropriate name or button.

Space can be added between the image buttons of an `ImageButtonPanel` by specifying a pixel size for the space.

```
public void addSpacer(int sizeInPixels) {
  Assert.notFalse(sizeInPixels > 0);
  Canvas spacer = new Canvas();
  spacer.resize(sizeInPixels, sizeInPixels);
  add(spacer);
}
```

`addSpacer()` creates a `Canvas`, sizes it to the size passed in, and adds the `Canvas` to itself in order to provide spacing.

Now that we have a high-level understanding of `ImageButtonPanel`, let's take a look at its implementation in Example 23-1.

Example 23-1 `gjt.ImageButtonPanel` **Class Source Code**

```
package gjt;
import java.awt.*;
import java.util.Enumeration;
import java.util.Hashtable;
```

3. For more information about insets, see the discussion of *Peers and Insets* on page 379.

```java
public class ImageButtonPanel extends Panel {
   static private int _defaultGap = 5;
   private Hashtable nameAndButtonPairs = new Hashtable();

   public ImageButtonPanel(Orientation orient) {
      this(orient, Orientation.CENTER,
                   Orientation.CENTER, _defaultGap);
   }
   public ImageButtonPanel(Orientation orient, int gap) {
      this(orient, Orientation.CENTER,
                   Orientation.CENTER, gap);
   }
   public ImageButtonPanel(Orientation orient,
                           Orientation horient,
                           Orientation vorient, int gap) {
      Assert.notFalse(orient == Orientation.HORIZONTAL ||
                   orient == Orientation.VERTICAL);
      if(orient == Orientation.VERTICAL)
         setLayout(new ColumnLayout(horient, vorient, gap));
      else
         setLayout(new RowLayout(horient, vorient, gap));
   }
   public Insets getInsets() { return new Insets(10,10,10,10); }

   public ImageButton add(Image image, String name) {
      ImageButton button = new ImageButton(image);
      add(button);
      nameAndButtonPairs.put(name, button);
      return button;
   }
   public ImageButton add(Image image) {
      return add(image, "noname");
   }
   public void add(ImageButton button) {
      add(button, "noname");
   }
   public void add(ImageButton button, String name) {
      nameAndButtonPairs.put(name, button);
      super.add(button);
   }
   public ImageButton getButtonByName(String name) {
      return (ImageButton)nameAndButtonPairs.get(name);
   }
   public String getButtonName(ImageButton button) {
      Enumeration e = nameAndButtonPairs.keys();
      ImageButton nbutt;
      String nstr;
      while(e.hasMoreElements()) {
         nstr = (String)e.nextElement();
```

```
        nbutt = (ImageButton)nameAndButtonPairs.get(nstr);
        if(nbutt.equals(button))
            return nstr;
      }
      return null;
   }
   public void addSpacer(int sizeInPixels) {
      Assert.notFalse(sizeInPixels > 0);
      Canvas spacer = new Canvas();
      spacer.setSize(sizeInPixels, sizeInPixels);
      add(spacer);
   }
}
```

At this point, you may be scratching your head wondering, where's the toolbar? In fact, there isn't a toolbar without the ImageButtonPanel (the superclass of ToolbarButtonPanel). Now that we've covered ImageButtonPanel, we're ready to take a look at the implementation of gjt.Toolbar.

gjt.Toolbar Associations and Responsibilities

As pointed out in the previous sections, gjt.Toolbar is a simple class that delegates a good deal of its functionality to an enclosed ToolbarButtonPanel. Table 23-3 lists the responsibilities of the Toolbar class.

Table 23-3 gjt.Toolbar **Responsibilities**

Methods	Description
ImageButton add(Image image)	Creates, adds, and returns an image button.
void add(ImageButton button)	Adds a new image button.
void addSpacer(int sizeInPixels)	Adds space between image buttons.

Table 23-4 lists the associations of a gjt.Toolbar.

Table 23-4 gjt.Toolbar **Associations**

Variables	Description
static int _defaultGap	Specifies the default gap as 5 pixels.
static int _defaultLeftInset	Specifies the default left inset to 0 pixels.
ToolbarButtonPanel buttonpanel	Is the panel in which the buttons reside.

Now, let's take a look at the gjt.Toolbar source code in Example 23-2. Notice that Toolbar uses a BorderLayout and specifies a ToolbarButtonPanel as the north component and a separator as the south component.

Example 23-2 gjt.Toolbar **Class Source Code**

```
public class Toolbar extends Container {
   static private int _defaultGap      = 0;
   static private int _defaultLeftInset = 0;
   private ToolbarButtonPanel buttonPanel;

   public Toolbar() {
      this(_defaultLeftInset, _defaultGap);
   }
   public Toolbar(int leftInset, int gap) {
      buttonPanel = new ToolbarButtonPanel(leftInset, gap);

      setLayout(new BorderLayout());
      add(buttonPanel, "North");
      add(new Separator(), "South");
   }
   public ImageButton add(Image image) {
      return buttonPanel.add(image);
   }
   public void add(ImageButton button) {
      buttonPanel.add(button);
   }
   public void addSpacer(int sizeInPixels) {
      Assert.notFalse(sizeInPixels > 0);
      buttonPanel.addSpacer(sizeInPixels);
   }
}
```

Both add() methods simply delegate responsibility to the associated image button panel.

Toolbar delegates its responsibilities to a ToolbarButtonPanel, which extends ImageButtonPanel, hardcodes its orientation to horizontal, and hardcodes the orientation of the buttons that it contains to left in the horizontal direction and centered in the vertical direction. ToolbarButtonPanel also overrides insets to (5, leftInset, 5, 5), where leftInset is specified by the Toolbar. Here is the implementation of ToolbarButtonPanel:

```
class ToolbarButtonPanel extends ImageButtonPanel {
   private int leftInset;
   public ToolbarButtonPanel(int leftInset, int gap) {
      super(Orientation.HORIZONTAL,
            Orientation.LEFT,
            Orientation.CENTER,
            gap);
      this.leftInset = leftInset;
   }
```

```
   public Insets getInsets() {
      return new Insets(5,leftInset,5,5);
   }
}
```

ExclusiveImageButtonPanel

The idea behind `ExclusiveImageButtonPanel` is to provide an extension of `ImageButtonPanel` that fits each image button in the panel with a sticky listener, and ensures that only one image button in the panel is painted inset at any given time (thus the rationale for *exclusive*).

Notice that `ExclusiveImageButtonPanel` has nothing to do with toolbars, per se, but it is a useful extension of `ImageButtonPanel`, and is used in the `Toolbar` unit test, so we'll take the opportunity to discuss it here.

`ExclusiveImageButtonPanel` overrides the `add()` methods implemented by `ImageButtonPanel` in order to set each of its image button's listeners to a `StickyImageButtonListener`.

Additionally, each image button has the `ExclusiveImageButtonPanel` added to the image button as an action listener—`ExclusiveImageButtonPanel` implements the `ActionListener` interface—more about this in a moment.

The implementation of `ExclusiveImageButtonPanel` is pretty straightforward, so let's take a look at the entire listing and then discuss it afterwards.

Example 23-3 `gjt.ExclusiveImageButtonPanel` **Class Source Code**

```
public class ExclusiveImageButtonPanel extends ImageButtonPanel
                           implements ActionListener {
   private EventQueue q = new EventQueue();
   private ImageButton insetButton;
   private ImageButtonListener stickyListener =
            new StickyImageButtonListener();

   public ExclusiveImageButtonPanel(Orientation orient) {
      this(orient, 5);
   }
   public ExclusiveImageButtonPanel(Orientation orient,
                                    int gap) {
      super(orient, gap);
   }
   public ExclusiveImageButtonPanel(Orientation orient,
                                    Orientation horient,
                                    Orientation vorient,
```

```
                                        int gap) {
        super(orient, horient, vorient, gap);
    }
    public void actionPerformed(ActionEvent event) {
        ImageButton button = (ImageButton)event.getSource();
        if(button.isRaised() && button == insetButton) {
            insetButton = null;
        }
        else {
            if(insetButton != null && insetButton != button) {
                MouseEvent mouseEvent =
                    new MouseEvent(insetButton,
                            MouseEvent.MOUSE_PRESSED,
                            System.currentTimeMillis(),
                            0, 0, 0, 1, false);

                q.postEvent(mouseEvent);
            }
            insetButton = button;
        }
    }
    public void add(ImageButton button) {
        super.add(button);
        attachListeners(button);
    }
    public ImageButton add(Image image) {
        ImageButton button = super.add(image);
        attachListeners(button);
        return button;
    }
    public ImageButton add(Image image, String name) {
        ImageButton button = super.add(image, name);
        attachListeners(button);
        return button;
    }
    protected void attachListeners(ImageButton button) {
        button.setListener(stickyListener);
        button.addActionListener(this);
    }
}
```

Each of the ExclusiveImageButtonPanel add() methods invokes the attachListeners() method.

```
protected void attachListeners(ImageButton button) {
  button.setListener(stickyListener);
  button.addActionListener(this);
}
```

`attachListeners()` sets the image button's listener to a sticky listener, and adds the `ExclusiveImageButtonPanel` as an action listener of the image button. As a result, when one of the image buttons in the panel is activated, `ExclusiveImageButtonPanel.actionPerformed()` is invoked.

```
private EventQueue q = new EventQueue();
...
public void actionPerformed(ActionEvent event) {
   ImageButton button = (ImageButton)event.getSource();

   if(button.isRaised()) {
      insetButton = null;
   }
   else {
      if(insetButton != null && insetButton != button) {
         MouseEvent mouseEvent =
            new MouseEvent(insetButton,
                          MouseEvent.MOUSE_PRESSED,
                          System.currentTimeMillis(),
                          0, 0, 0, 1, false);

         q.postEvent(mouseEvent);
      }
      insetButton = button;
   }
}
```

If the button that fired the action event is raised, then we know that it was the button that was previously inset. As a result, the `insetButton` is set to `null` and no further action is taken.

However, if the button is not painted raised (meaning it is inset), we must cause the button that was previously painted inset[4] to be painted raised. Remember, we want only one button to be painted inset at any given time, so if one button is currently painted inset and another button is clicked, causing it to be painted inset, we want the button previously painted inset to pop up.

In any event, to cause the button previously painted inset to pop up, we could just invoke `insetButton.paintRaised()` to achieve the desired visual effect. However, remember that when a button equipped with a sticky listener is popped up, it fires an action event, and therefore painting the button raised will not cause the button to fire the action event.

---

4. This has nothing to do with The Artist Formerly Known As Prince.

In order to pop the button up and fire an action event, we create a mouse event, and add it to our own private event queue. Posting the event to the event queue[5] will cause the button's listener to handle the mouse down event, which will paint the button raised and fire an action event.

Exercising the Toolbar

Now that we have a fairly detailed understanding of `Toolbar` and `ExclusiveImageButtonPanel`, let's take a look at the unit test that exercises them both. Figure 23-3 shows the unit test for the `Toolbar` class.

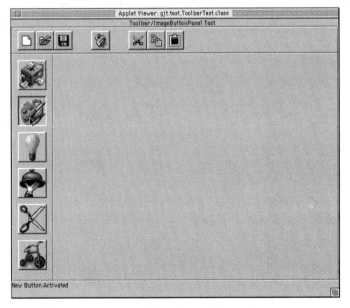

Figure 23-3 `gjt.Toolbar` Unit Test (screenshot from 1.02 GJT on Mac)
Notice the sticky button painted inset, second button from the top.

To see how the `ToolbarTest` is laid out, refer to Figure 23-4.

---

5. See "Propagating Events to Containers" on page 145.

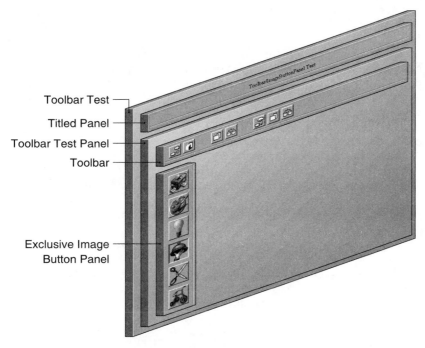

Figure 23-4 `ToolbarTest` Layout Diagram

Now that we've seen the layout characteristics of the unit test, let's take a look at its implementation. As usual, to make the most out of this discussion, you will want to run `appletviewer` on `ToolbarTest.html` in order to see the unit test in action. You may also want to refer back to Figure 23-3 and Figure 23-4 as you read through the code.

As you look through the unit test in Example 23-4 on page 711, notice that the `ToolbarTest` class sets its layout manager to a `BorderLayout` and specifies a `Toolbar` as the north component and an `ExclusiveImageButtonPanel` as its west component. Remember from our earlier discussion (see *ExclusiveImageButtonPanel* on page 705) that an `ExclusiveImageButtonPanel` fits all of its image buttons with a `StickyImageButtonListener`, so when an image button is activated, it stays painted inset until another image button is activated.

There are a couple methods worth pointing out before we look at the code in its entirety. To begin with, the `makeToolbar()` method is used to create a `Toolbar` and add image buttons to it.

```java
private Toolbar makeToolbar(Applet app, URL cb) {
Toolbar tb  = new Toolbar(10, 0);

newButton   = tb.add(app.getImage(cb, "gifs/new.gif"));
openButton  = tb.add(app.getImage(cb, "gifs/open.gif"));
diskButton  = tb.add(app.getImage(cb, "gifs/disk.gif"));

newButton.setBubbleHelp("create");
newButton.setBubbleInterval(0);
openButton.setBubbleHelp("open");
diskButton.setBubbleHelp("save");

tb.addSpacer(newButton.getPreferredSize().width);

printButton = tb.add(app.getImage(cb, "gifs/print.gif"));

tb.addSpacer(newButton.getPreferredSize().width);

cutButton   = tb.add(app.getImage(cb, "gifs/cut.gif"));
copyButton  = tb.add(app.getImage(cb, "gifs/copy.gif"));
pasteButton = tb.add(app.getImage(cb, "gifs/paste.gif"));

cutButton.setBubbleHelp  ("cut it out");
copyButton.setBubbleHelp ("copy");
pasteButton.setBubbleHelp("paste");
printButton.setBubbleHelp("print");

newButton.addActionListener  (this);
openButton.addActionListener (this);
diskButton.addActionListener (this);
printButton.addActionListener(this);
cutButton.addActionListener  (this);
copyButton.addActionListener (this);
pasteButton.addActionListener(this);

return tb;
}
```

The `Applet` is passed in order to use its `getImage()` method. As a convenience, we don't have to create the image buttons that will reside in the toolbar; we just pass the toolbar the images we want associated with the image buttons, and the toolbar creates and returns the image buttons.

Bubble help is also specified for each image button in the toolbar[6]. We specify zero as the bubble interval for the "new" button, so that it pops up without a delay.

The `makePalette()` method creates a new `ExclusiveImageButtonPanel`— the west component—which is constructed with vertical, center, and top orientations. The vertical orientation specifies the orientation of the panel itself. The center and top orientations specify the horizontal and vertical orientations of the image buttons within the `ExclusiveImageButtonPanel`:

```
iconPalette = new ExclusiveImageButtonPanel(
                        Orientation.VERTICAL,
                        Orientation.CENTER,
                        Orientation.TOP, 10);
```

Example 23-4 lists the unit test for toolbars in its entirety.

Example 23-4 `gjt.test.ToolbarTest` **Class Source Code**

```
package gjt.test;
import java.net.URL;
import java.awt.*;
import java.awt.event.*;
import java.applet.Applet;
import gjt.*;

public class ToolbarTest extends UnitTest {
  public String title() {
     return "Toolbar/ImageButtonPanel Test";
  }
  public Panel centerPanel() {
     return new ToolbarTestPanel(this);
  }
}
class ToolbarTestPanel extends Panel implements ActionListener {
  Applet       applet;
  ImageButton newButton,   openButton, diskButton,
  printButton, cutButton,   copyButton,
  pasteButton;

  public ToolbarTestPanel(Applet applet) {
     this.applet = applet;
     setLayout(new BorderLayout());
     add(makeToolbar(applet, applet.getCodeBase()), "North");
     add(makePalette(applet, applet.getCodeBase()), "West");
  }
```

6. See "Bubble Help" on page 675.

```
public void actionPerformed(ActionEvent event) {
   Object target = event.getSource();
   String s = null;

   if(target == newButton)   s = "New Button Activated";
   if(target == openButton)  s = "Open Button Activated";
   if(target == diskButton)  s = "Disk Button Activated";
   if(target == printButton) s = "Print Button Activated";
   if(target == cutButton)   s = "Cut Button Activated";
   if(target == copyButton)  s = "Copy Button Activated";
   if(target == pasteButton) s = "Paste Button Activated";

   applet.showStatus(s);
}
private Toolbar makeToolbar(Applet app, URL cb) {
   Toolbar tb  = new Toolbar(10, 0);

   newButton  = tb.add(app.getImage(cb, "gifs/new.gif"));
   openButton = tb.add(app.getImage(cb, "gifs/open.gif"));
   diskButton = tb.add(app.getImage(cb, "gifs/disk.gif"));

   newButton.setBubbleHelp("create");
   newButton.setBubbleInterval(0);
   openButton.setBubbleHelp("open");
   diskButton.setBubbleHelp("save");

   tb.addSpacer(newButton.getPreferredSize().width);

   printButton = tb.add(app.getImage(cb, "gifs/print.gif"));

   tb.addSpacer(newButton.getPreferredSize().width);

   cutButton   = tb.add(app.getImage(cb, "gifs/cut.gif"));
   copyButton  = tb.add(app.getImage(cb, "gifs/copy.gif"));
   pasteButton = tb.add(app.getImage(cb, "gifs/paste.gif"));

   cutButton.setBubbleHelp  ("cut it out");
   copyButton.setBubbleHelp ("copy");
   pasteButton.setBubbleHelp("paste");
   printButton.setBubbleHelp("print");

   newButton.addActionListener  (this);
   openButton.addActionListener (this);
   diskButton.addActionListener (this);
   printButton.addActionListener(this);
   cutButton.addActionListener  (this);
   copyButton.addActionListener (this);
   pasteButton.addActionListener(this);
```

```
        return tb;
    }
    private Panel makePalette(Applet app, URL cb) {
        ExclusiveImageButtonPanel iconPalette;
        ImageButton                ballotButton;
        Panel                      iconPalettePanel = new Panel();

        iconPalette = new ExclusiveImageButtonPanel(
                        Orientation.VERTICAL,
                        Orientation.CENTER,
                        Orientation.TOP, 10);
        ballotButton =
        iconPalette.add(app.getImage(cb,"gifs/ballot_box.gif"));

        iconPalette.add(app.getImage(cb,"gifs/palette.gif"));
        iconPalette.add(app.getImage(cb,"gifs/light_bulb1.gif"));
        iconPalette.add(app.getImage(cb,"gifs/Dining.gif"));
        iconPalette.add(app.getImage(cb,"gifs/scissors.gif"));
        iconPalette.add(app.getImage(cb,"gifs/tricycle.gif"));

        iconPalettePanel = new Panel();
        iconPalettePanel.setLayout(new BorderLayout());
        iconPalettePanel.add      (iconPalette, "Center");
        iconPalettePanel.add      (new Separator(), "East");

        return iconPalettePanel;
    }
}
```

Summary

We've discussed the implementation of the GJT's `Toolbar` class, along with the
`ImageButtonPanel` and `ExclusiveImageButtonPanel` classes. Image
buttons and toolbars are staples of user interface design, and since they are absent
from the AWT, we've chosen to provide them with the Graphic Java Toolkit.

CHAPTER

24

Dialogs

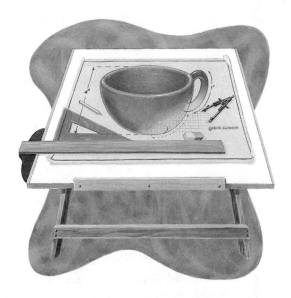

We introduced dialogs in the first half of *Graphic Java*—see "java.awt.Dialog" on page 286, where we mentioned that the AWT is pretty thin when it comes to dialogs. The AWT provides a basic `Dialog` class and only one `Dialog` extension: a `FileDialog` for selecting a file.

The Graphic Java Toolkit (GJT) provides six custom dialogs that are commonly found in user interface toolkits:

- `FontDialog`
- `ProgressDialog`
- `WorkDialog`
- `MessageDialog`
- `YesNoDialog`
- `QuestionDialog`

We will discuss all of the GJT dialogs in this chapter, with the exception of `FontDialog`, which is covered in "FontDialog" on page 755. Not only does the GJT fill the dialog gap created by the AWT, but discussing the dialogs listed above should considerably enhance your understanding of dialogs and their nuances. Additionally, we will introduce a couple of custom components used by the dialog classes that you may find useful in other contexts, namely `ButtonPanel` and `Postcard`.

The ProgressDialog displays a bargauge[1] that tracks a time-consuming task.

The MessageDialog displays a message and comes equipped with a lone button for dismissing the dialog.

Both YesNoDialog and QuestionDialog pose a question. The YesNoDialog provides two buttons (a *yes* button and a *no* button) for dismissing the dialog, while the QuestionDialog provides a textfield for typing in a response.

The WorkDialog class is the superclass of the YesNoDialog, MessageDialog, and QuestionDialog classes and provides a button panel and a work area in which to display a panel.

The GJT Dialog Classes

Figure 24-1 illustrates the relationships between the GJT dialog classes. Three fundamental abstractions are implemented in the GJT's dialog classes:

- GJTDialog takes care of low-level dialog gruntwork.
- ButtonPanel is a Panel extension that maintains a row of buttons centered at the bottom of the panel.
- WorkDialog is composed of a ButtonPanel to provide a dialog that has a work panel centered in the dialog and a row of buttons at the bottom of the dialog.

1. See "Separators and Bargauges" on page 575.

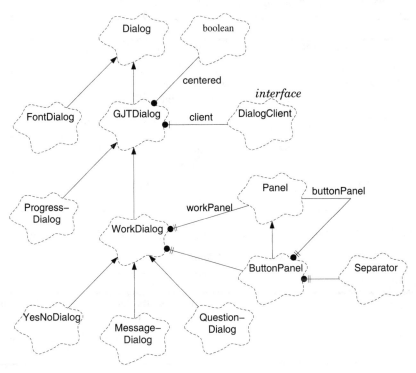

Figure 24-1 GJT Dialog Overview

GJTDialog

GJTDialog represents the most general abstraction embodied by the GJT dialog classes. GJTDialog takes care of a pair of primitive dialog responsibilities—centering itself in its parent's frame, and notifying a client when it has been dismissed or cancelled.

The responsibilities (public methods) of the GJTDialog class are listed in Table 24-1.

Table 24-1 `gjt.GJTDialog` **Responsibilities**

Methods	Description
`void setCentered(boolean b)`	Determines whether the dialog should be centered in its frame when shown.
`void setClient(DialogClient c)`	Associates an instance of `DialogClient` with the dialog.
`void dispose()`	Brings the dialog's frame to the front of other windows when the dialog is dismissed and notifies the dialog client of the dialog's dismissal.
`void setVisible(boolean b)`	Optionally centers the dialog in its frame and shows the dialog.

Table 24-2 lists the associations (class members) for the `GJTDialog` class.

Table 24-2 `gjt.GJTDialog` **Associations**

Variable	Description
`DialogClient client`	An object that is notified when the dialog is dismissed or cancelled.
`boolean centered`	If `true`, the dialog will be centered in its frame.

We'll come back to `GJTDialog` shortly to discuss its implementation, but first we must take a short detour to discuss non-modal dialogs and the `DialogClient` interface.

Non-modal Dialogs and the DialogClient Interface

Notice that the `GJTDialog` class maintains an association with a `DialogClient`. `DialogClient` is a simple interface that defines two methods:

- `void dialogDismissed(Dialog)`
- `void dialogCancelled(Dialog)`

As we discussed previously in "java.awt.Dialog" on page 286, dialogs are distinguished from frames and windows in that a dialog can be modal. Being modal means that while the dialog is being shown, input to other windows within the dialog's ancestry is blocked. Additionally, and more importantly from our immediate perspective, a modal dialog also blocks execution of the thread that showed the dialog in the first place. For instance, consider the hypothetical `someMethod()` below:

```
public void someMethod() {
  Dialog dialog = new Dialog(Util.getFrame(this), false);
  dialog.setVisible(true);
  // do something interesting
}
```

If the dialog being shown is modal, then the "do something interesting" part of
someMethod() is not executed until after the dialog is dismissed. However, if
the dialog is non-modal, the "do something interesting" part of someMethod()
will be executed immediately after the dialog is shown.

This leaves somewhat of a dilemma for non-modal dialogs, namely, how does the
class that showed the non-modal dialog get notified when the dialog is cancelled[2]
or dismissed? The answer, of course, is that the class responsible for showing the
dialog implements the DialogClient interface, so that it can be notified of the
dialog's impending dismissal or cancellation.

An instance of DialogClient may be associated with a GJTDialog. If a
GJTDialog has a non-null instance of DialogClient, the dialog client will be
notified when the dialog is dismissed or cancelled.

gjt.GJTDialog Revisited

Now that we have a basic understanding of modality, and thus the need for the
DialogClient interface, let's take a look at the implementation of the
GJTDialog class.

First of all, GJTDialog provides two constructors.

```
public GJTDialog(Frame        frame,
                 String       title,
                 DialogClient aClient,
                 boolean      modal) {
  this(frame, title, aClient, true, modal);
}
```

The first constructor merely invokes the second, passing a default value of true
signifying that the dialog will be centered in its frame when shown.

```
public GJTDialog(Frame        frame,
                 String       title,
                 DialogClient aClient,
                 boolean      centered,
                 boolean      modal) {
  super(frame, title, modal);
```

2. By cancelled, we mean closed via the system menu or the close box of the dialog, if
    the dialog is so equipped. See "java.awt.Frame" on page 283.

```
setClient(aClient);
setCentered(centered);

addWindowListener(new WindowAdapter() {
    public void windowClosing(WindowEvent event) {
        dispose();
        if(client != null)
            client.dialogCancelled(GJTDialog.this);
    }
});
}
```

The second constructor sets the client and the centered variables by invoking the setClient() and setCentered() methods, respectively. setClient() and setCentered() exist so that the dialog's client and centered status can be set after construction.

```
public void setCentered(boolean centered) {
    this.centered = centered;
}
public void setClient(DialogClient client) {
    this.client = client;
}
```

The second constructor also adds a window listener to the dialog that listens for window closing events. Recall from "java.awt.Frame" on page 283, that a window closing event is generated whenever a window is closed via the system menu or the window's close box (if the window is so equipped). Also, recall from the AWT Tip "Frames Don't Close By Default" on page 286, that the window must have dispose() invoked on it in response to a window closing event for the window to actually close, which is exactly what the window listener does. Also, notice that if the dialog has a non-null dialog client associated with it, the window listener invokes the dialog client's dialogCancelled() method after the dialog is disposed of.

GJTDialog overrides Window.dispose() and Component.setVisible(). Notice that both methods simply embellish their counterparts in Window and Component, respectively.

```
public void dispose() {
    Frame f = Util.getFrame(this);

    super.dispose();
    f.toFront();
    if(client != null)
        client.dialogDismissed(this);
```

```
      }
      public void setVisible(boolean visible) {
        pack();
        if(centered) {
          Dimension frameSize = getParent().getSize();
          Point     frameLoc  = getParent().getLocation();
          Dimension mySize     = getSize();
          int        x,y;
          x = frameLoc.x + (frameSize.width/2) -
                            (mySize.width/2);
          y = frameLoc.y + (frameSize.height/2) -
                            (mySize.height/2);
          setBounds(x,y,getSize().width,getSize().height);
        }
        super.setVisible(visible);
      }
```

GJTDialog overrides dispose() in order to bring the dialog's frame to the front of all other windows and to invoke the dialog client's dialogDismissed() method if the dialog client is non-null.

setVisible() is overridden in order to pack[3] the dialog before it is shown and to center the dialog in its frame if the centered variable is true.

As we stated previously, GJTDialog is the ancestor of all the GJT custom dialogs. Before we move on to the rest of the GJT's dialogs, let's summarize the functionality encompassed by the GJTDialog class. The GJTDialog class:

- can be associated with an instance of DialogClient. The dialog client associated with a GJTDialog can be null, which is typically the case for modal dialogs. Non-modal dialogs usually have a non-null dialog client.
- notifies its dialog client when the dialog is dismissed or cancelled if the dialog client is non-null.
- optionally centers the dialog in its frame when the dialog is shown.
- brings the dialog's frame to the front of all other windows when the dialog is dismissed or cancelled.
- provides methods for setting the dialog client and the centering status after construction.

Example 24-1 lists the GJTDialog class in its entirety.

---

3.   pack() sizes the dialog so that it is just big enough to encompass the components it contains. See "Splash Screen" on page 276.

Example 24-1 gjt.GJTDialog **Class Source Code**

```java
package gjt;

import java.awt.*;
import java.awt.event.*;

public class GJTDialog extends Dialog {
  protected DialogClient client;
  protected boolean      centered;

  public GJTDialog(Frame         frame,
                   String        title,
                   DialogClient aClient,
                   boolean       modal) {
    this(frame, title, aClient, true, modal);
  }
  public GJTDialog(Frame         frame,
                   String        title,
                   DialogClient aClient,
                   boolean       centered,
                   boolean       modal) {
    super(frame, title, modal);

    setClient(aClient);
    setCentered(centered);

    addWindowListener(new WindowAdapter() {
       public void windowClosing(WindowEvent event) {
          dispose();
          if(client != null)
              client.dialogCancelled(GJTDialog.this);
       }
    });
  }
  public void setCentered(boolean centered) {
    this.centered = centered;
  }
  public void setClient(DialogClient client) {
    this.client = client;
  }
  public void dispose() {
    Frame f = Util.getFrame(this);

    super.dispose();
    f.toFront();

    if(client != null)
```

```
            client.dialogDismissed(this);
   }
   public void setVisible(boolean visible) {
      pack();

      if(centered) {
         Dimension frameSize = getParent().getSize();
         Point     frameLoc  = getParent().getLocation();
         Dimension mySize    = getSize();
         int       x,y;

         x = frameLoc.x + (frameSize.width/2) -
                       (mySize.width/2);
         y = frameLoc.y + (frameSize.height/2) -
                       (mySize.height/2);
         setBounds(x,y,getSize().width,getSize().height);
      }
      super.setVisible(visible);
   }
}
```

The ProgressDialog Class

The `ProgressDialog` is a simple dialog that displays a bargauge for the purpose of tracking progress made in a time consuming task. Figure 24-2 shows the progress dialog in action; Figure 24-3 is a class diagram for the `ProgressDialog` class.

Figure 24-2 `gjt.ProgressDialog`

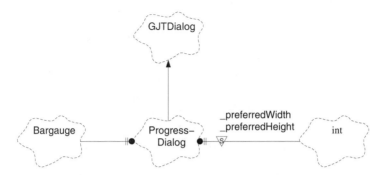

Figure 24-3 ProgressDialog Class Diagram

ProgressDialog directly extends GJTDialog. Since it has a simple implementation, thanks to the gjt.Bargauge class, we'll show you the entire listing and then point out a few highlights of its implementation. Example 24-2 lists the gjt.ProgressDialog class in its entirety.

Example 24-2 gjt.ProgressDialog **Class Source Code**

```java
package gjt;

import java.awt.*;

public class ProgressDialog extends GJTDialog {
   static private int _preferredWidth  = 400;
   static private int _preferredHeight = 75;

   private Bargauge bargauge;

   public ProgressDialog(Frame frame, DialogClient client,
                    String title, Color color) {
      this(frame, client, title, color, false);
   }
   public ProgressDialog(Frame frame, DialogClient client,
                    String title, Color color,
                    boolean modal) {
      super(frame, title, client, true, modal);

      bargauge = new Bargauge(color);
      setLayout(new BorderLayout());
      add(bargauge, "Center");
   }
   public void setPercentComplete(double percent) {
      bargauge.setFillPercent(percent);
      bargauge.fill();
```

```
      if(percent == 100) {
          dispose();
      }
   }
   public void reset() {
      bargauge.setFillPercent(0);
   }
   public Dimension getPreferredSize() {
      return new Dimension(_preferredWidth, _preferredHeight);
   }
}
```

A `ProgressDialog` must be constructed with a color to be displayed in the bargauge, in addition to a frame, which is required to construct an AWT dialog. Additionally, the title of the dialog and a dialog client must be specified, although the dialog client may be `null`. A second constructor is provided for specifying the modality of the dialog.

`ProgressDialog.getPreferredSize()` returns a preferred size of 400 pixels wide and 75 pixels high, which are values chosen purely for aesthetic reasons.

Notice that `ProgressDialog` by default, is non-modal, which is the case for `java.awt.Dialog` as well. Like `java.awt.Dialog`, all of the GJT dialogs are non-modal by default, and also like `java.awt.Dialog`, all allow their modality to be set at or after construction time.

AWT TIP ...

Dialogs Are Non-modal By Default

AWT dialogs allow their modality to be set either at construction time or after the dialog is constructed by invoking setModal(). The Graphic Java Toolkit dialogs follow suit and are non-modal by default. Of course, since the GJT dialogs ultimately extend the java.awt.Dialog class, setModal() can be invoked on any of the GJT dialogs to set modality after construction.

Notice that it is up to another object to update the bargauge's fill percentage by invoking `ProgressDialog.setPercentComplete()`.

gjt.ProgressDialog Unit Test

Like all of the GJT's custom dialogs, the progress dialog comes with its own unit test. Also, like all of the unit tests for the GJT's dialogs, the unit test for the progress dialog allows the modality of the dialog to be set. The unit test for gjt.ProgressDialog is shown in Figure 24-4.

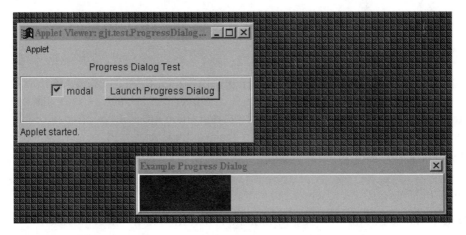

Figure 24-4 gjt.ProgressDialog Unit Test

Like all GJT unit tests, ProgressDialogTest extends the gjt.test.UnitTest class and provides a title for the unit test and a panel to be displayed in the center of the applet[4].

```
public class ProgressDialogTest extends UnitTest {
  public String title() {
    return "Progress Dialog Test";
  }
  public Panel centerPanel() {
    return new ProgressDialogLauncher(this);
  }
}
```

The ProgressDialogLauncher class is where all of the interesting action takes place. Notice that ProgressDialogLauncher implements the DialogClient interface for notification when the dialog is dismissed and the ActionListener interface for handling action events fired by the Launch Progress Dialog button. In addition, a checkbox is provided to set the modality of the progress dialog.

---

4. See "The GJT test Package" on page 571.

The `ProgessDialogLauncher` constructor is passed an instance of the applet, to which it maintains a reference, in order to call `Applet.showStatus()` when the dialog is dismissed or cancelled. The constructor adds the `modal` checkbox to the applet, along with the button that will cause the dialog to be shown.

```
class ProgressDialogLauncher extends Panel
                            implements DialogClient,
                            ActionListener {
  private ProgressDialog progressDialog;
  private ProgressDialogThread thread;
  private Checkbox        modal = new Checkbox("modal");
  private Applet          applet;

  private Button progressDialogButton;

  public ProgressDialogLauncher(Applet applet) {
    this.applet = applet;
    add(modal);
    add(progressDialogButton =
          new Button("Launch Progress Dialog"));

    progressDialogButton.addActionListener(this);
  }
  ...
```

The last thing the `ProgressDialogLauncher` constructor does is add itself as an action listener for the Launch Progress Dialog button, which results in `ProgressDialogLauncher.actionPerformed()` being invoked when the button is activated.

If the `progressDialog` has not been created, the `actionPerformed()` method constructs an instance of `ProgressDialog`. Notice the last argument to the `ProgressDialog` constructor: `modal.getState()`. The `Checkbox.getState()` method returns `true` if the checkbox is checked[5], and `false` if it is not. Also notice that the `gjt.Util.getFrame()` method[6] is used to obtain a reference to the frame in which the applet resides, which is passed along to the `ProgressDialog` constructor.

```
public void actionPerformed(ActionEvent event) {
  if(progressDialog == null) {
    progressDialog = new ProgressDialog(
                  Util.getFrame(this), this,
                  "Example Progress Dialog",
```

5. See "java.awt.Checkbox" on page 196.
6. See "The gjt.Util Class" on page 570.

```
                     Color.blue, modal.getState());
  }
  else {
    progressDialog.reset();

    if(modal.getState()) progressDialog.setModal(true);
    else                 progressDialog.setModal(false);
  }
  thread = new ProgressDialogThread(progressDialog);
  thread.start();
  progressDialog.setVisible(true);
}
```

If the progressDialog has already been constructed, then its state is reset with a call to ProgressDialog.reset(), which sets the bargauge's fill percent to zero. The modality of the progress dialog is then set to reflect the current state of the modal checkbox.

After either creating the progress dialog or updating its parameters, an instance of ProgressDialogThread is constructed, and the thread is started.

The last thing the actionPerformed() method does is to invoke setVisible() on the progress dialog, which of course invokes GJTDialog.setVisible(), which packs the dialog and centers it within its frame. The upshot of the call to setVisible() is that the dialog is packed and centered in the dialog's frame, and shown. You may have noticed that the dialog is not centered in its frame in Figure 24-4—that's because we moved it before taking the snapshot, so that you could see both the applet window and the dialog in their entirety.

One important point to note is that we start the progress dialog thread *before* we set the visibility of the dialog to true (thus showing the dialog). Remember, if the dialog is modal, it will block execution of the thread that showed the dialog, so if we start the thread *after* showing the dialog, the thread will not start until the dialog is dismissed if the dialog is modal.

Since ProgressDialogLauncher implements the DialogClient interface, it implements the two methods required of DialogClient implementors.

```
public void dialogDismissed(Dialog d) {
  applet.showStatus("Progress Dialog Dismissed");
}
public void dialogCancelled(Dialog d) {
  applet.showStatus("Dialog Cancelled");
  thread.stop();
}
```

We don't have much to do when the dialog is dismissed or cancelled, other than updating the applet's status line to indicate that the dialog was dismissed or cancelled, respectively. However, if the dialog was cancelled, then the ProgressDialogThread was not allowed to run its course, so we call its stop() method in order to ensure that the thread restarts the next time the dialog is shown.

All that's left is the implementation of the ProgressDialogThread class.

```
class ProgressDialogThread extends Thread {
  private ProgressDialog dialog;
  private double          percentComplete = 0;

  public ProgressDialogThread(ProgressDialog dialog) {
     this.dialog = dialog;
  }
  public void run() {
     while(percentComplete <= 100) {
         try { Thread.currentThread().sleep(250); }
         catch(InterruptedException e) { }

         if(dialog.isShowing()) {
            dialog.setPercentComplete(percentComplete);
            percentComplete += 10;
         }
     }
  }
}
```

Notice that the thread runs until percentComplete reaches 100%. Also notice that since the thread is started before the dialog is shown, the completion percentage for the dialog is not updated unless the dialog is showing.

There's one important point to note about the ProgressDialog unit test before we move on. The progress dialog is only constructed the first time the Launch Progress Dialog button is activated; however, its dispose() method is called repeatedly: whenever the call to ProgressDialog.setPercentComplete() is passed a value of 100. Recall that ProgressDialog.setPercentComplete() is implemented like so:

```
// ProgressDialog.setPercentComplete()
public void setPercentComplete(double percent) {
  bargauge.setFillPercent(percent);
  bargauge.fill();

  if(percent == 100) {
     dispose();
  }
}
```

Your first inclination, upon realizing that the dialog is disposed of repeatedly but only constructed once, may be that the dialog should be reconstructed after every call to dispose(). However, the dispose() method only disposes of the native resources of the window with which the dialog is associated, not the dialog itself. In fact, we have provided an AWT Tip that stresses this very point in our earlier coverage of frames, windows and dialogs. See "Window.dispose() Disposes of the Window's Resources, Not the AWT Component" on page 283.

For the sake of completeness, the gjt.test.ProgressDialogTest implementation is listed in its entirety in Example 24-3.

Example 24-3 gjt.test.ProgressDialogTest **Class Source Code**

```
package gjt.test;

import java.awt.*;
import java.awt.event.*;
import java.applet.Applet;

import gjt.*;

public class ProgressDialogTest extends UnitTest {
  public String title() {
     return "Progress Dialog Test";
  }
  public Panel centerPanel() {
     return new ProgressDialogLauncher(this);
  }
}
class ProgressDialogLauncher extends Panel
                             implements DialogClient,
                             ActionListener {
  private ProgressDialog progressDialog;
  private Checkbox       modal = new Checkbox("modal");
  private Applet         applet;

  private Button progressDialogButton;

  public ProgressDialogLauncher(Applet applet) {
     this.applet = applet;
     add(modal);
     add(progressDialogButton =
           new Button("Launch Progress Dialog"));

     progressDialogButton.addActionListener(this);
  }
  public void actionPerformed(ActionEvent event) {
```

```
        progressDialog = new ProgressDialog(
                            Util.getFrame(this), this,
                            "Example Progress Dialog",
                            Color.blue, modal.getState());

        ProgressDialogThread thread =
                    new ProgressDialogThread(progressDialog);
        thread.start();
        progressDialog.setVisible(true);
    }
    public void dialogDismissed(Dialog d) {
        applet.showStatus("Progress Dialog Dismissed");
    }
    public void dialogCancelled(Dialog d) {
        applet.showStatus("Dialog Cancelled");
    }
}
class ProgressDialogThread extends Thread {
    private ProgressDialog dialog;
    private double          percentComplete = 0;

    public ProgressDialogThread(ProgressDialog dialog) {
        this.dialog = dialog;
    }
    public void run() {
        while(percentComplete <= 100 && dialog.isShowing()) {
            try { Thread.currentThread().sleep(250); }
            catch(InterruptedException e) { }

            if(dialog.isShowing()) {
                dialog.setPercentComplete(percentComplete);
                percentComplete += 10;
            }
        }
    }
}
```

gjt.WorkDialog

Probably 90 percent of all dialogs contain a row of buttons along the bottom of the dialog and a work area above the buttons for user input—that is the rationale for the gjt.WorkDialog.

gjt.WorkDialog is an extension of GJTDialog that contains two panels—a work area into which a panel may be placed by extensions, and a button panel that may be populated with buttons.

WorkDialog has no unit test of its own. Since MessageDialog, YesNoDialog and QuestionDialog all extend WorkDialog it gets enough of a workout in the unit tests of its extensions.

The implementation of WorkDialog is straightforward, although it is somewhat lengthy because WorkDialog goes out of its way to implement a number of constructors in order to provide maximum flexibility for its extensions. As a result, we'll show you the entire implementation in one shot. WorkDialog employs an instance of ButtonPanel for managing its row of buttons; after taking a look at the WorkDialog implementation, we'll present the ButtonPanel class.

Example 24-4 gjt.WorkDialog **Class Source Code**

```
package gjt;
import java.awt.*;
import java.awt.event.*;

public class WorkDialog extends GJTDialog {
  private ButtonPanel buttonPanel;
  private Panel        workPanel;

  public WorkDialog(Frame          frame,
                    DialogClient client,
                    String         title) {
    this(frame, client, title,
         null, Orientation.CENTER, false);
  }
  public WorkDialog(Frame          frame,
                    DialogClient client,
                    String         title,
                    boolean        modal) {
    this(frame, client, title,
         null, Orientation.CENTER, modal);
  }
  public WorkDialog(Frame          frame,
                    DialogClient client,
                    String         title,
                    Orientation  buttonOrientation,
                    boolean        modal) {
    this(frame, client, title,
         null, buttonOrientation, modal);
  }
  public WorkDialog(Frame          frame,
                    DialogClient client,
                    String         title,
                    Panel          workPanel,
```

```
                Orientation   buttonOrientation,
                boolean       modal) {
      super(frame, title, client, modal);
      this.workPanel = workPanel;

      setLayout(new BorderLayout(0,2));

      if(workPanel != null)
         add(workPanel, "Center");

      add("South", buttonPanel =
            new ButtonPanel(buttonOrientation));
   }
   public void setWorkPanel(Panel workPanel) {
      if(workPanel != null)
         remove(workPanel);

      this.workPanel = workPanel;
      add(workPanel, "Center");

      if(isShowing())
         validate();
   }
   public Button addButton(String string) {
      return buttonPanel.add(string);
   }
   public void addButton(Button button) {
      buttonPanel.add(button);
   }
}
```

We'll touch upon a couple of interesting points about WorkDialog, then move on to the implementation of ButtonPanel.

WorkPanel provides four constructors, so that extensions can construct a WorkPanel with a minimum of three arguments and a maximum of six. As is typically the case with GJT classes that provide multiple constructors, all of the constructors turn around and invoke the constructor with the most arguments (except for the one with the most arguments, of course). Notice from looking at the first constructor that a WorkDialog, like all GJT dialogs, is non-modal by default.

The work panel (the panel above the button panel) can be set after construction. If a work panel is already in place, it is removed from the dialog and the new panel is subsequently added to the dialog. Then, if the dialog is showing, a call to validate() is made, which causes the dialog to be laid out—see "Forcing a Container to Lay Out Its Components" on page 385.

gjt.ButtonPanel

`WorkDialog` provides two methods for adding a button to the button panel—one that takes a string and another that takes a button. Notice that the `WorkDialog` `add()` methods simply delegate to their enclosed instance of `ButtonPanel`, so without further ado, let's take a look at the implementation of `ButtonPanel` in Example 24-5.

Example 24-5 `gjt.ButtonPanel` **Class Source Code**

```
package gjt;

import java.awt.*;

public class ButtonPanel extends Panel {
   Panel       buttonPanel = new Panel();
   Separator separator   = new Separator();

   public ButtonPanel() {
      this(Orientation.CENTER);
   }
   public ButtonPanel(Orientation orientation) {
      int buttonPanelOrient = FlowLayout.CENTER;
      setLayout(new BorderLayout(0,5));

      if(orientation == Orientation.CENTER)
         buttonPanelOrient = FlowLayout.CENTER;
      else if(orientation == Orientation.RIGHT)
         buttonPanelOrient = FlowLayout.RIGHT;
      else if(orientation == Orientation.LEFT)
         buttonPanelOrient = FlowLayout.LEFT;

      buttonPanel.setLayout(new FlowLayout(buttonPanelOrient));
      add(separator, "North");
      add(buttonPanel, "Center");
   }
   public void add(Button button) {
      buttonPanel.add(button);
   }
   public Button add(String buttonLabel) {
      Button addMe = new Button(buttonLabel);
      buttonPanel.add(addMe);
      return addMe;
   }
   protected String paramString() {
      return super.paramString() + "buttons=" +
      getComponentCount();
   }
}
```

ButtonPanel is a simple panel that contains a row of buttons. The orientation of the buttons can be specified at construction time by passing an instance of gjt.Orientation to the ButtonPanel constructor[7]. Additionally, ButtonPanel provides a default constructor that defaults the orientation of the buttons to center-justified. ButtonPanel sets its layout manager to an instance of FlowLayout with the appropriate orientation.

ButtonPanel provides two methods to add buttons to the panel—one that takes a java.awt.Button, and another that takes a String. The method that takes a string creates a button and returns the button in case the caller has need of a reference to the button itself.

With the implementations of ButtonPanel and WorkDialog under our belts, let's take a look at the rest of the dialogs provided by the Graphic Java Toolkit. First, however, we need to take one final detour—the gjt.Postcard class.

gjt.Postcard

MessageDialog, QuestionDialog, and YesNoDialog all extend WorkDialog, and all provide the means to add not only text to the dialog, but an image as well. Figure 24-5 shows instances of MessageDialog, QuestionDialog and YesNoDialog doing their thing.

Naturally, we don't want to reimplement the code for placing an image next to a panel in each dialog class, so that functionality is embedded in the gjt.Postcard class, which is listed in Example 24-6.

---

7.   See "Type-Checked Constants" on page 568.

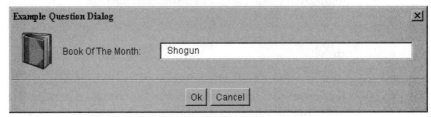

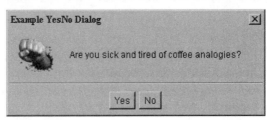

Figure 24-5 Message, Question, and Yes/No Dialogs
Message, question, and yes/no dialogs can be fitted with an image and a panel.

Example 24-6 `gjt.Postcard` **Class Source Code**

```
package gjt;

import java.awt.*;

public class Postcard extends Panel {
  private Panel        panel, panelContainer = new Panel();
  private ImageCanvas canvas = new ImageCanvas();

  public Postcard(Image image, Panel panel) {
     if(image != null) setImage(image);
     if(panel != null) setPanel(panel);

     setLayout(new RowLayout());
     add(canvas);
     add(panelContainer);
  }
  public Panel getPanel() {
```

```
      if(panelContainer.getComponentCount() == 1)
          return (Panel)panelContainer.getComponent(0);
      else
          return null;
   }
   public void setImage(Image image) {
      Util.waitForImage(this, image);
      canvas.setImage(image);
   }
   public void setPanel(Panel panel) {
      if(panelContainer.getComponentCount() == 1) {
         panelContainer.remove(getComponent(0));
      }
      this.panel = panel;
      panelContainer.add(panel);
   }
   public Insets getInsets() {
       return new Insets(10,10,10,10);
   }
}
```

The `Postcard` class gets its name from the fact that postcards usually have an image on one side and text on the other. While our `Postcard` class could be construed as somewhat of a misnomer because it cannot be turned over, it nevertheless was the best name that we could come up with.

At any rate, the `Postcard` class contains a panel and an image canvas[8]. Both the panel and the image can be set at construction time or anytime afterwards. The `Postcard` class also defines insets of ten pixels all the way around.

gjt.MessageDialog

Object-oriented development typically results in classes that stand on the shoulders of a number of other classes—`MessageDialog` is a case in point. As you can see from Figure 24-6, `MessageDialog` extends `WorkDialog`, which in turn extends `GJTDialog`; all of the functionality wrapped up in the ancestry of `MessageDialog` is, of course, inherited. Additionally, `MessageDialog` employs an extension of `Postcard` which it places in its work panel. As a result, the implementation of `MessageDialog` is simple enough to show in one fell swoop. `MessageDialog` is listed in its entirety in Example 24-7.

---

8.   See "Scrollers" on page 781.

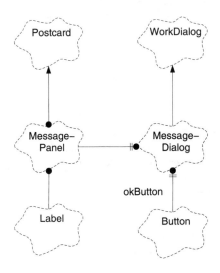

Figure 24-6 `MessageDialog` Class Diagram

Example 24-7 `gjt.MessageDialog` **Class Source Code**

```
package gjt;

import java.awt.*;
import java.awt.event.*;

public class MessageDialog extends WorkDialog
                     implements ActionListener{
    private Button        okButton;
    private MessagePanel messagePanel;

    public MessageDialog(Frame  frame, DialogClient client,
                   String title, String        message,
                   Image  image) {
        this(frame, client, title, message, image, false);
    }
    public MessageDialog(Frame  frame, DialogClient client,
                   String title, String        message,
                   Image  image, boolean       modal) {

        super(frame, client, title, modal);

        messagePanel = new MessagePanel(image, message);
        okButton     = addButton("Ok");

        okButton.addActionListener(this);
```

```
        setWorkPanel(messagePanel);
    }
    public void doLayout() {
        okButton.requestFocus();
        super.doLayout();
    }
    public void actionPerformed(ActionEvent event) {
        dispose();
    }
    private void setMessage(String message) {
        messagePanel.setMessage(message);
    }
    private void setImage(Image image) {
        messagePanel.setImage(image);
    }
}
class MessagePanel extends Postcard {
    private Label label;

    public MessagePanel(String message) {
        this(null, message);
    }
    public MessagePanel(Image image, String message) {
        super(image, new Panel());
        getPanel().add(label = new Label(message,Label.CENTER));
    }
    public void setMessage(String message) {
        label.setText(message);
    }
}
```

MessageDialog sets its work panel to an instance of MessagePanel, a simple extension of Postcard that adds a label representing the message to be displayed in the postcard's panel. (getPanel() is a ButtonPanel method). The image to be displayed in the postcard is passed along to the Postcard constructor.

MessageDialog adds a lone button to the button panel contained in the work dialog. When the button is activated, dispose() is invoked on the dialog, which of course, invokes GJTDialog.dispose().

One point of interest is the overridden doLayout() method.

```
public void doLayout() {
    okButton.requestFocus();
    super.doLayout();
}
```

The intent behind overriding `doLayout()` is to give the Ok button focus, so that the dialog can be dismissed without mousing around. `doLayout()` is invoked whenever the container is laid out—therefore all of the components in the dialog have been created, and more importantly, the components have had their peers created[9]. As a result, the Ok button can receive focus. Note that we are careful to invoke `super.doLayout()` to ensure that the actual laying out of the components takes place.

Finally, note that `MessageDialog`, like its counterparts that extend `WorkDialog`, allows both its image and text to be reset after construction.

gjt.MessageDialog Unit Test

Figure 24-7 shows the unit test for `MessageDialog`; Example 24-8 lists the unit test.

Figure 24-7 `gjt.MessageDialog` Unit Test

Example 24-8 `gjt.test.MessageDialogTest` **Class Source Code**

```
package gjt.test;

import java.awt.*;
import java.awt.event.*;
import java.applet.Applet;

import gjt.*;
```

9. See "java.awt.Component Methods That Depend Upon Peers" on page 158.

```
public class MessageDialogTest extends UnitTest {
  public String title() {
      return "MessageDialog Test";
  }
  public Panel centerPanel() {
      return new MessageDialogLauncher(this);
  }
}
class MessageDialogLauncher extends Panel
                               implements
                               DialogClient, ActionListener {
  private Applet         applet;
  private Button         messageDialogButton;
  private MessageDialog  messageDialog;
  private Image          image = null;
  private Checkbox       modal = new Checkbox("modal");

  public MessageDialogLauncher(Applet applet) {
     this.applet = applet;
     add(modal);
     add(messageDialogButton =
               new Button("Launch Message Dialog"));

     messageDialogButton.addActionListener (this);
  }
  public void actionPerformed(ActionEvent event) {
     Image image = applet.getImage(applet.getCodeBase(),
                              "gifs/information.gif");
     if(messageDialog == null) {
        messageDialog = new MessageDialog(
              Util.getFrame(this), this,
              "Example Message Dialog",
              "This is an example of a message dialog.",
              image, modal.getState());
     }
     else {
        if(modal.getState()) messageDialog.setModal(true);
        else                 messageDialog.setModal(false);
     }
      messageDialog.setVisible(true);
  }
  public void dialogDismissed(Dialog d) {
     applet.showStatus("MessageDialog Dismissed");
  }
  public void dialogCancelled(Dialog d) {
     applet.showStatus("Message Dialog Cancelled");
  }
}
```

`MessageDialogTest` is very similar to the `ProgressDialogTest` applet listed in Example 24-3 on page 730. A checkbox controls the modality of the dialog, and `MessageDialogLauncher` implements the `DialogClient` interface in order to update the applet's status line when the dialog is dismissed or cancelled.

gjt.YesNoDialog

The `YesNoDialog` poses a question and provides two buttons for answering it—a yes button and a no button.

Like `MessageDialog`, `YesNoDialog` extends `WorkDialog`, and employs an extension of `Postcard` which is displayed in its work panel. The class diagram for the YesNoDialog class is shown in Figure 24-8.

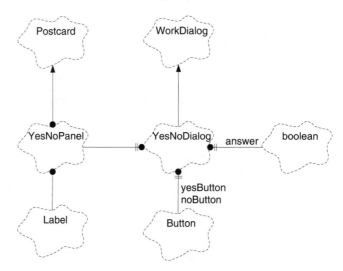

Figure 24-8 `YesNoDialog` Class Diagram

`YesNoDialog` is listed in Example 24-9.

Example 24-9 `gjt.YesNoDialog` **Class Source Code**

```
package gjt;

import java.awt.*;
import java.awt.event.*;

public class YesNoDialog extends WorkDialog {
    private Button      yesButton;
    private Button      noButton;
```

```
private boolean    answer    = false;
private ButtonPanel buttonPanel = new ButtonPanel();
private YesNoPanel  yesNoPanel;

public YesNoDialog(Frame  frame, DialogClient client,
                String title, String       question,
                Image  image) {
   this(frame, client, title, question, image, false);
}
public YesNoDialog(Frame  frame, DialogClient client,
                String title, String       question,
                Image  image, boolean       modal) {
   super(frame, client, title, modal);

   ButtonListener buttonListener = new ButtonListener();

   yesButton = addButton("Yes");
   noButton  = addButton("No");

   yesButton.addActionListener(buttonListener);
   noButton.addActionListener(buttonListener);
   setWorkPanel(yesNoPanel = new YesNoPanel(image,question));

   if(image != null)
      setImage(image);
}
public void doLayout() {
   yesButton.requestFocus();
   super.doLayout();
}
public void setYesButtonLabel(String label) {
   yesButton.setLabel(label);
}
public void setNoButtonLabel(String label) {
   noButton.setLabel(label);
}
public boolean answeredYes() {
   return answer;
}
private void setMessage(String question) {
   yesNoPanel.setMessage(question);
}
private void setImage(Image image) {
   yesNoPanel.setImage(image);
}
class ButtonListener implements ActionListener {
   public void actionPerformed(ActionEvent event) {
      if(event.getSource() == yesButton) answer = true;
```

```
                else                                answer = false;

            dispose();
        }
    }
}
class YesNoPanel extends Postcard {
  private Label label;

  public YesNoPanel(String question) {
     this(null, question);
  }
  public YesNoPanel(Image image, String question) {
     super(image, new Panel());
     getPanel().add(label = new Label(question,Label.CENTER));
  }
  public void setMessage(String question) {
     label.setText(question);
  }
}
```

Since `YesNoDialog` has two buttons, it implements an inner class implementation of `ActionListener`[10], which deciphers which button was activated and records whether the answer to the question was yes or no. One instance of `ButtonListener` is instantiated, which serves as the action listener for both buttons.

`YesNoDialog.answeredYes()` returns `true` if the Yes button was activated, and `false` if the No button was activated, thereby providing a means for discovering the answer to the question posed by the dialog.

gjt.YesNoDialog Unit Test

The unit test for the YesNoDialog is shown in Figure 24-9, while the listing for the unit test is shown in Example 24-10.

---

10. See "Encapsulating Event Handling in a Separate Listener Class" on page 121.

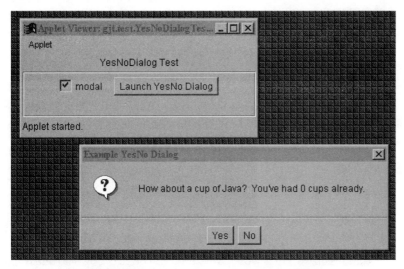

Figure 24-9 gjt.YesNoDialog Unit Test

Example 24-10 gjt.test.YesNoDialogTest **Class Source Code**

```java
package gjt.test;

import java.awt.*;
import java.awt.event.*;
import java.applet.Applet;

import gjt.*;

public class YesNoDialogTest extends UnitTest {
  public String title() {
     return "YesNoDialog Test";
  }
  public Panel centerPanel() {
     return new YesNoDialogLauncher(this);
  }
}
class YesNoDialogLauncher extends Panel
                     implements DialogClient, ActionListener {
  private Applet          applet;
  private YesNoDialog     yesNoDialog;
  private int             cupCnt = 0, coffeeLimit = 3;
  private Image           image = null;
  private Checkbox        modal = new Checkbox("modal");

  private Button yesNoDialogButton;

  public YesNoDialogLauncher(Applet applet) {
```

```java
        this.applet = applet;

        add(modal);
        add(yesNoDialogButton = new Button("Launch YesNo Dialog"));

        yesNoDialogButton.addActionListener(this);
    }
    public void actionPerformed(ActionEvent event) {
        String question = "How about a cup of Java?";
        Image image = applet.getImage(applet.getCodeBase(),
                                "gifs/question.gif");

        if(cupCnt >= 0 && cupCnt < coffeeLimit) {
            question += "  You've had " + cupCnt;
            if(cupCnt == 1) question += " cup already.";
            else            question += " cups already.";
        }
        else {
            question = "Are you sick and tired of coffee analogies?";
        }
        if(cupCnt >= 0 && cupCnt < coffeeLimit) {
            image = applet.getImage(applet.getCodeBase(),
                                "gifs/questionMark.gif");
        }
        else {
            image = applet.getImage(applet.getCodeBase(),
                                "gifs/punch.gif");
        }
        if(yesNoDialog == null) {
            yesNoDialog = new YesNoDialog(
                            Util.getFrame(this),
                            this, "Example YesNo Dialog",
                            question, image, modal.getState());
        }
        else {
            if(modal.getState()) yesNoDialog.setModal(true);
            else                 yesNoDialog.setModal(false);

            yesNoDialog.setImage(image);
            yesNoDialog.setMessage(question);
        }
        yesNoDialog.setVisible(true);
    }
    public void dialogDismissed(Dialog d) {
        if(yesNoDialog.answeredYes()) {
            ++cupCnt;

            if(cupCnt <= coffeeLimit)
                applet.showStatus("Cups Of Coffee:  " + cupCnt);
            else
```

```
              applet.showStatus("Me too");
      }
      else {
          if(cupCnt == 0)
              applet.showStatus("No coffee yet.");
          else if(cupCnt >= coffeeLimit)
              applet.showStatus("Me too");
      }
  }
  public void dialogCancelled(Dialog d) {
      applet.showStatus("Yes No Dialog Cancelled");
  }
}
```

Nearly all of the implementation of the unit test is wrapped up in the YesNoDialogLauncher.actionPerformed() method, which concerns itself with counting how many times the YesNoDialog has been shown. Once the coffeeLimit is reached, both the image and the text displayed in the dialog are modified.

gjt.QuestionDialog

Our final dialog is the gjt.QuestionDialog, which, like the YesNoDialog poses a question. Unlike the YesNoDialog, QuestionDialog provides a textfield for a response to the question instead of buttons. The class diagram for the QuestionDialog class is shown in Figure 24-10.

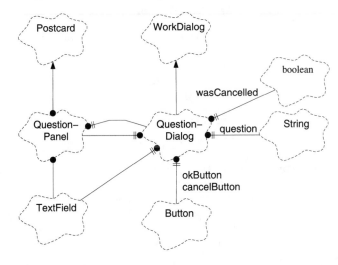

Figure 24-10 QuestionDialog Class Diagram

QuestionDialog is listed in Example 24-11.

Example 24-11 gjt.QuestionDialog **Class Source Code**

```java
package gjt;

import java.awt.*;
import java.awt.event.*;

public class QuestionDialog extends WorkDialog
                           implements ActionListener{
    static private int  _defaultTextFieldSize = 20;
    private Button       okButton;
    private Button       cancelButton;
    private String       question;
    private TextField    textField;
    private boolean      wasCancelled;
    private ButtonPanel buttonPanel = new ButtonPanel();

    public QuestionDialog(Frame  frame, DialogClient client,
                    String title, String       question,
                    String initialResponse,
                    Image image) {
        this(frame, client, title, question, initialResponse,
            _defaultTextFieldSize, image);
    }
    public QuestionDialog(Frame  frame, DialogClient client,
                    String title, String       question,
                    Image image) {
        this(frame, client, title,
        question, null, _defaultTextFieldSize, image);
    }
    public QuestionDialog(Frame  frame, DialogClient client,
                    String title, String       question,
                    int     textFieldSize,
                    Image image) {
        this(frame, client, title,
        question, null, textFieldSize, image);
    }
    public QuestionDialog(Frame  frame, DialogClient client,
                    String title, String       question,
                    String initialResponse,
                    int textFieldSize,
                    Image image) {
        this(frame, client, title, question, initialResponse,
        textFieldSize, image, false);
    }
    public QuestionDialog(Frame  frame, DialogClient client,
```

```
                  String title, String          question,
                  String initialResponse,
                  int textFieldSize,
                  Image image, boolean modal) {
   super(frame, client, title, modal);

   QuestionPanel questionPanel;

   okButton    = addButton("Ok");
   cancelButton = addButton("Cancel");

   okButton.addActionListener(this);
   cancelButton.addActionListener(this);

   questionPanel = new QuestionPanel(this, question,
                                 initialResponse,
                                 textFieldSize,
                                 image);
   textField = questionPanel.getTextField();
   setWorkPanel(questionPanel);
}
public void actionPerformed(ActionEvent ae) {
   if(ae.getSource() == cancelButton)
      wasCancelled = true;
   else
      wasCancelled = false;

   dispose();
}
public void setVisible(boolean b) {
   textField.requestFocus();
   super.setVisible(b);
}
public void returnInTextField() {
   okButton.requestFocus();
}
public TextField getTextField() {
   return textField;
}
public String getAnswer() {
   return textField.getText();
}
public boolean wasCancelled() {
   return wasCancelled;
}
private void setQuestion(String question) {
   this.question = question;
}
```

```java
}
class QuestionPanel extends Postcard {
  private TextField      field;
  private QuestionDialog dialog;

  public QuestionPanel(QuestionDialog dialog,
                       String question, Image image) {
    this(dialog, question, null, 0, image);
  }
  public QuestionPanel(QuestionDialog dialog, String question,
                       int columns, Image image) {
    this(dialog, question, null, columns, image);
  }
  public QuestionPanel(QuestionDialog myDialog, String question,
                       String initialResponse, int cols,
                       Image image) {
    super(image, new Panel());

    Panel panel = getPanel();
    this.dialog = myDialog;

    panel.setLayout(new RowLayout());
    panel.add(new Label(question));

    if(initialResponse != null) {
       if(cols != 0)
          panel.add(field =
                      new TextField(initialResponse, cols));
       else
          panel.add(field =
                      new TextField(initialResponse));
    }
    else {
       if(cols != 0) panel.add(field = new TextField(cols));
       else          panel.add(field = new TextField());
    }

    field.addActionListener(new ActionListener() {
       public void actionPerformed(ActionEvent event) {
          dialog.returnInTextField();
       }
    });
  }
  public TextField getTextField() {
    return field;
  }
}
```

Although the listing for QuestionDialog is long-winded, it is nonetheless quite straightforward.

QuestionDialog provides five constructors for flexibility in specifying the size of the textfield and the initial response (if any) to be displayed in the textfield. QuestionDialog also provides a number of accessors for obtaining a reference to the textfield, finding out the response typed in the textfield, determining whether the Ok or Cancel button was activated, and so on.

The work panel for the QuestionDialog is set to an instance of QuestionPanel, which is where most of the complexity of the implementation resides. QuestionPanel constructs the textfield according to the parameters passed to its constructor, and listens for action events in the textfield[11]. When the enter key is typed in the textfield, QuestionPanel invokes QuestionDialog.returnInTextField(), which gives the focus to the Ok button.

gjt.QuestionDialog Unit Test

Figure 24-11 shows the QuestionDialog unit test in action, while Example 24-12 lists the unit test.

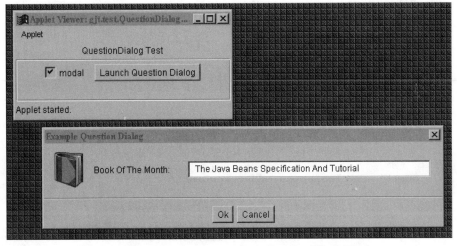

Figure 24-11 gjt.QuestionDialog Unit Test

---

11. See "Action Events" on page 106.

Example 24-12 `gjt.test.QuestionDialogTest` **Class Source Code**

```java
package gjt.test;

import java.awt.*;
import java.awt.event.*;
import java.applet.Applet;

import gjt.*;

public class QuestionDialogTest extends UnitTest {
  public String title() {
     return "QuestionDialog Test";
  }
  public Panel centerPanel() {
     return new QuestionDialogLauncher(this);
  }
}
class QuestionDialogLauncher extends Panel
                            implements DialogClient,
                            ActionListener {
  private Applet          applet;
  private QuestionDialog  questionDialog;
  private Image           image = null;
  private Checkbox        modal = new Checkbox("modal");

  private Button questionDialogButton;

  public QuestionDialogLauncher(Applet applet) {
     this.applet = applet;

     add(modal);
     add(questionDialogButton =
           new Button("Launch Question Dialog"));

     questionDialogButton.addActionListener(this);
  }
  public void actionPerformed(ActionEvent event) {
     Image image = applet.getImage(applet.getCodeBase(),
                               "gifs/book.gif");
     if(questionDialog == null) {
        questionDialog =
              new QuestionDialog(Util.getFrame(this), this,
                              "Example Question Dialog",
                              "Book Of The Month:  ",
                              "Shogun",
                              45, image, modal.getState());
     }
```

```
      if(modal.getState()) questionDialog.setModal(true);
      else                  questionDialog.setModal(false);

        questionDialog.setVisible(true);
    }
  public void dialogDismissed(Dialog d) {
      if(questionDialog.wasCancelled())
         applet.showStatus("CANCELLED");
      else
         applet.showStatus("Book Of The Month:  " +
                   questionDialog.getTextField().getText());
    }
  public void dialogCancelled(Dialog d) {
      applet.showStatus("Dialog Cancelled");
    }
  }
```

The `dialogDismissed()` method obtains a reference to the textfield in the
`QuestionDialog` to find out the text typed in the textfield.

Summary

In addition to an introduction to dialogs in "java.awt.Dialog" on page 286, we've
explored the intricacies of extending `java.awt.Dialog` by discussing the
custom dialogs provided by the Graphic Java Toolkit.

The GJT provides a handful of custom dialogs typically found in user interface
toolkits, but lacking in the AWT. We hope that you will find the dialogs useful in
your own development, in addition to gaining some insights into AWT dialogs
from our discussions in this chapter.

In the next chapter, we'll explore the `gjt.FontDialog` class—a dialog that
allows the selection of a font.

CHAPTER
25

FontDialog

This chapter discusses the implementation of the Graphic Java Toolkit `FontDialog`—a dialog that is used to select a font. Although a font dialog is not as generally useful as a general-purpose custom component such as an image button, it is nonetheless handy for applets and applications that manipulate fonts. Furthermore, the `gjt.FontDialog` implementation illustrates a number of useful techniques for developing custom components, such as:

- Overriding `addNotify()`
- Forcing a container to lay out its components
- Obtaining a list of available system fonts
- Requesting focus for a component

Finally, we provide yet another example that illustrates the use of `GridBagLayout`.

gjt.FontDialog

To begin with, look at Figure 25-1, which shows the gjt.FontDialog class diagram.

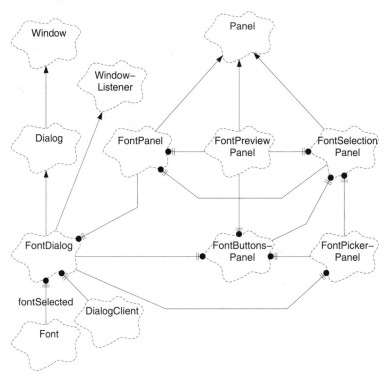

Figure 25-1 gjt.FontDialog Class Diagram

gjt.FontDialog extends awt.Dialog and maintains associations with a FontPanel, a DialogClient, and a Font. Note that FontDialog does not inherit from GJTDialog because we are not interested in inheriting the positioning of the dialog as implemented in GJTDialog.setVisible(). (Refer to our chapter on *Dialogs* for a discussion of GJTDialog). The responsibilities of gjt.FontDialog are listed in Table 25-1.

Table 25-1 gjt.FontDialog **Responsibilities**

Methods	Description
String[] getFontNames()	Returns a list of font names.
String[] getFontSizes()	Returns a list of font sizes.
String getPreviewButtonLabel()	Returns the text displayed in the preview button.
String getOkButtonLabel()	Returns the text displayed in the Ok button.
String getCancelButtonLabel()	Returns the text displayed in the Cancel button.
void setVisible(boolean b)	Explicitly shapes dialog and calls super.setVisible().
void done(Font font)	Invokes client's dialogDismissed() method and disposes of the dialog.
Font getFontSelected()	Returns the font selected. If the font dialog was cancelled, returns null.
void listSelectedInPicker()	Invoked when an item in a list contained in the FontPicker panel is selected. Requests focus for preview button.

Table 25-2 lists the associations of a gjt.FontDialog.

Table 25-2 gjt.FontDialog **Associations**

Variables	Description
private FontPanel fontpanel	Panel housing FontPreview panel and FontSelectionPanel.
private Font fontSelected	The font selected. Returns null if the font dialog is cancelled.
private DialogClient client	Client that gets notified when font dialog is dismissed.

The font dialog comes equipped with a preview panel that displays the name of the currently selected font, in the currently selected font. The preview panel only updates manually, when the preview button is activated.

When a font is selected and the preview button is subsequently activated, the size of the preview area will change if the new font is a different size from the current font. Notice that not only does the preview area have to change size, but all of the other components in the dialog must also be reshaped. The effect of resizing the preview panel can be seen by looking at Figure 25-2.

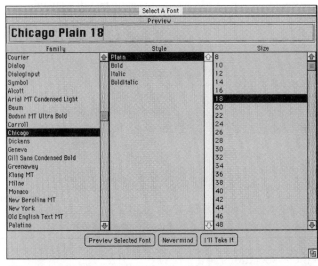

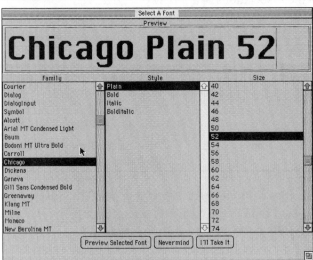

Figure 25-2 `FontDialog` in Action (screenshot from 1.02 GJT on Mac)

Figure 25-3 shows the layout of the `FontDialog`.

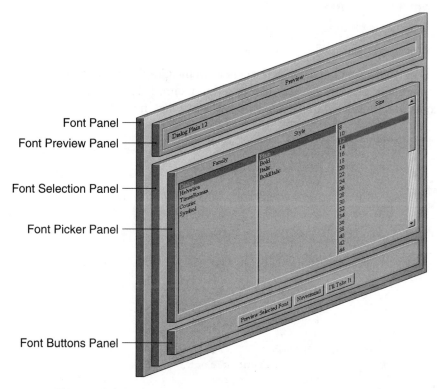

Font Panel

Font Preview Panel

Font Selection Panel

Font Picker Panel

Font Buttons Panel

Figure 25-3 `FontPanel` Layout Diagram

`FontDialog` uses a `BorderLayout` layout manager, which centers an instance of `FontPanel`. `FontPanel` likewise employs a `BorderLayout` to lay out an instance of `FontPreviewPanel` in the north and an instance of `FontSelectionPanel` in the center. Finally, `FontSelectionPanel` also uses a `BorderLayout` and lays out a `FontPickerPanel` instance in the center and a `FontButtonsPanel` in the south.

As an aside, this layout, along with others in the GJT, attests to the versatility of `BorderLayout`. It is the layout manager of choice for many layout situations, as mentioned in the chapter on *Separators and Bargauges*.

Now that you have a good grasp of the anatomy of the `FontDialog`, we are ready to take a look at its implementation. Specifically, we'll be looking at:

- `FontDialog`
- `FontPanel`
- `FontPreviewPanel`

- `FontSelectionPanel`
- `FontPickerPanel`
- `FontButtonsPanel`

`gjt.FontDialog`, like many of the classes in the Graphic Java Toolkit, has a fairly simple implementation, as illustrated in Example 25-1. Take a look through the code, and then we'll make a few points about how it works.

Example 25-1 `gjt.FontDialog` **Class Source Code**

```java
package gjt;

import java.awt.*;
import java.awt.event.*;

public class FontDialog extends Dialog {
    private static String _defaultSizes[] =
                { "8", "12", "14", "16", "18", "24", "48", "64" };

    private FontPanel      fontPanel;
    private Font           fontSelected;
    private DialogClient    client;

    public FontDialog(Frame          frame,
                      DialogClient client,
                      Font           font,    // initial font
                      boolean        modal) {
        super(frame, "Select A Font", modal);
        this.client = client;

        setLayout(new BorderLayout());
        add(fontPanel = new FontPanel(this, font), "Center");

        addWindowListener(new WindowAdapter() {
            public void windowClosing(WindowEvent event) {
                done(null);
            }
        });
    }
    public String[] getFontNames() {
        return getToolkit().getFontList();
    }
    public String[] getFontSizes() {
        return _defaultSizes;
    }

    public String getPreviewButtonLabel() { return "Preview"; }
```

```
   public String getOkButtonLabel     () { return "Ok";      }
   public String getCancelButtonLabel () { return "Cancel";  }

   public void setVisible(boolean b) {
      if(b == true) {
         Point frameLoc = getParent().getLocation();
         setBounds(frameLoc.x + 50, frameLoc.x + 50, 550, 450);
      }
      super.setVisible(b);
   }
   public void done(Font font) {
      fontSelected = font;

      if(client != null)
         client.dialogDismissed(this);

      dispose();  // hides dialog and disposes of system
                  // resources associated with the dialog.
   }
   public Font getFontSelected() {
      return fontSelected;
   }
   public void listSelectedInPicker() {
      fontPanel.getPreviewButton().requestFocus();
   }
}
```

A `FontDialog` can be modal or non-modal. If the font dialog is non-modal, it is expected that a non-null reference will be passed to the `FontDialog` constructor, so that the client can be notified when the dialog is disposed of[1].

`FontDialog` also adds an anonymous inner class representation of a `WindowListener` that handles window closing events by invoking the `done()` method. Recall that a window closing event is generated when the window is closed via the system menu or the close box[2], if the dialog is so equipped. Therefore, the `done()` method is passed a null reference for the selected font when a window closing event occurs, as this signifies that the dialog was cancelled.

The `FontDialog` does not employ the singleton pattern, as do some of the other dialogs in the GJT. We decided not to implement `FontDialog` as a singleton because we expect `FontDialog` to be subclassed fairly often, which makes implementing the singleton pattern somewhat problematic.

---

1.   See "Non-modal Dialogs and the DialogClient Interface" on page 718.
2.   See "java.awt.Frame" on page 283.

`FontDialog` implements five methods that subclasses may wish to override in order to customize the look of the `FontDialog`:

```
public String[] getFontNames() {
  return getToolkit().getFontList();
}
public String[] getFontSizes() { return _defaultSizes; }
public String getPreviewButtonLabel() { return "Preview"; }
public String getOkButtonLabel () { return "Ok"; }
public String getCancelButtonLabel () { return "Cancel"; }
```

By invoking the `static Toolkit.getFontList()`, the `getFontNames()` method returns a list of system fonts available. Should subclasses wish to expand or restrict this list, they can do so by overriding `getFontNames()`.

The `getFontSizes()` method returns the `FontDialog` list of default sizes, which includes only a handful of sizes: 8, 12, 14, 16, 18, 24, 48, and 64. Subclasses can substitute a different list of sizes by overriding the `getFontSizes()` method. As we shall see, our unit test for `FontDialog` does exactly this in order to provide an expanded list of font sizes.

`FontDialog` also implements three methods that define the labels on the buttons that reside in the `FontButtonsPanel`; subclasses can override these methods to customize the labels of the buttons.

The `setVisible()` method of `FontDialog` positions the dialog 50 pixels to the left and 50 pixels below the upper left-hand corner of the frame designated as its parent. Additionally, `setVisible()` hardcodes the initial size of the dialog as 550 pixels wide and 450 pixels high:

```
public void setVisible(boolean b) {
  if(b == true) {
    Point frameLoc = getParent().getLocation();
    setBounds(frameLoc.x + 50, frameLoc.x + 50, 550, 450);
  }
  super.setVisible(b);
}
```

In general, it is not a good idea to hardcode sizes of anything in the AWT. For windows and dialogs, it is much better to use `Window.pack()` to pack the contents of the window or dialog instead of hardcoding the size. However, using `pack()` for the font dialog results in a tiny dialog that we thought looked ridiculous and would probably be resized immediately anyway. Therefore, we've elected to indulge in a small bit of bad practice and hardcode the size to something that we find aesthetically appealing.

Note the `listSelectedInPicker()` method, which is called in response to a selection that is made in the `FontPickerPanel`:

```
public void listSelectedInPicker() {
  fontPanel.getPreviewButton().requestFocus();
}
```

`FontPickerPanel`, as you can see from the layout diagram in Figure 25-3 on page 759, contains three lists: one for font names, one for font styles, and one for font sizes[3]. Whenever a selection is made from one of the lists, `FontPickerPanel` calls `FontDialog.listSelectedInPicker()`, which requests focus for the font panel's preview button. Essentially, we are trying to implement a cornerstone of good user interface design—anticipation of the user's next move. Most likely, when a selection is made from one of the three lists, the user will want to preview the selection. As a result, we give the focus to the preview button so that the user does not have to mouse around to preview the new selection. (You may remember that we employed the same technique with the Graphic Java Toolkit's `QuestionDialog`, described in "gjt.QuestionDialog" on page 747.)

Lastly, `FontDialog` implements the simple, but crucial `getFontSelected()` method, which clients can invoke to obtain the font selected in the dialog.

```
public Font getFontSelected() {
  return fontSelected;
}
```

The FontPanel Class

Of course, `gjt.FontDialog` is a mere shell of a dialog that contains an instance of `FontPanel`:

```
class FontPanel extends Panel {
  private static Font defaultFont =
                          new Font("TimesRoman", Font.PLAIN, 12);
  private FontPreviewPanel    preview;
  private FontSelectionPanel fsp;

  public FontPanel(FontDialog dialog, Font f) {
     Font font = f == null ? defaultFont : f;

     setLayout(new BorderLayout());
     add(preview = new FontPreviewPanel(), "North");
```

---

3.   See "Two Applets for Selecting a Font" on page 202, for an alternative design that uses choices instead of lists.

```
add(fsp = new FontSelectionPanel(dialog, preview, font),
    "Center");
    }
    public Button getPreviewButton() {
        return fsp.getPreviewButton();
    }
}
```

FontPanel is a panel extension that contains the preview panel and the selection panel. FontPanel is constructed with an initial font to be displayed in the font selection panel. If the font passed to the FontPanel constructor is null, FontPanel defaults the initial font to TimesRoman PLAIN 12.

The FontSelectionPanel (the FontPanel center component), as its name implies, enables selection of a font, while the FontPreviewPanel (the FontPanel north component), previews the font before it is selected. Note that the functionality of both panels is easily gleaned from their names. Coming up with good names for classes is one of the most overlooked activities of solid object-oriented design and can sometimes be one of the more difficult part of designing a set of classes.

In any event, we digress, so let's take a look at the implementation of FontPreviewPanel:

```
class FontPreviewPanel extends Panel {
    TextField textField = new TextField();
    Box        box      = new Box(textField, "Preview");

    public FontPreviewPanel() {
        textField.setEditable(false);
        setLayout(new BorderLayout());
        add(box, "Center");
    }
    public void setPreviewFont(Font font) {
        String name  = font.getName();
        String size  = String.valueOf(font.getSize());
        String style = new String();

        if(font.isPlain () == true) style = "Plain";
        else {
            if(font.isBold  () == true) style += "Bold";
            if(font.isItalic() == true) style += "Italic";
        }
        textField.setFont(font);
        textField.setText(name + " " + style + " " + size);
        retrofitPreviewPanel();
    }
```

```
private void retrofitPreviewPanel() {
    Dimension tfps, tfs;
    FontPanel fontPanel = (FontPanel)getParent();

    tfps = textField.getPreferredSize();
    tfs  = textField.getSize();

    if(tfps.width != tfs.width || tfps.height != tfs.height) {
        fontPanel.invalidate();
        fontPanel.getParent().validate();
    }
  }
}
```

FontPreviewPanel uses a BorderLayout to lay out an instance of the versatile gjt.Box[4], which contains a TextField that will display the currently selected font.

In setPreviewFont(), the style of the font passed in is determined by invoking the Font class isPlain(), isBold(), and isItalic() methods.

After determining the style of the font, the textfield's font is set by invoking the Component method setFont(), and then the textfield's text is set to a string that displays the name, style, and size of the font selected. After we are done with the TextField, we then invoke retrofitPreviewPanel(), discussed next.

Forcing a Container to Lay Out Its Components—Revisited

The retrofitPreviewPanel() method forces a layout of the contents of the font dialog. Note that we discussed the technique of forcing a layout at some length in "Forcing a Container to Lay Out Its Components" on page 385, but it's worth the effort to revisit in the context of a real-world situation.

Realize that setting the font of the textfield in setPreviewFont() may cause the textfield to resize when its text is set. In response to this change in size, we must force a layout of the contents of the dialog; otherwise, we may only see a fraction of the text in the textfield or the textfield may be too big for the text. Either way, when the font of the preview panel is set, we want to cause the dialog to lay out its components. In practice, forcing containers to lay out their components is common in the world of the AWT.

4. See "Boxes and Borders" on page 601.

Forcing a layout is accomplished by invoking `validate()` on a container. However, calling `validate()` will result in a no-op if the components contained in the container are all valid. In reality, forcing a layout is accomplished by a two-step process:

1.   Invalidating components, either explicitly with the `invalidate()` method or implicitly with the `Container` methods that invalidate a component (see "Component and `Container` Methods That Invalidate the Component." on page 388).

2.   Calling `validate()` on the container that contains those components.

This is exactly what we do in the `retrofitPreviewPanel()` method:

```
private void retrofitPreviewPanel() {
  Dimension tfps, tfs;
  FontPanel fontPanel = (FontPanel)getParent();

  tfps = textField.getPreferredSize();
  tfs  = textField.getSize();

  if(tfps.width != tfs.width || tfps.height != tfs.height) {
     fontPanel.invalidate();
     fontPanel.getParent().validate();
  }
}
```

Notice that we get the textfield's preferred size and its actual size. If the preferred size is different from the actual size, then we know that the dialog needs to be laid out. This is accomplished by invalidating the font panel and then invoking `validate()` on the font panel's parent. (A component's parent is its container.)

Although you will want to run the unit test applet for `FontDialog`, you can see the forced layout in action in Figure 25-4.

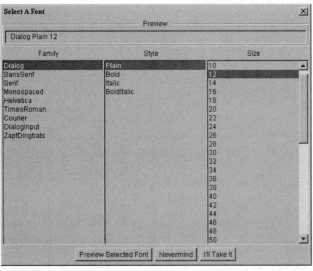

Figure 25-4 `FontDialog` With Preview Panel Resized

The Font Selection Panel

Next, let's take a look at the `FontSelectionPanel` implementation:

```
class FontSelectionPanel extends Panel {
  private FontPickerPanel  picker;
  private FontButtonsPanel buttons;
  private FontPreviewPanel preview;
  private Font                 initialFont;

  public FontSelectionPanel(FontDialog        dialog,
                            FontPreviewPanel preview,
                            Font initialFont) {
    this.preview     = preview;
    this.initialFont = initialFont;
    picker  = new FontPickerPanel (dialog, initialFont);
    buttons = new FontButtonsPanel(dialog, picker, preview);

    setLayout(new BorderLayout());
    add(picker, "Center");
    add(buttons, "South");
  }
  public void addNotify() {
    super.addNotify();
    preview.setPreviewFont(initialFont);
  }
  public Button getPreviewButton() {
    return buttons.getPreviewButton();
  }
}
```

`FontSelectionPanel` lays out a `FontPickerPanel` in the center and a `FontButtonsPanel` in the south. The `FontSelectionPanel` is passed the initial font, which it passes along to the preview panel's constructor.

Note that `addNotify()` is overridden, which ensures that all of the underlying peers have been created and that setting the font will work correctly. See "java.awt.Component Methods That Depend Upon Peers" on page 158 for information on `Component` methods that require peers to be created in order to work properly.

769

AWT TIP ...

Overriding addNotify()

The misnamed Component.addNotify() method creates the component's peer (createPeer() would have been a much better choice for a name). Therefore, if you need to ensure that the peer is created before performing some function, you can override addNotify() and take care of business. However, you must *always* call super.addNotify() when overriding addNotify() or else the platform-specific peers will not be created. Only after invoking super.addNotify() can you be assured that the component's peer has been created.

The Font Picker Panel

Now we've come to the most complicated panel contained in our `FontDialog` — the `FontPickerPanel`. The `FontPickerPanel` has a fairly long-winded implementation—in general, something we like to avoid. However, the `FontPickerPanel` has a good deal of work to do and a number of components to contain, so it merits being the heavyweight among its associates. Let's look at some of the particulars of its implementation before dropping you into the entire source code.

As mentioned before, and as you can see from the Figure 25-2 on page 758 and Figure 25-3 on page 759, `FontPickerPanel` contains lists for:

- Font names
- Font styles
- Font sizes

`FontPickerPanel` also has more complicated layout needs, so we turn to the powerful `GridBagLayout` to lend a hand. Here is how `GridBagLayout` is used:

```
❶   gbc.anchor    = GridBagConstraints.NORTH;
❷   gbc.gridwidth = 1;
    gbl.setConstraints(family, gbc); add(family);
    gbl.setConstraints(style,  gbc); add(style);
❸   gbc.gridwidth = GridBagConstraints.REMAINDER;
    gbl.setConstraints(size,   gbc); add(size);

    gbc.gridwidth = 1;
❹   gbc.weighty   = 1.0;
❺   gbc.weightx   = 1.0;
❻   gbc.fill      = GridBagConstraints.BOTH;
    gbl.setConstraints(fonts,  gbc); add(fonts);
    gbl.setConstraints(styles, gbc); add(styles);
    gbl.setConstraints(sizes,  gbc); add(sizes);
```

First, we set the constraints for each of the labels (family, style, and size) to NORTH in line ❶. In line ❷, we set the gridwidth for the first two labels to 1. By default, gridwidth is set to 1, but we like being explicit as to our intentions here. We set the constraints for the size label in line ❸ to REMAINDER so that it will be the last component in its row.

We once again set the gridwidth to 1, and then in lines ❹, ❺ and ❻, we set weightx and weighty to 1.0, and fill to BOTH. Setting weightx and weighty to 1.0, along with setting fill to BOTH, ensures that each list will fill all available extra space equally when a resize occurs, which is just the effect that we desire.

Now, with this background on how FontPickerPanel employs GridBagLayout, let's look at the class in its entirety:

```
class FontPickerPanel extends Panel implements ItemListener {
  private FontDialog dialog;
  private Button     previewButton;
  private List       fonts  = new List();
  private List       styles = new List();
  private List       sizes  = new List();
  private Font       initialFont;

  public FontPickerPanel(FontDialog dialog,
                         Font       initialFont) {
    GridBagLayout        gbl    = new GridBagLayout();
    GridBagConstraints   gbc    = new GridBagConstraints();
    Label                family = new Label("Family");
    Label                style  = new Label("Style");
    Label                size   = new Label("Size");

    this.initialFont = initialFont;
    this.dialog      = dialog;

    populateFonts ();
    populateStyles();
    populateSizes ();

    setLayout(gbl);

    gbc.anchor    = GridBagConstraints.NORTH;
    gbc.gridwidth = 1;
    gbl.setConstraints(family, gbc); add(family);
    gbl.setConstraints(style,  gbc); add(style);
    gbc.gridwidth = GridBagConstraints.REMAINDER;
    gbl.setConstraints(size,   gbc); add(size);
```

```
   gbc.gridwidth = 1;
   gbc.weighty   = 1.0;
   gbc.weightx   = 1.0;
   gbc.fill      = GridBagConstraints.BOTH;
   gbl.setConstraints(fonts,  gbc); add(fonts);
   gbl.setConstraints(styles, gbc); add(styles);
   gbl.setConstraints(sizes,  gbc); add(sizes);

   fonts.addItemListener (this);
   styles.addItemListener(this);
   sizes.addItemListener (this);
}
public void itemStateChanged(ItemEvent ie) {
   dialog.listSelectedInPicker();
}
public void addNotify() {
   super.addNotify();
   String initialFamily = initialFont.getName();
   int    initialSize   = initialFont.getSize();
   int    initialStyle  = initialFont.getStyle();

   styles.select(initialStyle);

   for(int i=0; i < fonts.getItemCount(); ++i) {
      String nextFamily = fonts.getItem(i);

      if(nextFamily.equals(initialFamily))
         fonts.select(i);
   }
   for(int i=0; i < sizes.getItemCount(); ++i) {
      String nextSize = sizes.getItem(i);
      if(nextSize.equals(String.valueOf(initialSize)))
         sizes.select(i);
   }
}
public String fontSelected() {
   return fonts.getSelectedItem ();
}
public String styleSelected() {
   return styles.getSelectedItem();
}
public int sizeSelected() {
   String szstring = sizes.getSelectedItem();
```

```
        if(szstring != null) {
            Integer integer = new Integer(szstring);
            return integer.intValue();
        }
        else
            return 0;
    }
    private void populateFonts() {
        String names[] = dialog.getFontNames();

        for(int i=0; i < names.length; ++i) {
            fonts.add(names[i]);
        }
    }
    private void populateSizes() {
        String sizeArray[] = dialog.getFontSizes();

        for(int i=0; i < sizeArray.length; ++i) {
            sizes.add(sizeArray[i]);
        }
    }
    private void populateStyles() {
        styles.add("Plain");
        styles.add("Bold");
        styles.add("Italic");
        styles.add("BoldItalic");
    }
}
```

Note that `FontPicker` also overrides `addNotify()` for the express purpose of selecting the appropriate items in each list corresponding to the initial font. `FontPicker` needs to ensure that the lists are created before selecting items in them; overriding `addNotify()` and invoking `super.addNotify()` guarantees that the lists and their associated peers are accessible and that we can select items in the lists.

The Font Buttons Panel

Now let's take a look at the last panel of which the `gjt.FontDialog` is composed—the `FontButtonsPanel`:

```
class FontButtonsPanel extends Panel implements ActionListener {
  private FontDialog        dialog;
  private FontPickerPanel  picker;
  private FontPreviewPanel preview;
  private Button              previewButton,
                         okButton,
  cancelButton;

  public FontButtonsPanel(FontDialog        dialog,
                      FontPickerPanel  picker,
                      FontPreviewPanel preview) {
    this.picker  = picker;
    this.preview = preview;
    this.dialog  = dialog;

    add(previewButton =
            new Button(dialog.getPreviewButtonLabel()));
    add(cancelButton  =
            new Button(dialog.getCancelButtonLabel()));
    add(okButton      =
            new Button(dialog.getOkButtonLabel()));

    previewButton.addActionListener(this);
    cancelButton.addActionListener (this);
    okButton.addActionListener      (this);
  }
  public void addNotify() {
    super.addNotify();
    cancelButton.requestFocus();
  }
  public void actionPerformed(ActionEvent event) {
    Button  button = (Button)event.getSource();

    if(event.getSource() == previewButton) {
      Font selectedFont = fontSelected();

      if(selectedFont != null) {
        preview.setPreviewFont(selectedFont);
        okButton.requestFocus();
      }
    }
    else if(event.getSource() == okButton)
      dialog.done(fontSelected());
    else if(event.getSource() == cancelButton)
      dialog.done(null);
  }
  public Button getPreviewButton() {
    return previewButton;
```

```
    }
    private Font fontSelected() {
        String font    = picker.fontSelected ();
        String style   = picker.styleSelected();
        int    size    = picker.sizeSelected ();
        int    istyle = Font.PLAIN;

        if(font != null && style != null && size > 0) {
            if(style.equals("Bold"))    istyle = Font.BOLD;
            if(style.equals("Plain"))   istyle = Font.PLAIN;
            if(style.equals("Italic"))  istyle = Font.ITALIC;

            if(style.equals("BoldItalic"))
                istyle = Font.BOLD + Font.ITALIC;

            return new Font(font, istyle, size);
        }
        else
            return null;
    }
}
```

There are a few points we should make about FontButtonsPanel. First, notice that we override addNotify() with the express purpose of giving the Cancel button focus. When the FontDialog first comes up, since a font has not yet been selected, the user has no need for either the preview button or the Ok button, so we give the Cancel button the initial focus. As we indicated in our previous discussion, the preview button is given focus when a list selection is made from the font picker panel.

Second, we override the actionPerformed() method to give the Ok button focus after the font has been set in the preview panel. Presumably, the next logical task after previewing a font is to choose it, which is done by activating the Ok button. Therefore, after a preview is complete, we give focus to the Ok button in anticipation of the user selecting the font previewed. If the user decides that the previewed font is not desirable, no harm has been done in giving the Ok button focus—the user is still free to choose a different font or select the Cancel button. Once again, we are just trying to make the font dialog user's life a little easier.

Exercising the gjt.FontDialog

Figure 25-5 shows sample output from the unit test implementation of the FontDialog class.

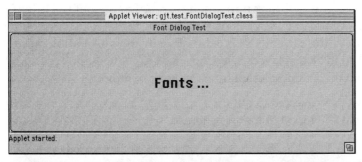

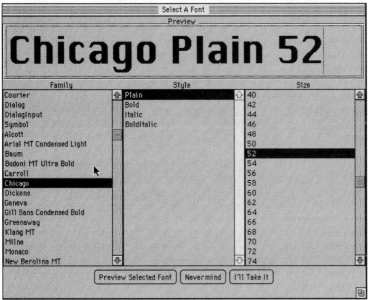

Figure 25-5 `gjt.FontDialog` Unit Test
This series of pictures shows the unit test in its initial state and
then final state after a Chicago 52 point font is selected from the
font dialog. (screenshot from 1.02 GJT on Mac)

Now, given Figure 25-5, look through the FontDialog unit test listed in
Example 25-2 and Example 25-3. As you do, notice that it creates a button that is
used to display the currently selected font. Activating the button causes the
FontDialog to be displayed. Selecting a font from the FontDialog sets the
button's font to the font selected from the FontDialog.

Note that we have elected to put the FontDialogTestPanel in its own file so
that it is available for other unit tests to use.

Example 25-2 `gjt.test.FontDialogTest` **Class Source Code**

```
package gjt.test;

import java.awt.*;

import gjt.*;

public class FontDialogTest extends UnitTest {
  public String title() { return "Font Dialog Test"; }
  public Panel centerPanel() {
     return new FontDialogTestPanel();
  }
}
```

Example 25-3 `gjt.test.FontDialogTest` **Class Source Code**

```
package gjt.test;

import java.awt.*;
import java.awt.event.*;

import gjt.*;

class LotsOfSizesFontDialog extends FontDialog {
  private static String _defaultSizes[] =
     { "8", "10", "12", "14", "16",
        "18", "20", "22", "24",
        "26", "28", "30", "32", "34",
        "36", "38", "40", "42", "44",
        "46", "48", "50", "52", "54",
        "56", "58", "60", "62", "64",
        "66", "68", "70", "72", "74",
        "76", "78", "80", "82", "84",
        "86", "88", "90", "92", "94",
        "96", "98", "100" };

  public LotsOfSizesFontDialog(Frame        frame,
                              DialogClient client,
```

```
                               Font        font) {
    super(frame, client, font, true);
  }
  public String getPreviewButtonLabel() {
    return "Preview Selected Font";
  }
  public String getOkButtonLabel () {
    return "I'll Take It";
  }
  public String getCancelButtonLabel() {
    return "Nevermind";
  }
  public String[] getFontSizes () {
    return _defaultSizes;
  }
}
public class FontDialogTestPanel extends    Panel
                                 implements DialogClient,
                                 ActionListener {
  private Button fontButton;

  public FontDialogTestPanel() {
    setLayout(new BorderLayout());
    add(fontButton = new Button("Fonts ..."), "Center");
    fontButton.addActionListener(this);
  }
  public void actionPerformed(ActionEvent event) {
    LotsOfSizesFontDialog d;
    d = new LotsOfSizesFontDialog(Util.getFrame(this),
                                  this,
                                  fontButton.getFont());
    d.setVisible(true);
  }
  public void dialogDismissed(Dialog d) {
    FontDialog fontDialog   = (FontDialog)d;
    Font       fontSelected = fontDialog.getFontSelected();

    if(fontSelected != null)
       fontButton.setFont(fontSelected);

    Util.getFrame(this).toFront();
    fontButton.requestFocus();
  }
  public void dialogCancelled(Dialog d) {
  }
}
```

Notice that `LotsOfSizesFontDialog` extends `FontDialog` and overrides a number of methods to customize the dialog, namely:

- `getPreviewButtonLabel()`
- `getOkButtonLabel()`
- `getCancelButtonLabel()`
- `getFontSizes()`

The `FontDialogTestPanel` adds a centered `Button`, whose activation causes the `LotsOfSizesFontDialog` to be displayed in the `actionPerformed()` method. The `dialogDismissed()` method casts the `Dialog` reference passed to a `FontDialog` and calls `FontDialog.getFontSelected()` to obtain the font selected in the `LotsOfSizesFontDialog`. Lastly, the `fontButton` has its font set to the font selected in the `LotsOfSizesFontDialog` and requests focus.

Summary

In this chapter, we've introduced the Graphic Java Toolkit `FontDialog` class and a number of supporting classes. Besides discussing the general utility of the `FontDialog`, we've spent some time highlighting exactly how to force a container to lay out its components—a commonly required task in response to an event within an applet. We've also taken yet another pass at showing the powerful `GridBagLayout` layout manager in use. Finally, we have discussed overriding `addNotify()` in order to perform functions that require a component's peer to exist.

CHAPTER 26

Scrollers

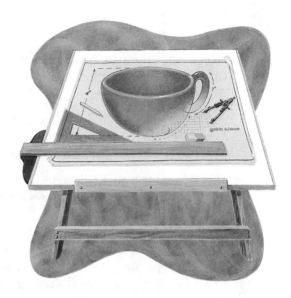

The 1.1 version of the AWT provides a ScrollPane class for scrolling a component and a more general Scrollbar class. We have discussed both the ScrollPane and Scrollbar classes at some length in "java.awt.ScrollPane" on page 256 and "java.awt.Scrollbar" on page 243, respectively.

If you just need to scroll a set of components in a container, then the ScrollPane class is for you. Although a scrollpane can scroll only one component, that component can be a container which of course, can contain multiple components, so in reality a scrollpane can scroll multiple components.

However, there are times when specialized scrolling needs arise, where ScrollPane is not quite up to the task.

For instance, one of the drawbacks to using a scrollpane is that most windowing systems have a limit as to how big a window (and therefore an AWT container) can be. Admittedly, that limit is usually pretty darn big, but the limit is there, nonetheless. If you were to implement a tree control, for example, limiting the size of the control would probably not be acceptable.

Another drawback to using a scrollpane is that in order to scroll an image, you must place the image in a container (since an image is not a component) and scroll the container in which the image resides. We have found that this technique gives

acceptable performance, but if you run the `ScrollImage` applet provided on the CD and discussed in "Scrolling Images" on page 260, you may notice a slight flickering around the edges of the image as the image is scrolled.

As a result, the Graphic Java Toolkit provides a framework for scrolling that does not suffer from the scrollpane drawbacks discussed above. The GJT provides two classes: a `Scroller` base class and an `ImageScroller` class[1].

The GJT scrollers are implemented entirely in Java, as opposed to the `ScrollPane` class which employs a native peer to do its grunt work. `gjt.Scroller` provides a base class that can be extended in order to implement scrolling without having to scroll one large container. For instance, you could limit the size of the viewport to the size of the scroller itself and react to scrollbar events by repainting the fixed size viewport with the appropriate contents. Doing so would allow you to scroll a seemingly infinite-sized area, which is just the effect desired for a tree control, for example.

Now that we've discussed the rationale behind the GJT scrolling classes, let's start by with an overview of the scrolling classes provided by the GJT.

Scrolling With the Graphic Java Toolkit

The GJT provides three classes that relate to scrolling: `ScrollerLayout`, `Scroller` and `ImageScroller`. Figure 26-1 shows the relationships between the GJT scroller classes.

---

1.   The first version of the GJT also provided a `ComponentScroller` class, but it is no longer needed with the advent of `java.awt.ScrollPane`.

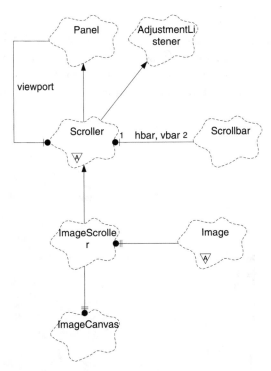

Figure 26-1 gjt.Scroller Class Diagram

ImageScroller extends Scroller. Scroller is a very general class that handles most aspects of scrolling, without regard for the object being scrolled. Notice that Scroller extends Panel. Since an ImageScroller is a component, it can be added to containers and laid out just like any other component.

Each Scroller contains three components:

- Horizontal scrollbar
- Vertical scrollbar
- A panel (viewport)

From here on, we will generically refer to the panel contained in a scroller as its *viewport*. The viewport displays the visible portion of whatever is being scrolled.

gjt.Scroller Layout

Each `Scroller` has a `ScrollerLayout` layout manager. `ScrollerLayout` is a good place to begin our discussion because it illustrates the components contained in a `Scroller` and, of course, how they are laid out. In order to better visualize a scroller, take a look at the diagram in Figure 26-2 showing its components.

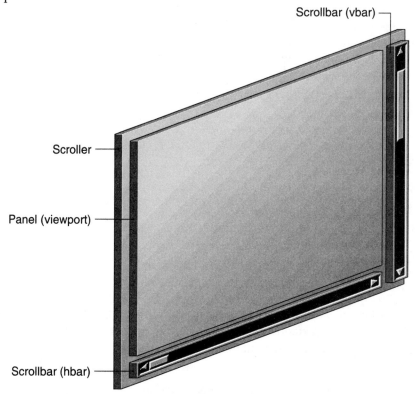

Figure 26-2 `ScrollerLayout` Diagram

A `gjt.ScrollerLayout` is responsible for placing and sizing the scrollbars and viewport associated with its `Scroller`. We'll dissect `ScrollerLayout` in the next few pages and then show the entire implementation in Example 26-1 on page 789.

A `ScrollerLayout` maintains references to its scroller, along with the scroller's scrollbars and viewport.

```
public class ScrollerLayout implements LayoutManager {
   private Scroller   scroller;
   private Scrollbar hbar, vbar;
   private String    hbarPosition, vbarPosition;
   private Component viewport;
   private int       top, bottom, right, left;

   public ScrollerLayout(Scroller scroller) {
      this.scroller = scroller;
   }
```

ScrollerLayout must be handed a scroller at construction time. Let's look at how components are added to and removed from a scroller layout:

```
public void addLayoutComponent(String name,Component comp) {
   Assert.notFalse(comp != null);

   if(comp instanceof Scrollbar) {
      Scrollbar sbar = (Scrollbar)comp;

      if(sbar.getOrientation() == Scrollbar.VERTICAL) {
         Assert.notFalse("East".equals(name) == true ||
                         "West".equals(name) == true);
         vbar          = sbar;
         vbarPosition = name;
      }
      else {
         Assert.notFalse("North".equals(name) == true ||
                         "South".equals(name) == true);
         hbar          = sbar;
         hbarPosition = name;
      }
   }
   else {
      Assert.notFalse("Scroll".equals(name) == true);
      viewport = comp;
   }
}
```

If the component to be added is an instance of `Scrollbar`, then we proceed to check the scrollbar's orientation. If it is vertical, then we assert that the name passed in is either East or West. If it is horizontal, we assert that the name is either North or South.

If the component is not a `Scrollbar`, an assertion is made to ensure that the name passed in is equal to "Scroll."[2]

---

2. In retrospect, "Viewport" would have been a better choice.

Let's cover the `ScrollerLayout` implementations of
`preferredLayoutSize()` and `minimumLayoutSize()`:

```
public Dimension preferredLayoutSize(Container parent) {
   Assert.isTrue(parent == scroller);
   Dimension ps = new Dimension(0,0);
   Insets     insets = parent.getInsets();

   if(vbar != null && vbar.isVisible()) {
      Dimension d = vbar.getPreferredSize();
      ps.width  = d.width;
      ps.height = d.height;
   }
   if(hbar != null && hbar.isVisible()) {
      Dimension d = hbar.getPreferredSize();
      ps.width  = d.width;
      ps.height = d.height + ps.height;
   }
   if(viewport != null && viewport.isVisible()) {
      Dimension d = viewport.getPreferredSize();
      ps.width  = Math.max(d.width, ps.width);
      ps.height = Math.max(d.height, ps.height);
   }
   ps.width  += insets.left + insets.right;
   ps.height += insets.top + insets.bottom;
   return ps;
}
public Dimension minimumLayoutSize(Container parent) {
   Assert.isTrue(parent == scroller);
   Dimension ps = new Dimension(0,0);
   Insets     insets = parent.getInsets();

   if(vbar != null && vbar.isVisible()) {
      Dimension d = vbar.getMinimumSize();
      ps.width  = d.width;
      ps.height = d.height;
   }
   if(hbar != null && hbar.isVisible()) {
      Dimension d = hbar.getMinimumSize();
      ps.width  = d.width;
      ps.height = d.height + ps.height;
   }
   if(viewport != null && viewport.isVisible()) {
      Dimension d = viewport.getMinimumSize();
      ps.width  = Math.max(d.width, ps.width);
      ps.height = Math.max(d.height, ps.height);
   }
   ps.width  += insets.left + insets.right;
```

```
    ps.height += insets.top + insets.bottom;
    return ps;
}
```

Notice that, as is typically the case, `preferredLayoutSize()` and `minimumLayoutSize()` are mirror images of each other with the exception that `preferredLayoutSize()` uses the preferred sizes of the components it lays out in order to calculate the preferred layout size, while `minimumLayoutSize()` uses the minimum sizes of the components. Notice also that both methods are careful to factor in the insets of the container.

The most interesting part of the `ScrollerLayout` is the `layoutContainer()` method:

```
public void layoutContainer(Container target) {
    Insets insets        = target.getInsets();
    Dimension targetSize = target.getSize();

    top    = insets.top;
    bottom = targetSize.height - insets.bottom;
    left   = insets.left;
    right  = targetSize.width - insets.right;

    scroller.manageScrollbars();

    reshapeHorizontalScrollbar();
    reshapeVerticalScrollbar  ();
    reshapeViewport           ();

    scroller.setScrollbarValues();
}
private void reshapeHorizontalScrollbar() {
    if(hbar != null && hbar.isVisible()) {
        if("North".equals(hbarPosition)) {
            Dimension d = hbar.getPreferredSize();
            hbar.setBounds(left, top, right - left, d.height);
            top += d.height;
        }
        else {  // South
            Dimension d = hbar.getPreferredSize();
            hbar.setBounds(left, bottom - d.height,
                           right - left,d.height);
            bottom -= d.height;
        }
    }
}
private void reshapeVerticalScrollbar() {
    if(vbar != null && vbar.isVisible()) {
```

```
    if("East".equals(vbarPosition)) {
        Dimension d = vbar.getPreferredSize();
        vbar.setBounds(right - d.width, top,
                        d.width, bottom - top);
        right -= d.width;
    }
    else { // West
        Dimension d = vbar.getPreferredSize();
        vbar.setBounds(left, top,
        d.width, bottom - top);
        left += d.width;
    }
  }
}
private void reshapeViewport() {
  if(viewport != null && viewport.isVisible()) {
    viewport.setBounds(left, top,
                        right - left, bottom - top);
  }
}
```

After we calculate the `top`, `left`, `bottom`, and `right` sides of the container, given the container's size and insets, we have the scroller manage its scrollbars. `Scroller.manageScrollbars()` determines whether each of its two scrollbars should be visible and ensures that their visibility is set appropriately.

Once the two scrollbars have been either hidden or shown, as appropriate, `ScrollerLayout` commences to reshape each component it is responsible for laying out.

After each of the three components has been laid out, the scroller sets the values for each of its scrollbars.

The only mystery left to uncover is how each component is laid out. First, notice that each reshape method uses the `top`, `left`, `bottom`, and `right` class members that were set in `layoutContainer()`. Furthermore, the scrollbar reshape methods (`reshapeHorizontalScrollbar()` and `reshapeVerticalScrollbar()`) potentially modify all four variables, so the order of invocation in `layoutContainer()` is important.

First, `reshapeHorizontalScrollbar()` checks to see if there's a horizontal scrollbar and if it is visible. If so, `reshapeHorizontalScrollbar()` reshapes the scrollbar and updates either the `top` or `bottom` dimension, depending upon whether the scrollbar is in the north or the south.

Second, `reshapeVerticalScrollbar()`, which is almost a mirror image of `reshapeHorizontalScrollbar()`, reshapes the vertical scrollbar and adjusts either the `right` or `left` dimensions.

By the time we get to `reshapeViewport()`, `left`, `top`, `bottom`, and `right` have all been adjusted to account for the horizontal and vertical scrollbars. (Notice that `reshapeViewport()` is invoked after the scrollbar reshape methods in `layoutContainer()`). All that is left, then, is to reshape the viewport, assuming that it is non-`null` and visible.

Now that we've thoroughly discussed the manner in which `ScrollerLayout` performs its duties, we're ready to take a look at its complete implementation in Example 26-1.

Example 26-1 `gjt.ScrollerLayout` **Class Source Code**

```java
package gjt;

import java.awt.*;

public class ScrollerLayout implements LayoutManager {
    private Scroller   scroller;
    private Scrollbar  hbar, vbar;
    private String     hbarPosition, vbarPosition;
    private Component  viewport;
    private int        top, bottom, right, left;

    public ScrollerLayout(Scroller scroller) {
        this.scroller = scroller;
    }
    public void addLayoutComponent(String name,
                                   Component comp) {
        Assert.notFalse(comp != null);

        if(comp instanceof Scrollbar) {
            Scrollbar sbar = (Scrollbar)comp;

            if(sbar.getOrientation() == Scrollbar.VERTICAL) {
                Assert.notFalse("East".equals(name) == true ||
                               "West".equals(name) == true);
                vbar         = sbar;
                vbarPosition = name;
            }
            else {
                Assert.notFalse("North".equals(name) == true ||
                               "South".equals(name) == true);
                hbar         = sbar;
```

```
                hbarPosition = name;
            }
        }
        else {
            Assert.notFalse("Scroll".equals(name) == true);
            viewport = comp;
        }
    }
    public void removeLayoutComponent(Component comp) {
        if(comp == vbar)     vbar     = null;
        if(comp == hbar)     hbar     = null;
        if(comp == viewport) viewport = null;
    }
    public Dimension preferredLayoutSize(Container parent) {
        Assert.isTrue(parent == scroller);
        Dimension ps = new Dimension(0,0);
        Insets    insets = parent.getInsets();

        if(vbar != null && vbar.isVisible()) {
            Dimension d = vbar.getSize();
            ps.width  = d.width;
            ps.height = d.height;
        }
        if(hbar != null && hbar.isVisible()) {
            Dimension d = hbar.getSize();
            ps.width  = d.width;
            ps.height = d.height + ps.height;
        }
        if(viewport != null && viewport.isVisible()) {
            Dimension d = viewport.getSize();
            ps.width  = Math.max(d.width, ps.width);
            ps.height = Math.max(d.height, ps.height);
        }
        ps.width  += insets.left + insets.right;
        ps.height += insets.top + insets.bottom;
        return ps;
    }
    public Dimension minimumLayoutSize(Container parent) {
        return preferredLayoutSize(parent);
    }
    public void layoutContainer(Container target) {
        Insets insets      = target.getInsets();
        Dimension targetSize = target.getSize();

        top    = insets.top;
        bottom = targetSize.height - insets.bottom;
        left   = insets.left;
        right  = targetSize.width - insets.right;
```

```
        scroller.manageScrollbars();

        reshapeHorizontalScrollbar();
        reshapeVerticalScrollbar  ();
        reshapeViewport           ();

        scroller.setScrollbarValues();
    }
    private void reshapeHorizontalScrollbar() {
        if(hbar != null && hbar.isVisible()) {
            if("North".equals(hbarPosition)) {
                Dimension d = hbar.getPreferredSize();
                hbar.setBounds(left, top, right - left, d.height);
                top += d.height;
            }
            else {  // South
                Dimension d = hbar.getPreferredSize();
                hbar.setBounds(left, bottom - d.height,
                                right - left,d.height);
                bottom -= d.height;
            }
        }
    }
    private void reshapeVerticalScrollbar() {
        if(vbar != null && vbar.isVisible()) {
            if("East".equals(vbarPosition)) {
                Dimension d = vbar.getPreferredSize();
                vbar.setBounds(right - d.width, top,
                                d.width, bottom - top);
                right -= d.width;
            }
            else { // West
                Dimension d = vbar.getPreferredSize();
                vbar.setBounds(left, top,
                d.width, bottom - top);
                left += d.width;
            }
        }
    }
    private void reshapeViewport() {
        if(viewport != null && viewport.isVisible()) {
            viewport.setBounds(left, top,
                                right - left, bottom - top);
        }
    }
}
```

gjt.Scroller

Table 26-1 lists the gjt.Scroller class responsibilities and Example 26-2 on page 798 lists its implementation.

Table 26-1 gjt.Scroller **Responsibilities**

Methods	Description
void scrollTo(int x, int y)	**Abstract** method. Passed current values for horizontal scrollbar's value and vertical scrollbar's value.
Dimension getScrollAreaSize()	**Abstract** method. Returns size of object being scrolled.
Scrollbar getHorizontalScrollbar()	Returns the horizontal scrollbar.
Scrollbar getVerticalScrollbar()	Returns the vertical scrollbar.
Panel getViewport()	Returns the viewport.
void adjustmentValueChanged(AdjustmentEvent event)	Reacts to scrollbar adjustment events.
void paint(Graphics g)	Calls scroll().
void update(Graphics g)	Calls update().
void manageScrollbars()	Sets visibility of scrollbars.
void setScrollbarValues()	Sets values of scrollbars.
void setScrollPosition(int x, int y)	Implements programmatic scrolling.

Table 26-2 lists the associations of a gjt.Scroller.

Table 26-2 gjt.Scroller **Associations**

Variables	Description
protected Panel viewport	Panel in which object being scrolled is displayed.
protected Scrollbar hbar	Horizontal scrollbar
protected Scrollbar vbar	Vertical scrollbar

There are a number of details worth pointing out before we show you the complete source code for the Scroller class.

`gjt.Scroller` is an abstract class that encapsulates all aspects of scrolling that are independent of the object being scrolled. As it turns out, that includes just about all of the scrolling functionality. Extensions of `gjt.Scroller` are left to implement but two methods:

```
abstract public void      scrollTo(int x, int y);
abstract public Dimension getScrollAreaSize();
```

Each extension of `Scroller` must be able to scroll to a given location. The x and y values passed to `scrollTo()` represent the current values for the horizontal and vertical scrollbars, respectively. It is up to extensions of `gjt.Scroller` to do the actual work of scrolling to those coordinates.

Each extension of `gjt.Scroller` must also be able to report the size of whatever it is that is being scrolled. Note that this is very much dependent upon what is being scrolled. The size of an `Image`, for instance, is obtained by invoking the `Image` methods:

- `Image.getWidth(ImageObserver)`
- `Image.getHeight(ImageObserver)`

The size of a `Container` is obtained by invoking `Container.size()`. Also note that the size can be a *virtual* size—it may not be the actual physical size of anything in particular.

Now that we understand the responsibilities of extensions of `gjt.Scroller`, let's take a look at how the `Scroller` class works.

The Scroller class extends Panel and implements the `AdjustmentListener` interface[3]. In its constructor, `Scroller` creates the viewport and two scrollbars and adds itself as an adjustment listener for each scrollbar. `Scroller` also provides accessors for each component.

```
public Scroller() {
  setLayout(new ScrollerLayout(this));

  add("Scroll", viewport = new Panel());
  add("East", vbar = new Scrollbar(Scrollbar.VERTICAL));
  add("South",hbar = new Scrollbar(Scrollbar.HORIZONTAL));

  hbar.addAdjustmentListener(this);
  vbar.addAdjustmentListener(this);
}
public Scrollbar getHorizontalScrollbar() {return hbar;    }
public Scrollbar getVerticalScrollbar () {return vbar;    }
public Panel     getViewport          () {return viewport;}
```

3. See "Adjustment Events" on page 108.

You may think it somewhat wasteful to always create both horizontal and vertical scrollbars, when one or both may be unnecessary, and you would be correct—we are wasting the space of an object or two once in a while. However, the clarity of the code would suffer if we were always checking to see if a scrollbar existed before we did anything with it, so we've taken the liberty to waste an object or two.

By the way, ScrollerLayout is very careful to check that a component is not null before it goes about laying it out. As Scroller is currently implemented, of course, ScrollerLayout need not be so cautious about invoking a method on a null scrollbar or viewport, because they are always there. However, ScrollerLayout is careful *not* to rely upon the implementation of Scroller (even though the author of Scroller and ScrollerLayout are one and the same).

Now, let's look at the adjustmentValueChanged() method:

```
public void adjustmentValueChanged(AdjustmentEvent event) {
  switch(event.getAdjustmentType()) {
    case AdjustmentEvent.BLOCK_INCREMENT:
        scrollLineUp();
        break;
    case AdjustmentEvent.BLOCK_DECREMENT:
        scrollLineDown();
        break;
    case AdjustmentEvent.UNIT_INCREMENT:
        scrollPageUp  ();
        break;
    case AdjustmentEvent.UNIT_DECREMENT:
        scrollPageDown();
        break;
    case AdjustmentEvent.TRACK:
        scrollAbsolute();
        break;
  }
}
protected void scrollLineUp   () { scroll(); }
protected void scrollLineDown() { scroll(); }
protected void scrollPageUp   () { scroll(); }
protected void scrollPageDown() { scroll(); }
protected void scrollAbsolute() { scroll(); }

protected void scroll() {
  scrollTo(hbar.getValue(), vbar.getValue());
}
```

Every type of adjustment event results in a helper method being invoked, each of which turns around and invokes scroll()! Of course, you may be wondering why we chose to take such an indirect route to invoke the scroll() method. The answer is that we want extensions of Scroller to be able to redefine the meaning of each of the different types of adjustment events if so desired. In practice, most extensions of Scroller will be perfectly content with the default behavior and will never override the intermediary methods. Nonetheless, it's a nice touch to provide them with the option.

Now let's take a look at the Scroller implementation of paint() and update():

```
public void paint (Graphics g) {
  scroll();
}
public void update(Graphics g) {
  paint(g);
}
```

We've overridden update() so that it just calls paint(). Normally, update() paints the entire component with the background color and then invokes paint(). Overriding update() to call paint() directly dispenses with erasing the scroller before painting, thus eliminating some distracting flashing.

The paint() method, is overridden to simply call scroll(), which of course, calls the scrollTo() method. Note that the scrollTo() method is an abstract method in Scroller and therefore must be implemented by Scroller extensions.

The result of all this maneuvering is that a call to either paint() or update() results in a call to the scrollTo() method, which is implemented by Scroller extensions. scrollTo() is passed the current values for each scrollbar.

This brings us to the management (that is, the hiding and showing) of the scroller's scrollbars. Remember that Scroller.manageScrollbars() is invoked from ScrollerLayout.layoutContainer(Container).

```
public void manageScrollbars() {
  manageHorizontalScrollbar();
  manageVerticalScrollbar   ();
}
protected void manageHorizontalScrollbar() {
  Dimension size           = getSize();
  Dimension scrollAreaSize = getScrollAreaSize();

  if(vbar.isVisible())
     size.width -= vbar.getSize().width;
```

```
    if(scrollAreaSize.width > size.width) {
       if( ! hbar.isVisible())
          hbar.setVisible(true);
    }
    else if(hbar.isVisible()) {
       hbar.setVisible(false);
       hbar.setValue(0);
       repaint();
    }
 }
 protected void manageVerticalScrollbar() {
    Dimension size            = getSize();
    Dimension scrollAreaSize = getScrollAreaSize();

    if(hbar.isVisible())
       size.height -= hbar.getSize().height;

    if(scrollAreaSize.height > size.height) {
       if( ! vbar.isVisible())
          vbar.setVisible(true);
    }
    else if(vbar.isVisible()) {
       vbar.setVisible(false);
       vbar.setValue(0);
       repaint();
    }
 }
```

Each of the scrollbar management methods determines whether its particular scrollbar is necessary at the moment by comparing the scroll area size to the size of the scroller. (Remember that getScrollAreaSize() is to be implemented by extensions of Scroller). Notice also that each of the scrollbar management methods must be careful to check whether the other scrollbar is visible and factor that into their calculations.

If the width of the scroll area is greater than the width of the scroller (adjusted for the presence of the other scrollbar), then the scrollbar should be visible. In such a case, we check to see if the scrollbar is currently not visible; if that is the case, we call setVisible(true).

If the width of the scroll area is less than the width of the scroller (adjusted for the presence of the other scrollbar), then the scrollbar should not be visible. In such a case, we check to see if the scrollbar is currently visible; if so, we call setVisible(false), set its value to 0, and then invoke repaint() for the scroller.

Now let's take a look at the other Scroller methods invoked from ScrollerLayout.layoutContainer(Container):

```
public void setScrollbarValues() {
  if(hbar.isVisible()) setHorizontalScrollbarValues();
  if(vbar.isVisible()) setVerticalScrollbarValues();
}
protected void setHorizontalScrollbarValues() {
  Dimension vsize          = viewport.getSize();
  Dimension scrollAreaSize = getScrollAreaSize();
  int max = scrollAreaSize.width;

  hbar.setValues(hbar.getValue(), // value
                 vsize.width,     // amt visible/page
                 0,               // minimum
                 max);            // maximum

  setHorizontalLineAndPageIncrements();
}
protected void setVerticalScrollbarValues() {
  Dimension vsize          = viewport.getSize();
  Dimension scrollAreaSize = getScrollAreaSize();
  int max = scrollAreaSize.height;

  vbar.setValues(vbar.getValue(), // value
                 vsize.height,    // amt visible/page
                 0,               // minimum
                 max);            // maximum

  setVerticalLineAndPageIncrements();
}
```

Notice that `setHorizontalScrollbarValues()` and
`setVerticalScrollbarValues()` have nearly identical implementations.
Each sets its scrollbar's value to the current value and sets the amount visible to
the size of the viewport. The minimum value is set to 0, and the maximum value
is set to the size of the scroll area.

Finally, we have two methods that set the line and page increments for the
scrollbars:

```
protected void setHorizontalLineAndPageIncrements() {
  Dimension size = getScrollAreaSize();
  hbar.setUnitIncrement(size.width/10);
  hbar.setBlockIncrement(size.width/5);
}
protected void setVerticalLineAndPageIncrements() {
  Dimension size = getScrollAreaSize();
  vbar.setUnitIncrement(size.height/10);
  vbar.setBlockIncrement(size.height/5);
}
```

Notice that all of the methods that react to scrolling events are protected, meaning you are free to override them in extensions of `Scroller`. For instance, if you are unhappy with a line increment that is one tenth of the scroll area size, you can override `setHorizontalLineAndPageIncrements()` in an extension of `Scroller`. On the other hand, if you need to customize the reaction to a scroll-line up event, you are free to override `scrollLineUp()` in a `Scroller` extension. Now that we've seen the significant parts of the `gjt.Scroller`, let's look at the entire implementation in Example 26-2.

Example 26-2 `gjt.Scroller` **Class Source Code**

```
package gjt;

import java.awt.*;
import java.awt.event.*;

public abstract class Scroller extends     Panel
                                implements AdjustmentListener {
  protected Panel      viewport;
  protected Scrollbar hbar, vbar;

  abstract public void        scrollTo(int x, int y);
  abstract public Dimension getScrollAreaSize();

  public Scroller() {
     setLayout(new ScrollerLayout(this));

     add("Scroll", viewport = new Panel());
     add("East", vbar = new Scrollbar(Scrollbar.VERTICAL));
     add("South",hbar = new Scrollbar(Scrollbar.HORIZONTAL));

     hbar.addAdjustmentListener(this);
     vbar.addAdjustmentListener(this);
  }
  public Scrollbar getHorizontalScrollbar() {return hbar;     }
  public Scrollbar getVerticalScrollbar  () {return vbar;     }
  public Panel     getViewport           () {return viewport;}

  public void adjustmentValueChanged(AdjustmentEvent event) {
     switch(event.getAdjustmentType()) {
        case AdjustmentEvent.BLOCK_INCREMENT:
           scrollLineUp();
           break;
        case AdjustmentEvent.BLOCK_DECREMENT:
           scrollLineDown();
           break;
     case AdjustmentEvent.UNIT_INCREMENT:
```

```java
              scrollPageUp  ();
              break;
     case AdjustmentEvent.UNIT_DECREMENT:
              scrollPageDown();
              break;
     case AdjustmentEvent.TRACK:
              scrollAbsolute();
              break;
      }
}
public void paint (Graphics g) { scroll(); }
public void update(Graphics g) { paint(g); }

public void manageScrollbars() {
   manageHorizontalScrollbar();
   manageVerticalScrollbar  ();
}
protected void manageHorizontalScrollbar() {
   Dimension size          = getSize();
   Dimension scrollAreaSize = getScrollAreaSize();

   if(vbar.isVisible())
      size.width -= vbar.getSize().width;

   if(scrollAreaSize.width > size.width) {
      if( ! hbar.isVisible())
         hbar.setVisible(true);
   }
   else if(hbar.isVisible()) {
      hbar.setVisible(false);
      hbar.setValue(0);
      repaint();
   }
}
protected void manageVerticalScrollbar() {
   Dimension size          = getSize();
   Dimension scrollAreaSize = getScrollAreaSize();

   if(hbar.isVisible())
      size.height -= hbar.getSize().height;

   if(scrollAreaSize.height > size.height) {
      if( ! vbar.isVisible())
         vbar.setVisible(true);
   }
   else if(vbar.isVisible()) {
      vbar.setVisible(false);
      vbar.setValue(0);
```

```
            repaint();
        }
    }
    public void setScrollPosition(int x, int y) {
        scrollTo(x,y);
        hbar.setValue(x);
        hbar.setValue(y);
        repaint();
    }
    public void setScrollbarValues() {
        if(hbar.isVisible()) setHorizontalScrollbarValues();
        if(vbar.isVisible()) setVerticalScrollbarValues();
    }
    protected void setHorizontalScrollbarValues() {
        Dimension vsize          = viewport.getSize();
        Dimension scrollAreaSize = getScrollAreaSize();
        int max = scrollAreaSize.width;

        hbar.setValues(hbar.getValue(), // value
                    vsize.width,      // amt visible/page
                    0,                // minimum
                    max);             // maximum

        setHorizontalLineAndPageIncrements();
    }
    protected void setVerticalScrollbarValues() {
        Dimension vsize          = viewport.getSize();
        Dimension scrollAreaSize = getScrollAreaSize();
        int max = scrollAreaSize.height;

        vbar.setValues(vbar.getValue(), // value
                    vsize.height,     // amt visible/page
                    0,                // minimum
                    max);             // maximum

        setVerticalLineAndPageIncrements();
    }
    protected void scrollLineUp   () { scroll(); }
    protected void scrollLineDown () { scroll(); }
    protected void scrollPageUp   () { scroll(); }
    protected void scrollPageDown () { scroll(); }
    protected void scrollAbsolute () { scroll(); }

    protected void setHorizontalLineAndPageIncrements() {
        Dimension size = getScrollAreaSize();
        hbar.setUnitIncrement(size.width/10);
        hbar.setBlockIncrement(size.width/5);
    }
```

```
   protected void setVerticalLineAndPageIncrements() {
      Dimension size = getScrollAreaSize();
      vbar.setUnitIncrement(size.height/10);
      vbar.setBlockIncrement(size.height/5);
   }
   protected void scroll() {
      scrollTo(hbar.getValue(), vbar.getValue());
   }
}
```

gjt.ImageCanvas and gjt.ImageScroller

Before we look at ImageScroller, we must take a slight detour and introduce another GJT component: ImageCanvas, which is a canvas onto which an image is painted. It exists solely because Image is not a component, which leaves us hanging, for instance, when we want to add an image to a container. Example 26-3 shows how it is implemented.

Example 26-3 gjt.ImageCanvas **Class Source Code**

```
package gjt;

import java.awt.*;

public class ImageCanvas extends Component {
  private Image image;

  public ImageCanvas() {
  }
  public ImageCanvas(Image image) {
     Assert.notNull(image);
     setImage(image);
  }
  public void paint(Graphics g) {
     if(image != null) {
        g.drawImage(image, 0, 0, this);
     }
  }
  public void update(Graphics g) {
     paint(g);
  }
  public void setImage(Image image) {
     Util.waitForImage(this, image);
     this.image = image;

     setSize(image.getWidth(this), image.getHeight(this));

     if(isShowing()) {
```

```
            repaint();
        }
    }
    public Dimension getPreferredSize() {
        if(image != null) {
            return new Dimension(image.getWidth(this),
            image.getHeight(this));
        }
        else
            return new Dimension(0,0);
    }
}
```

gjt.ImageCanvas can be constructed with or without an image. If an image is specified, gjt.Util.waitForImage() is called to wait for the image to load, and ImageCanvas adjusts its size to accommodate the image. When told to paint, the ImageCanvas draws the image at 0,0. Notice that ImageCanvas overrides update() for the same reason we override it in Scroller—to eliminate erasing of the background when an update occurs. Also notice that the image may be set after construction by invoking setImage(), which repaints the image canvas if it is showing.

Now we are ready to take a look at gjt.ImageScroller in Example 26-4.

Example 26-4 gjt.ImageScroller **Class Source Code**

```
package gjt;

import java.awt.*;

public class ImageScroller extends Scroller {
  private Image  image;
  private ImageCanvas canvas;

  public ImageScroller(Image image) {
    viewport.setLayout(new BorderLayout());
    setImage(image);
  }
  public void resetImage(Image image) {
    viewport.remove(canvas);
    setImage(image);
  }
  public void scrollTo(int x, int y) {
    Graphics g = canvas.getGraphics();
    if(g != null) {
        g.translate(-x,-y);
        g.drawImage(image, 0, 0, this);
        g.dispose();
```

```
        }
    }
    public Dimension getScrollAreaSize() {
        return new Dimension(image.getWidth(this),
                             image.getHeight(this));
    }
    private void setImage(Image image) {
        this.image = image;
        hbar.setValue(0);
        vbar.setValue(0);
        viewport.add("Center", canvas = new ImageCanvas(image));

        if(isShowing()) {
            canvas.invalidate();
            validate();
        }
    }
}
```

An `ImageScroller` is constructed with an image. After the constructor sets the viewport's layout manager to an instance of `BorderLayout`, the image is sent to the private `setImage()` method.

The `setImage()` method sets the initial values of the scrollbars to 0,0.

The `scrollTo()` method is overridden as follows:

```
public void scrollTo(int x, int y) {
  Graphics g = canvas.getGraphics();

  if(g != null) {
     g.translate(-x,-y);
     g.drawImage(image, 0, 0, this);
     g.dispose();
  }
}
```

The `scrollTo()` method obtains the `Graphics` object for the `ImageCanvas` and translates the `Graphics` object before drawing the image at 0,0. The `g.translate()` method translates the origin of the `Graphics` object, which results in all subsequent graphics operations being relative to the translated origin. Notice that we are careful to dispose of the graphics obtained by the call to `getGraphics()`—see "Disposing of a Graphics Object" on page 29.

Exercising the gjt.ImageScroller

`ImageScrollerTest` creates images and cycles through them when the "Advance Image" button is activated, as illustrated in Figure 26-3.

Figure 26-3 `gjt.ImageScroller` Unit Test
Activating the Advance Image button causes a new image to be displayed. Scrollbars appear only when an image is larger than the display area.

`ImageScrollerTest` extends `UnitTest` and supplies an instance of an `ImageScrollerTestPanel`. Figure 26-4 shows the unit test layout.

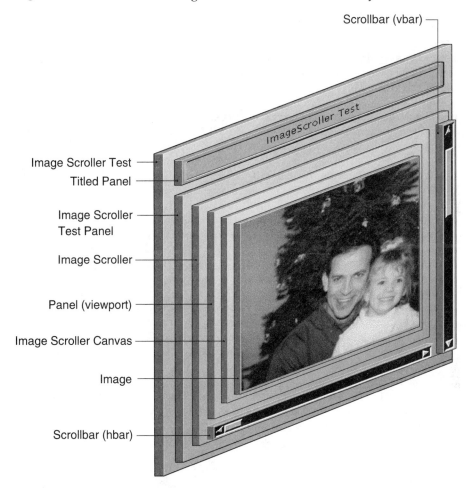

Figure 26-4 `ImageScrollerTest` Layout Diagram

Example 26-5 lists the source code for the `ImageScrollerTest` class.

Example 26-5 `gjt.test.ImageScrollerTest` **Class Source Code**

```java
package gjt.test;
import java.awt.*;
import java.awt.event.*;
import java.applet.Applet;
import java.net.URL;
import gjt.ImageScroller;
import gjt.Util;

public class ImageScrollerTest extends UnitTest {
  public String title() {
     return "ImageScroller Test";
  }
  public Panel centerPanel() {
     return new ImageScrollerTestPanel(this);
  }
}
class ImageScrollerTestPanel extends Panel implements
                                        ActionListener {
  private Image[]      images     = new Image[4];
  private int          imageIndex = 0;
  private ImageScroller scroller;
  private ImageScrollerAdvancePanel advancePanel;
  private Button       advance = new Button("Next Image");

  public ImageScrollerTestPanel(Applet applet) {
     URL cb = applet.getCodeBase();

     images[0]=applet.getImage(cb,"gifs/ashleyAndRoy.gif");
     images[1]=applet.getImage(cb,"gifs/ashleyAndSabre.gif");
     images[2]=applet.getImage(cb,"gifs/anjinAndMariko.gif");
     images[3]=applet.getImage(cb,"gifs/ashleyAndAnjin.gif");

     advancePanel = new ImageScrollerAdvancePanel(this);
     setLayout(new BorderLayout());
     add("North", advancePanel);
     add("Center", scroller = new ImageScroller(images[0]));
  }
  public void actionPerformed(ActionEvent event) {
     if(imageIndex == images.length-1) imageIndex = 0;
     else                              imageIndex++;

     Util.setCursor(Frame.WAIT_CURSOR, this);
     scroller.resetImage(images[imageIndex]);
     Util.setCursor(Frame.DEFAULT_CURSOR, this);
     scroller.getViewport().invalidate();
     scroller.validate();
```

```
    }
  }
  class ImageScrollerAdvancePanel extends Panel {
    private Button advanceButton = new Button("Advance Image");

    public ImageScrollerAdvancePanel(ImageScrollerTestPanel p) {
      add(advanceButton);
      advanceButton.addActionListener(p);
    }
  }
```

The `ImageScrollerTestPanel` constructor uses a `BorderLayout` and places an `ImageScroller` in the center of the panel.

This applet illustrates the ease with which an image can be scrolled with the Graphic Java Toolkit. As clients of `ImageScroller`, our only responsibilities are to ensure that `ImageScroller` is passed a valid image at construction time and that a valid image is also passed to the `ImageScroller.resetImage(Image)` method.

Summary

The AWT provides a `ScrollPane` class for scrolling a component, but there are times when a different approach to scrolling is necessary, specifically, when scrolling an image or scrolling a large *virtual* container. The GJT scrolling classes provide a framework for scrolling and also provide an image scroller that scrolls images more smoothly than does the java.awt.ScrollPane class.

CHAPTER
27

Sprite Animation

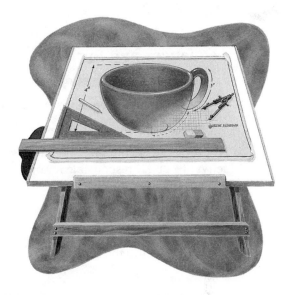

The Graphic Java Toolkit provides an animation package that encapsulates many of the low-level details of implementing animations. This chapter explores the `gjt.animation` package and discusses a number of animation-related topics, such as animation sequences, sprites, and collision detection.

The Participants

There are four major participants in the GJT `animation` package:

- `Playfield` — Is an extension of `gjt.DoubleBufferedContainer` on which sprite animation takes place.
- `Sprite` — Is a lightweight component that is animated on a `Playfield`.
- `Sequence` — Maintains a sequence of images.
- `CollisionDetector` — Detects collisions between two sprites and collisions between sprites and the boundaries of a `Playfield`.

The premise behind the `gjt.animation` package is simple: sprites are animated on a playfield and can collide with other sprites and with the boundaries of their playfield. The rate at which sprites cycle through their images and the speed at which they move can both be set.

We'll begin our discussion with sprites and sequences and then describe playfields and collision detection.

Sequences and Sprites

Sprites must be able to perform two major functions:

- Cycle through a sequence of images
- Move about on a double buffered container

As previously mentioned, the rate at which each of these functions occurs can be set. A Sprite is responsible for moving itself about and timing its movement; however, it delegates the responsibility for cycling through a sequence of images to another object: a Sequence.

gjt.animation.Sequence

Figure 27-1 shows the Sequence class diagram.

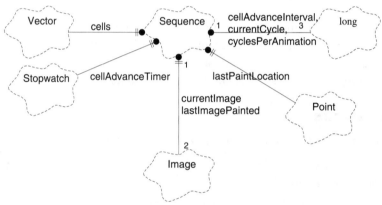

Figure 27-1 Sequence Class Diagram

As you can see, a Sequence maintains a vector of images that it cycles through. It also uses a stopwatch to control the rate at which it cycles through its images. The cellAdvanceInterval member of the Sequence class defines the elapsed time (in milliseconds) between the display of one image and the next.

If all Sequence objects simply cycled through their images only once, they wouldn't be of much use. Therefore, the number of cycles (defined as one complete pass through all the images) that a Sequence runs through can be set and is maintained in the cyclesPerAnimation member of the Sequence class.

Additionally, an instance of `Sequence` keeps track of its current cycle and is able to report whether its animation is over. The responsibilities of `gjt.animation.Sequence` are listed in Table 27-1.

Table 27-1 `gjt.animation.Sequence` **Responsibilities**

Methods	Description
`void start()`	Starts the sequence.
`Image getLastImage()`	Returns last image painted.
`Point getLastLocation()`	Returns location of last image painted.
`int getNumImages()`	Returns the number of images in the sequence.
`long getCurrentCycle()`	Returns the number of the current cycle.
`void setCurrentCycle(long)`	Sets the current cycle.
`long getCyclesPerAnimation()`	Returns the number of cycles for one complete animation.
`void setCyclesPerAnimation(long cyclesPerAnimation)`	Sets the number of cycles per animation.
`Image getFirstImage()`	Returns the first image in the sequence.
`Image getCurrentImage()`	Returns the current image.
`int getCurrentImagePosition()`	Returns the position of the current image.
`Image getNextImage()`	Returns the next image in the sequence.
`void setAdvanceInterval(long)`	Sets the interval between image updates in milliseconds.
`void addImage(Component, Image)`	Adds an image to the sequence.
`void removeImage(Image)`	Removes an image from the sequence.
`boolean needsRepainting(Point)`	Whether the sequence needs to repaint at a particular location.
`boolean isAtLastImage()`	Whether the sequence is on the last image.
`boolean timeToAdvanceCell()`	Whether it is time to advance to the next image.
`boolean animationOver()`	Whether the animation is over.
`void advance()`	Advances to the next image.

Table 27-2 lists the associations of a `gjt.animation.Sequence`.

Table 27-2 `gjt.animation.Sequence` **Associations**

Variables	Description
`private static long infiniteCycle`	Defines an infinite cycle.
`private Vector cells`	Images used in sequence
`private Point lastPaintLocation`	Location at which last image was painted.
`private Stopwatch cellAdvanceTimer`	Timer for timing interval between image advances.
`private Image currentImage`	The current image.
`private Image lastImagePainted`	The last image painted.
`private long cellAdvanceInterval`	The delay between image updates, in milliseconds.
`private long currentCycle`	The current cycle.
`private long cyclesPerAnimation`	The number of cycles per animation.

Now that we have a basic understanding of the inner workings of a `Sequence`, let's take a look at the implementation of the `Sequence` class in Example 27-1.

Example 27-1 `gjt.animation.Sequence` **Class Source Code**

```
package gjt.animation;

import java.util.Vector;
import java.awt.*;
import java.awt.image.ImageObserver;
import gjt.Util;
import gjt.Stopwatch;

public class Sequence {
  private static long infiniteCycle = -1;

  private Vector    cells               = new Vector();
  private Point     lastPaintLocation   = new Point(0,0);
  private Stopwatch cellAdvanceTimer    = new Stopwatch();
  private Image     currentImage, lastImagePainted;
  private long      cellAdvanceInterval = 0,
                    currentCycle        = 0,
                    cyclesPerAnimation  = 0;

  public Sequence() { }
```

```java
public Sequence(Component component, Image[] images) {
   for(int i=0; i < images.length; ++i) {
      addImage(component, images[i]);
   }
   cyclesPerAnimation = infiniteCycle;
}
public void  start           () { cellAdvanceTimer.start(); }
public Image getLastImage    () { return lastImagePainted;  }
public Point getLastLocation () { return lastPaintLocation; }
public int   getNumImages    () { return cells.size();      }

public long getCurrentCycle()           { return currentCycle; }
public void setCurrentCycle(long c) { currentCycle = c;     }

public long getCyclesPerAnimation() {
   return currentCycle;
}
public void setCyclesPerAnimation(long cyclesPerAnimation) {
   this.cyclesPerAnimation = cyclesPerAnimation;
}
public Image getFirstImage() {
   return (Image)cells.firstElement();
}
public Image getCurrentImage() {
   return currentImage;
}
public int getCurrentImagePosition() {
   return cells.indexOf(currentImage);
}
public Image getNextImage() {
   int    index = cells.indexOf(currentImage);
   Image image;

   if(index == cells.size() - 1)
      image = (Image)cells.elementAt(0);
   else
      image = (Image)cells.elementAt(index + 1);

   return image;
}
public void setAdvanceInterval(long interval) {
   cellAdvanceInterval = interval;
}
public void addImage(Component component, Image image) {
   if(currentImage == null)
      currentImage = image;

   Util.waitForImage(component, image);
```

```
         cells.addElement(image);
      }
      public void removeImage(Image image) {
         cells.removeElement(image);
      }
      public boolean needsRepainting(Point point) {
         return (lastPaintLocation.x != point.x ||
                 lastPaintLocation.y != point.y ||
                 lastImagePainted   != currentImage);
      }
      public boolean isAtLastImage() {
         return getCurrentImagePosition() == (cells.size() - 1);
      }
      public boolean timeToAdvanceCell() {
         return cellAdvanceTimer.elapsedTime() > cellAdvanceInterval;
      }
      public boolean animationOver() {
         return (cyclesPerAnimation != infiniteCycle) &&
                (currentCycle >= cyclesPerAnimation);
      }
      public void advance() {
         if(isAtLastImage())
             ++currentCycle;

         currentImage = getNextImage();
         cellAdvanceTimer.reset();
      }
   }
```

A Sequence can be constructed with a component and an array of images. The sequence waits for all the images in the array to be loaded before returning from its constructor. The component's only role is as an accomplice to image loading; it is passed to gjt.Util.waitForImage(Component, Image).

Additionally, a Sequence can be constructed with no arguments. Presumably, images will be added to such a sequence through its addImage() method before sequencing through its images when the default constructor is used.

A Sequence is also able to report whether it needs to be repainted at a given location. If the last paint location is different from the given location or if the last image painted is not equal to the current image, then the current image in the sequence needs to be repainted.

A Sequence also has methods that return information about the sequence:

- isAtLastImage()
- timeToAdvanceCell()
- animationOver()

gjt.animation.Sprite

It is important to realize that a Sequence is something of a simpleton that will continuously cycle through its sequence of images, no matter what its cyclesPerAnimation has been set to. It is up to another object to monitor the sequence's progress and determine if it is time to end the sequence. That object is a Sprite, as diagrammed in Figure 27-2.

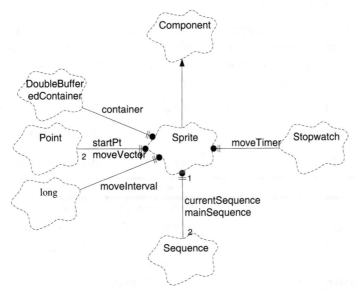

Figure 27-2 Sprite Class Diagram

Sprites are lightweight components[1] that can be animated on a DoubleBufferedContainer[2]. Because Sprite extends Component, it inherits all of the functionality provided by the java.awt.Component class.

The first thing that may strike you about the Sprite class is that it actually maintains two sequences: one main sprite sequence and one temporary one. Our sprites would be pretty boring if they endlessly cycled through only one sequence; thus, it is imperative that we give sprites the ability to change their sequence for a period of time. As a result, each sprite has a main sequence that it

---

1. See "Lightweight Components" on page 475.
2. See "DoubleBufferedContainer" on page 489.

cycles through endlessly and a temporary sequence that upstages the main sequence for a specific number of cycles. Upstaging the main sequence is accomplished by the play(Sequence sequence, long cycles) method.

As we previously mentioned, a sprite is responsible for moving itself, so it is not surprising to see that a sprite has both a stopwatch, which is used to time its movement, and an interval, specified in milliseconds, which times its movements from one location to the next.

Of course, in addition to timing its movements, a sprite must know the direction in which to move. The direction in which a sprite moves is stored in its moveVector, a point that defines how many pixels the sprite moves in the x and y directions each time it is told to move.

A sprite also keeps track of its width, height, current location.

The responsibilities of gjt.animation.Sprite are listed in Table 27-3.

Table 27-3 gjt.animation.Sprite **Responsibilities (public methods)**

Methods	Description
void reverseX()	Reverses the sprite's horizontal direction.
void reverseY	Reverses the sprite's vertical direction.
void reverse()	Reverses both the horizontal and vertical directions of the sprite.
void setMoveVector(Point p)	Sets the direction the sprite moves.
Point getMoveVector()	Returns the move vector.
void play(Sequence sequence, long cycles)	Plays a sequence other than the main sequence for a specified number of cycles
void animate()	Animates the sprite.
void setMainSequence(Sequence sequence)	Sets the sprite's main sequence.
Sequence getMainSequence()	Returns the sprite's main sequence.
void setSequence(Sequence sequence)	Sets a temporary sequence.
Sequence getSequence()	Gets the current sequence.
boolean willIntersect(Sprite otherSprite)	Determines if the sprite will intersect with another sprite the next time they are moved.
void setMoveInterval(long interval)	Sets the interval between movements.

Table 27-3 gjt.animation.Sprite **Responsibilities (public methods) (Continued)**

Methods	Description
void setImageChangeInterval(long interval)	Sets the interval between image advancement.
Point getNextLocation()	Returns the next location the sprite will be moved to.
Rectangle getNextBounds()	Returns the bounds the sprite will occupy when it is moved to its next location.
void paint(Graphics g)	Overridden Component method that paints the sprite.
void update(Graphics g)	Overridden Component method that invokes paint() directly to avoid erasing its background.
Dimension getPreferredSize()	Overridden Component method that returns the width and height of the current image in the sprite's sequence.
void setLocation()	Overridden Component method that resets move timer in addition to setting location.

Table 27-4 lists the associations of a gjt.animation.Sprite.

Table 27-4 gjt.animation.Sprite **Associations**

Variables	Description
private DoubleBufferedContainer container	The double buffered container that the sprite animates over.
private Sequence currentSequence	The sprite's current sequence.
private Sequence mainSequence	The sprite's main sequence.
private Stopwatch moveTimer	Timer used to time movements.
private Point startPoint	The starting location for the sprite.
private Point moveVector	The direction in which the sprite moves.
private long moveInterval	Interval, in milliseconds, between movements.

Example 27-2 shows the implementation of the Sprite class.

Example 27-2 gjt.animation.Sprite **Class Source Code**

```
package gjt.animation;

import java.awt.*;
import java.util.Vector;
import gjt.*;

public class Sprite extends Component {
  private DoubleBufferedContainer container;
  private Sequence currentSequence, mainSequence;
  private Stopwatch moveTimer = new Stopwatch();

  private Point startPt      = new Point(0,0);
  private Point moveVector    = new Point(1,1);
  private long  moveInterval = 0;

  public Sprite(DoubleBufferedContainer container,
                Sequence                  sequence,
                Point                     ulhc) {
    this.container = container;
    setSequence          (sequence);
    setMainSequence      (sequence);
    moveTimer.start      ();
    currentSequence.start();
    setLocation(ulhc);
  }

  public void  reverseX () { moveVector.x = 0-moveVector.x;  }
  public void  reverseY () { moveVector.y = 0-moveVector.y;  }
  public void  reverse  () { reverseX(); reverseY();         }

  public void  setMoveVector (Point p) { moveVector = p;     }
  public Point getMoveVector()          { return moveVector; }

  public void paint(Graphics g) {
    if(isVisible()) {
      Image image = currentSequence.getCurrentImage();
      g.drawImage(image, 0, 0, this);
    }
  }
  public void update(Graphics g) {
    paint(g);
  }
  public Dimension getPreferredSize() {
    Image image = currentSequence.getCurrentImage();
    return new Dimension(image.getWidth(this),
                         image.getHeight(this));
```

```
}
public void play(Sequence sequence, long cycles) {
   setSequence(sequence);
   sequence.setCyclesPerAnimation(cycles);
   sequence.setCurrentCycle(0);
}
public void animate() {
   if(currentSequence.animationOver())
      currentSequence = mainSequence;

   if(timeToChangeImage()) currentSequence.advance();

   if(timeToMove()) {
      advance();
   }
   else {
      if(needsRepainting()) {
         container.paintComponent(this);
      }
   }
}
public void setMainSequence(Sequence sequence) {
   mainSequence = sequence;
}
public Sequence getMainSequence() {
   return mainSequence;
}
public void setSequence(Sequence sequence) {
   currentSequence = sequence;
}
public Sequence getSequence() {
   return currentSequence;
}
public boolean willIntersect(Sprite otherSprite) {
   return getNextBounds().intersects(
                        otherSprite.getNextBounds());
}
public void setLocation(int x, int y) {
   super.setLocation(x, y);
   moveTimer.reset();
}
public void setMoveInterval(long interval) {
   moveInterval = interval;
}
public void setImageChangeInterval(long interval) {
   currentSequence.setAdvanceInterval(interval);
}
public Point getNextLocation() {
```

```
        Rectangle bounds = getBounds();
        return new Point(bounds.x + moveVector.x,
                         bounds.y + moveVector.y);
    }
    public Rectangle getNextBounds() {
        Rectangle bounds = getBounds();
        Point nextLoc    = getNextLocation();

        return new Rectangle(nextLoc.x,    nextLoc.y,
                             bounds.width, bounds.height);
    }
    protected boolean timeToChangeImage() {
        return currentSequence.timeToAdvanceCell();
    }
    protected boolean timeToMove() {
        return moveTimer.elapsedTime() > moveInterval;
    }
    protected boolean needsRepainting() {
        Rectangle bounds = getBounds();

        return currentSequence.needsRepainting(
                         new Point(bounds.x, bounds.y));
    }
    protected void advance() {
        Rectangle bounds = getBounds();
        container.blitBackgroundToWorkplace(bounds);

        Image image = currentSequence.getCurrentImage();
        setBounds(bounds.x + moveVector.x,
                  bounds.y + moveVector.y,
                  image.getWidth(this), image.getHeight(this));

        container.paintComponents(bounds.union(getBounds()),true);
    }
}
```

A Sprite must be constructed with a DoubleBufferedContainer, a main
Sequence, and a starting location:

```
public Sprite(DoubleBufferedContainer container,
              Sequence sequence, Point ulhc) {
```

An instance of a Sprite, of course, keeps track of its
DoubleBufferedContainer, main Sequence, and location; we leave nothing
to chance by requiring that each of these is supplied at construction time.

Notice that a sprite also implements a number of convenience methods. It is able to reverse its x direction, y direction, or both, and it may have its move vector and sequence set anytime after construction. Additionally, a sprite can tell whether will intersect with another sprite the next time it is moved.

One last thing to note about our implementation of the `Sprite` class is that it requires that each image in its current sequence be the same size. While this may seem restrictive, in practice it is usually not a problem; if a sprite is to grow or shrink, it can always be fitted with a new sequence with images that are larger or smaller. The only requirement is that each image in the sequence must have the same size.

Playfield and DoubleBufferedContainer

Of course, a sprite is useless without a `DoubleBufferedContainer` upon which to frolic, so let's turn our attention to the `Playfield` class and discuss the animation functionality it provides.

gjt.animation.Playfield

A `Playfield` is a double buffered container that adds animation capabilities to the double buffering functionality implemented by the `DoubleBufferedContainer` class. The class diagram for `gjt.animation.Playfield` is shown in Figure 27-3.

The `Playfield` class extends `gjt.DoubleBufferedContainer`. We've already discussed the implementation of `gjt.DoubleBufferedContainer` in "DoubleBufferedContainer" on page 489, so we won't bother to rehash that discussion here, other than to provide a brief recap of the `DoubleBufferedContainer` class.

`DoubleBufferedContainer` is a lightweight *container* that lightweight *components* can be rendered upon. `DoubleBufferedContainer`, as its name implies employs double buffering to smoothly move lightweight components over its surface. See "Dragging Lightweight Components" on page 496, for a discussion of dragging lightweights over the surface of a double buffered container.

In any event, a playfield implements functionality specific to animation over and above the double buffering capabilities implemented by its superclass. The `Playfield` class implements two interfaces:

* `Runnable`
* `CollisionArena`

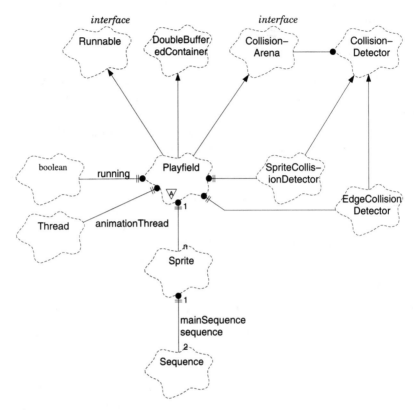

Figure 27-3 Playfield Class Diagram

A playfield creates and maintains a thread that is used to animate the sprites that reside in the playfield; thus it fulfills its obligations as a Runnable. Additionally, a playfield employs two collision detectors: a sprite collision detector and an edge collision detector. As their names suggest, the detectors detect collisions either between two sprites or between a sprite and the boundary of the playfield. The collision detectors merely *detect* collisions—they call back to the playfield to *handle* the collision. We will expound on this relationship more when we discuss collision detection.

Each playfield keeps track of the sprites that are currently animating on it. Because the double buffering functionality is implemented by its superclass, Playfield is a simple class. Table 27-5 lists the responsibilities of the gjt.animation.Playfield.

Table 27-5 `gjt.animation.Playfield` **Responsibilities**

Methods	Description
void spriteCollision(Sprite, Sprite)	A no-op implementation of a CollisionArena method.
void edgeCollision(Sprite, Orientation)	A no-op implementation of a CollisionArena method.
void start()	Starts the animation.
void stop()	Signifies that the animation is to stop.
boolean running()	Returns whether the animation is currently running.
Vector getSprites()	Returns the sprites in the playfield.
void animateSprites()	Animates the sprites in the playfield.
void run()	Animation loop.

Table 27-6 lists the associations of a `gjt.animation.Playfield`.

Table 27-6 `gjt.animation.Playfield` **Associations**

Variables	Description
private boolean running	Whether the animation is running.
private Thread animationThread	Thread controlling the animation.
private CollisionDetector edgeCollisionDetector	Detects collisions between sprites and boundaries of the playfield.
private CollisionDetector spriteCollisionDetector	Detects collisions between sprites.

The `Playfield` constructor creates its collision detectors and sets its layout manager to an instance of `gjt.BulletinLayout`[3], which simply positions components at their current location and shapes them to their preferred size.

```
public Playfield() {
  edgeDetector   = new EdgeCollisionDetector(this);
  spriteDetector = new SpriteCollisionDetector(this);
  setLayout(new BulletinLayout());
}
```

As we'll see when we discuss collision detectors, the `CollisionArena` interface that is implemented by the `Playfield` class defines two abstract methods, both of which `Playfield` implements as no-ops.

3. See "gjt.BulletinLayout" on page 444.

```
public void spriteCollision(Sprite sprite, Sprite other) { }
public void edgeCollision  (Sprite sprite, Orientation o){ }
```

By default then, the `Playfield` class takes no action when a collision occurs. Extensions of `Playfield` may override the methods in order to handle collisions if they so desire.

`Playfield` has both a `start()` and a `stop()` method, which start and stop the animation, respectively, along with a `running()` method that can be used to determine if the animation is currently running. The `start()` method creates a thread whose constructor is passed a reference to the `Playfield` so that the `Playfield` `run()` method is invoked when the thread is started. [4]

```
public void start() {
  animationThread = new Thread(this);
  running = true;
  animationThread.start();
}
public void    stop    ()  { running = false;  }
public boolean running()  { return running;    }
```

The implementation of the `stop()` method may seem odd, since it merely sets a `boolean` variable (`running`) to `false` and does nothing else. In reality, it does not stop anything. However, the `run()` method runs as long as the `running` member is `true`; this is checked at the top of the `run()` method's `while` loop. If `running` has been set to `false`, `run()` returns after setting `animationThread` to `null`. The reason for this seemingly roundabout way of stopping the animation thread is to ensure that the thread is not stopped in the middle of painting one of the playfield's sprites.

Let's take a closer look at the `run()` method to see exactly what it is that a `Playfield` does over and over until someone calls the `stop()` method:

```
public void run() {
  while(running == true) {
    edgeDetector.detectCollisions   ();
    spriteDetector.detectCollisions();

    animateSprites();

    try { Thread.currentThread().sleep(50); }
    catch(Exception e) { e.printStackTrace(); }
  }
  animationThread = null;
}
```

4.   A number of Java language books discuss threads in more detail.

First, each of the `Playfield` collision detectors is told to detect collisions. If a collision is detected, the detectors invoke either
`Playfield.spriteCollision()` or `Playfield.edgeCollision()`, depending upon the type of collision that was detected. Next, the playfield animates the sprites and then invokes `sleep(50)` on the current thread to give other processes some breathing room. (After all, when the boss walks by while you're playing the hottest new Internet game, a `Playfield` must be able to quickly allow someone else to take over the display.)

`Playfield.animateSprites()` runs through each `Component` contained in the playfield[5], and, if the component is a sprite, invokes the sprite's `animate()` method:

```
protected void animateSprites() {
   int         ncomps = getComponentCount();
   Component   comp;

   for(int i=0; i < ncomps; ++i)
      if((comp = getComponent(i)) instanceof Sprite)
         ((Sprite)comp).animate();
   }
}
```

That's about all there is to the Playfield class. The entire implementation of the `Playfield` class is listed in Example 27-3.

Example 27-3 `gjt.animation.Playfield` **Class Source Code**

```
package gjt.animation;

import java.awt.*;
import java.util.*;
import gjt.*;

public class Playfield extends DoubleBufferedContainer
                       implements Runnable, CollisionArena {
   private   boolean running = false;
   private   Thread  animationThread;
   private   CollisionDetector spriteDetector, edgeDetector;

   public Playfield() {
      edgeDetector   = new EdgeCollisionDetector(this);
      spriteDetector = new SpriteCollisionDetector(this);
      setLayout(new BulletinLayout());
   }
   public void spriteCollision(Sprite sprite, Sprite other) { }
```

5. Remember, `Playfield` ultimately extends `java.awt.Container`.

```java
public void edgeCollision  (Sprite sprite, Orientation o){ }

public void     stop   ()  { running = false;   }
public boolean running()   { return running;    }

public void start() {
   animationThread = new Thread(this);
   running = true;
   animationThread.start();
}
public void run() {
   while(running == true) {
      edgeDetector.detectCollisions  ();
      spriteDetector.detectCollisions();

      animateSprites();

      try { Thread.currentThread().sleep(50); }
      catch(Exception e) { e.printStackTrace(); }
   }
   animationThread = null;
}
public Vector getSprites() {
   int          ncomps = getComponentCount();
   Component    comp;
   Vector       vector = new Vector();

   for(int i=0; i < ncomps; ++i) {
      if((comp = getComponent(i)) instanceof Sprite)
         vector.addElement(comp);
   }
   return vector;
}
protected void animateSprites() {
   int          ncomps = getComponentCount();
   Component    comp;

   for(int i=0; i < ncomps; ++i)
      if((comp = getComponent(i)) instanceof Sprite)
         ((Sprite)comp).animate();
}
}
```

Collision Detection

Now that we've covered the Sequence, Sprite, and Playfield classes, the only topic left to discuss is collision detection. Collision detection is defined by an interface and an abstract class: CollisionArena and CollisionDetector, respectively. As we discuss collision detection, don't forget that Playfield implements CollisionArena, so everything we say concerning CollisionArena goes for Playfield.

gjt.animation.CollisionArena

The CollisionArena interface defines the behavior of an arena in which collisions take place, as you can see in Example 27-4.

Example 27-4 gjt.animation.CollisionArena **Interface Source Code**

```
package gjt.animation;

import java.awt.Dimension;
import java.awt.Insets;
import java.util.Vector;
import gjt.Orientation;

public interface CollisionArena {
  Vector     getSprites();
  Dimension getSize    ();
  Insets     getInsets ();

  void spriteCollision(Sprite sprite, Sprite other);
  void edgeCollision(Sprite sprite, Orientation orient);
}
```

A CollisionArena is responsible for producing a Vector of sprites that it contains, reporting its size and insets, and handling collisions between two Sprite objects and between a Sprite and a boundary. Notice that the CollisionArena is not responsible for actually *detecting* collisions but is responsible for handling the aftermath of a collision by implementing spriteCollision() and edgeCollision().

gjt.animation.CollisionDetector

The abstract CollisionDetector class establishes the relationship between itself and a CollisionArena but leaves the actual collision detection to extensions, as illustrated in Example 27-5.

Example 27-5 `gjt.animation.CollisionDetector` **Class Source Code**

```
package gjt.animation;

abstract public class CollisionDetector {
  protected CollisionArena arena;

  abstract public void detectCollisions();

  public CollisionDetector(CollisionArena arena) {
    this.arena = arena;
  }
}
```

A `CollisionDetector` must be constructed with a reference to a `CollisionArena`. Remember that a `CollisionArena` is responsible for handling the aftermath of a collision, whereas a `CollisionDetector` is only responsible for detecting collisions.

gjt.animation.SpriteCollisionDetector

`CollisionDetector` has two subclasses that do the grunt work of actually detecting collisions: `SpriteCollisionDetector` and `EdgeCollisionDetector`. Let's first look at `SpriteCollisionDetector` in Example 27-4, which detects collisions between sprites.

Example 27-6 `gjt.animation.SpriteCollisionDetector` **Class Source Code**

```
package gjt.animation;

import java.awt.*;
import java.util.Enumeration;
import java.util.Vector;
import gjt.Orientation;

public class SpriteCollisionDetector extends CollisionDetector {
  public SpriteCollisionDetector(CollisionArena arena) {
    super(arena);
  }
  public void detectCollisions() {
    Enumeration sprites = arena.getSprites().elements();
    Sprite      sprite;

    while(sprites.hasMoreElements()) {
      sprite = (Sprite)sprites.nextElement();

      Enumeration otherSprites = arena.getSprites().elements();
      Sprite otherSprite;
```

```
            while(otherSprites.hasMoreElements()) {
                otherSprite=(Sprite)otherSprites.nextElement();

                if(otherSprite != sprite)
                    if(sprite.willIntersect(otherSprite))
                        arena.spriteCollision(sprite,otherSprite);
            }
        }
    }
}
```

Simply put, `SpriteCollisionDetector` gets all of the sprites from its associated `CollisionArena` and cycles through each one to see if it will intersect with any of the other sprites the next time they are moved. If so, `SpriteCollisionDetector` invokes its collision arena's `spriteCollision()` method, passing along the sprites involved in the collision.

gjt.animation.EdgeCollision

`EdgeCollisionDetector` in Example 27-7 detects collisions between a sprite and the boundaries of its collision arena.

Example 27-7 `gjt.animation.EdgeCollisionDetector` **Class Source Code**

```
package gjt.animation;

import java.awt.*;
import java.util.Enumeration;
import java.util.Vector;
import gjt.Orientation;

public class EdgeCollisionDetector extends CollisionDetector {
  public EdgeCollisionDetector(CollisionArena arena) {
    super(arena);
  }
  public void detectCollisions() {
    Enumeration sprites    = arena.getSprites().elements();
    Dimension  arenaSize   = arena.getSize();
    Insets     arenaInsets = arena.getInsets();
    Sprite     sprite;

    while(sprites.hasMoreElements()) {
        sprite = (Sprite)sprites.nextElement();

        Point nl    = sprite.getNextLocation ();
        Point mv    = sprite.getMoveVector();
        int   width = sprite.getBounds().width;
```

```
    int    height = sprite.getBounds().height;

    int    nextRightEdge    = nl.x + width;
    int    nextBottomEdge   = nl.y + height;

    int    arenaBottomEdge = arenaSize.height -
                                  arenaInsets.bottom;
    int    arenaRightEdge  = arenaSize.width -
                                  arenaInsets.right;

    if(nextRightEdge > arenaRightEdge)
        arena.edgeCollision(sprite, Orientation.LEFT);
    else if(nl.x < arenaInsets.left)
        arena.edgeCollision(sprite, Orientation.RIGHT);

    if(nextBottomEdge > arenaBottomEdge)
        arena.edgeCollision(sprite, Orientation.BOTTOM);
    else if(nl.y < arenaInsets.top)
        arena.edgeCollision(sprite, Orientation.TOP);
    }
  }
}
```

Note that when a sprite collides with the boundary of the collision arena, it is not enough to simply state that a particular sprite ran into a boundary. We must also tell the collision arena which edge of the sprite collided with the boundary. This is the reason for the orientation argument in the arena's edgeCollision() method.

We've now covered the details of the Sprite, Playfield, and Sequence classes and collision detection and double buffering; it's time to have a little fun and take a look at the unit test for the gjt.animation package.

Exercising the gjt.animation Package

When animations are created using the GJT animation package, Playfield is typically extended and spriteCollision() and edgeCollision() are overridden in order to handle sprite-on-sprite and sprite/boundary collisions, respectively. The only other coding necessary is to create the sprites and their associated sequences, which are added to the playfield.

Simple Animation

To start off, we'll look at a simple animation applet that you can use as a starting point for your own animations. Our simple animation will have one instance of Sprite that will bounce off the walls of the Playfield. Figure 27-4 shows the unit test, but, of course, you can see the full animation by running the unit test included on the CD yourself. Simply run `appletviewer` on the `SimpleAnimationTest.html` file.

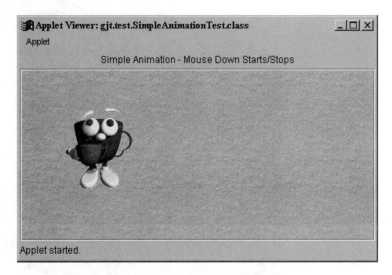

Figure 27-4 Simple Animation Unit Test
This sprite moves on the playfield and bumps off the walls.

As you look through the animation unit test in Example 27-8, notice that `SimpleAnimationTestPanel` centers a `SimplePlayfield` instance; once that is done, all that is left is to implement `SimplePlayfield`.

`SimplePlayfield.edgeCollisions()` is implemented such that our sprite bounces off the walls of the `Playfield`. If the orientation of the collision is right or left, then we know the sprite has bumped into a vertical wall, and we reverse its x direction. If the orientation is anything else (top or bottom), then we know the sprite has collided with the floor or ceiling of the `Playfield`, and we reverse its y direction.

`makeSequencesAndSprites()` first loads the 19 images used in the `Sprite` object's main sequence and then creates a sequence from the images loaded. Next, it creates the sprite itself (`javaDrinker`), passing a reference to the `Playfield`, the main sequence, and the starting location for `javaDrinker`. We set the move vector to (2,2), meaning the `Sprite` will move 2 pixels in the x direction and 2 pixels in the y direction every time it moves. Lastly, we add the `Sprite` to the `Playfield`. Figure 27-5 depicts the layout for all three of the sprite animation unit tests.

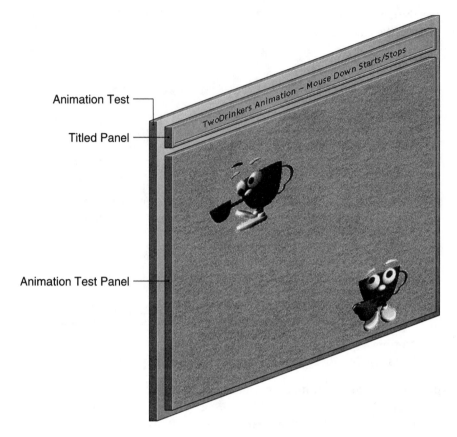

Figure 27-5 Sprite Animation Unit Tests Layout.

Now let's look at the unit test in Example 27-8.

Example 27-8 gjt.test.SimpleAnimationTest **Class Source Code**

```
package gjt.test;

import java.net.URL;
import java.applet.Applet;
import java.awt.*;
import java.awt.event.*;

import gjt.Util;
import gjt.Orientation;
import gjt.animation.*;

public class SimpleAnimationTest extends UnitTest {
  public String title() {
```

```
         return "Simple Animation - Mouse Down Starts/Stops";
    }
    public Panel centerPanel() {
        return new SimpleAnimationTestPanel(this);
    }
}
class SimpleAnimationTestPanel extends Panel {
    public SimpleAnimationTestPanel(Applet applet) {
        setLayout(new BorderLayout());
        add(new SimplePlayfield(applet), "Center");
    }
    public void update(Graphics g) {
        paint(g);
    }
}
class SimplePlayfield extends Playfield {
    private Applet    applet;
    private URL       cb;
    private Sprite    javaDrinker;
    private Sequence  spinSequence;

    public SimplePlayfield(Applet applet) {
        this.applet = applet;
        cb = applet.getCodeBase();

        makeSequencesAndSprites();

        setWallpaperImage(
            applet.getImage(cb, "gifs/background.gif"));

        addMouseListener(new MouseAdapter() {
            public void mousePressed(MouseEvent event) {
                if(running() == true) stop ();
                else                  start();
            }
        });
    }
    public void edgeCollision(Sprite       sprite,
                              Orientation orientation) {
        if(orientation == Orientation.RIGHT ||
           orientation == Orientation.LEFT)
            sprite.reverseX();
        else
            sprite.reverseY();
    }
    private void makeSequencesAndSprites() {
        String  file;
        Point   startLoc   = new Point(10, 10);
```

```
Image[] spinImages = new Image[19];

for(int i=0; i < spinImages.length; ++i) {
    file = "gifs/spin";

    if(i < 10) file += "0" + i + ".gif";
    else       file += i + ".gif";

    spinImages[i] = applet.getImage(cb, file);
}
spinSequence = new Sequence(this, spinImages);
javaDrinker  = new Sprite(this, spinSequence, startLoc);

javaDrinker.setMoveVector(new Point(1,1));
add(javaDrinker);
    }
}
```

Notice that SimplePlayfield implements an animation that can be stopped and started with a mouse down, complete with collision detection, in a mere 50 lines of code. All that was necessary on our part was to:

1. Subclass Playfield in order to handle collisions.
2. Set the wall paper image for painting the background.
3. Create the sprites and their associated sequences.
4. Add the sprites to the playfield.

Bump Animation

Now, let's add some more behavior to our javaDrinker when he bumps into the boundaries of the Playfield. We will create another sequence that javaDrinker will play when he bumps into a wall. Just to make things a little more interesting, we will have our javaDrinker cycle through the *bump* sequence once for collisions with the left wall and twice for collisions with the right wall. We will also slow down the rate at which javaDrinker cycles through its images. You can see a picture of the bump sequence in Figure 27-6.

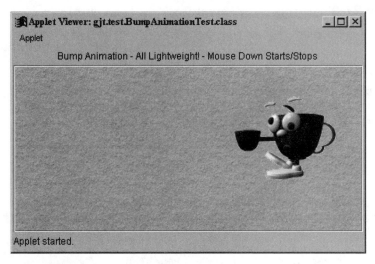

Figure 27-6 Bump Animation Unit Test
This sprite goes through a bump sequence after bumping into a wall.

Our applet in Example 27-9 looks exactly the same as the one in Example 27-8, except the names of the classes have changed. Pay attention to the differences between BumpPlayfield and SimplePlayfield. In BumpPlayfield, we create a second sequence, bumpSequence, and set the advance interval for the spin sequence to 100 milliseconds and the advance interval for the bump sequence to 200 milliseconds.

We've modified the edgeCollision() method so that a bump into the right or left walls causes javaDrinker to play the bump sequence the appropriate number of times. When the orientation is RIGHT, our javaDrinker has run into the left wall, and vice versa. The orientation specifies the side of the Sprite that hits the edges of the Playfield.

Example 27-9 `gjt.test.BumpAnimationTest` **Class Source Code**

```
package gjt.test;

import java.net.URL;
import java.applet.Applet;
import java.awt.*;
import java.awt.event.*;

import gjt.*;
import gjt.animation.*;

public class BumpAnimationTest extends UnitTest {
   public String title() {
      return
      "Bump Animation - All Lightweight! - Mouse Down Starts/Stops";
   }
   public Panel centerPanel() {
      return new BumpAnimationTestPanel(this);
   }
}
class BumpAnimationTestPanel extends Panel {
   public BumpAnimationTestPanel(Applet applet) {
      setLayout(new BorderLayout());
      add(new BumpPlayfield(applet), "Center");
   }
   public void update(Graphics g) {
      paint(g);
   }
}
class BumpPlayfield extends Playfield {
   private Applet   applet;
   private URL      cb;
   private Sprite   javaDrinker;
   private Sequence spinSequence, bumpSequence;

   public BumpPlayfield(Applet applet) {
      this.applet = applet;
      cb          = applet.getCodeBase();

      makeSequencesAndSprites();
      setWallpaperImage(
      applet.getImage(cb, "gifs/background.gif"));
```

```java
   addMouseListener(new MouseAdapter() {
      public void mousePressed(MouseEvent event) {
         if(running() == true) stop ();
         else                  start();
      }
   });
}
public void edgeCollision(Sprite     sprite,
                   Orientation orientation) {
   if(orientation == Orientation.RIGHT ||
      orientation == Orientation.LEFT) {
      if(sprite.getSequence() != bumpSequence) {
         sprite.reverseX();

         if(orientation == Orientation.RIGHT)
            sprite.play(bumpSequence, 1);
         else
            sprite.play(bumpSequence, 2);
      }
   }
   else
      sprite.reverseY();
}
private void makeSequencesAndSprites() {
   String  file;
   Point   startLoc  = new Point(10, 10);
   Image[] spinImages = new Image[19];
   Image[] bumpImages = new Image[6];

   for(int i=0; i < spinImages.length; ++i) {
      file = "gifs/spin";

      if(i < 10) file += "0" + i + ".gif";
      else       file += i + ".gif";

      spinImages[i] = applet.getImage(cb, file);
   }
   for(int i=0; i < bumpImages.length; ++i) {
      file = "gifs/bump0" + i + ".gif";
      bumpImages[i] = applet.getImage(cb, file);
   }
```

```
        spinSequence = new Sequence(this, spinImages);
        bumpSequence = new Sequence(this, bumpImages);
        javaDrinker  = new Sprite(this, spinSequence, startLoc);

        spinSequence.setAdvanceInterval(100);
        bumpSequence.setAdvanceInterval(200);
        javaDrinker.setMoveVector(new Point(1,1));
        javaDrinker.setImageChangeInterval(50);
        add(javaDrinker);
    }
}
```

Now, let's make one final iteration over our unit test to illustrate sprite-on-sprite collisions.

Two-Sprite Collision

This unit test adds another `javaDrinker` to the `Playfield`. We'll have one of the `javaDrinker` objects spin fast and move slow, while the other will spin slow and move fast. We will also create two bump sequences, one fast and the other slow. When the two `javaDrinker` objects collide, we'll have one of them play the slow bump sequence and the other the fast bump sequence. You can see the unit test in action in Figure 27-7.

We've added one additional twist to our unit test—we've added a choice that toggles collision detection on and off. Realize that since `Playfield` extends `gjt.DoubleBufferedContainer`, and `DoubleBufferedContainer` extends `java.awt.Container`, we can add AWT components to a playfield, as well as sprites.

Also, when collision detection is turned off, the sprites move over each other. Since sprites are components, the sprite that is on top is the sprite that has the highest zorder, or the sprite that was added to the container first. See "Components and Zorder" on page 159 for more on components and zorder.

Example 27-10 lists the unit test with two sprites. It is identical to the previous animation tests, except that this one creates a `TwoDrinkersPlayfield`. This time around, we will just show you the code without any accompanying commentary; it should be apparent what we're up to with the `TwoDrinkersPlayfield`.

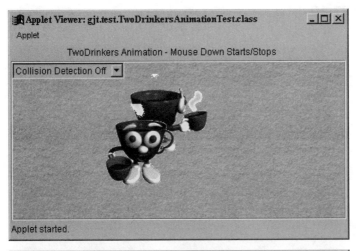

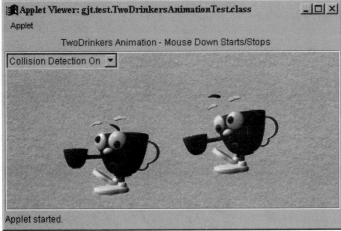

Figure 27-7 Two-Sprite Collision Animation Unit Test
The sprites each go through their individual bump sequences when
they collide if collision detection is turned on, and pass over each
other when it is turned off.

Example 27-10 `gjt.test.TwoDrinkersAnimationTest` **Class Source Code**

```
package gjt.test;

import java.net.URL;
import java.applet.Applet;
import java.awt.*;
import java.awt.Panel;

import gjt.Util;
import gjt.Orientation;
import gjt.animation.*;

public class TwoDrinkersAnimationTest extends UnitTest {
  public String title() {
    return "TwoDrinkers Animation - Mouse Down Starts/Stops";
  }
  public Panel centerPanel() {
    return new TwoDrinkersAnimationTestPanel(this);
  }
}
class TwoDrinkersAnimationTestPanel extends Panel {
  public TwoDrinkersAnimationTestPanel(Applet applet) {
    setLayout(new BorderLayout());
    add(new TwoDrinkersPlayfield(applet), "Center");
  }
  public void update(Graphics g) {
    paint(g);
  }
}
```

Example 27-11 `gjt.test.TwoDrinkersPlayfield` **Class Source Code**

```
package gjt.test;

import java.applet.Applet;
import java.net.URL;
import gjt.*;
import gjt.animation.*;
import java.awt.*;
import java.awt.event.*;

public class TwoDrinkersPlayfield extends Playfield
                               implements ItemListener {
  private Applet    applet;
  private Choice    collisionChoice;
  private boolean   collisionsEnabled = true;
  private URL       cb;
  private Sprite    moveFastSpinSlow, moveSlowSpinFast;
```

```java
private Sequence fastSpinSequence,
                slowSpinSequence,
                fastBumpSequence,
                slowBumpSequence;

public TwoDrinkersPlayfield(Applet applet) {
   this.applet = applet;
   cb          = applet.getCodeBase();

   makeSequencesAndSprites();
   add(collisionChoice = new Choice());

   collisionChoice.add("Collision Detection On");
   collisionChoice.add("Collision Detection Off");

   collisionChoice.addItemListener(this);

   addMouseListener(new MouseAdapter() {
      public void mousePressed (MouseEvent event) {
         if(running() == true) stop ();
         else                  start();
      }
   });
}
public void paintBackground(Graphics g) {
   Image bg = applet.getImage(cb, "gifs/background.gif");
   Util.wallPaper(this, g, bg);
}
public void itemStateChanged(ItemEvent event) {
   if(event.getSource() == collisionChoice) {
      if(collisionChoice.getSelectedIndex() == 0) {
         collisionsEnabled = true;
      }
      else {
         collisionsEnabled = false;
      }
   }
}
public void spriteCollision(Sprite sprite, Sprite sprite2) {
   if(collisionsEnabled) {
      if(moveSlowSpinFast.getSequence() != fastBumpSequence) {
         sprite.reverse();
         sprite2.reverse();

         moveSlowSpinFast.play(fastBumpSequence, 3);
         moveFastSpinSlow.play(slowBumpSequence, 3);
      }
   }
```

```java
    }
    public void edgeCollision(Sprite sprite,
                              Orientation orientation) {
       if(orientation == Orientation.RIGHT ||
          orientation == Orientation.LEFT)
          sprite.reverseX();
       else
          sprite.reverseY();
    }
    private void makeSequencesAndSprites() {
       String  file;
       Image[] spinImages = new Image[19];
       Image[] bumpImages = new Image[6];
       Image[] volleyball = new Image[4];

       for(int i=0; i < spinImages.length; ++i) {
          file = "gifs/spin";

          if(i < 10) file += "0" + i + ".gif";
          else       file += i + ".gif";

          spinImages[i] = applet.getImage(cb, file);
       }
       for(int i=0; i < bumpImages.length; ++i) {
          file = "gifs/bump0" + i + ".gif";
          bumpImages[i] = applet.getImage(cb, file);
       }
       fastSpinSequence = new Sequence(this, spinImages);
       slowSpinSequence = new Sequence(this, spinImages);

       fastBumpSequence = new Sequence(this, bumpImages);
    slowBumpSequence = new Sequence(this, bumpImages);

       moveFastSpinSlow = new Sprite(this,
       slowSpinSequence, new Point(25, 75));

       moveSlowSpinFast = new Sprite(this,
       fastSpinSequence, new Point(250,250));

       fastSpinSequence.setAdvanceInterval(50);
       slowSpinSequence.setAdvanceInterval(300);

       fastBumpSequence.setAdvanceInterval(25);
       slowBumpSequence.setAdvanceInterval(200);

       moveFastSpinSlow.setMoveVector(new Point(2,3));
       moveSlowSpinFast.setMoveVector(new Point(-1,-1));
```

```
    moveSlowSpinFast.setMoveInterval(100);

    add(moveFastSpinSlow);
    add(moveSlowSpinFast);
  }
}
```

Summary

By introducing the `gjt.animation` package, we have covered a number of animation-related topics, such as creating sprites, playfields, and animation sequences.

After exploring a number of animation unit tests in this chapter, it should be apparent how to go about creating your own animations, using the Graphic Java Toolkit. The first unit test, "`gjt.test.SimpleAnimationTest` Class Source Code" on page 832, is simple enough that it should be a good starting point for developing your own animations.

Appendixes

PART THREE

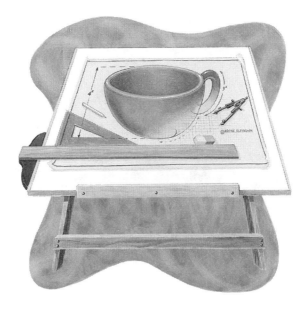

APPENDIX A

AWT Class
Diagrams

Imagine a world where architects write volumes of prose describing their buildings instead of drawing blueprints. While such a scenario would certainly be absurd, many software engineers are quick to eschew the software developer's equivalent of blueprints: the class diagram.

Class diagrams are to software development what blueprints are to the world of architecture. Class diagrams are essential for succinctly communicating one's design to others *Graphic Java* uses class diagrams extensively for documenting the classes from the Graphic Java Toolkit and the Abstract Window Toolkit.

The class diagrams throughout *Graphic Java* are of the *Booch* variety.[1] For those of you unfamiliar with Booch diagrams, we show a legend on the next page and then discuss a simple, yet fairly complete class diagram.

---

1. See Booch, Grady. *Object-Oriented Analysis And Design*. Benjamin/Cummings.

Legend

The following is a legend of the elements used in our class diagrams.

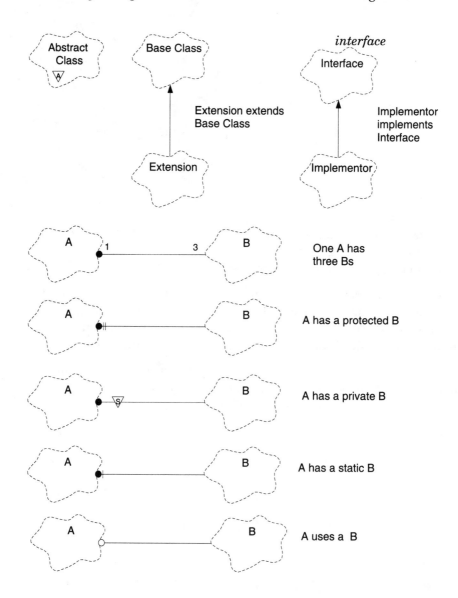

A Look at an Example Class Diagram

The class diagram below is for the `java.awt.Component` class.

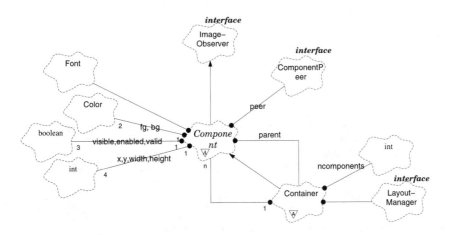

`Container` extends `Component`. Both `Container` and `Component` are abstract classes, meaning they have either declared or inherited abstract methods that they have not implemented. `Component`, on the other hand, implements the `ImageObserver` interface[2] and maintains an association with a `ComponentPeer`. Each `Component` has:

- Four `integer` values, named `x`, `y`, `width`, and `height`
- Three `boolean` values, named `visible`, `enabled`, and `valid`
- Two colors, `fg` and `bg`, and one `Font`

Note that the relationship between `Component` and `Font` is not labeled—we do not label relationships unless the name of the object adds some value. We to label the `int`, `boolean`, and `Color` relationships because the roles of those particular objects are not apparent without a label. Also note that `int` and `boolean` are not really objects; they are intrinsic types. We denote intrinsic types by changing the font of their "class" names.

One `Container` has potentially many `Components`. A `Container` also maintains a relationship with a `LayoutManager` and keeps track of the number of components it currently contains with an `integer` named `ncomponents`.

---

2. We denote interfaces by adorning them with an "interface" label. There is currently no notation in the Booch method for depicting interfaces.

APPENDIX
B

- Using the CD-ROM on Windows 95 and Windows NT

- Using the CD-ROM on Unix

- Using the CD-ROM on The Macintosh

- Source Code for the Part I of the Book

- Using the Graphic Java Toolkit (GJT)

The Graphic
Java CD-ROM

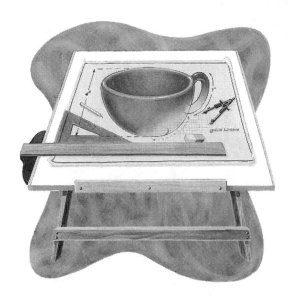

The CD that comes with *Graphic Java* contains the following:

- The 1.02 version of the Java Development Kit (JDK)
- The 1.12 version of the JDK
- A 1.1 version of the Graphic Java Tookit (GJT) for all platforms, except for the Macintosh
- A 1.02 version of the GJT for the Macintosh
- The source code in the first half of the book that is identified by a CD-ROM icon

As we went to press, the 1.1 JDK was not yet available for the Macintosh. As a result, we have included the 1.02 version of the JDK and a 1.02 version of the GJT for Macintosh users. When the 1.1 version of the JDK is available for the Macintosh, the 1.1 GJT should work without modification on the Macintosh.

Using the CD-ROM on Windows 95 and Windows NT

In addition to the JDK and Java applets and applications from the first half of the book, the Win95nt directory contains shareware versions of WinEdit and WinZip.

NOTE: This CD-ROM does not support Windows 3.1.

The Win95nt directory structure is shown in Figure B-1.

Figure B-1 The Win95nt directory on the *Graphic Java* CD.

Directory/FileContents

Gjt_1.02	A zip file for the 1.02 version of the GJT
Gjt_1.1	A zip file for the 1.02 version of the GJT
Grfxjava	Source code for part I of the book
Winedit	A zip file for WinEdit
Winzip	WinZip95 application

The versions of the GJT will work with any operating system that supports the appropriate version of the Java Virtual Machine (JVM). The GJT and JDK files are duplicated for Win95nt, Unix and Macintosh (minus the 1.1 versions on the Mac) on the CD-ROM for convenience.

Using the CD-ROM on Unix

The Unix directory on the CD-ROM is shown in Figure B-2.

Figure B-2 The Unix directory on the *Graphic Java* CD.

The Gjt_1.1 and Grfxjava directories contain zip files, while the Jdk_1.12 contains shell scripts for installing the JDK.

Using the CD-ROM on The Macintosh

Double clicking on the CD-ROM icon and the subsequent folders that are opened on the Macintosh desktop will result in the folders shown in Figure B-3.

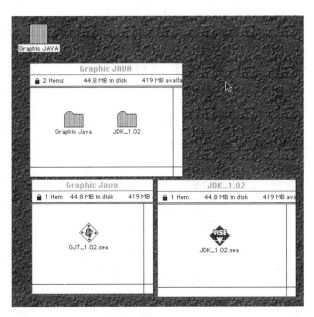

Figure B-3 Folders from the *Graphic Java* CD on the Macintosh.

The Graphic Java and JDK_1.02 folders contain StuffIt archive files. Double click on the icons to extract the contents of each. (Note that you must have the Stuffit archiver installed on the Macintosh). If you already have the 1.02 JDK installed, then just extract the GJT_1.02.sea file.

Extracting the GJT_1.02.sea file will result in a folder whose contents is shown in Figure B-4.

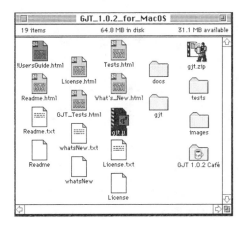

Figure B-4 The GJT folder on the Macintosh.

The GJT folder for the Mac contains additional documentation for the Macintosh and also contains project files for Symantec Cafe and CodeWarrior.

Source Code for the Part I of the Book

Under the Unix and Win95nt directories, you will find a zip file named Grfxjava, which contains all of the source code (and compiled class files) for all of the code in the first part of the book that is marked with a CD-ROM icon. Unzipping the file results in the directory structure shown in Figure B-5.

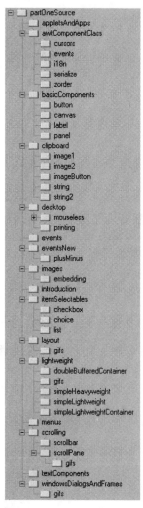

Figure B-5 The grfxjava directory.

The directories are named in accordance with the chapter names in the book. Again, note that duplicates of the Grfxjava zip file are provided under the Unix and Win95nt directories for convenience only. Also, when the 1.1 version of the JDK is available on the Macintosh, all of the source code should work as advertised, Macintosh-specific JDK bugs notwithstanding.

Be sure to read the README.txt file in the partOneSource directory.

Using the Graphic Java Toolkit (GJT)

Unzipping the zip file found in the Gjt_1.1 directories under either the Unix or Win95nt directories (the zip files are identical) results in the directory structure shown in Figure B-6.

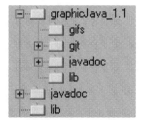

Figure B-6 The Gjt_1.1 directory.

Under the graphicJava_1.1 directory, you will find the following files:

- README.txt
- License.txt
- WhatsNew.txt

The README.txt file contains important information on using and compiling the Graphic Java Toolkit. The License.txt file contains the license for the Graphic Java Toolkit. Finally, the WhatsNew.txt file documents changes to the GJT from the 1.02 version to the 1.1 version.

Index

Java™ Development Kit
Version 1.1.x
Binary Code License

This binary code license ("License") contains rights and restrictions associated with use of the accompanying software and documentation ("Software"). Read the License carefully before installing the Software. By installing the Software you agree to the terms and conditions of this License.

1. Limited License Grant. Sun grants to you ("Licensee") a non-exclusive, non-transferable limited license to use the Software without fee for evaluation of the Software and for development of Java™ compatible applets and applications. Licensee may make one archival copy of the Software. Licensee may not re-distribute the Software in whole or in part, either separately or included with a product. Refer to the Java Runtime Environment Version 1.1 binary code license (http://www.javasoft.com/products/JDK/1.1/index.html) for the availability of runtime code which may be distributed with Java compatible applets and applications.

2. Java Platform Interface. Licensee may not modify the Java Platform Interface ("JPI", identified as classes contained within the "java" package or any subpackages of the "java" package), by creating additional classes within the JPI or otherwise causing the addition to or modification of the classes in the JPI. In the event that Licensee creates any Java-related API and distributes such API to others for applet or application development, Licensee must promptly publish an accurate specification for such API for free use by all developers of Java-based software.

3. Restrictions. Software is confidential copyrighted information of Sun and title to all copies is retained by Sun and/or its licensors. Licensee shall not modify, decompile, disassemble, decrypt, extract, or otherwise reverse engineer Software. Software may not be leased, assigned, or sublicensed, in whole or in part. **Software is not designed or intended for use in on-line control of aircraft, air traffic, aircraft navigation or aircraft communications; or in the design, construction, operation or maintenance of any nuclear facility. Licensee warrants that it will not use or redistribute the Software for such purposes.**

4. Trademarks and Logos. This License does not authorize Licensee to use any Sun name, trademark or logo. Licensee acknowledges that Sun owns the Java trademark and all Java-related trademarks, logos and icons including the Coffee Cup and Duke ("Java Marks") and agrees to: (i) to comply with the Java Trademark Guidelines at http://java.com/trademarks.html; (ii) not do anything harmful to or inconsistent with Sun's rights in the Java Marks; and (iii) assist Sun in protecting those rights, including assigning to Sun any rights acquired by Licensee in any Java Mark.

5. Disclaimer of Warranty. Software is provided "AS IS," without a warranty of any kind. ALL EXPRESS OR IMPLIED REPRESENTATIONS AND WARRANTIES,

INCLUDING ANY IMPLIED WARRANTY OF MERCHANTABILITY, FITNESS FOR A PARTICULAR PURPOSE OR NON-INFRINGEMENT, ARE HEREBY EXCLUDED.

6. Limitation of Liability. SUN AND ITS LICENSORS SHALL NOT BE LIABLE FOR ANY DAMAGES SUFFERED BY LICENSEE OR ANY THIRD PARTY AS A RESULT OF USING OR DISTRIBUTING SOFTWARE. IN NO EVENT WILL SUN OR ITS LICENSORS BE LIABLE FOR ANY LOST REVENUE, PROFIT OR DATA, OR FOR DIRECT, INDIRECT, SPECIAL, CONSEQUENTIAL, INCIDENTAL OR PUNITIVE DAMAGES, HOWEVER CAUSED AND REGARDLESS OF THE THEORY OF LIABILITY, ARISING OUT OF THE USE OF OR INABILITY TO USE SOFTWARE, EVEN IF SUN HAS BEEN ADVISED OF THE POSSIBILITY OF SUCH DAMAGES.

7. Termination. Licensee may terminate this License at any time by destroying all copies of Software. This License will terminate immediately without notice from Sun if Licensee fails to comply with any provision of this License. Upon such termination, Licensee must destroy all copies of Software.

8. Export Regulations. Software, including technical data, is subject to U.S. export control laws, including the U.S. Export Administration Act and its associated regulations, and may be subject to export or import regulations in other countries. Licensee agrees to comply strictly with all such regulations and acknowledges that it has the responsibility to obtain licenses to export, re-export, or import Software. Software may not be downloaded, or otherwise exported or re-exported (i) into, or to a national or resident of, Cuba, Iraq, Iran, North Korea, Libya, Sudan, Syria or any country to which the U.S. has embargoed goods; or (ii) to anyone on the U.S. Treasury Department's list of Specially Designated Nations or the U.S. Commerce Department's Table of Denial Orders.

9. Restricted Rights. Use, duplication or disclosure by the United States government is subject to the restrictions as set forth in the Rights in Technical Data and Computer Software Clauses in DFARS 252.227-7013(c) (1) (ii) and FAR 52.227-19(c) (2) as applicable.

10. Governing Law. Any action related to this License will be governed by California law and controlling U.S. federal law. No choice of law rules of any jurisdiction will apply.

11. Severability. If any of the above provisions are held to be in violation of applicable law, void, or unenforceable in any jurisdiction, then such provisions are herewith waived to the extent necessary for the License to be otherwise enforceable in such jurisdiction. However, if in Sun's opinion deletion of any provisions of the License by operation of this paragraph unreasonably compromises the rights or increase the liabilities of Sun or its licensors, Sun reserves the right to terminate the License and refund the fee paid by Licensee, if any, as Licensee's sole and exclusive remedy.

IMPORTANT — READ CAREFULLY BEFORE OPENING SEALED CD-ROM. By opening the sealed package containing the CD-ROM, you indicate your acceptance of the following Sun Microsystems, Inc. License Agreement.

SUN MICROSYSTEMS LICENSE AGREEMENT

This is a legal agreement between the purchaser of this book/CD-ROM package ("You") and Sun Microsystems, Inc. By opening the sealed CD-ROM you are agreeing to be bound by the terms of this agreement. If you do not agree to the terms of this agreement, promptly return the unopened book/CD-ROM package to the place you obtained it for a full refund.

SOFTWARE LICENSE

1. Grant of License: Sun Microsystems grants to you ("Licensee") a non-exclusive, non-transferable license to use the Sun Microsystems software programs included on the CD-ROM without fee. The software is in "use" on a computer when it is loaded into the temporary memory (i.e. RAM) or installed into the permanent memory (e.g. hard disk, CD-ROM, or other storage device). You may network the software or otherwise use it on more than one computer or computer terminal at the same time.

2. Copyright: The CD-ROM is copyrighted by Sun Microsystems, Inc. and is protected by United States copyright laws and international treaty provisions. Therefore, you must treat the CD-ROM like any other copyrighted material. Individual software programs on the CD-ROM are copyrighted by their respective owners and may require separate licensing. The Java Development Kit is copyrighted by Sun Microsystems, Inc. and is covered by a separate license agreement provided on the CD-ROM.

3. Graphic Java Toolkit (GJT) and Sample Code: Sun Microsystems, Inc. grants you a royalty-free right to reproduce and distribute the GJT and sample code provided that you: (a) distribute the GJT and sample code only in conjunction with and as a part of your software application; (b) do not use Sun Microsystems, Inc. or its authors' names, logos, or trademarks to market your software product; and (c) agree to indemnify, hold harmless and defend Sun Microsystems, Inc. and its authors and suppliers from and against any claims or lawsuits, including attorneys fees, that arise or result from the use or distribution of your software product.

DISCLAIMER OF WARRANTY

The SOFTWARE (including instructions for its use) is provided "AS IS" WITHOUT WARRANTY OF ANY KIND. SUN MICROSYSTEMS and any distributor of the SOFTWARE FURTHER DISCLAIM ALL IMPLIED WARRANTIES INCLUDING WITHOUT LIMITATION ANY IMPLIED WARRANTIES OF MERCHANTABILITY OR OF FITNESS FOR A PARTICULAR PURPOSE. THE ENTIRE RISK ARISING OUT OF THE USE OR PERFORMANCE OF THE SOFTWARE OR DOCUMENTATION REMAINS WITH YOU.

IN NO EVENT SHALL SUN MICROSYSTEMS, ITS AUTHORS, OR ANY ONE ELSE INVOLVED IN THE CREATION, PRODUCTION, OR DELIVERY OF THE SOFTWARE BE LIABLE FOR ANY DAMAGES WHATSOEVER (INCLUDING, WITHOUT LIMITATION, DAMAGES FOR LOSS OF BUSINESS PROFITS, BUSINESS INTERRUPTION, LOSS OF BUSINESS INFORMATION, OR OTHER PECUNIARY LOSS) ARISING OUT OF THE USE OF OR INABILITY TO USE THE SOFTWARE OR DOCUMENTATION, EVEN IF SUN MICROSYSTEMS HAS BEEN ADVISED OF THE POSSIBILITY OF SUCH DAMAGES, BECAUSE SOME STATES/COUNTRIES DO NOT ALLOW THE EXCLUSION OF LIMITATION OF LIABILITY FOR CONSEQUENTIAL OR INCIDENTAL DAMAGES, THE ABOVE LIMITATION MAY NOT APPLY TO YOU.

U.S. GOVERNMENT RESTRICTED RIGHTS

The SOFTWARE and documentation are provided with RESTRICTED RIGHTS. Use, duplication, or disclosure is subject to restrictions as set forth in subparagraph (c)(1)(ii) of The Rights in Technical Data and Computer Software clause at DFARS 252.227-7013 or subparagraphs (c)(1) and (2) of the Commercial Computer Software -- Restricted Rights 48 CFR 52.227-19.

Should you have any questions concerning this Agreement, or if you desire to contact Sun Microsystems for any reason, please write: Sun Microsystems, Inc., 2550 Garcia Avenue, Mountain View, CA 94043.

SUN MICROSYSTEMS PRESS BOOKS
Bringing Sun's Expertise to You!

PRENTICE HALL PTR is pleased to publish **SUN MICROSYSTEMS PRESS** books. This year's **SUN MICROSYSTEMS PRESS** catalog has unprecedented breadth and depth, covering not only the inner workings of Sun operating systems, but also guides to intranets, security, Java™, networking, and other topics important to anyone working with these technologies.

CORE JAVA 1.1
Volume I: Fundamentals
CAY S. HORSTMANN and GARY CORNELL

672 pages; (includes CD-ROM)
ISBN 0-13-766957-7

Now in its third revision, Core Java is still the leading Java book for software developers who want to put Java to work on real problems. Written for experienced programmers with a solid background in languages ranging from Visual Basic to COBOL to C and C++, CORE JAVA 1.1, VOLUME 1 concentrates on the underlying Java 1.1 language along with the fundamentals of using the cross-platform graphics library supplied with the JDK 1.1.

This must-have reference features comprehensive coverage of the essentials for serious programmers:

- Encapsulation
- Classes and methods
- Inheritance
- The Java 1.1 event model
- Data structures
- Exception handling

The accompanying CD is packed with sample programs that demonstrate key language and library features — no toy code! The CD also includes the Windows 95/NT and Solaris™ versions of the JDK 1.1 and shareware versions of WinEdit, WinZip and TextPad for Windows95/NT.

CORE JAVA 1.1
Volume 2: Advanced Features
CAY S. HORSTMANN and GARY CORNELL

750 pages; (includes CD-ROM)
ISBN 0-13-766965-8

For programmers already familiar with the core features of the JAVA 1.1 language, VOLUME 2: ADVANCED FEATURES includes detailed and up-to-date explanations of topics such as:

- Streams
- Multithreading
- Network programming
- JDBC, RMI, JavaBeans™
- Distributed objects

The accompanying CD includes useful sample programs (no toy code!), Windows 95/NT and Solaris™ versions of JDK 1.1, and shareware versions of WinEdit, TextPad, and WinZip.

"Cornell and Horstmann make the details of the powerful and expressive language understandable and they also furnish a conceptual model for its object-oriented foundations."

— GRADY BOOCH

GRAPHIC JAVA 1.1
Mastering the AWT, Second Edition
DAVID M. GEARY

900 pages; (includes CD-ROM)
ISBN 0-13-863077-1

- Revised and expanded to cover 1.1 AWT features: the new event model, lightweight components, clipboard and data transfer, etc.
- Includes more than 40 custom components—convenience dialogs, rubber-banding, image filters, etc.
- A comprehensive guide to the Abstract Window Toolkit for JDK 1.1

GRAPHIC JAVA 1.1 (Second Edition) has been completely revised to cover all of the AWT features provided by the 1.1 JDK. It provides detailed descriptions of every aspect of the AWT, including:
- Lightweight components
- Graphics Colors and Fonts
- Event Handling
- Image Manipulation
- Clipboard and data transfer
- Menus
- Printing
- Dialogs
- AWT Layout Managers

In addition, GRAPHIC JAVA 1.1 comes with the Graphic Java Toolkit (GJT)—a set of freely reusable Java packages that extend the functionality of the AWT. The GJT provides over 45 high-level components, ranging from image buttons and scrollers to toolbars and convenience dialogs.

The accompanying CD-ROM includes all of the example code from the book, ready to run on Solaris, Windows 95 and Windows NT along with the JDK1.1 for those platforms. The complete source code for the GJT for Solaris, Windows 95/NT, and Macintosh is also included for JDK 1.0.2 and JDK 1.1.

JUST JAVA 1.1,
Third Edition

PETER van der LINDEN

700 pages; (includes CD-ROM)
ISBN 0-13-784174-4

In JUST JAVA 1.1, the author of the classic Expert C Programming: Deep C Secrets brings his trademark enthusiasm, straight talk, and expertise to the challenge of learning Java and object-oriented programming.

In this updated Third Edition, you'll find all the fundamentals of Java programming, including Java object-oriented techniques, types, statements, string processing, as well as more sophisticated techniques like networking, threads, and using the Abstract Window Toolkit. You'll also discover more examples than ever, along with updated coverage of future Java APIs—including the Java Database Connectivity (JDBC) API completely updated to include coverage of JDK 1.1.

TOPICS INCLUDE:
- The Story of O—object-oriented programming
- Applications versus applets
- Identifiers, comments, keywords, and operators
- Arrays, exceptions, and threads
- GIGO—Garbage In, Gospel Out
- On the Internet No One Knows You're a Dog

The CD-ROM includes all source code for examples presented in the book along with the latest JDK for Solaris, Windows 95, Windows NT, and Macintosh.

JAVA BY EXAMPLE,
Second Edition
**JERRY R. JACKSON and
ALAN L. McCLELLAN**

380 pages; (includes CD-ROM)
ISBN 0-13-272295-X

There's no better way to learn Java than by example. If you're an experienced programmer, JAVA BY EXAMPLE is the quickest way to learn Java. By reviewing example code written by experts, you'll learn the right way to develop Java applets and applications that are elegant, readable, and easy to maintain.

Step-by-step, working from examples, you'll learn valuable techniques for working with the Java language. The Second Edition provides even more extensive coverage.

TOPICS INCLUDE:
- Memory and constructors
- Input/output
- Multithreading
- Exception handling
- Animation
- Remote methods invocation (RMI)
- Networking
- Java Database Connectivity (JDBC) API

The CD-ROM includes all source code for examples presented in the book along with Java WorkShop 1.0 30-Day Free Trial from Sun Microsystems and the latest JDK for Solaris, Windows 95, Windows NT, and Macintosh.

INSTANT JAVA, Second Edition
JOHN A. PEW

398 pages; (includes CD-ROM)
ISBN 0-13-272287-9

INSTANT JAVA™ applets—no programming necessary! Now anyone can use Java to add animation, sound, and interactivity to their Web pages! Instant Java is your guide to using more than 75 easy-to-customize Java applets. The Second Edition

contains even more applets and examples—plus updated, foolproof instructions for plugging them into your Web pages.

APPLETS INCLUDE:
- Text applets
- Image applets
- Animation applets
- Slide shows
- Tickers

You'll find all the applets on the cross-platform CD-ROM—along with sample HTML pages and valuable tools including Java™ WorkShop™ 1.0 30-Day Free Trial from Sun Microsystems and the latest JDK for Solaris,™ Microsoft Windows 95, Microsoft Windows NT, and Macintosh. This is an invaluable tool for adding Java special effects to your HTML documents!

NOT JUST JAVA
PETER van der LINDEN

313 pages; ISBN 0-13-864638-4

NOT JUST JAVA is the book for everybody who needs to understand why Java and other Internet technologies are taking the software industry by storm. Peter van der Linden, author of the best-selling JUST JAVA, carefully explains each of the key technologies driving the Internet revolution and provides a much-needed perspective on critical topics including:
- Java and its libraries—present and future
- Security on intranets and the Internet
- Thin clients, network computers, and webtops
- Multi-tier client/server system
- Software components, objects and CORBA
- The evolution and role of intranets
- JavaBeans™ versus ActiveX

Also included are case studies of leading-edge companies that show how to avoid the pitfalls and how to leverage Java and related technologies for maximum payoff.

"...the most complete and effective treatment of a programming topic since Charles Petzold's classic Programming Windows."

— COMPUTER SHOPPER

"Fantastic book/CD package for HTML authors...practical, hands-on instructions get you off to a fast start."

— COMPUTER BOOK REVIEW

EXPERT C PROGRAMMING:
Deep C Secrets
PETER van der LINDEN

352 pages; ISBN 0-13-177429-8

EXPERT C PROGRAMMING is a very different book on the C language! In an easy, conversational style, the author reveals coding techniques used by the best C programmers. EXPERT C PROGRAMMING explains the difficult areas of ANSI C, from arrays to runtime structures, and all the quirks in between. Covering both IBM PC and UNIX systems, this book is a must read for anyone who wants to learn more about the implementation, practical use, and folklore of C!

CHAPTER TITLES INCLUDE:

- It's not a bug, it's a language feature!
- Thinking of linking
- You know C, so C++ is easy!
- Secrets of programmer job interviews

THREADS PRIMER
A Guide to Multithreaded Programming
BIL LEWIS and DANIEL J. BERG

319 pages; ISBN 0-13-443698-9

Written for developers and technical managers, this book provides a solid, basic understanding of threads—what they are, how they work, and why they are useful. It covers the design and implementation of multithreaded programs as well as the business and technical benefits of writing threaded applications.

The THREADS PRIMER discusses four different threading libraries (POSIX, Solaris, OS/2, and Windows NT) and presents in-depth implementation details and examples for the Solaris and POSIX APIs.

PROGRAMMING WITH THREADS
STEVE KLEIMAN, DEVANG SHAH, and BART SMAALDERS

534 pages; ISBN 0-13-172389-8

Multithreaded programming can improve the performance and structure of your applications, allowing you to utilize all the power of today's high performance computer hardware. PROGRAMMING WITH THREADS is the definitive guide to multithreaded programming. It is intended for both novice and experienced threads programmers, with special attention given to the problems of multithreading existing programs. The book provides structured techniques for mastering the complexity of threads programming with an emphasis on performance issues.

TOPICS INCLUDE:

- Synchronization and threading strategies
- Using threads for graphical user interfaces and client-server computing
- Multiprocessors and parallel programming
- Threads implementation and performance issues

"[Expert C Programming] is essential, instructive, light-relief for C programmers... Five stars for Peter van der Linden."

— STAN KELLY-BOOTLE, Contributing Editor, *UNIX Review*

"[The authors] explain clearly the concepts of multithreaded programming as well as the useful little tricks of the trade."

—GUY L. STEELE JR. Distinguished Engineer, Sun Microsystems Laboratories

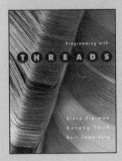

CONFIGURATION AND CAPACITY PLANNING FOR SOLARIS SERVERS

BRIAN L. WONG

448 pages; ISBN 0-13-349952-9

A complete reference for planning and configuring Solaris servers for NFS, DBMS, and timesharing environments, featuring coverage of SPARC station 10, SPARC center 2000, SPARC server 1000, and Solaris 2.3.

PANIC!
UNIX System Crash Dump Analysis

CHRIS DRAKE and KIMBERLEY BROWN

480 pages; (includes CD-ROM)
ISBN 0-13-149386-8

"...This book could be a lifesaver."

— MILES O'NEAL,
UNIX Review, January 1996

UNIX systems crash—it's a fact of life. Until now, little information has been available regarding system crashes. PANIC! is the first book to concentrate solely on system crashes and hangs, explaining what triggers them and what to do when they occur. PANIC! guides you through system crash dump postmortem analysis towards problem resolution. PANIC! presents this highly technical and intricate subject in a friendly, easy style that even the novice UNIX system administrator will find readable, educational, and enjoyable.

TOPICS COVERED INCLUDE:

- What is a panic? What is a hang?
- Header files, symbols, and symbol tables
- A comprehensive tutorial on adb, the absolute debugger
- Introduction to assembly language
- Actual case studies of postmortem analysis

A CD-ROM containing several useful analysis tools—such as adb macros and C tags output from the source trees of two different UNIX systems—is included.

SUN PERFORMANCE AND TUNING:
SPARC and Solaris

ADRIAN COCKCROFT

254 pages; ISBN 0-13-149642-5

This book is an indispensable reference for anyone working with Sun workstations running the Solaris environment. Written for system administrators and software developers, it includes techniques for maximizing system performance through application design, configuration tuning, and system monitoring tools. The book provides detailed performance and configuration information on all SPARC™ machines and peripherals and all operating system releases from SunOS™ 4.1 through Solaris 2.4.

HIGHLIGHTS INCLUDE:

- Performance measurement and analysis techniques
- Uni- and multiprocessor SPARC system architectures and performance
- Hardware components: CPUs, caches, and memory management unit designs
- Kernel algorithms and tuning rules

Second Edition coming early 1998!

WABI 2:
Opening Windows

SCOTT FORDIN and SUSAN NOLIN

383 pages; ISBN 0-13-461617-0

WABI™ 2: OPENING WINDOWS explains the ins and outs of using Wabi software from Sun Microsystems to install, run, and manage Microsoft Windows applications on UNIX systems. Easy step-by-step instructions, illustrations, and charts guide you through each phase of using Wabi—from getting started to managing printers, drives, and COM ports to getting the most from your specific Windows applications.

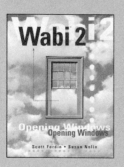

AUTOMATING SOLARIS INSTALLATIONS
A Custom Jumpstart Guide
PAUL ANTHONY KASPER and ALAN L. McCLELLAN

282 pages; (includes a diskette)
ISBN 0-13-312505-X

AUTOMATING SOLARIS INSTALLATIONS describes how to set up "hands-off" Solaris installations for hundreds of SPARC™ and x86 systems. It explains in detail how to configure your site so that when you install Solaris, you simply boot a system and walk away—the software installs automatically! The book also includes a diskette with working shell scripts to automate pre- and post-installation tasks, such as:

- Updating systems with patch releases
- Installing third-party or unbundled software on users' systems
- Saving and restoring system data
- Setting up access to local and remote printers
- Transitioning a system from SunOS™ 4.x to Solaris 2

SOLARIS IMPLEMENTATION
A Guide for System Administrators
GEORGE BECKER, MARY E. S. MORRIS, and KATHY SLATTERY

345 pages; ISBN 0-13-353350-6

Written by expert Sun™ system administrators, this book discusses real world, day-to-day Solaris 2 system administration for both new installations and for migration from an installed Solaris 1 base. It presents tested procedures to help system administrators improve and customize their networks and includes advice on managing heterogeneous Solaris environments. Provides actual sample auto install scripts and disk partitioning schemes used at Sun.

TOPICS COVERED INCLUDE:

- Local and network methods for installing Solaris 2 systems
- Configuring with admintool versus command-line processes
- Building and managing the network, including setting up security
- Managing software packages and patches
- Handling disk utilities and archiving procedures

SOLARIS PORTING GUIDE, Second Edition
SUNSOFT DEVELOPER ENGINEERING

695 pages; ISBN 0-13-443672-5

Ideal for application programmers and software developers, the SOLARIS PORTING GUIDE provides a comprehensive technical overview of the Solaris 2 operating environment and its related migration strategy.

The Second Edition is current through Solaris 2.4 (for both SPARC and x86 platforms) and provides all the information necessary to migrate from Solaris 1 (SunOS 4.x) to Solaris 2 (SunOS 5.x). Other additions include a discussion of emerging technologies such as the Common Desktop Environment from Sun, hints for application performance tuning, and extensive pointers to further information, including Internet sources.

TOPICS COVERED INCLUDE:

- SPARC and x86 architectural differences
- Migrating from common C to ANSI C
- Building device drivers for SPARC and x86 using DDI/DKI
- Multithreading, real-time processing, and the Sun Common Desktop Environment

"This book is a must for all Solaris 2 system administrators."
— TOM JOLLANDS,
Sun Enterprise Network Systems

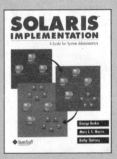

"[This book] deals with daily tasks and should be beneficial to anyone administering Solaris 2.x, whether a veteran or new Solaris user."
— SYS ADMIN,
May/June 1995

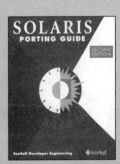

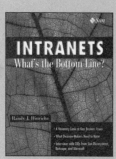

INTRANET SECURITY:
Stories From the Trenches
LINDA McCARTHY

300 pages; ISBN 0-13-894759-7

Do you have response procedures for systems break-ins? Is your e-mail encrypted? Is your firewall protecting your company? Is your security staff properly trained? These are just a few of the security issues that are covered in INTRANET SECURITY: STORIES FROM THE TRENCHES. Author Linda McCarthy, who in her job as a worldwide security team leader at Sun has broken into thousands of corporate intranets, presents detailed case studies of real-life break-ins that will help you make your systems safer. She explains how each breach occurred, describes what steps were taken to fix it, and then provides a practical and systematic solution for preventing similar problems from occurring on your network!

CREATING WORLDWIDE SOFTWARE
Solaris International Developer's Guide, Second Edition
BILL TUTHILL and DAVID SMALLBERG

ISBN 0-13-494493-3

A new edition of the essential reference text for creating global applications, with updated information on international markets, standards organizations, and writing international documents. This expanded edition of the Solaris International Developer's Guide includes new chapters on CDE/Motif, NEO/OpenStep, Universal codesets, global internet applications, code examples, and studies of successfully internationalized software.

INTRANETS:
What's the Bottom Line?
RANDY J. HINRICHS

420 pages; ISBN 0-13-841198-0

INTRANETS: WHAT'S THE BOTTOM LINE? is for decisions makers, who want bottom line information in order to figure out what an Intranet is and how it will help their organizations. It's a compelling case for the corporate Intranet. This book will give you a high-level perspective on Intranets and will answer your questions: What is an Intranet? What is it made of? What does it buy me? How much does it cost? How do I make it work? How do I know it's working?

HANDS-ON INTRANETS
**VASANTHAN S. DASAN and
LUIS R. ORDORICA**

ISBN 0-13-857608-4

This hands-on guide will show you how to implement a corporate Intranet, or a private network comprised of the open, standards-based protocols and services of the Internet. IS professionals and others interested in implementing an Intranet will learn the key Intranet protocols, services, and applications. The book also describes the technical issues such as security, privacy, and other problems areas encountered in Intranet implementation and integration, while providing practical solutions for each of these areas. You will learn how to realize the Intranet's potential.

RIGHTSIZING THE NEW ENTERPRISE:
**The Proof, Not the Hype
HARRIS KERN and Randy JOHNSON**

326 pages; ISBN 0-13-490384-6

The "how-to's" of rightsizing are defined in this detailed account based on the experiences of Sun Microsystems as it re-engineered its business to run on client/server systems. This book covers rightsizing strategies and benefits, management and system administration processes and tools, and the issues involved in transitioning personnel from mainframe to UNIX support. RIGHTSIZING THE NEW ENTERPRISE presents you with proof that rightsizing can be done...and has been done.

MANAGING THE NEW ENTERPRISE:
**The Proof, Not the Hype
HARRIS KERN, RANDY JOHNSON,
MICHAEL HAWKINS, and
ANDREW LAW, with
WILLIAM KENNEDY**

212 pages; ISBN 0-13-231184-4

MANAGING THE NEW ENTERPRISE describes how to build a solid technology foundation for the advanced networking and systems of the enterprise. Learn to re-engineer your traditional information technology (IT) systems while reducing costs! As the follow-up to RIGHTSIZING THE NEW ENTERPRISE, this volume is about relevant, critical solutions to issues challenging corporate computing in the 1990s and beyond. Topics include:

- Creating reliable UNIX distributed systems
- Building a production-quality enterprise network
- Managing a decentralized system with centralized controls
- Selecting the right systems management tools and standards

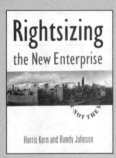

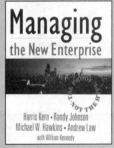

"This book has helped me clarify the essence of UNIX systems management in Client/Server technologies. It's a most valuable addition to our reference library."

— KEVIN W. KRYZDA, Director, Information Services Department Martin County, Florida

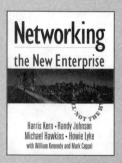

Use of this software is subject to the Binary Code License terms and conditions on page 876. Read the license carefully. By opening this package, you are agreeing to be bound by the terms and conditions of this license from Sun Microsystems, Inc.

The Graphic Java 1.1 CD-ROM is a standard ISO-9660 disc. Software on this CD-ROM requires Windows 95, Windows NT, Solaris 2, or Macintosh (System 7.5).

Windows 3.1 IS NOT SUPPORTED